U
m
fo
B
a

UE

1 9

Distribution of
Matrimonial Assets
on Divorce

Distribution of Matrimonial Assets on Divorce

Michael L. Rakusen
MA (Cantab), Solicitor

D. Peter Hunt
MA (Oxon), Barrister of
Gray's Inn and the
North-Eastern Circuit

London
Butterworths
1982

England Butterworth & Co. (Publishers) Ltd
London 88 Kingsway, WC2B 6AB

Australia Butterworths Pty Ltd
Sydney 586 Pacific Highway, Chatswood, NSW 2067
Also at Melbourne, Brisbane, Adelaide and Perth

Canada Butterworth & Co. (Canada) Ltd
Toronto 2265 Midland Avenue, Scarborough, M1P 4S1

New Zealand Butterworths of New Zealand Ltd
Wellington 33–35 Cumberland Place

South Africa Butterworth & Co. (South Africa) (Pty) Ltd
Durban 152–154 Gale Street

USA Butterworth (Publishers) Inc
Boston 10 Tower Office Park, Woburn, Mass. 01801

ISBN Casebound 0 406 35101 5

Thomson Litho Ltd, East Kilbride, Scotland

Preface

'I appreciate the point...that it is difficult for practitioners to advise clients in these cases because the rules are not very firm. That is inevitable when the courts are working out the exercise of the wide powers given by a statute like the Matrimonial Causes Act 1973. It is the essence of such a discretionary situation that the court should preserve, so far as it can, the utmost elasticity to deal with each case on its own facts. Therefore, it is a matter of trial and error and imagination on the part of those advising clients. It equally means that decisions of this court can never be better than guidelines. They are not precedents in the strict sense of the word.'

Those words, extracted from the judgment in the Court of Appeal of Ormrod LJ in the now well-known case of *Martin v Martin* [1977] 3 All ER 762, prefaced the first edition of this work. The words are no less relevant to this new edition of the book, because they express an important caveat as to how to treat the voluminous case law which has arisen since the enactment of the Matrimonial Proceedings and Property Act 1970. To that extent they are important words to bear in mind when endeavouring to understand what this book is and what it is not.

A casebook on matrimonial finance cannot, for the very reasons stated by Ormrod LJ, set out the leading cases on any given topic and thereby trace the gradual development of an area of law. 'Utmost elasticity' must and does prevail in the judicial exercise of the powers conferred by the modern matrimonial legislation. No doubt it is because of that elasticity that a plethora of reported cases, from diverse sources and publications, continues to emerge at such a rate that even the most meticulous practitioner has difficulty in keeping up to date. Some cases are widely reported but then quickly forgotten. Others are neither. *Mesher v Mesher* (which assumed an almost biblical authority in many registrars' courts) failed to appear in any extensive law report until seven years after it saw the light of day. In the meantime, the potential dangers of the order made in that case have now become all too obvious (see, for example, *Carson v Carson* (1981) Times, 7 July, CA), and the effects of *Mesher* orders, which were so fashionable in the mid-1970's, will not be forgotten by the parties involved for a long time. This book, it is hoped, brings together notes on most of the relevant cases in the area which we seek to tackle. In spite of the proper reminder that none of the cases are precedents in the strict sense of the word, it seems to us that to compile a summary of these cases is a useful exercise for the following reasons:

1. Although the cases do not acquire the status of legal precedent, a significant number of the cases clarify or redefine the principles according to which the modern jurisdiction is applied. It is, for example, difficult to understand the principles to be followed when allocating the matrimonial home without knowing what was said by the Court of Appeal in *Wachtel v Wachtel*, *Martin v Martin* or *Hanlon v Hanlon*. It would be difficult to know what is meant by the 'clean break' principle without knowing of the existence of *Minton v Minton*.
2. Even the experienced practitioner in this area of law will occasionally feel the need to refresh his memory as to how the superior courts have defined the various principles or guidelines, and this book is designed

to provide something of a directory reference for every useful case.

3. The inexperienced or occasional practitioner in this area of law should find some inspiration as to the nature and categories of orders available to the court which, given careful comparison with the facts of the case in hand, ought to provide a starting point for the preparation of that case and its ultimate presentation to the court.

4. There are frequently important areas of policy where the superior courts have left practitioners and registrars to contemplate an unfortunate balance of conflicting decisions. A topical example is whether a court has the power to dismiss an application for periodical payments without the consent of the applicant. It is only by careful recourse to the cases that a conscientious practitioner, registrar or judge can determine where the balance of judicial authority lies.

The first edition of this book started as a series of notes which were used to assist in advising clients and in the preparation of papers for counsel. The scope of the book has been widened to deal with important areas such as the relevance of third parties, private agreements entered into by the parties and the 'clean break'. Unhappily, lack of time and space has meant that the book does not consider the subjects of costs, evidence, tax or avoidance of dispositions.

All aspects of matrimonial finance are interrelated, and there is an inevitable degree of overlapping and repetition in the categories of cases; in any event, the aim of the book is to provide a short summary of the salient points of all the reported cases following any particular line. To that extent the book may be regarded as a directory or source of references and cross-references. The reader will find short introductory texts to some of the Parts and most of the Chapters, although it must be stressed that the book is not offered up as a text book but principally as a work of reference.

As regards the system of reference, each case is identified by reference to the appropriate Chapter and Section. For example, 23-101 means Chapter 23, Section 1, the first case under that Section.

We are obliged to those who have gone before us, in particular to Mr. George G. Brown, the author of 'Brown on Divorce', and we are most grateful to Shaw & Sons Ltd for permission to quote from that work. We are also most grateful to The Incorporated Council of Law Reporting for England and Wales for permission to quote extracts from *The Law Reports* and *The Weekly Law Reports* and to the publishers of *Family Law Reports, Family Law, New Law Journal, The Law Society's Gazette, The Solicitor's Journal* and *The Times* for allowing us to utilise material contained in those publications.

The law is stated as at 30th September 1981. However, in Appendix II we have managed to insert brief summaries of *Furniss v Furniss* and *Stockford v Stockford*, reported in *The Times* on 28th October and 5th November 1981 respectively, and in Appendix III we have set out those provisions relating to orders for sale of property contained in the Matrimonial Homes and Property Act 1981 which came into force on 1st October 1981.

Michael L. Rakusen
D. Peter Hunt
December 1981

Contents

Abbreviations

The following are the abbreviations
used for the principal legal journals
cited in this book.

All ER	All England Law Reports
Fam	Family Division
Fam Law	Family Law
FLR	Family Law Reports
LS Gaz R	Law Society's Gazette Reports
NLJ	New Law Journal
Sol Jo	Solicitors' Journal
WLR	Weekly Law Reports

Table of statutes

References in this Table to *Statutes* are to Halsbury's Statutes of England (Third Edition) showing the volume and page at which the annotated text of the Act will be found.
Page references printed in bold type indicate where the section of an Act is printed in part or in full.

Table of cases

Page numbers printed in **bold type** indicate where a case is set out.

PART 1

Meaning of 'matrimonial assets'

The starting point for any definition of the assets which go to make up the 'matrimonial assets' is still, we respectfully submit, the judgment of Lord Denning MR in *Wachtel v Wachtel* (1–101). Assets of a capital nature were one of two aspects of a concept which Lord Denning chose in 1973 to express as 'family assets' (the other being revenue-producing assets). The continued use of the phrase 'family assets' has more recently been seriously criticised by Ormrod LJ in *P v P* (13–015). It was pointed out that the phrase 'family assets' does not occur in the Matrimonial Causes Act 1973 and has nothing at all to do with section 25 of the Act. However, it is respectfully suggested that provided that the precise words of section 25 (1) (a) are properly borne in mind (and viewed in the overall context of the whole section) there is nothing intrinsically misleading in what has been hitherto used as the short and convenient phrase 'family assets'. It seems that what Ormrod LJ was seeking to do was to quash once and for all the simplistic notion that the court should approach each case according to the question of whether any particular financial item is a 'family asset' and thereafter exclude it from account if it is not. Whether the continued use of the phrase is of any particular value or not, the judgment of Lord Denning MR remains the definitive explanation of the court's role under the modern legislation, and the Matrimonial Causes Act 1973 is to be interpreted in the light of that case and the cases subsequent to it.

The cases provide specific examples of instances where a particular item of financial resources has been treated as 'property' within the meaning of section 25. In *Calderbank v Calderbank* (1–203), *Dennis v Dennis* (1–302) and *P v P* (1–207) inherited wealth and assets acquired by gift were taken into account. In both *Calderbank v Calderbank* and *P v P* the inherited wealth had already been applied to the matrimonial finances. However, in *Dennis v Dennis* the gift from the husband's father to the husband was not made until after the break-up of the marriage; accordingly, it must have been open to the husband to argue that the gift was made to him very much as a single man rather than as a married man. The fact that this argument was apparently ignored demonstrates the very wide interpretation of section 25 (1) (g) of the Matrimonial Causes Act 1973 which this and other decisions have entailed.

CHAPTER 1

Capital assets

In deciding whether to exercise its powers to order various forms of financial relief to a spouse and, if so, in what manner, the court is required by section 25 (1) of the Matrimonial Causes Act 1973 to have regard to all the circumstances, including '(a) the income, earning capacity, property and other financial resources which each of the parties to the marriage has or is likely to have in the foreseeable future'.

Insofar as the title of this book raises the obvious question: 'what does the phrase "matrimonial assets" mean?' then, in the context of the modern divorce legislation, section 25 (1) (a) of the 1973 Act provides the only answer. The briefest perusal of the cases brought under the modern legislation is sufficient to disclose the wide scope of the financial resources which have been determined to fall within the definition of section 25 (1) (a). In the ordinary case, the areas of finance which fall to be considered by the court do indeed neatly fit into three simple categories, namely, income, capital (which in most cases is invested principally in the matrimonial home and thus acquires a separate and paramount significance) and any other ordinary financial resources such as pensions, insurance policies, etc. But what of the extraordinary features such as, for example, capital sums awarded to one spouse as compensation for personal injury, or a prospective inheritance? It is only by recourse to the cases that guidance may be obtained as to which assets or prospective assets might be considered by the court in the exercise of its powers. This and the following two chapters follow the simple logic of the statute in considering cases which cast some light on the applied meaning of the term 'matrimonial assets' in three separate aspects. It cannot be stressed too early or too highly, however, that the mere fact that the different categories of matrimonial assets can be examined separately should in no sense be taken as an indication of the way in which the court approaches its task in the exercise of its various powers. In reality and in practice all of the numerous and frequently complex strands of family finance go to make up a composite or global picture. Therefore, quite properly and realistically, the court will not look at any individual aspect, such as capital or income, in isolation from the overall picture, but rather, an attempt is made to obtain a result of objective overall fairness, if possible. Therefore the purpose of enumerating cases which cast some light on the meaning of phrases such as 'matrimonial assets' or 'family assets' is entirely definitive and not, at this stage, explanatory of the method by which the diverse strands can be manipulated in the task of distribution. An attempt is made to explain that aspect of the court's function by the introductory text to Part 3.

1   Family assets: the matrimonial home, etc.

A. *The meaning of 'family assets'*

CASE SUMMARIES

1–101 Wachtel v Wachtel

[1973] 1 All ER 829, CA

Meaning of 'family assets'.   Lord Denning MR said (at page 836): 'The phrase "family assets" is a convenient short way of expressing an important concept. It refers to those things which are acquired by one or other or both of the parties, with the intention that they should be continuing provision for them and their children during their joint lives, and used for the benefit of the family as a whole. It is a phrase, for want of a better, used by the Law Commission, and is well understood. The family assets can be divided into two parts: (i) those which are of a capital nature, such as the matrimonial home and the furniture in it; (ii) those which are of a revenue-producing nature, such as the earning power of husband and wife. When the marriage comes to an end, the capital assets have to be divided: the earning power of each has to be allocated.'

1–102 Trippas v Trippas

[1973] 2 All ER 1, CA

Distinction between family assets and business assets.   Lord Denning MR said (at page 4): '...The wife cannot claim a share *in the business as such*. She did not give any active help in it. She did not work in it herself. All she did was what a good wife does do. She gave moral support to her husband by looking after the home. If he was depressed or in difficulty, she would encourage him to keep going. That does not give her a share.'

However, his lordship continued (at page 5): '...if this marriage had continued, it is plain that the wife had a good chance of receiving a financial benefit on the sale of the business...Now that there has been a divorce, she should be compensated for the loss of that chance.'

Notes

1. It is therefore clear that there is a distinction between family assets as such and business assets. When the husband and wife parted they came to an arrangement about the matrimonial home. The husband bought out the wife's interest. The furniture was divided between the parties and their adult children. The argument over the proceeds of sale of the husband's family business remained. It is clear that these proceeds of sale were not family assets. Nevertheless, the wife was entitled to a share.

2. See also case summary 1–401, and the case summaries following.

1–102A P v P (financial provision: lump sum)

[1978] 3 All ER 70, CA

(1) *Use of the phrase 'family assets' criticised as obsolete.*   Not referred to in s. 25 of the Matrimonial Causes Act 1973 – see case summary 13–015.

(2) *Quantification of parties' strict interests in matrimonial assets under Married Women's Property Act 1882, s. 17 irrelevant under modern legislation.*   Ormrod LJ said (at page 75): '...For my part I do not find it particularly helpful to try to ascertain and quantify [the husband's] so-called interests. It is useful to ascertain these interests in a broad way so that one can see the justice of each side's case, but I would prefer to avoid quantifying or seeking to quantify these rights in terms of figures, because the moment one quantifies them people begin to do arithmetic with the figures, and it is a well-known statistical fallacy that if you

start with an estimate and you multiply it and divide it you multiply and divide the error as well.'

1-103 Bennett v Bennett

(1978) 9 Fam Law 19, CA

Investments owned by the parties taken into account. See case summary 5-108.

1-104 Richardson v Richardson

(1978) 9 Fam Law 86, CA

Investments under monthly savings plan scheme. Orr LJ said that the judge at first instance had been wrong to leave the value of the savings plan out of account. The savings plan was being built up in order to supplement the husband's pension and, had the marriage subsisted, the wife would have had the benefit of it together with the husband. See case summary 14-012.

1-105 Page v Page

(1981) Times, 30 January, CA

Assets no longer in party's possession. The husband transferred £124,000 to his secretary, who removed it out of the jurisdiction. Ormrod LJ said that the husband had, very wisely, agreed that the sum should be treated as still part of his assets. For further details, see Appendix II.

B. *The matrimonial home*

CASE SUMMARIES

1-131 Wachtel v Wachtel

[1973] 1 All ER 829, CA

Matrimonial home purchased in the husband's name but acquired and maintained by the joint efforts of both parties – contributions to the family in kind equal to contributions in money or money's worth. Lord Denning MR said (at page 838): '...we may take it that Parliament recognised that the wife who looks after the home and family contributes as much to the family assets as the wife who goes out to work. The one contributes in kind. The other in money or money's worth. If the court comes to the conclusion that the home has been acquired and maintained by the joint efforts of both, then, when the marriage breaks down, it should be regarded as the joint property of both of them, no matter in whose name it stands. Just as the wife who makes substantial money contributions usually gets a share, so should the wife who looks after the home and cares for the family for 20 years or more.'

Note. See also *Griffiths v Griffiths* (1-132A).

1-132 Kowalczuk v Kowalczuk

[1973] 2 All ER 1042, CA

Matrimonial home purchased by husband before marriage contemplated. The Court of Appeal held that the registrar had been wrong to take into account the wife's contributions in kind in looking after the home and family when dealing with an application under the Married Women's Property Act 1882. Such contributions could only be taken into account under the 1970 Act. Liberty to either party to make further application for a transfer of property order under the 1970 Act.

Notes

1. For the 1970 Act see now section 24 of the Matrimonial Causes Act 1973 – see Appendix I.
2. This case deals in great detail with the ascertainment of a proprietary interest in the matrimonial home under the 1882 Act, but contains no argument under the modern legislation.
3. See also *P v P* (1–102A) – valuation of parties' interests in matrimonial assets irrelevant under modern legislation.

1–132A Griffiths v Griffiths

[1974] 1 All ER 932, CA

Matrimonial home acquired almost entirely by husband's efforts alone – conveyance to wife in return for nominal sum – legal ownership irrelevant.   Roskill LJ said (at page 941): '... Some importance has been attached to the fact that the house was in the wife's name. It is suggested that different considerations may apply because the house is in the wife's name from what would apply if the house were in the husband's name. It is necessary to refer to what was said on this point in the judgment in *Wachtel v Wachtel* (1–131):

> "If the court comes to the conclusion that the home has been acquired and maintained by the joint efforts of both, then, when the marriage breaks down, it should be regarded as the joint property of both of them, no matter in whose name it stands."

'I do not think that the word "joint" was being used there in any technical sense. What the court was saying was that the actual legal title is not the material consideration. So, in the present case, to my mind, the mere fact that the house is in the wife's name is not the determinative factor, any more than it would be if the house were in the husband's name. The purpose for which the house may previously have been conveyed to the wife may in this case (and indeed in other cases) be a material factor; but, for my part, I think one starts from the fact that one has to look at the totality of the family assets. It does not matter who is actually the legal owner of the asset in question.'

Note. See also *P v P* (1–102A) – valuation of parties' interests in matrimonial assets irrelevant under modern legislation

1–132B Cumbers v Cumbers

[1975] 1 All ER 1, CA

Matrimonial home purchased by husband prior to marriage ceremony.   Wife awarded lump sum provision. See case summary 14–003A.

1–133 McDonnell v McDonnell

(1976) Times, 17 February, CA

Matrimonial home a gift to the husband from his family.   See case summary 23–905.

1–134 Dallimer v Dallimer

(1978) 8 Fam Law 142, CA

Wife's half share in matrimonial home settled on husband for life.   Required as a home for husband in his old age. Wife securely housed with third party. See case summary 5–106.

Notes

1. Wife's half share treated as a family asset, available for redistribution.

2. Wife's half share reduced to one-third.
3. See also *Eshak v Nowojewski* (17–007) in which, again, the wife's half share was treated as a family asset and settled on the husband for life. However, in view of the fact that there was no order for maintenance, on the husband's death the proceeds of sale were to be divided equally between his estate and the wife or her estate.
4. See also *Browne v Pritchard* (4–104), in which the point at issue was the need to provide a home for the children living with the husband. On the house no longer being required as a home for the children it was to be sold and the proceeds divided as to two-thirds to the husband and one-third to the wife. Again, the wife's half share was treated as a family asset, available for redistribution.
5. See also *P v P* (1–102A) – valuation of parties' interests in matrimonial assets irrelevant under modern legislation.

1–135 Bennett v Bennett

(1978) 9 Fam Law 19, CA

Matrimonial home purchased in husband's name and acquired almost entirely by his efforts alone. See case summary 5–108.

2 Assets brought into the marriage, or acquired during the marriage by inheritance or gift, and the possibility of future inheritance

CASE SUMMARIES

1–201 Kowalczuk v Kowalczuk

[1973] 2 All ER 1042, CA

Matrimonial home purchased by husband before marriage contemplated. See case summary 1–132.

1–202 O'Donnell v O'Donnell (sub nom. O'D v O'D)

[1975] 2 All ER 993, CA

Capital resources made available by the husband's father. The husband and his mother jointly purchased a lease of a hotel. The husband received substantial financial backing from his father, which enabled him, in partnership with his father after his mother's death, to acquire the freehold of the hotel, to enlarge it and to become the manager of that increasingly profitable business. The wife worked in the hotel and by her efforts contributed to the success of the business, but the scale and speed of the development of the business was largely due to the capital resources made available by the husband's father.

Ormrod LJ said that *Wachtel v Wachtel* (1–101) was essentially a case of two people starting their married life with little or nothing but their earning capacities; and together founding a family and building up, by their joint efforts, such capital as they were able to save; but that in other cases the situation is different. *One or other or, perhaps, both spouses may bring into the marriage substantial capital assets, or may acquire such assets during the marriage by inheritance or by gift from members of their families. In such cases the expressions 'family assets' and 'the wife earning her share' cannot be applied without modification.*

The Court of Appeal (Ormrod LJ and Sir George Baker P) considered that the case did not fall properly into the same class as *Wachtel v Wachtel* but that it fell somewhere between that and the other class of case described above. In the circumstances they did not amend the judgment of the judge at first instance who had treated all the assets as family assets and had then applied the one-third ratio.

Ormrod LJ stated that in cases on the scale of this case this ratio may produce results which may seem to be too high; but inflation had already altered values very considerably, bringing many cases into the class in which the one-third ratio would not have been accepted in the past.

Note. Compare *McDonnell v McDonnell* (23–905) where the capital asset brought into the marriage was the matrimonial home.

1–203 Calderbank v Calderbank

[1975] 3 All ER 333, CA

Assets acquired during the marriage by inheritance.   See case summary 18–001.

1–204 McDonnell v McDonnell

(1976) Times, 17 February, CA

Matrimonial home a gift to the husband from his family.   See case summary 23–905.

1–205 Calder v Calder

(1976) Times, 29 June, CA

The possibility of future inheritance.   The husband's mother, now domiciled in Monaco, enjoyed a large income from two very substantial Canadian settlements. The trustees in Canada had refused to disclose any information concerning the settlements, but the husband appeared to have a vested interest of one-third in one of the settlements, whose assets were not less than 200,000 Canadian dollars, provided he survived his mother, and also a contingent interest in the other settlement which could be of far greater value.

Ormrod LJ said that the judge at first instance had been wrong to ignore the husband's interest in the Canadian settlements, because, on a balance of probabilities, he could become a wealthy man when the interests of the various life tenants eventually fell in. See case summary 16–103.

1–206 Morgan v Morgan

[1977] 2 All ER 515

The possibility of future inheritance.   During the marriage the parties lived on a farm owned by the husband. He and the wife had lived there for 23 years. There were no children. In 1973 the wife left the farm and the husband. In September 1975 she obtained a decree nisi, which was duly made absolute. Following the final decree the husband remarried and was joined at the farm by his new wife.

On leaving the farm the wife went to live in a house owned by her father, Mr. Evans, who was a widower aged 74 and was not in robust health. The wife was his only child. She applied for periodical payments and for a lump sum settlement. The husband alleged that, if after her father's death the wife were to become the sole beneficiary of her father's estate, she might become better off financially than the husband. The husband therefore maintained that accurate evidence of Mr. Evans' assets should be available so that the court might decide (a) if a lump sum award should be made at all and (b) if so, its size.

Watkins J stated that in his opinion the evidence Mr. Evans could give would be both relevant and admissible: 'I have said that Mr. Evans' evidence would be relevant. No judge would be entitled to ignore it having regard to section 25 of the Matrimonial Causes Act 1973. But is the respondent entitled to force that evidence out of Mr. Evans? Is the privacy of a person to be so invaded? Must he reveal, when he may not desire it, his testamentary dispositions and details of his wealth? I have been referred to *Calder v Calder* (1–205). There the husband had a vested and a contingent interest under a settlement, and Ormrod LJ said that it would be wrong to ignore those prospects because on a balance of probabilities the husband could become a wealthy man.'

However, in the opinion of Watkins J it would have been oppressive to cause Mr. Evans to come under the duress of a subpoena to give evidence to the court. The order setting aside the subpoena was accordingly upheld.

Note. Compare *H v H* (2nd June 1981) – see Appendix II.

1–207 P v P (financial provision: lump sum)

[1978] 3 All ER 70, CA

Capital resources made available by the wife's father – husband and wife in partnership in farming enterprise.   See case summary 1–408.

Note. Compare *O'Donnell v O'Donnell* (1–202) – capital resources made available by the husband's father – but parties not in partnership in the hotel business.

1–208 Hardy v Hardy

(1981) Times, 11 June, CA

Husband's very substantial expectations – wife's application for lump sum adjourned generally at her request.   See Appendix II.

3   Assets acquired after breakdown of the marriage

CASE SUMMARIES

1–301 Trippas v Trippas

[1973] 2 All ER 1, CA

The parties separated in 1968. In 1969 the husband's family business was taken over for £350,000 and he received as his half share £80,000 in cash and the balance in shares. He gave each of his sons £5,000. It was held that section 5 (1) (g) of the Matrimonial Proceedings and Property Act 1970 (now section 25 (1) (g) of the Matrimonial Causes Act 1973) could apply to acquisitions of capital subsequent to the breakdown of the marriage; and that in all the circumstances the wife was entitled to a lump sum award out of the husband's capital from the sale of the business, for it fell exactly within paragraph (g) as a benefit which, but for the divorce, the wife would have had the chance of acquiring. See case summary 13–002.

1–302 Dennis v Dennis

(1975) 6 Fam Law 54, CA

Shortly after the separation the husband's father gave the husband £90,000 in order to purchase a farm, which the husband bought after the wife had presented a petition for divorce. Sir John Pennycuick said that there was no doubt that the court could take into account an accession of wealth after the break-up of the marriage, and he cited *Trippas v Trippas* (1–301) as an example. Stamp LJ agreed.

1–303 Dallimer v Dallimer

(1978) 8 Fam Law 142, CA

The matrimonial home was purchased in the parties' joint names, with a deposit which the husband borrowed from his employers and from members of his family. The balance was on mortgage. The husband made all the mortgage repayments. The husband, aged 75, was now retired and living upon a state pension and social security benefit. *The wife was now living with the co-respondent, who had transferred to the wife the house in which they both lived.*

The value of the wife's house was £15,000 subject to a mortgage of £6,000. So far as the matrimonial home was concerned, the mortgage had now been paid off by the husband and the house was now worth some £14,000.

The wife's half share in the matrimonial home was reduced to one-third, not to be payable except on the husband's death or on his voluntarily ceasing to reside in the house.

Note. For further details, see case summary 5–106. See also *W v W* (6–204).

4   Business assets

CASE SUMMARIES

1–401   Trippas v Trippas

[1973] 2 All ER 1, CA

The parties separated in 1968. In 1969 the husband's family business was taken over for £350,000 and he received as his half share £80,000 in cash and the balance in shares. He gave each of his sons £5,000. It was held that section 5 (1) (g) of the 1970 Act (now section 25 (1) (g) of the Matrimonial Causes Act 1973) could apply to acquisitions of capital subsequent to the breakdown of the marriage; and that in all the circumstances the wife was entitled to a lump sum award out of the husband's capital from the sale of the business, for it fell exactly within paragraph (g) as a benefit which, but for the divorce, the wife would have had the chance of acquiring.

The husband, now out of work, argued that he needed his capital to live on. The lump sum award having been increased to £10,000, the husband was left with free capital, i.e. apart from his house, of £30,000, which earned him an income of £2,100 per annum, less tax. The wife's free capital (including the award of £10,000) amounted to £12,000, and her income (including her earnings from employment) to £2,460. The net result was that the wife's capital position was much weaker than the husband's, but her income position was slightly better and would remain so provided she remained in employment. Scarman LJ (as he then was) said (at page 9): 'There is nothing in the so-called one-third rule or in the language of the 1970 Act which precludes this court from doing rough justice on the basis of equality, provided it is, on the whole, just to both parties, as in my opinion it is in this case ... I think a lump sum of £10,000 goes as far as practicable towards doing just that.'

Note. For the distinction between business assets and family assets see case summary 1–102.

1–402   Strelley-Upton v Strelley-Upton

(1973) 4 Fam Law 9, CA

During the marriage the parties had lived on a farm, owned by the husband. When this was sold the proceeds largely went to pay debts. After the breakdown of the marriage the husband bought a farm jointly with his mother for £32,000. The mother contributed £15,000 while the husband borrowed his share from the bank. At the time of the hearing at first instance he had an overdraft of £19,500. The equipment and livestock of the farm was worth about £2,000. The county court judge ordered the husband to pay (inter alia) a lump sum of £2,000 to the wife within four months.

The husband appealed against the lump sum order, contending that, had the marriage survived, there would have been no capital sum available; further, that the farm should not be regarded as a capital asset. By the time of the appeal the husband's overdraft had increased to £23,000 and in order to pay the £2,000 to the wife he would have had to borrow further from the bank.

Orr LJ said that the wife's argument was that the court should have regard not only to the present circumstances, but to the foreseeable circumstances, that the farm was a growing business, and that here was a husband who had already been able to obtain a substantial overdraft from the bank. His lordship said that this was a marriage which had lasted 17 years and an application by a wife who had undoubtedly helped the husband in his previous farming business. His lordship thought that the judge had been right in thinking that the circumstances called for a lump sum payment. However, in view of the husband's financial circumstances the sum was reduced to £1,000 and the husband would be given one year in which to pay the money.

1–402A Bothe v Amos

[1976] Fam 46, [1975] 2 All ER 321, CA

Valuation of share in partnership assets – Married Women's Property Act 1882, s. 17. Wife's interest assessed as at the date she deserted the husband and abandoned the family business, thereby renouncing the partnership by her conduct. See case summary 8–703.

1–402B O'Donnell v O'Donnell (sub nom. **O'D v O'D**)

[1975] 2 All ER 993, CA

The husband and his mother jointly purchased a lease of a hotel. The husband received substantial financial backing from his father, which enabled him, in partnership with his father after his mother's death, to acquire the freehold of the hotel, to enlarge it and to become the manager of that increasingly profitable business. One-third ratio applied. See case summary 1–202.

Note. The wife had assisted in the business.

1–403 Sopher v Sopher

(1975) 6 Fam Law 12, CA

The husband was by profession a chartered accountant. He was employed as an attaché by a firm of stockbrokers, his earnings comprising the commission he earned on share dealings. He also engaged in share dealings on his own account, but had so far been unsuccessful, and his capital had been steadily decreasing. He had remarried, and was living in a house worth £41,000 belonging to his new wife, together with his son and his new wife's daughter by a previous marriage. The wife was living in a one-room furnished flat.

The husband's capital had been reduced to £5,100. The wife asked for a lump sum order to enable her to put down a deposit for a house. The judge at first instance considered that the husband's capital represented his 'stock-in-trade'. Counsel for the wife argued that this was the wrong way of looking at it. Shaw LJ said that the husband needed a capital reserve to draw on, for example, for school fees, and that whichever way one looked at it, whether as 'stock-in-trade' or as a necessary family reserve, the sum of £5,100 ought not to be diminished. Browne and Stamp LJJ concurred.

1–404 Smith v Smith

(1976) 6 Fam Law 245, CA

The husband was managing director of a family company. There was £15,289 standing to the credit of his loan account. Stamp LJ said that it was true that this sum was not realisable and should be regarded as being frozen indefinitely. Nevertheless, the county court judge had been right to bring it into account. The husband's appeal against the order that he should transfer his interest in the former matrimonial home to the wife was dismissed.

1-405 Martin v Martin

[1976] 3 All ER 625, CA

Neither of the parties had brought substantial assets into the marriage, but by successful property transactions they had acquired a farm now worth £53,770. The wife left in 1967, but after a reconciliation in 1968 an agreement was made whereby the husband should transfer into their joint names not only the matrimonial home but also another property in which the husband's mother lived and various bank balances and insurance policies. The husband did not implement the agreement.

In 1969 the husband left and bought a Post Office business, charging the farm to the extent of £14,000 to do so. He subsequently purchased another farm for £90,000 and stock for £10,000 by means of a bank overdraft of £89,000. This property had to be sold for £65,000 in 1975.

It was argued on behalf of the husband that his conduct since the separation was not relevant, and on behalf of the wife that the husband's dissipation of £33,000 of the family's assets following the separation should be taken into consideration.

Purchas J took into account the following facts:
1) the wife had maintained, if not enhanced, the value of the farm since the separation;
2) the husband had saddled the farm with a burdensome charge which would oblige the wife to sell the farmhouse and possibly move into a caravan;
3) the husband had had the use of further capital sums and had pledged insurance policies.

On those factors alone the husband had had more than his entitlement of the capital assets. He was ordered to make the wife a lump sum payment of £5,000 and to transfer to her the whole of his interest in the farm.

Note. On appeal the lump sum payment was reduced to £2,000 because this was all the husband could find. Cairns LJ said that but for the husband's inability to pay his lordship would have been in favour of awarding a higher figure. Stephenson and Bridge LJJ agreed.

1-406 Penman v Penman

(1976) 7 Fam Law 46, CA

The parties had three children, now aged ten, seven and four. The matrimonial home was the farmhouse on a farm, both of which were owned by the wife. The parties were partners in the farming enterprise. The partnership assets consisted of the livestock and dead stock. The husband had no other assets. The marriage broke down and the wife petitioned for divorce. She then applied for an interim injunction to exclude the husband from the matrimonial home. The judge found it proved that the husband had been violent. He concluded that it was impossible for the couple to live in the same house and ordered the husband to vacate the house. In view of the fact that the husband had no other home, no other job, was suffering from a back ailment and had no assets other than his share in the partnership, the judge ordered that the husband need not vacate the house until 14 days after the wife had fulfilled one of three conditions:
a) that she paid to the husband a sum of £10,000 on account of his share in the partnership, such sum being an estimate of what he would receive on a final division of the partnership assets, or

b) that she paid him an agreed sum representing one-half of the value of the partnership assets, such sum to be ascertained, or

c) that she paid him such sum as was due to him in respect of his share of the partnership assets.

The wife appealed on the ground that she could not raise £10,000, that there was no incentive to the husband to agree to any transfer of property order and that it looked as though he might stay on in the farmhouse indefinitely.

Lord Denning MR referred to *Bassett v Bassett* (4–203) with approval. The court, when dealing with cases of excluding a spouse from the matrimonial home should essentially think in terms of a home for the children and only then consider the balance of hardship. The property rights between the spouses were of comparative minor importance. The wife should be allowed to remain on the farm and ought not to be required to find the £10,000. The court had been told that the dispute as to the parties' property rights could be determined within six months. The right course was to see that the husband was reasonably provided for before he vacated the house. The way to do that was to order the wife to make weekly payments of £50 to the husband until such time as the parties' property rights were determined.

1–407 Porter v Porter

(1978) 8 Fam Law 143, CA

In 1973 the wife had obtained a decree of divorce based on the husband's adultery. The husband had remarried and there were two children of that union. In 1975 the second wife died. The husband owned a freehold shop worth about £13,000 above which he lived with his children by his second wife. It was subject to a mortgage of £1,690. He carried on his business in the shop, which produced an income of about £1,100 per annum. He owed National Insurance fines and arrears of about £800. The wife lived in council accommodation and was supported by social security and unemployment benefit.

The registrar ordered the husband to pay to the wife a lump sum of £3,500 within six months, and this order was upheld by the county court judge. Stamp LJ said that the registrar had apparently taken the view that this sum could be raised without selling the shop. That assumption having been shown to be incorrect, the registrar's order was wrong. It would be unjust to order the payment of a sum which would involve either a sale or, even, an increase in the mortgage on the property. The husband's only other asset was a life policy with a surrender value of £1,416, and the lump sum order was accordingly reduced to £1,400. Orr and Eveleigh LJJ agreed.

1–408 P v P (financial provision: lump sum)

[1978] 3 All ER 70, CA

Shortly after the parties married the wife's father bought them a farm for £15,000 which he eventually conveyed to the wife by deed of gift. The farm was very run down at the time and the husband did a lot of work on it, improving the farmhouse and the land. He succeeded in building up a successful farm business which he and his wife ran as partners. The valuation of the farm came to approximately £102,000. The judge at first instance awarded the husband a lump sum of £15,000 payable by three instalments, and made nominal orders for periodical payments by the husband to the wife and three children. The husband appealed.

Ormrod LJ said that the wife must be allowed to keep the farm in order to derive income from it to keep the children. The sum of £15,000 was the largest capital amount she could be expected to raise from the farm business without being obliged to sell it, and it would suffice to supply the husband's principal need of a home.

Notes
1. The wife had applied her wealth towards the family good: see Lord Denning MR's judgment in *Wachtel v Wachtel* (1–101).
2. Ormrod LJ's remarks at page 73 on the valuation of business assets are worthy of note. See case summary 26–010A.

1–408A B v B (matrimonial proceedings: discovery)

[1979] 1 All ER 801

Order for disclosure of company documents.   See Appendix II.

1–409 Hudson v Hudson

(1979) 10 Fam Law 23, CA

The parties owned the former matrimonial home in equal shares. It was purchased in 1972 for £2,500 in poor condition. The parties rehabilitated it with the aid of a mortgage of £3,400. The parties also purchased three derelict properties, reconstructed them and converted them into a hotel at a cost of over £30,000, raised in various ways. The hotel business was successful and the parties were partners in it.

Ormrod LJ said that the parties were agreed in principle that the wife should have the house and the husband the hotel, subject to an 'equalisation payment' by the husband to the wife. All the relevant figures were agreed.

Hotel and stock	£	*House and contents*	£
Gross asset value	81,421	Gross asset value	40,418
Less liabilities	17,809	Less mortgage	15,645
	63,612		24,773
Less capital gains tax (estimated)	16,400		
	47,212		

If there were to be an exact division in equal shares the husband would have to pay the wife £11,219. This, subject to some minor adjustments, was the sum which counsel for the wife submitted should be paid to the wife. The judge at first instance thought that the basis of division should be 50:50 and the Court of Appeal saw no reason to differ from that view. Prima facie, therefore, on these figures, the wife should receive a lump sum of £11,219 or thereabouts. But the husband could not afford to pay more than £7,000 at present, which was the sum the judge had ordered to be paid. The Court of Appeal awarded the wife an additional sum of £4,000, charged on the hotel and payable in five years' time or on the sale of the hotel if earlier. To help the husband's income position, interest would not be payable annually but would be capitalised, and the total charge was accordingly fixed at £6,000 (including capitalised interest).

Note. Ormrod LJ said that the equalisation payment to the wife would have been considerably higher if no reduction had been made in the value of the hotel for estimated capital gains tax. Counsel for the wife conceded that this was a proper deduction. But his lordship stated that he would like to reserve his opinion on the point until it arose in a contested case. There was no evidence that either party was contemplating selling the hotel.

1–410 Kokosinski v Kokosinski

[1980] 1 All ER 1106

The husband escaped to Britain from Poland in 1939, leaving behind his Polish wife. During the war he met the wife and in 1947 they started to live together. A son was born in 1950. The wife knew it would be impossible for the husband to obtain a divorce in Poland unless his wife there divorced him, and the husband had always promised that as soon as he could he would marry the wife.

The husband started an engineering business with some friends in 1946. When the child was old enough to go to playschool the wife commenced working in the business. Over the years the business became a successful concern and the wife occupied an important position.

In 1969 the husband was divorced by the wife in Poland and in 1971 he and the wife were married. In 1972 the marriage broke down and the parties separated. The wife and son, now an adult, bought out the husband's shares in the business.

Wood J considered that he could not do justice between the parties unless he took into account the wife's contribution to the family in kind and to the running of the family business during those years, prior to the marriage ceremony, when the husband had been unable to marry her. The estimated value of the business was £120,000. Wood J considered that a figure of £8,000, or one-fifteenth of that value, was a reasonable proportion for the wife to have earned, bearing in mind the fact that she was receiving a regular salary. The husband was ordered to pay the wife a lump sum of £8,000.

Note. For further details see case summary 8–310.

1–411 S v S

(1980) Times, 10 May

The value of the husband's assets had been agreed at £2.1 m. Balcombe J said that the one-third starting point would be inappropriate. On that basis the lump sum would have been around £700,000. His lordship did not find the one-third approach of much assistance in a case where the capital assets were so large. However, the sum of £200,000 offered by the husband was too low. It was more than adequate for the wife's needs, but to award her such a sum would not adequately take into account her very substantial contributions to the farming business. The husband was ordered to make a lump sum payment of £375,000.

For further details, see case summary 16–104.

Note. Balcombe J said that one of the most important matters to be taken into account was the effect of any order on the husband's farming enterprise. It would not be right to make an order which would have the effect of destroying the husband's successful business, thereby causing hardship to his employees and their families, in order to provide the wife with more than she reasonably required for her own needs.

1–412 W v W

(1981) Times, 20 March and 21 March

Order for disclosure against husband's business associates.   See Appendix II.

1–413 H v H (2nd June 1981)

[1981] LS Gaz R 786

Subpoena issued against family company.   See Appendix II.

5   Damages for personal injury

CASE SUMMARIES

1–501 Armstrong v Armstrong

(1974) 118 Sol Jo 579, CA

Buckley LJ said that though the judgment of the judge at first instance was not explicit, in deciding to deduct the damages for personal injury from the sum to be divided between the husband and wife he must have taken the view that the damages had been awarded for *pain and suffering and loss of amenity,* which were *personal to the husband* and which the husband should not be required to share with the wife. Buckley LJ thought that it would not be justifiable to interfere with that part of the decision, and Stephenson LJ agreed.

1–502 Jones v Jones (sub nom. **Jones (MA) v Jones (W)**)

[1975] 2 All ER 12, CA

Orr LJ said: '. . . I mention briefly a third argument which has been addressed to us on behalf of the wife. It is that the judge was wrong to take into account the prospect of the wife receiving compensation from the Criminal Injuries Compensation Board – an expectation which, as I have said, has in the event been realised. Reliance was placed as to that matter on the decision of this court in *Armstrong v Armstrong* (1–501). That was a case in which the judge had refused to take into account, in ascertaining what were the assets of the two spouses, a sum of damages received by the husband in respect of an industrial accident. It is clear from the judgment of the court that the court assumed in that case that those damages had been awarded for pain and suffering and loss of amenity, and on that basis the court took the view that that sum of damages was not to be regarded as a family asset which the husband ought to share with the wife. It is by no means clear, and I for my part would not be prepared to assume, that the court would have taken the same view had there been evidence that the damages figure was wholly or in part in respect of loss of future earnings.

'In the present case we do not know whether and to what extent the figure of £1,800 which I have mentioned, and any further sum that may be received from the Criminal Injuries Compensation Board, represents loss of earnings as distinct from pain and suffering and loss of amenity. For my part, I would not be prepared to lay down that a sum of compensation of the former kind is necessarily to be left out of account for the purposes of proceedings between spouses as to matrimonial property and periodical payments.'

Megaw LJ said: '. . . It is said that the award which the wife has received from the Criminal Injuries Compensation Board, which we are told has resulted in an interim payment of £1,800, is something which can properly be weighed in the balance here. Let me assume, for the purpose of this appeal, that it can properly be taken into account as a factor. In my judgment, it could only be a relevant factor if and insofar as that £1,800 is attributable to the prospect of the wife's future loss of earnings. I cannot see that any part of it which is properly attributable to what is known in another sphere as pain and suffering and loss of amenity should be a relevant factor in the question which the court has to consider here.'

1–503 **Daubney v Daubney**

[1976] 2 All ER 453, CA

Scarman LJ said (at page 459): 'There is, as Cairns LJ has described, a conflict of judicial opinion on the point whether damages for pain and suffering should be brought into account under section 25 of the 1973 Act. I need not analyse the cases as Cairns LJ has already done that. Suffice it to say that this is not, as I see it, a conflict of decisions, but solely a conflict of judicial opinion. The two cases on which reliance has been placed for the submission that damages of this character are not to be regarded are *Armstrong v Armstrong* (1–501) and *Jones v Jones* (1–502), both of them decisions of the Court of Appeal, though in *Armstrong v Armstrong* only two judges were sitting.

'As I understand the decision in *Armstrong v Armstrong,* it proceeded on the basis that the court would not in the circumstances of that case interfere with the discretion of the judge. Expressions of opinion, therefore, on the point now under consideration were obiter. In *Jones v Jones*, as Cairns LJ has pointed out, the expressions of opinion on the point were plainly obiter as the decision turned on the conduct [i.e. the conduct of the husband, who assaulted his wife, resulting in the award of compensation in respect of her injuries] and circumstances giving rise to the compensation paid by the Criminal Injuries Compensation Board to the wife. As I understand *Smith v Smith* (1974) 28 November (unreported), Bar Library Transcript No. 380A, to which Cairns LJ referred, it was a decision by the Court of Appeal that damages for pain and suffering are to be considered in the exercise of the duty imposed on the court by sections 24 and 25 of the 1973 Act.

'In this conflict of opinion I unhesitatingly agree with Cairns LJ. I think that the Act is capable of no other interpretation than that damages of this class fall to be considered as part of the resources or property, as the case may be, of one of the parties to the marriage.'

Sir Gordon Willmer agreed.

Note. The report of *Smith v Smith* at (1974) 5 Fam Law 125 does not mention the question of damages for personal injury.

CHAPTER 2

Revenue-producing assets

The cases quoted in this chapter are, in their individual origin, of diverse breed. In other words, they are by no means all cases under the modern law; some of them were cases in which the only issue for determination was the question of periodic maintenance, whether originating in magistrates' courts or the divorce courts. To that extent they can only be read with the extremely important caveat that they illustrate only the various lines of approach adopted by the courts when considering the division of income. Again, they are at this stage intended to be illustrative not of how the precise division is calculated but, rather, of the factors which may be taken into account in arriving at the starting point. For example the court, when considering the question of income and earning capacity, will often be faced with problems. How far do the details of income disclosed accord with the reality as evidenced by spending power and lifestyle? How far do the actual details of income compare and contrast with the actual earning capacity? What, if any, is the relevance of the earning capacity of a party's new spouse or cohabitee? It is the general approach to questions such as these that these cases, it is hoped, will illustrate.

1   Earning capacity of the husband

CASE SUMMARIES

2–101 N v N

(1928) 138 LT 693

Year of exceptional prosperity.   Lord Merrivale P said (at page 697) that an order for maintenance should not be based on the income of the husband during a year of exceptional prosperity.

2–102 Klucinski v Klucinski

[1953] 1 All ER 683

Overtime pay.   The justices based their award of maintenance on the husband's basic wage, ignoring his overtime earnings. The wife appealed to the Divisional Court.

Lord Merriman P said: 'In my opinion, the justices have gone wrong on a matter of principle, and we must make that clear. They say: "Experience in dealing with such cases has shown us that, if we base the amount of our order on [a husband's total earnings, including his overtime earnings], the man more often than not stops working overtime, as he feels he has no longer any incentive to do so." That is a plain misdirection in law. It is elementary law that, in assessing the amount of maintenance, justices ought to take into account, just as we are bound to do here, not merely the husband's basic wage, but his *earning capacity . . .*'

His lordship said that it would not be satisfactory to send the case back for a re-hearing, and the present court did not have sufficient evidence to decide the proper amount to be awarded. He continued: 'The obvious solution is to leave the wife, if it proves that she has not sufficient to live on under the order, to apply to the justices for a revision, in which event I hope that they will take note of the view I am expressing, namely, that it is wrong to eliminate from their calculations overtime pay *or the capacity to earn it.*'

2–103 McEwan v McEwan

[1972] 2 All ER 708

Early retirement – husband's potential earning capacity.   The husband, aged about 59, was a retired detective constable. The justices found that he had deserted his wife and ordered him to pay maintenance. At a subsequent hearing the amount of maintenance was reduced. At yet another hearing a further application by the husband to vary the maintenance order was dismissed. The justices held that he had not made a genuine effort to obtain and retain work suitable to his intelligence and experience, and that it would be wrong for them to ignore his earning potential as a fit and capable retired detective constable. The husband appealed.

The Divisional Court dismissed the husband's appeal. The justices were entitled to take into account not only the husband's actual earnings, but also his potential earning capacity. Dicta of Lord Merrivale P in *N v N* (2–201), of Lord Merriman P in *Klucinski v Klucinski* (2–102) and of Scarman J (as he then was) in *W v W (No. 3)* (2–204) applied.

2–104 Wachtel v Wachtel

[1973] 1 All ER 829, CA

Earning capacity of the husband.   Lord Denning MR said (at page 841): 'So far as *the husband's earning capacity* is concerned, we venture to think that the learned judge's findings are self-contradictory; for, if the husband was spending at the rate of £4,000 to £5,000 per annum without incurring debts and was, in fact, at the same time making savings, his gross taxable income must have been considerably more than the £4,000 to £5,000 found by the judge. We propose to proceed on the basis of the husband's earning capacity (i.e. his gross taxable income) being not less than £6,000 per annum. This may well be too favourable to the husband who appears not to have disclosed part of his income as a dentist.'

2–105 Billington v Billington

[1974] 1 All ER 546

Bonus payments.   The justices had found that a bonus earned by the husband in effect added £5 per week to his income. In the absence of evidence that the employer paid it as a gift out of profits after tax, the Divisional Court held that it was part of the husband's earnings to be brought into account when fixing the amount of maintenance which he should pay his ex-wife. The fact that it was not paid weekly was irrelevant.

2–106 Williams (LA) v Williams (EM) (sub nom. Williams v Williams)

[1974] 3 All ER 377

Husband unemployed and in receipt of supplementary benefit – whether genuinely unemployed. In divorce proceedings the husband had been ordered to pay the wife £4 per week. The order had been registered in the magistrates' court. The husband had subsequently been made redundant and was now in receipt of supplementary benefit. The husband applied to the justices for a variation of the maintenance order on the ground that it was impossible for him to pay £4 per week to the wife out of the amount he was receiving from the Supplementary Benefits Commission. The justices were not satisfied that the husband had genuinely attempted to find employment and dismissed the application. The husband appealed.

The Divisional Court held that because the officials of the DHSS (who had a duty to investigate such matters) had not reduced or stopped the payments of supplementary benefit to the husband, it was possible to infer that he was genuinely and not voluntarily unemployed. That was a matter which the justices ought to have taken into account, and the case would be remitted to a fresh panel of justices for rehearing.

2–107 Adams v Adams

(1978) 8 Fam Law 141, 122 Sol Jo 348

Husband resigned from job on grounds of ill-health – whether genuinely unable to work. The husband was a company secretary earning £6,600 a year. The justices found that the husband had deserted the wife and ordered him to pay her maintenance for herself and for the child of the family. A few weeks after the making of the orders the husband resigned from his job on the grounds of ill-health. On the husband's application, the justices accordingly reduced the orders. The wife appealed to the Divisional Court, on the grounds, inter alia, that the justices had been wrong to accept the husband's poor health as the reason for his resignation; he had given evidence that he had resigned because he was angry with the decision of the justices.

Sir George Baker P said (inter alia) that the justices were entitled to conclude that the husband had genuinely resigned his position on the grounds of ill-health.

2–108 Eshak v Nowojewski

(1980) Times, 19 November, CA

Earning capacity of spouse bringing up children. There were two children of the marriage, aged 10 and 5. The parties contemplated that they would remain in the husband's care. The wife had now remarried and was provided for by her new husband. The husband, aged 38, now lived on social security. Because the wife had remarried, no question of periodical payments arose. However, the husband's earning capacity was relevant to the question of housing.

Sir John Arnold P said that the husband was severely restricted in his ability to earn a living by virtue of having to look after the children. He might not be free to work until the younger child attained 18 years, when he would be 51. He might not work until he was 54 if the child continued in further education. He would thus be handicapped in relation to the mortgage market. It seemed to his lordship that the judge had failed to attach due importance to the husband's need for housing after the children had grown up. The transfer of property order made by the judge was varied so as to allow the husband to live in the house for the rest of his life. Thereafter the property would be sold and the proceeds divided equally between the husband's estate and the wife or her estate.

2 Husband's resources: looking at the realities

CASE SUMMARIES

2–201 N v N

(1928) 138 LT 693

Husband divesting himself of assets – looking at the realities. Lord Merrivale P said (at page 696): '. . . It was contended by Mr. Middleton for the husband that there was not in truth an increase of the husband's means . . . and that it was contrary to the principles laid down in the authorities . . . to hold that there had been an increase in his means. It was said that by effectual legal process he had divested himself of funds which would otherwise have been his, and the court must take that into account. It is true that he has effectually divested himself, at any rate for the time being, of his control over assets and his interest in assets which would have been his. What effect does that have? The Ecclesiastical Courts showed a degree of practical wisdom which well justified their existence, and which anybody who considers their proceedings will attribute perhaps to the fact that those who conducted what were called ecclesiastical proceedings were very learned lawyers skilled in civil law. They were not misled by appearances. When they considered what maintenance . . . a husband should provide for a wife from whom he was separated by a decree of the court, they looked at the realities. It is quite true that if the husband became voluntarily a pauper, or if he entered into religious orders in another Church and had divested himself of his means, it might have been said that he had got nothing. So far as I am aware there is not a case in which the judge in the Ecclesiastical Courts had to deal with that kind of respondent. They were more worldly minded. But this emerges: the court not only ascertained what moneys the husband had, but what moneys he could have had if he liked, and the term "faculties" describes the capacity and the ability of the respondent to provide maintenance. And the principle went to this extent, that if a man were living at ease upon an income which was given him voluntarily by other parties, that income could be taken into account. And it went further than that: if a man were living in idleness and chose to refuse to earn money, his "faculties" were not treated as non-existent for that reason. The court considered, having regard to the substance of the matter, what was the ability of the respondent to provide for the wife . . . I conceive that I must take into consideration the position in which the parties were, and the position in which the wife was entitled to expect herself to be and would have been, if her husband had properly discharged his marital obligation . . .'

2–202 J v J (sub nom. J–PC v J–AF)

[1955] 2 All ER 617, CA

Looking at husband's expenditure – looking at the realities. This was an appeal by the husband against an order for the payment of interim maintenance. The husband's total income, according to his income tax returns, was £44 for 1951/52, £69 for 1952/53 and £60 for 1953/54, these sums being derived from insurance commissions. He had, however, in the past earned a salary of £3,500 annually plus expenses. Before the order under appeal was made, he had been engaged in the development of a freehold estate of 50 acres in Buckinghamshire and a leasehold property at South Kensington. The value of the Buckinghamshire property on completion of the development was estimated to be £34,800. The South Kensington property had been acquired for £10,800; no estimate had been given of its developed value. The husband had taken out substantial loans in order to finance these developments and was living by means of bank loans.

The Court of Appeal held that the correct way of assessing the husband's ability to pay maintenance in these circumstances was to look at his current expenditure.

Hodson LJ quoted with approval from Lord Merrivale P's judgment in *N v N* (2–201) where he had said: 'The ecclesiastical courts showed a degree of practical wisdom . . . They were not misled by appearances . . . they looked at the realities . . . The court not only ascertained what moneys the husband had, but what moneys he could have had if he liked . . .' His lordship said that Lord Merrivale's words were applicable in such a case as this, where the husband was able to maintain a consistent standard of living over a substantial period by means of bank loans. His lordship concluded that a proper estimate of the husband's ability to pay, based on his current expenditure, was to treat him as a £1,500 a year man who (because he had virtually no taxable income) paid no income tax. The husband was living according to a standard appropriate to one having not less than £1,200 per annum as free income, after tax had been paid, and the figure of £800 per annum, which had been originally taken by the registrar was certainly too low. The judge had been correct to increase the registrar's award.

Note. Sir Raymond Evershed MR said that the judge had been correct in finding that the husband was a man whose *capabilities* ranked him as a £3,000 a year man who was living according to the standard appropriate to one having not less than £1,200 per annum as free income after tax. The wife had not cross-appealed against the judge's order. Had she done so, might the Court of Appeal perhaps have been inclined to increase the judge's award on the basis that the husband, because of his capabilities, could have paid more? Two points should be noted; firstly, that the husband was not sitting idly by and allowing his talents to go to waste; secondly, that the order appealed against was an interim order only. The authors are accordingly of the opinion that it would have been wrong to have based the award on the assumption that the husband was a £3,000 a year man, because (as the Court of Appeal stated) the correct approach was to assess the husband's ability to pay in the light of his current expenditure. On completion of the developments the award could be (and no doubt was) increased. As Hodson LJ said (at page 620): 'The date when the husband's ambitious schemes will fructify and yield a substantial profit may not be long distant, but the learned judge came to the conclusion, which is not challenged and with which I agree, that no order for maintenance, interim or otherwise, could sensibly be made at this time based on a capital valuation and a notional income attributed thereto.'

2–203 Donaldson v Donaldson

[1958] 2 All ER 660

Assets transferred to third party – looking at the realities. On retiring from the RAF the husband had received a gratuity; he had commuted as much of his pension as possible, and he had handed the whole of the cash which he had thus received to the woman whom he wished to marry. She had purchased a mink farm with the money, which she and the husband ran together, living as man and wife. The husband received no wages but lived rent-free at the farm. The farm did not yet show a profit, and the husband's only income was that portion of his pension which he had not been allowed to commute (amounting to £385 per annum) and £90 per annum payable under an insurance policy, totalling £475 per annum. The wife applied for maintenance on the ground that the husband had wilfully neglected to maintain her and the two children of the family (See now section 27 of the Matrimonial Causes Act 1973 – see Appendix I).

Karminski J said (at page 663): 'I was at one stage doubtful whether I could order a husband to provide maintenance for a wife or children out of capital. I think that there is no objection, either in practice or in law, to such a course when the circumstances permit it. My attention was drawn to the judgment of Lord Merrivale P in *N v N* (2–201) . . . Lord Merrivale dealt with the practical wisdom of the ecclesiastical courts who, he said, were not misled by appearances but looked at the realities. He summed up the matter in this way: "The court not only ascertained what moneys the husband had, but what moneys he could have had if he liked, and the term 'faculties' describes the capacity and the ability of the respondent to provide maintenance." That is the test which, I think, the Court of Appeal approved in *J v J* (2–202) . . .'

The husband was ordered to pay over in maintenance the whole of his remaining income of £475 per annum.

Note. See also *Page v Page* (see Appendix II) and *W v W* (ibid.).

2–204 W v W (No. 3)

[1962] 1 All ER 736

Looking at all the circumstances – looking at the realities. The wife had obtained a decree absolute and a high court judge had made an interim order for maintenance in her favour. The husband now applied to discharge or vary that order.

Scarman J (as he then was) said (at page 737): 'The husband's case is that because of her conduct the wife does not deserve maintenance, and, because of her resources, does not need it. When he passes from attack to defence, he says that, although wealthy in the past, he is now a poor man, beggared by ill-health, ill luck, and the persecution of the wife. The wife's case is that there has been nothing in her conduct to disentitle her to maintenance, that she is in genuine need, living, in the absence of any regular or substantial help from him, by selling her assets, such as her jewellery, on a small income derived from student lodgers in her flat, and on the generosity of her friends and relatives. She is convinced that he is still a man of some wealth, adept at concealing his true financial position and determined to stop at nothing, ready, indeed, to commit perjury, so that he may avoid maintaining her.'

Regarding the husband, his lordship continued (at page 738): 'I do not wholly reject the picture that he paints of his present difficulties and way of life; but I think it is necessary to put them in correct focus. *His ability to pay maintenance must be judged in the light of all his circumstances. Absence of regular income, though an important circumstance, is not, by itself, decisive: J v J* (sub nom. *J–PC v J–AF*) (2–202). *One must look also at the man's mental and physical resources, the money at his disposal, however it may be used, his capital position, and the rate of his current personal expenditure.* I do not pretend this list is exhaustive, but it serves to emphasise the points that the ability of a husband to make provision for a wife falls to be determined not by a cash calculation but by an evaluation of all his circumstances and resources (see *Klucinski v Klucinski* (2–102), *J v J* and *Donaldson v Donaldson* (2–203).'

2–205 Ette v Ette

[1965] 1 All ER 341

(1) *Third party nominally in control of business partnership – looking at the realities.* The husband was living with a Mrs. Johnson in a comfortable and commodious country house belonging to Mrs. Johnson. They were partners in a business which provided a more than adequate income. The wife, who was virtually without money, applied for an order for periodical payments on the ground that the husband had wilfully neglected to provide reasonable maintenance for herself and for their three children (See now section 27 of the Matrimonial Causes Act 1973 – see Appendix I). The husband stated that he worked for a company formed by Mrs. Johnson and received no salary but lived rent free, that he had no official position in the company and could not sign cheques.

Lloyd-Jones J held that in reality, the husband and Mrs. Johnson were living as husband and wife and that the person in charge of the business was the husband, notwithstanding the fact that Mrs. Johnson's signature was required on cheques. Accordingly, a fair estimate of the husband's earnings as the person in control of the business should be taken into account.

His lordship said (at page 344): 'In my judgment it is wholly unrealistic and misleading to view the husband as a man depending for his living on his mistress. At all material times they were living as husband and wife. They have two children of that union and, even more to the present purpose, have been business partners, with the husband in charge of the business and in a position to draw whatever sums he has required at all times and at his bidding. The only sense in which Mrs. Johnson had any say or control was that her signature to cheques was necessary.'

Note. The person who ran the business was the husband, not Mrs. Johnson, and the court was concerned with the husband's earning capacity, not that of Mrs. Johnson. Compare *Lombardi v Lombardi* (2–302) in which the husband's mistress jointly managed the husband's business together with the husband, and in which the Court of Appeal discounted her contribution to the profits.

(2) *Lack of full and frank disclosure.* His lordship further held that in the absence of full and frank information by the husband as to his financial position, the court was entitled to draw inferences adverse to the husband as to his capacity or faculties and to treat him as a man in a position to command a substantial income.

2–206 Brett v Brett

[1969] 1 All ER 1007, CA

Husband divesting himself of assets – looking at the realities. The husband (who did not make a full disclosure of his capital assets and income) formerly had substantial holdings in a group of textile companies, which he had disposed of in order to settle the proceeds on a discretionary trust in the Bahamas, which he said he was not in a position to control and from which (he said) he obtained no benefit. However, the wife informed the court that he had told her that, excluding what he had put into the Bahamas trust, he still had assets in the United Kingdom worth some £50,000. Furthermore, he had become a member of Lloyds (for which he would have to show that he was good for £75,000). He had an income somewhat in excess of £4,000 per annum on the latest figures available. The county court judge had awarded the wife a lump sum, and maintenance of £1,000 per annum.

The Court of Appeal held that, having regard (inter alia) to the advantage to husbands possessed of large capital assets of so arranging their affairs that they had little or no apparent income while still enjoying a high standard of living by the skilful use of their capital assets, and to the possibility of this husband further removing his capital assets out of the jurisdiction, it would be absurd to award maintenance merely on the basis that the husband had an income of something in the region of £4,000 a year. The Court of Appeal increased the award to £2,000 a year.

Note. The wife had an earning capacity of £1,250 per annum.

2–206A Wachtel v Wachtel

[1973] 1 All ER 829, CA

Lack of full and frank disclosure – looking at the realities – looking at husband's expenditure. See case summary 2–104.

Note. See also *Ette v Ette* (2–205).

2–207 Rodewald v Rodewald

[1977] 2 All ER 609, CA

(1) *Children's contributions to household expenses;* (2) *employees' benefits in kind.* See case summary 19–009.

2–208 Cann v Cann

[1977] 3 All ER 957

Interest from investments. See case summary 3–203.

2–209 Cain v Cain

(1976) Times, 4 December

Capital savings. Sir George Baker P said that justices could take into account capital savings of either a husband or wife when considering whether to make or vary a matrimonial order. Capital savings were part of 'all the circumstances'.

3 Husband's resources: relevance of earning capacity of third parties

CASE SUMMARIES

2–301 Grainger v Grainger

[1954] 2 All ER 665

The old law – earning capacity of second wife taken into account. Husband refused to consider suggestion that his present wife might let off surplus rooms so as to increase the family's income. Lord Merriman P said that this suggestion was merely a common-sense comment on the realities of this particular case.

2–302 Lombardi v Lombardi

[1973] 3 All ER 625, CA

The modern law – third party's earnings discounted when calculating one-third ratio. See case summary 19–004.

2–303 Campbell v Campbell

[1977] 1 All ER 1

The modern law – one-third ratio applied without having regard to second wife's earnings – but taken into account in the overall picture. See case summary 6–333.

2–304 Ward v Ward and Greene (sub nom. Ward v Ward)

[1980] 1 All ER 176, CA

The modern law – third party's earnings taken into account in the overall picture. See case summary 6–303.

2–305 Wilkinson v Wilkinson

(1979) 10 Fam Law 48

The modern law – second wife's earnings to be taken into account in the overall picture. Dame Margaret Booth referred to *Grainger v Grainger* (2–301), and said that in order to discharge its duty under section 25 (1) of the Matrimonial Causes Act 1973 (see Appendix I) the Court had to know how the means of the second wife were deployed within the husband's household.

Note. See, however, the Court of Appeal's decision in *Wynne v Wynne* (2–306).

2–306 Wynne v Wynne and Jeffers (sub nom. **W v W**)

[1980] 3 All ER 659, CA

Husband's mistress can be ordered to attend court and give evidence but cannot be ordered to file affidavit of means.   See case summary 6–362.

2–307 Brown v Brown

(1981) Times, 14 July

The modern law – third party's earnings to be excluded.   See Appendix II.

2–308 Macey v Macey

(1981) Times, 14 July

The modern law – third party's earnings to be excluded – but to be taken into account in the overall picture.   See Appendix II.

4   Husband's resources: relevance of social security benefits

CASE SUMMARIES

2–401 Ivory v Ivory

[1954] 1 All ER 898

See case summary 22–000.

2–402 Winter v Winter

(1972) 140 JP Jo 597

See case summary 22–003.

2–403 Williams (LA) v Williams (EM) (sub nom. **Williams v Williams**)

[1974] 3 All ER 377

See case summary 22–005.

2–404 Tovey v Tovey

(1977) 8 Fam Law 80, CA

See case summary 22–008.

2–405 Walker v Walker

(1978) Times, 3 March, 8 Fam Law 107

See case summary 22–008A.

2–406 Fitzpatrick v Fitzpatrick

(1978) 9 Fam Law 16, CA

See case summary 22–009.

2–407 Brown v Brown

(1981) Times, 14 July

See case summary 22–016.

5   Potential earning capacity of the wife

CASE SUMMARIES

2–501 Rose v Rose

[1950] 2 All ER 311, CA

Potential earning capacity of the wife.   The husband was a chief assistant civil engineer with a local authority. The wife, aged 41, had no means of her own and was not trained for any work, and during the period of the marriage, which had lasted for 21 years, she had not been required to earn any money. After the divorce, as a temporary measure, she obtained board and lodgings with a friend who owned a school, where she assisted in cooking meals and her child obtained free education. It was contended for the wife that, in arriving at the amount of maintenance ordered to be paid to her, the judge had wrongly attributed a notional earning capacity to her and based his calculation on the husband's earnings plus that notional figure. The Court of Appeal allowed the wife's appeal.

Denning LJ (as he then was) said: '. . . A very important matter in awarding maintenance is the conduct of the parties. In this case it has been established that the husband broke up the marriage after twenty-one years of married life, leaving the wife with two children, one of them very young. It was a particularly bad case because the husband committed adultery with a Swiss student help who came to the house. After the divorce the wife claimed maintenance, and the question is whether she ought to go out to work. *I agree that no general rule can be laid down on the matter, but this wife is certainly under no legal duty to go out to work in order to reduce the maintenance that her husband should pay. It would be quite unreasonable to expect her to do so when she has to look after a young child. If a wife does earn, then her earnings must be taken into account; or if she is a young woman with no children, and obviously ought to go out to work in her own interest, but does not, then her potential earning capacity ought to be taken into account; or if she has worked regularly during the married life and might reasonably be expected to work after the divorce, her potential earnings ought to be taken into account. Except in cases such as those, however, it does not as a rule lie in the mouth of a wrongdoing husband to say that the wife ought to go out to work simply in order to relieve him from paying maintenance.'*

Note. This was a case under the old law. Under the modern law, conduct is generally ignored. However, the courts are still reluctant, when dealing with an application for maintenance by a wife whose station in life has been such that she has not been required to work during her married life, to suggest that she should now obtain employment. See, for instance, the judgment of the Divisional Court in *Adams v Adams* (2–508).

2–502 Le Roy-Lewis v Le Roy-Lewis

[1954] 3 All ER 57

Potential earning capacity of the wife.   Before the marriage the wife had worked as a shop assistant. The husband was of independent means. The wife applied to the Divisional Court for an order for maintenance, alleging that the husband had wilfully neglected to provide her with reasonable maintenance. The husband contended that, there being no children and the wife being young, there was no reason why she should not return to the position in which she had been prior to the marriage and again go out and earn her living.

Barnard J said: 'It has been suggested that because she was working before the marriage, that because she is still young and there are no children of the marriage, she ought at once to go back into the position she was in before the marriage and start earning her living – as far as I can see with only one object, to reduce the amount of money that the husband should pay her. I do not accept that view at all. She may have been lucky, or at any rate thought that she was lucky at the time, in marrying someone who brought about an improvement in her financial, and, possibly, her social position, but it has been through no fault of hers that their married life together has come to an end and I see no reason whatever why the wife should go back to earning to reduce the husband's liability to maintain her.'

Note. This was a case under the old law. The headnote reads: 'Held: *the marriage having ended through no fault of the wife,* there was no reason why she should go back to earning her living in order to reduce the husband's liability to maintain her.' In *Rose v Rose* (2–501) Denning LJ (as he then was) said: '... it does not as a rule lie in the mouth of a wrongdoing husband to say that the wife ought to go out to work simply in order to relieve him from paying maintenance.' However, Lord Denning prefaced those words with the following: 'If a wife does earn, then her earnings must be taken into account; *or if she is a young woman with no children, and obviously ought to go out to work in her own interest, but does not, then her potential earning capacity ought to be taken into account*; or if she has worked regularly during the married life and might reasonably be expected to work after the divorce, her potential earnings ought to be taken into account. *Except in cases such as those,* however, it does not as a rule lie in the mouth of a wrongdoing husband to say that the wife ought to go out to work simply in order to relieve him from paying maintenance.' Thus it would seem that Lord Denning might have been inclined to take into account the wife's earning capacity even under the old law. However, the courts have always been reluctant, when dealing with an application for maintenance by a wife whose station in life has been such that she has not been required to work during her married life, to suggest that she should now obtain employment. And this is so whether or not she worked prior to the marriage.

2–503 J v J (sub nom. J-PC v J-AF)

[1955] 2 All ER 617, CA

Potential earning capacity of the wife.   This was an appeal by the husband against an order for the payment of interim maintenance. Hodson LJ said (at page 621): 'There remains ... the question whether the learned judge misdirected himself in any way as to the fortune of the wife ... As to her fortune, the wife had worked before her marriage at the age of twenty. After marriage, her position, as found by the judge, was as follows: "... I note that at no stage during her married life did the wife enter into employment outside the matrimonial home, except in so far as she assisted the husband in the joint enterprise of running a country club ... Having regard to her duties towards the children and the fact that the husband was previously earning a considerable salary this is not surprising. After the marriage broke up there came a time when the wife of her own initiative sought training to become a saleswoman with a well-known firm, but this employment she had to give up in August 1954, owing to an operation affecting her feet ... From then onwards there has been a period when she has been unable to work. So far as can be gathered from the evidence she is now available for sedentary work, but so far has secured only a temporary post at £8 a week at the Ideal Home Exhibition. She has no other income ..."

'Having regard to a decision of this court in *Rose v Rose* (2–501) ... the judge stated his conclusion as follows: "I take the view that the wife is not under an obligation in the circumstances to go out and earn, and that if she does obtain employment the husband is not entitled to have the whole amount of what she earns taken into account in any calculations which affect maintenance. On the other hand, I propose to assume that she will work when she can and that there should accordingly be some 'discount' applied to whatever amount would otherwise be ordered against the husband as regards maintenance." I agree with this view.'

Notes

1. The courts are still reluctant, when dealing with an application for maintenance by a wife whose station in life has been such that she has not been required to work during her married life, to suggest that she should now obtain employment. And this is so whether or not she worked prior to the marriage. See, for instance, the judgment of the Divisional Court in *Adams v Adams* (2–508).
2. In *Rove v Rose*, Denning LJ (as he then was) said: 'If a wife does earn, then her earnings must be taken into account'. Hodson LJ's view was that although the wife's earnings must be taken into account, in these circumstances the husband was not entitled to have the whole amount of what she earned taken into account. Hodson LJ's judgment was followed by Sir Jocelyn Simon P in *Attwood v Attwood* (2–505).

2–504 Griffith v Griffith

[1957] 1 All ER 494

Potential earning capacity of the wife. The wife applied for maintenance pending suit. She had worked prior to the marriage but had not worked since then. Sachs J held that although the court had an unfettered discretion to award what sum it considered just, the wife's earning capacity ought not, in the present case, to be taken into account. *The husband's financial position was such that his wife would not normally be expected to go out to work. Rose v Rose* (2–501) and *Le Roy-Lewis v Le Roy-Lewis* (2–502) applied.

Notes

1. The courts are still reluctant, when dealing with an application for maintenance by a wife whose station in life has been such that she has not been required to work during her married life, to suggest that she should now obtain employment. And this is so whether or not she worked prior to the marriage. See, for instance, the judgment of the Divisional Court in *Adams v Adams* (2–508).
2. Surprisingly, *J v J* (2–503) was not referred to in the judgment.

2–505 Attwood v Attwood

[1968] 3 All ER 385

Earnings of the wife and potential earning capacity of the wife. The wife had worked before the marriage but gave up on marrying the husband. She again obtained a job shortly after the separation, earning £9 per week. The magistrates found that the wife had re-commenced employment solely because of the breakdown of the marriage and they ordered the husband to pay her £6 per week, so that her income totalled £15 per week; this reduced the husband's income to £8.15.0 per week. The husband appealed to the Divisional Court.

Sir Jocelyn Simon P said (at page 387): 'The finding of the justices which disturbs me is the final one. It reads as follows:

"Although the [wife] was earning £9 a week at the date when the order was made, she had undertaken this work solely on account of the break-up of the marriage, and the [husband] was not entitled to be relieved of his obligation to maintain the [wife] on account of her own industry."

'Those words, as well as the order that emerged from the figures which I have rehearsed, suggest to me that the justices discounted the whole of the wife's earnings. If they did so, I am satisfied that they misdirected themselves. A scrutiny of the figures also suggests that they plainly went wrong: the wife would, after payment of the maintenance ordered, have some £15 a week income; the husband £8.15.0.

'In my view the general considerations which should be borne in mind in this type of case are as follows . . . (vi) *If the wife is earning an income, or if she has what should in all the circumstances be considered as a potential earning capacity, that must be taken into account . . .*'

The Divisional Court reduced the award to £4.10.0 per week.

Note. Here the wife was in employment following the breakdown of the marriage. In *Rose v Rose* (2–501) Denning LJ (as he then was) said: 'If a wife does earn, then her earnings must be taken into account'. What relevance was the fact that the wife had not been required to work during the marriage? Sir Jocelyn Simon P referred to the judgment of Hodson LJ in *J v J* (2–503) and said that the wife's income need not be wholly brought into account, inter alia, if she would not reasonably have been expected to have obtained employment if the marriage had not been disrupted by the husband.

2–506 Wachtel v Wachtel

[1973] 1 All ER 829, CA

Potential earning capacity of the wife. Giving the unanimous judgment of the Court of Appeal, Lord Denning MR said (at the foot of page 841): '. . . We put the wife's *potential earning capacity* on part-time work as a dental nurse at £15 per week gross – say £750 per annum.'

2–507 Gengler v Gengler

[1976] 2 All ER 81

Earnings of the wife. Sir George Baker P said that the court need not bring into account all the wife's earnings, and that this was so irrespective of whether or not she had worked during the marriage. His lordship cited *Attwood v Attwood* (2–505), and said that it was not correct to say that if the wife had been working during the marriage then the full amount of her earnings were necessarily to be brought into account.

Note. Sir George Baker's assertion that in applying the one-third ratio the husband's *gross* income should be added to the wife's *net* income was disapproved by the Court of Appeal in *Rodewald v Rodewald* (19–009).

2–508 Adams v Adams

(1978) 8 Fam Law 141, 122 Sol Jo 348

Potential earning capacity of the wife. The husband was a company secretary with a salary of £6,600 per year. The wife had not worked since the marriage. The Justices found that the husband had deserted the wife and ordered him to pay her £220 per month maintenance for herself and £50 per month maintenance for the child of the family. A few weeks after the making of the orders the husband resigned from his job on the grounds of ill-health. On the husband's application, the justices accordingly reduced the orders. The wife appealed to the Divisional Court.

Sir George Baker P said (inter alia) that because the wife had not worked since the beginning of the marriage, it was necessary for the husband to prove that there had been such a change in the family circumstances that it was reasonable for the court to consider whether the wife had an earning capacity. Furthermore, where a husband is going to allege that a wife should obtain employment he should make that allegation in the application to vary so that the wife has notice; the husband failed to do this. The justices had accordingly been wrong to give as one of their reasons for reducing the order their conclusion that the wife should obtain employment. The wife's appeal would be allowed and the case remitted to a fresh panel of justices.

2–509 Bateman v Bateman

[1979] 2 WLR 377

Potential earning capacity of the wife – relevance of grave misconduct. See case summary 8–309.

2–510 Ward v Ward and Greene (sub nom. **Ward v Ward**)

[1980] 1 All ER 176, [1980] 1 WLR 4, CA (these notes taken from transcript of shorthand notes of Association of Official Shorthandwriters Limited.)

Potential earning capacity of the wife. The wife, aged 51, had worked substantially throughout the marriage, but shortly after commencing proceedings had given up her employment. Medical evidence was called, the effect of which was that she was suffering from high blood pressure and depression which, at her age, made it very difficult for her to continue to work. Dunn J stated that he felt it would probably be a good thing for her to take part-time employment so as to take her mind off her troubles, but he found it impossible to put any figure on her likely earning capacity.

Speaking of the wife's earning capacity, Dunn J said: 'I find it quite impossible, on the evidence, to put any figure on her likely earning capacity, in view of the evidence of Dr. Frankel; but the fact that she is, in my judgment, probably capable of some such work as I have described, is something that I take into account in considering what financial provision her husband should make her.' Ormrod LJ said: 'With that conclusion I find myself entirely in agreement; it seems to me purely theoretical to attribute any actual cash earning capacity to the wife in the present circumstances – obviously it is very difficult for her to do more than earn very little.'

2–511 Khan v Khan

[1980] 1 All ER 497

Potential earning capacity of wife – Moslem practice. Both parties were Moslems and formerly natives of India, although the wife had come to England at an early age. It was urged on behalf of the wife that it is not Moslem practice for a married woman to go out to earn an income. On appeal to the Divisional Court from the decision of the stipendiary magistrate, Waterhouse J stated that he was unable to accept the argument that he should take judicial notice of the Moslem practice in this regard. It was a matter about which there should be evidence if it was to be relied on as a relevant factor.

2–512 Eshak v Nowojewski

(1980) Times, 19 November, CA

Earning capacity of spouse bringing up children. See case summary 2–108.

6 The young able-bodied wife

CASE SUMMARIES

2–601 Mathias v Mathias

[1972] 3 All ER 1, CA

Divorce on ground of five years' separation – grave financial hardship – loss of widow's pension – young able-bodied wife. See case summary 3–302.

2–602 Graves v Graves

(1973) 4 Fam Law 124, 117 Sol Jo 679

Short childless marriage between young parties.   See case summary 7–231.

2–603 W-S v W-S (sub nom. **Whyte-Smith v Whyte-Smith**)

(1974) Times, 25 October, 119 Sol Jo 46

Short childless marriage between young parties.   See case summary 7–233.

2–604 Khan v Khan

[1980] 1 All ER 497

Short childless marriage between young parties.   See case summary 7–234.

2–605 H v H (15 May 1981)

(1981) Times, 16 May

Short childless marriage between young parties – desirability of the clean break.   See Appendix II.

7   Wife's resources other than her earning capacity

CASE SUMMARIES

2–700 Trippas v Trippas

[1973] 2 All ER 1, CA

Investment income – adjustment of capital position so as to equalise income position.   See case summary 16–101.

2–701 Griffiths v Griffiths

[1974] 1 All ER 932, CA

Investment income – adjustment of capital position so as to equalise income position.   See case summary 15–303.

2–701A Rodewald v Rodewald

[1977] 2 All ER 609, CA

(1) *children's contibutions to household expenses.*

(2) *employees' benefits in kind.*

See case summary 19–009.

2–702 Cain v Cain

(1976) Times, 4 December

Capital savings.   Sir George Baker P said that justices could take into account capital savings of either a husband or wife when considering whether to make or vary a matrimonial order. Capital savings were part of 'all the circumstances'.

8 Wife's resources: relevance of social security benefits

2–801 Barnes v Barnes

[1972] 3 All ER 872, CA

See case summary 19–001A. For further details, see case summary 22–002.

2–802 Reiterbund v Reiterbund

[1975] 1 All ER 280, CA

See case summary 3–403.

2–803 Walker v Walker

(1978) Times, 3 March, 8 Fam Law 107

See case summary 19–012A. For further details, see case summary 22–008A.

2–804 M v M (sub nom. Moon v Moon)

(1979) 10 Fam Law 114

See case summary 19–014.

2–805 C v W

(1980) Times, 16 February

See case summary 19–015.

CHAPTER 3

Pensions, insurance policies etc.

Pensions, savings schemes and life insurance policies are to be taken into account by the court. It would seem that section 25 of the Matrimonial Causes Act 1973 directs the court to have regard to these particular resources by the reference to 'other financial resources' in subsection 1 (a), and in subsection 1 (g) (applicable only to proceedings for divorce or nullity) by the reference to 'the value to either of the parties to the marriage of any benefit (for example, a pension) which, by reason of the dissolution or annulment of the marriage, that party will lose the chance of acquiring'.

In practice, the effect of what might be called these ancillary financial resources is not necessarily complex. Any income under a pension or similar scheme is treated simply as income in the ordinary way.

Alternatively, these ancillary resources may in reality be of a capital nature, such as pension rights commutable to a lump sum or the accrued surrender value of an insurance policy. The court's ability to take full account of all these elements of capital, be they actual or prospective, provides due reflection on the flexibility of the court's powers under the modern legislation. For example, the surrender value of an insurance policy can quite simply be taken into account when making a compilation of the total value of the parties' capital assets. The fact that the benefit of any particular insurance policy may more conveniently reside in the hands of one party rather than the other would then simply mean that the other party is likely to be given credit for this in the overall division of capital. Alternatively, the court may, for example, order that capital invested in a fixed-term savings plan be held on trust for the parties in equal shares. However, recently the Court of Appeal in *Milne v Milne* (3–105) has directed that an order that a husband should execute a life insurance policy on his own life, assign the benefit to his wife and make all payments due thereunder is outside the orbit of the powers given under section 23 (1) (c) of the 1973 Act.

The ability of the court to accommodate the mere prospect of a lump sum retirement benefit again pays tribute to the proper flexibility of the powers under section 23 of the 1973 Act. A husband's prospect of a capital sum on retirement is, by its very nature, usually entirely speculative at the time of the hearing of the remainder of the financial claims. The size of the capital sum is something which is frequently at the husband's own election. The husband may not even survive to qualify for a lump sum. All these contingencies are catered for by the court's power to award a 'lump sum or sums', giving the power to award more than one sum within a single application; there could be an order for an immediate sum and another payable on the happening of a future event – for example, on the payment to the husband of a capital sum on retirement.

1 Pensions, insurance policies etc. as capital assets

CASE SUMMARIES

3–101 Donaldson v Donaldson

[1958] 2 All ER 660

Husband's ability to provide maintenance.   See case summary 2–203.

3–102 Bennett v Bennett

(1978) 9 Fam Law 19, CA

Accrued surrender value of insurance policy treated as a capital asset. Commutable pension rights treated as a capital asset.   See case summary 5–108.

3–103 Richardson v Richardson

(1978) 9 Fam Law 86, CA

Lump sum payable on husband's retirement in three years' time.   See case summary 14–012.

3–104 Priest v Priest

(1978) 9 Fam Law 252, CA

Gratuity contingent on completion of military contract.   Wife awarded lump sum amounting to one-third of current expected value, payable on receipt of gratuity. See case summary 14–013.

    Note. Compare *Milne v Milne* (3–105) – order for payment of share rather than fixed sum.

3–105 Milne v Milne

(1981) Times, 6 February, CA

(1) *Commutable pension rights – form of order.*   The husband was a member of a pension scheme under which on retirement or at pensionable age he could commute one quarter of the pension into a lump sum. On present calculations, this would yield about £16,000. If he died before then, a lump sum of about £15,000 would be payable to his estate. The Court of Appeal ordered that, provided the wife was still alive at the material time, she should receive a lump sum equal to one-half the amount the husband or his estate would be entitled to on his retirement or earlier death.

    Note. The fraction of one-half was not based on any formula. It was simply that their lordships considered that this would be an appropriate amount in this particular case.

(2) *No power to order payment of life insurance premiums.*   The Court of Appeal held that the judge's order that the husband should execute a life insurance policy on his life, assign the benefit to the wife and make all payments due thereunder was outside the ambit of the powers given under section 23 (1) (c) of the Matrimonial Causes Act 1973, to pay 'such lump sum or sums as may be so specified' (see Appendix I).

3–106 Auty, Mills, Rogers and Popow v National Coal Board

(1981) Times, 1 July

Assessing pension losses in accident claims – future inflation disregarded.   Tudor Evans J held that if future inflation was not to be taken into account in claims for loss of future earnings, it should not be taken into account in claims for loss of pension benefits. His lordship valued each claim according to the method used in *Lim Poh Choo v Camden and Islington Area Health Authority* [1979] QB 196, [1979] 2 All ER 910, HL with the variation of using a multiplier at the date of retirement.

Note. In Lim v Camden Health Authority the judge's award in respect of loss of pension rights was not contested. See page 925 at letter h.

2   Pensions as revenue-producing assets

CASE SUMMARIES

3–201 Donaldson v Donaldson

[1958] 2 All ER 660

Husband's ability to provide maintenance.   See case summary 2–203.

3–202 S v S

[1977] 1 All ER 56, CA

Wife nearing retirement – state retirement pension – occupational pension – calculation of one-third ratio.   The parties had married when both were aged over 50. Each had been married previously. The marriage lasted only two years. The husband was a doctor and the wife a part-time teacher. Both were aged 59. The wife had accrued pension rights arising from her employment amounting to £350 per annum. On reaching 60 she would receive the pension of £350 per annum plus the usual state retirement pension of £676 per annum, making a total of about £1,000 a year, or a little over that if the amount of the retirement pension increased. The husband was ordered to make periodical payments of £2,000 per annum less tax, which would give the wife about £3,000 less tax when she retired and got her pensions. This was under one-third of the joint income of the parties, and both parties agreed that this was right in view of the length of the marriage.

3–203 Cann v Cann

[1977] 3 All ER 957

Neither party earning – calculation of one-third ratio.   Following his retirement the husband (aged 67) applied for variation of the magistrates' order made in favour of the wife. He was in receipt of pensions amounting to £23.46 a week and, after paying outgoings of £19.61 plus the £7 maintenance, he had a deficit of £3.15 a week. He had a capital sum of £830, which, if invested, could increase his income by about £1.50 per week, and a car valued at £250. The wife was in receipt of a pension of £13.30 and the maintenance of £7. Her outgoings were £13.37 a week.

On appeal from the magistrates' court, the Divisional Court reduced the award by £2 per week. This would leave the husband with a deficit of £1.15 per week, which could be financed out of interest on his capital sum.

Note. It was held that in cases where neither party is earning the one-third ratio is inappropriate; instead, the court has to look at the parties' needs and see what can best be done in all the circumstances.

3   Relevance on divorce on ground of five years' separation

CASE SUMMARIES

3–301 Parker v Parker

[1972] 1 All ER 410

Divorce on ground of five years' separation – grave financial hardship – wife aged 47 – acceptable alternative proposals – decree granted.   The husband, a police officer, brought a petition for divorce on the ground of five years' separation. The wife, aged 47, opposed the petition on the ground that a divorce would result in grave financial hardship to her in that she would lose her right to a police widow's pension. Cumming-Bruce J held that, although the loss of the pension would amount to grave financial hardship, because the petitioner could afford to compensate the respondent for the loss of her pension rights (either by the purchase of a deferred annuity or by means of a policy producing a specified sum on maturity) the petitioner would be granted a decree nisi.

3–302 Mathias v Mathias

[1972] 3 All ER 1, CA

Divorce on ground of five years' separation – grave financial hardship – young able-bodied wife aged 32 – decree granted.   The husband, a non-commissioned officer in the army, brought a petition for divorce on the ground of five years' separation. The wife, aged 32, opposed the petition on the ground that a divorce would result in grave financial hardship to her in that she would lose her right to an army widow's pension and the state widow's pension. The Court of Appeal held that, bearing in mind the fact that the wife was young and could take a part-time job, the loss of the pensions would not constitute 'grave financial hardship' sufficient to warrant keeping alive an empty shell of a marriage.

Stephenson LJ said that it must be harder for a wife aged 32 to succeed in the statutory defence to a decree on the ground of five years' separation than it is for a wife aged 47: see *Parker v Parker* (3–301). However, this was not to say that no young able-bodied wife could hope to succeed in resisting a petition on this ground.

3–303 Julian v Julian

(1972) Times, 4 October, 116 Sol Jo 763

Divorce on ground of five years' separation – grave financial hardship – wife aged 58 – husband unable to afford adequate compensation for loss of widow's pension – petition dismissed.   The husband, a retired senior police officer, brought a petition for divorce on the ground of five years' separation. The wife, aged 58, opposed the petition on the ground that a divorce would result in grave financial hardship to her in that she would lose her right to a police widow's pension. Cusack J agreed, in view of the fact that the husband was unable to afford adequate compensation to the wife for the loss of the pension. Petition dismissed.

3–304 Lee v Lee

(1973) 117 Sol Jo 616

Divorce on ground of five years' separation – grave financial hardship – wife aged 62 – alternative proposals not acceptable in the circumstances – petition dismissed.   The husband, a retired civil servant aged 67, brought a petition for divorce on the ground of five years' separation. The wife, aged 62, opposed the petition on the ground that a divorce would result in grave financial or other hardship to her in that she would lose her right to a civil servant's widow's pension. The husband proposed that the matrimonial home should be sold and the wife be given half the proceeds of sale, that he should pay the wife periodical payments and buy her an annuity to compensate her for the loss of this pension. Stirling J said that the husband's proposals were not ungenerous. However, his lordship was forced to come to the conclusion that the wife would suffer grave hardship (whether it was called financial hardship or other hardship) because of the difficulty of rehousing herself and her invalid son. The local authority had not been helpful. If and when the circumstances changed the husband would be able to present a fresh petition. Petition dismissed.

3–305 Brickell v Brickell

[1973] 3 All ER 508, CA

Divorce on ground of five years' separation – grave financial hardship – wife aged 58 – loss of widow's pension of £232 per annum – decree granted. The husband brought a petition for divorce on the ground of five years' separation. The wife, who was nine years older than the husband and then aged 58, opposed the petition on the ground that it would result in grave financial hardship to her in that she would lose her right to a civil servant's widow's pension of £232 per annum.

When the suit was originally heard before Cusack J the wife had not at that stage filed an answer to the petition. Cusack J granted the husband a decree nisi on the basis that he had no pension rights which would affect his widow, and he granted leave to the wife to apply to the court to rescind the decree nisi if such rights were subsequently discovered. It was only thereafter that evidence came to light of a pension which the husband would receive from his former employment in the Ministry of Defence which would give pension rights to his widow. The wife accordingly filed an answer to the husband's petition alleging grave financial hardship. When the suit came before Park J on the wife's application to rescind the decree nisi, he in effect reheard the husband's petition. He found that the wife would suffer grave financial hardship by the loss of the pension, but that nevertheless, in all the circumstances, it would not be wrong to dissolve the marriage.

The wife appealed to the Court of Appeal, contending (inter alia) that, having come to the conclusion that she would suffer grave financial hardship, the judge had erred in holding that it would not be wrong to dissolve the marriage. Her appeal was dismissed.

3–306 Carpenter v Carpenter

(1973) 3 Fam Law 169, CA

Divorce on ground of five years' separation – grave financial hardship – practice. The husband brought a petition for divorce on the ground of five years' separation. The wife signed an acknowledgement of service indicating her intention to oppose the petition on the ground that a divorce would result in grave financial hardship to her in that she would lose pension rights of £4 a week. She applied for legal aid but was not granted a legal aid certificate until two days before the hearing and was unable to file her answer in time. The wife appealed against the grant of the decree nisi and applied for leave to file an answer out of time. The Court of Appeal held that the judge ought to have stood the case out of the list. Appeal allowed.

3–307 Le Marchant v Le Marchant

[1977] 3 All ER 610, CA

Divorce on ground of five years' separation – grave financial hardship – (1) index-linked pension (2) practice. The husband, who was employed by the Post Office and was about to retire, brought a petition for divorce on the ground of five years' separation. The wife filed an asnwer opposing the petition on the ground that a divorce would result in grave financial hardship to her in that she would lose her right to a widow's pension under the husband's occupational pension scheme. At the time of the appeal this was worth £1,300 a year; it was index-linked and therefore protected against inflation. By his reply the husband pleaded that he had made reasonable proposals to mitigate that hardship but that the wife had rejected them. The correspondence containing the husband's proposals was not served with the pleadings and was not produced by the husband at the hearing of the petition.

The Court of Appeal held that, at the conclusion of the hearing before the judge, the wife had established a prima facie case of grave financial hardship and the husband had not rebutted that case; accordingly the judge should have dismissed the petition, or at least adjourned the case and warned the husband that unless he produced reasonable proposals to relieve the wife's hardship the petition would be dismissed.

However, at the appeal the husband had put forward proposals to mitigate the wife's financial hardship. These were that his interest in the matrimonial home be transferred to the wife forthwith, that he should pay her a lump sum of £5,000 when he received the capital sum payable to him on his retirement, and that he should take out a life insurance policy on his life to provide the wife with a further lump sum of £5,000 on his death if she survived him. The Court of Appeal agreed that these proposals were reasonable. Accordingly, the decree granted by the judge would be allowed to stand, on the formal undertaking of the husband to implement those proposals.

Note. The Court of Appeal held that, where an answer to a petition alleges that a decree would result in grave financial hardship to the respondent, the onus is in the first place on the respondent to set up a prima facie case of grave financial hardship. The respondent having shown a prima facie case, the petition should be dismissed unless the petitioner can meet the answer in his reply, by putting forward a proposal which is acceptable to the court as reasonable in the circumstances and which is sufficient to remove the element of grave financial hardship.

3–308 **Purse v Purse**

[1981] 2 All ER 465, CA

Divorce on ground of five years' separation – grave financial hardship – wife's loss of pension rights by being divorced without her knowledge – decrees granted to dead husband set aside. The husband filed a petition for divorce on the ground of five years' separation. He did not know the wife's whereabouts. He swore an affidavit, stating that he had not seen her since she left the matrimonial home over ten years ago and exhibiting an enquiry agent's report that he had been unable to trace her. On the basis of the affidavit and supporting documents, and without further enquiry, the registrar made an order dispensing with service. Decrees nisi and absolute were pronounced without the wife's knowledge. The husband then died.

The wife's application for the decrees to be set aside was granted by the Court of Appeal. The wife had suffered a serious injustice in that she had been divorced by her husband without her knowledge and, in consequence, had lost her rights to a widow's pension from her husband's employers. The husband's efforts to discover the wife's whereabouts had been quite inadequate. Since the petition never came to the wife's notice by reason of service being dispensed with after inadequate enquiry by both the husband and the registrar, and since the wife would have had a serious prospect of resisting the decree nisi (under section 5 of the Matrimonial Causes Act 1973) and the decree absolute (under section 10 of the Act), the case was one in which the discretion of the court should be exercised in favour of setting both decrees aside. There was no reason for the intervening death to restrict the court's power to do this. Decree nisi and decree absolute rescinded.

4 Divorce on ground of five years' separation: relevance of social security benefits

CASE SUMMARIES

3–401 Dorrell v Dorrell

[1972] 3 All ER 343

Divorce on ground of five years' separation – grave financial hardship – (1) loss of widow's pension (2) social security benefits. The husband brought a petition for divorce on the ground of five years' separation. The wife, aged over 60 and living on social security benefits, opposed the petition on the ground that a divorce would result in grave financial hardship to her in that *she would lose her right to a widow's pension of £2 per week from her husband's employers.* Sir George Baker P said that the fact that social security is available to a wife is not a reason for a man refusing to carry out, or being excused from carrying out, his obligations to maintain his wife. The fact that such maintenance as he can pay will go to repay in whole or in part the social security paid to the wife is not a reason for reducing the sum which the husband ought to pay. When a woman is living on £6 or £8 a week, £2 a week is a third or a quarter of her income. The loss of this pension, small though it is, would be grave financial hardship to the wife.

However, the petition was adjourned rather than dismissed so as to give the husband the opportunity of making proposals for financial provision for the wife.

Note. Disapproved in *Reiterbund v Reiterbund* (3–403), in which Megaw LJ said: '. . . Sir George Baker P appears to have taken the view that supplementary benefit or other social security benefit ought, as a matter of principle, to be ignored in deciding the question of "grave financial hardship" under section 5 of the 1973 Act. I am far from sure that Sir George Baker P was indeed intending to state that as being a principle. The facts in *Dorrell v Dorrell* were different from the facts with which we are here concerned, and, it may be, materially different. But, if and insofar as anything which was said in that case ought to be construed to mean that, on the facts such as exist in the present case, the fact and the amount of supplementary benefit must be ignored in assessing financial hardship under section 5, I would respectfully disagree. I agree with Finer J's conclusion that, on the facts of the present case, there cannot be grave, or indeed any, financial hardship to the wife, by reason of the divorce decree, because, *in the event of the husband's death . . . while the wife would lose the contribution from public funds consisting of the widow's benefit, she would be entitled to a larger contribution from public funds consisting of supplementary benefit.*'

3–402 Burvill v Burvill '

(1974) 4 Fam Law 121

Divorce on ground of five years' separation – grave financial hardship – (1) loss of widow's pension (2) national insurance contributions (3) social security benefits. The husband, a local authority employee earning £25 per week, brought a petition for divorce on the ground of five years' separation. The wife, who was employed as a part-time cleaner at a wage of £7 per week and who paid 4p per week under the national insurance scheme, opposed the petition on the ground that a divorce would result in grave financial hardship to her in that she would have to pay an increased national insurance contribution of £1.67 per week and *would lose her right to a local authority's widow's pension of £192 per annum.*

Ormrod J (as he then was) rejected her answer to the petition and granted the husband a decree nisi for the following reasons. Firstly, the change in the amount of national insurance contributions payable would affect all divorced wives under the age of 60; the increased contributions could not properly be regarded as grave financial hardship and should not be allowed to frustrate the intention of the modern divorce legislation. Secondly, to compensate the wife for the loss of the widow's pension the husband would have to pay £3 a week to an insurance company in order to purchase her an annuity, which he could not afford to do. He was at present paying her £4.75 a week under a magistrates' order. His offer to pay her £4.75 a week while he was earning and £3 a week after his retirement was the best that could be arranged in the circumstances. If, following the husband's death, the state retirement pension proved inadequate for the widow's support she would be entitled to social security benefit; this being the case, any local authority widow's pension would simply reduce the amount of the social security benefit. His lordship said that it was doubtful whether the courts could go on ignoring the availability of social security benefits; otherwise the beneficent provisions of the new divorce legislation would be withheld from those with limited means.

3–403 Reiterbund v Reiterbund

[1975] 1 All ER 280, CA

Divorce on ground of five years' separation – grave financial hardship – (1) loss of state widow's pension (2) state retirement pension (3) supplementary benefits. The husband brought a petition for divorce on the ground of five years' separation. The wife opposed the petition on the ground that a divorce would result in grave financial hardship to her in that *she would lose her right to the state widow's pension.*

The wife, aged 52, lived on supplementary benefits of £7.75 a week, out of which she paid £4.55 for her keep to a charitable institution which was looking after her. It was unlikely that she would be capable of supporting herself financially.

The husband, aged 54, was himself dependent for the most part on state benefits. He was disabled. It was similarly unlikely that he would be capable of supporting himself financially in the future either.

Finer J found that the wife would not suffer grave financial hardship since the supplementary benefits to which she was entitled (then £7.75 per week) would not be less than the widow's pension (then £6.75 per week up to the age of 60) which she would lose the chance of acquiring. The wife appealed contending, inter alia, that in determining whether she would suffer grave financial hardship the court was not entitled to take account of the social security benefits.

The Court of Appeal affirmed Finer J's decision. The loss of the wife's right to a widow's pension would only occur on the husband's death. The husband being dead, there could be no question of public funds being used to relieve him of his duty to maintain her. Accordingly, there was no reason to ignore the wife's right to social security benefits. Since the sums which she would receive in supplementary benefits after his death would not be less than those which she would otherwise receive in the form of a widow's pension, it could not be said that she would suffer any financial hardship as a result of the divorce.

Ormrod LJ said (at page 287): 'The case as it was presented to the learned judge below seems to have been put on the general proposition which is often put forward – that, as a result of the divorce, the wife would lose her widow's pension. The first thing to be noticed about the learned judge's judgment, I think, in this context, is the distinction which he draws, and which is now accepted as entirely valid, between the widow's pension, properly so called, and the retirement pension; because, as he fully demonstrates and counsel for the wife now accepts, after the wife has reached the age of 60 the dissolution of her marriage will not have any adverse effect on her retirement pension situation, on the facts of this case. On the other hand, the learned judge pointed out the different considerations which concern the widow's pension, the widow's pension being a pension which is payable on widowhood and, on facts like these at any rate, which becomes absorbed in the retirement pension at the age of 60.'

He continued (at page 288): 'In the event that the husband dies during the next eight years and the marriage is still subsisting, the widow (as she would be then) would receive £6.75, plus any increments subsequently ordered by the government, by way of widow's pension, and, by way of supplementary benefit, such sum as brought her up to whatever is the going rate for supplementary benefit at the time. If, on the other hand, her marriage had been dissolved, she would continue to receive precisely the same sum . . . from social security. So that she would be in precisely the same financial position as to income whether her marriage was dissolved or whether it was not.'

PART 2

CHAPTER 4

Overriding requirements of dependent children

It will be suggested in Chapter 5 that one of the greatest factors influencing the distribution of matrimonial assets is the very large emphasis that is to be placed by the courts on the provision of homes. However, if there is one consideration which is more than emphatic and might be said to be paramount, it is the need to consider what are herein described as the 'overriding requirements of dependent children'. Accordingly, it may safely be stated that in nearly every case which comes before the courts where there are children, there is a simple and unalterable starting point. It is that the availability of the house as a home for the wife and children should ordinarily be ensured while the children are being educated. The reason for this clear policy is self-evident. But as well as the desire to protect children as much as possible from the consequences of divorce, there may also be seen to be a desire on the part of many courts to protect and compensate the party (usually the wife) who is left with the financial, mental and physical burden of caring for the children of the family.

1   A home for the children

A. *Proceedings under Matrimonial Causes Act 1973*

CASE SUMMARIES

4–101 Mesher v Mesher (sub nom. Mesher v Mesher and Hall)

(1973) Times, 13 February, [1980] 1 All ER 126n, CA

Sale not to take place until child has reached age 17 or until further order.   The former matrimonial home had been purchased by the husband and wife in joint names in 1966 for £6,750. There was £3,500 outstanding on mortgage in June 1970 when the husband left to go to live with Mrs. Hall, with whom he had been committing adultery since 1968. The wife remained in the house with the child of the marriage, a girl approaching nine.

The house where the husband was now living with Mrs. Hall was bought in April 1971 for £6,200 in their joint names. Mrs. Hall had provided £3,000, the balance being covered by a mortgage. The husband and Mrs. Hall, who was free to marry, intended to marry when the decree was made absolute. The wife intended to marry a Mr. Jones, who was also free to marry. He was previously married and had to support his former wife. He had no house, having transferred his former matrimonial home to his former wife.

The husband appealed against an order transferring the former matrimonial home wholly to the wife.

Davies LJ said that the income positions of the two families – treating the husband and Mrs. Hall as one family and the wife and Mr. Jones as another, which was convenient in view of the impending marriages – were remarkably similar. One had to take a broad approach to the whole case. *What was wanted here was to see that the wife and daughter, no doubt together with Mr. Jones in the near future, should have a house in which to live rather than that the wife should have a large sum of available capital.* With that end in view, his Lordship had come to the conclusion that it would be wrong to strip the husband entirely of any interest in the house. He would set aside the judge's order so far as concerned the house and substitute a declaration that it was to be held by the parties in equal shares on trust for sale, and that it was not to be sold until the child of the marriage reached a specified age or with the leave of the Court. Cairns and Stamp LJJ agreed. The wife was ordered to discharge all outgoings, including mortgage interest; any capital repayments to be discharged equally by the husband and wife.

Appeal allowed. Transfer order set aside. Order that the matrimonial home to be held on trust for sale to hold the net proceeds of sale and rents and profits until sale in equal shares, provided that as long as the child of the marriage be under the age of 17 or until further order the house not be sold; the wife to be at liberty to live there rent-free, paying and discharging all rates, taxes and outgoings, including mortgage interest, and indemnifying the husband therefor; any repayments of capital to be borne in equal shares.

Note. *Mesher* orders are not always appropriate – see *Carson v Carson* (5–115).

4–102 Chamberlain v Chamberlain

[1974] 1 All ER 33, CA

A home for grown-up children – sale not to take place until children have completed full-time education or thereafter without consent. Following the separation the wife was living in the former matrimonial home with the three children. Scarman LJ (as he then was) said, at page 39: '. . . *I am satisfied that it would be wrong to sell the house at any rate before the children have completed their full-time education. When that moment comes, there may well be a difference of interest between the husband and wife. One cannot tell, but it is possible that at that time the wife will want to go on living in the house and providing a sort of family centre for her grown-up children and, conceivably, for their families.* This is a very human wish. On the other hand, the husband has an interest: he may wish, and again legitimately wish, to realise his capital at that time . . .'

'Nobody at this date can say what would be the appropriate order in those circumstances. The order that I would propose, in respect to the delaying of the sale of this house, is that the house should not be sold until the children have completed their full-time education *or thereafter without either the consent of the parties or the order of the court.*'

Appeal allowed. Order below varied by declaring that the beneficial interest in the former matrimonial home be jointly held in the proportions of two-thirds to the wife and one-third to the husband, to be so held on trust for sale, such sale not to take place until every child of the family has ceased to receive full-time education, or thereafter without the consent of the parties or order of the court.

Notes
1. Compare Ormrod LJ's judgment in *Hanlon v Hanlon* (4–106): '. . . A family like this will not simply dissolve completely on the 17th birthday of the youngest child. In fact, of course, [the wife] will be, as the mother of this family, maintaining the nucleus of the home effectively for a considerable number of years until the girls are married and settled on their own, and the boys are similarly married and settled on their own; that is what it really means in real life.'
2. In view of the decision in *Martin v Martin* (5–103) it is now very unlikely that on any application by such a husband when the children have completed their full-

time education that the court would order a sale, unless the wife will have enough capital to rehouse herself out of the sale proceeds or has other secure accommodation available.

4-103 Allen v Allen

[1974] 3 All ER 385, CA

A home for the children – form of order. Buckley LJ said (at page 387): 'The form of order made by the learned judge was this. He first of all granted joint custody of the two boys to the husband and the wife – and no attack is made upon that part of the order on this appeal – with care and control to the wife, and ordered that the matrimonial home should be transferred by the husband to the wife and himself on trust for sale, in trust for themselves in equal shares, directing that the property should remain unsold until such time as Nigel, the younger boy, should reach the age of 17 or finish his full time education, whichever date should be earlier. *The learned judge then ordered that the husband should leave the matrimonial home within two months from the date of the order.* There then followed an order for payments for maintenance of the two boys, and a direction that from the time that the husband left the matrimonial home, the wife should be responsible for making the mortgage repayments of £22 monthly in respect of the house and for paying all other outgoings.

'That form of order has been attacked by counsel for the husband on the ground that the judge had no power, as he submits, under any of the statutory provisions that are available, to order the husband to leave the matrimonial home; *and he says that this was not a case in which circumstances existed in which the granting of a mandatory injunction of that kind would be justified.* The case which was referred to in the course of the argument was *Hall v Hall* (4-202). *It has not really been suggested that this is the type of case for a mandatory injunction requiring one spouse to leave the matrimonial home in order that the other spouse might be able to live there in tolerable conditions.* What is said is that under section 42 of the Matrimonial Causes Act 1973 the court has jurisdiction to "make such order as it thinks fit for the custody and education of any child of the family under the age of 18"; and it is also said that under section 24 of the 1973 Act the judge had power to make such an arrangement as he considered to be a proper arrangement in the present case. For my own part, I do not find very much assistance from section 42.

'An order excluding one spouse from beneficial enjoyment of the matrimonial home does not seem to me to fit very conveniently into the description of "such order as the court thinks fit for the custody or education of any child". *But it does seem to me that under section 24 (1) (b) it was within the judge's power to so arrange matters that the objective which he thought was a practical solution to this problem should be attained . . .*'

His lordship continued (at page 389): '*Taking all the circumstances into consideration, I have come to the conclusion that the solution favoured by the learned judge was in fact a solution which would be most satisfactory for these boys in particular and for the family as a whole.* I think the judge, therefore, arrived at the right conclusion. But I think it would be better that his order should be varied in its terms (the precise drafting can be considered later) to provide that the former matrimonial home should be transferred to the husband and wife, to be held on trust for sale, with a direction that the sale should not take place until the younger child had attained the age of 17 years, or had finished his full time education, whichever date should be the earlier, without either the consent of both the parents or under an order of the court, *and that during that limited period the property should be held in trust for the wife to the exclusion of the husband for the purpose of her providing a home there for the children of the family, and, in particular, the two boys, and that at the expiration of that limited period it should then be held on trust for the two spouses in equal shares.*

'Now it would follow from that that the husband would no longer have any right to reside in the home during the limited period which I have referred to, and I think it right that the order should be so framed as to give him a reasonable time to get out. The learned judge ordered him to leave within two months from the date of his order, and I think it would be right, if the order is altered on the lines I suggest, that he should still be given a reasonable time, whatever might now be a reasonable time, to find other accommodation and to make his move.'

Note. Hall v Hall was a case in which the Court of Appeal allowed the husband's appeal against the grant of an injunction excluding him from the matrimonial home *pending determination of the suit for judicial separation brought by the wife*, because there was no evidence that the order was necessary for the wife's protection or that it was in the children's interests.

4–104 Browne v Pritchard

[1975] 3 All ER 721, CA

A home for children by a former association. The matrimonial home was purchased for £4,500 in 1968 and conveyed into joint names; the husband borrowed £500 from his parents and invested the proceeds of sale of a house owned by him prior to the marriage, and the rest was borrowed on mortgage. In 1971 the wife left the house taking the youngest child with her. The husband stayed in the house with the two elder children of the family *who were his by a former association.*

The judge at first instance held that the wife, who was living on social security in a council house, had a one-third interest in the house, and made an order for its sale unless the husband, who was also on social security, paid £1,885, the value of her interest in the house, to her within six months.

The husband's appeal was allowed. *The house was needed as a home for the two elder children*; the wife's joint interest should be replaced by a charge in her favour for one-third of the net proceeds of sale, the charge not to be realised until six months after the younger of the two elder children became 18, with liberty to apply for the charge to be realised sooner if circumstances made that desirable.

The judge at first instance said:

> 'Although the wife is joint owner, it would not be right to say that she should be entitled to a half interest. The marriage only lasted three years and [the husband] owned the previous house, the proceeds of sale of which provided the deposit. One third is the proper proportion: see *Wachtel v Wachtel.*' (14–001)

Lord Denning MR said: 'I think the judge was quite entitled to assess it at one-third. But the question arises as to when and how the wife should receive her one-third.' He continued (at page 723): '*Section 25 of the 1973 Act requires the court, so far as practicable, to place the parties in the financial position in which they would have been if the marriage had not broken down. Now this wife, if the marriage had continued, would never have received her share in cash at all. She would have remained with the family in the house looking after the children until they were all grown up. It was she who left the house. The husband and the two boys are still there. It is their home. They have nowhere else to go. And although the wife's new husband has deserted her, she is quite well off. She has a council house and is being maintained by the state. So each has a home. In the circumstances it would not be right to order a sale of the house at this stage.*'

4–104A Potts v Potts

(1976) 6 Fam Law 217, CA

A home for children of husband's new wife by her previous husband – interests of husband's second family equal to interests of husband's first family – delay in applying for financial relief – further delay in hearing of appeal – circumstances altering during passage of time.   The parties were married in June 1961. There were two children of the family, born in June 1963 and June 1965 respectively. In March 1971 the wife left the home, taking the children with her, and rented a one-bedroomed flat, where she and the two girls were still living at the time of the appeal before the Court of Appeal. Such accommodation was obviously unsatisfactory, yet there was a history of delay on the part of the wife in bringing the matter before the court.

The wife's petition for divorce was filed in August 1972. Cross decrees were granted in March 1973. The wife obtained custody of the children. At the hearing in March 1973 the wife obtained leave to include in her petition a prayer for a transfer and/or settlement of property order in respect of the matrimonial home. In the November of that year, no application for such an order having been made by the wife, the husband made application to the court for determination of the matter. It was then over 2½ years since the wife had left the home.

In March 1975, i.e. four years after the wife had left the home, the case came before the county court judge. The judge ordered the husband to pay the wife a lump sum of £7,500 as consideration for the wife's interest in the property being extinguished. The husband failed to pay the sum within the time stipulated, and the wife applied to another county court judge for the property to be transferred into her name. The judge made an order that the wife should have the use and occupation of the property until the younger child attained the age of eighteen. Both parties appealed to the Court of Appeal.

The case came before the Court of Appeal in February 1976. It was now five years since the wife had left the home. Much of the delay had been unavoidable, but the Court of Appeal considered that the wife's delay in pursuing her claim was of relevance, if only because of the fact that with the passing of time the circumstances of the case had altered. *The husband had now remarried. His new wife was living with him in the former matrimonial home together with the two children of her former marriage. The house was now their home, and it would be a hard thing to drive them from it. The husband had made an offer to pay the wife a lump sum not exceeding £8,100 in order to enable her to purchase a new home. It being agreed that a three-bedroomed semi-detached house could be purchased in the vicinity for such a sum, the Court of Appeal ordered that the wife's interest in the former matrimonial home should be extinguished on payment of this amount.*

Stamp LJ said that, had the wife's application come before the court within a reasonable time after her departure from the matrimonial home, no court could have properly refused her the relief she sought. The question arose, therefore, whether the court ought now to make the order which would have been made had the matter come before a court within a reasonable time. His lordship thought not. In the first place, the home had to all intents and purposes ceased to be the children's home. Five years was a very long time in the life of a child. Secondly, after five years the house had inevitably become very much more the husband's home; and his lordship agreed with the county court judge that it would be unfair to the husband to turn him out after all this time unless there were no other satisfactory alternative from the point of view of the wife. Thirdly, it would be wrong to ignore the fact that the home had become the home of the husband's new wife and her children, and it would be a hard thing to drive them from it.

Counsel for the wife had urged that the wife and her children ought not to be prejudiced by the delay in pursuing her claim; but the answer to that (said his lordship) was that with the passing of time there had inevitably emerged a new situation. Nor was it as though the wife and children were going to have to live in the very limited and unsatisfactory situation of the last five years. One of the agreed facts in the case was that a three-bedroomed semi-detached house with central heating but without a garage in the same locality as the matrimonial home could be purchased for £8,100. If, therefore, the wife received £8,100 she would be able to buy a not too unsatisfactory house which would be hers even after the younger child attained the age of eighteen; she would not be turned out of it as she would be out of the matrimonial home upon that event.

Before the county court judge, the husband had said that he would pay such sum as the court thought right, with a ceiling of £8,100. His lordship would allow the appeal to the extent of substituting for the figure of £7,500 in the original order the sum of £8,100.

Notes

1. Delay alone was not the ground of this decision. With the passing of time resulting from the wife's delay in applying for financial relief and the further delay in the hearing of the appeal the circumstances of the case had changed. The result was that when the appeal was heard the court had the interests of two sets of children to consider, not one.

2. See *Backhouse v Backhouse* (4–105) for a further example of the court considering the needs of the husband's new family.

4–105 Backhouse v Backhouse

[1978] 1 All ER 1158

A home for child of husband's by his new wife. The marriage broke down owing to the adulterous affair of the wife. Both parties remarried, the husband remaining in the former matrimonial home with the younger child of the marriage, now 13. (The elder child was now married.) The wife was now living in a new house she had purchased together with the co-respondent. Balcombe J held that, having regard to the substantial contribution made by the wife to the purchase of the former matrimonial home, it would be repugnant to deprive her of all interest in it. However, it would also be repugnant to justice if her interest were to be such that the husband would be required to sell the house, *which was required as a home for himself and the younger child of the marriage and for his new wife and her child.* Justice would be done by giving the wife a share in the house, but not by reference to any increase in its value which had occurred after she had left the husband. Husband ordered to pay a lump sum of £3,500 which, having regard to his income, he would be able to raise by mortgage without crippling him financially.

Note. See also *Potts v Potts* (4–104A).

4–106 Hanlon v Hanlon

[1978] 2 All ER 889, CA

A home for grown-up children – Mesher v Mesher (4–101) distinguished. The matrimonial home had been purchased in the sole name of the husband although during the 14 years of the marriage the husband and wife had contributed equally in money and work to the family. The parties separated in 1971 and had now lived apart for over five years. *The wife remained in the house with the four children while the husband, a police officer, now lived in a flat provided rent-free by his employers. The judge at first instance ordered that the house be transferred into joint names on trust for sale in equal shares, the sale to be postponed until the youngest child, then 12, had attained 17.*

Ormrod LJ said that it was not right to regard the interests of the husband and wife in the house as being equal because the wife had, in the five years since the separation, maintained it and looked after the family and would continue to do so until they left home, and had therefore made a very large contribution to the family. *As one-half of the equity on the eventual sale of the house could not produce a sum sufficient to enable the wife to buy another home for herself and such of the children as were still with her, it would be wrong to make an order which would have the result of forcing the wife to leave the house when the youngest child attained the age of 17. As she was willing to forgo any further periodical payments for the two children who were under 17 the proper order was to transfer the house to the wife absolutely.*

Ormrod LJ at page 893: '*I think it is right to say once again that the* Mesher v

Mesher *type of order is not, in a great many cases, a satisfactory way of solving these cases. The facts in* Mesher v Mesher *(4–101) were very different; in that case both parties had in fact remarried before the case came before the court, and the primary concern in the case was to preserve the home for the children.*

'In my judgment it is as well in this case to have another look at the history. Up to now everybody has been approaching the case on the footing that the interests of these two parties in this property were equal. That seems to me to be a doubtfully accurate assumption, or premise. Putting them as shortly as I can, the facts are these. Over 14 years of cohabitation these two parties no doubt contributed broadly equally to this family in terms of money, in terms of work and so on. From 1971 onwards, that is now for over five years, the wife has had the upbringing of these four children and has been working full time as a community nurse. She has maintained the house as well as she could during those years, and on any view she has taken a considerable load off the shoulders of the husband over a period of five years, and she will continue to take a large load off his shoulders from now until the youngest child leaves home, which of course will not necessarily by any manner of means be in five years' time. *A family like this will not simply dissolve completely on the 17th birthday of the youngest child. In fact, of course, she will be, as the mother of this family, maintaining the nucleus of the home effectively for a considerable number of years until the girls are married and settled on their own, and the boys are similarly married and settled on their own; that is what it really means in real life.* So in my view she has made a very large contribution to this family. She has much less good prospects than the husband's so far as her future is concerned, because he will be able to retire when he is 58 and, like many police officers, will be able to take other employment, certainly for another seven years or maybe longer if he wishes. He is a completely free agent so far as his life is concerned; he is living to all intents and purposes a bachelor existence, at the moment contributing £7 per week, under the judge's order, for each of these two children. As I have said before, on any view £7 a week for girls, one of 14 and one of 12, is manifestly inadequate to cover the cost of feeding and clothing and all the other expenses which are unavoidable.

'So the view I take of the case is that, as the cards have fallen, apart no doubt from his being unhappy at being on his own, in financial terms he has done a lot better than his wife, and is likely to go on doing a lot better than his wife.'

Counsel for the husband argued that it was essential that the husband should, to use his own phrase, get on the 'property escalator' as soon as possible, and that the best way of doing this was for the wife to raise £5,000 on mortgage to pay to the husband so that he could purchase a house on mortgage. But there was no clear evidence that the husband had any intention whatever of giving up his police flat so long as his employment in the police force continued.

Notes

1. Compare the judgment of Scarman LJ (as he then was) in *Chamberlain v Chamberlain* (4–102): '. . . I am satisfied that it would be wrong to sell the house at any rate before the children have completed their full-time education. When that moment comes, there may well be a difference of interest between the husband and wife. One cannot tell, but it is possible that at that time the wife will want to go on living in the house and providing a sort of family centre for her grown-up children and, conceivably, for their families.'
2. The wife was not precluded from applying for variation of the order for maintenance of the children, which was not discharged but was reduced to a nominal sum. The principle of the clean break does not apply as far as maintenance for children is concerned. See note 6 to the summary of *Minton v Minton* at 10–205.
3. Regarding the wife's acceptance of a clean break in this case see notes to case summary 10–102.

4–107 Scott v Scott

[1978] 3 All ER 65, CA

Sale not to take place until children have reached age 18 or ceased full-time education, whichever is the later.   There were three children of the marriage, twin girls aged 4 and a boy aged 6. The wife was residing with the children in the former matrimonial home while the husband was living in a bed-sitting room. The house had been purchased in the husband's name the year before the marriage with the aid of a mortgage granted to the husband by his employers at an unusually low rate of interest. Both parties had contributed to the deposit, and the wife had worked and contributed to the family expenses until the birth of the eldest child. The wife had capital of her own of £2,000.

The registrar ordered that the house be settled on trust for sale, the sale to be postponed until the younger children attained 18 or ceased full-time education whichever was later, i.e. in effect postponing the sale for some 14 years, and that on the sale of the property the proceeds were to be divided as to 60 per cent for the husband and 40 per cent for the wife. The county court judge having affirmed the registrar's order, the husband appealed to the Court of Appeal.

The Court of Appeal also upheld the order in respect of the house. The order would enable the wife, with the help of her own capital, to be in a slightly better capital position than the husband when the house was sold in about 14 years' time, in order to compensate her for the fact that she would not be in as strong a position as the husband to raise a mortgage and rehouse herself; the husband, who would then be 45, would have less difficulty in obtaining a mortgage. The division of the capital had nothing to do with the one-third ratio; it was an attempt to deal with the rehousing of the parties in 14 years' time after the children had grown up.

The court expressed sympathy for the husband, who was living in poor accommodation, but the wife's standard of living in the former matrimonial home was also extremely restricted; this was a 'small income situation' and a 'small capital situation'; the house had first to be appropriated for the use of the children and the parent who had the responsibility of bringing them up; in this case, the wife.

4–107A Porter v Porter

(1978) 8 Fam Law 143, CA

A home for children of husband's by his new wife.   See case summary 1–407.
   Note. See also *Potts v Potts* (4–104A).

4–108 Bateman v Bateman

[1979] 2 WLR 377

'Guilty wife' – mortgage repayments, maintenance and repairs.   The wife inflicted a serious chest wound on the husband with a knife. After that incident the parties separated. The wife and children went to live in a house the husband had bought as a matrimonial home. The husband now intended to purchase another house for himself and the woman he wished to marry; he agreed that the former matrimonial home should be settled on the wife for life or until her remarriage, and thereafter should pass to the children absolutely. Of the three children, only one was still at school, and would be leaving school the following year.

It was ordered that the house should be settled on trust for sale, postponed until the wife ceased to use the home as her main place of residence or remarried or died. Thereafter the house should be sold and the proceeds distributed as to 25 per cent to the wife if still alive and 75 per cent to be divided equally among the surviving children or their issue. *The husband should pay a lump sum of £3,000 as a contribution towards the urgent repairs required to the house.*

Regarding maintenance, Purchas J said (at page 388): '. . . the figure should reflect two aspects, namely, a figure which would allow the wife to live in a modest way if she persists in her attitude of not working, *and should also include an element which would enable her to maintain the mortgage repayments on the house so long as she remains in it, and also a small element to assist but not wholly discharge the cost of maintenance on that house. I consider that the last two elements are justifiable because the children of the family will, to a large extent, eventually benefit from these payments and from the proper maintenance of the house, and of course they ought not to be prejudiced in claims against their father by the conduct of their mother.* The figure which I consider should be awarded includes £1,000 per annum for the wife for herself, less tax, and a further sum of £800, to cover not only the liability to meet the mortgage payments, but also to contribute partly towards the on-going maintenance and upkeep of the house. If at any time the house is sold, then the periodical payments will reduce to the sum of £1,000 less tax. On the same token, however, if the wife elects to engage in gainful employment, then this should not be a reason for the husband to apply to vary this order by way of reduction. The basis upon which I make this order is that any money earned by the wife should inure to her benefit and enjoyment.'

Note. The husband agreed that the matrimonial home should be settled on the wife for her life or until remarriage and that it should thereafter pass to the children, and he had adequate capital and income to rehouse himself and the woman he intended to marry.

4–109 Blezard v Blezard

(1978) 9 Fam Law 249, CA

Completion of education at present school. The husband deserted the wife and children (then aged 13 and 11) for a younger woman, and the wife obtained a divorce on the ground of his adultery. The husband married the co-respondent, and they were living in a house which they had purchased jointly. The wife was living in the former matrimonial home with the children, a boy now aged 16 who had left school and obtained employment, and a girl now aged 14. The house had an equity of at least £48,000. It was owned jointly by the parties. *Orr LJ said that had there been no children, he would have ordered an immediate sale of the property, subject only to allowing the wife sufficient time to find a new home. But the interests of the children had to be considered, and in his judgment it was best that they should remain in their present home until the younger child attained 18 and that she should complete her education at her present school.* The Court of Appeal ordered that the husband would have a charge of two-fifths of the net proceeds of sale of the house, such charge not to be enforced until January 1980 or unless the wife remarried or cohabited with another man.

4–110 Tilley v Tilley

(1979) 10 Fam Law 89, CA

A home for children takes precedence over consent order entered into with benefit of legal advice.   The parties owned a pet shop. They lived above the premises. They purchased the adjoining house, which was then not in a habitable condition. Following the breakdown of the marriage and pronouncement of a decree nisi, a consent order was made vesting both properties, then worth about £30,000, in the wife in consideration of the wife making instalment payments to the husband, £4,000 to be paid within three months and a further £3,500 to be paid over a period of six years thereafter. It was part of the order that the husband's maintenance liability should be merely a nominal 5p per year. The wife made the payment of £4,000. Subsequently the pet shop business became unsuccessful. The wife sold the shop and used the money to make the adjoining house fit to live in. The house was now worth about £10,000. The wife applied for variation of the consent order on the basis that she could not pay the £3,500 owing without selling the house and thereby rendering herself and the children homeless.

Donaldson LJ said that counsel for the husband had urged on the court the necessity of maintaining the sanctity of consent orders, particularly where consent was given with the aid of skilled advice. However, the fact that execution of the order would render a family and, above all, the children homeless was the paramount consideration in this case. The husband certainly had an obligation to maintain his mistress and the child of that union. However, he also had a continuing obligation to maintain his four children by his wife, and this obligation would remain whether he received the £3,500 or not. The order would be varied by providing that there should be no further payments made to the husband, but if there was any future application for maintenance for the children, any court faced with such an application ought to take into consideration the £3,500 which the husband would have in effect contributed towards their maintenance.

Ormrod LJ, agreeing, said that it should be plainly borne in mind that the husband had a continuing obligation to the children which offset the consent order. However, had execution of the agreement not been going to lead inevitably to the eviction of the children from their home, the result of the case might have been very different.

B. *Proceedings under Married Women's Property Act 1882, etc.*

CASE SUMMARIES

4–131 Burke v Burke

[1974] 2 All ER 944, [1974] 1 WLR 1063, CA

Married Women's Property Act 1882, section 17 – the old approach. The matrimonial home had been purchased in the sole name of the husband. The husband left the home. The wife remained in the house with the children. The husband obtained a divorce on the ground of two years' separation, with the consent of the wife. The wife was granted custody of the children. By consent, no maintenance was ordered for the wife but the husband was ordered to pay £3 a week in respect of each of the two children. That order was made as a result of negotiations between the parties whereby the wife agreed to purchase the equity of redemption in the house (or the husband's share in it) for £2,250. The wife was unable to raise the money. The husband commenced proceedings under the Married Women's Property Act 1882, section 17. The husband asserted that he owned the sole beneficial interest in the property. The registrar held that the property was held by the husband on trust for himself and the wife in equal shares. The husband did not appeal against that finding. *Consequently the position was that the property was held under the statutory trust for sale under the Law of Property Act 1925.* The husband applied for a sale of the property. The wife wished the sale to be postponed. The registrar gave leave for both parties to file affidavits on the question of whether there should be a sale or not. The husband's application again came before the registrar, at which time he had the two affidavits before him. He ordered that the house be put up for sale within two months, but he gave liberty to the wife to apply for further postponement of the sale on filing a further affidavit setting out what further attempts she had made to find alternative accommodation or to raise the money to buy out the husband. The wife filed a further affidavit and the matter came back before the registrar. The registrar ordered that the wife's application for a further postponement of the sale should be refused. However, a stay of the earlier order for sale was ordered for a further six weeks in order to enable the wife to appeal. The wife's appeal was dismissed.

Buckley LJ said that the personal problems of beneficiaries connected with the question of whether or not the property should be sold were matters which fell to be taken into account, and that the interests of the children were to be taken into consideration so far as they affected the equities in the matter as between the two persons entitled to the beneficial interests in the property. However, his lordship continued (at page 948): '... *But it is not, I think, right to treat this case as though the husband was obliged to make provision for his children by agreeing to retain the property unsold.* To do this is, as I think, and as was urged on us by counsel for the husband, to confuse with a problem relating to property, considerations which are relevant to maintenance. Those are two different things. If the property is sold and the means available to the husband in the present case are enhanced by his receiving his share of the proceeds of sale, it may well be that he may find himself exposed to an application for an order for increased maintenance; but that does not seem to me to be a good ground for refusing to give effect to *the trust for sale* which is *the primary provision applicable to this property*.'

Lawton LJ, agreeing, said: '... During the course of the argument a question arose as to what was meant by the term "matrimonial home", which was used in all three cases to which the court was referred. I asked counsel whether the term "matrimonial home" might not mean, when there are children either in being or in contemplation, a home for them. *If the circumstances are such that the parents buy a house in which to accommodate themselves and any children of the marriage, for my part I cannot see why the children should not be beneficiaries under any implied trust which may come into existence on the purchase of the home; and if that is the position on the evidence in any particular case, then it may well be that the position of the children has to be considered.* But when I raised this question Buckley LJ pointed out that the order of the registrar dated 13th April 1972 *had in fact decided what the trust was in this case.* It is pertinent to bear in mind that the registrar had heard the evidence of the parties and of such witnesses as they called. He then adjudged and declared that *the property was held in trust for the husband and the wife in equal shares.* It follows from that moment onwards (the order not having been appealed) that the learned registrar was concerned [*solely*] *with the position of a trust for the spouses,* and in those circumstances I agree with what has been said already, that the personal problems were factors to be taken into consideration but nothing more.'

Note. The word 'solely' in the final sentence of Lawton LJ's judgment is omitted in the report of the case in the All England Law Reports. The report at [1974] 1 WLR 1063 at 1068 reads: 'It follows from that moment onwards (the order not having been appealed) that the registrar was concerned solely with the position of a trust for the spouses, and in those circumstances I agree with what has been said already, that the personal problems were factors to be taken into consideration but nothing more.' The case is not reported in The Law Reports.

4–132 Brown v Brown

(1974) 5 Fam Law 51, 119 Sol Jo 166, CA

Married Women's Property Act 1882, section 17 – the modern approach.   The parties had purchased the matrimonial home in their joint names. There were two children, a boy of eight and a girl of four. The wife left the house with the girl. The marriage was dissolved. The husband remained in the house with the boy who went to school locally. Another woman lived in the house with the husband. The wife applied for an order for sale of the house, under the Married Women's Property Act 1882, section 17.

Lord Denning MR said that the legal position was that the wife had a joint interest with the husband in the house, and so long as they lived together they could jointly occupy it. After she left she still had her joint interest but she was not entitled to a sale unless the court in its discretion ordered a sale. The court had often expressed the view that in such cases it was the intention of the parties that the house should be the matrimonial home for the parties and for any children they might have. When an application for sale was made, the interests of the children had to be taken into account as well as those of the two parties. *Burke v Burke* (4–131) laid down nothing to the contrary. The right approach was that of Lawton LJ in *Burke v Burke,* who said:

'If the circumstances are such that the parents buy a house in which to accommodate themselves and any children of the marriage ... I cannot see why the children should not be beneficiaries under any implied trust which may come into existence on the purchase of the house; and *if that is the position* ... then it may well be that the position of the children has to be considered.'

The judge had rightly exercised his discretion not to order a sale in view of the need to retain the house as a home for the boy.

Notes

1. The authors find it difficult to reconcile this case with *Burke v Burke.* Lawton LJ's judgment in *Burke v Burke* continues: 'But when I raised this question Buckley LJ pointed out that the order of the registrar dated 13th April 1972 *had in fact decided what the trust was in this case.* It is pertinent to bear in mind that the registrar had heard the evidence of the parties and of such witnesses as they called. He then adjudged and declared that *the property was held in trust for the husband and the wife in equal shares.* It follows from that moment onwards (the order not having been appealed) that the learned registrar was concerned [*solely*] *with the position of a trust for the spouses,* and in those circumstances I agree with what has been said already, that the personal problems were factors to be taken into consideration but nothing more.'

2. Lord Denning MR went on to say that it was undesirable that such applications should be made under s. 17 of the 1882 Act alone; they ought to be heard with applications under s. 4 of the Matrimonial Proceedings and Property Act 1970 whereby the court could deal with the whole matter. [See now s. 24 of the Matrimonial Causes Act 1973 – see Appendix I.] The authors' advice to any client faced with proceedings under s. 17 of the 1882 Act would be to counter with proceedings for a divorce or judicial separation, coupled with an application under s. 24 of the 1973 Act – see *Williams v Williams* (4–133).

4–133 Williams v Williams

[1977] 1 All ER 28, CA

Law of Property Act 1925, section 30 – the modern approach. The matrimonial home had been conveyed to the parties as beneficial tenants in common in equal shares. Following the breakdown of the marriage, the wife remained in the house with the children. The husband moved a few miles away. The husband took out a summons in the Chancery Division under section 30 of the Law of Property Act 1925, asking for the house to be sold and for his half share to be made available to him. The judge ordered a sale in order that the husband should have his money even though it meant that the wife would have to leave. That is the old approach which was taken in *Jones v Challenger* [1960] 1 All ER 785, where Devlin LJ said at 789:

'The position is the same if the marriage is ended by divorce, for the court is not concerned under section 30 with the reasons for the ending of the marriage or the rights and wrongs of it; it can only take note that the object of the trust, so far as it required the preservation of the realty, has been fulfilled.'

A similar approach was taken in *Burke v Burke* (4–131) [1974] 2 All ER 944, where Buckley LJ said at 948:

'... it is not, I think, right to treat this case as though the husband was obliged to make provision for his children by agreeing to retain the property unsold ... the trust for sale ... is the primary provision applicable to this property.'

Lord Denning MR said (at page 30): 'I must say that that approach is now outdated. *When judges are dealing with the matrimonial home, they nowadays have great regard to the fact that the house is bought as a home in which the family is to be brought up. It is not treated as property to be sold, nor as an investment to be realised for cash. That was emphasised by this court in the recent case of Browne v Pritchard (4–104). The court, in executing the trust, should regard the primary object as being to provide a home and not a sale. Steps should be taken to preserve it as a home for the remaining partner and children, but giving the outgoing partner such compensation, by way of a charge or being bought out, as is reasonable in the circumstances.'*

His lordship concluded (at page 31): 'I would therefore be in favour of allowing the appeal; to set aside the order for sale made by Foster J; to remit the matter for further consideration by a judge of the Family Division when an application is taken out under the matrimonial property legislation. I would allow the appeal accordingly.'

Roskill LJ said (at page 32): 'I am clearly of the view that the order for sale should be set aside. Whether, after the matter has been gone into further, an order for sale should be made, and if so on what terms, or whether the husband's share should be vested in the wife, and if so on what terms . . . I do not know. All those are matters which are fit for determination . . . by a judge of the Family Division.'

Note. The Chancery Division is not the correct forum for matrimonial disputes. Such cases should be commenced in the Family Division. If no divorce proceedings are contemplated, a suit for judicial separation should be instituted so that the court has the necessary powers to deal with the matter fully under section 24 of the Matrimonial Causes Act 1973 (see Appendix I). But see also *Bigg v Bigg* (5–133), in which an application for an adjournment of the section 30 proceedings pending the commencement of divorce proceedings was refused by the Court of Appeal, on the ground that the judge had considered the matter fully and had exercised his discretion in a proper manner.

4–134 Re Evers's Trust, Papps v Evers

[1980] 3 All ER 399, CA

Law of Property Act 1925, section 30 – unmarried couple.   The 'matrimonial home' had been conveyed to the parties on trust for sale with power to postpone the sale. Both had contributed to the purchase price. They had lived there as man and wife for over 4 years. Following the separation, the respondent remained in the house with the child of the parties and her two children by her former marriage. The appellant applied under section 30 of the Law of Property Act 1925 for an order for sale of the property. The judge ordered that the property be sold but postponed the sale until the child of the parties reached the age of 16. The appellant appealed.

Ormrod LJ said that the irresistible inference from the facts was that the parties had purchased the property as a family home for themselves and three children. There was no evidence that the appellant needed to realise his investment, whereas a sale would put the respondent in a very difficult position. The judge was right to exercise his discretion not to order an immediate sale, but the form of the order was unsatisfactory. The form of the order had been derived from orders made under section 24 of the Matrimonial Causes Act 1973. Under section 30 of the Law of Property Act 1925 the question was whether the court should aid the applicant at the particular time and in the peculiar circumstances when the application was made. His lordship added that it might not be appropriate to order a sale when the child reached the age of 16. It would be wiser simply to dismiss the application for a sale, and the order should be varied to that extent.

4–135 Dennis v McDonald

[1981] 2 All ER 632

Law of Property Act 1925, section 30 – unmarried couple.   The three eldest children now lived with the defendant in the former family home; the two youngest lived with the applicant in rented property. Order for sale refused. *Re Evers's Trust* (4–134) followed.

C. *Bankruptcy proceedings*

CASE SUMMARIES

4–161 Re Densham (a bankrupt), ex parte the trustee of the bankrupt v Densham

[1975] 3 All ER 726

Law of Property Act 1925, section 30 – bankruptcy – matrimonial home vested in husband's name alone – wife's contributions towards purchase price – wife entitled to beneficial share proportionate to contributions – husband declared bankrupt – application by trustee in bankruptcy for order for sale – factors governing exercise of discretion – children – Burke v Burke (4–131) applied – order for sale granted.
Notes
1. See also *Re Bailey (a bankrupt)* (4–162).
2. Both section 2 (5) of the Matrimonial Homes Act 1967 and section 39 of the Matrimonial Causes Act 1973 make it clear that the obligation to pay one's debts should prevail over one's obligations to maintain one's wife and family. See the judgment of Walton J in *Re Bailey (a bankrupt)*.

4–162 Re Bailey (a bankrupt), ex parte the trustee of the bankrupt v Bailey

[1977] 2 All ER 26

Law of Property Act 1925, section 30 – bankruptcy – matrimonial home held by husband and wife on trust for sale as beneficial joint tenants – husband declared bankrupt – application by trustee in bankruptcy for order for sale – factors governing exercise of discretion – children – Burke v Burke (4–131) and Re Densham (a bankrupt) (4–161) applied – order for sale granted. Counsel for the wife relied on *Williams v Williams* (4–133) and argued that the interests of the family as a whole should outweigh those of the husband's creditors. Megarry V-C said that, although the court had a discretion whether or not to order a sale for the benefit of the husband's creditors, on the facts of the case the claim of the wife and child was not such as to outweigh the claim of the creditors.

4–163 Re Holliday (a bankrupt), ex parte the trustee of the bankrupt v the bankrupt

[1980] 3 All ER 385, CA

Law of Property Act 1925, section 30 – bankruptcy – matrimonial home held by husband and wife on trust for sale – filing of own bankruptcy petition by husband in order to frustrate claim for transfer of property order by wife – application by trustee in bankruptcy for order for sale – discretion of court whether to order sale – overriding requirements of dependent children – order for sale postponed*. The former matrimonial home had been conveyed to the parties as beneficial joint tenants. Following the breakdown of the marriage, the wife remained in the house with the children. The wife was granted a divorce on the ground of the husband's adultery and was granted custody of the children. She gave notice of her intention to proceed with her application for a property adjustment order. On the same day the husband filed a bankruptcy petition and asked for an immediate adjudication order. In accordance with section 6 of the Bankruptcy Act 1914 he was at once adjudicated bankrupt. He subsequently filed a statement of affairs disclosing that he was unable to pay his debts. His trustee in bankruptcy applied for an order for sale of the house under section 30 of the Law of Property Act 1925. The wife

---

*Distinguished by Walton J in *Re Lowrie (a bankrupt)* [1981] 3 All ER 353 on the grounds that it was an exceptional case.

claimed that the bankruptcy petition was nothing more than a device to prevent her from obtaining a property adjustment order under section 24 of the Matrimonial Causes Act 1973 and was therefore an abuse of the process of the court. She applied for annulment of the adjudication order. The judge dismissed her application, and subsequently made an order for sale. The wife appealed.

The Court of Appeal held that, balancing the interests of the husband's creditors and the interest of the wife, who was burdened with an obligation to provide a home for the children of the marriage, the house should not be sold before 1st July 1985. By that time the problems confronting the wife would be very different. The eldest child, then 15, would be 20; the middle child, then almost 12, would have just attained 17, and the youngest child, then 7, would be 12. When that date was reached, it would be open for any party to apply to enforce the trust for sale, or to seek to have the trust for sale still not carried into effect. In the meantime, there would be liberty to apply.

Sir David Cairns said (at page 398): 'I agree with Buckley LJ that in all the circumstances here the voice of the wife, on behalf of herself and the children, should prevail to the extent that the sale of the house should be deferred for a substantial period. I reach that view because I am satisfied that it would at present be very difficult, if not impossible, for the wife to secure another suitable home for the family in or near Thorpe Bay; because it would be upsetting for the children's education if they had to move far away from their present schools, even if it were practicable, having regard to the wife's means, to find an alternative home at some more distant place; because it is highly unlikely that postponement of the payment of the debts would cause any great hardship to any of the creditors; and because none of the creditors thought fit themselves to present a bankruptcy petition and it is quite impossible to know whether any one of them would have done so if the debtor had not himself presented such a petition.

'Although there is apparently no previous reported case in which the interests of a debtor's family have been held to prevail over those of creditors in a bankruptcy, there have certainly been earlier cases in which family interests have been considered and set against those of the creditors: see *Re Turner* (5–161) where it was the wife's interest that was considered, and *Re Bailey* (4–162) where it was the interests of a son of the family.

'In the earlier cases the trustee has succeeded, because no sufficiently substantial case of hardship of dependants was established. That is where, in my judgment, this case differs from the earlier ones. It may well be, however, that the hardship for the wife and children would be much less, or would have disappeared altogether, in five years' time or possibly even earlier. I therefore agree that it is appropriate that we should not at this stage defer sale for longer than five years or thereabouts, and that we should leave a loophole for earlier sale to be applied for if the circumstances change in such a way as to warrant it.'

Note. In *Re McCarthy* (5–161A) the fact that the bankrupt and his wife had said that they would co-operate with the trustee in bankruptcy if a sale were ordered, and the fact that one of their four children was suffering from a disablement, led Goff J to say that he did not think it right to exercise his discretion to make an order for immediate possession in favour of the trustee, as opposed to an order for sale. His lordship said that an order for possession should only be made when the facts justified it. If the parties in possession should obstruct the sale, the trustee could restore the matter to the court, whereupon an order for possession could be made. It was not suggested that the interests of the debtor's family should prevail over those of the creditors; merely that the family should be spared unnecessary hardship.

2 Exclusion of party from matrimonial home in the interests of children

It is not within the ambit of this book to deal with injunctions, or with proceedings under the Domestic Violence and Matrimonial Proceedings

Act 1976 or the Domestic Proceedings and Magistrates' Courts Act 1978. However, in order that the reader may obtain a better understanding of how the courts deal with the vexed question of who is to remain in occupation of the matrimonial home on divorce, selected cases on the exclusion of a party to the marriage from the matrimonial home are included in this section. Some of the case summaries in this section are very brief, and the reader is referred to the standard textbooks for further information. *For cases in which the question of providing a home for the children was not an issue, see Chapter 5/2.*

CASE SUMMARIES

4–201 Gurasz v Gurasz

[1969] 3 All ER 822, CA

If the court concludes that it is impossible for the parties to live together in the matrimonial home, and that the property is required as a home for the wife and children, the court will order the husband to leave without proof of violence. See case summary 5–202.

4–202 Hall v Hall

[1971] 1 All ER 762, CA

An order excluding a spouse from the matrimonial home is a drastic order and ought not to be made unless it is proved to be impossible for the spouses to live together *or that it is necessary in the interests of the children.* There was no real difficulty in both parties living in the same house. Neither had it been shown to be necessary to exclude the husband in the interests of the children. Order for injunction discharged.

4–203 Bassett v Bassett

[1975] 1 All ER 513, CA

(1) *Evidence of violence inconclusive – welfare of children the paramount consideration – injunction excluding husband from matrimonial home upheld.*

(2) *The court should think essentially in terms of homes, especially for children.*

Ormrod LJ said (at page 519): '*My conclusion is that the court, when dealing with these cases,* particularly where it is clear that the marriage has already broken down, *should think essentially in terms of homes, especially for the children, and then consider the balance of hardship as I have indicated,* being careful not to underestimate the difficulties which even single men have these days in finding somewhere to live, *bearing in mind* that the break will have to be made in the relatively near future and *that property rights as between the spouses are of comparatively minor importance.*'

Cumming-Bruce J (as he then was), agreeing, added (at page 521): '*Where there are children, whom the mother is looking after, a major consideration must be to relieve them of the psychological stresses and strains imposed by the friction between their parents, as the long-term effect on a child is liable to be of the utmost gravity. This factor ought to weigh at least as heavily in the scales as the personal protection of the parent seeking relief.*'

4–204 Walker v Walker

[1978] 3 All ER 141, CA

Blame irrelevent – children the deciding factor – wife had care of children – husband ordered to vacate matrimonial home.

4–205 Wood v Wood

(1978) 9 Fam Law 254, CA

Exclusion order quashed pending determination of issue of custody.

Note. See also *Smith v Smith* (4–206).

4–206 Smith v Smith

(1978) 10 Fam Law 50, CA

Exclusion order refused pending determination of issue of custody.
Note. See also *Wood v Wood* (4–205)

4–207 S v S

(1980) Times, 21 February

Court's inherent power to protect children in absence of any legal right. The parties came to the UK from Pakistan. The wife returned to Pakistan for a supposedly short holiday. She went on a single ticket because the husband, a businessman, was short of funds. The husband prevaricated about her return, and she eventually returned three years later, without the husband's assistance, to find that the husband had in the meantime purchased a house and set up home there with an Italian mistress. The wife applied to the court for an order under its inherent jurisdiction to allow her to live in part of the house. She could not invoke the Matrimonial Homes Act 1967 because the house had never been the matrimonial home.

French J said that there was no legal right which could be invoked in favour of the wife because the house had never been the matrimonial home. *His lordship added (obiter) that where the interests of children were concerned the court had power to protect them in the absence of any legal right.* But as the parties had no children the court did not have to consider the interests of children.

Note. French J said that in his opinion Lord Denning MR's statement in *Gurasz v Gurasz* (5–202) that a husband had a duty to allow his wife to remain in the matrimonial home did not apply to properties which had never been the matrimonial home.

4–208 Beard v Beard (sub nom. B v B)

[1981] 1 All ER 783, CA

Exclusion order granted on making of interim care order.

3   Capital provision for children

CASE SUMMARIES

4–301 Wachtel v Wachtel

[1973] 1 All ER 829, CA

Settlement of matrimonial home on wife and children. Lord Denning MR read the judgment of the Court, and said, at page 841: '. . . suppose the husband leaves the house and the wife stays in it. If she is likely to be there indefinitely, arrangements should be made whereby it is vested in her absolutely, free of any share in the husband; or, *if there are children, settled on her and the children.*'

Note. See, however, *Chamberlain v Chamberlain* (4–303) and *Alonso v Alonso* (4–305) – settlement on wife and children disapproved.

4–302 Marsden (JL) v Marsden (AM)

[1973] 2 All ER 851

Settlement of adulterous party's assets on children disapproved.   See case summary 6–162.

4–303 Chamberlain v Chamberlain

[1974] 1 All ER 33, CA

Settlement of matrimonial home on wife and children disapproved.   The decision of Latey J, extinguishing the husband's half interest in the former matrimonial home and settling the property on the wife for life and then on the children in equal shares, was set aside by the Court of Appeal. Scarman LJ (as he then was) said, at page 37: 'There is no doubt that the learned judge, in making the order that he did in respect of the interests in the house, had in mind, as indeed he said he had in mind, a passage in the judgment of Lord Denning MR in *Wachtel v Wachtel* (4–301) in which he said:

> "Conversely, suppose the husband leaves the house and the wife stays in it. [If I may digress, that is the factual situation in this case.] If she is likely to be there indefinitely, arrangements should be made whereby it is vested in her absolutely, free of any share in the husband; or, *if there are children, settled on her and the children . . .*"

'I have no doubt, having read carefully the judgment of Latey J, that he did model his order on that passage in the judgment of Lord Denning MR. I think one may make this observation about judgments given in this court as to the application of the provisions of the Matrimonial Proceedings and Property Act 1970: they must be studied in the light of the particular circumstances of the case before the court. It would, I believe, be unfortunate if the very flexible and wide-ranging powers conferred on the court by the 1970 Act should be considered by the profession to be cut down or forced into this or that line of decision by the courts. I have no doubt that the passage that I have quoted from the judgment of Lord Denning MR is valuable guidance for a large number of cases; but, for reasons associated with the particular finances of this family, I do not think the passage is helpful to resolve the problem with which we are in the present case confronted.' His lordship continued (at page 38): '*Equally, I think the learned judge erred in this case in settling the house so that the beneficial interest at the end of the day became that of the children in equal shares. The order that the registrar made provided for the care and upbringing of the children in this house until they should finish full-time education. I think that that was an appropriate order. There are no circumstances in this case to suggest that any of these children had special circumstances that required them to make demands on their parents after the conclusion of their full-time education. The capital asset, the house, was acquired by the work and by the resources of their parents, and, provided their parents meet their responsibilities to their children as long as their children are dependent, this seems to me an asset that should revert then to the parents.*'

   Note. The relevant provisions of the Matrimonial Proceedings and Property Act 1970 have been re-enacted in sections 23, 24 and 25 of the Matrimonial Causes Act 1973 (see Appendix I).

4–304 Harnett v Harnett

[1973] 2 All ER 593; affd. [1974] 1 All ER 764, CA

'*. . . shelter, food and education, according to the means of his parents.*'   Custody of the children was given to the husband, with care and control to the wife. Bagnall J (at page 598) referred to section 5 (1) and (2) of the Matrimonial Proceedings and

Property Act 1970, which has been re-enacted without amendment as section 25 (1) and (2) of the Matrimonial Causes Act 1973 (see Appendix I). His lordship said: 'Section 5 (1) governs the manner in which the powers conferred by ss 2 and 4 are to be exercised. First the court is to have regard to all the circumstances of the case including specific matters set out in paras (a) to (g), many of which by virtue of decisions of the court were taken into account under the old law, but which do not expressly include conduct, except insofar as conduct is inherent in the duration of the marriage (para (d)) and in para (f).

'At that stage the legislature might well have directed the court in quite general terms to exercise its power so as to achieve a fair, or equitable, or just (or any other synonymous epithet) division of the capital and income resources of the parties. It did not do so; it set up a specific target. The court is:

> "so to exercise those powers as to place the parties, so far as it is practicable and, having regard to their conduct, just to do so, in the financial position in which they would have been if the marriage had not broken down and each had properly discharged his or her financial obligations and responsibilities towards the other".

'The same form of words is used, mutatis mutandis, in sub-s (2) dealing with orders in relation to a child, though *in the vast majority of cases the financial position of a child of a subsisting marriage is simply to be afforded shelter, food and education, according to the means of his parents.*'

Note. This passage was referred to by Orr LJ in *Lord Lilford v Glynn* (4–307).

4–305 Alonso v Alonso

(1974) 4 Fam Law 164, CA

Settlement of matrimonial home on wife and children disapproved. The first instance decision settling the husband's share in the matrimonial home on the children was set aside by the Court of Appeal and the house was ordered to be held on trust for sale, one-third for the husband and two-thirds for the wife. The trust for sale was not to be executed except by agreement or by order of the court until the wife's death, the end of each child's full-time education or the youngest child attaining 21, whichever was the earliest.

Buckley LJ said that he thought the judge had been influenced by remarks made in *Wachtel v Wachtel* (4–301). However, the court's attention had been called to section 29 of the Matrimonial Causes Act 1973, which placed limits on the kind of benefit courts should consider making available in this situation; also to *Chamberlain v Chamberlain* (4–303) in which the Court of Appeal had held that it was inappropriate to make an order which conferred a beneficial interest on the children of a kind which they would have been unlikely to have obtained if the marriage had remained unbroken. These considerations satisfied his lordship that the judge was in error in taking the husband's share and settling it on the children.

Notes

1. Section 29, so far as material, provides:

    '(1) Subject to subsection (3) below, no financial provision order and no order for a transfer of property under section 24 (1) (a) above shall be made in favour of a child who has attained the age of eighteen . . .

    '(3) Subsection (1) above . . . shall not apply in the case of a child, if it appears to the court that – (a) the child is, or will be, or if an order were made . . . would be, receiving instruction at an educational establishment . . .'

2. Although section 29 does not apply to *settlements* made for the benefit of children, the court nevertheless considered that the general tenor of the section was relevant. The court took a similar line in *Lord Lilford v Glynn* (4–307) (*q.v.*).

4–306 McKay v Chapman

[1978] 2 All ER 548

Unreasonable to require father to make capital provision for children.   The wife presented a petition for divorce in 1969 claiming, inter alia, custody of the three children, and in the prayer 'such sums by way of alimony pending suit, maintenance, child maintenance, a lump sum and/or secured provision as may be just'. Under the Matrimonial Causes Act 1965 which was then in force, it was not open to the wife to apply for a lump sum for the children. The decree was made absolute in 1970, the wife having obtained orders for periodical payments for herself and each of the children and, by agreement, custody of the children and a transfer of the matrimonial home. In 1976 the wife issued a summons under the Matrimonial Causes Act 1973 seeking a lump sum for the children.

Lionel Swift QC, sitting as a deputy judge of the High Court, held that leave was required to make the application on behalf of the children and that leave would be refused. The wife contended that the children should have a nest egg and that the implication in the husband's affidavit was that he was a rich man, in whose capital the children would have shared had the marriage continued. It was held that, bearing in mind the dicta of Scarman LJ in *Chamberlain v Chamberlain* (4–303), it would not be reasonable to require the husband to make capital provision for the children. At the time of the divorce the parties had arranged the disposition of capital on the basis that no further claims would be made on the husband. *There was no financial need on the part of the children that could not adequately be met by a periodical payments order. And there was no evidence that the husband had failed to comply with the existing periodical payments order or would fail to comply with an increased order in the future, or that the husband was so unreliable that a lump sum was desirable to secure the children's future.*

4–307 Lord Lilford v Glynn

[1979] 1 All ER 441, CA

No obligation upon millionaire father to make capital provision for children over and above trust fund for their education.   In 1969 the marriage between the husband and wife was dissolved, and the husband, who was a millionaire, made substantial financial provision for the wife and provided a trust fund of £30,000 to meet the cost of educating the two children of the marriage, daughters then aged 15 and 13, who were to remain in the wife's care. The fund proved insufficient to pay the school fees and provide for the children's maintenance at home. The wife therefore applied to the court for periodical payments for the benefit of the children. In 1973 the court made an order by consent for such maintenance, incorporating an increase in 1976 to provide for inflation, the maintenance to cease on each child attaining 18. However, in 1976, the wife sought a further increase, security for the payments, a lump sum for the benefit of the children and a settlement on each child, on the ground that the current periodical payments did not make reasonable provision for the children in the ,light of the expenditure required to maintain them at the standard they would have enjoyed if the marriage had continued. The judge's order provided for a further increase in the maintenance, that this increased maintenance be secured, that in addition the husband should pay the children's school fees and that he should settle a sum of £25,000 on each child. The husband, having already provided a trust fund for the purposes of the children's education, appealed against the part of the order requiring him to pay the school fees and provide a further settlement for each child.

The Court of Appeal allowed the husband's appeal for the following reasons:
1) *Since the husband had created the trust fund of £30,000 to provide for the cost of educating the children, it would be unjust for him, and would defeat the object of the trust, to place on him the primary liability for the school fees and to leave the*

trustees to accumulate the income of the fund for the prospective benefit of the children after their education was completed. Accordingly, the order to pay the school fees was revoked on the husband undertaking to pay each term the balance of the fees outstanding over and above the amount available from the trust fund.

2) *Having regard to the restrictions imposed by section 29 of the Matrimonial Causes Act 1973 on the making of orders in favour of children beyond the age of 18, the court should not exercise its powers under section 24 (1) so as to order the additional settlements making provision for the payment of income to the children during the whole of their lives.*

The relevant parts of section 24 (1) read:

'On granting a decree of divorce . . . or at any time thereafter (whether, in the case of a decree of divorce . . . before or after the decree is made absolute), the court may make any one or more of the following orders . . .
'. . . (b) an order that a settlement of such property as may be so specified, being property to which a party to the marriage is so entitled, be made to the satisfaction of the court for the benefit of the other party to the marriage and of the children of the family or either or any of them . . .'

The proviso which follows applies to transfer of property orders under section 24 (1) (a) but not to settlements made under section 24 (1) (b). The proviso reads:

'subject, however, *in the case of an order under paragraph (a) above*, to the restrictions imposed by section 29 (1) and (3) below *on the making of orders for a transfer of property* in favour of children who have attained the age of eighteen.'

Section 29, so far as material, provides:

'(1) Subject to subsection (3) below, *no financial provision order* and *no order for a transfer of property under section 24 (1) (a) above* shall be made in favour of a child who has attained the age of eighteen . . .
'(3) Subsection (1) above . . . shall not apply in the case of a child, if it appears to the court that – (a) the child is, or will be, or if an order were made . . . would be, receiving instruction at an educational establishment . . .'

Thus, the court was *empowered* under section 24 (1) (b) to order the additional settlements to be made on the children, and the settlements, if made, would not be subject to the restrictions imposed by section 29. But having regard to those restrictions, the court held that it would be wrong to exercise those powers so as to order settlements making provision for the payment of income to the children during the whole of their lives.

3) *Even the richest father was not to be regarded as under a financial obligation or responsibility to provide the settlements envisaged by the judge on children who were under no disability and whose maintenance and education were secure.* Section 25 (2), which lays down the duty of the court in deciding whether to exercise its powers under sections 23 and 24 states that the court is 'so to exercise those powers as *to place the child . . . in the financial position in which the child would have been* if the marriage had not broken down and each of those parties [to the marriage] had properly discharged his or her financial obligations and responsibilities towards him'.

Orr LJ referred to the judgment of Bagnall J in *Harnett v Harnett* (4–304) in which he had said: '. . . *in the vast majority of cases the financial position of a child of a subsisting marriage is simply to be afforded shelter, food and education, according to the means of his parents.*' *Chamberlain v Chamberlain* (4–303) (*q.v.*) was also cited with approval.

Reading the judgment of the court, Orr LJ concluded: 'There is not, in this context, one rule for millionaires and another for less wealthy fathers and, in our judgment, there was no means of judging whether the father, if the marriage had continued, would or would not have made a settlement in favour of the daughters.'

4–308 D v D (sub nom. **Drascovic v Drascovic**)

(1980) Times, 23 December

In the absence of special circumstances property should not be settled on children.   The husband requested that his interest in the former matrimonial home be settled on the infant children of the marriage. Balcombe J said that if the court acceded to the request there would be no property on which the Law Society could attach a charge for costs. His lordship cited *Chamberlain v Chamberlain* (4–303) as authority for the principle that property should not be settled on children in the absence of special circumstances. In the present case there were no special circumstances, and it was in the public interest that the public purse should be reimbursed.

Quaere. What would have been the position had the parties agreed a compromise which necessitated a court order only in respect of the agreed periodical payments? Suppose the house had been owned in equal shares, and it was agreed that in consideration of the wife accepting agreed periodical payments (and agreed periodical payments payable direct to the children) that the husband's share was to be settled on the children with no benefit under the settlement in favour of the wife, in full and final settlement of all claims under sections 23 and 24 of the Matrimonial Causes Act 1973. Assuming the ownership of the wife's share had never been at issue, her share would be neither 'property recovered' nor 'property preserved', and so would escape the Law Society's charge. The parties having agreed to the husband's share being settled on the children, his share would not be 'property recovered' as far as the wife was concerned because she would not have obtained the ownership of it. Presumably, because the transfer would be part of a compromise of a divorce action, no liability to capital transfer tax would arise. What would be the attitude of the Law Society to such a compromise? Would they claim that the wife had 'recovered' the husband's share in the house by virtue of the fact that she would be living in the property with the children and thus obtaining the benefit of their equitable interest in the property?

4–309 Page v Page

(1981) Times, 30 January, CA

Desire to make provision by will for adult children not relevant.   Ormrod LJ said that it was not legitimate to take into account, under section 25 of the Matrimonial Causes Act 1973 (see Appendix I), the wife's wish to be in a position to make provision by will for her adult children who were in no way dependent on either her or the husband. Dunn LJ added that the scheme of the Act was to give the court jurisdiction to make orders for the benefit of wives and *dependent* children. For further details, see Appendix II.

Note. This was a 'large assets' case. See also *Lord Lilford v Glynn* (4–307).

4   Maintenance for children

CASE SUMMARIES

4–400 P(JM) v P(LE)

[1971] 2 All ER 728

(1) *Permanent maintenance for child can be ordered before granting decree.*

(2) *Permanent maintenance for child can be ordered notwithstanding dismissal of petition.*

Section 23 of the Matrimonial Causes Act 1973 reads as follows:

> '(1) *On granting a decree* of divorce, a decree of nullity of marriage or a decree of judicial separation *or at any time thereafter* (whether, in the case of a decree of divorce or of nullity of marriage, before or after the decree is made absolute), *the court may make any one or more of the following orders,* that is to say . . .
>
> > (d) an order that a party to the marriage shall make *to such person as may be specified in the order for the benefit of a child of the family, or to such a child,* such periodical payments, for such term, as may be so specified . . .
>
> subject, however, in the case of an order under paragraph (d), (e), or (f) above [relating to orders for children], to the restrictions imposed by section 29 (1) and (3) below on the making of financial provision orders in favour of children who have attained the age of eighteen.
>
> '(2) *The court may also,* subject to those restrictions, *make any one or more of the orders mentioned in subsection (1) (d), (e) and (f) above* [relating to children] –
>
> > (a) in any proceedings for divorce, nullity of marriage or judicial separation, *before granting a decree; and*
> >
> > (b) *where any such proceedings are dismissed after the beginning of the trial, either forthwith or within a reasonable period after the dismissal* . . .
>
> '(4) The power of the court under subsection (1) or 2 (a) above to make an order in favour of a child of the family shall be exercisable from time to time; *and where the court makes an order in favour of a child under subsection 2 (b) above, it may from time to time,* subject to the restrictions mentioned in subsection (1) above [on the making of financial provision orders in favour of children who have attained the age of eighteen], *make a further order in his favour of any of the kinds mentioned in subsection (1) (d),(e) or (f) above . . .*'

In 1967 the marriage of the parties was dissolved by a court in the State of Virginia at the suit of the wife. In May 1969 the husband presented a petition to the High Court for a declaration that the Virginian decree was valid; at the same time his petition for dissolution of marriage was filed in a county court but subsequently transferred to the High Court. The suit for a declaration was heard first and the judge held that the Virginian decree had validly dissolved the marriage. The divorce suit was then called on, and in view of the declaration in the preceding suit the petition was dismissed.

On the question whether the court had jurisdiction to entertain an application by the wife for maintenance for the child of the marriage, it was held that the divorce suit had been dismissed 'after the beginning of the trial', because the trial had begun at the moment the divorce suit was called on. Accordingly the court had jurisdiction (under what is now section 23 (2) (b) of the 1973 Act) to make a maintenance order for the child.

Notes

1. Accordingly, under what is now section 23 (4) of the 1973 Act, the court would have power to make a further order in favour of the child from time to time.

2. As a result of section 23 (2) of the 1973 Act, the court has power to back-date orders for *maintenance of children* to the date of the filing of the application, notwithstanding the fact that the application may have been filed before the *decree nisi* was pronounced. Under section 23 (5) of the Act, orders under section 23 (1) (a), (b) and (c) *in favour of the parties to the marriage themselves* cannot take effect unless the decree has been made *absolute.* Accordingly, an order for *permanent maintenance for the wife herself* cannot be back-dated beyond the date of the *decree absolute.* If it is intended to give the husband the benefit of tax relief in respect of maintenance for the wife herself paid prior to decree absolute, an additional application for *maintenance pending suit* will have to be lodged under section 22 of the Act. However, although it is not necessary to make two applications in respect of maintenance for children, one for maintenance pending suit and the other for permanent maintenance, it should be remembered that *no order for*

maintenance can be back-dated beyond the date of lodging the application in the court. See IR Statement of Practice dated 8.9.81 – see Appendix II. From the husband's point of view, therefore, it is of benefit to him that the application for maintenance for the children and for maintenance pending suit for the wife is filed at the time of filing the petition. The wife also benefits from filing the application at the earliest possible date, because on filing the application the court will issue a pro forma summons ordering the husband to file an affidavit of means, so ordering disclosure at an early date.

3.   The significance of the words in brackets in subsection (1) of section 23 is that the decree pronounced in the first instance upon a petition for divorce or nullity is a decree nisi, not to be made absolute until after the expiration of six weeks. This does not apply where the petition is for judicial separation.

4–401 Wachtel v Wachtel

[1973] 1 All ER 829, CA

One-third of joint income for wife plus additional sum for child.   See case summary 19–002.

4–402 Downing v Downing (Downing intervening)

[1976] 3 All ER 474

Maintenance for child over 18 while education is continuing.   The parents of the intervener, Miss Downing, were divorced when she was ten. Both parents remarried. After leaving school she obtained a place at a university. She received a full education grant for the year 1974–75 but both parents refused to make a statement of their financial means for 1975–76. They were assessed for parental contribution but refused to pay it. The intervener, now no longer a minor, was granted leave to intervene in the parents' divorce suit and applied for an order for financial provision against both parents. The district registrar held that the court had no jurisdiction to hear her application. The intervener appealed.

Payne J held that the court had jurisdiction to make a financial provision order in favour of a child who had attained the age of 18 if the child was receiving instruction at an educational establishment.

The relevant parts of section 23 (1) of the Matrimonial Causes Act 1973 read:

> 'On granting a decree of divorce . . . or at any time thereafter (whether, in the case of a decree of divorce . . . before or after the decree is made absolute), the court may make any one or more of the following orders . . .
> '. . . (d) an order that a party to the marriage shall make to such a person as may be specified in the order for the benefit of a child of the family, or to such a child, such periodical payments, for such term, as may be so specified . . .'

Paragraphs (e) and (f) refer to similar orders relating to secured maintenance and lump sum provision respectively. There follows a proviso:

> 'subject, however, in the case of an order under paragraph (d), (e) or (f) above, to the restrictions imposed by section 29 (1) and (3) below on the making of financial provision orders in favour of children who have attained the age of eighteen.'

The relevant parts of section 29 of the Act read:

> '(1) Subject to subsection (3) below, no financial provision order . . . shall be made in favour of a child who has attained the age of eighteen . . .
> '(3) Subsection (1) above . . . shall not apply in the case of a child, if it appears to the court that – (a) the child is, or will be, or if an order were made . . . would be, receiving instruction at an educational establishment . . .'

4–403 West v West

[1978] Fam 1, [1977] 2 All ER 705, CA

Children not to be prejudiced by parents' conduct.   Counsel for the wife's argument before the Court of Appeal was: the judge having found that the wife's conduct was not 'obvious or gross', it was wrong for the judge to take her conduct into account at all; therefore there was no reason why he should not have given her something like the normal one-third of the combined income, whereas what she got was something like one-eighth.

Sir John Pennycuick said (at page 8): '... Once it is accepted that the court is bound to take into account the failure of the wife to set up a [married] life at all, then the judge's conclusion is perfectly unexceptionable ...

'*Given those circumstances, it was, I think, entirely right that the judge, while directing maintenance sufficient for the wife to keep a home for the two children, should have awarded her very considerably less than would have been proper to award her apart from that all-important circumstance, namely, that she failed from the start to get this marriage going.*'

Note. Children are not to be prejudiced by their parents' conduct. For a further example of this principle see *Bateman v Bateman* (4–108).

4–404 Lewis v Lewis

[1977] 3 All ER 992, CA

Variation – the right approach.   The parties had been divorced some time ago. The original maintenance order in respect of the children had been made in 1972. In 1975 the wife applied to the court for variation on the ground that the husband's means had increased and also on the ground that her expenses in looking after the children had increased. The registrar increased the order. On appeal to the county court judge, the judge further increased the order by grossing up the payments ordered by the registrar, so as to leave in the wife's hands, as a net sum after tax, the amount ordered by the registrar. The total amount of the order for the three children now amounted to £2,400 a year less tax; in addition, the husband was liable for school fees, which he had to pay out of net income.

The husband appealed to the Court of Appeal. The only point taken by counsel for the husband was that the judge's approach had been incorrect in that, instead of bearing in mind that he was being asked to vary an existing order – that of 1972 – he approached the matter as if he had been fixing periodical payments de novo.

The Court of Appeal held that, on the true construction of section 31 of the Matrimonial Causes Act 1973, the court, in considering an application for variation, is not confined to looking at changes in the means of the parties since the original order was made, but has an unfettered discretion to deal with the situation as it is when the matter comes before it. The court here had to deal with maintenance for three growing children. The judge was perfectly right to look at the matter as it stood at the time when the case was before him.

Note. On the question of payment of school fees, see now *Practice Direction dated 10th November 1980* (4–418).

4–405 Dennett v Dennett

(1977) Times, 24 March, CA

Maintenance of child out of public funds.   The wife brought a petition for divorce on the ground of the husband's unreasonable behaviour. At the hearing the judge was informed that the parties had made an agreement: that the husband would not defend the petition, that the wife would not claim costs against him or periodical payments for herself, and would accept the £4 a week offered by the husband for the maintenance of the child. The wife was living on social security; the judge considered the agreement to be contrary to public policy and refused to grant a decree nisi.

The Court of Appeal held that the court could not insist on the wife pursuing her claim for periodical payments. The marriage had broken down irretrievably, and the judge was under a duty to grant a decree.

However, the judge had also said that he would refuse to certify that he was satisfied with the arrangements for the child's welfare. He took the view that, as there was no provision of periodical payments for the wife, £4 a week was not a satisfactory financial provision for the child. The Court of Appeal agreed that the judge, not having adequate information about the husband's means, was entitled to question whether the child's maintenance was sufficient. Scarman LJ said that the judge had performed a public service in refusing to grant the certificate. The matter would be remitted back to the judge with an instruction that the registrar should investigate the husband's means and report to him so as to enable him to decide whether the arrangements made for the child were satisfactory.

Notes
1. The Court of Appeal also held that it was not possible for the wife by agreement to bar herself from bringing a claim for periodical payments. Such an agreement was null and void. The case was heard prior to *Minton v Minton* (4–409) and this statement must now be read in the light of the principle of the 'clean break' enshrined in the judgment of the House of Lords in that case. Although a wife cannot bar herself from bringing a claim before the court for periodical payments, she can agree to her claim for periodical payments being dismissed so as to provide a clean break between the parties. See Chapter 10 – 'The clean break'.
2. A husband cannot shift the burden of his responsibilities towards his dependent children wholly onto the State when he has the means (however slender) to contribute towards the support of those children; see *Tovey v Tovey* (4–406). For further cases on the relevance of social security benefits see Chapter 22 – 'Relevance of social security benefits'.
3. It was apparent that the husband had exerted undue influence over the wife at a time of emotional stress. See also the judgment of Balcombe J in *Backhouse v Backhouse* [1978] 1 All ER 1158 at 1164 et seq. At 1166 Balcombe J said: 'When a marriage has broken down, both parties are liable to be in an emotional state. The party remaining in the matrimonial home, as the husband did in this case, has an advantage. The wife is no doubt in circumstances of great emotional strain. It seems to me that she should at least be encouraged to take independent advice so that she may know whether or not it is right for her, whatever the circumstances of the breakdown of the marriage may be, to transfer away what is her only substantial capital asset.' The same surely applies equally to the question of a wife forgoing her right to pursue her claim for periodical payments, either for herself or for the maintenance of the children. But in the case of maintenance for the children the court has additional powers under its inherent jurisdiction, and will not, for instance, allow a clean break to be applied as far as the children's maintenance is concerned – see *Minton v Minton* (4–409), *Carter v Carter* (4–413) and *Moore v Moore* (4–415).
4. See also *Cook v Cook* (4–407), *England v England* (4–409A) and *McDermott v McDermott* (4–411A).

4–406 Tovey v Tovey

(1977) 8 Fam Law 80, CA

The husband's two families – maintenance of children out of public funds.   Following the separation, the husband had gone to live with an unmarried woman (whom he intended to marry) who had two children. A decree absolute of divorce had now been pronounced and the wife had obtained custody of the three children of the marriage. The husband's income was £51.50 per week gross, £39 per week net. The wife earned £7 per week as a part-time barmaid, drawing £40 per week from the DHSS. Ormrod LJ said that if the husband were out of work he would be entitled to supplementary benefit at the rate of £39 per week, and that figure, his lordship said, must be taken as being more or less the minimum that he could live on; the minimum figure was not a fixed figure, but obviously a sum of £39 per week was very near the minimum.

The Court of Appeal approved the registrar's award of a nominal sum for the maintenance of the wife herself. However, regarding the children, Ormrod LJ said that the question was: *should the husband be able to off-load the whole of his obligation to his wife and his three children on to the State, simply by taking on the responsibility of providing for another woman and her two children? His lordship said that it seemed to him a startling proposition that a man who was in regular work should be required to make no contribution at all to the maintenance of his own children. It was true that it could be argued that he had relieved the DHSS from having to support another woman and her two children. However, it was undesirable as a matter of public policy that a man should not continue to contribute even in a purely formal sense towards the upkeep of his own children, who were his primary liability.*

On the figures here, it was clear that the husband could not afford anything much for the children, but in his lordship's opinion the husband should at least pay £1 per week for each child.

Note. For further details and comments, see case summary 22–008.

4–407 Cook v Cook

[1978] 3 All ER 1009, CA

Maintenance of child out of public funds.   Following the separation the wife rented a two-bedroomed council house and lived there with the child of the family, a girl aged just under 7. She went out to work and earned £9.15 a week. She also received a little over £20 a week by way of supplementary benefit from the DHSS. In addition, the DHSS paid her rent. A magistrates' court awarded her custody and ordered the husband to pay her maintenance of £3 a week for herself and £5 a week for the child. These moneys were paid direct to the DHSS. The husband was in arrears with his payments.

The wife subsequently filed a petition for divorce and applied for legal aid in order to apply for increased maintenance. Decree nisi was pronounced, but the judge refused to make a declaration that he was satisfied with the arrangements for the child, because he considered that the arrangements for financial provision for the child were inadequate and it was not in the public interest that a child should be supported out of public funds.

The wife appealed against the judge's refusal to make the declaration. The Court of Appeal held that the judge had exercised his discretion on wrong grounds and allowed the appeal. *Dennett v Dennett* (4–405) distinguished.

Note. The judge, His Honour Judge Hill-Smith, tried another way of achieving what he failed to do in *Cook v Cook* in a later case, *England v England* (4–409A) which came before him in 1979; this time by granting a decree nisi and making a declaration of satisfaction but ordering that the decree was not to be made absolute until a maintenance order had been made in favour of the children. The wife appealed to the Court of Appeal, which again ruled against him. Brandon LJ said that once the judge had declared his satisfaction as to the arrangements for the children, the fact that the children were being provided for out of public funds afforded no good or sufficient reason for delaying the decree absolute.

4–408 Fitzpatrick v Fitzpatrick

(1978) 9 Fam Law 16, CA

The husband's two families – husband assuming responsibility for children not his own.   The husband appealed to the Court of Appeal on the ground (inter alia) that on the basis of the judge's order of £15 per week for the wife and £5 per week for each child, the husband and his second family were left with approximately £2 per week less than the supplementary benefits (including child benefit) to which the family would be entitled if he were unemployed. Order reduced to £12 per week.

See case summary 22–009.

4–409 Minton v Minton

[1979] 1 All ER 79, HL

Clean break principle does not apply to financial provision for children. Lord Scarman said (at page 87): '. . . There are two principles which inform the modern legislation. One is the public interest that spouses, to the extent that their means permit, should provide for themselves and their children. But the other, of equal importance, is the principle of "the clean break". The law now encourages spouses to avoid bitterness after family breakdown and to settle their money and property problems. An object of the modern law is to encourage the parties to put the past behind them and to begin a new life which is not overshadowed by the relationship which has broken down.'

However, his lordship also said (at page 82): '. . . *No question arises in this appeal as to the provision for the children, for whom it is recognised that the husband has a continuing responsibility, and the court a continuing jurisdiction (until they reach the age of 18) to make such orders as it thinks appropriate.*'

The principle of the clean break does not apply as far as maintenance for the children of the family is concerned. *Section 23 (4) of the Matrimonial Causes Act 1973 says that 'The power of the court under subsection (1) or (2) (a) [of section 23] to make an order in favour of a child of the family shall be exercisable from time to time . . .'* His lordship said (at page 87): '. . . *When Parliament wished to make it clear that no previous dismissal of an application or discharge or termination of an order could displace the court's power to make maintenance orders in favour of children, it added, by subsection (4), the words "from time to time" to the words "at any time thereafter" which it had used in subsection (1). No plainer indication could be given of the intention of Parliament.*' There is no subsection equivalent to subsection (4) qualifying the words used in subsection (1) in respect of maintenance orders in favour of the parties to the marriage themselves.

Notes

1. See also *Carter v Carter* (4–413) and *Moore v Moore* (4–415).
2. In *Hanlon v Hanlon* (10–102) the matrimonial home was transferred to the wife absolutely, partly because she was willing to forgo any further periodical payments in respect of the two children who were under 17. The order for the maintenance of the children was not discharged, but merely reduced to a nominal sum. In this way the wife was not precluded from applying for variation of the order for the children's maintenance in the future. However, even if the order for the children's maintenance had been discharged, the wife would still have been able to apply afresh for an order for their maintenance in the future.

4–409A England v England

(1979) 10 Fam Law 86, CA

Maintenance of children out of public funds. The wife filed a petition for divorce. Her evidence as to the arrangements for the children of the family who were under 16 was that the husband was unemployed and that she and the children were living on social security. The judge granted decree nisi and made a declaration of satisfaction as to the arrangements for the children under section 41 of the Matrimonial Causes Act 1973, but ordered that the decree was not to be made absolute until a maintenance order had been made in favour of the children. The wife appealed, contending that the provision as to the making of the decree absolute should never have been included in the judge's order.

The wife's appeal was allowed. Brandon LJ said that the judge's order was no more than a device to get round the decision of the Court of Appeal in *Cook v Cook* (4–407). Once the judge had declared his satisfaction under section 41, the fact that the children were being provided for out of public funds was no good or sufficient reason for delaying the decree absolute.

4–410 Re L

(1979) 9 Fam Law 152

Minimum order £5 per week. Sir George Baker P said that it was generally accepted that there should be no order under £5 per week and increased the order accordingly. See case summary 6–232.

4–411 M v M (sub nom. **Moon v Moon**)

(1979) Law Society's Gazette 27 February 1980

(Transcript of official tape recording provided by Messrs. Cater Walsh & Co. of 10 Victoria Avenue, Halesowen, West Midlands)

DHSS single parent allowance disregarded. This was an appeal against a magistrates' order for the maintenance of two of the children of the family, girls aged 10 and 11, in the custody of the wife. A third child had now reached 18 years.

The husband had remarried since the decree absolute. His gross income was approximately £4,300 per annum. His second wife was currently working as a secretary, earning £2,100 per annum. She was pregnant, and intended to give up work in about a month's time. However, Waterhouse J added, it might well be that she would be able to resume her earnings when the child was able to attend school. The husband was purchasing a house with the aid of a mortgage. Waterhouse J said: '... *It is right for me to bear in mind the outgoings and commitments of the father in these circumstances; but I am bound to say that I regard his responsibility for the two young girls of his former marriage as a primary responsibility in his life. It is wrong for Justices to be over-influenced in deciding matters of this kind by detailed calculations of the outgoings of each household. It is the father here who has set the standard on his life in his new marriage and it is part of his responsibilities and duties to cut his coat appropriately in the light of his existing responsibilities. The Divisional Court has said over and over again, in considering appeals from Magistrates, that it is essential, whether one is considering the wife's maintenance or a child's maintenance, to take as the starting point the actual earnings of the parties in gross terms and to make basic calculations on that footing without being unduly influenced by detailed calculations of the outgoings on either side. Outgoings are not wholly irrelevant, but the primary calculation and the essential starting point is the gross earning capacity or actual earnings on the one hand of the father and on the other hand of the mother.*

'When one adopts that approach one sees how surprising it is that a man with an earning capacity in excess of £4,000 per annum gross should contribute only £3 a week each to the maintenance of his two dependent children.

'The other side of the picture is the mother's present position. She is employed as a solicitor's secretary and she is earning £2,850 per annum gross ... She has a substantial household to look after. There is the eldest child, Suzanne, who is a university student and who is not being maintained by Mr. Moon. There are the two young children in addition to herself. She has only a small amount of capital, £1,200, in a building society, her share of the net proceeds of sale of a house in which she had an interest. She now lives in a Council house.

'*There seems to have been some confusion in the minds of the Justices about the amount of the wife's income derived from allowances. The realistic position is that she now gets £4 per week per child as child benefit. In addition, she gets £2 per week as single parent allowance.* At the time of the hearing before the Justices she was receiving £3 per child for three children because Suzanne had not then reached the age of 18 years. That was in addition to the single parent allowance.

'In some way the Justices seem to have rolled these figures together and created confusion because they came to the conclusion that she was receiving in all £700 per annum for the children. That was not true at the time and never would have been true because Suzanne was dropping out of the picture. *In any event, I should add that I do not myself regard it as appropriate to take account of the single parent allowance in these calculations. The essential basis of the single parent allowance is that this additional sum paid by the state is intended to compensate a parent for the special difficulty of bringing up a family without the aid of a spouse. It is wrong to regard it as part of the income of a wife in the ordinary way to be contrasted with the income of a husband because it is a special allowance for a special purpose. If it is included in the wife's income, the whole purpose of the allowance is negatived.*

'*The proper approach in this case is to say that the mother is receiving £4 a week as the contribution from the State to the cost of bringing up each child. In total, she receives £8 per week. That is the relevant figure.*

'As for the actual cost of bringing up children, the husband concedes that it must be of the order of £15 to £20 a week, having regard to the high rate of inflation that has occurred in recent years. That is not, of course, the cost of bringing up a baby but it is certainly the cost of bringing up children entering their teens, especially in the case of girls, who have rather greater demands in terms of clothing.

'*I think that it is right that the wife should make a contribution from her own salary to the maintenance of the children.* She is, of course, making a very substantial contribution in work and effort; she is also making a contribution indirectly by providing light, heating and the home in which the children are being maintained. These are expenses additional, at least in part, to the cost of £15/£20 per week to which I have referred.

'Doing the best I can in these circumstances, I have come to the conclusion that the fairest order that I can make is that the appeal should be allowed and that I should substitute the figure of £7.50 per week maintenance in respect of each child. That will mean that the wife will receive a total contribution of £11.50 per week for each child from the state and from her former husband. *She will be left to meet the balance out of her own income.* Bearing in mind the comparative earnings of the parties and their obligations, I think that is the best solution that I can devise in this case.'

Note. See also *C v W* (4–414).

4–411A McDermott v McDermott

(1979) 10 Fam Law 145, CA

Maintenance of children out of public funds.   The wife filed a petition for divorce. Her statement as to the arrangements for the children of the family was that 'the children shall be maintained by both parties and a maintenance order against the respondent shall be obtained'. She was at present wholly dependent on social security payments. The husband was in regular employment. The judge granted decree nisi and expressed satisfaction with the arrangements for the accommodation and education of the children, but refused to grant a declaration of satisfaction as to the arrangements for the children under section 41 of the Matrimonial Causes Act 1973 pending the supply of further information as to the husband's means. The wife appealed.

Ormrod LJ referred to *Cook v Cook* (4–407), and said that the judge was perfectly correct in holding that further information was required before he could make a decision. In *Cook v Cook*, Goff LJ said (at page 1015):

'I would like to add a few words of my own on the question of general principle which has been argued before us as to what the judge should do under section 41 when he finds that the family is being supported by social security payments. In my judgment he should nevertheless grant a certificate unless either (i) he has reasonable grounds for supposing that a maintenance order could be obtained, or an existing order varied, so as to make provision for the child and the family significantly in excess of that which they obtained from social security; or (ii) he has before him no sufficient evidence to enable him to form any realistic opinion on that question; or (iii) that there is some particular circumstance, or event, to arouse his suspicion, as of course there was in *Dennett v Dennett* (4–405) . . .'

The case was an example of the second instance quoted by Goff LJ. The application for a declaration of satisfaction would stand adjourned pending the supply of further information.

Notes

1. Ormrod LJ added that a husband can be asked to provide an affidavit of means at any time after the filing of the divorce petition. [All that is necessary is for the wife to file a notice of intention to proceed with her application for maintenance pending suit and/or her application for maintenance for the children. The court will then issue a pro forma summons ordering the husband to file an affidavit of means. See *P (JM) v P (LE)* (4–400).] It is not a very expensive exercise and would provide the judge with a little more information.

2. In *Cook v Cook* (4–407) the question was not whether the judge had before him the necessary information, but whether he had exercised his discretion on wrong grounds in holding that it was not in the public interest that a child should be supported by public funds. It was held that the public interest was not a factor which the judge should have taken into account.

4–411B Tilley v Tilley

(1979) 10 Fam Law 89, CA

Husband's continuing liability for maintenance of children. Following the pronouncement of the decree nisi, a consent order was made vesting two properties in the wife in consideration of the wife making instalment payments to the husband. It was part of the order that the husband's maintenance liability should be merely a nominal 5p per year. The wife fell into financial difficulties and applied for variation of the consent order on the basis that she could not pay the balance of the instalments amounting to £3,500 now due without selling the roof over her head and rendering herself and the children homeless. Donaldson LJ said that the husband had a continuing obligation to maintain the children. The order would be varied by providing that there should be no further payments made to the husband, but that if there were any future application for maintenance for the children, any court faced with such an application ought to take into consideration the £3,500 which the husband would in effect have contributed towards their maintenance. Ormrod LJ, agreeing, said that it should be plainly borne in mind that the husband had a continuing obligation to the children which offset the consent order. However, had execution of the agreement not inevitably been going to lead to the eviction of the children from their home, the result of the case might have been very different.

Note. For further details, see case summary 4–110.

4–412 Gandolfo v Gandolfo (Standard Chartered Bank Ltd., garnishee)

[1980] 1 All ER 833, CA

School fees – garnishee order. The husband had been ordered to pay the wife periodical payments for herself and, on the basis of the husband's undertaking to the court to pay the school fees of the child of the marriage, was ordered to make further periodical payments to the wife for the benefit of the child. The husband fell into arrears with the periodical payments and the payment of the school fees.

The wife issued a garnishee summons against the husband's bank, applying for an order that the bank pay to the wife a sum in respect of the arrears of school fees and a further sum in respect of the arrears of maintenance. The husband appealed against the garnishee order in respect of the arrears of school fees. His appeal was on the grounds that the judge had no jurisdiction to make such an order in favour of the wife *because the school fees were payable by virtue of the husband's undertaking to the court and were not payable under any judgment or order obtained by the wife within the meaning of Order 27, rule 1 of the County Court Rules.*

The Court of Appeal held *that the court would in an appropriate case treat an undertaking given to the court as equivalent to an order in the terms of the undertaking. Furthermore, the undertaking was equivalent to an order 'obtained' by the wife because it was not an undertaking to pay the fees to the school.*

Note. It has now been settled that the courts have power to make orders for the payment of school fees direct to the school – see *Practice Direction dated 10th November 1980* (4–418). In such a case, possibly the school could obtain a garnishee order. However, the school would not have been a party to the proceedings. Could it be said to have 'obtained' the order for the payment of the school fees? But if the school could not obtain a garnishee order, could the mother? Could the mother be said to have 'obtained' the order for the payment of the school fees if the order was that they be paid direct to the school? In *Gandolfo v Gandolfo* the husband's argument had two limbs; the first was that there was no *order* against him for the payment of school fees; the second was that the undertaking was really an undertaking to pay the school fees *to the school* and so could not be regarded as an order obtained *by the wife*. The Court of Appeal's judgment in answer to the first limb of the husband's argument was that his undertaking was equivalent to an order. Their lordships' answer to the second limb of the argument was that the husband's undertaking did not say that the husband would pay the school fees *to the school*; it was merely an undertaking to pay them; therefore it could be regarded as an order obtained by the wife because it was in effect in her favour.

4–413 Carter v Carter

[1980] 1 All ER 827, CA

Clean break principle does not apply to financial provision for children.   The county court judge transferred the matrimonial home to the wife, subject to a charge in favour of the husband, and dismissed the wife's claim for periodical payments for herself and the children.

Ormrod LJ said that section 23 (1) of the Matrimonial Causes Act 1973 gives a right to apply for periodical payments on the granting of a decree or at any time thereafter (see Appendix I). That right cannot be taken away by the court unless the party concerned consents. The wife had not consented to her claim for periodical payments being dismissed in consideration of the matrimonial home being transferred into her name subject to the charge, *and no one could consent on behalf of the children.*

Note. See also *Minton v Minton* (4–409) and *Moore v Moore* (4–415).

4–414 C v W

(1980) Times, 16 February

DHSS single parent allowance disregarded.   Bush J endorsed Waterhouse J's statement in *M v M* (4–411) that it was not appropriate to take into account when calculating maintenance for children the additional single parent allowance paid by the DHSS to single parent families (i.e. over and above child benefit, which is payable to all families). The report in *The Times* reads as follows:

> A statement on the nature of the single parent allowance in the judgment of Mr. Justice Waterhouse in *M v M* (unreported, October 9, 1979) was endorsed by Mr. Justice Bush in the Family Division.
>   Mr. Justice Waterhouse said:
> '*I do not regard it as appropriate to take account of the single parent allowance in these calculations (for maintenance of children). The essential basis of the*

allowance is that this additional sum paid by the state is intended to compensate a parent for the special difficulty of bringing up a family without the aid of a spouse. It is wrong to regard it as part of the income of a wife in the ordinary way, to be contrasted with the income of a husband, because it is a special allowance for a special purpose. If it is included in the wife's income the purpose of the allowance is negatived.'

4–415 Moore v Moore

(1980) Times, 10 May, CA

Single parent raising young child unable to support herself – clean break not applicable. Ormrod LJ said that the 'clean break' principle as expounded in *Minton v Minton* (4–409) had caused misunderstanding. In that case a clean break was possible because a comprehensive settlement of the parties' finances was possible; it was not applicable where the financial resources of the parties were insufficient. It was nonsense to talk about a clean break where there were young children; it could not apply as the parties had to continue to co-operate because of the children. Moreover, it did not apply where one party was earning and the other could not earn; the effect of a clean break in such cases would mean people living on social security.

In the present case the wife was severely handicapped in that she was raising a small child on her own. She was entitled to a substantive order for periodical payments.

4–415A Hulley v Thompson

[1981] 1 All ER 1128

Husband's continuing liability to maintain children notwithstanding consent order transferring his interest in matrimonial home to wife.   See Appendix II.
   Note. See also *Tilley v Tilley* (4–411B).

4–416 Supplementary Benefits Commission v Jull

[1980] 3 All ER 65, HL

Maintenance order payable direct to child to be taken into account when calculating mother's entitlement to supplementary benefit.   Mrs. Jull was divorced. Her former husband had been ordered to make periodical payments of £21 a week to her and £12 a week direct to the child who lived with her. He had paid the child's order regularly but had not paid anything on Mrs. Jull's order, so that she had to have recourse to supplementary benefit. The Supplementary Benefits Commission took into account as part of her resources the £12 per week payable direct to the child. The result was that she received £6.70 less benefit than she would have received had the child's order not been taken into account. Woolf J held that the child's maintenance, because it was payable direct to the child, should not be included as part of Mrs. Jull's resources. Hence Mrs. Jull would be entitled to a further £6.70 benefit each week. The House of Lords allowed the Commission's appeal.
Notes
1. In June 1979 the Commission changed its policy and decided to take into account maintenance payable direct to children when assessing the mother's entitlement to benefit, so ending the advantage of direct payments of maintenance to children so far as supplementary benefits are concerned. The decision of the House of Lords upholds the Commission's new policy.
2. Under the Social Security Act 1980, the Supplementary Benefits Commission is abolished.
3. Paragraph 3 (2) of Schedule 4 to the Act reads: 'Where a person is responsible for, and is a member of the same household as, another person ... (a) if the other person is a

child . . . their requirements and resources shall be aggregated and treated as those of the first-mentioned person.'

4–417 Y v Supplementary Benefits Commission

[1980] 3 All ER 65, HL

Affiliation order payable to mother in respect of her illegitimate child to be taken into account when calculating mother's entitlement to supplementary benefit. The House of Lords upheld the views of the Supplementary Benefits Commission that maintenance payments are resources to be taken into account whether they are payable to the mother for the child or payable direct to the child. For further details, see *Supplementary Benefits Commission v Jull* (4–416).

4–418 Practice Direction 10th November 1980 – Payment of school fees

[1980] 3 All ER 832

Where a maintenance order to a child includes an element in respect of school fees, which is paid direct to the school (because, eg it is feared that the other spouse might dissipate it), the Inland Revenue has agreed, subject to the condition hereafter set out, that tax relief will be given on that element. The wording of the order should be *'that that part of the order which reflects the school fees shall be paid to the (headmaster) (bursar) (school secretary) as agent for the said child and the receipt of that payee shall be sufficient discharge'*. The school fees should be paid in full and should be paid out of the net amount under the maintenance order after deduction of tax. Certificates for the full tax deduction should continue to be provided to the other spouse (or other person referred to in r. 69 of the Matrimonial Causes Rules 1977 (S.I. No 344)) in the normal way.

It is a condition of such an order being acceptable for tax purposes that the contract for the child's education (which should preferably be in writing) should be between the child (whose income is being used) and the school and that the fees are received by the officer of the school as the appointed agent for the child.

A form of contract which is acceptable to the Inland Revenue is as follows:

> THIS AGREEMENT is made between THE GOVERNORS OF . . . by their duly authorised officer . . . (hereinafter called 'the school') of the first part; . . . and the (headmaster) (bursar) (school secretary) of the second part, and . . . (hereinafter called 'the child') of the third part.
>
> WHEREAS it is proposed to ask the . . . court to make an order/the . . . court has made an order/in cause No . . . that the father do make periodical payments to the child at the rate of £ . . . per annum less tax until the child completes full time education (or as the case may be) and that that part of the order which reflects the school fees shall be paid to the (headmaster) (bursar) (school secretary) as agent for the said child and the receipt of that agent shall be a sufficient discharge.
>
> 1 The child hereby constitutes the (headmaster) (bursar) (school secretary) to be his agent for the purpose of receiving the said fees and the child agrees to pay the said fees to the said school in consideration of being educated there.
>
> 2 In consideration of the said covenant the (headmaster) (bursar) (school secretary) agrees to accept the said payments by the father as payments on behalf of the child and the school agrees to educate the child during such time as the said school fees are paid.

Notes

1. In an article in *The Law Society's Gazette* published on 11th February 1981 Mr. K. M. Kirby suggested that clause 2 of this form of contract is unsatisfactory from the school's point of view and that the closing words of clause 2 should be revised to read: 'and the school agrees to educate the child during such time as the school fees at the appropriate rate for the time being in force and incidentals are paid'.
2. In an article in *The Law Society's Gazette* published on 10th December 1980 Mr.

Sebastian Cullwick suggested that an additional clause be added in order that the tax relief might be back-dated:

The (headmaster) (bursar) (school secretary) acknowledges that the first payment by the father on behalf of the child was made on the ... day of ... 19 ... and that since that date until the date hereof all such payments in respect of the child's education have been paid. It is acknowledged that such payments amount in total to £ ... (gross).

Mr. Cullwick argues that there has been no change in the law; therefore, if tax relief is available now it ought to have been available from the date the court ordered the payment of the school fees.

The Law Society Gazette published the following letter from Mr. R. L. Bayne-Powell, Senior Registrar at the Principal Registry, on 21st January 1981.

Dear Mr. Cullwick,

Payment of School Fees

Thank you for your letter of 7 January.

As you are aware it is not possible for the court to order payment of school fees as such. The normal practice is to obtain a maintenance order which is large enough to cover those fees. Tax relief is available on maintenance payments. It is not available on payments of school fees even if a respondent has undertaken to the court to pay these.

In some cases, a payer under a maintenance order, which includes an element in respect of school fees, and which is expressed to be payable direct to a child, may pay part of it to the school and the balance to the child after deduction of tax. At the stage at which payment is made to the school, the payment is still one of maintenance and forms part of the child's income.

The Inland Revenue takes the view that as payment is to be made out of the child's income, the responsibility for the payment of the fees must be the child's. The Revenue therefore requires it to be clear that a contract exists between the child and the school; hence the suggested form of agreement contained in the Direction of 10 November 1980.

It is, of course, still possible for all of the amount ordered to be paid direct to the child, including the element for school fees, as has been the practice in the past, deducting tax as appropriate.

The arrangement for the diversionary payment is merely an alternative.

As I have said, tax relief is not available on payment of school fees and the Revenue would never agree to it. In my opinion, if there are cases in which tax relief is not available because of the way in which the order has been worded, consideration ought to be given to having the order appropriately varied.

You may publish this letter if you wish.

Yours sincerely,

R. L. Bayne-Powell Senior Registrar

3. In the light of Mr. Bayne-Powell's letter to Mr. Cullwick the authors would suggest the following alternative arrangement where the parties are of a mind to co-operate over their children's education: that the child's maintenance, including an amount sufficient to cover the school fees, be ordered to be paid direct to the child, with the usual provision that the receipt of the parent having care and control shall be sufficient discharge. The recipient parent will then be in a position to pay the school fees without necessitating any written contract between the child and the school which the child may refuse to sign!

4. Halsbury's Laws of England (4th Edition) Volume 24: Infants, Children and Young Persons states at para. 407: 'In accordance with the principle that an infant is of immature intelligence and discretion, an infant's contract is at common law generally voidable at the instance of the infant, although it is binding upon the other party. Exceptions to this rule are contracts for necessaries and certain other contracts such as contracts of service and apprenticeship, if they are clearly for the infant's benefit; such contracts are valid and binding upon an infant. In such cases the question to be judged is whether the contract is or is not on the whole beneficial at the date when it is made.' And at para. 417: '... Education suitable to the infant's prospects in life is a necessary for which he can bind himself.' Alternatively, a contract for the provision of education can be valid as a contract for the infant's benefit: *Mackinlay v Bathurst* (1919) 36 TLR 31, CA.

4-419 Brown v Brown

(1981) Times, 14 July

Maintenance of children – third party's earnings to be excluded.   See Appendix II.

Note. This husband had no resources. Compare *Tovey v Tovey* (4–406) – husband ordered to pay maintenance of £1 per week for each of the children of his first marriage out of his meagre resources. And compare *Macey v Macey* (see Appendix II) – third party's earnings to be taken into account in the overall picture.

4-420 Macey v Macey

(1981) Times, 14 July

Maintenance of children – third party's earnings to be excluded – but to be taken into account in the overall picture.   See Appendix II.

CHAPTER 5

A home for the parties to the marriage

As was suggested in the last chapter, the provision of a home for both parties to the marriage has now reached a stage of some considerable emphasis. Probably the most important case is *Martin v Martin* (5–103). Prior to *Martin v Martin*, it had generally been assumed that a wife who remained in the jointly-owned matrimonial home with the children would be allowed to remain there until the children reached their late teens, when the husband could obtain an order for its sale so as to get his money out; whereas where there were no children, or the children had reached adulthood, there would be no reason for not ordering an immediate sale of the property. In *Martin v Martin* there were no children, and the husband would ordinarily have expected an order for sale to be made. Purchas J ordered that the house should be held on trust for sale for the wife during her life or until remarriage or such earlier date as she ceased to live there, and thereafter upon trust for the parties in equal shares. The husband's appeal was dismissed by the Court of Appeal, which emphasised that the primary consideration is that each party should have a roof over his or her head, whether or not there are children of the family.

If there are children of the family, then it can be argued that, if the wife obtains custody, the house is required as a home for them. But if there are no children, or if the children have grown up, the argument will frequently turn on the question of whether a sale of the house will enable both parties to be adequately rehoused. In *Goodfield v Goodfield* (5–102) this was possible; accordingly, there was no reason to deny the husband the use of his capital tied up in the house. In *Martin v Martin* a sale of the house would have left the wife homeless, because she did not have the means to rehouse herself; consequently the husband was denied an order for sale. [See generally the introduction to Part 6.]

1 A roof over the heads of both parties

A. *Proceedings under Matrimonial Causes Act 1973*

CASE SUMMARIES

5–101 Thompson v Thompson
[1975] 2 All ER 208, CA

Council tenancy – wife and child adequately housed with wife's parents – husband's housing difficulties the decisive factor. The former matrimonial home was a council house. The husband was the tenant. The wife obtained custody of the child of the marriage. She applied for a transfer of property order under section 24 of the Matrimonial Causes Act 1973. She was living with her parents and was adequately housed, although the accommodation was neither very suitable nor convenient. However, the decisive factor in the judge's opinion was that the husband would have difficulty in rehousing himself if he lost his home. The Court of Appeal held that the judge had carefully weighed all the relevant considerations, and had properly exercised his discretion in refusing to make the order.

5–102 Goodfield v Goodfield

(1975) 5 Fam Law 197, CA

Matrimonial home owned in equal shares – one half of net sale proceeds sufficient to rehouse wife – sale ordered. The parties had agreed before the hearing for ancillary relief that the beneficial interest in the former matrimonial home should be divided between them in equal shares. There was one child of the marriage, now over 17 years of age, but still living with the mother in the house. The registrar ordered that the wife be permitted to remain in the house until her remarriage or death or the sale of the property, such sale not to take place without her express consent.

Scarman LJ (as he then was) said that the problem before the court was whether the husband, who was entitled to an equal share of the one capital asset of the family, should be subject to an order which in all likelihood would deprive him of the benefit of his share of that asset. Since the wife's case was largely based on the difficulties she would have in finding other accommodation, there was a very strong probability that if the wife were allowed to remain in the house, she would continue to do so for a very considerable period. While the wife would be in a difficult accommodation market, it was really inconceivable that a single woman with £4,750 behind her (half the equity in the house) and a steady job could not find accommodation if she were forced to. That accommodation might not be the accommodation to which she had been accustomed for 20 years. It was a sadness of matrimonial breakdown that neither side was able to maintain quite the standard of life they were able to maintain when they were united. The wife must accept a measure of disadvantage if the Matrimonial Causes Act 1973, section 25 were to be applied and justice be done to the husband as well as to her. A matrimonial home for a family such as this was not only a place in which both could live; it was a security for old age, a capital resource to which they could turn in times of trouble or emergency. Postponing the sale indefinitely meant that the husband was deprived of the backing of that capital asset. That was clearly a very serious problem for him, causing genuine hardship. It might be otherwise if he had other capital or was earning a substantial income. The fact that he had acquired what appeared to be a stable home with the lady with whom he was living went only to his accommodation problem, whereas the hardship imposed by the order was the deprivation of immediate access to his capital asset. A postponement of the benefit of the capital asset for a period of time was often a reasonable burden to place on a spouse, e.g. where there were young children living with the wife. The menace of this order to the husband was the prolonged and indefinite nature of the postponement and the possibility that he might require the asset and be unable to realise it. Cairns LJ agreed.

The court ordered that the house be sold, but not before the elapse of one year from the date of the order unless in the meantime the wife died or remarried or consented to such sale; until such sale the wife was to be entitled to remain in occupation but with the duty to pay the rates and mortgage instalments. Upon sale the proceeds were to be divided equally between the parties.

Notes

1. A recital of the facts (taken from the judgment of the county court judge) and of the

judgment of the Court of Appeal is also to be found in the judgment of Stamp LJ in *Martin v Martin* (5–103).

2. *Goodfield v Goodfield* was distinguished in *Martin v Martin* on the ground that in *Goodfield v Goodfield* the sale of the house and division of the sale proceeds would not leave the wife without a roof over her head.

3. In *Blezard v Blezard* (5–111) it was argued by counsel for the husband that *Goodfield v Goodfield* was not consistent with the judgment of the Court of Appeal in *Martin v Martin*. Orr LJ said that there was no inconsistency between the two cases. *Martin v Martin* was a case in which the registrar had found that the wife's share in the equity of the matrimonial home was insufficient to enable her to find alternative accommodation.

5–102A Mentel v Mentel

(1975) 6 Fam Law 53, 119 Sol Jo 808, CA

Matrimonial home owned in equal shares – wife living with new husband in secure accommodation – husband's inability to raise sufficient on mortgage to purchase wife's half share – order for sale refused. In 1963 the parties purchased a matrimonial home for £3,600, financed as to £1,600 out of their joint savings, the balance being raised by mortgage. In 1968 the wife left the home and shortly afterwards started living with a man, whom she later married; the man became a police officer and secured rent-free accommodation. The wife applied under section 17 of the Married Women's Property Act 1882 for an order that the house be sold and the equity be divided equally between the parties. The husband applied for a transfer of property order under the modern legislation.

Roskill LJ said that the right way to approach the problem was to start by asking what the assets of the parties were when the marriage broke up and what property each had in those assets. The only property was a one-half interest in the house subject to the mortgage. It was all very well in these cases to talk about the matrimonial home as if it were a capital asset, but anything less readily and quickly realisable than a matrimonial home was difficult to imagine. If the property were to be sold, then there would be the question not only of providing a roof over the head of the party who had left the home, but also the problem of rehousing the party who remained in the home.

Applying each of the paragraphs of section 25 (1) (g) of the Matrimonial Causes Act 1973 item by item to the parties, certain things stood out clearly. The first was that the husband was undoubtedly worse off than he was before the marriage broke up. He was having to pay the whole of the mortgage interest and principal. Whereas if the marriage had lasted, if his wife had gone on working while living with him, he would have received a contribution towards that liability. That was an extra burden on him. On the other hand, he still had the house as a home.

If the wife had not left the husband, the husband would have been hard put to have resisted an order for a 50:50 division. In that event the house would almost certainly have had to be sold in order to realise the requisite cash for payment to the wife, but that was not now the position. The wife had remarried and had got a home. Therefore, if she had her full half share made over to her or its equivalent in terms of cash, she would be getting half the value of the house at a time when she had the benefit of a completely new home, rent free, as a result of her remarriage.

It would not be right to say that the wife should receive anything approaching that one half interest. That would not produce a just result when one took all the relevant considerations into account. The judge's award to the wife of a lump sum of £1,750 might be on the low side, but there was great force in counsel for the husband's argument that if this figure were substantially raised by requiring the husband to borrow a much larger sum in order to buy the wife out, he would be being asked to accept an unfair burden. The judge's figure was one with which the court ought not to interfere.

Ormrod and Stamp LJJ agreed.

5–103 Martin v Martin (sub nom. **Martin (BH) v Martin (D)**)

[1977] 3 All ER 762, CA

Matrimonial home owned in equal shares – husband living with another woman in council house – one half of net sale proceeds insufficient to rehouse wife – order for sale refused. After a childless marriage lasting 15 years the husband left the matrimonial home which he had bought during the first year of the marriage and went to live with another woman who had a tenancy of a council house. The wife remained in the matrimonial home, obtained a divorce and applied for a property adjustment order in respect of the husband's interest in the house. The equity in the house was worth approximately £10,000 and the parties' solicitors agreed that the equity belonged to the parties in equal shares. Purchas J ordered that the house should be held on trust for the wife during her life or until her remarriage or such earlier date as she should cease to live there and thereafter upon trust for the parties in equal shares. The husband's appeal was dismissed.

Stamp LJ said (at page 765): '*It is of primary concern in these cases that on the breakdown of the marriage the parties should, if possible, each have a roof over his or her head. That is perhaps the most important circumstance to be taken into account in applying section 25 of the Matrimonial Causes Act 1973 when the only available asset is the matrimonial home. It is important that each party should have a roof over his or her head whether or not there be children of the marriage.*'

Stamp LJ distinguished *Goodfield v Goodfield* (5–102) on the ground that an order for sale and division of the proceeds of the matrimonial home in that case did not involve leaving the wife without a roof over her head (see page 767).

Note. In *Blezard v Blezard* (5–111) it was argued by counsel for the husband that *Goodfield v Goodfield* was not consistent with the judgment of the Court of Appeal in *Martin v Martin*. Orr LJ said that there was no inconsistency between the two cases. *Martin v Martin* was a case in which the registrar had found that the wife's share in the equity of the matrimonial home was insufficient to enable her to find alternative accommodation.

5–104 Hanlon v Hanlon

[1978] 2 All ER 889, CA

Husband living in secure accommodation – one half of net sale proceeds insufficient to rehouse wife in 5 years' time on youngest child attaining 17 – desirability of crystallising parties' interests now – transfer to wife absolutely. The matrimonial home had been purchased in the sole name of the husband, although during the 14 years of the marriage the husband and wife had contributed equally in money and work to the family. The parties had now lived apart for over five years. The wife remained in the house with the four children while the husband, a police officer, now lived in a flat provided rent-free by his employers. The judge at first instance ordered that the house be transferred into joint names on trust for sale in equal shares, the sale to be postponed until the youngest child, then 12, had attained 17.

Ormrod LJ said that it was not right to regard the interests of the husband and wife in the house as being equal because the wife had, in the five years since the separation, maintained it and looked after the family and would continue to do so until they left home, and had therefore made a very large contribution to the family. *As one-half of the equity on the eventual sale of the house could not produce a sum sufficient to enable the wife to buy another home for herself and such of the children as were still with her, it would be wrong to make an order which would have the result of forcing the wife to leave the house when the youngest child attained the age of 17. As she was not claiming any maintenance for herself, and was willing to forgo any further periodical payments for the two children who were under 17, the proper order was to transfer the house to the wife absolutely.*

Ormrod LJ said (at page 895): '. . . In my judgment it would be a quite wrong exercise of the discretion in accordance with the principles of section 25 [of the

Matrimonial Causes Act 1973 – see Appendix I] to make any order which had the result of forcing [the wife] to leave that property in the foreseeable future. It was suggested that this might be the kind of case which could be met by postponing the sale indefinitely until further order, and then distributing the proceeds of sale, not necessarily on a 50–50 basis; but I do not think that that, in this case, would be in the least satisfactory; it would leave the wife in a state of perpetual uncertainty and neither party would know where ultimately they were going to be. It seems to me far better that the parties' interests should be crystallised now, once and for all, so that the wife can know what she is going to do about the property and the husband can make up his mind about what he is going to do about rehousing.'

Note. This is the principle of the clean break. Regarding the wife's acceptance of a clean break in this case, see notes to case summary 10–102.

5–105 Scott v Scott

[1978] 3 All ER 65, CA

One-third of net sale proceeds insufficient to rehouse wife in 14 years' time on youngest child attaining 18 – wife's share increased accordingly. There were three children of the marriage, twin girls aged 4 and a boy aged 6. The wife was residing with the children in the former matrimonial home while the husband was living in a bed-sitting room. The house had been purchased in the husband's name the year before the marriage with the aid of a mortgage granted to the husband by his employers at an unusually low rate of interest. Both parties had contributed to the deposit, and the wife had worked and contributed to the family expenses until the birth of the eldest child. The wife had capital of her own of £2,000.

The registrar ordered that the house be settled on trust for sale, the sale to be postponed until the younger children attained 18 or ceased full-time education whichever was later, i.e. in effect postponing the sale for some 14 years, and that on the sale of the property the proceeds were to be divided as to 60 per cent for the husband and 40 per cent for the wife. The county court judge having affirmed the registrar's order, the husband appealed to the Court of Appeal.

The Court of Appeal also upheld the order in respect of the house. *The order would enable the wife, with the help of her own capital, to be in a slightly better capital position than the husband when the house was sold in about 14 years' time, in order to compensate her for the fact that she would not be in as strong a position as the husband to raise a mortgage and rehouse herself; the husband, who would then be 45, would have less difficulty in obtaining a mortgage. The division of the capital had nothing to do with the one-third ratio; it was an attempt to deal with the rehousing of the parties in 14 years' time after the children had grown up.*

The court expressed sympathy for the husband, who was living in poor accommodation, but the wife's standard of living in the former matrimonial home was also extremely restricted; this was a 'small income situation' and a 'small capital situation'; the house had first to be appropriated for the use of the children and the parent who had the responsibility of bringing them up; in this case, the wife.

5–106 Dallimer v Dallimer

(1978) 8 Fam Law 142, CA

Wife living with co-respondent – wrong to force husband to leave house. The matrimonial home was purchased in the parties' joint names in 1956 for £2,200, with a deposit of £450 which the husband borrowed from his employers and from members of his family. The balance of £1,750 was on mortgage. The husband made all the mortgage repayments. The husband, aged 75, was now retired and living upon a state pension and social security benefit. His only asset apart from his interest in the house was a sum of £300, which represented his savings. The wife was now living with the co-respondent, by whom she had three children. The husband contended that the wife should be given a one-third interest in the property, not to be realised until he should die or voluntarily cease to reside in the house. The wife conceded that the husband should remain in the house but contended that her share should be a one-half interest.

The co-respondent had transferred to the wife the house in which they both lived. Its value was about £15,000 and it was subject to a mortgage of £6,000. So far as the matrimonial home was concerned, the mortgage had now been paid off by the husband and the house was now worth some £14,000.

Eveleigh LJ emphasised that it would be wholly wrong to make any order which would cause the husband to leave the house. But considering what proportion of the interest in the house should belong to the wife – and these matters were never easy – his Lordship came to the conclusion that the fair and just apportionment was one-third to the wife and two-thirds to the husband.

Orr and Stamp LJJ agreed. Stamp LJ added that the wife had a roof over her head and had not suffered any financial loss as a result of the breakdown of the marriage.

Note. See also *Eshak v Nowojewski* (5–114).

5–107 Cawkwell v Cawkwell

(1978) 9 Fam Law 25, CA

One-half of net sale proceeds insufficient to rehouse wife in 5 years' time on youngest child attaining 17 – wife's share increased accordingly.   There were three children of the marriage, two boys who were now adults, and a girl now aged 12. The girl resided with the wife in the former matrimonial home while the husband lived in a bed-sitting room. The house had been purchased with the aid of compensation received by the husband for an industrial injury and with the aid of a mortgage. The wife had contributed to its purchase by assisting with the mortgage repayments and by paying the rates, out of her income from part-time employment and from providing bed and breakfast accommodation to visitors during the holiday season. The county court judge ordered the house to be transferred to the husband and wife in equal shares and that the wife should be allowed to remain there until the daughter attained 17 or ceased full-time education.

The wife appealed on the basis that she would have to vacate the house in five years' time when the daughter reached 17 and that her half share of the proceeds would not be enough to rehouse herself.

Orr LJ said that the Court of Appeal had pointed out in *Hanlon v Hanlon* (5–104) that a serious problem arose where a sale of the former matrimonial home would not produce sufficient to rehouse both parties. In *Hanlon v Hanlon* the husband was a police officer living in police accommodation. In addition, he would be entitled to a lump sum by way of gratuity on his retirement. Similarly, in *Martin v Martin* (5–103) the husband was living with a woman he intended to marry in a council house of which she was the tenant. Therefore, in both of these cases the husbands in effect had a degree of security of tenure. In the present case the husband had none.

The Court of Appeal ordered that the house be held on trust for sale, two-thirds to the wife and one-third to the husband, the trust not to be executed until the daughter reached 17 or ceased full-time education, which would produce a larger sum for the wife than the order made by the county court judge, and would give her a substantially better chance of obtaining secure accommodation when the house was sold. Furthermore, it would also provide a modest capital sum for the husband which he might be able to use so as to obtain secure accommodation for himself.

Notes

1. Compare *Hanlon v Hanlon* in which the husband's share was extinguished, firstly,

because he was in secure accommodation and, secondly, because the wife was willing to agree to a clean break.

2. Compare *Martin v Martin* in which the order made allowed the wife to remain in the house for the rest of her life, the house then to be sold and the proceeds divided equally. As in *Hanlon v Hanlon*, the husband was living in secure accommodation.

3. It can now be seen that in cases where the wife is going to have difficulty in rehousing herself with her share of the sale proceeds the court has three courses open to it: (i) allow the wife to remain in the house for the rest of her life and then divide the proceeds (*Martin v Martin*); (ii) vest the house in the wife alone in return for her agreeing to a clean break (*Hanlon v Hanlon*); (iii) increase the wife's share in the property and order a sale, either on the children attaining 17 or ceasing their full-time education (*Cawkwell v Cawkwell* and *Scott v Scott* (5–105)) or, if the children are grown up, immediately (*Bennett v Bennett* (5–108)).

4. Orr LJ said that it was unfortunate that the court did not have before it evidence as to the level of property values in the area and evidence as to whether the wife could have found accommodation for herself with a half share of the sale proceeds. The court had therefore to deal with the matter on an uncertain basis.

5–108 Bennett v Bennett

(1978) 9 Fam Law 19, CA

One-third of capital assets insufficient to rehouse wife – wife's share increased accordingly. Both parties were now aged 50. Their elder child was already at university and their younger child was about to go to university. The wife remained in the former matrimonial home with the younger child. The husband was living with the co-respondent in a house she had bought out of the proceeds of sale of her former matrimonial home.

The wife earned £3,000 per annum. The husband had resigned his job as a financial director earning between £7,000 and £8,000 per annum two years ago following the appointment of a new managing director. He was unwilling to accept a lower paid appointment. Unless he found a job offering more than £6,000, by virtue of the one-third ratio, he would not be liable to pay any maintenance other than a nominal payment. The husband owned the house, valued at £30,250, subject to a mortgage of £4,000, an insurance policy with a surrender value of £2,850 which was mortgaged as collateral in connection with the mortgage of the house, and he had commutable pension rights of the value of £5,268, producing a total of £34,368. The wife had investments totalling some £4,000.

The judge accepted that if the wife obtained the whole interest in the house she might appear to be getting more than she was entitled to, but he considered it would be wrong to order a sale of the house because the wife needed somewhere to live. He had already warned the husband at an earlier hearing that unless he obtained a job he would order the house to be transferred into the wife's name, which was duly done. The husband appealed against this order.

The wife's advisers agreed that if the wife were to obtain a sum of the order of £17,000 she would be in a position to purchase a suitable home in the locality. The Court of Appeal substituted an order for the immediate sale of the house, the wife to obtain two-thirds of the net proceeds of sale or £17,000, whichever was the greater. The husband would retain for his own benefit the life policy mortgaged as collateral security. Nominal order for periodical payments.

Notes

1. It would seem surprising if the court had not considered a *Martin v Martin* (5–103) order, vesting the house in the wife for her life and dividing the proceeds on its sale; the wife could have used her £4,000 worth of investments to pay off the mortgage, and she was earning enough to support herself. The benefit to the husband of the order which was made was that he would get some of his money out of the house in the immediate future.

2. The order which was made follows the line taken by Stamp and Orr LJJ in *Cawkwell v Cawkwell* (5–107).

5–109 Kurylowicz v Kurylowicz

(1978) 9 Fam Law 119, CA

Two-thirds of net sale proceeds insufficient to rehouse wife – sale refused.   The wife was now living in the matrimonial home with her son aged 18 who was paying her £8 per week for his keep. The husband was living in an alcoholics' hospital. The matrimonial home had an equity of approximately £10,000.

The registrar had ordered that the house be transferred to the wife subject to a charge of £3,500 in the husband's favour, the charge to be enforceable after five years or on the wife's earlier death. Following an appeal to the county court judge there was an appeal to the Court of Appeal.

Orr LJ said that it would not be right for the wife to have to sell the house and rehouse herself. She was now 60 and was living in a house which was near the bottom of the housing market. She would be in a worse position in five years' time, when she would be 65. It would be impossible for her to satisfy the charge without selling the house, and she had no other capital to assist in rehousing herself.

On the other hand, his lordship considered that it would be wrong to strip the husband entirely of his interest in his sole capital asset.

The Court of Appeal ordered that the house be held on trust for sale but not to be sold during the lifetime of the wife, that the wife should have the right to live there during her life, and that after her death the net proceeds of sale be divided as to two-thirds to the wife's estate and one-third to the husband if he survived her.

5–110 Chinnock v Chinnock

(1978) 9 Fam Law 249, CA

Wife and children living in council house – three fifths of net sale proceeds insufficient to rehouse husband – sale refused.   The husband had once left the matrimonial home and had gone to live with another woman, but that association had only lasted three months. The wife went to live with her parents. She now lived with the children in a council house and was wholly maintained by social security. The husband was now living in the matrimonial home.

The matrimonial home was valued at £11,000 with an equity of £5,000. The husband conceded that the wife had a one-third interest in it. The county court judge ordered the husband to pay the wife a lump sum of £2,000 within six months. The husband appealed.

Ormrod LJ said that the husband could not possibly raise any such sum, and that to make such an order would mean that the house would have to be sold immediately. There was no evidence that the husband could obtain other accommodation once he had lost his home, and in his lordship's view such an order would cause a real injustice to the husband.

His lordship referred to *Browne v Pritchard* (4–104), but in that case two of the children of the family were living with the husband in the matrimonial home. Therefore, the two cases were not directly comparable. However, in his lordship's judgment, the reasoning of Lord Denning MR in that case was applicable here, and the fact that the children were with the wife in this case and not with the husband (as in that case) did not really alter the argument. Both parties and the children had a home. The wife's argument was that she should be allowed her share of the capital now; but the Court of Appeal had held in many cases [e.g. *Martin v Martin* (5–103), *Dallimer v Dallimer* (5–106)] that so long as one spouse was living in the house no order should be made which would displace that spouse unless there was some way of adjusting the housing arrangements fairly. One circumstance in which the wife might expect to realise her interest in the property would be when the husband chose to sell it. If he chose to sell it, then it would seem reasonable that he should account to her for her interest in it. But if he were required to sell the house in other circumstances it was bound to cause him a large degree of hardship.

The husband's appeal was allowed. The husband would hold the property subject to a charge of one-third of the net proceeds of sale, such charge to be free of interest and not to be enforceable unless and until the husband either sold the property or died.

5–111 Blezard v Blezard

(1978) 9 Fam Law 249, CA

Matrimonial home owned in equal shares – three fifths of net sale proceeds sufficient to rehouse wife – order for sale on youngest child completing education. The former matrimonial home, now valued at at least £52,000 with an equity of £48,000, had been purchased in joint names. There were two children of the marriage, a boy aged 16 who had left school and obtained employment, and a girl aged 14. Both were living with their mother in the house. The judge had ordered that there should be an immediate sale of the property and that a lump sum of £32,500 be paid to the wife out of the proceeds of sale. The wife appealed.

Orr LJ referred to *Goodfield v Goodfield* (5–102) which, his lordship said, was similar inasmuch as in both cases the husband had left the wife in order to live with another woman. However, in that case the child living with the wife was a boy aged 17 and able to look after himself whereas in the present case the younger child was still at school. In *Goodfield v Goodfield* the Court of Appeal had made an order for sale in a year's time, that being, in the view of the court, an appropriate time to afford the wife an opportunity of obtaining fresh accommodation. Orr LJ said that he was satisfied that in the present case the judge had been correct in deciding that the sale of the house should not be postponed until the death or remarriage of the wife; but the remaining question was whether he had been right to order an immediate sale.

His lordship said that the interests of the children had to be considered, and that in his judgment it was in their best interests that they should remain in their present home until the younger child attained 18 and that she should complete her education at her present school. His lordship would therefore vary the judge's order to provide for a sale on January 1st 1983, which would be some months after the younger child attained the age of 18. Had there been no children, his lordship would have ordered an immediate sale, subject only to allowing the wife sufficient time to find a new home.

Order varied to provide that the husband should have a charge of two-fifths of the net proceeds of sale, such charge not to be enforced until January 1st 1983 or unless the wife remarried or cohabited with another man.

Notes
1. The wife had agreed to make the mortgage repayments. Orr LJ thought it right that the husband should have less than a half share of the sale proceeds in view of this.
2. Orr LJ stated that there was no inconsistency between the decisions in *Goodfield v Goodfield* and *Martin v Martin* (5–103). The latter case was one in which the registrar had found that the wife's share in the equity of the matrimonial home was insufficient to enable her to find alternative accommodation.

5–112 Ward v Ward and Greene (sub nom. Ward v Ward)

[1980] 1 All ER 176, [1980] 1 WLR 4, CA (these notes taken from transcript of shorthand notes of Association of Official Shorthandwriters Limited)

Matrimonial home owned in equal shares – husband and co-respondent securely housed – one half of net sale proceeds insufficient to rehouse wife – transfer to wife absolutely. During the course of proceedings agreement was reached that the jointly-owned matrimonial home, a flat where the wife was now living, should be transferred to her absolutely. It was common ground that the flat would have to be sold because it was too expensive to keep up. After repayment of the three mortgages secured on the property, together with the arrears which had accrued, it was apparent that the wife would not have enough capital to purchase even modest accommodation without recourse to borrowing.

The husband was now living with a Mrs. Greene in rented accommodation. Both of them were earning substantial sums.

The husband appealed against Dunn J's order for periodical payments on the ground (inter alia) that the wife had already received all the capital of the family.

Ormrod LJ said that one should not look just at the fact that the wife had obtained all of the family's capital, but at what that really meant in real life terms – i.e. that she would be in a position to buy herself a very modest flat, so reducing her cost of living in so far as she would not have to pay a high rent. All she was in a position to do was to rehouse herself more cheaply than she otherwise would have been able. It would be cheaper for her to be housed in this way than to divide the capital equally. This would leave her with too little with which to rehouse herself and would not help the husband at all because he would then have to pay her increased maintenance to cover the cost of rented accommodation.

His lordship said that the order balanced the needs of the one against the needs of the other, and that Dunn J was fully entitled to take into account the fact that the husband had the advantage of living with a lady who had a substantial income of her own which plainly reduced his cost of living.

For further details, see case summary 6–303.

5–113 Dunford v Dunford

[1980] 1 All ER 122, CA

Desirability of crystallising parties' interests now.   The matrimonial home had been purchased in the parties' joint names with the aid of a 100 per cent mortgage. The parties separated, the wife remaining in the house with the children, the husband going into lodgings. The county court judge ordered the husband to transfer his half share to the wife subject to a charge of 25 per cent of the net sale proceeds should the wife vacate the property or die. The husband appealed, contending that the house should be sold on the youngest child completing her full-time education or on the wife's remarriage, and that he should be ordered to transfer to the wife not 50 per cent of his interest in the property but only such interest as would be necessary for the wife's future needs. The wife cross-appealed, contending that the husband's interest should be extinguished. The Court of Appeal approved the judge's order in respect of the matrimonial home.

Lord Denning MR said that when the matter had first come before the registrar the registrar had applied *Mesher v Mesher* (4–101) and had ordered that the house was not to be sold until the youngest child had finished her schooling. Presumably, after that time, it could be sold and the proceeds divided equally between the parties. His lordship continued (at page 124): 'That order left the parties in complete uncertainty as to the future. After six or seven years the house would have to be sold and the husband would take a half share of the proceeds, and the wife would be left with insufficient money to buy another house. The wife's solicitors appealed. The judge made a different order. He ordered that the whole of the interest in the house should be transferred to the wife within three months. He realised that if it were transferred, the wife would have to pay the mortgage instalments, the rates, and all the other outgoings on the house. But the judge realised that the wife might die or might sell the house some time in the future. If that should happen, the judge ordered that the husband should then have 25 per cent of the equity . . .

'By making that order, the parties would know exactly where they stood with regard to the future. In so ordering, the judge applied the principle which is now flowing through these cases. It was indicated in the recent case of *Hanlon v Hanlon* (5–104) by Ormrod LJ. When it was suggested that there should be a postponement of the sale and then a distribution on a fifty-fifty basis, he said:

"... I do not think that that, in this case, would be in the least satisfactory; it would leave the wife in a state of perpetual uncertainty and neither party would know where ultimately they were going to be. It seems to me far better that the parties' interests should be crystallised now, once and for all, so that the wife can know what she is going to do about the property and the husband can make up his mind about what he is going to do about rehousing."

That principle was expressed again in the recent case of *Minton v Minton* (10–205) by Lord Scarman. He drew attention to the principle of the clean break. He said:

"The law now encourages spouses to avoid bitterness after family breakdown and to settle their money and property problems. An object of the modern law is to encourage the parties to put the past behind them and to begin a new life which is not overshadowed by the relationship which has broken down."

'There is only one variation which I think should be made to the order of the judge. He ordered that the order for periodical payments for the wife should be 5p per annum, a nominal sum. That should not be included in an order when you want a clean break ... so I think in this case the order of the judge should be varied by striking out the order for periodical payments of 5p per year. In that way we have the "clean break". The wife knows exactly where she stands. The house is vested in her. She has the property in it, and she can keep the family together. She can keep it as a home for the family as they grow up. She can keep it going indefinitely, knowing exactly where she stands. But if it should happen that she should sell the house (or should die) then the husband is to have one-quarter of the net proceeds.'

Eveleigh LJ, agreeing, said: 'It is true that the husband is losing his share in the equity of the house, but it is a house where the mortgage is still at the original figure and the wife has the obligation of paying that off. The husband's capital prospects are very much greater than those of the wife. He has a superior earning capacity; and, in the not too distant future when the children's payments come to an end, the difference between their earning capacity or their income will be even more pronounced.

'In those circumstances, I think that his prospects, as I say, of acquiring a house in due course are really quite good.'

Notes

1. In *Hanlon v Hanlon* the husband, who was paying no maintenance for the wife, and in return for the maintenance order for the children being reduced to a nominal sum, was deprived of his share of the house. In *Dunford v Dunford* the husband still retained a reversionary interest in the house, but its value (at the time of the appeal to the Court of Appeal, at least) was nil, so that the position of both husbands was similar.
2. The clean break does not apply as far as children's maintenance is concerned. The wife in *Hanlon v Hanlon* could always apply for an increase in the order for maintenance for the children in the future. The wife in *Dunford v Dunford* would continue to receive substantial maintenance for the children.
3. The Court of Appeal has now decided that *Dunford v Dunford* was wrongly decided in so far as it imposed a clean break on the wife by striking out the nominal order for the wife's maintenance. It is now settled law that, although a wife can agree to her application for maintenance being dismissed, a clean break cannot be imposed by striking out her application for maintenance against her express wishes: see notes to case summary 10–103.

5–113A Curtis v Curtis

(1980) 11 Fam Law 55, CA

Lump sum of £4,000 of very little value where inadequate to rehouse recipient party. The parties' only capital asset was the matrimonial home, valued at

£40,000, purchased wholly out of the wife's money. The husband, now aged 69 and living on a retirement and disability pension, had nowhere else to live. The Court of Appeal allowed his appeal against an order that he vacate the property on the wife paying him a lump sum of £4,000. There was substituted an order for the settlement of sufficient to purchase an alternative residence for the husband for life with remainder to the wife absolutely. Ormrod LJ said that in these days lump sums of the order of £4,000 were of very little value where they were inadequate to rehouse the recipient party. The problem to be faced was to see that both parties had a roof over their heads; the award of £4,000 would have been disastrous to the husband because it failed to meet the problem.

5–114 Eshak v Nowojewski

(1980) Times, 19 November, CA

Husband remaining in matrimonial home with infant children – wife provided for by new husband – 60 per cent of net sale proceeds insufficient to rehouse husband in 13 years' time on youngest child attaining 18 – husband to occupy house for life. The marriage broke down in 1975, some six months after the birth of the younger of the two children of the family. The husband had looked after the children since. They were now aged 10 and 5. The parties contemplated that both would remain in the husband's care. The husband required the former matrimonial home as a home for the children. The wife had now remarried and had a secure home.

The judge ordered that the jointly-owned matrimonial home should be sold when the youngest child attained 18 or completed full-time education, 60 per cent of the net sale proceeds to go to the husband and 40 per cent to the wife. The husband's appeal, on the ground that he would be severely handicapped in acquiring a new house when the youngest child attained 18 in 13 years' time and when he would then be 51, was allowed.

It was urged for the husband that the proper order would be an outright transfer to him. Sir John Arnold P disagreed. While it seemed to his lordship that the judge had failed to attach due importance to the husband's housing needs after the children had grown up, these could be provided for by allowing him to live in the house for the rest of his life. However, as the husband was to have this additional right of occupation, the judge's order should be revised so that on the sale of the house on the husband's death the proceeds would be divided equally between the husband's estate and the wife or her estate.

Notes
1. The wife had remarried. Therefore no question of periodical payments arose. Sir John Arnold said that, in a case where there was no question of periodical payments, the general approach was to start with the idea of an equal division of the property, while bearing in mind that this would yield to a different solution if the circumstances of the case so required. Compare, therefore, *Dallimer v Dallimer* (5–106), in which the jointly-owned former matrimonial home had similarly been purchased entirely by the husband. In *Dallimer v Dallimer* the Court of Appeal decided that on the husband's death the proceeds of sale should be divided as to two-thirds to the husband's estate and one-third to the wife or her estate.
2. Sir John Arnold said that the husband would be severely restricted in his ability to earn a living in view of the fact that he would have to look after the children, the youngest of which was only five. (This goes without saying.) However, his lordship went on to say that the husband might not be free to work until the younger child attained 18 years, when the husband would be 51, and that he might not work until he was 54 if the child continued in further education. With all due respect to Sir John Arnold, the authors find this hard to accept.

5–115 Carson v Carson

(1981) Times, 7 July, CA

No power to vary Mesher order once made – 50 : 50 division of assets on sale of matrimonial home rarely appropriate. Ormrod LJ said the case was a good example of the dangers of *Mesher* orders (see case summary 4–101). On the wife being obliged to sell the house on the children attaining 18 or completing their education she would find herself in a most unfavourable position with only half the proceeds of sale.

Notes
1. For further details, see case summary 10–107.
2. Compare *Goodfield v Goodfield* (5–102).

B. *Proceedings under Married Women's Property Act 1882, etc.*

CASE SUMMARIES

5–131 Bedson v Bedson

[1965] 3 All ER 308, CA

Husband's duty to provide wife with a roof over her head – severance of beneficial joint tenancy of matrimonial home not possible so long as wife is in possession. However, Russell LJ's dissenting judgment is generally accepted to be the better opinion. See *Emmet on Title.*

5–132 Jackson v Jackson

[1971] 3 All ER 774, CA

Law of Property Act 1925, section 30 – one half of net sale proceeds sufficient to rehouse wife – order for sale granted. The matrimonial home had been conveyed to the parties as beneficial joint tenants. They had one daughter, now married and living in Canada. Following the breakdown of the marriage, the husband left the home and went to live with the daughter. He wished to emigrate to Canada and to take with him his half share in the house in cash. The wife would not agree to a sale of the property. The husband served notice on the wife severing the joint tenancy and took out a summons in the Chancery Division under section 30 of the Law of Property Act 1925, asking for the house to be sold and for his half share to be made available to him. The parties agreed that they owned the beneficial interest in the property in equal shares.

Although neither party intended to seek a divorce, the judge found that the marriage had irretrievably broken down, and that there was no prospect of the husband returning to the matrimonial home. He ordered that the house should be sold. The wife appealed.

Counsel for the wife argued that the wife had been deserted by the husband and that, as a deserted wife, she was entitled to remain in the matrimonial home. He relied on *Gurasz v Gurasz* (4–201), in which Lord Denning MR said:

> 'Some features of family life are elemental in our society. One is that it is the husband's duty to provide his wife with a roof over her head . . . So long as the wife behaves herself, she is entitled to remain in the matrimonial home.'

Counsel for the husband argued that the house was joint property held under a trust for sale; the marriage had irretrievably broken down; therefore, the primary object of the trust – the provision of a matrimonial home – had broken down; therefore, the house should be sold so that each party could have their share. He relied on *Rawlings v Rawlings* [1964] 2 All ER 804, CA, in which Salmon LJ (as he then was) said (at page 813):

'Where parties acquire property jointly there is a statutory trust for sale with power to postpone. If one party wishes to postpone the sale and the other does not, the court has a wide discretion to do what is right and proper in all the circumstances. Where the parties are husband and wife and the property has been acquired as a matrimonial home, neither party has the right to demand a sale whilst that purpose still exists.'

But, counsel for the husband argued, that purpose no longer existed; the marriage had irretrievably broken down; therefore, the court should exercise its discretion in favour of a sale.

Lord Denning MR said (at page 778): 'On what principles should the court act in ordering a sale? In a straight case of desertion by the husband – as, for instance, where he leaves the home to go and live with another woman – the court will not usually order the wife to go out. It is his duty to provide her with a roof over her head. No matter in whose name the house stands – in the husband's name or in them both jointly – the court will not in the ordinary way order her out unless he provides her with suitable alternative accommodation ... But when it is the wife who deserts the husband – when it is she who leaves the house – it is rather different. The courts have not laid down a similar principle in favour of a deserted husband. It is not a wife's duty to provide a roof over the husband's head. But the courts have given the husband considerable protection. If he is in occupation, they do not order a sale or turn him out – at the behest of a deserting wife – unless it is just and equitable so to do ...

'In truth, all these cases depend on the discretion of the court. The cases about desertion are only instances of the way in which the conduct of the parties will influence the exercise of discretion ... *in all these cases when the husband or the wife has an equitable interest in a dwelling-house or in the proceeds of sale thereof, the court will make such order about the occupation as it thinks just and reasonable having regard to the conduct of the parties and the circumstances of the case.*'

Lord Denning MR said that if the house were sold and the wife got half the net sale proceeds, she ought to have sufficient money to find accommodation for herself. This would enable the husband to go to spend the rest of his life in Canada with the daughter. The wife's appeal was dismissed.

Note. See *Williams v Williams* (5–134) however, in which the Court of Appeal not only considered it right to exercise its discretion to refuse a sale in the circumstances, but ordered that the whole matter be remitted for further consideration by a judge in the Family Division, so that the court's wider powers under sections 23 and 24 of the Matrimonial Causes Act 1973 (see Appendix I) could be exercised.

5–133 Bigg v Bigg

(1976) 6 Fam Law 56, CA

Law of Property Act 1925, section 30 – one half of net sale proceeds sufficient to rehouse husband – order for sale granted – no divorce proceedings yet instituted – application for adjournment pending commencement of divorce proceedings refused. The matrimonial home had been conveyed to the parties as beneficial joint tenants. The presumption was, therefore, that they had equal interests in it. They had married late in life. The husband was a bachelor in his sixties and the wife, who had been previously married, was in her fifties. Three or four years after the date of the marriage the wife developed an illness which required her to live in a warmer climate. She purchased a house in Menorca with her own money. The parties had it in mind to retire there, but a year or so later the marriage broke down.

The wife was now living in Menorca. She had capital of over £10,000 and lived on the interest of £1,000 per annum which it produced. The husband, now nearly 70, remained in the former matrimonial home. He ran a small driving school from the property. The wife applied to the county court under section 30 of the Law of Property Act 1925 for an order for sale of the house. The parties had lived apart for two years but divorce proceedings had not been commenced. The husband's appeal against the order for sale was dismissed.

Lord Denning MR said that on a sale of the house the husband's half share would be sufficient to enable him to rehouse himself, and he ought to be able to move his driving school to other premises. Accordingly, there was no reason for keeping the wife out of her money.

Counsel for the husband argued that there would soon be a divorce, and that the proceedings should be adjourned so as to enable the whole matter to be considered in the light of the Matrimonial Proceedings and Property Act 1970. (See now the Matrimonial Causes Act 1973, sections 23, 24 and 25 – see Appendix I.) Lawton LJ said that if a divorce was likely it was often wise and convenient to adjourn section 30 proceedings; but the judge had borne this factor in mind when exercising his discretion, and had expressly said so. Lord Denning MR said that the judge had considered the matter carefully and had exercised his discretion in a proper manner.

Notes
1. Compare *Williams v Williams* (5–134), in which the house was required as a home for the children, and an order for sale was refused.
2. Compare *Williams v Williams* (ibid.), in which divorce proceedings had already been commenced. The husband's application to the Chancery Division under section 30 was refused and the case remitted for further consideration by a judge of the Family Division.
3. Lord Denning MR was the presiding judge in both cases.

5–134 Williams v Williams (sub nom. Williams (JW) v Williams (MA))

[1977] 1 All ER 28, CA

Law of Property Act 1925, section 30 – divorce proceedings already instituted – order for sale refused – case remitted to Family Division. The Court of Appeal allowed the wife's appeal against the order for sale. Lord Denning MR said (at page 30): '*The court, in executing the trust, should regard the primary object as being to provide a home and not a sale.*' His lordship continued (at page 31): '*. . . the approach to these cases has been transformed since the Matrimonial Proceedings and Property Act 1970 and the Matrimonial Causes Act 1973, which have given the power to the court, after a divorce, to order the transfer of property. In exercising any discretion under section 30 of the 1925 Act, those Acts must be taken into account. The discretion should be exercised on the principles stated by this court in Jackson v Jackson*' (5–132). In view of the fact that proceedings for divorce had already been instituted the case was remitted for further consideration by a judge in the Family Division, so that the court's wider powers under sections 23 and 24 of the Matrimonial Causes Act 1973 (see Appendix I) could be exercised.

Notes
1. The wife's case was particularly strong because the house was required as a home for the children. See case summary 4–133. However, the approach of the court *(The court, in executing the trust, should regard the primary object as being to provide a home and not a sale . . . the approach to these cases has been transformed since the Matrimonial Proceedings and Property Act 1970 and the Matrimonial Causes Act 1973)* is now the same whether there are children or not. The courts no longer treat the primary object of the trust as being to sell the property.
2. The Chancery Division is not the correct forum for matrimonial disputes. Such cases should be commenced in the Family Division. If no divorce proceedings are contemplated, a suit for judicial separation should be instituted so that the court has the necessary powers to deal with the matter fully under sections 23, 24 and 25 of the 1973 Act.
3. But see also *Bigg v Bigg* (5–133), in which an application for an adjournment of the section 30 proceedings pending the commencement of divorce proceedings was refused by the Court of Appeal, on the ground that the judge had considered the matter fully and had exercised his discretion in a proper manner.

C. *Bankruptcy proceedings*

5–161 Re Turner (a bankrupt), ex parte the trustee of the bankrupt v Turner

[1975] 1 All ER 5

Law of Property Act 1925, section 30 – bankruptcy – matrimonial home held by husband and wife on trust for sale – husband declared bankrupt – application by trustee in bankruptcy for order for sale – discretion of court whether to order sale – trustee's claim the stronger – order for sale granted.

5–161A Re McCarthy (a bankrupt), ex parte the trustee of the bankrupt v McCarthy

[1975] 2 All ER 857

Law of Property Act 1925, section 30 – bankruptcy – matrimonial home held by husband and wife on trust for sale – husband declared bankrupt – application by trustee in bankruptcy for order for possession – discretion of court – no reason to order that immediate possession be given – order for sale granted.

5–162 Re Bailey (a bankrupt), ex parte the trustee of the bankrupt v Bailey

[1977] 2 All ER 26

Law of Property Act 1925, section 30 – bankruptcy – matrimonial home held by husband and wife on trust for sale – husband declared bankrupt – application by trustee in bankruptcy for order for sale – discretion of court whether to order sale – trustee's claim the stronger – order for sale granted.

5–163 Re Holliday (a bankrupt), ex parte the trustee of the bankrupt v the bankrupt

[1980] 3 All ER 385, CA

Law of Property Act 1925, section 30 – bankruptcy – matrimonial home held by husband and wife on trust for sale – filing of own bankruptcy petition by husband in order to frustrate claim for transfer of property order by wife – application by trustee in bankruptcy for order for sale – discretion of court whether to order sale – overriding requirements of dependent children – order for sale postponed.   See case summary 4–163.

2   Exclusion of party from matrimonial home

It is not within the ambit of this book to deal with injunctions, or with proceedings under the Domestic Violence and Matrimonial Proceedings Act 1976 or the Domestic Proceedings and Magistrates' Courts Act 1978. However, in order that the reader may obtain a better understanding of how the courts deal with the vexed question of who is to remain in occupation of the matrimonial home on divorce, selected cases on the exclusion of a party to the marriage from the matrimonial home are included in this section. Some of the case summaries in this section are very brief, and the reader is referred to the standard textbooks for further information. *For cases in which the question of providing a home for the children was the dominant consideration, see Chapter 4/2.*

CASE SUMMARIES

5–201 Miles v Bull

[1968] 3 All ER 632

Matrimonial Homes Act 1967 – right of wife to remain in occupation. Until the middle of June 1965, the defendant, Mrs. Bull, was cohabiting with her husband in the matrimonial home. Following the breakdown of the marriage, the husband left the home. In June 1967 the wife filed a petition for judicial separation. The house was vested in the husband and his brother as part of the property of their farming partnership. On 23rd January 1968 they entered into a contract to sell the house and other land to the plaintiff, Mr. Miles. The contract contained a special condition, which read:

> 'The dwellinghouse forming part of the property hereby agreed to be sold is subject to such rights of occupation as may exist in favour of [the wife], provided that this shall not be deemed to imply that [the wife] has, or after completion will have, any such rights as against the [plaintiff]; but as to the remainder of the property vacant possession shall be given at completion.'

Completion of the purchase took place on the same day.

The next day the wife called on her solicitors and told them that she thought the house was being sold over her head. *The solicitors then registered a Class F land charge under the Matrimonial Homes Act 1967. Unfortunately, this was to no avail. Firstly, it was not registered until after completion of the sale had already taken place. Secondly, the land was registered land; therefore, what should have been registered was a notice or caution in the Land Registry, not a land charge in the Land Charges Registry.* Megarry J (as he then was) said (at page 634): '*The Act of 1967 contains nothing to require prior notice of any proposed transaction to be given to the occupying spouse, and so where, as here, that spouse does not learn of the transaction until too late, the Act provides no protection. Those advising such a spouse should accordingly consider whether a precautionary registration should be made as soon as the matrimonial affairs reach a stage in which there appears to be any risk of a dealing with the home to the disadvantage of the occupying spouse.*'

The plaintiff issued a writ in the Queen's Bench Division claiming possession of the premises and applied for summary judgment under Order 14 of the Rules of the Supreme Court. The master gave the wife unconditional leave to defend. The plaintiff appealed.

His lordship continued (at page 635): '*The leading case on this branch of the law is National Provincial Bank Ltd v Ainsworth [1965] 2 All ER 472, HL. There the House of Lords held that the so-called deserted wife's equity to occupy the matrimonial home did not exist, and that as against third parties the wife had no right of occupation. As against her husband, a wife has a right to occupy the matrimonial home by virtue of her status as a wife; but this is a mere personal right which does not amount to any proprietary interest or clog on the husband's ownership of the home, and so will not bind a purchaser from the husband, even if he has full knowledge of the wife's claims.*

'*To this general rule there is one qualification relevant to this case; that is where the sale of the matrimonial home is not a genuine sale, but is a mere sham. In National Provincial Bank Ltd v Ainsworth, Lord Hodson said this (at page 479):*

>> "The court can protect itself against sham sales ... and the court now has power to set aside transfers of property made to defeat claims for alimony or maintenance as happened in this case." '

The wife contended that she should have leave to defend because she had an arguable prospect of establishing that the sale to the plaintiff was a mere sham. She argued that the plaintiff was at all times aware that there was a matrimonial dispute; the plaintiff denied this. Megarry J said that the price paid was not a derisory price and there was no evidence that the sale was not what it appeared to be. Accordingly, his lordship could perceive no arguable defence to the plaintiff's claim.

However, his lordship continued (at page 638): '... By carrying through a transaction at unusual speed the defendant's husband is seeking to enable the plaintiff to do what he cannot do, namely, evict the defendant from her home. The husband has whatever rights the law gives him, and so has the plaintiff; but in the circumstances of the case I do not think it would be just if the plaintiff were able to enforce the rights that he claims without being put to strict proof that they do enable him to evict the defendant ... RSC Ord. 14 is for the plain and straightforward, not for the devious and crafty. There is here a case for investigation, and so not for summary decision.'

The plaintiff's appeal was dismissed, so allowing the wife to defend the action, to apply for discovery and to cross-examine the plaintiff and his witnesses.

Notes
1. On applying to register a Class F land charge in the Land Charges Registry, application should also be made for an index map search, in order to determine whether the Class F land charge should be superseded by a notice or caution at the Land Registry. The application to register the Class F land charge should be accompanied by a letter to the effect that the application is being made before the result of the index map search is known.
2. See also *Whittingham v Whittingham* (26–011) – house never occupied as matrimonial home – Class F land charge of no effect – application for transfer of property order registrable as a pending action.
3. See also *Barnett v Hassett* (26–016) – it is a misuse of the Matrimonial Homes Act 1967 for a spouse who has no intention of occupying the matrimonial home to register a Class F land charge on the property solely in order to freeze the assets of the other spouse – registration set aside.

5–202 Gurasz v Gurasz

[1969] 3 All ER 822, CA

1. *Common law imposes duty on husband to provide wife and children with roof over their heads.*
2. *Common law may be invoked when court otherwise lacks jurisdiction, e.g. when jurisdiction under Matrimonial Homes Act 1967 lacking because legal estate in matrimonial home vested in both spouses jointly.*
3. *Court will restore wife and children to matrimonial home where necessary to solve housing problem.*
4. *If husband's conduct so outrageous as to make it impossible for parties to live together in matrimonial home, court will order husband to leave.*
5. *If court concludes that impossible for parties to live together in matrimonial home and that property required as home for wife and children court will order husband to leave without proof of violence.*
6. *Matrimonial home owned jointly by the parties – court's inherent jurisdiction to exclude party from matrimonial home exercisable irrespective of property rights.*
7. *Inherent jurisdiction to exclude party from matrimonial home vested both in High Court and county court.*

The wife left the jointly-owned matrimonial home on account of the husband's alleged conduct, taking the children with her. She and the children were now living in accommodation which was 'utterly unsuitable'. Pending the hearing of her petition for divorce, she applied to the Southampton County Court under the Matrimonial Homes Act 1967 for an order that the husband's right to occupy the matrimonial home be terminated. The county court judge thought it urgent to find a solution to the housing problem particularly in view of the unsuitability of the accommodation as far as the children were concerned. He made an order under the Matrimonial Homes Act 1967 ordering the husband to vacate the property. The husband appealed. Counsel for the husband said that the county court judge had no jurisdiction under the Act to order the husband to vacate the house. Counsel for the wife said that the judge had jurisdiction under the Act or, alternatively, at common law.

Lord Denning MR said (at page 823): 'I propose first to deal with the position at common law, because it is an essential preliminary to understanding the import of the Act.

'*Some features of family life are elemental in our society. One is that it is the husband's duty to provide his wife with a roof over her head; and the children too. So long as the wife behaves herself, she is entitled to remain in the matrimonial home. The husband is not at liberty to turn her out of it, neither by virtue of his command, nor by force of his conduct. If he should seek to get rid of her, the court will restrain him. If he should succeed in making her go, the court will restore her. In an extreme case, if his conduct is so outrageous as to make it impossible for them to live together, the court will order him to go out and leave her there.*'

His lordship continued (at page 824): '. . . The Matrimonial Homes Act 1967 gave either spouse (when the house was owned by the other) a right to occupy which, on being registered, would operate as a charge on the property and be available against third persons. The Act did not take away or diminish the wife's personal right to occupy the matrimonial home. That was left intact. It is still available to her as against her husband, and the courts will protect her in her occupation, just as they did before the Act. It is available, irrespective of the title to the house, no matter whether it is in her name, or her husband's name, or in joint names. The only thing is that, if it is in her own name, or in joint names, she is in so much the stronger position; because she can add to her personal right against her husband, a proprietary right which is available against third persons . . .

'Such being the protection afforded to the wife by the common law, I think that the order of the county court judge can be justified on that footing.'

Notes

1. The husband's alleged conduct was hardly discussed, and was certainly not treated as proven. The point at issue was the jurisdiction of the court to deal with the housing problem, rather than any question of protecting the wife or children from the husband.

2. In *S v S* (5–207), French J said that in his opinion Lord Denning MR's statement that a husband had a duty to provide his wife with a roof over her head and thus to remain in the matrimonial home did not apply to properties which had never been the matrimonial home. However, his lordship added (obiter), that the court's jurisdiction is not limited in this way when seeking to protect the interests of children.

3. It was clear that the court had no jurisdiction under the Matrimonial Homes Act 1967, because the house had been conveyed into the joint names of the parties. The Act gives either spouse rights of occupation in the matrimonial home when the legal estate in the property is vested solely in the other. The legal estate in the property being vested in the parties jointly, the Act did not apply. (The wife's rights of occupation were enforceable against third parties by virtue of the fact that she held the legal estate, without requiring protection and registration under the Act.) The Matrimonial Homes Act 1967 has been amended by the Matrimonial Proceedings and Property Act 1970 in order to enable the provisions of the Matrimonial Homes Act to apply where the legal estate in the matrimonial home is vested solely in one spouse but the other spouse owns an equitable interest in the property (or in the proceeds of sale thereof).

4. Both Edmund Davies and Fenton Atkinson LJJ were troubled by the fact that the appeal was against an order *made under the Matrimonial Homes Act 1967*. It was therefore clear that the county court judge had no jurisdiction to have made the order. Should the husband's appeal have been allowed and the wife left to make a further application to the county court judge for an order under the court's inherent jurisdiction? Their lordships agreed with Lord Denning MR that in the interests of justice the husband's appeal should be dismissed.

5. It is possible to argue that the county court has no inherent jurisdiction. However, in

Gurasz v Gurasz, Edmund Davies LJ said (at page 826): '. . . counsel for the wife has
submitted that, even if he cannot succeed under the Act of 1967, the court had power
under its general jurisdiction to grant the wife relief of the nature granted by the county
court judge and that, accordingly, the order made ought not to be disturbed. That such a
general power unquestionably existed has, if I may say so, been amply and convincingly
demonstrated by Lord Denning MR.' In any event, the question of the county court's
inherent jurisdiction is now probably only of academic importance in view of the wide
powers now possessed by the county court under the Domestic Violence and
Matrimonial Proceedings Act 1976.

5–203 Jones v Jones

[1971] 2 All ER 738, CA

*Husband installing mistress in matrimonial home shortly after wife's departure – if
husband's conduct so outrageous as to make it impossible for parties to live together in
matrimoniial home court will order husband to leave without proof of violence or
cruelty.   Gurasz v Gurasz (5–202) applied.*

   Note. Compare *S v S* (5–207), in which the property concerned had never been the
matrimonial home; French J held that the wife had no implied licence to occupy a property
which had never been the matrimonial home; hence there was no legal right which could be
invoked in her favour; the wife's application for an injunction was refused.

5–204 Bassett v Bassett

[1975] 1 All ER 513, CA

The balance of hardship – difficulties of single men in finding accommodation.
Ormrod LJ said (at page 519): 'My conclusion is that the court, when dealing
with these cases, particularly where it is clear that the marriage has already
broken down, should think essentially in terms of homes, especially for the
children, and then consider the balance of hardship as I have indicated, *being
careful not to underestimate the difficulties which even single men have these days in
finding somewhere to live,* bearing in mind that the break will have to be made in
the relatively near future and that property rights as between the spouses are of
comparatively minor importance.'

   Note. See also his lordship's judgment in *Harding v Harding* (5–206).

5–205 Hoggett v Hoggett

(1979) 39 P & CR 121, CA, 1980 Halsbury's Abridgment para. 1491

*Matrimonial Homes Act 1967 – purported surrender of tenancy by husband in order
to defeat wife's claim – right of wife to remain in occupation.*

5–206 Harding v Harding

(1979) 10 Fam Law 146, CA

*Domestic Violence and Matrimonial Proceedings Act 1976 – the balance of hardship
– difficulties of single men in finding accommodation.*   Ormrod LJ referred to his
own judgment in *Bassett v Bassett* (5–204). His lordship said that the county court
judge had been right to think in terms of a home for the child, while bearing in
mind that the husband's difficulties as a single man in finding accommodation
were very real. Had the wife been able to provide accommodation for herself and
the child without involving turning the husband out of the home, that would have
been another matter. But in this case the only relevant question was: which of
them was going to look after the child? Clearly the mother. Therefore the father
would have to leave.

5–207 S v S

(1980) Times, 21 February

Power to exclude party from matrimonial home does not extend to property which has never been the matrimonial home. The parties came to the UK from Pakistan. The wife returned to Pakistan for a supposedly short holiday. She went on a single ticket because the husband, a businessman, was short of funds. The husband prevaricated about her return, and she eventually returned three years later, without the husband's assistance, to find that the husband had in the meantime purchased a house and set up home there with an Italian mistress. The wife applied to the court for an order under its inherent jurisdiction to allow her to live in part of the house. *She could not invoke the Matrimonial Homes Act 1967 because the house had never been the matrimonial home. French J held that neither could she invoke the inherent jurisdiction of the court.*

His lordship said that in *Gurasz v Gurasz* (5–202) Lord Denning MR referred to a husband's duty to provide his wife with a roof over her head, but that it was clear from Lord Denning MR's judgment that he was contemplating the husband's duty to allow the wife to remain in the matrimonial home. The court would only grant an injunction to support or protect a legal right. In the present case, because the house had never been the matrimonial home, the wife had no implied licence to occupy the property. Therefore there was no legal right which could be invoked in her favour.

Notes

1. Compare *Jones v Jones* (5–203) where, because the property in question was the matrimonial home, the court granted an injunction ordering the husband and his mistress to leave.
2. French J added (obiter) that where the interests of children are concerned, the court has power to protect them in the absence of any legal right. Had the wife had care and control of any children of the family, the court would have had the necessary power to make the order applied for.

CHAPTER 6

Relevance of third parties

In the vast majority of contested cases the court will be invited to consider the fact that one party or the other is, by the time of the hearing, financially affected by the existence of a third party (usually a cohabitee or new spouse). In this chapter are assembled cases where the courts have had to consider what effect, if any, the financial benefit or burden of a third party ought to have on the eventual order. Also included in this chapter are cases where the courts have considered the prospects of remarriage of a wife; in all these cases the courts have reached the clear conclusion that the prospects or even likelihood of remarriage are of virtually no consequence. Remarriage itself, on the other hand, will debar any application for financial relief if not filed prior to the remarriage of the applicant spouse. Cases on the practice in this area of the law are to be found in Section 1C of this chapter. The question of whether a new spouse or cohabitee can be compelled to give evidence before the court is dealt with in Section 3C.

The manner in which the cases have been subdivided will again be, it is hoped, largely self-explanatory. It will be readily apparent that there is a very clear distinction between the relevance of a third party on an application for capital provision and that on an application for maintenance. Broadly speaking, the relevance of a third party, in so far as it affects the capital position, is considerably more limited than its effect on the matter of maintenance. That is because the court, when considering the capital and property position, is often faced with the task of implementing strict property rights, or is considering the claim of a spouse to be entitled to an interest in property because of many years of marital assistance and involvement. Accordingly, the fact that a spouse who is claiming a share in capital has already prospered by finding new circumstances with an affluent third party is to a large extent irrelevant. However, the court does have the duty under section 25 of the Matrimonial Causes Act 1973 to look at the financial needs, obligations and responsibilities which each of the parties has or is likely to have in the foreseeable future. The existence of a cohabitee or a new spouse is clearly relevant to the proper implementation of that clause. But, on the whole, the courts more frequently are inclined to a result which places the parties, so far as it is practicable, in the financial position in which they would have been if the marriage had not broken down. If the court chooses to be directed along those lines, the existence of third parties is not of great effect on the distribution of capital. That proposition, however, cannot and does not extend to the position where the court is determining the fate of the matrimonial home. Where there are arguments over the question of sale or the occupation of the home, the fact that a party has acquired a new home because of his or her remarriage or cohabitation can be, and frequently is, of the highest significance. It should also be noted that where an order for settlement postpones the sale of a former matrimonial home so that a wife can continue to live there, the events on which the sale is to take place normally include not only her remarriage but also her cohabiting with another man.

See *Blezard v Blezard* (23–405) for an example of such an order.

So far as maintenance is concerned, the straightforward rule of practice is that periodic maintenance is assessed without regard to the prospects of remarriage. If, for example, a wife does in fact remarry, periodic maintenance ceases. If she cohabits, maintenance may be reviewed and, in practice, it normally ceases.

1 Relevance of remarriage of the wife, or the possibility of the wife remarrying

A. *Relevance on application for capital provision*

CASE SUMMARIES

6–101 Wachtel v Wachtel

[1973] 1 All ER 829, CA

Relevance of possibility of wife remarrying. Lord Denning MR said (at page 841): 'In making financial provision, ought the prospects of remarriage to be taken into account? The [Matrimonial Proceedings and Property Act 1970] says in terms that periodical payments shall cease *on remarriage*: see section 7 (1) (b). [See now section 28 of the Matrimonial Causes Act 1973.] *But it says nothing about the prospects of remarriage. The question then arises: ought the provision for the wife to be reduced if she is likely to remarry?*

'So far as the capital assets are concerned, we see no reason for reducing her share. After all, she has earned it by her contribution in looking after the home and caring for the family. It should not be taken away from her by the prospect of remarriage...'

Note. Compare *H v H (financial provision: remarriage)* (6–105), which deals with the situation where the wife has in fact remarried and its relevance on the distribution of capital assets.

6–102 Trippas v Trippas

[1973] 2 All ER 1, CA

Relevance of possibility of wife remarrying – wife living with married man. The wife left the matrimonial home and went to live with a married man. Subsequently, the husband formed an association with another woman. Cross-petitions on the grounds of adultery were dropped in favour of a petition based on two years' separation with mutual consent. The wife applied for a lump sum order and was awarded £8,000 by the county court judge. The husband appealed, contending that because the wife might marry the man with whom she was living this was not a case where a lump sum order would be appropriate, and the wife cross-appealed.

Lord Denning MR referred to section 5 (1) of the Matrimonial Proceedings and

Property Act 1970 (see now section 25 (1) of the Matrimonial Causes Act 1973 – see Appendix I) and said (at page 5): 'If this marriage had continued, it is plain that the wife had a good chance of receiving a financial benefit on the sale of the [husband's family] business . . . Now that there has been a divorce, she should be compensated for the loss of that chance.

'Counsel for the husband submits that she should have no compensation for the loss of that chance. She is living with another man and may marry him. She has thrown in her lot with him. She has severed her connection with her husband. So she should not have any share in this sum [i.e. the proceeds of sale of the family business amounting to £80,000] which only came into being after they had separated. That argument would have been acceptable before the Act of 1970, but is not acceptable now. Section 5 (1) (g) [see now section 25 (1) (g) of the 1973 Act – see Appendix I] covers the position exactly . . . supposing the man with whom she is living dies. Suppose he is killed in a car accident. She would need all the help she can get. The subsection tells the court to do what it can to put them both in the same position as if the marriage had not broken down. It is also to do what is just considering that she looked after the home and brought up the family over those 27 years. It seems to me only just that, having regard to the capital sum received by the husband, he should provide a lump sum for her.'

The lump sum award was increased by the Court of Appeal to £10,000, which left the husband, who was not in employment, with investment income approximately equal to the wife's total income from her earnings and invested capital. 'Rough justice on the basis of equality' – see case summary 13–002.
Notes
1.   See also *Marsden (JL) v Marsden (AM)* (6–103).
2.   Compare *H v H (financial provision: remarriage)* (6–105).

6–103 Marsden (JL) v Marsden (AM)

[1973] 2 All ER 851

Relevance of remarriage of wife – wife taking assets with her into her new marriage.   Sir George Baker P said that it would be undesirable for the court to settle an adulterous wife's share in the former matrimonial home on the children solely in order that she should not take such an asset with her into her new marriage. See case summary 6–162.

Note. See also *Trippas v Trippas* (6–102).

6–104 Smith v Smith (sub nom. S v S)

[1975] 2 All ER 19, CA

No evidence of likelihood of wife remarrying.   The former matrimonial home had been purchased jointly by the parties. On the separation the husband left to live with his parents; the wife remained in the house with the child of the marriage. The husband conceded that the wife and child should be allowed to reside in the house until the child reached 17. Latey J reviewed (inter alia) *Wachtel v Wachtel* (6–101) and *Mesher v Mesher* (4–101) and extracted from them four guidelines: '. . . (4) *If the wife has remarried or is going to remarry her financial position on remarriage must be considered. If it is guesswork whether she will or will not remarry prospective remarriage should be ignored.*' There being no evidence to suggest a likelihood of the wife remarrying, Latey J did not consider her prospects of remarrying when making his decision.

The husband appealed against Latey J's order transferring his half share in the house to the wife; the husband's appeal was dismissed by the Court of Appeal. For details see case summary 23–902.

Note. Cited with approval in *H v H (financial provision: remarriage)* (6–105).

6–105 H v H (financial provision: remarriage)

[1975] 1 All ER 367

Relevance of remarriage of wife to wealthy man. The wife left the husband and went to live with the co-respondent. An agreed custody order was made under which the husband obtained care and control of the children with access to the wife. After the making of the decree absolute the wife married the co-respondent, who was a wealthy man. She applied for a one-third interest in the former matrimonial home.

Sir George Baker P quoted that part of the passage from Lord Denning MR's judgment in *Wachtel v Wachtel* relating to capital assets quoted in case summary 6–101, and continued (at page 371): '*Lord Denning was careful to deal with the prospects, the likelihood, of remarriage. He said nothing of the fact of remarriage in relation to capital assets . . . In Trippas v Trippas (6–102) the wife was living with another man whom she might marry. That did not affect her entitlement. The prospect, chance or hope of remarriage is I think irrelevant, but the fact of remarriage, which does not admit of speculation, is in my judgment something which the court must consider in the course of its statutory duty under section 25* [of the Matrimonial Causes Act 1973]: *"to have regard to all the circumstances of the case".*' [See Appendix I.]

Sir George Baker said that this accorded with Latey J's conclusion in *Smith v Smith* (6–104) where Latey J had said:

'(4) If the wife has remarried or is going to remarry her financial position on remarriage must be considered. If it is guesswork whether she will or will not remarry prospective remarriage should be ignored.'

His lordship continued: 'To ignore remarriage entirely would be to ignore the financial needs of the parties in the foreseeable future: see section 25 (1) (b).

'It seems to me that the real problem in any particular case is to decide how to translate a new marriage into money. How is it to be regarded and what part is to play in the financial provision? Counsel for the wife argues that a wife who remarries a poor man should get no more, and therefore a wife who remarries a rich man gets no less. I do not accept this submission. Remarriage to a poor man would reflect in her financial resources and financial needs, and would probably result in her receiving the full share of what she had earned. Equally, marriage to a wealthy man has a bearing on her financial needs and resources just as her own capital would be taken into account, for as Bagnall J said in *Harnett v Harnett* (14–002): "Where the wife has some capital that must be taken into account in determining what she should be given by the husband." The Matrimonial Causes Act 1973, section 25 (1) gives the court the widest possible power to achieve the statutory object, namely –

"to place the parties, so far as it is practicable and . . . just to do so, in the financial position in which they would have been if the marriage had not broken down . . ."

'First, in my opinion, justice must be done in all cases, not only in those in which conduct is relevant. That is a matter of construction. Then, it is not the wife alone who is to be placed in the same position but "the parties". Too often the husband's position tends now to be disregarded.'

Having dealt with the relative financial positions of the two families, his lordship continued (at page 373): '. . . I think, first, that it is unjust and impracticable to make the husband pay a lump sum. He cannot raise more money on the house, he has to pay for the four children and he has little other capital . . . She needs no flat or house and I think most people would find it distasteful and unjust that a lump sum should be given to a wife for the probable benefit of the new family.

'But, she says, she has earned a share, and will accommodate her first family by allowing it to remain with them till the youngest is 18. She now says that share should be one-third of the house . . . Any payment will in fact put her in a better financial position than if the marriage had continued and I would give her one-twelfth of the unencumbered value of the house . . . her entitlement to rank after the present charges for the bank overdrafts and not to be payable until the youngest child is 18.'

Note. Compare Sir George Baker's own judgment in *Marsden (JL) v Marsden (AM)* (6–103). There are two differences between the cases. First, the wife in *Marsden* already owned a half share in the house, whereas the wife in *H v H* was asking the court to award her a share of the matrimonial assets in view of her contributions to the family in kind over 15 years of married life. Secondly, the parties in *Marsden* had agreed that the house should be sold, and there was no shortage of cash on either side. The point at issue in *H v H* was whether the fact that the wife had remarried was relevant or not. The court held that it was. It followed that evidence as to the relative financial positions of the two families was relevant.

6–106 Cumbers v Cumbers

[1975] 1 All ER 1, CA

Relevance of possibility of wife remarrying.   The former matrimonial home had been purchased by the husband three months before the marriage. Following the separation it was sold, realising a sum of £1,600. The husband remarried and used the proceeds of sale for the purpose of buying a new house.

Lord Denning MR said (at page 3): 'It was said for the husband that this was not a case for capital provision at all. It was pointed out that the marriage had been very short. The wife had no proprietary right in the matrimonial home. She had no case under section 17 of the Married Women's Property Act 1882. So no part of the £1,600 should be allocated to her.

'I can see the force of that argument. But, looking once again at *Wachtel v Wachtel* (6–101), it is important to remember that, *in addition to the income provision, there should be, in a proper case, a capital provision. During the argument in this case Ormrod LJ pointed out that an income provision comes to an end automatically if the wife remarries. So it may sometimes be wise to make some capital provision for her which will not cease on her remarriage. That is, in a case where she has really played a part in the marriage which deserves compensation of a capital nature.* It seems to me that this case is properly one in which a capital provision – a lump sum – should be ordered. But I think the sum of £800 [half the proceeds of sale of the former matrimonial home] is too large. The better figure would be one-third or thereabouts. I would put it at £500, in regard to the capital provision.'

Note. See also case summary 6–402.

B. *Relevance on application for maintenance*

CASE SUMMARIES

6–131 Wachtel v Wachtel

[1973] 1 All ER 829, CA

Relevance of possibility of wife remarrying.   Lord Denning MR said (at page 841): 'So far as periodical payments are concerned, they are, of course, to be assessed without regard to the prospects of remarriage. If the wife does in fact remarry, they cease. If she goes to live with another man – without marrying him – they may be reviewed.'

6–132 Campbell v Campbell

[1977] 1 All ER 1

No evidence of immediate likelihood of wife remarrying. The husband appealed to the county court judge against an award of maintenance pending suit. At the hearing of the appeal it was agreed that, as the wife now intended to marry a Mr. Stalker, the appeal would be adjourned on the wife undertaking to claim no further financial provision for herself from the husband after a certain date. The judge suggested that there should be a provision in the order to cover the situation in case the wife should not in fact remarry. That was done by inserting that there should be liberty to apply.

The wife did not remarry and applied to be released from her undertaking. The husband contended that, since the wife might still remarry, that possibility should be taken into account.

Sir George Baker P gave the wife leave to apply for maintenance. His lordship said (at page 6): 'The question then is what is the proper amount of an order for the wife? The question of remarriage is not yet finally resolved. Mr. Stalker, who was in court but from whom there is no affidavit, has not given evidence. There is no criticism about that at all; it is, I think, the right course. He is said to be in some financial difficulties in resolving the problems of his former marriage and, *temporarily at least, the question of further matrimony for Mrs. Campbell is on the shelf.*

'Counsel for Mr. Campbell suggests that there is here a contemplation of remarriage and I should take that into account. I do not agree. Whatever may be the situation where one is considering a transfer of property or lump sum payment, *where the question is the amount of the periodical payments, I have to deal with the fact that the wife has not yet remarried. If she does remarry, of course, the order will end and that is the finality of the matter. So I put aside all questions of remarriage; that is not something which I shall take into consideration.* Then it is said that I ought to draw the inference that Mr. Stalker is in fact keeping her. At the present position, she is still living with her old mother . . . She accepts that she was investigated, and apparently Mr. Stalker was investigated, no doubt at the instigation of Mr. Campbell, by the social security authorities. She says that she has got a clean bill and they have agreed that she was not being kept and were quite prepared to pay, but she has not been claiming any social security. She has been living on a loan of £10 a week from one of her sons but that is going to cease. From that I am asked to draw the inference that she is in fact being kept by Mr. Stalker, but to my mind that is suspicion and guesswork and there is not sufficient evidence from which I could draw any proper inference.'

In considering the order for periodical payments, the possibility of the wife remarrying was excluded from consideration.

Note. Sir George Baker P was out of sympathy with both parties. First, there were many allegations and counter-allegations regarding conduct, leading his lordship to conclude: '. . . I seem to be faced with the profitless investigation which might well end with the question: Who fornicated first?' Next, counsel for the wife attempted to persuade his lordship that the 3½ years of premarital cohabitation should be taken into account in assessing the length of the marriage, to which he replied: 'Well that is, to my mind, an entirely misconceived outlook. It is the ceremony of marriage and the sanctity of marriage which count; rights, duties and obligations begin on the marriage and not before. It is a complete cheapening of the marriage relationship . . .' The wife's award was accordingly reduced in view of the shortness of the marriage. Counsel for the husband argued that the wife's maintenance should be reduced because of the possibility of the wife marrying Mr. Stalker and because of the presumption (in his eyes) that Mr. Stalker was already keeping her. His lordship was not impressed by that argument. Counsel for the husband then suggested that because the husband had remarried and had a child of six to support there should only be a nominal order for maintenance of the wife. His lordship said: '. . . I am invited not to put a burden on him which would prejudice him in his future life. I ask myself why should the public (social security) keep his ex-wife, whom he, not the public, married, rather than that he should make his fair and proper contribution, whatever the effect may be on him. Husbands, even very young husbands [such as Mr. Campbell], must realise that in matrimony they are taking on themselves a financial obligation . . .' Finally, counsel for the wife suggested that the earnings of the husband's new wife should be brought into account when calculating the maintenance payable to her under the one-third ratio. She too got short shrift. His lordship said that although the new wife's earnings were something to bear in mind in the overall picture, the one-third ratio was always taken on the husband's gross earnings without having regard in the calculation to the new wife's earnings.

Perhaps these points should be borne in mind when reading the President's words: 'So I put aside all questions of remarriage; that is not something which I shall take into consideration.' In any event, if the wife went to live with Mr. Stalker in the future, or if it looked as though they were now about to marry, the position could be reviewed – see *Wachtel v Wachtel* (6–131).

c. *Practice*

CASE SUMMARIES

6–161 Jackson (SM) v Jackson (EL)

[1973] 2 All ER 395

Wife's application for financial relief contained in her petition not barred by subsequent remarriage. In her petition the wife applied for financial relief. She was granted a decree of divorce which was duly made absolute, and she then remarried. At a subsequent hearing of the wife's application for financial relief the registrar expressed doubts whether he had jurisdiction to make any order in favour of the wife owing to the fact that section 7 (4) of the Matrimonial Proceedings and Property Act 1970 prohibited a person whose marriage had been dissolved and who had remarried from applying for financial relief. (See now section 28 (3) of the Matrimonial Causes Act 1973.) The matter was referred to Bagnall J, who held that the word 'apply' referred to the petition, summons, notice or other process which initiated the application. Accordingly, the court could entertain an application for financial relief by a former spouse who had since remarried provided that the application was initiated before the remarriage.

Note. It is still easy for a respondent to fall foul of section 28 (3) of the Matrimonial Causes Act 1973 – see *Jenkins v Hargood* (6–167).

6–162 Marsden (JL) v Marsden (AM)

[1973] 2 All ER 851

Application for leave to apply for financial relief omitted from petition in order to prevent wife taking family asset into new marriage – remarriage of wife irrelevant – husband's application refused. The matrimonial home, valued in September 1972 at £58,000, had been purchased by the husband. It had been placed in the parties' joint names in order to save estate duty. The husband commenced a petition for divorce on the ground of the wife's adultery with the co-respondent. The petition did not contain any application for financial relief.

Terms were agreed between the parties regarding the custody and schooling of the children, and for the transfer of the ownership of an aeroplane to the husband. The wife's solicitors wrote to the husband's solicitors reminding them that the house was in joint names and requesting a valuation and suggestions as to the payment to the wife of her half share. In the meantime the decree was made absolute and the wife married the co-respondent.

The husband applied for leave to apply for a transfer of property order and a variation of settlement order in respect of the house. His original proposal was that the order should be in favour of himself or the children. The application was dismissed by the registrar. On appeal the husband restricted the proposed application to an order for the benefit of the children.

Sir George Baker P said (at page 854): '*The rule is clear. The application must be made in the petition. If it is not, the leave of the court is required. This cannot mean that leave is to be given for the asking.* . . . No excuse or reason has been given for the omission of the application from the petition, and there is certainly no satisfactory explanation of the husband's change of mind . . . *In my opinion there must be some reason or explanation before the court gives leave* . . . The husband may have started off with the belief that he was the sole owner [of the house], although this is disputed by the wife, but he was very soon aware that the house was in their joint names. *It is now said that this is an adulterous wife going off with a substantial asset*; but that was true at the time of the divorce. Moreover, this is a dangerous argument. Damages awarded for adultery used often to be settled on the children. Such damages can now no longer be recovered, since the law, for better or worse, has been changed. *It would, I think, be very undesirable for a court to appear to be trying to reintroduce the concept of damages, now against the wife, by taking away her share in the matrimonial home, or any other asset, and settling it on the children, solely in order that she should not take such an asset with her into her new marriage, to the possible benefit of her new husband; and particularly is this so where the wife and the new husband have the care of the children. A woman should be allowed to use her assets in her own way, just as a former husband, subject to his duty to maintain the children, can use his assets in his own way* . . .'

Appeal dismissed.

6–163 H v H (financial provision: remarriage)

[1975] 1 All ER 367

Respondent wife's application for financial relief made prior to remarriage not barred by remarriage. After the making of the decree absolute the wife married the co-respondent, who was a wealthy man. She applied for a one-third interest in the former matrimonial home.

Sir George Baker P said (at page 369): 'Counsel for the wife rightly points out that continuing financial provision orders . . . end on remarriage, but that a property adjustment order can be made after remarriage. The sole prohibition, contained in section 28 (3) of the [Matrimonial Causes Act 1973], is that a party to a remarriage shall not be entitled to apply for a financial provision order, and the courts have consistently held that that means "make a new application". An application which has already been made can be pursued: see *Jackson v Jackson* (6–161) . . .'

However, his lordship was of the opinion that to ignore the wife's remarriage would be to ignore the financial needs of the parties in the foreseeable future. Any payment would put her in a better financial position than if the marriage had continued. He accordingly awarded her only a one-twelfth interest in the property. For further details see case summary 6–105.

6–164 Campbell v Campbell

[1977] 1 All ER 1

(1) *Possibility of remarriage of wife – liberty to apply.* The husband appealed to the county court judge against an award of maintenance pending suit. At the hearing of the appeal it was agreed that, as the wife now intended to marry a Mr. Stalker, the appeal would be adjourned on the wife undertaking to claim no further financial provision for herself from the husband after a certain date. The judge suggested that there should be a provision in the order to cover the situation in case the wife should not in fact remarry. That was done by inserting that there should be liberty to apply. Sir George Baker P thought this a wise course. Mr.

Stalker was unable to marry the wife and the wife applied to be released from her undertaking. His lordship gave the wife leave to apply for maintenance.

(2) *Possibility of remarriage of wife – no evidence given by third party.*   Sir George Baker P said (at page 6): '... Mr. Stalker, who was in court but from whom there is no affidavit, has not given evidence. There is no criticism about that at all; it is, I think, the right course. He is said to be in some financial difficulties in resolving the problems of his former marriage and, temporarily at least, the question of further matrimony for Mrs. Campbell is on the shelf... So I put aside all questions of remarriage; that is not something which I shall take into consideration.'

6–164A Pace v Doe

[1977] 1 All ER 176

Wife barred by remarriage from obtaining lump sum by way of application to vary maintenance agreement.   In 1971 the husband petitioned for divorce. The wife filed an answer, in which she applied for a lump sum order. In June 1972 an agreement was concluded under which the husband transferred to the wife a freehold house subject to the existing mortgage, and agreed to pay the mortgage repayments and maintenance for her and for the children. A decree nisi was granted and made absolute in October 1972. In October 1973 the wife remarried.

The wife applied under section 35 of the Matrimonial Causes Act 1973 to vary the maintenance agreement. She asked that the children's maintenance be increased and secured. By a further application she asked that the agreement be varied to provide a lump sum for herself and the children. Sir George Baker P said that to make an original application to the court for a lump sum under section 23 of the Matrimonial Causes Act 1973 after remarriage is expressly prohibited by section 28 (3) of the Act, and it would be contrary to the philosophy of the Act to permit the wife to obtain a lump sum after remarriage by means of an application to vary the maintenance agreement. Even if there were jurisdiction, his lordship would not allow such a variation in the present case in view of the wife's remarriage. See case summary 9–016.

Quaere. The wife had already made an original application for a lump sum order in her answer. Why did she not pursue this?

6–165 Wales v Wadham

[1977] 2 All ER 125

Duty to disclose intention to remarry.   A consent order had been made prior to the filing of affidavits of means. Neither party had made full disclosure. The wife had not been asked if she intended to remarry. The husband had not disclosed all his income and had not disclosed the financial position of the woman with whom he was living. On the facts of the case it was held that the wife had been under no obligation to disclose her intention, and that there were no grounds to set aside the consent order. For further details, see case summary 9–017.

Notes
1. Counsel for the wife accepted that as soon as a duty to file an affidavit of means arises a firm intention to remarry must be disclosed.
2. Tudor Evans J said that there might be circumstances in which there is a duty to make full disclosure even before a duty to file an affidavit of means arises.

6–166 Nixon v Fox

(1978) Times, 7 March

Failure of respondent wife to file application for financial relief prior to remarriage fatal to application.   Section 28 (3) of the Matrimonial Causes Act 1973 expressly bars a former wife from applying for financial relief from a former husband after her remarriage. Before the dissolution of her marriage, the wife had given notice on Form 11 that she intended to apply for periodical payments for the children of the marriage. After her remarriage, she applied for leave to amend the application to add an application for ancillary relief for herself. The registrar granted leave. The husband appealed. Dunn J held that the amendment was in reality a fresh application made after remarriage, and was therefore contrary to section 28 (3).

Note. It is the filing of the formal application for financial relief (whether contained in a petition, answer or on Form 11) which must precede the remarriage. The fact that the hearing of the application takes place after remarriage is irrelevant: *Jackson v Jackson* (6–161).

6–167 Jenkins v Hargood

[1978] 3 All ER 1001

Failure of respondent wife to file application for financial relief prior to remarriage fatal to application.   Section 28 (3) of the Matrimonial Causes Act 1973 expressly bars a former wife from applying for financial relief from a former husband after her remarriage. Wood J dismissed the former wife's application for leave to amend her acknowledgement of service to her former husband's petition so as to incorporate a formal application for financial relief. Such an application was an attempt to defeat section 28 (3), his lordship said.

His lordship suggested that if, on receipt of a petition, a decision is reached not to file an answer, the respondent (whether husband or wife) should file an application for financial relief on Form 11 in lieu of an answer.

Notes
1. It is the filing of the formal application for financial relief (whether contained in a petition, answer or on Form 11) which must precede the remarriage. The fact that the hearing of the application takes place after remarriage is irrelevant: *Jackson v Jackson* (6–161).
2. Compare *Nixon v Fox* (6–166).

2   The wife's new family: relevance of third party's resources

A. *Relevance on application for capital provision*

CASE SUMMARIES

6–201 White v White

(1972) Times, 10 March, 116 Sol Jo 219, CA

Home provided by wife's new husband.   The wife left the husband and child of the family and, following the divorce, married the co-respondent, whose house provided better accommodation than the former matrimonial home. The wife's interest in the property was extinguished.

Notes
1. In *Cuzner v Underdown* (8–204) Davies LJ said: 'there are ... certain distinctions between *White v White* and the present case. But, apart from two matters, namely, that the co-respondent's house in that case provided better accommodation and that the only child of the marriage was with the husband, that case is extraordinarily close to the present one [*Cuzner v Underdown*] ... Following the observations that Lord Denning MR made in that case I think it would be quite wrong that the husband should be turned out of the house which he himself has provided ...' The authors are of the

opinion that in view of the fact that the husband in *White v White* required the house as a home for himself and the child of the family whereas the wife was housed in secure accommodation, indeed, better accommodation than the former matrimonial home in which the husband was residing, the Court of Appeal's decision in *White v White* cannot be thought of as anything but fair-minded. Section 25 (1) of the Matrimonial Causes Act 1973 states that in exercising its powers under the Act the court should endeavour to place the parties 'so far as it is practicable and, having regard to their conduct, just to do so, in the financial position in which they would have been if the marriage had not broken down and each had properly discharged his or her financial obligations and responsibilities towards the other'. This, the authors consider, is exactly what the Court of Appeal did in *White v White*. For the authors' comments on the much more difficult and controversial decision in *Cuzner v Underdown* see case summary 8–204.

2. For further details see case summary 8–201.

6–202 H v H (financial provision: remarriage)

[1975] 1 All ER 367

Wife's new husband a wealthy man.   The wife left the husband and went to live with the co-respondent. An agreed custody order was made under which the husband obtained care and control of the children with access to the wife. After the making of the decree absolute the wife remarried the co-respondent, who was a wealthy man. She applied for a one-third interest in the former matrimonial home but was awarded only one-twelfth. Sir George Baker P said that any payment would put the wife in a better financial position than if the marriage had continued.

Note. For further details see case summary 6–105.

6–203 Dopson v Cherry

(1974) 5 Fam Law 57, CA

Home provided by wife's new husband.   The wife left the husband and went to live with the co-respondent, whom she subsequently married. Both children were now living with their mother in a house provided for the family by the co-respondent. The husband remarried a woman who had a child of her own. He argued that he required the former matrimonial home for his new family.

Lord Denning MR said that the fact that the husband had remarried and had a new wife and her child was relevant. Orr LJ agreed, saying that the harm to the husband which would be caused by the sale of the former matrimonial home would outweigh any which the wife might suffer. The Court of Appeal ordered the joint interest in the property to be transferred into the husband's sole name, an immediate payment of £3,000 to be made to the wife and a further £2,000 to be raised on the house, the house not to be sold except on an application to the court.

6–204 W v W (financial provision: lump sum)

[1975] 3 All ER 970

Home provided for wife by third party.   The third party had put the house into the joint names of himself and the wife. Sir George Baker P said that the wife had earned a share in the former matrimonial home, which had an equity value of £8,100. Applying the one-third ratio that share would have been £2,700, but the fact that she now had a joint interest in her new house was relevant. The law relating to the proprietary rights of a mistress was still in a state of development, and it could be argued that the third party might be able to establish that the new house was held on a resulting trust for himself absolutely, the wife having contributed nothing towards its purchase. It would therefore be wrong to take into account the full value of her joint interest in the new house. After consideration of the figures the wife's lump sum order was reduced to £2,400. See case summary 13–009.

Note. In *Leake v Bruzzi* (24–202) the Court of Appeal held that where the conveyance makes an express declaration as to the proportions in which the beneficial title to the property is to vest, that declaration is conclusive in the absence of fraud or mistake and the parties cannot go behind it; because a beneficial joint tenancy had been expressly created the wife was accordingly held to be entitled to one-half of the net proceeds of sale.

6–205 Mentel v Mentel

(1975) 6 Fam Law 53, CA

Home provided by wife's new husband. The wife left the husband to go to live with another man and brought a petition for divorce. By the time of the hearing of the appeal the wife had married the third party, who was a police officer who had the benefit of rent-free accommodation provided by his employers. The former matrimonial home had been purchased in the joint names of the husband and the wife. It had an equity of £7,770. The Court of Appeal upheld an order that the wife's interest in the property be extinguished in return for a payment of £1,750.

6–206 Backhouse v Backhouse

[1978] 1 All ER 1158

Home purchased by wife together with new husband. The wife left the husband and children of the family and, following the divorce, married the co-respondent. They together purchased a new home. The husband remained in the former matrimonial home with the younger child of the marriage. The elder child was now married. The husband remarried, and had a child by his second wife. Balcombe J held that having regard to the substantial contribution made by the wife to the purchase of the former matrimonial home it would be repugnant to deprive her of all interest in it. However, it would also be repugnant to justice if her interest were to be such that the husband were required to sell the house, which was required as a home for his new family. Justice would be done by giving the wife a share in the house, but not by reference to any increase in its value which had occurred after she had left the husband. The husband was ordered to pay a lump sum of £3,500 which, having regard to his income, he would be able to raise by mortgage without crippling him financially.

6–207 Dallimer v Dallimer

(1978) 8 Fam Law 142, CA

Home provided for wife by third party. The husband was living in the jointly-owned matrimonial home. He was now retired and living upon a state pension and social security benefit. He contended that the wife should be given a one-third interest in the property, not to be realised until he should die or voluntarily cease to reside there. The wife conceded that the husband should remain in the house, but contended that her share should be a one-half interest. The wife's half share was reduced to one-third and settled on the husband for life. See case summary 5–106.

6–208 Eshak v Nowojewski

(1980) Times, 19 November, CA

Home provided by wife's new husband. The husband was living in the former matrimonial home with the two children of the family, aged 10 and 5. The parties contemplated that the children would remain in the husband's care.

The judge ordered that the jointly-owned matrimonial home should be sold when the youngest child attained 18 or completed full-time education, 60 per cent of the net sale proceeds to go to the husband and 40 per cent to the wife. The husband's appeal, on the ground that he would be severely handicapped in acquiring a new home when the youngest child attained 18 in 13 years' time and when he would then be 51, was allowed. The Court of Appeal ordered that the husband would be permitted to reside in the house for the rest of his life. On its sale after his death the proceeds would be divided equally between his estate and the wife or her estate.

Note. Compare *Dallimer v Dallimer* (6–207)

B. *Relevance on application for maintenance*

CASE SUMMARIES

6–231 Wachtel v Wachtel

[1973] 1 All ER 829, CA

Relevance of cohabitee's resources.   Lord Denning MR said (at page 841): 'So far as periodical payments are concerned, they are, of course, to be assessed without regard to the prospects of remarriage. If the wife does in fact remarry, they cease. If she goes to live with another man – without marrying him – they may be reviewed.'

6–232 Re L

(1979) 9 Fam Law 152

Maintenance of children – resources of wife's household.   The wife, who had obtained custody of the child of the marriage, was now cohabiting with a man and his two children. The husband had remarried and his new family comprised a wife and two children. The wife sought an increase in the order for the maintenance of the child of the family, now aged five.

The amount coming into the wife's household was £52 per week plus family benefits for three children. The amount coming into the husband's household was £68 per week plus family benefits for two children. The existing order was for £3 per week.

Sir George Baker P said that it was generally accepted that there should be no order under £5 per week and his lordship increased the order accordingly, adding, however, that this was no more than an attempt to get justice for the child by having regard both to the father's and the mother's obligations towards the child.

Note. In other words, Sir George Baker considered all the circumstances of the case, including not only the needs of the child in financial terms, but also the financial circumstances of both the husband's family and the wife's family.

6–233 Re L (Minors)

(1979) 123 Sol Jo 404

Maintenance of children – third party's earnings to be excluded.   The wife departed from the matrimonial home and went to live with another man, leaving the children with the husband. In proceedings under the Guardianship of Minors Act 1971 the father was awarded custody. The justices ordered the wife to pay to the husband maintenance of £4 per week for each child. The wife appealed.

Dunn J said that the wife had no job and no money. She could only pay maintenance if she was put in funds by the third party, who was not a party to the suit and had not accepted the children as members of his family. The justices had misdirected themselves in taking into account the third party's earnings. Appeal allowed.

Note. This case is the converse of *Brown v Brown* (see Appendix II), in which the roles were reversed.

c. *Practice*

CASE SUMMARIES

6–261 Campbell v Campbell

[1977] 1 All ER 1

No sufficient evidence of maintenance of wife by third party – no evidence given by third party. The husband appealed to the county court judge against an award of maintenance pending suit. At the hearing of the appeal it was agreed that, as the wife now intended to marry a Mr. Stalker, the appeal would be adjourned. Mr. Stalker was unable to marry the wife. Sir George Baker P gave the wife leave to apply for maintenance.

Sir George Baker P said (at page 6): '... Mr. Stalker, who was in court but from whom there is no affidavit, has not given evidence. There is no criticism about that at all; it is, I think, the right course. He is said to be in some financial difficulties in resolving the problems of his former marriage and, temporarily at least, the question of further matrimony for Mrs. Campbell is on the shelf.'

His lordship continued (at page 7): '... So I put aside all questions of remarriage; that is not something which I shall take into consideration. Then it is said that I ought to draw the inference that Mr. Stalker is in fact keeping her. At the present position, she is still living with her old mother ... She accepts that she was investigated, and apparently Mr. Stalker was investigated, no doubt at the instigation of Mr. Campbell, by the social security authorities. She says that she has got a clean bill and they have agreed that she was not being kept and were quite prepared to pay, but she has not been claiming any social security. She has been living on a loan of £10 a week from one of her sons but that is going to cease. From that I am asked to draw the inference that she is in fact being kept by Mr. Stalker, but to my mind that is suspicion and guesswork and there is not sufficient evidence from which I could draw any proper inference.'

6–262 Tomlinson v Tomlinson

[1980] 1 All ER 593

No sufficient evidence of maintenance of wife by third party – no evidence given by third party. The husband applied to the justices for an order reducing the amount of maintenance payable to the wife, on the ground that the wife was cohabiting with and being maintained by another man, a Mr. Holmes. The wife and third party attended the hearing of the application. The wife was unrepresented. At the outset the husband drew the justices' attention to the presence of the third party in court but they made no order excluding him. The third party was present when the husband was giving his evidence and was being cross-examined by the wife, and also when the wife was giving her evidence. The wife denied that she was being maintained by the third party. She wanted to call him as a witness in support of her case but, when the husband's solicitor pointed out that he had been present throughout the hearing, the justices refused to allow her to do so. The wife appealed to the Divisional Court against the order reducing her maintenance to a nominal sum, on the grounds, inter alia:

1) That there was no sufficient evidence to enable the justices to find that she was being maintained by the third party. [Sir John Arnold P said that there was no

doubt that there was sufficient evidence for the justices to find that she was cohabiting with the third party.]

2) That the justices had been wrong in law or, alternatively, in the exercise of their discretion to refuse to permit the wife to call the third party in support of her contention that she was neither cohabiting with him nor being maintained by him.

Sir John Arnold P said (at page 594): 'The facts which were adduced in evidence as regards the proposition that the wife was being maintained by Mr. Holmes were two, and two only. One was that Mr. Holmes from time to time bought toys for the wife's children, and the other was that on occasions he left his van at the wife's premises to enable her to run her mother about ...

'It is for consideration whether, without more, those two matters could really be enough to enable justices to hold that they were facts from which the inference of some degree of maintenance could be drawn.

'But they are very much bound up with the rest of the matter, because if Mr. Holmes had been called those two matters could, and could with propriety, have been more deeply investigated. For my part, I have preferred to place my judgment in this appeal on the basis not of the first ground, that is, there being no evidence from which the justices could legitimately infer the fact of maintenance, but on the matter of the evidence of Mr. Holmes ...'

The Divisional Court held:

1) A witness in matrimonial proceedings in the magistrates' courts is not under any obligation to leave the court unless the justices make an order excluding him. Where such an application is made they should, unless they are satisfied that it would not be an appropriate step to take in the circumstances, order the witness to withdraw. If a party is not represented then they should in appropriate circumstances suggest to that party that he should make an application to that effect.

2) The justices had exceeded their powers in refusing to allow the wife to call the third party as a witness, because no order had been made requiring him to withdraw.

Because the third Party's evidence might have influenced the justices' decision in respect of the maintenance order, the case was remitted for rehearing.

3   The husband's new family: relevance of third party's resources

A.   *Relevance on application for capital provision*

CASE SUMMARIES

6–301   Goodfield v Goodfield

(1975) 5 Fam Law 197, CA

Home provided by third party.   The wife was living in the former matrimonial home with the child of the marriage, now over 17 years of age. The husband was living with a third party. The parties had already agreed that the beneficial interest in the property was owned by them in equal shares, and the wife was earning as much as the husband. The wife's case was largely based on the difficulties she would have in finding other accommodation. Scarman LJ said that, while she would be in a difficult accommodation market, it was inconceivable that with half the equity in the house behind her and a steady job she could not find accommodation if she were forced to, and he ordered the house to be sold. For further details see case summary 5–102.

Note. This case was distinguished in *Martin v Martin* (6–302) on the ground that the sale of the house would not leave the wife without a roof over her head.

6–302 Martin v Martin (sub nom. **Martin (BH) v Martin (D)**)

[1977] 3 All ER 762, CA

Home provided by third party. After a childless marriage lasting 15 years the husband left the matrimonial home and went to live with another woman who had a tenancy of a council house. Purchas J ordered that the house should be held on trust for the wife during her life or until her remarriage or such earlier date as she should cease to live there, and thereafter upon trust for the parties in equal shares. The husband's appeal was dismissed.

Stamp LJ distinguished *Goodfield v Goodfield* (6–301) on the ground that an order for sale and division of the proceeds of the matrimonial home in that case did not involve leaving the wife without a roof over her head.

For further details, see case summary 5–103.

6–302A Foster v Foster

(1977) 7 Fam Law 112, CA

Assets built up by joint efforts of husband and second wife discounted. The parties were married in 1937. The marriage lasted twelve years, during which there were periods of separation. The final parting took place in 1949. There were no children. The husband went to live with another woman. He voluntarily gave the wife £2,000 at the time of the final separation and had since voluntarily paid her £3 per week. He ceased work because of ill-health in 1963. Since then he had been living on payments received on the winding-up of his former business. He also had investment income.

In 1972 the husband obtained a decree nisi of divorce on the ground of five years' separation. The wife applied for her financial position following the divorce to be considered. On the husband giving the necessary undertaking, the decree was made absolute and the husband married the woman with whom he had been living since the time of the final separation.

The wife's application came before the registrar in 1974. The husband was then 62 and the wife about 66. The registrar held that the husband had insufficient funds to justify making a lump sum order against him, but that he should continue to pay the wife maintenance of £3 per week. The wife appealed to the county court judge, who ordered the husband to pay a lump sum of £7,500. The husband appealed to the Court of Appeal. The appeal was heard in 1977.

Ormrod LJ described the marriage as a short unhappy marriage. It was 28 years since the parties separated, which was half a lifetime, and the husband had lived with his second wife much longer than with his first wife. Furthermore, the husband's present assets had been built up by the joint efforts of him and the second wife. The first wife could have taken action earlier to divorce him or could have brought proceedings for wilful neglect to maintain. It would not be right to deal with the matter now, after all these years, on the basis of the husband's current financial position.

The husband's liquid assets comprised investments of some £8,000, against which had to be set a tax liability of between £500 and £2,000. There was also his house. But it was wrong to convert homes into cash and then order a lump sum unless they were so large that they could be sold to provide a lump sum while leaving sufficient to provide another home. Furthermore, the husband at his age was in no position to borrow money on the security of the house. The husband's appeal should be allowed and the registrar's order reinstated.

Stamp LJ, agreeing, added that the husband's gift of £2,000 to the wife when the parties separated was an additional factor to take into consideration.

Note. See also *Lombardi v Lombardi* (19–004) – earnings from business carried on by joint efforts of husband and third party – third party's earnings discounted when calculating one-third ratio.

6–303 Ward v Ward and Greene (sub nom. Ward v Ward)

[1980] 1 All ER 176, [1980] 1 WLR 4, CA (these notes taken from transcript of shorthand notes of Association of Official Shorthandwriters Limited)

Third party's earnings taken into account in the overall picture.   During the course of proceedings agreement was reached that the jointly-owned matrimonial home, a flat where the wife was now living, should be transferred to her absolutely. It was common ground that the flat would have to be sold because it was too expensive to keep up. After repayment of the three mortgages secured on the property, together with the arrears which had accrued, it was apparent that the wife would not have enough capital to purchase even modest accommodation without recourse to borrowing. The husband, now living with the third party in rented accommodation, was adequately housed.

Medical evidence was produced to the effect that the wife had little or no present earning capacity (see case summary 2–510). The husband was earning £9,200 per annum gross, and he and the third party had a gross annual income of some £14,000 between them. The husband appealed against Dunn J's order for periodical payments of £3,500 a year on the ground (inter alia) that the wife had already received all the capital of the family.

Ormrod LJ said that one should not look just at the fact that the wife had obtained all of the family's capital, but at what that really meant in real life terms – i.e. that she would be in a position to buy herself a very modest flat, so reducing her cost of living in so far as she would not have to pay a high rent. All she was in a position to do was to rehouse herself more cheaply than she otherwise would have been able. It would be cheaper for her to be housed in this way than to divide the capital equally. That would leave her with too little with which to rehouse herself and would not help the husband at all because he would then have to pay her increased maintenance to cover the cost of rented accommodation.

His lordship said that the order balanced the needs of the one against the needs of the other, and that Dunn J was fully entitled to take into account the fact that the husband had the advantage of living with a lady who had a substantial income of her own which plainly reduced his cost of living.

Ormrod LJ said: 'So in summary the position is that the husband and Mrs. Greene are living together in a joint household, with no other person dependent upon them, with a gross income now of something of the order of £14,000 a year; the wife who, in the last two years, has undoubtedly had a difficult time over money, is going to have to sell her flat and find a modest flat for herself and will need enough money to live on. On present figures it looks as though she may have to borrow some money, perhaps only a small amount, to find herself accommodation.

'. . . I think the learned judge did exactly what he said he was doing on page 10 of his judgment; that is, balancing the needs of one of the parties against the needs of the other, and bearing in mind, as he was fully entitled to do, the fact that the husband has the advantage of living with a lady who has a substantial income of her own, which must, looking at it in the most limited way, reduce his cost of living substantially.'

6–304 Page v Page

(1981) Times, 30 January, CA

Relevance of gift by husband to third party.   The husband transferred £124,000 to his secretary, who removed it out of the jurisdiction. Ormrod LJ said that the husband's conduct in regard to the transfer was a highly relevant consideration, and that the husband had, very wisely, agreed that the sum should be treated as still part of his assets.

However, his lordship said that it was clear from the judgment that the judge had been comparing and contrasting the wife's position with that of the third party and, in effect, saying that if the third party had received £124,000 from the husband the wife should get more. The judge had not exercised his discretion in accordance with section 25 of the Matrimonial Causes Act 1973 (see Appendix I), said his lordship. The Court of Appeal reduced the lump sum payment from £165,000 to £90,000. For further details, see Appendix II.

Note. See also *Donaldson v Donaldson* (2–203).

B. *Relevance on application for maintenance*

CASE SUMMARIES

6–331 Grainger v Grainger

[1954] 2 All ER 665

The old law – earning capacity of second wife taken into account. Husband refused to consider suggestion that his present wife might let off surplus rooms so as to increase the family's income. Lord Merriman P said this suggestion was merely common-sense comment on the realities of this particular case.

6–332 Lombardi v Lombardi

[1973] 3 All ER 625, CA

The modern law – third party's earnings discounted when calculating one-third ratio. See case summary 19–004.

6–333 Campbell v Campbell

[1977] 1 All ER 1

The modern law – one-third ratio applied without having regard to the second wife's earnings – but taken into account in the overall picture. The husband left the wife to live with a third party, who subsequently had a child of which he was the father, and whom he later married. The husband's new wife was in employment. Sir George Baker P said that in his experience the one-third ratio was always calculated without having regard to the new wife's earnings. However, he continued (at page 7): 'But of course the new wife's earnings can be taken into account to this extent: that he has a person – a new wife – *a woman who is either keeping herself or contributing towards her own keep.* It is something to which one should have regard in the overall picture.'

Note. The punctuation and italics are the authors', who conclude that what Sir George Baker meant was that because the new wife was contributing towards her own keep she could not be spoken of as a dependant in the same way as a child or a new wife who was wholly dependent on the husband for her maintenance. See also *Rodewald v Rodewald* (19–009) – adult children.

6–334 Ward v Ward and Greene (sub nom. Ward v Ward)

[1980] 1 All ER 176, [1980] 1 WLR 4, CA

The modern law – third party's earnings taken into account in the overall picture. See case summary 6–303.

6–335 **Brown v Brown**

(1981) Times, 14 July

The modern law – maintenance of children – third party's earnings to be excluded. See Appendix II.

6–336 **Macey v Macey**

(1981) Times, 14 July

The modern law – third party's earnings to be excluded – but to be taken into account in the overall picture. See Appendix II.

c. *Practice*

CASE SUMMARIES

6–361 **Wilkinson v Wilkinson**

(1979) 10 Fam Law 48

Second wife ordered to file affidavit of means. Following the divorce the husband remarried. The wife applied for financial relief. In his affidavit of means the husband failed to disclose any income or capital of his second wife. The wife maintained that the husband's new wife had a substantial earning capacity and requested the registrar to order her to file an affidavit of means. The registrar refused to make the order and the wife appealed.

Booth J referred to *Grainger v Grainger* (6–331) and said that in order to discharge its duty properly under section 25 (1) of the Matrimonial Causes Act 1973 (see Appendix I) the court had to know how the means of the second wife were deployed within the husband's household. Appeal allowed.

Note. Compare Bush J's decision in *Wynne v Wynne and Jeffers* (6–362), which was upheld by the Court of Appeal. *Wilkinson v Wilkinson* must therefore be considered to have been decided per incuriam.

6–362 **Wynne v Wynne and Jeffers** (sub nom. **W v W**)

[1980] 3 All ER 659, CA

Husband's mistress can be ordered to attend court and give evidence but cannot be ordered to file affidavit of means. Shortly after separating from the wife, the husband, who was in lucrative employment, went to live with the co-respondent in a luxurious house belonging to his employers. Prior to the hearing of the wife's application for ancillary relief his employment was terminated in circumstances which aroused considerable suspicion on the part of the wife and her advisers. The husband continued to live in the house. He said he was under threat of eviction, but the threat never materialised. The wife thought he was being supported by the co-respondent, and argued that it would be relevant for the court to know the extent of such support when considering both his means and his needs under section 25 (1) (a) and (b) of the Matrimonial Causes Act 1973. [See Appendix I.] The wife applied for an order, under rule 77 (5) of the Matrimonial Causes Rules 1977, that the co-respondent file an affidavit of means.

Bridge LJ said (at the bottom of page 661): '. . . It is, of course, perfectly clear from the language of rule 77 (5) that when it comes to the effective hearing of this wife's claim for ancillary financial relief the co-respondent can be ordered to attend and to give evidence, to be examined or cross-examined, but the critical question is whether the concluding words of the rule on their true construction permit an order to be made now that she should make an affidavit of her means.'

His lordship continued (at page 662): 'Having been much assisted by the argument of counsel on both sides, in the end I have reached a clear conclusion in this matter that the registrar and the judge were right in the view that they reached that they had no jurisdiction to order an affidavit to be made by the co-respondent in this case. Counsel for the wife has put his argument boldly on the footing that the rule gives power to the court to order an affidavit to be made by any third party; any person, that is to say, who is not a party to the proceedings. In a subsidiary argument he did rely on the circumstance that this co-respondent was a party to the suit. In my judgment that really is quite irrelevant. Apart from the fact that there was no finding against her in the suit, on any view she cannot properly be regarded as a party to the lis which is involved in ancillary proceedings for financial relief.'

Cumming-Bruce and Eveleigh LJJ agreed. Cumming-Bruce LJ said (at page 664): '. . . I cannot find in para (5), as I interpret it, any power to require an affidavit from a stranger to the lis. There is a power on the hearing of the application to take evidence orally, to order the attendance of any person for the purpose of being examined or cross-examined, and, in my view, after the exercise of such powers on the hearing of the application, the court then has the power to take such steps as are necessary with a view to ordering the production of any document.

'. . . In my view there is no jurisdiction either to order an affidavit of means from a stranger to the suit or to order the more limited affidavit that counsel submitted might be more appropriate, namely an affidavit setting out the factual quantum of support . . .'

Notes

1. Bridge LJ (at page 661) referred to *Wilkinson v Wilkinson* (6–361). What was canvassed there, said his lordship, was the question whether the affidavit of means which the first wife was seeking from the second wife was one which would properly be *relevant*. The judge (Dame Margaret Booth) held that it was, and made an order requiring it. But it did not appear that the issue of *jurisdiction* was argued before her, said his lordship. Similarly, in *West v West* (1972) Times, 16 December there was nothing to indicate that the point was argued. Compare *Morgan v Morgan* (1–206) in which it was held that the evidence which the wife's aged father could give would be *relevant*, but that it would have been oppressive to cause him to come to court under the duress of a subpoena to give that evidence.
2. See also *W v W* (1981) Times, 21 March – see Appendix II.

6–363 Tebbutt v Haynes

[1981] 2 All ER 238, CA

On an application for a transfer of property order the court has jurisdiction to determine not only the interests of the parties to the marriage in the property in question but also the interests of third parties. Since the interests of the husband, wife and third party in the house in question had already been determined on the hearing of the application for a transfer of property order in the Family Division, it followed that those findings were conclusive as between the third party and the parties to the suit; the third party was accordingly estopped from reopening the issue in the Chancery Division.

6–364 W v W

(1981) Times, 20 March and 21 March

Husband's business associates ordered to produce documents. See Appendix II.

3–365 H v H (2nd June 1981)

[1981] LS Gaz R 786

Subpoena issued against family company. See Appendix II. And compare *B v B (matrimonial proceedings: discovery)* (see Appendix II).

4   The husband's new family: relevance of husband's new commitments

A. *Relevance on application for capital provision*

CASE SUMMARIES

6–401 H v H (financial provision: remarriage)

[1975] 1 All ER 367

The husband's new commitments – capital provision.   By the time of the hearing the wife had remarried the co-respondent, who was a wealthy man. The husband had also remarried; his new wife had no income or assets and the husband had the financial responsibility of educating all four children of the marriage, who were residing with him.

Sir George Baker P said (at page 371): 'The Matrimonial Causes Act 1973, section 25 (1) gives the court the widest possible power to achieve the statutory object, namely – "to place the parties, so far as it is practicable and . . . just to do so, in the financial position in which they would have been if the marriage had not broken down . . ." First, in my opinion, justice must be done in all cases, not only in those in which conduct is relevant . . . Then, it is not the wife alone who is to be placed in the same position but "the parties". Too often the husband's position tends now to be disregarded. In the present case I find that the husband, having remarried a lady of 29 with no income or assets and having to bring up and educate four young children, is near enough in the same financial position as he would have been if the marriage had not broken down . . .

'Now the wife . . .

'. . . She needs no flat or house and I think most people would find it distasteful and unjust that a lump sum should be given to a wife for the probable benefit of [her] new family.

'But, she says, she has earned a share . . . She . . . says that share should be one-third of the house . . . Any payment will in fact put her in a better financial position than if the marriage had continued and I would give her one-twelfth of the unencumbered value of the house . . . her entitlement to rank after the present charges for bank overdrafts and not to be payable until the youngest child is 18.'

6–402 Cumbers v Cumbers

[1975] 1 All ER 1, CA

A home for the husband's new family.   The former matrimonial home had been purchased by the husband three months before the marriage. Following the separation it was sold. The husband remarried and used the proceeds of sale for the purpose of buying another house for himself and his new wife. Lord Denning MR said that it would not be right that the wife should be able to sell up the husband's new house. The lump sum award in her favour was ordered to be charged on the new house at interest and payable by instalments.

6–403 Dopson v Cherry

(1974) 5 Fam Law 57, CA

A home for the husband's new family.   Lord Denning MR said that the fact that the husband had remarried and had a new wife and her child was relevant. Orr LJ agreed, saying that the harm to the husband which would be caused by the sale of the former matrimonial home would outweigh any which the wife might suffer. The Court of Appeal ordered the joint interest in the property to be transferred into the husband's sole name, an immediate payment of £3,000 to be made to the wife and a further £2,000 to be raised on the house, the house not to be sold except on an application to the court.

6–404 Daubney v Daubney

[1976] 2 All ER 453, CA

A home for the husband's new family. The wife had left the husband and purchased a flat. She subsequently obtained custody of the children. The husband was living in the jointly-owned matrimonial home together with a third party, her child by her previous marriage and a further child she had had by the husband. They planned to marry. The county court judge had ordered the house to be transferred to the husband subject to a charge of 30 per cent of the proceeds of sale in favour of the wife, postponed for 15 years. The husband appealed.

Scarman LJ said that one had to bear in mind that the husband had commitments to his new family, and Cairns LJ said that the judge had under-estimated the effect which should be given to the needs of the husband. The Court of Appeal reduced the wife's share to 15 per cent, postponed for 15 years.

Note. The husband and wife had been involved in a serious car accident. The husband had invested his damages in a business which had failed, and his earning capacity was expected to be limited in the future. The wife had invested her damages in the purchase of her flat. She was in employment, and earning as much as the husband.

6–405 Backhouse v Backhouse

[1978] 1 All ER 1158

A home for the husband's new family. The marriage broke down owing to the adulterous affair of the wife. The husband was ordered to pay a lump sum of £3,500 which, having regard to his income, he would be able to raise by mortgage without crippling him financially.

6–406 Porter v Porter

(1978) 8 Fam Law 143, CA

A home for the husband's new family. Following the divorce the husband had remarried and had two children of that marriage, but his second wife had now died. The former matrimonial home consisted of a flat above the shop which provided the husband's livelihood. The husband owned the freehold and resided in the flat with his new family. The wife lived in council accommodation.

Stamp LJ said that it would be wrong to order the husband to pay a sum which would involve a sale of the property, and he could not afford to take on the burden of an additional loan. The lump sum order made by the registrar was reduced by the Court of Appeal to a sum which the husband could raise by surrendering a life policy.

6–407 Blezard v Blezard

(1978) 9 Fam Law 249, CA

The husband's two families – conflict of interests. The husband deserted the wife and children (then aged 13 and 11) for a younger woman, and the wife obtained a divorce on the ground of his adultery. The husband married the co-respondent, and they were living in a house which they had purchased jointly. The wife was living in the former matrimonial home with the children, a boy now aged 16 who had left school and obtained employment, and a girl now aged 14. The house had an equity value of at least £48,000. It was owned jointly by the parties.

For the husband, it was urged that he was at present unemployed; he had no real prospect of early employment because of the recession in his industry; he had therefore registered at the labour exchange; in these circumstances, burdened as he was with obligations in respect of two homes, he badly needed the money which a sale of the matrimonial home would release.

Orr LJ said that had there been no children, he would have ordered an immediate sale of the property, subject only to allowing the wife sufficient time to find a new home. His lordship derived support for that conclusion from the judgment of Scarman LJ (as he then was) in *Goodfield v Goodfield* (5–102). There, reference was made to the fact that if a sale of the home was postponed so long as the wife chose to live in it, the husband would be deprived of the capital backing which he had every reason to expect would be his, and that a wife must accept *some measure* of disadvantage if justice were to be done between the parties. But the interests of the children had to be considered, and in his judgment it was best that they should remain in the house until the younger child attained 18 so that she could complete her education at her present school.

The Court of Appeal ordered that the husband would have a charge of two-fifths of the net proceeds of sale of the house, such charge not to be enforced until January 1980 or unless the wife remarried or cohabited with another man.

Lawton LJ, although agreeing with the judgment delivered by Orr LJ (who had ignored the question of conduct) said that one of the matters which he had taken into consideration was the conduct of the husband in leaving the wife for a younger woman. There were sufficient matrimonial assets to enable the first wife to be supported to a standard approaching her old standard of living while leaving the husband and the second wife with an adequate standard of living. The husband had made the new conjugal bed and he should not be allowed now to say that it was uncomfortable to lie in. The interests of the 'innocent' party and her family were to be given preference.

Note. For further details see case summary 8–214.

6–408 Tilley v Tilley

(1979) 10 Fam Law 89, CA

The husband's two families – conflict of interests.   Following the pronouncement of the decree nisi, a consent order was made vesting two properties in the wife in consideration of the wife making instalment payments to the husband. It was part of the order that the husband's maintenance liability should be merely a nominal 5p per year. The wife fell into financial difficulties and applied for variation of the consent order on the basis that she could not pay the balance of the instalments amounting to £3,500 now due without selling the roof over her head and rendering herself and the children homeless. Donaldson LJ said that the fact that execution of the order would render a family and, above all, the children homeless was the paramount consideration in this case. The husband certainly had an obligation to maintain his mistress and the child of that union. However, he also had a continuing obligation to maintain his four children by his wife, and this obligation would remain whether he received the £3,500 or not. The order would be varied by providing that there should be no further payments made to the husband, but that if there was any future application for maintenance for the children, any court faced with such an application ought to take into consideration the £3,500 which the husband would have in effect contributed towards their maintenance.

Note. For further details, see case summary 4–110.

B. *Relevance on application for maintenance*

CASE SUMMARIES

6–431 Barnes v Barnes

[1972] 3 All ER 872, CA

The husband's two families – conflict of interests.   Edmund Davies LJ said (at page 874): 'When the court adverts to the requirement imposed by section 5 (1) (b) of the Matrimonial Proceedings and Property Act 1970 [see now section 25 (1) (b) of the Matrimonial Causes Act 1973 – see Appendix I], to have regard to "the financial needs, obligations and responsibilities which each of the parties to the marriage has or is likely to have in the foreseeable future", then the fact that the husband has undertaken the legal responsibility of maintaining a new wife must be fully borne in mind *and be given the same degree and weight as his responsibility in any other financial respect.*'

Note. For further details, see case summary 22–002.

6–432 Winter v Winter

(1972) 140 JP Jo 597

The husband's two families – conflict of interests.   Payne J said that no order should be made against a husband which left him with an inadequate amount for the support of his second family; the result would be that in such circumstances the husband would decide to maintain his second family and to default on the court order, knowing that his first wife could look to the state for support, whereas his second wife or mistress could not.

Note. For further details, see case summary 22–003.

6–433 Campbell v Campbell

[1977] 1 All ER 1

Whether or not working wife a dependant.   The husband left the wife to live with a third party, who subsequently had a child of which he was the father, and whom he later married. The husband's new wife was in employment. Sir George Baker P said that in his experience the one-third ratio was always calculated without having regard to the new wife's earnings. However, he continued (at page 7): 'But of course the new wife's earnings can be taken into account to this extent: that he has a person – a new wife – *a woman who is either keeping herself or contributing towards her own keep.* It is something to which one should have regard in the overall picture.'

Note. The punctuation and italics are the authors', who conclude that what Sir George Baker meant was that because the new wife was contributing towards her own keep she could not be spoken of as a dependant in the same way as a child or a new wife who was wholly dependent on the husband for her maintenance.

6–434 Smethurst v Smethurst

[1977] 3 All ER 1110

The husband's several families – conflict of interests.   The county court registrar made a maintenance order against the husband in favour of his third wife, ordering him to pay £9 a week. At the time when the order was made the husband was earning approximately £34 a week net and, as the registrar knew, was liable under a previous maintenance order to pay his second wife £3.50 a week. The husband had married a fourth wife and she and her child were fully dependent on him.

Sir George Baker P said that whatever way one tested the husband's ability to pay he could not have afforded to pay £9 a week maintenance without falling below subsistence level.

Note. For further details, see case summary 22–006.

6–435 Tovey v Tovey

(1977) 8 Fam Law 80, CA

The husband's two families – conflict of interests. Following the separation, the husband had gone to live with an unmarried woman (whom he intended to marry) who had two children of her own. A decree absolute of divorce had now been pronounced and the wife had obtained custody of the three children of the marriage. The husband's income was £51.50 per week gross, £39 per week net. The wife earned £7 per week as a part-time barmaid, drawing £40 per week from the DHSS. Ormrod LJ said that if the husband were out of work he would be entitled to supplementary benefit at the rate of £39 per week, and that figure must be taken as being more or less the minimum that he could live on; the minimum figure was not a fixed figure, but obviously a sum of £39 per week was very near the minimum.

The Court of Appeal approved the registrar's award of a nominal sum for the maintenance of the wife herself. However, the husband was ordered to pay £1 per week for each child.

Note. For further details see case summary 22–008.

6–436 Fitzpatrick v Fitzpatrick

(1978) 9 Fam Law 16, CA

The husband's two families – conflict of interests. The wife lived in a council flat with the two children of the marriage. The husband lived with a Mrs. James, whom he intended to marry, together with her two children from her previous marriage, now dissolved.

The husband appealed to the Court of Appeal on the ground (inter alia) that on the basis of the judge's order of £15 per week for the wife and £5 per week for each child, the husband was left with £47.65 per week (including the child benefit in respect of Mrs. James's children), which sum was approximately £2 per week less than the supplementary benefits (including child benefit) to which he would be entitled if he were unemployed. Order reduced to £12 per week. See case summary 22–009.

6–437 Wagner v Wagner

(1978) 9 Fam Law 183, CA

The husband's two families – what would be fair in all the circumstances. Young childless couple married in November 1971 and divorced in May 1976. On the assumption that the wife was earning £30 per week and the husband £72 per week, a consent order of £1 per week was made in the wife's favour. In fact, the wife had not disclosed that she had stopped work, being pregnant by another man. She and the child were now living on social security.

The husband was now living with another woman who had given birth to a child of which he was the father. The judge having increased the wife's award to £10 per week, the husband appealed, contending that it was inequitable that the order should be increased when the wife's child was not his; alternatively, that in view of his finances the order was excessive.

Waller LJ said that it was not correct to state that there was any principle which applied in such a case; the court had to do what would be fair in all the circumstances. Taking all things into account, including the fact that whatever sum the court awarded it would make no difference to the wife because her sole income came from social security benefits, £10 per week was too much. However,

£1 per week was too little. After considering the living expenses of the husband's family his lordship reduced the order to £3 per week. Brandon and Ormrod LJJ agreed.

6–438 Re L

(1979) 9 Fam Law 152

The husband's two families – what would be fair in all the circumstances. The wife, who had obtained custody of the child of the marriage, was now cohabiting with a man and his two children. The husband had remarried and his new family comprised a wife and two children. The wife sought an increase in the order for the maintenance of the child of the family, now aged five.

The amount coming into the wife's household was £52 per week plus family benefits for three children. The amount coming into the husband's household was £68 per week plus family benefits for two children. The existing order was for £3 per week.

Sir George Baker P said that it was generally accepted that there should be no order under £5 per week and his lordship increased the order accordingly, adding, however, that this was no more than an attempt to get justice for the child by having regard both to the father's and the mother's obligations towards the child.

Note. In other words, Sir George Baker considered all the circumstances of the case, including not only the needs of the child in financial terms, but also the financial circumstances of both the husband's family and the wife's family.

6–439 Macey v Macey

(1981) Times, 14 July

Legal or moral obligation to support second wife or mistress relevant. Wood J said that the presence of a second wife or mistress might be relevant in two ways. The husband might be under a legal or moral obligation to support them, which would have some relevance on his ability to support the first wife and the children of the first marriage, or the husband might derive some benefit from the third party's income, which would mean that a greater part of his income would be available out of which to pay maintenance to his first wife and children. See Appendix II.

Note. Compare *Tovey v Tovey* (22–008), in which the husband was nevertheless ordered to pay maintenance of £1 per week for each of the children of his first marriage out of his meagre resources.

5 Remarriage/cohabitation by both parties: the two families: conflict of interests

CASE SUMMARIES

6–501 Mesher v Mesher and Hall

[1980] 1 All ER 126n, CA

See case summary 4–101.

6–502 Trippas v Trippas

[1973] 2 All ER 1, CA

See case summary 6–102.

6–503 H v H (financial provision: remarriage)

[1975] 1 All ER 367

See case summary 6–401.

6–504 Dopson v Cherry

(1974) 5 Fam Law 57, CA

See case summary 6–203.

6–505 Backhouse v Backhouse

[1978] 1 All ER 1158

See case summary 6–206.

6–506 Re L

(1979) 9 Fam Law 152

See case summary 6–232.

CHAPTER 7

Relevance of duration of marriage, etc.

Section 25 (1) (d) of the Matrimonial Causes Act 1973 requires the court to have regard to 'the age of each party to the marriage and the duration of the marriage'. In *Wachtel v Wachtel* (7–101) Lord Denning MR did in fact suggest that the one-third approach may not be applicable when the marriage has lasted only a short time, or where there are no children and the wife can go out to work. In cases where a spouse, more commonly the wife, is applying for a share in capital and/or property in which she has no strict legal interest, it is still to some extent relevant to talk of the wife 'earning her share' in these assets, either by direct or indirect contributions to their purchase, or by having contributed in kind to the family good throughout the marriage over a period of years. In those circumstances the duration of the marriage is of obvious relevance. Furthermore, if a marriage has broken down so soon after its inception that it would be repugnant to anyone's sense of justice not to take this factor into account, the court may not only refuse to make any award at all but may even extinguish altogether any interest which a spouse already owns in the capital assets. See *Taylor v Taylor* (7–201). But it would not avail a husband who had destroyed a marriage so soon after the ceremony to say that he was not obliged to pay any maintenance to the wife: see, for instance, *W-S v W-S* (7–361).

The case of *S v S* (7–462) illustrates that the court will not simply apply a discount merely because the marriage was a short one, but will consider all the circumstances in an attempt to do justice between the parties. The problems engendered by short marriages insofar as they affect the matrimonial home were raised in *Earley v Earley* (7–202) and *Browne v Pritchard* (7–103A).

1 The wife earning her share by her contributions to the family throughout the duration of the marriage: relevance of duration of the marriage, etc.

CASE SUMMARIES

7–101 Wachtel v Wachtel

[1973] 1 All ER 829, CA

Contributions to the family in kind over the years. Lord Denning MR, reading the unanimous judgment of the Court of Appeal, said (at page 837): 'In 1965 Sir

Jocelyn Simon P used a telling metaphor: "The cock can feather the nest because he does not have to spend most of his time sitting on it." He went on to give reasons in an address which he gave to the Law Society:

> "In the generality of marriages the wife bears and rears children and minds the home. She thereby frees her husband for his economic activities. Since it is her performance of her function which enables the husband to perform his, she is in justice entitled to share in its fruits."

But the courts have never been able to do justice to her. In April 1969 in *Pettitt v Pettitt* Lord Hodson said: "I do not myself see how one can correct the imbalance which may be found to exist in property rights as between husband and wife without legislation."

'Now we have the legislation. In order to remedy the injustice Parliament has intervened. The [Matrimonial Proceedings and Property Act 1970] expressly says that, in considering whether to make a transfer of property, the court is to have regard, among other things, to –

> "(f) the contributions made by each of the parties to the welfare of the family, including any contribution made by looking after the home or caring for the family"

'. . . *we may take it that Parliament recognised that the wife who looks after the home and family contributes as much to the family assets as the wife who goes out to work. The one contributes in kind. The other in money or money's worth. If the court comes to the conclusion that the home has been acquired and maintained by the joint efforts of both, then, when the marriage breaks down, it should be regarded as the joint property of both of them, no matter in whose name it stands. Just as the wife who makes substantial money contributions usually gets a share, so should the wife who looks after the home and cares for the family for 20 years or more.*'

His lordship concluded (at page 842): 'The wife undoubtedly contributed to the home for some 18 years and, as far as the evidence goes, was in every respect an excellent mother. This is clearly a case in which the wife has made a substantial contribution to the home [in kind], as of course the husband has out of his earnings.'

The one-third ratio was applied in respect of both capital and income provision.

Notes

1. Section 5 (1) (f) of the 1970 Act has been re-enacted without amendment as section 25 (1) (f) of the Matrimonial Causes Act 1973 – see Appendix I.
2. Compare *West v West* (7–103B), in which the wife had not earned any share in the matrimonial assets.
3. Compare *Browne v Pritchard* (7–103A), in which Ormrod LJ said, referring to the fact that the house was in joint names and the wife owned a one-half interest although the husband had provided the deposit and had paid the mortgage repayments: 'If it had not been in joint names I very much doubt whether any court, after a three-year marriage, would have given her as much as a one-third interest.'
4. Compare *Hanlon v Hanlon* (7–104), in which the fact of the wife's *very large* contribution to the family over a long period, and the fact that her contribution to the provision of a home for the children over the five years since the separation would continue for some years to come, were among the facts which led the Court of Appeal to give her an *increased share* in the matrimonial assets.

7–102 Trippas v Trippas

[1973] 2 All ER 1, CA

Wife, having earned her share, now living with married man – relevance of possible remarriage.   See case summary 6–102.

7–102A Flatt v Flatt

(1973) 4 Fam Law 20, 118 Sol Jo 183, CA

Wife earning her share – working wife – one third ratio applied.   The husband and wife were married in 1930. They had one child, a daughter, who was now married. The wife worked during the marriage. In 1956 the husband bought the house in which they had lived since 1935 for £1,130, of which he paid about one-half from his savings, the balance being on mortgage. The husband paid the mortgage instalments and the wife contributed to the housekeeping expenses. After the marriage had subsisted for some 34 years the wife left the husband to live with her married daughter. The husband remained in the matrimonial home by himself.

The husband obtained a decree nisi on the ground of five years' separation, and the wife made application for financial provision under the Matrimonial Proceedings and Property Act 1970. [See now sections 23 and 24 of the Matrimonial Causes Act 1973 – see Appendix I.]

Lord Denning MR said that both the capital position and the revenue position had to be considered. The sole capital asset was the matrimonial home. Under the 1970 Act [see now the 1973 Act] the court looked not merely at the wife's money contribution to the purchase, but at all the contributions she had made to bringing up the family, looking after the home and so forth, which were all set out in section 5 of the 1970 Act. [See now section 25 of the 1973 Act – see Appendix I.] In *Wachtel v Wachtel* (7–101) it was indicated that one-third of the capital assets and one-third of the revenue-producing assets was the starting point. That applied in this case. There was no reason to depart from it. The judge had decided the case before *Wachtel v Wachtel* and had made an order of some complication. The better order was that the house should be held by the parties in the proportion of two-thirds to the husband and one-third to the wife on trust for sale, with power to postpone the sale as long as the husband wished to remain there. In respect of the wife's one-third interest in the house, the husband should pay the wife £247 a year so long as he was in the house and having the whole benefit of it. If the husband wanted to sell the house the wife would have one-third of the proceeds. Periodical payments of £3 per week were awarded, amounting to one-third of the joint income of the parties.

Notes

1. The report at (1973) 118 Sol Jo 183 makes it clear that the property was vested solely in the name of the husband. Lord Denning MR's judgment clearly states that the wife earned her one-third share in the property by virtue of her contributions to the family in kind in looking after the home and family over 34 years of married life. What was the relevance of the fact that she had also contributed financially towards the purchase of the matrimonial home by working and contributing towards the housekeeping expenses? Apparently, this was of little significance. The report at (1973) 4 Fam Law 20 reads: 'Lord Denning MR said ... Under the 1970 Act, the court looked not merely at the wife's money contribution to the purchase, but at all the contributions she had made to bringing up the family, looking after the home and so forth ...' From this sentence one may perhaps deduce that the share in the property which the wife had earned through her indirect financial contributions towards its purchase was insignificant when compared with the share she had earned through her contributions to the family in kind over the years. Did her financial contributions earn her a larger share in the family assets than she would otherwise have earned through her contributions in kind? They did not; the one-third ratio was applied. One could *perhaps* argue that they did earn her a larger share, because the husband was ordered to pay her the sum of £247 a year, in addition to the maintenance, as a form of rent for so long as he remained in the house. But neither report states that this was awarded to the wife because of her financial contributions towards the family purse. Therefore one is forced to the conclusion that the wife's financial contributions were merely treated as part of her contributions towards the family as a whole.

2. The wife's indirect financial contributions towards the purchase of the house would also have earned her a share in the property under the Married Women's Property Act 1882, section 17. See *Kowalczuk v Kowalczuk* (1–132) for an explanation of this point. However, as Lord Denning MR said in *Hanlon v Law Society* ([1980] 1 All ER 763 at 770, quoted by Lord Simon on appeal to the House of Lords at [1980] 2 All ER 199 at 206): 'The court takes the rights and obligations of the parties all together, and puts the pieces into a mixed bag. Such pieces are the right to occupy the matrimonial home or

have a share in it, the obligation to maintain the wife and children, and so on. The court then takes out the pieces and hands them to the two parties, some to one party and some to the other, so that each can provide for the future with the pieces allotted to him or her. The court hands them out without paying any too nice a regard to their legal or equitable rights but simply according to what is the fairest provision for the future, for mother and father and the children.'

3. See now *S v S* (7–107) and *Preston v Preston* (7–109). It is now clear that active participation by the wife in the husband's business or her acceptance of a simple lifestyle so as to enable him to plough back the business profits, or where her earnings during the early stages of the business have contributed towards its success, are all important elements to be taken into account (see judgment of Ormrod LJ in *Preston v Preston*), assuming, that is, that there are enough assets to enable both parties to be adequately housed (see *Martin v Martin* (5–103)). *S v S* and *Preston v Preston* are both 'large assets' cases.

7–103 H v H (financial provision: remarriage)

[1975] 1 All ER 367

Wife earning her share – failing to finish the job.   After a marriage lasting 15 years the wife left the husband and four children and went to live with the co-respondent. An agreed custody order was made under which the husband obtained care and control of the children with access to the wife. After the making of the decree absolute the wife married the co-respondent, who was a wealthy man. She applied for a one-third interest in the former matrimonial home.

Sir George Baker P said (at page 373): '... I think, first, that it is unjust and impracticable to make the husband pay a lump sum. He cannot raise more money on the house, he has to pay for the four children and he has little other capital ... She needs no flat or house and I think most people would find it distasteful and unjust that a lump sum should be given to a wife for the probable benefit of the new family.

'But, she says, she has earned a share, and will accommodate her first family by allowing it to remain with them till the youngest is 18. She now says that share should be one-third of the house. If the concept of earning is to be applied to a domestic situation, then it should be applied with all its normal consequences. One is that if the job is left unfinished you do not earn as much. A builder agrees to build four houses. He goes off to a job which he prefers to do, leaving them in varying stages of completion. Leaving aside any question of special contractual terms, the best he could hope to receive is the value of work actually done, remembering also that the owner has to have the work completed. Is there any difference between four houses and four children? I think not. Any payment will in fact put her in a better financial position than if the marriage had continued and I would give her one-twelfth of the unencumbered value of the house ... her entitlement to rank after the present charges for the bank overdraft and not to be payable until the youngest child is 18.'

Notes

1. The wife's new husband was a wealthy man. The husband's needs were greater than the wife's. See case summary 6–401.

2. Notwithstanding the fact that the parties had agreed that conduct was not a relevant issue, Sir George Baker took into account the fact that the wife had left the matrimonial home and had left the children to be cared for by the husband. Compare *Trippas v Trippas* (6–102) where the parties separated after the children had grown up.

7–103A Browne v Pritchard

[1975] 3 All ER 721, CA

Wife earning her share – short marriage – house purchased by husband in joint names – relevance of wife's ownership of half share – house required as a home for children living with husband – wife living in council accommodation – comparative positions of the parties at the end of the day – wife's half share in house reduced to one-

third. Ormrod LJ said that, had the house not been in joint names, his lordship doubted whether any court, after a three-year marriage, would have given the wife as much as a one-third interest. His lordship summed it up by saying: 'Finally, let us compare the positions of these two adults. At the end of the day the wife will have a council flat plus £X,000. The husband will have no council flat or other accommodation, plus £2X,000. It does not require much consideration, I venture to think, to decide which of those two people will be the better off in five years' time when [the younger of the two children living in the house with the husband attains the age of 18 and] the house is sold. Quite obviously the wife. And so I think the order proposed is a fair and reasonable one, and represents the best that the court can do in the circumstances.'

Note. For further details, see case summary 4–104.

7–103B West v West

[1977] 2 All ER 705, CA

Wife, from outset of marriage, unreasonably refusing to cohabit with husband in house purchased by him as matrimonial home – duration of marriage nil to all intents and purposes – wife's contribution to the family nil to all intents and purposes. Periodical payments of £550 a year were awarded, which represented one-eighth of the joint income of the parties. The wife's appeal was dismissed. See case summary 13–013.

7–104 Hanlon v Hanlon

[1978] 2 All ER 889, CA

Wife's very large contributions to the family both in kind and financially. The matrimonial home had been purchased in the sole name of the husband. However, during the 14 years of married life the husband and wife had contributed equally in terms of money and work to the family. (The wife's current earnings as a community nurse were equal to those of the husband as a police officer, and no order was sought for her maintenance). The parties separated. The wife remained in the house with the four children while the husband now lived in a flat provided rent-free by his employers.

Ormrod LJ said that it was not right to regard the interests of the husband and wife in the house as being equal. In the five years since the separation the wife had continued to bring up the four children while continuing to work full-time. She had maintained the house as well as she could during those years, and had taken a considerable load off the shoulders of the husband during that period. She had therefore made a very large contribution to the family. As one-half of the equity on any future sale of the house would not produce a sum sufficient to enable the wife to buy another home for herself and such of the children as were still with her, it would be wrong to make any order which would have the result of forcing the wife to leave. As she was willing to forgo any further periodical payments for the two children who were under 17, the proper order was to transfer the house to the wife absolutely.

Quaere. A wife who contributes to the family in kind throughout the duration of the marriage without contributing financially in any way will usually be presumed to earn for herself a one-third interest in the family assets – see *Wachtel v Wachtel* (7–101). If she fails to finish the job of raising the children the court may, as in *H v H* (7–103), decide that she has failed to earn so large a share. If the matrimonial home has been conveyed into the joint names of the parties the law of Equity will presume that the wife owns a beneficial half interest in the property, or such other beneficial interest as is stipulated in the conveyance – see *Leake v Bruzzi* (24–202). If the matrimonial home, although conveyed into the sole name of the husband, has in effect been acquired by the parties' joint efforts with the aid of financial contributions from the wife towards the family purse, then Equity will impute a trust for her benefit according to the extent of her financial contributions – see *Kowalczuk v Kowalczuk* (1–132) in which the court was unable to impute any such trust because the house had been purchased by the husband prior to his contemplating marriage.

If, in order to provide a home for the children or a home for the parties themselves, it is then necessary to redistribute the parties' beneficial interests in the property (or such 'interests' in the property as the court might otherwise have held they were entitled to by virtue of their contributions towards the family, financial or otherwise), the court has the widest possible powers to do whatever it sees fit. This includes transferring the ownership of an asset vested in the sole name of one party into the sole name of the other party – see *Hanlon v Hanlon*.

If, however, both parties and the children are already adequately provided for without the necessity of a property transfer order, would it be correct to presume that a wife who goes out to work and contributes financially as well as in kind should earn for herself a greater share of the family assets than a wife who merely contributes in kind? *Hanlon v Hanlon* was a case, not so much on the point of the wife's *contributions* towards the family, as on the *future needs* of the wife when the family had grown up.* *S v S* (7–107) and *Preston v Preston* (7–109) would now seem to answer this question in the affirmative.

* In *Hanlon v Hanlon*, Ormrod LJ (at page 893) referred to the wife's very *large contribution* to the family. His lordship said that it would accordingly not be right to regard the interests of the parties in the house as being equal. Did the wife's *financial contributions* earn her a greater share in the property than she would have earned merely by virtue of her *contributions in kind*? And did the case turn on the wife's *very large contribution*, financial or otherwise, or on the wife's *future needs*?

In *Hanlon v Law Society* there was discussed whether the wife was entitled to an equitable interest in the house by virtue of her financial contributions. Lord Lowry said (at [1980] 2 All ER 199 at page 222): '... I am of the opinion that at no time proved or agreed, in either the matrimonial proceedings [i.e. *Hanlon v Hanlon*] or these proceedings [i.e. *Hanlon v Law Society*], that the appellant [Mrs. Hanlon], according to the principles laid down by your Lordships' House in cases such as *Pettitt v Pettitt* and *Gissing v Gissing* ..., had any equitable interest in the house. The issues which would have had to be decided in her favour by analogy with section 17 [of the Married Women's Property Act 1882] were neither raised nor conceded, and the courts which adjudicated under section 24 [of the Matrimonial Causes Act 1973] expressly did not consider them.' His lordship continued (at page 223): 'I do not ... find myself able to accept Arnold P's factual conclusion that the appellant had an equitable half-share ... On the evidence in the matrimonial proceedings and the present proceedings I must conclude that the effect of the [property transfer] order was to transfer the entire equitable estate from husband to wife. What Ormrod LJ said [in *Hanlon v Hanlon* at page 893] is ... consistent with this result, and I cannot accept the view that he was referring, or referring only, to the sort of financial contribution by the appellant which is regarded in *Gissing v Gissing* as justifying the inference of a common intention of spouses that the wife should share in the beneficial interest. On the contrary, many of the contributions (using that word in a broad sense) of the appellant to the welfare of the home were ... of a kind which does not satisfy the *Gissing* test.'

If the wife's *financial contributions* did not earn the wife a half share in the house, would it be correct to say that they influenced the Court of Appeal in *Hanlon v Hanlon* into giving the wife a greater share in the property than she would have earned merely by virtue of her *contributions in kind*? Possibly they did, but the report is by no means clear. The authors are of the opinion that, notwithstanding the passage in Ormrod LJ's judgment in *Hanlon v Hanlon* referred to by Lord Lowry in *Hanlon v Law Society*, the wife's *financial contributions* were merely *part of the contributions made by each of the parties to the welfare of the family*.

Furthermore, they would submit that, although the wife's *contributions to the welfare of the family*, including her financial contributions, were important considerations which were expressly taken into consideration by the Court of Appeal in *Hanlon v Hanlon*, the case of *Hanlon v Hanlon* did not turn on the wife's *contributions*, but, rather, on the wife's *future needs*, namely: (1) the necessity of the wife retaining the house as a home for the children, not only while they were dependent but also when they had grown up, for so long as they were still living with their mother and until they were settled on their own; (2) the necessity of the wife thereafter retaining the house as a home for herself, in view of the difficulties she would have in re-housing herself were the house to be sold in the future and the proceeds divided between the parties, and (3) the desirability of predicting the parties' interests in the property there and then, so that both parties could face the future knowing exactly where they stood.

7–105 Bateman v Bateman

[1979] 2 WLR 377

Wife earning her share – relevance of grave misconduct.   See case summary 8–309.

7–106 Hudson v Hudson

(1979) 10 Fam Law 23, CA

Wife earning her share – working wife – husband and wife in partnership in hotel business – 50:50 division of assets. See case summary 1–409.

    Note. See also *S v S* (16–104) for another case involving a wife's substantial contributions to the family business.

7–107 S v S

(1980) Times, 10 May

Wife earning her share – working wife – large assets. Balcombe J said that, although the sum of £200,000 offered by the husband was more than adequate for the wife's needs, to award her no more than this would be to fail to adequately take into account her very substantial contributions towards the success of the husband's farming business by her hard physical work on the farm and her acceptance of a simple lifestyle, which had contributed in no small way to the husband's ability to utilise the profits of the farm and buy more land.

    For further details, see case summary 16–104.

7–108 Page v Page

(1981) Times, 30 January, CA

40 years of marriage represents a large contribution by both parties, but does not earn a bonus – lump sum reduced from £165,000 to £90,000. Ormrod LJ said that the present case was not one in which the wife had been actively engaged in the husband's business. She had not 'earned' a share in that sense. Applying all the considerations set out in section 25 of the Matrimonial Causes Act 1973 (see Appendix I), his lordship came to the conclusion that the appropriate figure would be £90,000. Dunn LJ and Wood J concurred.

Notes

1. For further details, see Appendix II.
2. Compare *S v S* (16–104), in which Balcombe J said that although the sum of £200,000 offered by the husband in that case was more than adequate for the wife's needs, to award her no more than this would be to fail to adequately take into account her very substantial contributions to the husband's business. His lordship accordingly increased the lump sum to £375,000.

7–109 Preston v Preston

(1981) Times, 25 June, CA

Wife earning her share – contribution to success of husband's business by frugal living – large assets. The wife had lived frugally, so helping the husband to build up business assets valued at £2.3m. Ormrod LJ said that the judge was entitled to take into account the wife's contribution, which the judge had clearly regarded as a significant factor. The Court of Appeal held (Brandon LJ dissenting) that the award of a lump sum of £600,000 to the wife was not so excessively high as to warrant interference with the exercise of the judge's discretion.

    Ormrod LJ said that active participation by a wife, either by working in the family business or by providing finance, would greatly enhance her contribution to the welfare of the family and might lead to a substantial increase in the lump sum awarded, over and above her 'reasonable requirements'.

    Similarly, the acceptance of a frugal standard of living so as to enable the husband to plough back a large proportion of the profits.

    The same effect was produced, said his lordship, where a wife's earnings contributed to the husband's success, especially in the early stages where they might be an important element.

Notes

1. For further details, see case summary 13–018.
2. For the facts of the case, see the report on page 3 of *The Times*. These are omitted from the law report on page 28.

2   Short childless marriage between young parties

A.   *Relevance on application for capital provision*

CASE SUMMARIES

7–201 Taylor v Taylor

(1974) 119 Sol Jo 30

Husband aged 36 and wife 33 – no children – parties sleeping under same roof for only 20 nights. The matrimonial home had been purchased by the husband, a bank clerk, with the aid of a loan from his employers and conveyed into joint names. Because the wife was a doctor working at a hospital she had kept on her bed-sitter. The wife had contributed nothing to the marriage, either in cash or in kind, and had lost nothing as a result of its breakdown. She had contributed nothing towards the purchase of the house, next to nothing to the household expenses, and such furniture as she had provided had been returned to her. The wife's interest in the matrimonial home was extinguished, on the ground that her contributions to the marriage had been so small.

Cumbers v Cumbers (7–301) was distinguished. In that case the wife had borne a child and the parties' financial circumstances were very different. Here there was no child and the wife was earning much more than the husband. The husband could not be expected to provide either periodical payments or a capital sum.

Note. The fact that the husband obtained a divorce on the ground of the wife's desertion was irrelevant. Compare *Chesworth v Chesworth* (7–232) and *W-S v W-S* (7–233) in which the husband deserted the wife, and *Khan v Khan* (7–234) in which the husband's conduct caused the wife to leave the matrimonial home. In none of these cases was conduct a relevant factor.

7–202 Earley v Earley

(1975) Times, 20 June, CA

Husband aged 31 and wife 24 – no children – parties living together for less than four months. The parties married in June 1972. In September they were at loggerheads and separated. They attempted a reconciliation, and in October, while still living apart, they bought a house in joint names. They spent only one night together in the house, in February 1973, when the husband left.

The house had cost £5,348. A mortgage loan of £4,000 had been obtained, repayable by monthly instalments of £33. Of the balance purchase money, loans of £100 and £840 had been made to the couple by the wife's parents, and the balance had come from the wife's savings account to which the husband had contributed £50. The wife had repaid £100 to her parents.

Apart from two mortgage payments made by the husband in October and November 1972, the wife had been responsible for all the repayments to date. She wished to live in the house and to own it. The wife claimed a transfer of property order under the Matrimonial Causes Act 1973, section 24, and the judge had based his decision on the spouses' financial contributions to the purchase money. The husband had actually contributed only £116, made up of two mortgage instalments and his share of his wife's savings account. Adding a sum to take account of inflation, the judge decided that the husband was entitled only to £200, and made an order that the wife should pay him that amount in extinction of his interest in the house. The husband appealed.

Cairns LJ said that if the husband's entitlement was to be worked out by reference to his contributions so should the wife's, and on that basis the wife would get much less than the order gave her. His Lordship thought that the judge had approached the matter on the wrong basis. *The right approach was not merely to have regard to the cash contributions of the spouses, but also to look at their commitments in respect of the property. It had to be borne in mind that the wife had borne almost entirely the responsiblity for the mortgage instalments, that she would continue to do so, and that the house was increasing in value while she kept up the repayments.* Taking all those matters into account, his Lordship thought that a fair sum to which the husband was entitled was £750. The husband, however, remained liable to meet his commitments to his wife and her parents in respect of the loans of £100 and £840, which came to £470. This would mean that the cash sum the husband would receive would be £280.

Scarman LJ, concurring, said that before the capital asset could be realised, substantial burdens must be discharged. Regard must be had to the fact that the wife would have the obligation of discharging the repayments, and also to the fact that the husband would be getting an immediate cash payment without the house being sold.

7–203 H v H (15 May 1981)

(1981) Times, 16 May

Husband aged 35 and wife 26 – no children – neither party adversely affected by consequences of marriage – desirability of the clean break. If the wife was prepared to consent to the dismissal of her claim for periodical payments, the court was prepared to order the husband to make her a small lump sum payment. See Appendix II.

B. *Relevance on application for maintenance*

CASE SUMMARIES

7–231 Graves v Graves

(1973) 4 Fam Law 124, 117 Sol Jo 679

Parties in their early twenties – no children – marriage lasting only a year. Ormrod J (as he then was) stated that, *where a marriage was of short duration and the parties were young, a nominal order for periodical payments was the appropriate order unless there were children or the wife was handicapped in some way which prevented her from working.* At the time of the hearing before the justices the wife had not been working, but she was a state enrolled nurse and the justices should have taken into account her potential earning capacity. The wife was now employed full time in a hospital. The Divisional Court allowed the husband's appeal and substituted a nominal order.

Note. See *Khan v Khan* (7–234) [1980] 1 All ER 497 at 499 for a short summary of the judgment in this case.

7–232 Chesworth v Chesworth

(1973) 4 Fam Law 22, 118 Sol Jo 183

Parties in their early twenties – no children – marriage lasting less than a year. Sir George Baker P said that notwithstanding the fact that the magistrates had found the wife's complaints of desertion and persistent cruelty proved, counsel for the wife could justify only a nominal order.

The husband was willing to pay the wife £3 per week for nine months to enable the wife to re-organise her life. Sir George Baker P thought this a sensible course.

7–233 **W-S v W-S** (sub nom. **Whyte-Smith v Whyte-Smith**)

(1974) Times, 25 October, 119 Sol Jo 46

Parties in their late twenties – no children – marriage lasting less than six months.   Rees J said that it was not an attractive argument on behalf of a husband whose conduct had destroyed a marriage so soon after the ceremony to say that he was not obliged to provide any maintenance for his wife because she was capable of earning her own living and the marriage had not lasted long enough to warrant an award of maintenance in her favour. But the husband's conduct in this case had not been *gross and obvious* and therefore was not a factor to be taken into consideration. *However, as a result of the marriage breakdown and its sequel the wife had been unable to work for more than a year. Order to pay £250 per annum until a stated time, by which the wife should have recovered from the effects of a disastrous marriage, when the financial position could be reviewed.* For further details, see case summary 7–361.

7–234 **Khan v Khan**

[1980] 1 All ER 497

Wife in late teens and husband in late twenties – no children – marriage lasting only nine months.   The stipendiary magistrate found that the husband had constructively deserted the wife and that he had, since a date following the separation, wilfully neglected to maintain her. The husband appealed against the quantum of maintenance to the Divisional Court.

The wife's position was that she had never worked, although she was taking a correspondence course. After the parting she had gone to live with her parents.

Waterhouse J said that the general principle applicable to a case of this kind was stated in *Graves v Graves* (7–231). In that case, the parting had occurred only about 12 months after the marriage, there was no child, and both parties were in their early twenties; Ormrod LJ had stated that where a marriage was of short duration and the parties were young a nominal order was appropriate unless there were children *or the wife was handicapped in some way which prevented her from working.* Waterhouse J continued to say that the present case was distinguishable from *Graves v Graves* because the wife in that case had a profession. It was suggested on behalf of the husband that either the order should have been for a limited period in order to encourage the wife to train herself for employment at an early date or that it should have been assessed at such a modest level that there would be active encouragement to the wife to find employment at the earliest opportunity.

Looking at the whole of the facts, Waterhouse J said that he considered this a case in which it would be right to place a time limit on the order for maintenance. Although the award of £18 per week was rather less than one-third of the husband's income it was adequate for the wife in her present circumstances while she was seeking to train herself and obtain satisfactory employment. Waterhouse J considered that if the magistrate's order had been limited to a period of two years from the date of the desertion this would have been satisfactory, and he therefore allowed the appeal to the extent of inserting in the magistrates' court order a time limit of 12 months, so that the maintenance of £18 a week would terminate just over two years from the date of the separation. Thereafter the maintenance payable would be reduced to £5 per week.

Sir John Arnold P agreed, adding that it would be open to either party to apply for variation of the order at the end of the 12 months' period.

Note. It is perhaps surprising that a nominal order was not made, but their lordships considered that even after the wife had obtained employment some small subsidy from the husband would be appropriate (see Sir John Arnold's judgment). It should be noted that the case was not one of divorce. Compare *W-S v W-S* (7–233), a case under section 27 of the Matrimonial Causes Act 1973 (neglect to maintain) prior to the amendment of that section by the Domestic Proceedings and Magistrates' Courts Act 1978, in which, as a result of the marriage breakdown and its sequel the wife had been unable to work for more than a year; an order for maintenance was made, limited to a stated time, by which the wife should have recovered and when the financial position could be reviewed.

7–235 H v H (15 May 1981)

(1981) Times, 16 May

Husband aged 35 and wife 26 – no children – neither party adversely affected by consequences of marriage – desirability of the clean break. If the wife was prepared to consent to the dismissal of her claim for periodical payments, the court was prepared to order the husband to make her a small lump sum payment. See Appendix II.

3   Short marriage: young wife awarded financial provision

A. *Capital provision*

CASE SUMMARIES

7–301 Cumbers v Cumbers

[1975] 1 All ER 1, CA

Parties in their early twenties – one child – marriage lasting only 18 months. The matrimonial home had been purchased by the husband three months prior to the marriage. He had paid the deposit out of compensation he had received following an accident. The balance was on mortgage. Although the wife continued to work after the marriage, she acquired no interest in the house under the Married Women's Property Act 1882, section 17. [See *Kowalczuk v Kowalczuk* (1–132).] Following the husband's departure from the matrimonial home the wife obtained a maintenance order in the magistrates' court for herself and the child of the marriage. The husband sold the house. [The wife must have vacated the property.] The net sale proceeds amounted to £1,600. The husband used the money in order to purchase a new car and another house for his new family. He obtained a divorce on the ground of two years' separation by consent. The wife applied for financial provision. The judge ordered that, in addition to maintenance, the husband should pay the wife a lump sum of £800, to be paid by instalments and charged on the husband's new house. The husband appealed.

Lord Denning MR said (at page 3): '. . . It was said for the husband that this was not a case for capital provision at all. It was pointed out that the marriage had been very short. The wife had no proprietary right in the matrimonial home. She had no case under section 17 of the Married Women's Property Act 1882. So no part of the £1,600 should be allocated to her.

'I can see the force of that argument. But, looking once again at *Wachtel v Wachtel* (7–101), it is important to remember that, in addition to the income provision, there should be, in a proper case, a capital provision. During the argument in this case Ormrod LJ pointed out that an income provision comes to an end automatically if the wife remarries. So it may sometimes be wise to make some capital provision for her which will not cease on her remarriage. That is, in a case where she has really played a part in the marriage which deserves compensation of a capital nature. It seems to me that this case is properly one in which a capital provision – a lump sum – should be ordered. But I think that the sum of £800 [one-half of the family assets] is too large. The better figure would be one-third or thereabouts. I would put it at £500, in regard to the capital provision.

'Again it would not be right that the wife should be able to sell up the husband's new house. The right course would be to award her a sum of £500 to be a charge on the new house, but such charge not to be available or enforced except on further application to the court; but meanwhile interest to run at an appropriate rate which I would suggest to be ten per cent. The husband should pay that ten per cent on the balance outstanding by weekly instalments. He should repay the £500 gradually as he could – by instalments to be agreed or fixed – until the £500 is discharged. So far as maintenance is concerned, it would be better dealt with in the future by the registrar in the Family Division here. So I would replace the justices' order by an interim order in the High Court here. It should be at present the same amount, namely, £5 for the wife and the £2 for the child; but that that income provision could and should be reviewed on application to the Family Division here. The registrar is to be able to consider it in the light of all the circumstances.'

Notes

1. Distinguished in *Taylor v Taylor* (7–201).

2. Compare *Browne v Pritchard* (7–103A), in which Ormrod LJ said: 'If the matrimonial home had not been in joint names, I doubt very much whether any court, after a three years' marriage, would have given [the wife] as much as a one-third interest.' Strangely enough, Lord Denning MR and Ormrod LJ sat in the Court of Appeal on the hearing of both *Browne v Pritchard* and *Cumbers v Cumbers*. The authors are unable to reconcile their lordships' two decisions except on the basis that in *Cumbers v Cumbers* their lordships considered that, because the wife had worked during the marriage and had contributed to the housekeeping expenses, she had played such a part in the marriage that she had thereby earned a share of the capital assets, and that she therefore deserved *something* in the way of capital provision notwithstanding the shortness of the marriage. In any event, £500 payable by instalments is not very much.

3. The authors are of the opinion that *Cumbers v Cumbers* is not representative of the modern law. They are of the opinion that, where the marriage is short, the wife is unlikely to get as much as a one-third interest in the capital assets unless her financial contributions have been such as to warrant it (see *Earley v Earley* (7–202)) or her needs demand it (see *Scott v Scott* (4–107)). In all cases, the needs of the parties and, in particular, the needs of the children of the family, take precedence over all other considerations (see *Browne v Pritchard* and *Scott v Scott*).

7–302 **Earley v Earley**

(1975) Times, 20 June, CA

Husband aged 31 and wife 24 – no children – parties living together for less than four months – wife bearing almost entire responsibility for mortgage repayments on jointly-owned matrimonial home occupied by her. See case summary 7–202.

7–303 **M v M**

(1976) 6 Fam Law 243, CA

Husband aged 29 and wife 27 – two children – marriage lasting only 3½ years. The husband had purchased the matrimonial home out of money left to him by his late mother. The wife did not go out to work and made no financial contribution to the family. After only 3½ years of marriage the wife left the matrimonial home, taking the children with her. She obtained a divorce on the ground of two years' separation by consent, and applied for financial provision. The judge at first instance awarded her a lump sum of £1,500. Her counsel in the Court of Appeal suggested that the award should have been of the order of £5,000, which would be just under one-third of the present value of the house. The Court of Appeal held that, bearing in mind that the marriage had lasted only 3½ years, that the husband had purchased the matrimonial home entirely out of money left to him by his late mother, that the wife had at no time contributed to the family financially by going out to work, that the home was used by the husband for business purposes, that his only capital asset apart from the house was an insurance policy with a surrender value of £500 and a savings bond amounting to £500, and that to borrow further sums might well cripple the husband's business, the judge had been fully justified in awarding the wife a lump sum of only £1,500. Orr LJ said that, but for the fact that the wife had only a bare subsistence and capital resources of only £94, his lordship might have awarded an even lower figure.

Notes

1. See also *Browne v Pritchard* (7–103A). There the matrimonial home had been purchased by the husband in joint names; the wife's interest was reduced to one-third; Ormrod LJ said: 'If it had not been in joint names I very much doubt whether any court, after a three years' marriage, would have given her as much as a one-third interest.'
2. Notwithstanding the fact that the wife had custody of two young children, she was nevertheless awarded only nominal maintenance for herself. Compare *Cumbers v Cumbers* (7–301).

7-304 H v H (15 May 1981)

(1981) Times, 16 May

Husband aged 35 and wife 26 – no children – neither party adversely affected by consequences of marriage – desirability of the clean break.   If the wife was prepared to consent to the dismissal of her claim for periodical payments, the court was prepared to order the husband to make her a small lump sum payment. See Appendix II.

B. *Maintenance*

CASE SUMMARIES

7-331 Cumbers v Cumbers

[1975] 1 All ER 1, CA

Parties in their early twenties – one child – marriage lasting only 18 months.   Following the husband's departure from the matrimonial home the wife obtained a maintenance order in the magistrates' court for herself and the child of the marriage. Following the divorce an order for capital provision was made, against which the husband appealed (see case summary 7–301). The Court of Appeal held that so far as maintenance was concerned, this should be dealt with by a registrar in the Family Division. The Court of Appeal replaced the justices' order with an interim order for the same amount, pending further application to the Family Division.

Note. *The wife had custody of a young child. Her earning capacity was therefore limited.* Compare *M v M* (7–303), in which the wife also had custody of two young children; the Court of Appeal held that the judge had been wrong in finding that the wife's conduct was a relevant factor, but that in view of the fact that the marriage had lasted only 3½ years the wife was entitled to only a nominal order. The authors are of the opinion that the modern law as far as maintenance is concerned is as stated in *Graves v Graves* (7–231) and followed in *Khan v Khan* (7–333): following a short marriage between young parties a nominal order for periodical payments is the appropriate order *unless there are children or the wife is handicapped in some way which prevents her from working.*

7–332 W-S v W-S (sub nom. **Whyte-Smith v Whyte-Smith**)

(1974) Times, 25 October, 119 Sol Jo 46

Parties in their late twenties – no children – marriage lasting less than six months.   As a result of the marriage breakdown and its sequel the wife had been unable to work for more than a year. Order to pay £250 per annum until a stated time, by which the wife should have recovered from the effects of a disastrous marriage, when the financial position could be reviewed. See case summary 7–361.

7–333 Khan v Khan

[1980] 1 All ER 497

Wife in late teens and husband in late twenties – no children – marriage lasting only nine months.   The wife had never worked. She required maintenance while she was seeking to train herself for employment. See case summary 7–234.

7–334 H v H (15 May 1981)

(1981) Times, 16 May

Husband aged 35 and wife 26 – no children – neither party adversely affected by consequences of marriage – desirability of the clean break.   If the wife was prepared to consent to the dismissal of her claim for periodical payments, the court was prepared to order the husband to make her a small lump sum payment. See Appendix II.

C. *Effect of the marriage on the wife*

CASE SUMMARIES

7–361 W-S v W-S (sub nom. **Whyte-Smith v Whyte-Smith**)

(1974) Times, 25 October, 119 Sol Jo 46

Matrimonial Causes Act 1973, section 27 – neglect to maintain – parties in their late twenties – no children – marriage lasting less than six months.   Prior to the marriage the wife worked as a property manager earning £2,500 a year and lived rent-free in a London flat. On marrying the husband their flat became the matrimonial home. The husband was earning £5,000 a year, and during the marriage the parties enjoyed a high standard of living. *Three months after the date of the marriage the wife underwent a major operation. The husband deserted the wife the following month. The wife's convalescence was retarded by the shock and stress caused by the breakdown of the marriage. As a result of the breakdown of the marriage she was unable to work for over a year. During this period she was in receipt of supplementary benefit. Eventually, she got a clerical job paying less than half her previous salary. Furthermore, whereas prior to the marriage she had been living rent-free, she was now having to pay rent.*

Rees J said that no principle could be derived from the decided cases that a nominal order was the proper order in *all* cases where there was a childless marriage of short duration between young people, each of whom was capable of earning a living. In proceedings under section 27 it was the duty of the court to decide whether the wife had established that the husband had wilfully neglected to provide reasonable maintenance and, if so satisfied, then to make such an order as it thought just. In deciding what was just, the court would take into account all the circumstances, including the standard of living during cohabitation, length of cohabitation and the means and earning capacities of the parties. Conduct was relevant if it fell into the *Wachtel v Wachtel* category of being *gross and obvious* (see case summary 8–202). It was not an attractive argument on behalf of a husband whose conduct had destroyed a marriage so soon after the ceremony to say that he was not obliged to provide any maintenance for his wife because she was capable of earning her own living and the marriage had not lasted long enough to warrant an award of maintenance in her favour. But the husband's conduct in this case had not been *gross and obvious* and therefore was not a factor to be taken into consideration. However, as a result of the marriage breakdown and its sequel the wife had been unable to work for more than a year. The husband had promised to pay the wife £10 a week but had failed to keep up the payments. He had the means to make the agreed payments. *He should pay her £520 a year for the period during which she had been unable to work, credit to be given for the money already paid. Thereafter he should pay her £250 per annum until a stated time, by which the wife should have recovered from the effects of a disastrous marriage, when the financial position could be reviewed.*

Notes

1. Although section 27 of the Matrimonial Causes Act 1973 has now been amended by the Domestic Proceedings and Magistrates' Courts Act 1978, the passage from Rees J's judgment summarised above is still pertinent. For the amendments to section 27 made by the 1978 Act see *Gray v Gray* (8–602).
2. Compare *S v S* (7–462), in which Ormrod LJ said: 'I think it is of importance, with these short marriages, particularly where the people concerned are not young, to look very closely to see what the effect of the marriage has been, mainly on the wife, but of course also on the husband.'

7–362 **H v H** (15 May 1981)

(1981) Times, 16 May

Husband aged 35 and wife 26 – no children – neither party adversely affected by consequences of marriage – desirability of the clean break. If the wife was prepared to consent to the dismissal of her claim for periodical payments, the court was prepared to order the husband to make her a small lump sum payment. See Appendix II.

4 Short marriage where parties not young

A. *Relevance on application for capital provision*

CASE SUMMARIES

7–401 **Johnston v Johnston**

(1975) 6 Fam Law 17, CA

Husband a widower aged 68 and wife a widow aged 61 – parties living together for only six months – effect of the marriage on the wife. See case summary 7–461.

7–402 **S v S**
[1977] 1 All ER 56, CA

Husband a widower aged 59 and wife a divorced woman aged 58 – marriage lasting only two years – effect of the marriage on the wife. See case summary 7–462.

7–403 **Warder v Warder**

(1978) 122 Sol Jo 713

Husband a widower aged 61 and wife a divorced woman aged 51 – marriage lasting less than four months – effect of the marriage on the wife.   See case summary 7–464.

B. *Relevance on application for maintenance*

CASE SUMMARIES

7–431 **S v S**

[1977] 1 All ER 56, CA

Husband a widower aged 59 and wife a divorced woman aged 58 – marriage lasting only two years.   The husband was a medical practitioner earning £14,600 per annum. The wife, who had formerly worked full-time, was now working part-time as a teacher earning £450 per annum.

Ormrod LJ said that, in applying the Matrimonial Causes Act 1973, section 25 to a short marriage where the parties were not young, it was important to consider *the effect of the marriage on them, particularly the wife.* But for the marriage, the wife would have been living in her own house, continuing in her full-time employment and earning a larger pension. The court had to do broad justice between the parties. The husband was ordered to settle sufficient capital on the wife in order to enable her to purchase a house.

As regards income, the wife would shortly be 60 and would thereupon become entitled to a full retirement pension of £676 per annum together with a pension arising from her work of £350 per annum, which would give her an income of about £1,000 a year, or a little over that if the amount of the retirement pension increased. The husband was ordered to make periodical payments of £2,000 a year less tax, which would give the wife about £3,000 less tax when she retired and got her pensions, and would not seriously diminish the husband's spending money. This was under one-third, and both parties agreed that this was right.

Note. For further details, see case summary 7–462.

7–432 **Abdureman v Abdureman**

(1978) 122 Sol Jo 663

Husband a bachelor aged 45 and wife a widow of similar age – marriage lasting just under three months – effect of the marriage on the wife.   See case summary 7–463.

C. *Effect of the marriage on the wife*

CASE SUMMARIES

7–461 **Johnston v Johnston**

(1975) 6 Fam Law 17, CA

Husband a widower aged 68 and wife a widow aged 61 – parties living together for only six months.   The parties married in May 1974. In November of that year the husband went into hospital. They had lived apart ever since. In that same month the husband presented a petition for nullity on the ground of his own impotence, and the decree had now been made absolute.

At the time of the marriage the wife had been a protected tenant of a flat, living on social security. On giving up her tenancy to live with the husband she had received £1,000 from her landlord. She was still living in the matrimonial home, but her capital had now dwindled to £677. The husband owned the matrimonial home, a flat worth £11,000, which he held on a 99-year lease which had just begun to run, at a ground rent of £15.75 per annum. He was now living in a private hotel, but he had free capital of £5,589 and a gross income of £2,220 per annum.

The county court judge took the view that, because of the state of his health, the husband would be unable to continue living alone for long. He accordingly settled the flat on the wife for life with reversion to the husband absolutely. The husband appealed.

Counsel for the husband argued that this was a very short marriage, that the judge's order had conferred on the wife a large interest in property which had belonged entirely to the husband and that the husband was going to be physically excluded from the flat which he had made his home for his old age. Sir John Pennycuick said that he had every sympathy for the husband and, had there been any real possibility of the husband being able to live in the flat for any length of time, his lordship would have attempted to find the means of allowing the husband to do so. But looking at the evidence as a whole, the judge's conclusion that the husband would not be able to live in the flat for long because of ill-health was a reasonable conclusion. It was true that the wife had made no contribution, but she had most importantly given up her own flat.

His lordship said that the effect of the judge's order was that the husband would just about be able to manage, but with the inevitable dipping into capital. The wife would be adequately provided for by the use of the flat, the maintenance of £5 a week awarded by the judge and her state pension. The judge has exercised his discretion in a proper manner. However, the husband should be relieved of the obligation to pay the outgoings. Furthermore, the wording of the judge's order should be varied to make it clear that the wife would only have a personal right of residence, and that if she ceased to live in the flat her interest would revert to the husband. The husband's appeal was accordingly allowed in part.

7–462 S v S

[1977] 1 All ER 56, CA

Husband a widower aged 59 and wife a divorced woman aged 58 – marriage lasting only two years. The wife obtained a divorce on the ground of two years' separation by consent. The husband, a medical practitioner earning £14,600 per annum, owned free capital of £30,000. He also owned the matrimonial home, valued at £28,000. The wife, who had formerly worked full-time, was now working as a part-time teacher earning £450 per annum. She had sold her house after marrying the husband and had given the bulk of the £4,000 profit realised on the sale to her son, who had recently married and was setting up a home. She now had no capital. The registrar ordered a payment to the wife of £7,000 to provide her with a house. Her appeal was dismissed in the county court and she appealed to the Court of Appeal.

Ormrod LJ said that in applying the Matrimonial Causes Act 1973, section 25 to a short marriage where the parties were not young it was important to consider the effect of the marriage on them, particularly the wife. But for the marriage, the wife would have been living in her own house, continuing in her full-time employment and earning a larger pension. The court had to do broad justice between the parties. £7,000 could not buy a suitable house. The order would be £11,000 to be settled on the wife for her life or until remarriage to purchase a house, £2,000 with which to furnish it, plus a periodical payments order. Sir John Pennycuick and Stamp LJ agreed.

Ormrod LJ said at page 57: 'The case is unusual in one sense; it is a case in which the court is dealing with a second marriage between two persons of mature years, both of whom had previously been married and whose marriage lasted in fact a very short time, a total of about two years altogether or perhaps a little less. The case, therefore, is quite different from what one might call the average run of cases, the sort of cases that were dealt with by this court in *Wachtel v Wachtel* (7–101), and it requires a different approach.'

His lordship continued (at page 59): 'When the matter came before the learned registrar, the argument seems to have proceeded very largely on the footing of what was the right fraction to choose in this case. I think, with respect to the learned registrar and to the judge, that a lot of confusion has crept into this case by concentrating over-much on trying to find the right fraction, it being common ground, as the wife's counsel from the outset made it clear, that she was not asking for a one-third division, mainly on the ground that the marriage had lasted so short a time.'

And at page 60: '. . . In my view it is much easier, and better in these cases, to follow the Matrimonial Causes Act 1973, section 25 and to perform the exercise there required, namely, to ascertain the means of the parties and their resources and the charges and obligations that they have to meet; and also to take account of the needs of the parties and then to have regard to such other matters as are set out there, such as contribution to the family welfare: obviously, in a case like this, that contribution was not very great and counsel for the wife in this court has made no attempt to place any great reliance, or indeed any reliance, on that aspect of it. The length of the marriage has to be taken into account also; and again counsel for the wife has readily conceded that this was quite a short marriage.

'So it seems to me that the primary consideration is to look at the needs of the wife, first of all; and, having made some assessment of her needs, then to check the resulting figure that emerges against the resources of the husband, and at that stage see what the ratio of the one to the other is and to consider – assuming an order for £x, the lump sum, and £y for the periodical payments order – how the two parties will stand in relation one to the other, and relate that to all the circumstances of the case, including the shortness of the marriage . . .

'*I think it is of importance, with these short marriages, particularly where the people concerned are not young, to look very closely to see what the effect of the marriage has been, mainly on the wife, but of course also on the husband. There is no doubt that the fact of this marriage has been unfortunate as far as this wife was concerned. Had she not married, she would presumably still have been in her own house; she would probably still have been doing her full-time job; she would undoubtedly have earned a larger pension than she will now get, although she would not of course have enjoyed the very much higher standard of living that her husband could offer her in his house. But the result is that she has lost, as a result of the marriage, her house in circumstances [sic] which I think quite reasonable; she must be worse off pension-wise than she would have been. While there is no question of putting her back into the position in which she was before the marriage, or performing any hypothetical task of that kind, these are all factors which are to be borne in mind in making an order which is just in all the circumstances of the case, which is the primary requirement of the 1973 Act. As a result of the breakdown of the marriage she has lost substantial prospects of, at any rate, a comfortable old age which she would have had had the marriage subsisted. That is not a question of whose fault it is; it is a fact that she has lost that.*'

Note. Regarding the income position, see case summary 7–431.

7–463 Abdureman v Abdureman

(1978) 122 Sol Jo 663

Husband a bachelor aged 45 and wife a widow of similar age – marriage lasting just under three months – husband deserted wife. The parties married on 3 June 1977.

The husband earned £85 per week gross as a dock gatekeeper. After the marriage they went to live with the wife's father, who died five days later. The wife was then granted a rent-free life occupancy of the property. On 27 August 1977 the husband left the wife. On the wife's complaint of desertion, the justices found her complaint proved and ordered the husband to pay maintenance of £20 per week. The husband appealed, contending that as the marriage had only lasted some 12 weeks the justices should have made a nominal order.

Balcombe J said that on marriage the wife had given up her employment to look after the husband, whose hours were irregular. She had lost pension rights and her right to a widow's pension of £7.20 per week. She had been unable to find another job, and in monetary terms she had had a disastrous three months. The justices were right to consider the effect of the marriage on the wife. Appeal dismissed.

Note. Compare *W-S v W-S* (7–361), which was a case under the Matrimonial Causes Act 1973, section 27 – neglect to maintain – where Rees J said that it was not an attractive argument on behalf of a husband, who had destroyed a marriage so soon after the ceremony, to say he was not obliged to provide any maintenance for his wife.

7–464 Warder v Warder

(1978) 122 Sol Jo 713

Husband a widower aged 61 and wife a divorced woman aged 51 – marriage lasting less than four months. The wife had given up the tenancy of a council house on marrying the husband, and was now living on social security in a furnished flat. The husband was comparatively well off. *In view of the fact that the wife had lost the tenancy of her council house she was awarded a lump sum of £1,000 in full and final settlement.*

D. *Effect of the marriage on the husband*

CASE SUMMARIES

7–491 Johnston v Johnston

(1975) 6 Fam Law 17, CA

Husband a widower aged 68 and wife a widow aged 61 – parties living together for only six months. Counsel for the husband argued that this was a very short marriage, that the judge's order had conferred on the wife a large interest in property which had belonged entirely to the husband, and that the husband was going to be physically excluded from the flat which he had made his home for his old age. Sir John Pennycuick said that he had every sympathy for the husband and, had there been any real possibility of the husband being able to live in the flat for any length of time, his lordship would have attempted to find the means of allowing the husband to do so. But looking at the evidence as a whole, the judge's conclusion that the husband would not be able to live in the flat for long because of ill-health was a reasonable conclusion. See case summary 7–461.

7–492 S v S

[1977] 1 All ER 56, CA

Ormrod LJ said (at page 60): 'I think it is of importance, with these short marriages, particularly where the people concerned are not young, to look very closely to see what the effect of the marriage has been, mainly on the wife, but of course also on the husband.'

5 'Short marriage' defined

CASE SUMMARIES

7–501 Browne v Pritchard

[1975] 3 All ER 721, CA

Three-year marriage. The matrimonial home had been purchased by the husband and conveyed into the joint names of the parties. The Court of Appeal held that the house could not be sold for so long as it was required as a home for the two children living with the husband. Ormrod LJ then continued (at page 725): 'The next question is, *what sort of share ought the wife to have in this house,* the only asset of the couple? *If it had not been in joint names, I doubt very much whether any court, after a three years' marriage, would have given her as much as a one-third interest.*'

In view of the fact that the wife had the benefit of council accommodation the wife's half share was reduced to one-third. See case summary 7–103A.

7–502 Gengler v Gengler

[1976] 2 All ER 81

Three-year marriage. Sir George Baker P said (at page 82): 'I do not think, for myself, that this can properly be classed as a short marriage. Of course, it was not a very long marriage. I am not seeking to lay down what is short, what is not very short, what is not very long, and what is long; that would be trying to define the length of a piece of string. But it is, I think, to be noted that at the time, or just about the time of the parting, the three years had elapsed within which the wife could not have brought a divorce petition unless on the ground of exceptional depravity or exceptional hardship.' See case summary 19–007A.

7–503 M v M

(1976) 6 Fam Law 243, CA

$3\frac{1}{2}$- *year marriage.* Orr LJ said that bearing in mind that the marriage had lasted only $3\frac{1}{2}$ years and (inter alia) the fact that the husband required the matrimonial home for the purposes of his business and was unable to borrow a substantial sum on the security of the house, the judge had been fully justified in awarding the wife a lump sum of only £1,500 rather than the £5,000 (just under one-third of the present value of the house) suggested by her counsel. See case summary 7–303.

7–504 Campbell v Campbell

[1977] 1 All ER 1

Two-year marriage. Sir George Baker P said that, applying the one-third ratio to the joint income of the parties, the wife should receive £13.44 a week, but scaling that figure down, as the marriage had lasted only two years, the proper figure would be £12 a week.

Notes
1. £5 a week was also payable in respect of the child of the family.
2. Sir George Baker P said that periods of pre-marital co-habitation were not to be taken into account when determining the duration of a marriage (see case summary 8–401).

7–505 S v S

[1977] 1 All ER 56, CA

Two-year marriage between mature parties. The Court of Appeal held that when considering a short marriage, particularly where the parties were not young, the primary consideration was the needs of the parties. As a result of the marriage and its breakdown the wife had lost her home and was worse off in respect of her pension rights. The court ordered a sum of £11,000 to be settled on the wife for her life or until remarriage in order to purchase a house, plus a lump sum of £2,000 with which to furnish it. She was also awarded a periodical payments order of £2,000 a year less tax. This was less than one-third of the joint income of the parties; in view of the shortness of the marriage both parties agreed that this was right.

Note. For further details, see case summary 7–462.

7–506 H v H (15 May 1981)

(1981) Times, 16 May

Premarital cohabitation lasting intermittently over period of six years followed by seven week marriage – intermittent cohabitation of no relevance – desirability of the clean break. See Appendix II.

6 Relevance of cohabitation prior to marriage

CASE SUMMARIES

7–601 Campbell v Campbell

[1977] 1 All ER 1

'A complete cheapening of the marriage relationship'.   See case summary 8–401.

7–602 Kokosinski v Kokosinski

[1980] 1 All ER 1106

Wife's contribution to running of family business during pre-marital cohabitation when husband unable to marry.   See case summary 8–402. For further details and commentary, see case summary 8–310.

7–603 H v H (15 May 1981)

(1981) Times 16 May

Premarital cohabitation lasting intermittently over period of six years followed by seven week marriage – intermittent cohabitation of no relevance – desirability of the clean break. See Appendix II.

7–604 Foley v Foley

[1981] 2 All ER 857, CA

Premarital cohabitation taken into account under 'all the circumstances of the case' but not counted as part of duration of marriage under section 25 (1) (d).   See Appendix II.

7 Relevance of lapse of time since separation

CASE SUMMARIES

7–701 Mathias v Mathias

[1972] 3 All ER 1, CA

Divorce on ground of five years' separation – grave financial hardship – marriage lasting less than three years – separation of almost eight years – ridiculous to keep alive shell of a marriage.   See case summary 3–302.

7–702 Krystman v Krystman

[1973] 3 All ER 247, CA

Parties living together for only two weeks – separation of 26 years – financial provision – 'all the circumstances of the case'.   The parties were married in Italy in December 1946 when the wife was 37 and the husband 26. At that time the husband, who was in the Polish army stationed in Italy, was awaiting repatriation to the United Kingdom. The wife was Italian. They had an affair, and when the wife told the husband that she was pregnant he married her out of a sense of duty. Two weeks later he was repatriated to England and the parties did not live together again. The basis of the marriage, the forthcoming child, did not materialise. The wife remained in Italy. From about 1948 the husband commenced to live in adultery with a Polish woman. There was some correspondence between the husband and wife in the early years but they lost contact. The husband never supported the wife financially and she never applied for support. In 1972 the husband presented a petition for divorce on the grounds of five years' separation. The wife applied to the court for the decree not to be made absolute until her financial position had been considered. The decree was made absolute on the husband undertaking to make such provision as the court should deem right. The Court of Appeal held that in all the circumstances of the case the husband should not be required to make any financial provision for the wife. Even a nominal order of 10p per year would not be appropriate. Even if the husband came into unexpected wealth it would not be just that the wife should share in it.

7–703 Lombardi v Lombardi

[1973] 3 All ER 625, CA

17-year separation – financial provision – 'all the circumstances of the case'.   Cairns LJ said (at page 629): 'Counsel says that the learned judge was wrong in taking into account the long lapse of time since the marriage broke up. I do not think it can be said as a matter of law that he was wrong to do so. This is one of "the circumstances of the case".' See case summary 13–003.

7–704 Chaterjee v Chaterjee

[1976] 1 All ER 719, CA

Relevance of delay in applying for financial relief.   The parties were married in 1952 and divorced in 1955. They lived together again as man and wife from 1961 to 1966. From 1966 to 1974 they lived separately under the same roof. During much of that time they ran the business of an old people's home in the house in which they lived. In 1974 the wife obtained leave from the registrar to apply for a lump sum order and/or a transfer of property order. The husband's appeal against leave being granted was dismissed by a High Court judge. His appeal to the Court of Appeal was also dismissed.

Ormrod J (as he then was) said (at page 725): '. . . *Delay, if it really is delay in the sense of prejudicing the other party, may have an important influence on the justice of the case. So may conduct which can be described as "lulling" the other party into the belief that all claims have already been dealt with. Similarly, it may be unjust to interfere with property rights after a lapse of time during which the other party has ordered his or her affairs in a reasonable and proper manner in the belief that the financial consequences of the divorce have been settled* . . .'

However, his lordship continued: 'Turning briefly to the facts of this case . . . it is enough to say that, extraordinary as it may seem, these parties lived together before the divorce for three years, and after it, for 12 or 13 years, for much of that time running together the business of an old people's home in the house at Baldslow Road, Hastings. Both now have very little to live on; the wife who is in her fifties lives on social security in a house which is said to belong to her mother and sister; the husband, who is 70 and in poor health, has the state retirement pension and a small pension from his former employers, but he owns two freehold properties. They have an illegitimate daughter aged 12, who lives with the wife. On the evidence before us the wife would seem to have a reasonably good claim on the husband's bounty. In my judgment, she has reasonable prospects of obtaining a property adjustment order, giving her an interest in Baldslow Road, subject, perhaps, to further investigation of her interest, if any, in the house in which she lives, or a lump sum, if the husband prefers to sell the property in the near future. As to conduct, they might as well have been a married couple up to 1974; all that was lacking was an appointment at the registry office. There is no delay in any relevant sense, nor can it be said that their financial affairs after the divorce were in any meaningful sense settled or concluded. In these circumstances I have no hesitation in holding that this is a proper case for granting leave to apply for a lump sum or a property adjustment order. I would dismiss the appeal.'

7–704A Potts v Potts

(1976) 6 Fam Law 217, CA

Circumstances altering during passage of time – house now required as a home for husband's second family.   See case summary 4–104A.

7–705 Foster v Foster

(1977) 7 Fam Law 112, CA

28-year separation – half a lifetime – not right to deal with the matter on the basis of the husband's current financial position.   See case summary 6–302A.

7–706 McGrady v McGrady

(1977) 8 Fam Law 15

Marriage lasting only 2½ years – separation of over 30 years – original order eroded by inflation – delay in application to vary.   The parties were married in July 1942 when the wife was 22 and the husband (who was then serving in the merchant navy) was 19. The parties separated at the end of December 1944. In 1945 the wife obtained a magistrates' order for the sum of £2 per week for herself plus an additional sum for the child of the marriage. The order was later varied to £1.50 per week. Following the separation the wife went out to work, but in 1970 she had to give up her employment because of her health. In 1977 she applied to the justices for an order for variation. Her application was refused and she appealed to the Divisional Court.

Arnold J (as he then was) said that this was a case of a relatively short marriage and a long separation. The order in force was now so eroded by inflation as to have no meaning at all. His lordship referred to *Krystman v Krystman* (7–702) and *Lombardi v Lombardi* (7–703). In both cases long delay had been relevant. But delay had been only one factor among other factors for consideration, and each case had turned on its own facts. His lordship said that the shortness of the marriage and the length of the separation were relevant, but that the matter was one of degree rather than principle, and there were other factors to be considered as well. One was the relative value of the original order in terms of today's purchasing power. Another was the difference between the wife's present means and her earnings before she was forced to give up work. To apply the one-third ratio would suggest a starting point of £24 per week. His lordship considered that the appropriate amount in view of all the circumstances of the case would be £12 per week.

7–707 Chambers v Chambers

(1979) 10 Fam Law 22

Marriage lasting 21 years – separation of over 20 years – financial provision – 'all the circumstances of the case'.   For the wife it was said that the marriage had lasted 21 years and she had brought up the three children of the family. Wood J said that the policy now was that on the breakdown of a marriage there should be, if possible, a clean break financially. After a certain lapse of time a party should be entitled to take the view that there would be no revival or institution of financial claims against them. Such considerations fell within 'all the circumstances of the case' under section 25 (1) of the Matrimonial Causes Act 1973. See case summary 13–017.

The wife was securely housed in a rented flat. His lordship stated that he did not believe that she was in any danger of losing her tenancy. The husband was a landscape gardener trading from his home address. He was unable to carry out any but essential repairs. His lordship rejected any suggestion of a sale of the husband's property, and considered that to raise a loan on the security of the property was not reasonable in the circumstances.

Note. Although the report does not specifically say so, it would appear that it would not have been feasible for the husband to raise capital on the security of the property.

7–708 Pearce v Pearce

(1980) 1 FLR 261, CA

Capital provision after delay of 10 years – bankruptcy of husband – subsequent inheritance – difficulty of wife in bringing up children unaided – leave granted to apply out of time for lump sum payment.   See case summary 10–106.

7–709 Brykiert v Jones

(1981) Times, 16 January, CA

Marriage lasting less than four years – separation of 30 years – Law of Property Act 1925, section 30 – declaration of trust contained in conveyance – wife entitled to half share.   See case summary 24–203.

CHAPTER 8
Relevance of conduct

Section 25 (1) of the Matrimonial Causes Act 1973 states that the court is to exercise its powers under sections 23 and 24 of the Act so as to place the parties (so far as is practicable and, having regard to their conduct, just to do so) in the financial position in which they would have been if the marriage had not broken down and each had properly discharged his or her financial obligations and responsibilities towards the other. There has been much discussion as to when conduct is sufficiently grave to warrant its being taken into consideration. In earlier cases, perhaps unfortunately, judges have used the rather obscure terms 'gross and obvious' to describe such misconduct as should be taken into consideration. In *West v West* (8–212), Sir John Pennycuick said that the word 'gross' did not carry any moral judgment; it meant no more than 'of the greatest importance', and Ormrod LJ agreed that it was quite wrong to read the word 'gross' in the context of *Wachtel v Wachtel* (8–301) as meaning gross in any moral sense. In *Backhouse v Backhouse* (8–308), after quoting from Lord Denning MR's judgment in *Wachtel v Wachtel* where he had used the words 'obvious and gross', Balcombe J went on to say that he did not find the words of Sir John Pennycuick in *West v West* of much assistance, and that he preferred to rely on the phrase in *Wachtel v Wachtel* where Lord Denning MR had used the words 'repugnant to anyone's sense of justice'. Perhaps it would be better if the words 'gross and obvious' were to be forgotten and Balcombe J's suggestion adopted.

This still leaves the essential problem, however, of what would be repugnant to anyone's sense of justice, and there is an unfortunate degree of uncertainty in this important area of matrimonial law. Not surprisingly, issues of conduct are frequently well to the fore in the minds of lay clients. Consequently, the task of advising them that the proceedings in which they are involved are to be contested along exclusively financial (rather than retributive or censorious) lines is not an easy one. This is the more so when advising in borderline cases in which such advice could be very wrong and conduct could play a significant part in any contest.

Adultery can present a particular problem in this area of matrimonial law. Now that the only ground for divorce is the irretrievable breakdown of the marriage, there is an increasing tendency to see adultery as a symptom of the breakdown of the marriage rather than as the cause of its breakdown, but this is not a view which always finds favour with lay clients or with judges. In *W v W* (8–305) it was held that an adulterous association by the wife after the dissolution of the marriage was not to be taken into account under section 25. It has sometimes been held otherwise in cases in which the court has blamed the breakdown of the marriage on the adulterous conduct of the party seeking financial relief.

It is respectfully submitted that the decision in *Cuzner v Underdown* (8–204) is outside the mainstream of the current judicial approach to issues of conduct. The case is unusual in that (as in *Backhouse v Backhouse*) the court blamed the breakdown of the marriage entirely on the adulterous conduct of the wife; no allegations were made by the wife against the husband. (Compare *Bateman v Bateman* (8–309) in which, notwithstanding the extreme conduct of the wife who had inflicted a serious chest wound on the husband with a knife, the judge upheld certain of the wife's cross-allegations and found a good deal to criticise in the husband's behaviour and, viewing the conduct of the parties as a whole, took the husband's conduct into account also.) In *Cuzner v Underdown* the wife had not obtained her one-half share of the matrimonial home by fraud or deception; but it was held that allowing the husband to purchase the house in their joint names while she was carrying on an adulterous affair amounted to 'gross' conduct that should be taken into consideration by the court, and the court extinguished her one-half interest. Although the wife had made no direct financial contribution to the purchase of the house she had clearly made a substantial indirect contribution, having been an appreciable wage-earner. She had also brought up the children of the family. The decision that she was entitled to nothing is difficult to reconcile with the whole philosophy of the current legislation, certainly as it was expressed in *Wachtel v Wachtel*.

In *Backhouse v Backhouse* Balcombe J was clearly at pains to distinguish *Cuzner v Underdown* by distinguishing the facts on what seems to be the narrowest of bases namely, that in the instant case the wife's financial contribution towards the purchase of the house had been direct rather than indirect. The authors are of the opinion that the position has to some extent been restored to what it was before *Cuzner v Underdown* (accepting, of course, that the decisions of the courts can only be treated as 'guidelines' and not as precedents to be strictly followed).

The reader is referred to the rather more recent decision of the Court of Appeal in *Blezard v Blezard* (8–214) as an example of the current judicial approach to adultery. It would appear that Orr LJ's view was that the conduct of the husband in deserting the wife for a younger woman was not a matter to take into consideration on the issues of financial relief. Lawton LJ, in his dissenting judgment, strongly disagreed, although he agreed with the order of the court.

One of the matters stressed by Lawton LJ in *Blezard v Blezard* (and by Purchas J in *Bateman v Bateman*) was the importance of comparing and contrasting the conduct of both parties. It is for this reason that we have divided this chapter into sections, including a section on what has been held to constitute grave misconduct (Chapter 8/2) and a further section (Chapter 8/3) which contains summaries of those cases in which the conduct of the parties has been compared and 'weighed in the balance', so to speak, the good against the bad. Chapter 8/1 acts as a directory of references and cross-references for handy use. The reader's attention is particularly drawn to Chapter 8/1B (the relevance of good conduct) and to Chapter 8/1C (the relevance of agreements between the parties, which the courts are now increasingly taking into account under the heading of 'conduct').

Chapter 8/1A contains a brief summary of all the reported cases in which misconduct has been taken into account under the modern law. The reader will observe that they are relatively few, and is referred to the judgment of Bagnall J in *Harnett v Harnett* (8–303), in which his lordship said that he thought there would be very few cases in which the test of 'gross and obvious misconduct' would be satisfied.

The question therefore arises: how should a respondent's advisers deal with a petition containing allegations of misconduct which the client wishes to contest or counter with cross-allegations?

Whenever an answer is filed, the matter is automatically transferred into the High Court. However, now that the definition of an 'undefended cause' contained in Rule 2 (2) of the Matrimonial Causes Rules 1977 has been amended by the Matrimonial Causes (Amendment) Rules 1978, it is common for directions to be given that the matter be re-transferred back into the county court where the grant of the decree is not opposed. Indeed, the authors' experience is that registrars endeavour to avoid contested suits for divorce and to relegate all contested issues to the hearing of the claims for ancillary relief if the parties' advisers will consent and provided that the issues pleaded necessary to prove irretrievable breakdown of marriage (the 'fact' of adultery, the 'fact' of desertion, etc.) are not opposed. (If, for example, an allegation of adultery, whether in a petition or cross-petition, is denied, then the matter will have to go forward for trial as a contested suit unless either the allegation is withdrawn or the pleading denying it withdrawn. If, on the other hand, an allegation of adultery in a petition is merely met with a counter-allegation of adultery in a cross-petition which the petitioner does not deny, then the matter can be re-transferred back to the county court as an undefended cause, where cross decrees will be granted.)

This, then, leads to a further question: if issues of conduct can be dealt with in chambers, is it necessary or, indeed, desirable to file an answer? The advantage of filing an answer is that the offending allegations of misconduct can be openly averred from the outset, but this may lead the registrar to exercise his discretion under Rule 32 (1) (which allows the transfer of undefended causes to the High Court if the registrar thinks it desirable). Issues of conduct may be investigated in ancillary proceedings whether or not they are pleaded in the petition and whether or not any answer is filed – see *Spill v Spill* (8–906). (See also *Rogers v Rogers* (8–908), however, in which the respondent was granted leave to file a cross-petition out of time.)

The practitioner's attention is drawn to the recent practice direction dated 4th June 1981 (see Appendix II) which states that where an issue of conduct is raised on the affidavits relating to financial relief, an appointment for directions should be taken out at which the registrar will enquire whether the issue is being pursued and, if so, will order particulars to be given of the precise allegations relied on. Again, the registrar has a discretion (under Rule 80) whether to hear the issue himself or whether to transfer the proceedings for ancillary relief to the High Court for trial before a High Court judge. (See *Greyson v Greyson* (8–911), in which it was held that it is for the registrar to decide whether to hear the issue himself or whether it would be better for it to be tried by a High Court judge.) Registrars' lists are crowded, and it may well be that the registrar will delete the case from his list on this ground alone.

1   Summary of cases in which conduct was taken into account

A. *Misconduct*

CASE SUMMARIES

8–101 Cuzner v Underdown

[1974] 2 All ER 351, CA

Wife had already committed adultery with co-respondent and was contemplating leaving husband for co-respondent at a time when husband and wife had decided to move house. Husband arranged for purchase of new house in joint names in order to benefit wife on his death. Husband, informed of adultery prior to completion of purchase, persuaded wife not to leave. Wife deserted husband six weeks later. Husband obtained divorce on ground of wife's adultery. Wife subsequently married co-respondent. Wife now claimed half share in new house under MWPA 1882 and applied for order for sale in order to purchase house for herself, co-respondent and children of their family. Wife's need of lump sum to solve impending housing crisis of co-respondent. Probability that any sale and payment of sufficient lump sum to wife would precipitate housing crisis for husband. Necessity of retaining home for husband's new family. Wife's share extinguished. Distinguished in *Backhouse v Backhouse* (8–109); and compare *McDonnell v McDonnell* (23–905). See case summary 8–204.

8–102 Armstrong v Armstrong

(1974) 118 Sol Jo 579, CA

Wife fired shotgun at husband; awarded nominal maintenance and one-quarter of capital assets. See case summary 8–205.

8–103 Dixon v Dixon

(1974) 5 Fam Law 58, CA

Husband living with daughter-in-law as man and wife. Husband a farmer; essential not to cripple his earning capacity; lump sum awarded to wife less than one-third of matrimonial assets. See case summary 8–206.

8–104 Jones v Jones (sub nom. Jones (MA) v Jones (W))

[1975] 2 All ER 12, CA

Husband attacked wife with knife, severing tendons of right hand. Wife unable to continue working. Husband's interest in matrimonial home extinguished. See case summary 13–006.

8–105 Weisz v Weisz

(1975) Times, 16 December, CA

Husband concealed existence of bank account and extent of his income. Held: husband clearly a dishonest man, and unless compelled to do so would not make any contribution for wife and daughter. Husband's share in matrimonial home extinguished and additional lump sum payment ordered. See case summary 8–209.

8–106 Bryant v Bryant

(1976) Times, 3 February, CA

Husband a persistent maintenance defaulter in prison. Husband's share in matrimonial home extinguished. See case summary 8–211.

8–107 Martin v Martin

[1976] 3 All ER 625, CA

Husband's dissipation of assets taken into consideration. Wife's award increased. See case summary 8–307.

8–108 West v West

[1977] 2 All ER 705, CA

Wife refused to set up home with husband; failure to set up a married life. Reduced award of periodical payments. See case summary 13–013.

8–109 Backhouse v Backhouse

[1978] 1 All ER 1158

Wife deserted husband and children (aged 17 and 8) and went to live with co-respondent. Wife's behaviour a substantial cause of breakdown of marriage and a relevant factor when considering distribution of matrimonial assets, but not the only factor to be considered: substantial contribution made by wife to purchase of matrimonial home: *Cuzner v Underdown* (8–101) distinguished on this ground. Husband ordered to pay lump sum which, having regard to his income, he could raise by mortgage without crippling him financially. See case summary 8–308.

8–110 Bateman v Bateman

[1979] 2 WLR 377

Wife wounded husband with knife on two occasions; in addition, wife's damaging attitude towards husband and his career very substantially contributed to eventual breakdown of marriage. Husband's behaviour also criticised. Conduct of the parties viewed as a whole. Valuable contribution to family in kind by wife over long period. Necessity of home for children and means to upkeep home; children should not be prejudiced by their mother's conduct. See case summary 8–309.

8–111 Blezard v Blezard

(1978) 9 Fam Law 249, CA

Husband deserted wife and children (aged 13 and 11) for younger woman. Lawton LJ criticised modern approach to conduct and considered that the interests of first wife should (if possible) take precedence over those of husband and second wife; sufficient matrimonial assets available to enable first wife to be supported to a standard approaching previous standard of living while leaving husband and second wife with adequate standard of living. Orr LJ considered that no question of conduct arose. Husband awarded charge on former matrimonial home amounting to two-fifths of net proceeds of sale, not to be enforced until after younger child completed her education or unless the wife remarried or co-habited with another man. See case summary 8–214.

Note. Lawton LJ considered conduct a relevant factor, but not the only factor to be considered: compare *Backhouse v Backhouse* (8–109).

8–112 J (HD) v J (AM) (sub nom. **Johnson v Johnson**)

[1980] 1 All ER 156

Persistent harassment of husband and second wife by first wife. First wife warned that if behaviour continued court would reduce or extinguish periodical payments. See case summary 8–504.

8–113 Page v Page

(1981) Times, 30 January, CA

Husband transferred £124,000 to his secretary, who removed it out of the jurisdiction. Husband's conduct in regard to such transfer a highly relevant consideration. Husband's assets calculated as if transfer had not been made. See Appendix II.

B. *Good conduct*

CASE SUMMARIES

8–131 Wachtel v Wachtel

[1973] 1 All ER 829, CA

Contribution to the family in kind. Parties 'roughly equally responsible' for breakdown of marriage; wife's misconduct ignored; one-third ratio applied. Lord Denning MR (at page 838): '. . . we may take it that Parliament recognised that the wife who looks after the home and family contributes as much to the family assets as the wife who goes out to work. The one contributes in kind. The other in money or money's worth.' And at page 842: 'The wife undoubtedly contributed to the home for some 18 years and, as far as the evidence goes, was in every respect an excellent mother. This is clearly a case in which the wife has made a substantial contribution to the home [in kind], as of course the husband has out of his earnings.' See case summary 7–101.

8–132 Martin v Martin

[1976] 3 All ER 625, CA

Contribution to the running of the family business. Following separation wife maintained value of farm comprising principal matrimonial asset whereas husband dissipated £33,000 in business ventures which failed; husband's interest in farm transferred to wife plus lump sum award to wife in addition. See case summary 8–307.

8–133 Backhouse v Backhouse

[1978] 1 All ER 1158

Financial contribution to the purchase of the matrimonial home. Wife's misconduct caused breakdown of marriage; repugnant to justice to ignore wife's very substantial contribution towards purchase of house. See case summary 8–308.

8–134 Bateman v Bateman

[1979] 2 WLR 377

Contribution to the family in kind. Wife wounded husband with knife on two occasions and also very substantially contributed to breakdown of marriage by her damaging attitude towards husband and his career; husband's conduct also criticised; conduct of parties viewed as a whole; wife's valuable contribution to family in kind over the years taken into account. See case summary 8–309.

8–135 Kokosinski v Kokosinski

[1980] 1 All ER 1106

Contribution to the running of the family business and to the family in kind prior to the marriage ceremony. Husband unable to marry wife until his first wife divorced him. See case summary 8–310. Compare *Campbell v Campbell* (8–401).

8–136 S v S

(1980) Times, 10 May

Contribution to the building up of the family business. Wife's hard physical work during early years of marriage and acceptance of very simple lifestyle contributed in no small way to husband's ability to utilize profits of farm and buy more land; contributions made by each party to the welfare of the family. See case summary 16–104.

8–137 Preston v Preston

(1981) Times, 25 June, CA

Contribution to the building up of the family business. Ormrod LJ said that the following were factors to be taken into account under section 25 (1) (f) of the Matrimonial Causes Act 1973 as contributions to the welfare of the family: active participation in the family business either by working or by providing finance, the acceptance of a frugal standard of living so as to enable profits to be ploughed back, and where the wife's earnings have contributed to the husband's success. See case summary 13–018.

C. *Agreements between the parties*

CASE SUMMARIES

8–161 Brockwell v Brockwell

(1975) 6 Fam Law 46, CA

Agreement to transfer interest in matrimonial home to spouse in return for granting of divorce. Ormrod LJ said that the agreement was a very important piece of conduct to be taken into account under section 25 of the Matrimonial Causes Act 1973. See case summary 9–013.

8–162 Backhouse v Backhouse

[1978] 1 All ER 1158

Time of stress – inequality of bargaining power – lack of independent legal advice. Transfer of interest in matrimonial home by wife to husband; application for financial provision dealt with as if transfer had not been made. See case summary 9–019.

8–163 Dean v Dean

[1978] 3 All ER 758

Agreement subject to approval of court taken into account under heading of conduct.   The agreement having been freely entered into with the benefit of legal advice, the wife was held to her bargain. See case summary 9–020.

8–164 Edgar v Edgar

[1980] 3 All ER 887, CA

Agreement not to claim lump sum taken into account under heading of conduct.   The agreement having been freely entered into with the benefit of legal advice, the wife was held to her bargain. See case summary 9–026.

2   Misconduct: whether sufficiently grave to take into account: the absolute test

Sections 23 and 24 of the Matrimonial Causes Act 1973 set out the powers of the court to re-distribute the family's assets. Section 25 of the Act lays down the manner in which those powers are to be exercised by the court. Section 25 (1) states that the court is 'so to exercise those powers as to place the parties, so far as it is practicable and, *having regard to their conduct, just to do so,* in the financial position in which they would have been if the marriage had not broken down and each had properly discharged his or her financial obligations and responsibilities towards the other'.

This section of Chapter 8 contains summaries of those cases in which there was discussion as to what conduct may or may not constitute grave misconduct. Compare Chapter 8/3, which contains summaries of those cases in which the conduct of the parties was compared and contrasted, that of the one against that of the other, the bad against the bad, the bad against the good.

CASE SUMMARIES

8–201 White v White

(1972) Times, 10 March, 116 Sol Jo 219, CA

The former matrimonial home had been purchased in the joint names of the husband and wife. The husband had paid the deposit and all the mortgage instalments. The wife left the husband and the child of the family. She later married the co-respondent, whose house provided better accommodation than the former matrimonial home.

In a defended suit, Dunn J granted the husband a decree on the ground of the wife's adultery, and ordered the co-respondent to pay £500 damages to the husband, execution being stayed pending determination of the property issues.

The husband applied for a property adjustment order under section 4 of the Matrimonial Proceedings and Property Act 1970 (see now section 24 of the Matrimonial Causes Act 1973 – see Appendix I) and the wife applied under section 17 of the Married Women's Property Act 1882 for an order for sale of the matrimonial home. Dunn J ordered that the wife's interest in the house be extinguished, but continued the stay of execution in respect of the award of damages.

The wife and the co-respondent appealed to the Court of Appeal. Lord Denning MR said that the courts now had very wide powers to deal with property after divorce, and care had to be taken not to use them as a means of punishing one or other party for any misconduct in the past, but to see what was fair and just to be done in the circumstances which had developed. The marriage had broken down because the wife had left the matrimonial home, and it would be altogether wrong for any order to be made which would have the effect of making the husband and the child of the family leave in order that it could be sold. The husband must be allowed to remain in the house because that was only just and equitable.

However, his lordship said that it was agreed that the wife had a joint interest in the property, and if the husband were to be allowed to remain there he ought to pay her something. The final order made by the judge had been that the wife's interest in the property would be extinguished but that execution of the award of £500 damages to the husband would be stayed indefinitely. On the making of that order the judge might have had in mind that the amount which ought fairly to be payable to the wife should have been about £500. His lordship thought that this might well be a case in which the husband should pay the wife a sum of £500 in respect of her share in the property. Although the judge's order had been a convenient order to make in the circumstances, his lordship was not sure how far it was legitimate to stay execution of the order for the payment of damages. Accordingly, although the wife's appeal against the order extinguishing her interest in the property would be dismissed, the co-respondent's appeal against the award of damages would be allowed.

Edmund Davies LJ, concurring, said that by relieving the co-respondent from paying the damages the court was helping the wife.

Notes
1. In *Cuzner v Underdown* (8–204) Davies LJ said: 'There are... certain distinctions between *White v White* and the present case. But, apart from two matters, namely, that the co-respondent's house in that case provided better accommodation and that the only child of the marriage was with the husband, that case is extraordinarily close to the present one [*Cuzner v Underdown*]... Following the observations that Lord Denning MR made in that case I think it would be quite wrong that the husband should be turned out of the house which he himself has provided...' The authors are of the opinion that in view of the fact that the husband in *White v White* required the house as a home for himself and the child of the family whereas the wife was housed in secure accommodation, indeed, better accommodation than the former matrimonial home in which the husband was residing, the Court of Appeal's decision in *White v White* cannot be thought of as anything but fair-minded. Section 25 (1) of the Matrimonial Causes Act 1973 states that in exercising its powers under the Act the court should endeavour to place the parties 'so far as it is practicable and, having regard to their conduct, just to do so, in the financial position in which they would have been if the marriage had not broken down and each had properly discharged his or her financial obligations and responsibilities towards the other'. This, the authors consider, is exactly what the Court of Appeal did in *White v White*. For the authors' comments on the much more difficult and controversial decision in *Cuzner v Underdown* see case summary 8–204.
2. Damages may not now be awarded, but a co-respondent may be made liable for the costs of the suit (but not for the costs of proceedings under sections 23 and 24 of the Matrimonial Causes Act 1973).
3. Dunn J had placed the whole of the blame for the breakdown of the marriage on the wife.
4. See also *H v H* (6–401) and *Backhouse v Backhouse* (6–206). In *H v H* the wife left the husband and went to live with the co-respondent, whom she subsequently married. It was agreed that conduct was not a relevant issue. The main question was the effect of the wife's remarriage to the co-respondent, who was a man of means. In *Backhouse v Backhouse* conduct was at issue, and Balcombe J found that the marriage had broken down owing to the adulterous affair of the wife. Nevertheless, his decision, as in *White v*

White and *H v H,* turned on the fact that the wife and co-respondent were now adequately re-housed, and that it would be contrary to justice to make any order which would be prejudicial to the well-being of the husband's new family.

8–202 Wachtel v Wachtel

[1973] 1 All ER 829, CA

Giving the unanimous judgment of the Court of Appeal, Lord Denning MR said (at the foot of page 835): '. . . There will no doubt be a residue of cases where the conduct of one of the parties is [in the words of Ormrod J] *"both obvious and gross",* so much so that to order one party to support another whose conduct falls into this category is *repugnant to anyone's sense of justice* . . . But, short of cases falling into this category, the court should not reduce its order for financial provision merely because of what was formerly regarded as guilt or blame. To do so would be to impose a fine for supposed misbehaviour in the course of an unhappy married life.'

However, this was not a case where the court had to decide whether one party's adulterous conduct was sufficiently grave to take into account. The one party's conduct was compared with that of the other. The court of first instance having found each spouse 'roughly equally responsible' for the breakdown of the marriage, the Court of Appeal upheld the decision of Ormrod J (as he then was) that the fact that one party bore a share of the responsibility for the breakdown should not affect that party's entitlement to a share of the family assets.

Notes

1. See case summary 8–301 for further details.
2. See also *Backhouse v Backhouse* (8–308), in which the meaning of the words 'obvious and gross' and 'repugnant to anyone's sense of justice' was discussed.
3. The above passage from Lord Denning MR's judgment should not be taken to mean that conduct is completely irrelevant in every case unless it is 'obvious and gross'. See Davies LJ's judgment in *Rogers v Rogers* (8–204A).

8–203 Marsden (JL) v Marsden (AM)

[1973] 2 All ER 851

Settlement of adulterous party's share in former matrimonial home on children disapproved. The husband's suggestion that the wife's half share in the house, valued at £58,000 in September 1972, be settled on the children, solely in order that she should not take such an asset with her into her new marriage, did not commend itself to Sir George Baker P. See case summary 6–162.

8–203A Harnett v Harnett

[1974] 1 All ER 764, CA

Adultery by wife with 20-year-old youth half her age. Conduct of both parties considered. Wife's conduct not 'gross and obvious misconduct'. See case summary 8–303.

8–204 Cuzner v Underdown

[1974] 2 All ER 351, CA

The husband had purchased the previous matrimonial home in his name alone. The wife had made no direct financial contribution to the purchase money or mortgage payments. The parties decided to sell that property and buy a larger one, and in due course contracts were exchanged. The husband contracted to purchase the new house in his name alone. In order to save estate duty on the husband's death and thus benefit the wife in the event of his predeceasing her, the husband's solicitor advised the husband to have the new house conveyed into the parties' joint names. The husband agreed, and instructed his solicitor accordingly.

Six days before completion of the purchase was due to take place the wife admitted to the husband that she had for some time been having an adulterous affair with the co-respondent. She was undecided whether to leave the husband; but the husband, who at first apparently did not believe her when she told him that she had committed adultery, did not want her to go and tried to persuade her to stay. Two days after the original disclosure, the wife told the husband that she had decided to stay with him and that she would move with him and the children into the new house. Accordingly, the house was duly conveyed into the parties' joint names. However, six weeks after they had moved into the house the wife left the husband and went to live with the co-respondent, taking the children with her. The eldest child subsequently returned to live with the husband.

The husband obtained a divorce on the ground of the wife's adultery with the co-respondent, whom the wife then married. The wife applied under section 17 of the Married Women's Property Act 1882 for a declaration that the house was jointly owned by the husband and herself in equal shares and for an order that it should be sold and the proceeds divided equally between them. The husband had paid the deposit in respect of the purchase of the house and all the mortgage repayments.

Dunn J found that the wife had been entirely to blame for the breakdown of the marriage. He refused her application under the Married Women's Property Act and granted the husband a property transfer order under section 4 of the Matrimonial Proceedings and Property Act 1970 (see now section 24 of the Matrimonial Causes Act 1973 – see Appendix I) transferring the wife's interest in the property to the husband. The wife appealed.

Even though the wife had not obtained her half share in the house by fraud or deception, the Court of Appeal (Davies LJ and Walton J) nevertheless held that *to have accepted the half share while she was committing adultery amounted to 'obvious and gross' misconduct.* Their lordships further held that *even allowing for the fact that the wife had brought up the children and for the fact that she had contributed a proportion of her earnings towards the family's expenses, it would not be just that she should have a share in the house, particularly* (per Walton J) *in view of the finding that she had been entirely to blame for the breakdown of the marriage.* The wife's appeal was dismissed.

Dunn J, in his judgment at first instance, said: 'The wife and the two younger children and the co-respondent and a baby born to the wife by the co-respondent...are living...[in a maisonette]...owned jointly by the co-respondent and his former wife... It had apparently been agreed between the co-respondent and his [former] wife that [the maisonette] should be sold and the proceeds of sale split equally between them. The wife in this case says that the equity in [the maisonette] is about £6,000, so that if and when [the maisonette] is sold, the co-respondent will receive about £3,000. She says that a new house large enough for the co-respondent, herself and the three children will cost about £13,000. The co-respondent earns about £2,000 a year; he is an engineer. So on the basis that he would not be able to obtain a mortgage in excess of three times his annual income, the maximum mortgage which he could obtain would be about £6,000. So that if the £3,000, his share of the proceeds of sale of [the maisonette], is added to that, there is still a shortfall of some £4,000 to enable the co-respondent and the wife to buy a suitable house for £13,000. Therefore, the wife asks that [the former matrimonial home] should be sold and that her half share [about £4,000] should be paid out of the proceeds...'

However, as his lordship went on to point out, if that were done, *the husband (a) would be deprived of the use and occupation of the former matrimonial home which he had entirely paid for, and (b) would probably have insufficient money to acquire a house suitable for himself, the woman whom he now wished to marry, her daughter and his own eldest daughter.*

Having recited the above facts, Davies LJ said (at page 354): 'As the wife admitted and the husband said before the learned judge, it is quite certain that if the husband had known at the time when this house was acquired [i.e. when contracts were being exchanged, and immediately afterwards, when estate duty was being discussed] that she was committing adultery with the co-respondent, the house would never have been put into joint names; it would have been put into the husband's name. I suppose learned counsel would say: well, even if that were so, it would not have stopped her coming along and asking for a half share or some share in the house. That is no doubt true. But *here is the case of a house entirely paid for by the husband, and transferred into joint names simply with the idea that the transfer would advantage the wife in some respect in the future . . . What she was doing was seeking to turn the husband out of this house so that she might have some share of it in order to contribute to the purchase of a house for herself and the co-respondent . . . I cannot see any justice in such an order as is asked for by the wife . . .*

'. . . In relation to *Wachtel v Wachtel* (8–301), . . . the learned judge took the view that in this case, though conduct, as we all know, does not often matter now, *the wife's conduct in taking a half share in the house while she was committing adultery with the co-respondent was*, within the words that Lord Denning MR used in that case, *"obvious and gross" misconduct*. For myself, I would not dream of interfering with the learned judge's order . . .'

In his judgment in the Court of Appeal, Walton J said (at page 355): 'I would only add one word in regard to *Wachtel v Wachtel* and that is this. The general principles which are there enunciated – and they are only general principles – are principles which govern the normal situation in 99 per cent of divorce cases: that is to say, cases in which some blame can be attached to both parties for the breakdown of the marriage. To my mind, *it is an important point here that the whole of the blame was placed by the learned judge on the wife.* He said: "It is true that in many cases when a marriage breaks down both parties have contributed to that breakdown, but it is remarkable in this case that no allegation of any kind has been made against the conduct of the husband" . . . "In my judgment, this marriage broke down entirely because of the wife's adultery with the co-respondent and because of her subsequent desertion without just cause or excuse."'

Notes

1. A few days after Dunn J's decision at first instance, Bagnall J delivered his judgment at first instance in *Harnett v Harnett* (8–303), which is another case involving adultery. In relation to the facts in *Harnett v Harnett* Bagnall J said: 'I think that before [the episode of the wife's adultery in] 1969 the marriage was foundering, and, if any serious crisis occurred, liable to break. This was due partly to misfortune in the husband's illness, mainly to the temperaments of the parties, partly even to the passage of time.' and it is clear that his lordship considered that the husband in *Harnett v Harnett* was much to blame for the breakdown of the marriage.

    Similarly, in a judgment delivered some seven months previously, Ormrod J, in his judgment at first instance in *Wachtel v Wachtel* (8–301), had said: 'On the face of it, the principal cause of the breakdown of this marriage was the wife's sudden decision to leave home and go to Dr. Fyvie, yet, as the history of the marriage unfolded, it became increasingly clear that the real cause of the breakdown lay in the personalities of the spouses and their behaviour to each other over the years. The Dr. Fyvie episode was, in fact, no more than a symptom, a conclusion which might have been guessed from the fact that the marriage had lasted 18 years. This case is yet another illustration of Vaisey J's favourite dictum . . . "it takes three to commit adultery".

    '. . . If I had to assess conduct in terms of responsibility for breakdown I would, with some doubts, regard each spouse as roughly equally responsible. My doubts are double-edged; in some ways the husband could be regarded as primarily to blame, in others the wife.'

    The marriage in *Cuzner v Underdown* had lasted over 11 years. Did it really break down because of the wife's adultery with the co-respondent and her subsequent desertion? Dunn J was never asked to look into the matter. No doubt relying (perhaps mistakenly) on the Court of Appeal's decision in *Wachtel v Wachtel*, the wife's advisers had made no cross-allegations against the husband. It was perhaps inevitable, therefore, that Dunn J should have found that the marriage broke down entirely because of the wife's adultery and her subsequent desertion.

This being so, it followed logically for Walton J in the Court of Appeal to distinguish *Wachtel v Wachtel* (inter alia) on the ground that in *Wachtel v Wachtel* Ormrod J had found the parties 'roughly equally responsible' for the breakdown of the marriage.

2. Both Dunn J at first instance and Davies LJ and Walton J in the Court of Appeal also distinguished *Wachtel v Wachtel* (8–301) on the ground that all three of their lordships found the conduct of the wife to be 'obvious and gross' misconduct. However, it should be noted that the conduct of the wife which their lordships found to be 'gross and obvious' was not her adultery and desertion per se, but the fact that she had allowed the husband to give her a half share in the house, in order to benefit her on his death, at a time when she was committing adultery with the co-respondent and was considering leaving the husband to go to live with the co-respondent.

3. The finding that the wife's adultery and her subsequent desertion was the sole cause of the breakdown of the marriage and the finding that her conduct in accepting the half share in the house was 'gross and obvious' misconduct were presumably the reasons why the Court of Appeal entirely ignored the contribution which the wife had made to the family over 11 years of married life.

    However, the reader is referred to *Bateman v Bateman* (8–309), a case heard in 1978. In *Bateman v Bateman* Purchas J held that, although the wife's conduct was a relevant factor to be taken into account, bearing in mind the husband's shortcomings and also that the wife had made a valuable contribution to the family in kind over the years, she should not be deprived of all financial provision. Notwithstanding the fact that Purchas J found that the husband had been to blame for the breakdown of the marriage to some extent, *Bateman v Bateman* is a particularly strong case. The wife had not only substantially contributed to the breakdown of the marriage by her damaging attitude towards the husband and his career but had also twice attacked the husband with a knife. The second attack had clearly been without provocation justifying the attack and had caused the husband to require hospital treatment for a serious chest wound.

    The reader is also referred to *Armstrong v Armstrong* (8–205), a case heard in 1974, which is perhaps an even stronger case than *Bateman v Bateman* because no allegations were made by the wife against the husband. There the wife fired a shotgun at her husband. Fortunately he sustained only a slight injury, and the wife was subsequently put on probation after pleading guilty to being in possession of a firearm with intent to endanger life, and assault. The Court of Appeal agreed with Cumming-Bruce J that, while the conduct of the wife was conduct which it was proper to take into account, her conduct was not so gross as to disentitle her to any financial relief; and Cumming-Bruce J's order awarding her one-quarter of the family assets was upheld by the Court of Appeal.

4. It could have been argued that the house had been put into the joint names of the parties in an attempt at reconciliation. In *McDonnell v McDonnell* (23–905), a case in 1976, the matrimonial home had been given to the husband by his family. During an unsuccessful attempt at reconciliation he had transferred it into joint names. Shortly afterwards the wife commenced divorce proceedings. The Court of Appeal, rather surprisingly in the authors' view, stated that there were no sufficient grounds for interfering with the arrangements made by the parties themselves for sharing the house equally. The approach of Davies LJ and Walton J in *Cuzner v Underdown* is difficult to reconcile with that of Ormrod and Stamp LJJ and Sir John Pennycuick in *McDonnell v McDonnell* without taking conduct into account. It is unfortunate that *McDonnell v McDonnell* has not been fully reported.

5. In *Backhouse v Backhouse* (8–308), a case heard in 1977, Balcombe J went to great lengths (perhaps not altogether logical) to distinguish *Cuzner v Underdown* so as not to do injustice to the wife before him. His lordship distinguished *Cuzner v Underdown* on the basis that, whereas the wife in *Backhouse v Backhouse* had made a direct contribution towards the purchase of the house plus substantial indirect contributions, the wife in *Cuzner v Underdown* had made none. But in point of fact the wife in *Cuzner v Underdown* had made contributions (although perhaps not substantial contributions) to the family's finances out of her earnings. In *Backhouse v Backhouse* the wife, whose adultery Balcombe J found had been a substantial cause of the breakdown of the marriage, was awarded such a lump sum as the husband could raise by mortgage without crippling him financially. His lordship said: '. . . it seems to me that this is not a case where, as in *Cuzner v Underdown*, the wife should be deprived of all interest in the matrimonial home. It does seem to me, and I so hold, that this is one of those cases where the conduct of the wife is *a*, but not the only, relevant factor to be taken into account.'

6. The authors would respectfully submit that the judgments in *Cuzner v Underdown* are

outside the mainstream of the current judicial approach to issues of conduct, and that *Cuzner v Underdown* is unlikely to be followed today.

8–204A Rogers v Rogers

[1974] 2 All ER 361, CA

Davies LJ said (at page 363): '. . . The passage on which, it would appear, both the legal aid authorities and the learned judge relied was in *Wachtel v Wachtel* (8–202). It is so well known and has been discussed so often that I do not think it necessary to read it. In effect, what Lord Denning MR was saying was that, in the light of the change in the law on a main suit, allegations of conduct or misconduct were really irrelevant and that those matters could be investigated in ancillary proceedings. But I do not think that Lord Denning MR could possibly have meant that in any and every case conduct was quite irrelevant unless (to use his words) it was "obvious and gross". I think he could not have meant that in the light of the wording of section 5 (1) of the Matrimonial Proceedings and Property Act 1970, which expressly provides, in the last few lines of the section, after sub-paras (a) to (g), dealing with ancillary proceedings:

> ". . . and so to exercise those powers as to place the parties, so far as it is practicable and, having regard to their conduct, just to do so . . ."

And it does seem to me that in ancillary proceedings it is right that by and large the court should, in the words of the statute, have regard to their conduct.'

8–205 Armstrong v Armstrong

(1974) 118 Sol Jo 579, CA

Relations between the parties deteriorated, culminating in an incident in which the husband refused to allow the wife into the house one night. She was eventually admitted by another member of the family. The following morning she got hold of the husband's shotgun and fired at him; fortunately, he sustained only a slight injury. The wife was subsequently put on probation after pleading guilty to being in possession of a firearm with intent to endanger life, and assault. There had also been an earlier shooting incident.

The wife left the matrimonial home and the husband obtained a decree nisi with her consent on the ground of two years' separation. Meanwhile he had sold the pig farm and matrimonial home. On the wife's applying for financial provision the judge made a nominal order for periodical payments of £1 a year and ordered the husband to pay her one-quarter of the net proceeds of sale of the farm.

The wife appealed, claiming, inter alia, that she was entitled to one-third of the net sale proceeds. Her appeal was dismissed.

Buckley LJ said that what the judge had in effect been saying was that, although the wife's conduct was not so gross as to disentitle her to any financial relief, it was conduct which it was proper for him to take into account. 'Gross and obvious' was not a definitive expression. In *Wachtel v Wachtel* (8–202) it had been said that conduct should be taken into account only if it would be repugnant to anyone's sense of justice not to do so. In *Harnett v Harnett* (8–303), it had been said that conduct should be taken into account only in a very broad way. *Here the question to which the judge had to apply his mind was whether, to a reasonable person, the wife's conduct as known to the court was such that it would really offend that reasonable person's sense of justice if no effect were given to it in arriving at the financial relief to be given to the wife.* The judge had done that and had taken the view that justice would be done by giving the wife a quarter share of the proceeds of the farm.

In the light of her plea of guilty to possessing a firearm with intent to endanger the husband's life that was not an unreasonable view. The judge had exercised his discretion in a proper manner.

8–206 Dixon v Dixon

(1974) 5 Fam Law 58, CA

The husband had committed adultery with his daughter-in-law and they had been living together as man and wife ever since. Salmon LJ said that such conduct could properly be stigmatised as shocking and stated that he would bear that conduct in mind in making the order he would propose. However, he referred to a passage in the judgment of Lord Denning MR in *Wachtel v Wachtel* (8–202) in which he had said: 'No order should be made for a lump sum unless the husband has capital assets out of which to pay it without crippling his earning power'. The husband was a farmer, and to award one-third of the family assets to his wife would do just that. A lump sum order was made which left the husband with sufficient of the farm to enable him to earn a living.

8–207 W-S v W-S (sub nom. Whyte-Smith v Whyte-Smith)

(1974) Times, 25 October, 119 Sol Jo 46

Desertion – marriage lasting less than six months – not 'gross and obvious misconduct'. See case summary 7–361.

8–208 Jones v Jones (sub nom. Jones (MA) v Jones (W))

[1975] 2 All ER 12, CA

Violent attack on wife. Husband convicted of causing grievous bodily harm. Wife's future prospects of employment doubtful. Wife's financial position exceptionally weak. *Smith v Smith* (23–902) followed. See case summary 13–006.

8–209 Weisz v Weisz

(1975) Times, 16 December, CA

The husband concealed the existence of a bank account and the extent of his income. The Court of Appeal upheld an order that he should transfer his interest in the former matrimonial home to the wife. He was further ordered to make a lump sum payment of an amount equal to one half of the value of his two additional properties. The total of the award amounted to three-quarters of the capital assets and one-sixth of the joint income. Held (Sir John Pennycuick dissenting), the husband was clearly a dishonest man, and unless compelled to do so would not make any contribution for the wife and daughter. The award was one which gave the wife financial security immediately and one which had the merit of finality. The husband's appeal was dismissed.

8–210 M v M

(1976) 6 Fam Law 243, CA

After only $3\frac{1}{2}$ years of marriage the wife left the matrimonial home, taking the children with her. With the husband's consent, she obtained a divorce on the ground of two years' separation. The judge at first instance came to the conclusion that the wife suffered from a quality of possessiveness which led her to regard the children as exclusively her own; she had plainly behaved badly with regard to the arrangements for access; furthermore, the judge was satisfied that her loss of interest in the sexual side of marriage was genuinely trying for the husband.

However, the Court of Appeal did not find it possible to say that the wife's conduct was such that it would be repugnant to anyone's sense of justice to exclude it from consideration; the judge had been wrong in holding that the wife's conduct was a relevant factor to be taken into account.

For further details, see case summary 7–303.

8–211 Bryant v Bryant

(1976) Times, 3 February, CA

The Court of Appeal upheld an order that the husband, a persistent maintenance defaulter who had been in prison at the time of the first instance decision, should convey his half share in the house to the wife. The wife was ordered to make the mortgage repayments.

8–211A Martin v Martin

[1976] 3 All ER 625, CA

Dissipation of assets taken into account.   See case summary 1–405.

8–212 West v West

[1977] 2 All ER 705, CA

Wife, from outset of marriage, unreasonably refusing to cohabit with husband in house purchased by him as matrimonial home.   See case summary 13–013.
   Note. Sir John Pennycuick said that it was difficult to think of any conduct by a wife that was more gross than failing, for reasons which were predominantly her own fault, to set up any married life at all. The word 'gross' did not carry any moral judgment. It meant no more than 'of the greatest importance'. Once it was accepted that the court was forced to take account of the failure of the wife to set up a married life at all, the judge's decision to reduce substantially the amount of periodical payments was unexceptional.
   Ormrod LJ said that it was quite wrong to read the word 'gross' in the context of *Wachtel v Wachtel* (8–202) as meaning gross in any moral sense. A refusal by a wife to join her husband in spite of his having bought a house for her must be described as gross unless it was found that the house was totally unsuitable. Alternatively, the judge's decision could be justified on the ground that the duration of the marriage was to all intents and purposes nil and the wife's contribution in looking after the home was also nil.

8–212A Backhouse v Backhouse

[1978] 1 All ER 1158

Adultery and desertion.   All the circumstances of the case. *Cuzner v Underdown* (8–204) not followed. See case summary 8–308.
   Note. See also *Blezard v Blezard* (8–214).

8–213 Abdureman v Abdureman

(1978) 122 Sol Jo 663

Desertion by husband after 12 weeks of marriage.   The wife did not argue that the husband's conduct should be taken into account; rather, that as a result of marrying him she was now worse off financially than she was before the marriage. See case summary 7–463.
   Note. Compare *W-S v W-S* 8–207.

8–213A Bateman v Bateman

[1979] 2 WLR 377

Wife's unprovoked attack on husband with knife.   Conduct of both parties taken into account. Home for the children the most important factor. Children not to be prejudiced by their mother's conduct. See case summary 8–309.

8–214 Blezard v Blezard

(1978) 9 Fam Law 249, CA

The husband deserted the wife and children (then aged 13 and 11) for a younger woman, and the wife obtained a divorce on the ground of his adultery. The husband married the co-respondent, and they were living in a house which they had purchased jointly. The wife was living in the former matrimonial home with the children, a boy now aged 16 who had left school and obtained employment, and a girl now aged 14. The house had an equity of at least £48,000. It was owned jointly by the parties. Orr LJ said that had there been no children, he would have ordered an immediate sale of the property, subject only to allowing the wife sufficient time to find a new home. But the interests of the children had to be considered, and in his judgment it was best that they should remain in the house until the younger child attained 18 so that she could complete her education at her present school. The Court of Appeal ordered that the husband would have a charge of two-fifths of the net proceeds of sale of the house, such charge not to be enforced until January 1983 or unless the wife remarried or cohabited with another man.

Orr LJ referred to the judgment of Scarman LJ (as he then was) in *Goodfield v Goodfield* (5–102). That too was a case, like this, in which the husband had left the wife in order to live with another woman, and in his judgment in that case Scarman LJ had expressly stated that no question of conduct arose. The report of Orr LJ's judgment at 9 Fam Law 249 makes no further reference to conduct.

Lawton LJ, although agreeing with the judgment delivered by Orr LJ, added *that one of the matters which he had taken into consideration was the conduct of the husband in leaving the wife for a younger woman.* In *Wachtel v Wachtel* (8–301) the Court of Appeal had decided that the word 'conduct' should not be construed so as to allow the parties to continue to fight out the sort of petty issues which many sensible people thought had brought the old law into disrepute. At first instance, Ormrod J (as he then was) had labelled such conduct as should properly be taken into consideration 'obvious and gross', and the Court of Appeal had approved that label. However, that did not mean that conduct had to be deplorable or depraved before it could be taken into account. As Sir John Pennycuick pointed out in *West v West* (8–212), it merely meant that for conduct to be relevant it must be 'of the greatest importance'. The idea had got around among some lawyers (but not, perhaps, amongst right-thinking members of the public, his lordship said) that nowadays, leaving one's spouse to set up home with another was a mere accident of life which should be borne by a wife without fuss, and which should not be taken into account when the court exercised its jurisdiction to rearrange the finances of the broken family. In his lordship's judgment that was not the law. Such conduct may be of the greatest importance, as in this case, where there were no allegations of misconduct against the wife.

Counsel for the husband had submitted that if a balance sheet were drawn up of the assets and liabilities of the parties, the first wife would be seen to have more assets and less liabilities than the husband and that, accordingly, an adjustment should be made. However, his lordship continued, *when, as in this case, the husband's conduct had brought about the first wife's present situation, and he had not alleged that she was responsible in any way for the breakdown of the marriage, his lordship could see no reason why her living standards should be reduced to the same level as his. The woman he married must have known that he had been married before and had left his first wife to marry her. The husband had made the new conjugal bed and he should not be allowed now to say that it was uncomfortable to lie in. When this kind of situation arose in cases where the husband could not support two women, both may have to suffer, because any other result would be impracticable. That was not this case. The first wife and the two children could be supported in something approaching the old standard of living.*

8–215 J (HD) v J (AM) (sub nom. Johnson v Johnson)

[1980] 1 All ER 156

Persistent harassment of husband and second wife. See case summary 8–504.

8–216 Page v Page

(1981) Times, 30 January, CA

Removal of assets out of the jurisdiction. Husband's assets calculated as if the transfer had not occurred. See Appendix II.

  Note. See also *Weisz v Weisz* (8–209).

3   Conduct of the parties compared: contributions to the family and financial contributions: all the circumstances of the case: the relative test

CASE SUMMARIES

8–301 Wachtel v Wachtel

[1973] 1 All ER 829, CA

The husband presented a divorce petition alleging adultery by the wife. In a contested suit, Ormrod J (as he then was) found that the adultery had not been proved but he granted the husband leave to amend the petition and subsequently granted both the husband and the wife cross-decrees on the ground that each had behaved in such a way that neither could be expected to live with the other. He assessed the conduct of the parties 'as roughly equally responsible' for the breakdown of the marriage.

  Ormrod J said in his judgment at first instance (reported at [1973] 1 All ER 113 at 118): 'The fact is that the forensic process is reasonably well-adapted to determining in broad terms the share of responsibility of each party for an accident on the road or at work because the issues are relatively confined in scope, but it is much too clumsy a tool for dissecting the complex interactions which go on all the time in a family. *Shares in responsibility for breakdown cannot be properly assessed without a meticulous examination and understanding of the characters and personalities of the spouses concerned, and the more thorough the investigation the more the shares will, in most cases, approach equality.* There are, of course, cases in which the contribution of one party *seems to be* either very marginal or quite clear, yet a more subtle approach will reveal how much the other has in fact contributed to the ultimate result. The present case illustrates this very clearly. *On the face of it,* the principal cause of the breakdown of this marriage was the wife's sudden decision to leave home and go to Dr. Fyvie, yet, as the history of the marriage unfolded, it became increasingly clear that the real cause of the breakdown lay in the personalities of the spouses and their behaviour to each other over the years. The Dr. Fyvie episode was, in fact, no more than a symptom, a conclusion which might have been guessed from the fact that the marriage had lasted 18 years. This case is yet another illustration of Vaisey J's favourite dictum in ward of court cases – "it takes three to commit adultery".

  'But the problem remains, because conduct must still be taken into account. In my judgment the [Matrimonial Proceedings and Property Act 1970] itself indicates the answer. As section 5 stands, conduct is to be taken into account as a factor which may modify the result which is arrived at after consideration of all the other factors specified in the section. [See now section 25 of the Matrimonial Causes Act 1973 (see Appendix I) which ends with the words: "and so as to exercise those powers as to place the parties, so far as it is practicable and, *having regard to their conduct, just to do so,* in the financial position in which they would have been if the marriage had not broken down..."] The court can only approach this issue in a broad way. It should bear in mind the new basis of divorce which recognises that, generally speaking, the causes of breakdown are complex and rarely to be found wholly or mainly on one side, and that the forensic process is not well-adapted to fine assessments or evaluations of behaviour, and that it is not only conduct in relation to the breakdown which may have to be considered. Conduct subsequent to the separation by either spouse may affect the discretion of the court in many ways, e.g. the appearance of signs of financial recklessness in the husband or of some form of socially unacceptable behaviour by the wife which would suggest to a reasonable person that in justice some modification to the order ought to be made. In my experience, however, conduct in these cases usually proves to be a marginal issue which exerts little effect on the ultimate result *unless it is both obvious and gross*.'

His lordship concluded (at page 120): 'If I had to assess conduct in terms of responsibility for [the] breakdown I would, with some doubts, regard each spouse as roughly equally responsible. My doubts are double-edged; in some ways the husband could be regarded as primarily to blame, in others the wife.'

Giving the unanimous judgment of the Court of Appeal, Lord Denning MR said (at page 835): 'It has been suggested that there should be a "discount" or "reduction" in what the wife is to receive because of her supposed misconduct, guilt or blame (whatever word is used). We cannot accept this argument. In the vast majority of cases it is repugnant to the principles underlying the new legislation, and in particular the [Divorce Reform Act 1969]. [See now the Matrimonial Causes Act 1973.] There will be many cases in which a wife (although once considered guilty or blameworthy) will have cared for the home and looked after the family for very many years. Is she to be deprived of the benefit otherwise to be accorded to her by section 5 (1) [of the Matrimonial Proceedings and Property Act 1970] [for having looked after the home and cared for the family] [see now section 25 (1) (f) of the Matrimonial Causes Act 1973 – see Appendix I] because she may share responsibility for the breakdown with her husband? There will no doubt be a residue of cases where the conduct of one of the parties is [in the words of Ormrod J] "both obvious and gross", so much so that to order one party to support another whose conduct falls into this category is repugnant to anyone's sense of justice. In such a case the court remains free to decline to afford financial support or to reduce the support which it would otherwise have ordered. But, short of cases falling into this category, the court should not reduce its order for financial provision merely because of what was formerly regarded as guilt or blame. To do so would be to impose a fine for supposed misbehaviour in the course of an unhappy married life. Counsel for the husband disputed this and claimed that it was but justice that a wife should suffer for her supposed misbehaviour. We do not agree. Criminal justice often requires the imposition of financial and indeed custodial penalties. But in the financial adjustments consequent on the dissolution of a marriage which has irretrievably broken down, the imposition of financial penalties ought seldom to find a place.'

The Court of Appeal held that the fact that the wife bore a share of the responsibility for the breakdown of the marriage should not affect the distribution of the family assets. The one-third ratio was applied.

8–302 Trippas v Trippas

[1973] 2 All ER 1, CA

The husband filed a petition on the ground of the wife's adultery. In answer, the wife cross-petitioned on the ground of the husband's adultery. When the new law came into force on 1st January 1971 those proceedings were dropped. The husband got leave to issue a second petition on the ground that they had been living apart continuously for two years, and both sides consented to a divorce. The wife applied for and was awarded a lump sum. The husband appealed.

Lord Denning MR (at page 3): 'Counsel for the husband says that that sum should be set aside or reduced. He relied before the judge, and before us, on the wife's conduct. He says that the wife went to live with another man four and a half years ago. She has lived with him ever since. That man is earning. So is she. Counsel relied on the words of Latey J in *Iverson v Iverson* [1966] I All ER 258 at 260:

> "*At one end of the scale her adultery may indeed disqualify her altogether. It may do so, for example, where her adultery has broken up the marriage, where it is continuing and where she is being supported by her paramour.*"

Those words cannot survive the recent decision of this court in Wachtel v Wachtel (8–301). This is a good instance where the conduct of the parties can be put on one side altogether. Since 1968 each has been living with another partner. There is nothing to choose between them. The financial dispositions must be made without regard to their conduct.'

Note. For a summary of the order made by the Court of Appeal see case summary 6–102.

8–303 Harnett v Harnett

[1973] 2 All ER 593; affd. [1974] I All ER 764, CA

In June 1969 the husband discovered the wife committing adultery with a youth half her age. The husband reacted violently, ordering the wife out of the home, and she left with the children. Her association with the youth did not survive, but the husband treated the marriage as at an end because of the wife's disloyalty and, in October 1969 (i.e. prior to the coming into effect of the Divorce Reform Act 1969 on I January 1971), he instituted proceedings for a divorce on the ground of her adultery. The wife cross-petitioned, alleging cruelty, but did not proceed with her cross-petition, and a decree nisi was granted to the husband in May 1970. The application for ancillary relief did not come before the registrar until November 1971 (i.e. after the coming into effect of the Matrimonial Proceedings and Property Act 1970 on I January 1971).

On appeal from the order of the registrar, Bagnall J reviewed *Wachtel v Wachtel* (8–301) and (at page 601) said: '. . . *It will not be just to have regard to conduct unless there is a very substantial disparity between the parties on that score.* Ormrod J and the Court of Appeal in *Wachtel v Wachtel* used the phrase "obvious and gross". In this phrase I think that "gross" describes the conduct; "obvious" describes the clarity or certainty with which it is seen to be gross. But *the conduct of both parties must be considered. If the conduct of one is substantially as bad as that of the other then it matters not how gross that conduct is; they will weigh equally in the balance. In my view, to satisfy the test the conduct must be obvious and gross in the sense that the party concerned must be plainly seen to have wilfully persisted in conduct, or a course of conduct, calculated to destroy the marriage in circumstances in which the other party is substantially blameless. I think that there will be very few cases in which these conditions will be satisfied.*'

He continued (at page 603): 'In deciding the question of conduct I do not think it necessary to make any findings on the specific allegations made by the wife. I think that before 1969 the marriage was foundering, and, if any serious crisis occurred, liable to break. This was due partly to misfortune in the husband's illness, mainly to the temperaments of the parties, partly even to the passage of time. The husband conceded that he was in part responsible for the breakdown. The wife clearly behaved foolishly and reprehensibly; I think that the need she sought to satisfy was solely physical, with no intention of destroying the marriage; she simply thought – if she thought at all – that she would not be found out. This behaviour was, in my view, susceptible of forgiveness by a reasonable and loving husband who thought his marriage worth preserving and who wanted to maintain the unity of his family. This husband did not preserve and maintain them because . . . he did not think them worth it and because of his wounded pride and self esteem. I am satisfied that the conduct of the wife fell far short of being gross and obvious, certainly in comparison with that of the husband, and, probably also, absolutely.'

Ignoring the conduct of either party, Bagnall J applied the one-third ratio. His decision was affirmed by the Court of Appeal. Except in respect of the sentence in Bagnall J's judgment where he had said: 'The husband conceded that he was in part responsible for the breakdown', Cairns LJ said that he thought it impossible to criticise the way Bagnall J had dealt with the case, and Roskill and Davies LJJ agreed.

8–304 Griffiths v Griffiths

[1974] 1 All ER 932, CA

The wife filed a petition alleging unreasonable behaviour by the husband; the husband filed an answer relying on adultery which had been alleged in earlier proceedings ten years before and on allegations of unreasonable behaviour by the wife. The wife then filed a supplemental petition and the husband filed an answer to that. The bundle of pleadings occupied 66 pages. Arnold J (as he then was) gave a judgment which occupied 64 pages of transcript.

His conclusion was that over 24 years of married life there had been two periods when the husband's behaviour had been callously unkind and, on a substantial number of occasions, brutal; but that during such other periods of the marriage as had been marked by disputes and storms there had been little disparity of conduct between the parties. Taking into account the fact that the husband had worked hard to provide for his family, his lordship came to the conclusion that, badly as the husband had behaved on occasions, it would not be right to refuse him all relief. However, he continued, this aspect of the matter had to be taken into account, and this might fairly be done by taking care to apply a somewhat strict limit to the husband's claim for financial relief.

The husband appealed against the award of capital assets in his favour. Counsel for the husband submitted that if and so far as Sir John Arnold had taken the husband's misconduct into account he had misdirected himself.

Roskill LJ said (at page 936): 'The parties having chosen to fight the case in this way, the judge was obviously bound to find, as he did find with the utmost care, where he thought the truth lay on every one of these allegations which had been launched before him by way of charge and countercharge over so long a period.

'... I would only pause to make this observation on one submission of counsel for the husband in relation to those findings. This marriage lasted, he said, for a total of some 300 months. On the judge's findings, in the first period there were ten months of misbehaviour by the husband and in relation to the second period there were five months of misbehaviour. Thus, argued counsel for the husband, there was a total of 15 months' misbehaviour out of the entire period of the marriage of 300 months, which he put at 5 per cent. He suggested that this represented a minute proportion of the total period. Of course, put like that, that is perfectly true; but matters of this kind cannot be settled ... as if the effect of such conduct can be calculated on a computer.'

His lordship continued (at page 938), agreeing with Sir John Arnold's treatment of the question of conduct: 'In my view all that the learned judge was saying ... was: "Well, when I come to consider what is the right sum to award, I am certainly not going to stretch any point in favour of the husband having regard to what I have found his behaviour to have been." That seems to me to be a legitimate approach, so long as the judge has not gone outside what I have ventured to call the "bracket" [i.e. within which any reasonable person might think that the right figure lay]. But to suggest that the learned judge has positively penalised the husband and has reduced the amount he would have otherwise ordered because of his misconduct seems to me, with all respect to counsel for the husband's argument, to be quite unjustified in the light of the language which the learned judge used.

'Accordingly, in my view, notwithstanding the days and days that have been spent – much of it at public expense – in seeking to make these allegations and cross-allegations, conduct in the end disappears from this case, and one is left with what is a by no means easy question of fact. The question in all these cases – which rarely raise any question of law but only questions of fact – is: what is the right answer to the problem which the court has to solve under sections 2, 4 and 5 of the 1970 Act [now sections 23, 24 and 25 of the 1973 Act] in terms of pounds and pence, on the facts which in this case the learned judge has found in his two most careful judgments?'

Note. For a summary of the order made see case summary 10–203.

8–305 W v W (financial provision: lump sum)

[1975] 3 All ER 970

The marriage had been a turbulent one, marked by acts of violence on the part of the husband, the last of which had led to him being charged with assault occasioning actual bodily harm and in consequence of which he had been bound over to keep the peace. The wife left the husband, taking the children with her, and obtained a decree of divorce based on the husband's conduct.

Sir George Baker P said (at page 972): '. . . . The decree was made absolute in August 1972.

'The following month the wife began to have intercourse with a Mr. Smith, a married man whose wife had divorced him naming the wife. In the present proceedings the husband has argued that the wife's conduct is relevant and that the court should award a lesser lump sum or less maintenance than she would have received had Mr. Smith not committed adultery with her.

'He called Mrs. Smith to try to establish that there had been an association from the autumn of 1971 but I cannot find any evidence of adultery before decree absolute. What the wife did after the dissolution of the marriage is no concern of the husband; conduct after the grant of decree absolute is irrelevant, except possibly in the rare case in which it directly affects the husband's finances.

'Even if there had been adultery in 1971, or some time before the wife left, it seems to me – and this is I think the first important point in this case – that as the law has been interpreted and followed since the decision in *Wachtel v Wachtel* (8–301), it would be quite impossible here to contend that that conduct is a matter to which the court should pay any attention. In my view, conduct does not even get to the starting gate. True, in some cases it is necessary for the court to enquire into the facts in order to discover whether the conduct is of the kind described conveniently in *Wachtel v Wachtel* as "gross and obvious", or of the kind that would cause the ordinary mortal to throw up his hands and say, "Surely that woman is not going to be given any money", or "is not going to get a full award".

'But here is a husband who has been found to have behaved unreasonably towards his wife, and who, on looking at the petition, must have been found to have used considerable violence in a not very calm marriage. He was a husband who regarded, and wanted, the marriage at an end by July 1971. It is quite impossible for him to seek to rely on conduct on the part of his wife, and I have deliberately tried to dissuade counsel from embarking and wasting time – because I think it has been a waste of time – on enquiries about conduct. In conclusion, counsel for the husband said that he accepted that both parties were to blame for the breakdown of this marriage and he was not putting his case any higher than that. That is exactly the case which in my opinion should not be investigated.'

However, the fact that the wife had a joint interest in the new house in which she was living with Mr. Smith was a relevant matter to be taken into consideration. After applying the one-third ratio this factor was taken into account so as to reduce the lump sum which would otherwise have been payable to the wife: see case summary 13–009.

Note. In *Jones v Jones* (8–208), after the decree had been made absolute, the husband attacked the wife with a knife and was convicted of causing grievous bodily harm with intent; the Court of Appeal held that conduct after decree absolute can be taken into consideration. Although *Jones v Jones* was cited in argument, Sir George Baker did not refer to it in his judgment. In *J (HD) v J (AM)* sub nom. *Johnson v Johnson* (8–215) Sheldon J, referring to *Jones v Jones*, said that the court was entitled to consider any conduct by one party after dissolution of the marriage, whether or not it affected the finances of the other party. However, Sir George was certainly correct in refusing to take account of the wife's behaviour with Mr. Smith following decree absolute, as was his statement that even if she had committed adultery with Mr. Smith before she left the matrimonial home it would still be impossible to contend that such conduct was a matter to which the court should pay attention.

8–306 Campbell v Campbell

[1977] 1 All ER 1

Sir George Baker P said (at page 4): 'Now the first point in the case is that Mr. Campbell has sought to raise Mrs. Campbell's conduct ... Of course one begins with the decision in *Wachtel v Wachtel* (8–301) that unless the conduct is "gross and obvious" the court should not have regard to it when considering the amount of the maintenance or the amount of any financial provision for the wife. But in this case, as in so many cases, the preliminary question is how can the court come to a conclusion whether the conduct falls within that grave category without a hearing; and in many cases in chambers I have been faced with the problem, as I have no doubt other judges have as well, how can one avoid a lengthy, costly and, most likely, profitless investigation stretching over days, when allegations and counter-allegations are made by the ex-spouses or spouses, one against the other.'

Having investigated the various charges and counter-charges, his lordship concluded: 'So there is the sorry story, and I seem to be faced with the profitless investigation which might well end with the question who fornicated first?'

His lordship continued (at page 6): 'Conduct in this case never got to the starting gate on any showing, if only on Mr. Campbell's own admissions that there was not a whit to choose between him and Mrs. Campbell, even if one accepts, which I do not, his story about Mrs. Campbell. When I say I do not accept it, it is simply not established, and it really is impossible to go into the affairs of these parties ten years ago, certainly without a very detailed enquiry which, in my view, would be entirely wrong. I disregard any question of conduct; and while I appreciate that in some cases it is impossible, particularly with litigants in person and often for counsel, to dissuade spouses or ex-spouses from pursuing conduct, I take the view that everything should be done by the court to avoid costly, indecent and time-wasting investigations.'

Note. For a summary of his lordship's order see case summary 8–401.

8–307 Martin v Martin

[1976] 3 All ER 625, CA

Dissipation of £33,000 in unsuccessful business ventures by husband – successful running of farm business by wife. Purchas J took into account:
1) the wife had maintained, if not enhanced, the value of the farm since the separation;
2) the husband had saddled the farm with a burdensome charge which would oblige the wife to sell the farmhouse and possibly move into a caravan;
3) the husband had had the use of further capital sums and had pledged insurance policies.

On those factors alone the husband had had more than his entitlement of the capital assets. He was ordered to make the wife a lump sum payment of £5,000 and to transfer to her the whole of his interest in the farm. See case summary 1–405.

8–308 Backhouse v Backhouse

[1978] 1 All ER 1158

Balcombe J summed up the question of conduct as follows (at page 1164): 'I do not accept that this is a case of six of one and half a dozen of the other. On the evidence that I have heard and having seen the witnesses, I am satisfied that the wife fell out of love with the husband. She fell in love with the co-respondent and she kept that a secret for two years. She then walked out leaving the husband with the responsibility for a young child [then only 8 and now 13] and an older one [then 17 and now married]. She now seeks to justify her actions ex post facto. I find that the wife's behaviour was a substantial cause of the breakdown of the marriage.'

The husband obtained custody of the younger daughter by consent. Following the divorce, both parties remarried. The husband remained in the former matrimonial home while the wife was now living in a new house she had purchased together with the co-respondent. Balcombe J held that having regard to the substantial contribution made by the wife to the purchase of the former matrimonial home it would be repugnant to deprive her of all interest in it. However, it would also be repugnant to justice if her interest were to be such that the husband would be required to sell the house, which was required as a home for himself and the younger child of the marriage and for his new wife and her child. Justice would be done by giving the wife a share in the house, but not by reference to any increase in its value which had occurred after she had left the husband. Husband ordered to pay lump sum of £3,500 which, having regard to his income, he would be able to raise by mortgage without crippling him financially.

Balcombe J (at page 1166): 'Next I have to decide the question of the effect of the wife's conduct. Of course, one starts, as one always does in these cases, from the decision of the Court of Appeal in *Wachtel v Wachtel* (8–301) and from the judgment of Lord Denning MR where he says:

> "There will no doubt be a residue of cases where the conduct of one of the parties is in the judge's words 'both obvious and gross', so much so that to order one party to support another whose conduct falls into this category is repugnant to anyone's sense of justice. In such a case the court remains free to decline to afford financial support or to reduce the support which it would otherwise have ordered."

I think it is unfortunate that so many cases now seem to turn on the meaning of the words "gross and obvious" so that they almost have to be construed as though they themselves were words in the statute. There was cited to me the recent case of *West v West* (8–212) where Sir John Pennycuick said that one should read "gross" as simply meaning "of the greatest importance". But that was said in the context of a marriage that never really got started at all and I do not derive very much assistance from that case. I prefer to rely on the phrase in *Wachtel v Wachtel* where Lord Denning MR said that an order would be "repugnant to anyone's sense of justice". It would be repugnant to my sense of justice in this case to deprive the wife of all interest in a house to the initial purchase of which she very substantially contributed ...

'I refer ... to *Cuzner v Underdown* (8–204), which was a case where, to put it very briefly, the husband had bought the house and had transferred it into the joint names of himself and his wife at a time when the wife, unbeknown to the husband, was carrying on an adulterous association. The difference between that case and the present one is primarily that the wife there had made no contribution towards the purchase of the house, and therefore it seems to me that this is not a case where, as in *Cuzner v Underdown*, the wife should be deprived of all interest in the matrimonial home. It does seem to me, and I so hold, that this is one of those cases where the conduct of the wife is *a*, but not the only, relevant factor to be taken into account.'

8–309 Bateman v Bateman

[1979] Fam 25, [1979] 2 WLR 377

Purchas J took into account (a) the fact that on two occasions the wife had wounded the husband with a knife and (b) the fact that she had also very substantially contributed to the eventual breakdown of the marriage by her damaging attitude towards the husband and his career.

The wife suggested that the cut on his wrist which the husband received during the first attack had been self-inflicted during a struggle; Purchas J rejected that contention. The wife admitted that there was no real provocation justifying the second attack, during which the husband suffered a serious chest wound requiring hospital treatment. After that incident the parties had lived apart.

Purchas J said that the allegations that the wife had prejudiced the husband's career by her damaging attitude and by undermining his position with his superiors (in respect of which his Lordship was satisfied that there was a great deal of truth) fell into an entirely different category from the two attacks on the husband's person, but nevertheless they could not be ignored without grave injustice to the husband.

The wife made numerous complaints about the husband's behaviour. She alleged that the time and effort spent upon his career was at the expense of the family and she also made other allegations. Purchas J decided that many of these were unjustified, but he also concluded that there was a good deal to criticise in the husband's behaviour, and he took this into account when viewing the conduct of the parties as a whole.

Following the separation, the wife and children went to live in a house which the husband had purchased as a matrimonial home. The husband now intended to purchase another house for himself and the woman he wished to marry; he agreed that the former matrimonial home should be settled on the wife for life or until her remarriage, and thereafter should pass to the children absolutely. The husband, at the time of the hearing, was earning £9,212 per annum, but he would probably renew his work overseas, whereupon his earnings would increase substantially. The wife was on social security.

Purchas J held that the wife's conduct was a relevant factor to be taken into account when applying the provisions of the Matrimonial Causes Act 1973, section 25 (1), but the conduct of both parties had to be viewed as a whole. Bearing in mind the fact that the wife had made a valuable contribution to the family in kind over the years, and also bearing in mind the husband's shortcomings, she should not be deprived of all financial provision. An order was made that the former matrimonial home should be held upon trust for sale, postponed until the wife ceased to use the home as her main place of residence or remarried or died; that thereafter the house should be sold and the proceeds distributed as to 25 per cent to the wife if still alive and 75 per cent to be distributed equally among the surviving children or their issue; that the husband should pay a lump sum of £3,000 as a contribution towards the urgent repairs required to the house; and that the wife should receive reduced periodical payments of £1,000 per annum only, plus a further £800 per annum out of which she should make the mortgage repayments on the house and pay for the maintenance of the property, on the basis that the children would eventually benefit from the proper maintenance of the house and should not be prejudiced by their mother's conduct.

His lordship said: 'When dealing with conduct, it is essentially to the conduct of the party making the claim for financial relief that attention must be paid, but it is impossible to ignore the general context of such allegations, including the behaviour of the other party.'

Note. Compare this statement of Purchas J with that of Bagnall J in his judgment in *Harnett v Harnett* (8–303) where he said: 'It will not be just to have regard to conduct unless there is a very substantial disparity between the parties on that score … the conduct of both parties must be considered. If the conduct of one is substantially as bad as that of the other then it matters not how gross that conduct is; they will weigh equally in the balance.' Bagnall J continued: 'In my view, to satisfy the test, the conduct must be obvious and gross in the sense that the party concerned must be plainly seen to have wilfully persisted in conduct, or a course of conduct, calculated to destroy the marriage *in circumstances in which the other party is substantially blameless.*' Perhaps this ought to be rephrased: 'in circumstances in which, taking into account the gravity of this conduct, the other party is relatively blameless.'

Regarding the income position, his lordship said: '. . . the figure should reflect two aspects, namely, a figure which would allow the wife to live in a modest way if she persists in her attitude of not working, and should also include an element which would enable her to maintain the mortgage repayments on the house so long as she remains in it, and also a small element to assist but not wholly discharge the cost of maintenance on that house. I consider that the last two elements are justifiable because the children of the family will, to a large extent, eventually benefit from these payments and from the proper maintenance of the house, and of course they ought not to be prejudiced . . . by the conduct of their mother. The figure which I consider should be awarded includes £1,000 per annum for the wife for herself, less tax, and a further sum of £800, to cover not only the liability to meet the mortgage payments, but also to contribute partly towards the on-going maintenance and upkeep of the house. If at any time the house is sold, then the periodical payments will reduce to the sum of £1,000 less tax. On the same token, however, if the wife elects to engage in gainful employment, then this should not be a reason for the husband to apply to vary this order by way of reduction. The basis upon which I make this order is that any money earned by the wife should inure to her benefit and enjoyment.'

Note. It is clear from this passage that Purchas J considered that the wife ought to return to work (being both capable of earning and in a position to go out to work) and, by the same token, that she should not be discouraged from returning to work by risking having her maintenance reduced if she did so.

8–310 Kokosinski v Kokosinski

[1980] 1 All ER 1106

Conduct is a relevant factor not only when the question is whether a claim for financial relief should be cut down but also when the question is whether it should be increased. The husband escaped to Britain from Poland in 1939, leaving behind a wife and baby son, Wojciech, now aged 40. During the War he met the wife and in 1947 they started to live together. A son, Christopher, was born in 1950. The wife knew it would be impossible for the husband to obtain a divorce in Poland unless his wife there divorced him, and the husband had always promised that as soon as he could he would marry the wife. Meanwhile, the wife changed her name to his by deed poll in 1955.

The husband started an engineering business with some friends in 1946. When Christopher was old enough to go to play school the wife commenced working in the business. Over the years the business became a successful concern and the wife occupied an important position. In 1959 the husband obtained control, and shares were transferred to Christopher for the purpose of avoiding estate duty.

The parties lived in a house in North London purchased by the husband. Later they bought a weekend bungalow in Berkshire, the wife contributing towards the purchase price from her savings. The bungalow was conveyed into the sole name of the husband. In order to save estate duty he conveyed both properties to trustees on behalf of Christopher in 1968.

In November 1969 the husband was divorced by his wife in Poland. This was something which the husband, the wife and Wojciech had been trying to achieve for many years. In September 1971 the husband and wife were married.

In January 1972 it was decided to purchase a fresh matrimonial home. This was purchased by the husband and was conveyed into Christopher's name. The husband refused to move into the new house. This was the ending of the cohabitation between the husband and the wife which had continued since 1947. The husband remained in the former matrimonial home while the wife and Christopher moved into the new house, together with the wife's mother. The husband did visit the new house, including during Christmas 1972, but he continued in his refusal to resume cohabitation.

Until about 1975 the relationship between Wojciech and Christopher was always cordial. Wojciech visited England and they went on holidays together. The husband sought to treat both sons equally. Substantial sums of money were transferred to Poland for Wojciech's benefit, and it was the husband's intention that Christopher and Wojciech would eventually take over the running of the business. Permission was sought for Wojciech to work here but this was always refused. [It appeared to the husband's advisers that the wife was deeply concerned to gain eventual control of the business for her son Christopher alone. She was instrumental in preventing Wojciech from obtaining permission to work here by writing to the Home Office. However, there are no such findings in the judgment of Wood J as reported.] The failure to obtain permission was a bitter disappointment to the husband. In 1975 he made a will leaving everything to Wojciech. He insisted on paying Wojciech from the company during Wojciech's visits to England. Eventually there came an occasion when the wife refused to sign a document which allotted a £4,000 bonus to Wojciech, and as a result she and Christopher took legal advice. The outcome of this advice was that the wife and Christopher presented a petition in the Companies Court alleging, inter alia, that the husband had misappropriated company funds. Ultimately, negotiations were concluded whereby the husband sold his shares to the wife and Christopher for £40,000. The money was raised by selling the matrimonial home purchased in 1972. This was owned by Christopher. As Christopher had provided the purchase price of the shares the wife executed a deed of trust in respect of those shares which were transferred into her name. Eventually these shares were transferred to Christopher in 1979.

The wife was now living in the bungalow in Berkshire. With her lived her sister and aged mother. She needed a lump sum in order to purchase a small flat near the factory.

The husband now lived in the former matrimonial home in North London. Christopher, appreciating that there was a moral obligation to house his father, was content to allow him to live there rent-free.

The husband, now 68, had £37,545 capital and a state retirement pension of £1,319 a year. The wife's capital consisted of her jewellery, valued at £16,000, and she earned £5,700 a year gross.

Wood J said (at page 1114): 'In support of his first main submission counsel for the husband relies strongly on *Campbell v Campbell* (8–401), and in particular the passage in the judgment of Sir George Baker P which reads:

"... Counsel for Mrs. Campbell attempts to persuade me that the 3½ years of pre-marital co-habitation should be taken into account in assessing the length of the marriage ... Now I entirely reject that argument ... There is an increasing tendency ... to regard and, indeed, to speak of the celebration of marriage as 'the paper work'. The phrase used is: 'We were living together but we never got round to the paper work'. Well that is, to my mind, an entirely misconceived outlook ... *It is a complete cheapening of the marriage relationship ... to suggest that premarital periods, particularly in the circumstances of this case* [*and I emphasise those words*], *should, as it were, by a doctrine of relation back of matrimony, be taken as a part of marriage to count in favour of the wife performing, as it is put, 'wifely duties before marriage' ...*"

'On the facts of that case it was abundantly clear that neither party was worthy of praise for his or her moral attitudes, nor for his or her contribution to a home, nor the upbringing of a family. Indeed there seemed to have been nothing to show for his or her efforts during their relationship. *I note that Sir George Baker P stressed in the passage which I have quoted that his decision related to the particular circumstances of that case.'*

His lordship continued (at page 1117): 'This wife has given the best years of her life to this husband. She has been faithful, loving and hard-working. She has helped him to build what is in every sense a family business. She has managed his home and been a mother to and helped him bring up a son of whom they are both justly proud. *I believe that she has earned for herself some part of the value of the family business.*

'Having set out those matters prior to the ceremony of marriage itself, which seem to me to be relevant, I ask myself whether I can do justice, that which is fair just and reasonable between these parties, if I ignore the earlier history and the wife's behaviour during those earlier years. To put the question in a different form: would it really offend a reasonable person's sense of justice to ignore those events and that behaviour? I have no doubt that the answer from the reasonable man would be that they must be taken into account and, in my judgment, not only can I take these matters into account, whether under the phrase "conduct" or "in all the circumstances of the case" in section 25 [of the Matrimonial Causes Act 1973], but that same section casts a duty on me to do so.'

Reverting to the question of the business assets, his lordship referred to *Trippas v Trippas* (1–401) and continued (at 1119): *'The estimated value of the business today is £120,000. In my judgment, a figure of £8,000, or one-fifteenth of that value, is a reasonable proportion for the wife to have earned ...*

'Bearing in mind what was said by Sir George Baker P in the passage which I have cited from *Campbell v Campbell*, it will be said by some that to recognise the relationship which existed before marriage as relevant to financial redistribution is to encourage relationships outside marriage. To them I would answer that the occasions on which a court is likely to feel that justice requires such recognition are likely to be few, possibly very few.'

Notes

1. The headnote reads: 'Held – (i) ... It was the function of the court to reach a financial resolution of the problems of the family which was fair, just and reasonable as between the parties, and "conduct" was a relevant factor not only when the question was whether a claim by a wife for financial relief should be cut down but also when the question was whether it should be increased ...'

2. For other examples of good conduct being brought into account see Chapter 8/IB.

3. *In Kokosinski v Kokosinski Wood J considered that he could not do justice between the parties unless he took into account the wife's contribution to the family in kind and to the running of the family business during those years, prior to the marriage ceremony, when the husband had been unable to marry her.*

4. It is interesting to speculate what might have been the conclusion of the court had the wife never worked in the family business. Would the court have taken into account the wife's contribution to the family in kind prior to the marriage ceremony? One of the authors has a client whose case bore a remarkable similarity to *Kokosinski v Kokosinski* in certain respects. She had lived with her husband, a Ukrainian émigré doctor, since 1949. They too were unable to marry because the husband was already married before he came to Britain and his first wife was still alive and living behind the Iron Curtain. He told her that his first wife would not divorce him, and they lived together for some seven years before they were married, at all times being known as Dr. and Mrs. X and their son Y. During the early part of this period she acted as his secretary/receptionist. Later she worked in the wholesale fashion trade, at one time earning almost as much as he was. Her earnings were applied towards a common housekeeping fund, thereby enabling his earnings to be applied towards the purchase of a commodious house in a fashionable part of London. The husband eventually obtained a divorce from his first wife, and the parties were subsequently married. The marriage broke down only a year later, in 1957. Because of the wife's substantial earning capacity, the award of maintenance at the time of the divorce in 1960 was only £2 per week. In 1977 the wife, having fallen on hard times and having learned of her right to apply for a property transfer order, brought proceedings for further financial relief. The application

eventually came before the master in December 1979. The master distinguished *Kokosinski v Kokosinski* on the ground that it was a special case turning on its own facts, and refused to take into account the wife's contributions to the family in kind during the seven years prior to the marriage ceremony.

5. The authors are grateful to Mr. Nicholas Price, counsel for the husband, and Mr. Nicholas Wilson, counsel for the wife, for their assistance in the preparation of this case summary.

4 Relevance of conduct during pre-marital co-habitation

CASE SUMMARIES

8–401 Campbell v Campbell

[1977] 1 All ER 1

Sir George Baker P said that the wife had not remarried and was entitled to an order for periodical payments. Applying the one-third ratio to the joint income, the wife should receive £13.78 a week. But scaling that figure down because the marriage had only lasted two years, the proper figure would be £12 a week.

Regarding the question of pre-marital co-habitation, his lordship said (at page 6): 'Counsel for Mrs. Campbell attempts to persuade me that the 3½ years of pre-marital co-habitation should be taken into account in assessing the length of the marriage. The way he puts it is: "She was for 3½ years performing wifely duties before marriage." Now I entirely reject that argument. This was a married woman with a large number of children, most of them in care, living with a youngster. There is an increasing tendency, I have found in cases in chambers, to regard and, indeed, to speak of the celebration of marriage as "the paper work". The phrase used is: "We were living together but we never got round to the paper work." Well that is, to my mind, an entirely misconceived outlook. It is the ceremony of marriage and the sanctity of marriage which count; rights, duties and obligations begin on the marriage and not before. It is a complete cheapening of the marriage relationship, which I believe, and I am sure many share this belief, is essential to the well-being of our society as we understand it, to suggest that pre-marital periods, particularly in the circumstances of this case, should, as it were, by a doctrine of relation back of matrimony, be taken as part of marriage to count in favour of the wife performing, as it is put, "wifely duties before marriage". So it comes to this that I take this as a marriage of two years and a month or two, and it ended.'

Note. Compare *Kokosinski v Kokosinski* (8–402) in which Wood J, referring to *Campbell v Campbell*, said: 'On the facts of that case it was abundantly clear that neither party was worthy of praise . . . I note that Sir George Baker P stressed . . . that his decision related to the particular circumstances of that case.' Wood J continued: 'This wife has given the best years of her life to her husband. She has been faithful, loving and hard-working. She has helped him to build what is in every sense a family business. She has managed his home and been a mother to and helped him bring up a son of whom they are both justly proud. I believe that she has earned for herself some part of the value of the family business.' Wood J therefore went on to say that he did not consider that he could do justice between the parties unless he took into account the wife's contribution to the family in kind and to the running of the family business during those years, prior to the marriage ceremony, when the husband had been unable to marry her because his first wife in Poland would not divorce him there.

8–402 Kokosinski v Kokosinski

[1980] 1 All ER 1106

The husband escaped to Britain from Poland in 1939, leaving his first wife behind. During the war he met the wife and in 1947 they started to live together. The wife knew it would be impossible for the husband to obtain a divorce in Poland unless his first wife divorced him, and the husband had always promised that as soon as he could he would marry the wife. The first wife divorced the husband in 1969, and in 1971 the husband married the wife. The parties separated in 1972.

The husband started an engineering business in 1946. As soon as her child was old enough to go to play school the wife commenced working in the business. Over the years the business became a successful concern and the wife occupied an important position.

Counsel for the husband argued that the marriage had lasted only a few months. He relied on *Campbell v Campbell* (8–401).

Wood J distinguished *Campbell v Campbell*. His lordship considered that the wife had earned a share in the family business and awarded her a lump sum of £8,000, being one-fifteenth of its value, in order to assist her to purchase a flat. His lordship did not consider that he could do justice between the parties unless he took into account the wife's contribution to the family in kind and to the running of the family business during those years, prior to the marriage ceremony, when the husband had been unable to marry her. See case summary 8–310.

8–403 H v H (15 May 1981)

(1981) Times, 16 May

Intermittent premarital cohabitation of no relevance.   See Appendix II.

8–404 Foley v Foley

[1981] 2 All ER 857, CA

Premarital cohabitation taken into account under 'all the circumstances of the case' but not counted as part of duration of marriage under section 25 (1) (d).   See Appendix II.

5   Relevance of conduct after separation

CASE SUMMARIES

8–501 Jones v Jones (sub nom. Jones (MA) v Jones (W))

[1975] 2 All ER 12, CA

After the decree had been made absolute the husband attacked the wife with a knife and inflicted a number of wounds on her, one of which severed the tendons of her right hand. The judge found that as a result of the husband's attack the wife would be unable to continue working as a nurse and that her future prospects of employment were doubtful.

Orr LJ said (at page 16): 'It has not been argued – certainly not pressed – on behalf of the husband that the word "conduct", where it appears in the closing words of section 25 (1) of the Matrimonial Causes Act 1973, is incapable of applying to something that has happened after the breakdown of the marriage, or indeed after the decree absolute. The wording in question is entirely general in its character and I would not be prepared to limit it in that way.'

The husband's interest in the former matrimonial home was extinguished.

Note. For further details see case summary 13–006.

8–502 W v W (financial provision: lump sum)

[1975] 3 All ER 970

Adultery after decree absolute irrelevant.   See case summary 8–305.
Notes
1. Sir George Baker P said that conduct after the grant of decree absolute is irrelevant, except possibly in the rare case in which it directly affects the husband's finances. See case summary 8–305.
2. But see *Jones v Jones* (8–501) and *J (HD) v J (AM)* (8–504).

8–503 Martin v Martin

[1976] 3 All ER 625, CA

Husband's dissipation of £33,000 of the family's assets following the separation taken into account. See case summary 8–307.

8–504 J (HD) v J (AM) (sub nom. Johnson v Johnson)

[1980] 1 All ER 156

Since the husband's remarriage the wife had persistently harassed both the husband and his second wife. She made numerous telephone calls to their home and to the husband's place of work. Following a violent attack by the wife on the second wife, the wife was convicted of assault.

  The husband now sought a variation of the periodical payments order which had been made on the divorce. Sheldon J referred to *Jones v Jones* (8–501) and said that the court could take into account the conduct of a party after dissolution of the marriage. His lordship said that the wife had deliberately set out to harass the husband and his second wife, and the character and gravity of her behaviour was of such a nature that it would be repugnant to anyone's sense of justice to ignore it. In view of the fact that the wife had custody of the child of the marriage his lordship did not vary the order, but he warned the wife that if such behaviour continued the stage might well be reached when it would be repugnant for a court to order the husband to continue making any periodical payments.

  Note. In *W v W* (8–502) Sir George Baker P said that conduct after the grant of decree absolute is irrelevant, except possibly in the rare case in which it directly affects the husband's finances. Referring to *Jones v Jones*, Sheldon J said that the court was entitled to consider any conduct by one party after dissolution of the marriage, whether or not it affected the finances of the other party.

6   Relevance of conduct in proceedings for neglect to maintain

CASE SUMMARIES

8–601 W-S v W-S (sub nom. Whyte-Smith v Whyte-Smith)

(1974) Times, 25 October, 119 Sol Jo 46

Desertion by respondent spouse after less than six months of marriage not 'gross and obvious misconduct'.   See case summary 7–361.

8–602 Gray v Gray

[1976] 3 All ER 225

Position prior to Domestic Proceedings and Magistrates' Courts Act 1978 – adultery

by applicant spouse.   The Domestic Proceedings and Magistrates' Courts Act
1978 has now radically amended section 27 of the Matrimonial Causes Act 1973.
This case was heard prior to the coming into force of the new Act. It was held
that the meaning of 'wilful neglect to provide reasonable maintenance' must be
equivalent whether it was considered by magistrates or in the High Court. The
Common Law rule that there was no duty to maintain a wife who had been guilty
of adultery which the husband had not condoned (provided that he had neither
connived at nor by his conduct conduced to such adultery) had not been mitigated
by the passage of time. The wife's application was dismissed.

Notes

1. The 1978 Act implements the Law Commission's recommendation to eliminate
    anomalies between the matrimonial jurisdiction of magistrates and the jurisdiction of
    the High Court under section 27 of the 1973 Act. Section 27 is amended so as to bring
    the powers of the High Court into line with the new powers conferred on magistrates by
    the 1978 Act. In both jurisdictions the law has previously been that a husband, and
    presumably a wife, could not be guilty of wilful neglect to maintain a spouse who had
    committed adultery unless such adultery had been connived at, condoned or conduced
    to by neglect or misconduct. This was confirmed as recently as *Gray v Gray*.
2. Subsection (1) of the 1973 Act as amended makes it clear that each spouse has a duty to
    support the other. See Appendix I.
3. The failure to provide reasonable maintenance need no longer be wilful. See the new
    subsection (1).
4. The court is now to take into account those matters mentioned in section 25 (1) (a) to
    (f). See the new subsection (3).
5. Conduct may be taken into account 'so far as it is just to take it into account'. See the
    new subsection (3).
6. Subsection (8) of the Act as originally enacted has been repealed. Adultery is thus no
    longer an absolute bar.
7. Section 63 of the 1978 Act, which amends section 27 of the 1973 Act, came into force
    on 1st February 1981.

8–603 Newmarch v Newmarch

[1978] 1 All ER 1

*Position prior to Domestic Proceedings and Magistrates' Courts Act 1978 – desertion
by applicant spouse*.   This case was another case heard prior to the coming into
force of the 1978 Act. (See notes to *Gray v Gray* (8–602).) Rees J said (at page
13): '... I respectfully agree with the decision of Purchas J in *Gray v Gray*. In
that case the learned judge held that the common law rule that a husband is not
bound to maintain a wife in default has been imported into the High Court
jurisdiction under section 27 of the 1973 Act to make orders for financial
provision for a wife on the ground of wilful neglect to maintain ... If, therefore,
the wife in the instant case were in desertion of her husband at any relevant time,
or were guilty of adultery not conduced to, nor condoned, by her husband, then it
would not be open to this court to make an order for financial provision under
section 27 of the 1973 Act.' However, his lordship continued: '... On the evidence
before me, I have found that she was not in desertion.'

7 Relevance of conduct in proceedings under Married Women's Property Act 1882, section 17

CASE SUMMARIES

8–701 Cracknell v Cracknell

[1971] 3 All ER 552, CA

The former matrimonial home had been purchased in the joint names of the parties and was held to be owned by the parties in equal shares. The wife formed an association with another man and left the house. The husband was subsequently granted a divorce on the ground of her adultery. During the $4\frac{1}{2}$ years which had elapsed since the wife's departure until the hearing in the Court of Appeal the husband had paid all the mortgage instalments. In proceedings under the Married Women's Property Act 1882, section 17 the wife claimed she was entitled to a half share in the property *without any deduction in respect of the mortgage instalments paid by the husband following her departure.*

Lord Denning MR said: 'Clearly the registrar took the wife's conduct into account. Was he entitled so to do? I think he was. There is a difference between, on the one hand, deciding the shares of husband and wife in a house; and, on the other hand, subsequently taking accounts between them. When deciding the shares, we look to their respective contributions and we see what trust is to be implied or imputed to them. We do not have regard to the rights and wrongs of the separation. But, after they have separated, and it comes to taking the accounts between them, we do have regard to their conduct . . .

'It seems to me, therefore, that when a wife, who owns half the house, voluntarily chooses to leave of her own accord – leaving the husband to pay the whole of the mortgage instalments – then, when the house is sold, in taking the accounts, she gets half the proceeds of sale, but it is subject to deduction of half the mortgage instalments, and these are added to his half. If the wife does not leave voluntarily but is virtually forced out by his conduct, then it is to be taken that the husband pays the whole of the mortgage instalments for his own benefit, as he has the use of the whole house. When the house is sold, she is entitled to one-half of the proceeds, without deduction.

'This case is one where the wife left voluntarily of her own accord. The registrar was quite right to allow the husband to set off against the wife's share of the equity (£1,033) a sum representing half the mortgage instalments (£432) which he paid since she left.'

Notes

1. Compare *Finch v Finch* (8–705) where the husband evicted the wife.
2. In *Suttill v Graham* (8–707) Stamp LJ said that Lord Denning MR's view of conduct propounded in *Cracknell v Cracknell* would hardly have been sustainable had the decision come after *Wachtel v Wachtel* (8–202), and that the decision in *Leake v Bruzzi* (8–702) was to be preferred to that in *Cracknell v Cracknell*.

8–702 Leake v Bruzzi

[1974] 2 All ER 1196, CA

The Court of Appeal held that, since the husband alone had paid the mortgage instalments after the separation, he should be given credit for half of the payments of the mortgage in respect of capital, but not in respect of interest because he had had the sole use of the house, and the interest payments could be regarded as equivalent to payment for use and occupation. Since it was undesirable that questions of conduct should be considered in proceedings under the Married Women's Property Act 1882, he was not to be deprived of that credit even though the wife had obtained a decree on the ground of his unreasonable behaviour.

Note. Approved in *Suttill v Graham* (8–707).

8–703 Bothe v Amos

[1975] 2 All ER 321, CA

The business premises, at which was situated the former matrimonial home, had been purchased in joint names. The business was a joint venture. The wife voluntarily left the matrimonial home after committing adultery, abandoning the business. The husband obtained a divorce on the ground of her adultery. Following the divorce the wife remarried. It was held that the wife's adultery was not relevant to the point at issue; when dealing with an application under section 17 of the Married Women's Property Act 1882 the court was not concerned with the matrimonial conduct of the parties; however, the wife's conduct in breaking up the business partnership should be taken into account; the wife's interest in the assets and goodwill of the family business was accordingly assessed as at the date when she left the matrimonial home and renounced the partnership by her conduct.

8–704 Coley v Coley

(1975) 5 Fam Law 195, CA

The wife obtained a divorce under the old law on the ground of the husband's cruelty, having asked the court to exercise its discretion in respect of her own adultery. Following the divorce, she applied under the Married Women's Property Act 1882, section 17 for an order for the sale of the matrimonial home. The judge found that the house was held in trust for the parties equally, and considered that he should treat the matter upon the footing that the wife had been driven from the house by the husband's conduct. Accordingly, applying *Cracknell v Cracknell* (8–701), the judge did not give the husband credit for the mortgage instalments which the husband had paid since the separation, and ordered that the house be sold and that the sale proceeds be divided equally. (See *Finch v Finch* (8–705).)

The Court of Appeal found that, on a true view of the facts, it was reasonable and fair to assume that the mortgage instalments had been paid out of rents received by the husband from the letting of rooms since the separation. Thus each mortgage instalment would have been paid out of money which belonged to the parties in equal shares. Accordingly, the husband should not be given credit for the mortgage instalments paid since the separation *for this reason*. Conduct was to be ignored.

8–705 Finch v Finch

(1975) 119 Sol Jo 793, CA

The matrimonial home was purchased in the husband's name, although both parties worked during the marriage and contributed towards its purchase. The balance purchase moneys were obtained by means of a building society mortgage, the capital being secured by a with-profits insurance policy on the husband's life. The husband evicted the wife from the house and the parties had lived apart ever since. Proceedings were instituted under section 17 of the Married Women's Property Act 1882.

Commenting that this was one of those cases where it was very difficult to say what the proportion borne by the contributions of the wife to the purchase price had been, Lord Denning MR came to the conclusion that the wife's share should be one-half and that the registrar had erred by considering the husband's contributions made after the separation of the parties.

Notes

1. In *Cracknell v Cracknell* (8–701) Lord Denning MR said: 'But suppose now that the wife does not voluntarily leave the house but is driven out by the husband, or his conduct is so intolerable that she cannot be expected to live there with him any longer;

then he himself has deprived her of her share, and she should not suffer on that account. Even though he does pay the whole of the mortgage instalments after she leaves, nevertheless he must be taken to pay it for his own benefit, especially when he is using her half of the house for himself. He cannot claim credit, as against her, for any part of those instalments. They are regarded as paid by him in lieu of rent for her half. If the house is afterwards sold, the wife is entitled to half the proceeds at the time of sale – without any deduction or credit to him at all.'

2. In *Suttill v Graham* (8–707) Stamp LJ said that Lord Denning MR's view of conduct propounded in *Cracknell v Cracknell* would hardly have been sustainable had the decision come after *Wachtel v Wachtel* (8–202). Therefore, not only is the decision in *Cracknell v Cracknell* now suspect, but so is that in *Finch v Finch* as an example of the effect of conduct.

8–706 Shinh v Shinh

[1977] 1 All ER 97

After leaving the matrimonial home the wife brought proceedings in the magistrates' court; the husband was found guilty of cruelty and constructive desertion. The wife, being a Hindu, did not wish to proceed with her petition for judicial separation, on religious grounds. The husband was unable to petition for divorce because three years had not elapsed from the date of the marriage. Therefore the parties could not make application under the Matrimonial Causes Act 1973, sections 23 and 24, and were anxious to have the matter disposed of under the Married Women's Property Act 1882, section 17. A preliminary question arose as to whether it was open to the wife to allege that, by reason of the husband's conduct, she had been obliged to leave the matrimonial home and that therefore he was not entitled to claim credit in respect of the mortgage repayments made by him since the separation.

Jupp J concluded that the court could not be hindered in its investigation of the circumstances of the case by any restriction placed on the investigation of the conduct of the parties as spouses.

Note. See, however, the Court of Appeal's judgment in *Suttill v Graham* (8–707), which would appear to cast doubt on Jupp J's conclusions.

8–707 Suttill v Graham

[1977] 3 All ER 1117, CA

Following the wife's departure from the jointly-owned matrimonial home the husband obtained a divorce on the ground of the wife's adultery and both parties remarried. The husband continued to live in the house and to pay the mortgage instalments. The wife applied for a declaration under section 17 of the Married Women's Property Act 1882 that she was entitled to half the beneficial interest in the house and for an order for sale. The Court of Appeal held that the county court judge had been right to ignore the question of conduct, and upheld the judge's decision that the husband should be given credit *for half the repayments of capital* made by him since the separation (because such payments increased the value of the equity in the jointly-owned property), *but not of interest* (because he had had the benefit of the use of the house, and such payments could be regarded as equivalent to rent or payment for use and occupation). The decision in *Leake v Bruzzi* (8–702) was to be preferred to that in *Cracknell v Cracknell* (8–701).

8   Relevance of conduct in proceedings in Chancery Division

8–801 Jackson v Jackson

[1971] 3 All ER 774, CA

Law of Property Act 1925, section 30 – application for order for sale of jointly-owned matrimonial home – the court's discretion.   Lord Denning MR said (at page 778): 'On what principles should the court act in ordering a sale? In a stright case of desertion by the husband – as, for instance, where he leaves the home to go and live with another woman – the court will not usually order the wife to go out. It is his duty to provide her with a roof over her head. No matter in whose name the house stands – in the husband's name or in them both jointly – the court will not in the ordinary way order her out unless he provides her with suitable alternative accommodation . . . But when it is the wife who deserts the husband – when it is she who leaves the house – it is rather different. The courts have not laid down a similar principle in favour of a deserted husband. It is not a wife's duty to provide a roof over the husband's head. But the courts have given the husband considerable protection. If he is in occupation, they do not order a sale or turn him out – at the behest of a deserting wife – unless it is just and equitable so to do . . .

'In truth, all these cases depend on the discretion of the court. The cases about desertion are only instances of the way in which the conduct of the parties will influence the exercise of discretion . . . *in all these cases when the husband or the wife has an equitable interest in a dwelling-house or in the proceeds of sale thereof, the court will make such order about the occupation as it thinks just and reasonable having regard to the conduct of the parties and the circumstances of the case.*'

Note. For further details, see case summary 5–132.

8–802 Hayward v Hayward

(1974) 237 Estates Gazette 577, 1976 Halsbury's Abridgment para. 1399

Law of Property Act 1925, section 30 – application for order for sale of jointly-owned matrimonial home – conduct taken into account.   Following the breakdown of the marriage, the wife left the home. She served a notice on the husband severing the joint tenancy and took out a summons in the Chancery Division under section 30 of the Law of Property Act 1925, asking for the house to be sold and for her half share to be made available to her.

Walton J held that, as the wife was responsible for the breakdown of the marriage, it would be inequitable for the husband to be turned out of the house for which he had provided all the money. Accordingly, the order for sale would be refused.

Notes

1. Compare Lord Denning MR's dictum in *Jackson v Jackson* (8–801): '. . . It is not a wife's duty to provide a roof over the husband's head. But the courts have given the husband considerable protection. If he is in occupation, they do not order a sale or turn him out – at the behest of a deserting wife – unless it is just and equitable so to do . . .'
2. There has been much judicial disagreement as to the relevance of conduct in proceedings brought under section 17 of the Married Women's Property Act 1882 and section 30 of the Law of Property Act 1925. This case follows the old approach. The modern approach is to deprecate this method of bringing conduct into divorce proceedings 'by the back door', so to speak. However, *Jackson v Jackson* was referred to with approval in *Williams v Williams* (8–803).

8–803 Williams v Williams (sub nom. **Williams (JW) v Williams (MA)**)

[1977] 1 All ER 28, CA

Law of Property Act 1925, section 30 – application for order for sale of jointly-owned matrimonial home – the court's discretion. Lord Denning MR said (at page 31) that the court should exercise its discretion under section 30 of the 1925 Act on the principles stated by the Court of Appeal in *Jackson v Jackson* (8–801).

Note. In view of the fact that proceedings for divorce had already been instituted, the case was remitted for further consideration by a judge in the Family Division, so that the court's wider powers under sections 23 and 24 of the Matrimonial Causes Act 1973 (see Appendix I) could be exercised. See case summary 5–134 for further details.

8–804 Hannible v Bridge

(1976) Times, 22 May, CA

Home in name of wife's parents – desertion by husband – no equitable interest remaining in husband. The Court of Appeal dismissed an appeal by a husband who claimed that he had an equitable interest in the former matrimonial home by a kind of proprietary estoppel. The house, which was in the joint names of the wife's parents, had been provided by the wife's father at a cost of £850 on the understanding that the parties could have the house for that sum when they could raise the money, and could live there in the meantime.

The parties had lived in the house until the husband had left in 1971. They had extended and improved the house at a cost of £550, of which £340 had come from a local authority improvement grant, the balance being jointly contributed. The husband, a joiner, had done a considerable amount of work to the house himself. No attempt had been made to pay off the £850 to the wife's father.

Lord Denning MR said that, had the parties paid the £850, had the marriage continued and had the wife's father then refused to transfer the house, they might have had an equitable interest. But he could not see that there was any equitable interest remaining in the husband when he had left the house and gone off with another woman. By doing so the husband had destroyed the whole purpose of the arrangement.

8–805 Jones v Jones (sub nom. **Jones (AE) v Jones (FW)**)

[1977] 2 All ER 231, CA

Tenant in common out of possession not entitled to claim occupation rent from co-tenant in occupation. They are both equally entitled to occupation, and one cannot claim rent from the other, said Lord Denning MR. However, his lordship continued, if there was an ouster, that would be another matter [see *Dennis v McDonald* (8–806)].

8–806 Dennis v McDonald

[1981] 2 All ER 632

Ousted tenant in common entitled to claim occupation rent. Purchas J said that the basic principle that a tenant in common was not liable to pay an occupation rent by virtue merely that he was in sole occupation did not apply where one party was wrongfully excluded from the family home. Dictum of Lord Denning MR in *Jones v Jones* (8–805) applied.

For part of the period since the separation the tenant in occupation had made all the mortgage repayments. In respect of this period, *Leake v Bruzzi* (24–305) was applied. (See case summary 24–311.) For the period during which no question of mortgage repayments arose, the rent would be one-half of the appropriate rent which would be payable were there a letting under the Rent Acts.

9   Practice

CASE SUMMARIES

8–901 Thoday v Thoday

[1964] 1 All ER 341, CA

Estoppel – res judicata.   Diplock LJ (as he then was) said, at page 351: 'Estoppel merely means that, under the rules of the adversary system of procedure on which the common law of England is based, a party is not allowed, in certain circumstances, to prove in litigation particular facts or matters which, if proved, would assist him to succeed as plaintiff or defendant in an action.'

Lord Diplock continued at page 352: '... The particular type of estoppel relied on by the husband is *estoppel per rem judicatam*. This is a generic term which in modern law includes two species. The first species, which I will call *"cause of action estoppel"*, is that which prevents a party to an action from asserting or denying, as against the other party, the existence of a particular *cause of action*, the non-existence or existence of which has been determined by a court of competent jurisdiction in previous litigation between the same parties ... If [the cause of action] was determined not to exist, the unsuccessful plaintiff can no longer assert that it does; he is estopped per rem judicatam ... The second species, which I will call *"issue estoppel"*, is an extension of the same rule of public policy. There are many *causes of action* which can only be established by proving that two or more different conditions are fulfilled. Such causes of action invoke as many separate *issues* between the parties as there are conditions to be fulfilled by the plaintiff in order to establish his cause of action; and there may be cases where the fulfilment of an identical condition is a requirement common to two or more different causes of action. If, in litigation on one such *cause of action*, any of such separate *issues* whether a particular condition has been fulfilled is determined by a court of competent jurisdication, either on evidence or on admission by a party to the litigation, neither party can, in subsequent litigation between them on any cause of action which depends on the fulfilment of the identical condition, assert that the condition was fulfilled if the court has in the first litigation determined that it was not, or deny that it was fulfilled if the court in the first litigation determined that it was.'

Notes

1. In *McIlkenny v Chief Constable of West Midlands Police Force* [1980] 2 All ER 227 at 255, CA, Sir George Baker referred with approval to the distinction drawn by Lord Diplock in *Thoday v Thoday* between *cause of action estopped* and *issue estoppel*. A further judgment by Lord Diplock emphasising the distinction between these two types of estoppel is to be found in the report of *Fidelitas Shipping Co Ltd v V/O Exportchleb* [1965] 2 All ER 4 at 9–10, CA.

2. In *Thoday v Thoday* Lord Diplock also distinguished *issue estoppel* from *fact estoppel*. The passage from his lordship's judgment quoted above continues: 'But "issue estoppel" must not be confused with "fact estoppel" ... The determination by a court of competent jurisdiction of the existence or non-existence of a fact, the existence of which is not itself a condition the fulfilment of which is necessary to the cause of action which is being litigated before that court, but which is only relevant to proving the fulfilment of such a condition, does not estop at any rate per rem judicatam either party in subsequent litigation from asserting the existence or non-existence of the same fact contrary to the determination of the first court ...' Lord Reid in *Carl-Zeiss-Stiftung v Rayner and Keeler Ltd* [1966] 2 All ER 536 at 554, HL, said that he found the distinction 'difficult to understand'. (See also the judgments of Lord Hodson, at page 560, Lord Guest, at page 565, Lord Upjohn, at page 573, and Lord Wilberforce, at page 583.) Indeed, the distinction drawn by Lord Diplock between *issue estoppel* and *fact estoppel* is hard to reconcile with Ormrod LJ's explanation of *estoppel per rem judicatam* in *Porter v Porter* (8–903) in which he said (at page 1039): '.... where the trial judge has made specific findings, e.g. that the husband did not strike the wife as alleged in a

particular paragraph of the pleading, that finding is conclusive', i.e. as far as subsequent ancillary proceedings are concerned. Ormrod LJ's statement of the law is generally accepted today. For instance, it is stated in *Jackson's Matrimonial Finance and Taxation* at page 82 of the Third Edition: '. . . nor can a party [to ancillary proceedings] attack the express findings of fact of the trial judge, although it is to be observed that most cases are undefended, and the trial judge gives no detailed judgment, in consequence of which it is not necessarily possible to ascertain what were his findings of fact . . .'
3. For a recent case on issue estoppel and matrimonial law (though nothing to do with the question of conduct and ancillary relief) see *Tebbutt v Haynes* (6–363).

8–902 Tumath v Tumath

[1970] 1 All ER 111, CA

Estoppel – res judicata – undefended petition by wife on ground of husband's adultery – evidence of wife's desertion sought to be adduced by husband in maintenance proceedings – husband not precluded from making such allegation in subsequent proceedings.   Sir Gordon Willmer said (at page 120): 'I have come to the clear conclusion that in cases, such as the present, where there is no ground for holding that there is an estoppel per rem judicatam, *there is no principle of public policy which inhibits the right of the parties to bring to light in maintenance proceedings all matters relevant to the conduct of the parties, whether or not they have been raised at the trial of the suit . . .*

'If there is any room for doubt, I think that that doubt is removed by the recent decision of *Porter v Porter* [1969] 3 All ER 640, CA . . . It was a case in which a wife had petitioned for divorce on the ground of cruelty. The husband by his answer denied that he had been guilty of cruelty, and cross-prayed for a decree of divorce on the ground of the wife's adultery, which she did not deny. Before the trial, as the result of discussions between the parties, a consent order was obtained whereby the wife's prayer for relief was struck out, although her allegations of cruelty remained on the file. The case then went undefended on the husband's answer, and he was granted a decree on the ground of the wife's adultery. At the trial evidence was given that the marriage had already broken down before the wife's adultery, but there was no investigation with regard to her charges of cruelty against the husband. In subsequent maintenance proceedings the wife again raised the same allegations which had formed the basis of her charge of cruelty as matter relevant to be considered in relation to the conduct of the parties. Sachs LJ in delivering the leading judgment, with which the other members of the court expressed their concurrence, said:

"... it is now commonly accepted that a decree based on a matrimonial offence, whilst of course establishing the factum of that offence, is often of little and sometimes of no importance in reaching conclusions as to whose conduct actually broke up the marriage. As early as 1950 Denning LJ in *Trestain v Trestain* [1950] P 198 at page 202 said: 'I desire to say emphatically that the fact that the husband has obtained this decree does not give a true picture of the conduct of the parties. I agree that the marriage has irretrievably broken down and that it is better dissolved. So let it be dissolved. But when it comes to maintenance, or any of the other ancillary questions which follow on divorce, then let the truth be seen'."

I have ventured to underline that last sentence, which seems to me to be of vital significance. Sachs LJ went on:

"The second factor is this, that the adultery of the wife against whom a decree has been granted may be of great or it may be of little significance according to the background . . . Next, the present case is one which, but for the consent order of May 1968, might have entailed a lengthy trial at great cost to the community and ended with decrees to both parties, had the findings been so warranted. It is important for it to be clear that counsel can properly advise, as they often do and as has been endorsed by this court, that, by taking a course of not pursuing a prayer, the spouse who takes it does not prejudice his or her chances of success on ancillary matters such as custody and maintenance, which will probably have to be investigated later. These ancillary (a euphemistic word) matters are often those which are at the very heart of the real issues with which the parties are concerned."

'Accepting, as I do, that this is a correct statement of the principle involved, I cannot think that there is any room for a rule of public policy inhibiting parties from raising in maintenance proceedings matters relating to the conduct of the parties, even where such matters could have been raised on the trial of the suit, provided that there is no ground for holding that there is an estoppel per rem judicatam as between the parties. This is a matter which, I apprehend, is likely to become one of increasing importance if and when the new Matrimonial Causes Act comes into force; it is likely that when decrees of divorce can be granted on mere proof of break-down of the marriage, the real disputes between the parties will only emerge in the course of subsequent ancillary proceedings.'

8–903 Porter v Porter

[1971] 2 All ER 1037

Estoppel – res judicata – defended petition by husband on ground of wife's desertion – wife's answer denying desertion and alleging cruelty by husband – agreement that suit should proceed undefended on husband's petition – evidence of husband's cruelty sought to be adduced by wife in maintenance proceedings – Matrimonial Proceedings and Property Act 1970, section 5 – wife precluded from making allegations of cruelty in subsequent proceedings but not precluded from bringing evidence of husband's conduct.   Under section 5 of the 1970 Act (as under section 25 of the Matrimonial Causes Act 1973 – see Appendix I) the court was required to have regard to the conduct of the parties. The registrar held on a preliminary point that the wife was estopped from raising the allegations of cruelty in the maintenance proceedings. Ormrod J (as he then was) allowed the wife's appeal. His lordship held:

(i)   Estoppel per rem judicatam in matrimonial causes arose to prevent a party in ancillary proceedings from (a) challenging the ground on which the decree in the suit had been pronounced and (b) attacking the trial judge's express findings of fact. Apart from these two categories of estoppel there was no estoppel in ancillary proceedings.

(ii)   It followed that in the maintenance proceedings the wife could not deny that she had deserted the husband without just cause as found by the trial judge in pronouncing the decree in the suit.

(iii)   Accordingly, she could not set up just cause for leaving the husband; nor could she assert that he had treated her with cruelty within the meaning of the Matrimonial Causes Act 1965, because that would be equivalent to asserting just cause for desertion.

(iv)   However, she could give evidence in the maintenance proceedings of the facts relied on in her answer in order that the court could properly assess the conduct of the parties, as it was bound to do under section 5 of the 1970 Act. She could not rely on such evidence in order to prove cruelty or just cause for leaving the husband, but she could invite the court to consider such evidence in mitigation of the inference which might otherwise have been drawn against her from the bare finding of desertion in the suit.

His lordship said (at page 1039): 'The principles involved have been fully discussed in two recent cases in the Court of Appeal, *Porter v Porter* [1969] 3 All ER 640, CA and *Tumath v Tumath* (8–902). In both cases the court recognised that the actual decree itself was sometimes a poor guide to the actual facts of the marital situation, and, if taken alone, was apt to produce an unreal picture of the relations between the spouses and, therefore, of their respective conduct.'

Concluding, his lordship said (at page 1040): 'I would not like anything which I have said so far to be taken as an encouragement to parties to raise issues of conduct in maintenance proceedings unless they are of a really serious nature. In this case where the marriage has lasted no less than 28 years and the wife has had at least one mental breakdown and is now aged 55 years, neither the finding of desertion nor proof of the matters pleaded in paras 5 to 15 of the answer can depress either side of the discretionary scale to more than a marginal extent . . .

'Finally, I would draw attention to the fact that this application has to be dealt with under section 5 of the Matrimonial Proceedings and Property Act 1970 which sets out very fully the matters which the court must consider in deciding to make a periodical payments order. Conduct is still a relevant matter, and in some cases may be very important, but it is only one among a number of other serious considerations.

'In my judgment, therefore, the wife may, if she thinks any useful purpose will be served, give evidence of the facts alleged in the answer but she may not rely on such evidence as proof of cruelty within the meaning of the Matrimonial Causes Act 1965 nor by way of just cause for leaving her husband. She can, however, invite the court to consider such matters in order properly to assess the conduct of the parties to one another on the level of human relations and in this way, possibly, mitigate the inference which might otherwise be drawn against her from the bare finding of desertion in the suit.'

8–904 Huxford v Huxford

[1972] 1 All ER 330

Leave to file answer out of time – petition by husband on ground of wife's adultery – leave to file answer containing cross-prayer alleging adultery by husband granted. It was contended by the husband that the wife's application for leave to file an answer out of time should not be granted. Counsel for the husband argued that by allowing the petition to proceed undefended the wife's right to maintenance would in no way be prejudiced, because she could bring up all matters of the husband's conduct (including the alleged adultery) in the subsequent ancillary proceedings.

Hollings J held:
(i) The wife had nothing to lose by allowing the husband's petition to remain undefended insofar as her rights to maintenance would be completely preserved.
(ii) However, the wife's interest in having her allegations against the husband considered by the court and, if established, made the subject of a public decree, outweighed the inconvenience of delay and extra costs incurred by the husband.

Note. Compare *Collins v Collins* (8–905), in which the petition was on the ground of five years' separation, and in which leave to file a cross-petition out of time on the ground of two years' desertion was refused.

8–905 Collins v Collins

[1972] 2 All ER 658, CA

Leave to file answer out of time – petition by husband on ground of five years' separation – leave to file answer containing cross-prayer alleging two years' desertion by husband refused. Davies LJ said (at page 660): '. . . Learned counsel admits that if the wife were to file an answer and to obtain a decree, or a cross-decree, it would make absolutely no difference to her financial position at all. Her right to periodical payments or to other ancillary relief would be completely preserved if the husband were to get his decree. All the controversy which there may very well be about the circumstances in which [the parties separated] can be fully investigated on her claim for periodical payments or other relief.

'But, as far as I can see, the main point of counsel's contention is that there is a stigma or taint in having a decree of dissolution pronounced against one. I am afraid that, particularly under section 2 (1) (e) [of the Divorce Reform Act 1969– now re-enacted as section 1 (2) (e) of the Matrimonial Causes Act 1973 – the ground of five years' separation], I do not agree with that view at all. There is no stigma at all . . .

'We were referred by learned counsel to *Huxford v Huxford* (8–904). But I think that that case is clearly distinguishable from the present . . . In that case the husband had based his petition on a charge of adultery, alleging that there had been irretrievable breakdown because of the wife's adultery. The wife, out of time, came along and wanted to file an answer to make a cross-charge of adultery, which application was granted by the learned judge. But even in these days there is a stigma in adultery: there is no doubt about that; and I think that that is quite different from the present case.'

Note. This distinction was upheld by Sir Gordon Willmer in *Rogers v Rogers* (8–908).

8–906 Spill v Spill

[1972] 3 All ER 9, CA

Leave to file answer out of time – petition by wife on ground of husband's behaviour – no right to defend merely as a tactical device – leave to file answer denying behaviour refused.   In his acknowledgment of service the husband stated that he did not intend to defend the wife's petition. Negotiations relating to financial matters were then taking place. These negotiations broke down and the husband took out a summons for leave to file an answer out of time. *The husband was not intending to make any counter-allegations against the wife, but merely to defend her allegations against him. The impression was that the husband's application was merely a tactical device to secure some benefit which he thought might not be secured were the petition to be left undefended.* He had not shown adequate grounds why the court should exercise its discretion in his favour. The husband's appeal against the judge's refusal to grant him leave to file an answer out of time was dismissed.

Davies LJ said (at page 10): 'Counsel for the husband has said everything that could be said on behalf of his client. He says that the husband ought to be entitled to defend this charge of cruelty because cruelty carries a certain stigma. That word came from some observations of mine in a fairly recent case, *Collins v Collins* (8–905) . . . I said that there is in these days still a stigma attached to adultery, and that that was the real justification for the decision of Hollings J in an earlier case, *Huxford v Huxford* (8–904), where the learned judge gave the respondent wife, who had been charged with adultery, an opportunity to make a counter-charge of adultery. There is some stigma, I suppose, in cruelty nowadays. But the husband is not wishing to make any counter-allegation here; he merely wishes to defend.

'I was, I confess, impressed by the considerations that counsel for the wife put before the court. I do not consider that we have had any satisfactory explanation in this court of the husband's change of mind. Counsel for the wife suggests, and there may be something in it, that the change of mind – and plainly there has been a change of mind – is due to the husband's wish in some way to fortify his position with regard to the house and possibly to embarrass the wife to some extent in that regard. As was pointed out by Roskill LJ during the argument, we have had no affidavit of merits at all, and no explanation on affidavit as to why the husband changed his mind. It is suggested that really he is not sincere now in his wish to defend the case. We have not even had put before us a draft answer. *The impression is inevitably left in one's mind that this is merely a tactical device in order to secure some benefit which he thinks he might not get if he leaves the case to go undefended. But it is quite obvious that if there are proceedings with regard to property, or if there are proceedings with regard to periodical payments, he will not be prevented in any way from asking the court to investigate the rights and wrongs of the case and the conduct of the parties.'*

Notes
1. Although the husband would not be able to deny in ancillary proceedings that his behaviour was such that the wife could not reasonably be expected to continue to live with him, by virtue of being estopped per rem judicatam from challenging the ground on which the decree would be pronounced (see *Porter v Porter* (8–903)), he would not be estopped from giving evidence in the ancillary proceedings so that the court could properly assess the conduct of both parties, as it was bound to do under section 25 of the Matrimonial Causes Act 1973 (ibid.).
2. Compare *Rogers v Rogers* (8–908), in which the respondent husband not only wished to deny the behaviour alleged in the wife's peition but also to cross-petition on the ground of the wife's adultery, and in which *Spill v Spill* was distinguished.

8–907 Morley v Morley

(1973) 117 Sol Jo 69

Right to pursue petition when not defending cross-petition – petition by husband on ground of wife's behaviour – cross-petition by wife on ground of husband's behaviour and on further ground of husband's adultery – admission of adultery by husband – husband not intending to raise question of conduct on wife's application for financial relief – all questions of conduct irrelevant – refusal to hear husband's petition based on behaviour – decree granted on wife's cross-petition. This case is referred to in the judgment of Arnold J (as he then was) in *Mustafa v Mustafa* (8–910). His lordship said ([1975] 3 All ER 355 at 356): '. . . That case [i.e. *Morley v Morley*] as reported is one in which the husband presented a petition for divorce on the ground that the marriage had irretrievably broken down, and that there had been conduct on the part of the wife such as was currently then described in section 2 (1) (b) of the Divorce Reform Act 1969. [Now re-enacted as section 1 (2) (b) of the Matrimonial Causes Act 1973.] The wife had put in an answer in which it was agreed that the marriage had irretrievably broken down, and she cross-prayed alternatively under section 2 (1) (a) and (b) of the 1969 Act. [Section 2 (1) (a) of the 1969 Act – adultery – has been re-enacted as section 1 (2) (a) of the 1973 Act.] There was then a reply by the husband in which he admitted the adultery, so that he admitted the fact alleged under section 2 (1) (a) insofar as it dealt with his own activities, and alleged that that was not the cause of the breakdown of the marriage; not, one might think, a very relevant plea as the law is now understood, but one which in November 1972, at any rate, was commonly seen. Sir George Baker P said, and he was plainly right, that both parties agreed that the marriage had irretrievably broken down. He went on in these terms [as reported at (1973) 117 Sol Jo 69]:

> "The husband had admitted the adultery and the wife had declared that she would never live with the husband again. That was the end of the matter. All questions of conduct were irrelevant. The court has a discretion to refuse to hear the petition based on section 2 (1) (b) [that was, of course, the husband's petition], as all the necessary material for the granting of a decree to the wife was before the court. In any event the husband did not propose to raise the question of conduct in any proceedings for financial provision by the wife and accepted that the wife was entitled to a periodical payments order."

And on that, without more, Sir George Baker P proceeded to grant the decree to the wife on the answer and heard no more of the husband's petition.'

Note. Sir John Arnold continued (at page 357): '. . . It is undoubtedly a very remarkable circumstance that in *Rayden on Divorce* [12th. Edn. (1974) at page 186], where the law is stated as at a period up to a year later than Sir George Baker P's decision in *Morley v Morley*, the case is cited once only for this proposition:

> "Where a petitioner alleges two facts [by facts what is intended is one of the five matters set forth now in section 1 (2) of the 1973 Act] and the respondent admits one of them and the petitioner is not prejudiced in any financial proceedings by having to rely on the admitted fact, the Court may decline to investigate the unadmitted fact and may grant a decree on the admitted one."

That proposition of course is totally different from that advanced by Sir George Baker P in *Morley v Morley* as reported in the Solicitors' Journal. For, according to *Rayden*, all that the case supports is this proposition, that if more than one allegation is made by a spouse as a ground for the grant to that spouse of a decree of dissolution, that spouse will not be permitted to pursue more than one of those allegations if that one is admitted or, I suppose, proved, *whereas the case as reported sustains a more far-reaching proposition, namely that where a spouse has admitted an allegation against him or her calculated to lead to a decree, he cannot or she cannot thereafter pursue an independent ground on which he or she claimed to be entitled also to a decree,* a wholly different proposition . . .

'*The obvious utility of the rule,* whether it be the more limited rule instanced in *Rayden,* or the more far-reaching rule embodied in the decision of Sir George Baker P, *is that it is wrong, wasteful and contrary to policy that more matters should be canvassed in litigation than are necessary to lead to a result of utility. In Morley v Morley it is plain that any further investigation of the allegations of the husband would have led to such a tautalogy . . .* because the party making the allegations, the investigation of which was prematurely terminated, was not minded to agitate the relevant considerations in ancillary proceedings . . . which were or were likely to be forthcoming in the future.'

8–908 Rogers v Rogers

[1974] 2 All ER 361, CA

Leave to file answer out of time – petition by wife on ground of husband's behaviour – leave to file answer containing cross-prayer alleging adultery by wife granted.   In his acknowledgment of service the husband stated that he intended to defend the wife's petition. During the next six months he made attempts to achieve a reconciliation. Meanwhile he lodged an application for a legal aid certificate to defend the suit. This was refused. The petition was set down for hearing. The husband had meanwhile failed to file his answer. However, he suspected that the wife had been committing adultery for some time and he eventually obtained satisfactory evidence of her adultery. He applied for leave to file an answer out of time, exhibiting a draft answer which denied the allegations concerning his behaviour and which contained a cross-prayer based on adultery. The judge refused the husband's application. The husband's appeal was allowed.

Davies LJ said (at page 363): 'Among the authorities cited to us was a case in this court, *Spill v Spill* (8–906), which indicated that in support of an application of this kind there should be a satisfactory explanation of the husband's change of mind (in that case he had not indicated an intention to defend in the first instance whereas of course this man had); the husband had not sworn an affidavit relating to the merits of his application (in the present case we have such an affidavit); nor was there a draft answer before the court (in the present case we have a draft answer exhibited). It seems to me that, quite apart from what counsel has told us, the husband here has got his tackle in proper order. The draft answer contains a denial of intolerable conduct; it contains an allegation of desertion; and, perhaps more importantly, it contains an allegation of adultery.

'As I have said, when the matter was before the legal aid authorities there was no suggestion of any cross-prayer but merely an indication that the husband was defending the charge of intolerable conduct. Before the county court, however, as I have just indicated, there was the draft answer, which contained, in addition to the husband's denial, this allegation of adultery. When the matter came before Judge Lloyd the case was argued by counsel on both sides, and the judge, like the legal aid authorities, took the view, in the light of the decision in *Wachtel v Wachtel* (8–202) that conduct was irrelevant, that whoever was right and whoever was wrong about the intolerable conduct made no difference and, it would appear, whether adultery against the wife was proved would make no difference either. The passage on which, it would appear, both the legal aid authorities and the learned judge relied was in *Wachtel v Wachtel.* It is so well known and has been discussed so often that I do not think it necessary to read it. In effect, what Lord Denning MR was saying was that, in the light of the change in the law on a main suit, allegations of conduct or misconduct were really irrelevant and that those matters could be investigated in ancillary proceedings. But I do not think that Lord Denning MR could possibly have meant that in any and every case conduct was quite irrelevant unless (to use his words) it was "obvious and gross". I think he could not have meant that in the light of the wording of section 5 (1) of the Matrimonial Proceedings and Property Act 1970, which expressly provides, in the last few lines of the section, after sub-paras (a) to (g), dealing with ancillary proceedings:

"... and so to exercise those powers as to place the parties, so far as it is practicable and, having regard to their conduct, just to do so ..."

And it does seem to me that in ancillary proceedings it is right that by and large the court should, in the words of the statute, have regard to their conduct.

'It is pointed out by counsel for the husband, quite apart from the cross-allegation of adultery, that if this suit as it stands at the moment were allowed to go undefended without an answer the husband would be estopped from alleging in ancillary proceedings that his conduct had not been intolerable. It seems to me that, in all the circumstances of this case, in the light of the efforts that the husband made from shortly after the filing of the petition to put his case forward, it would be wrong to debar him from defending the suit. It is perfectly true that he has not done very much since the acknowledgment of service and did not take any opportunity of filing an answer; but the evidence that would justify him in making a cross-charge only came into his possession, as I have indicated, towards the end of November, and there was really not much time to do anything between then and 7th December, when the case was down for hearing and he applied to file an answer.

'We have had other authorities cited to us. The facts in each are different from each other, and I think it is a truism to say that applications of this kind should be dealt with and decided on their individual facts. I cannot myself see that the husband could really have done very much more than he did. It is suggested that he stands to gain nothing by defending the suit. Well, his counsel made for him what I thought was a good point, and I think this is valid: he said that, if the case goes on as it stands at present and if the wife succeeds, as she might, the husband would be ordered to pay the costs. Counsel for the wife frankly says that he would be under a duty to ask on behalf of the legal aid fund that the husband be ordered to pay the costs. The husband says that if he wins he would not be ordered to pay the costs, and also that he might have a chance of getting the alleged adulterer ordered to pay the costs. I think there is substance in both of those matters.

'In all the circumstances of this case, realising as I do that of course it is not a matter of right that the husband should be allowed to file an answer out of time at this stage but is a matter of grace, in my opinion the learned judge ought to have made, and this court ought to make, the order prayed for; and I would allow the appeal and give leave to file an answer out of time.'

Sir Gordon Willmer: 'I agree and I venture to add only a very few words on one aspect of the case. We were in the course of the argument very properly referred to the decision of this court in *Collins v Collins* (8–905). It so happens that on that occasion this court was constituted in the same way as the court today, and the appeal was from the same learned judge, against a similar order. I only refer to the case to point out the difference. That was a case in which the learned judge, as here, had refused leave to file an answer; and we upheld the learned judge's refusal. But that was a case where the petition was presented on the ground of section 2 (1) (e) of the Act, that is to say a simple allegation of five years' separation. It was pointed out by Davies LJ in delivering the leading judgment that such an allegation in these days carries no stigma, whereas it would be quite different, and different considerations would apply, if there were an allegation of, for instance, adultery. Here we have just such a case, where there are allegations of misconduct by the wife and a proposed allegation of adultery by the husband. It seems to me that in those circumstances different considerations do apply as compared with those in *Collins v Collins,* and that for that reason it is proper to come to a conclusion opposite to that to which we came in that case.'

Notes

1. Section 2 (1) (e) of the Divorce Reform Act 1969 – five years' separation – has been re-enacted as section 1 (2) (e) of the Matrimonial Causes Act 1973.
2. Section 5 (1) of the Matrimonial Proceedings and Property Act 1970 has been re-enacted as section 25 (1) of the Matrimonial Causes Act 1973 – see Appendix I.
3. The headnote to the report in the All England Law Reports reads: 'Held... In the circumstances the husband's application should be allowed ... if the suit were allowed to proceed undefended he would be estopped from denying in the ancillary proceedings the allegations concerning his behaviour...' This is clearly incorrect. See *Porter v Porter* (8–903) and *Spill v Spill* (8–906). The only finding which the husband would be estopped from challenging would be the finding that he had behaved in such a way that the wife could not reasonably be expected to continue to live with him. There would be no other finding of fact by the judge; therefore no further estoppel could arise, and the husband would not be estopped from disputing individual allegations made by the wife in her petition. See the judgment of Davies LJ in *Spill v Spill,* in which his lordship said that notwithstanding the court's refusal to grant leave to the husband to file an answer out of time defending the allegations contained in the wife's petition: '... it is quite obvious that if there are proceedings with regard to property, or if there are proceedings with regard to periodical payments, he will not be prevented in any way from asking the court to investigate the rights and wrongs of the case and the conduct of the parties.'

8–909 Parsons v Parsons

[1975] 3 All ER 344

Right to defend conduct – petition by wife on ground of constructive desertion by husband for upwards of two years and on ground of five years' separation – answer by husband conceding breakdown of marriage, denying wife's allegation of constructive desertion, making counter-allegation of desertion by wife and cross-praying for divorce on ground of five years' separation – application by wife to strike out husband's answer – husband unable to oppose wife's prayer for divorce on ground of five years' separation but granted leave to defend wife's prayer for divorce on ground of constructive desertion. The wife alleged that the marriage had irretrievably broken down by virtue of the husband's constructive desertion since May 1949. Her petition also contained a prayer for divorce on the ground of five years' separation. The husband in his answer agreed that the marriage had broken down irretrievably but denied the behaviour alleged by the wife. He counter-charged that the wife had deserted him in October 1947, when she had left the matrimonial home of her own volition and not by reason of his conduct. His petition then stated that the parties had lived apart for a continuous period of upwards of five years immediately preceding its presentation, and contained the prayer (1) that the prayer in the wife's petition be rejected and (2) that the marriage be dissolved (i.e. on the prayer contained in the answer). The wife applied to the registrar to strike out the answer on the grounds that it disclosed no defence, was frivolous and was an abuse of the process of the court. The registrar dismissed her application and the wife appealed.

Sir George Baker P held that because the husband accepted that the marriage had irretrievably broken down and that the parties had been separated for over five years he could not oppose the wife's plea for a divorce on that ground. Accordingly, his prayer that her petition be rejected would be struck out, and her appeal would be allowed to that extent. However, since the wife also alleged constructive desertion by the husband, the husband should be allowed to dispute the grant of a decree on that ground and the registrar had been right to allow his answer to stand.

The wife's appeal was allowed on terms that the husband's answer be amended so as simply to deny the constructive desertion.

His lordship said (at page 347): 'The decisions in *Huxford v Huxford* (8–904), *Collins v Collins* (8–905) and *Spill v Spill* (8–906), which have been cited, all deal with leave to file answers out of time. Such leave is discretionary and will not be granted where there is no stigma and no obvious benefit to the respondent. The contrast is, for example, between a five years' separation case and an allegation of adultery: see Davies LJ in *Collins v Collins*. At first sight the present answer would seem to be unprofitable and useless as the law now stands, but the wife has elected, perhaps unwisely, to add a plea of desertion which the husband is entitled to deny and defend. He was not out of time with his answer.

'I would add a word about cross-decrees which, although not strictly relevant, have been discussed. In *Darvill v Darvill* (1973) 117 Sol Jo 223, Stirling J is reported to have said it was undesirable to encourage in any way that form of pettiness which arose when each party wanted a decree, and that cross-decrees under what was then section 2 (1) (d) of the Divorce Reform Act 1969 (two years' separation and consent) were a waste of time and money and a negation of good sense. With that I entirely agree, but there are some exceptional cases in which, as Counsel for the Queen's Proctor put it, logic is perhaps not the best guide. I have myself granted cross-decrees in consent cases, although rarely; more often I have made decrees for both parties where each has established unreasonable behaviour against the other. These are cases in which, after negotiation, each spouse is prepared to resolve the dispute on the basis of cross-decrees but not otherwise. Amour propre is involved, for each in fact had played a significant part in causing the failure of the marriage. Sometimes for the sake of peace, sometimes in the interests of the children so that the feelings of the parents may not be outraged, a decree to each party will pour oil on troubled waters. But in my judgment there can never be a cross-decree for the respondent when the petitioner establishes a five year separation; that would be contrary to the philosophy underlying the pronouncement of such a decree.'

8–910 Mustafa v Mustafa

[1975] 3 All ER 355

Right to pursue petition when not defending cross-petition – petition by husband on ground of wife's adultery – cross-petition by wife on ground of husband's adultery – admission of adultery by husband – denial of adultery by wife – application by wife for order dismissing husband's petition refused. Arnold J (as he then was) said that it was wrong, wasteful and contrary to public policy that more matters should be canvassed in litigation than were necessary. But the reason behind the wife's departure from the matrimonial home, leaving the husband to carry on the running of the restaurant in which she had previously been actively engaged, was something which would inevitably have to be investigated when considering the wife's application for a transfer of property order. To grant the wife's application for an order dismissing the husband's petition would only have the effect of avoiding an examination of matters which would inevitably have to be examined in ancillary proceedings. Accordingly, the husband would be allowed to pursue his petition.

Notes

1. The wife relied on *Morley v Morley* (8–907). In *Morley v Morley* the husband petitioned for divorce on the ground of the wife's behaviour while the wife cross-petitioned on the ground of the husband's behaviour and also his adultery. The husband's adultery was admitted. Sir George Baker P refused to hear the husband's petition and granted a decree on the wife's cross-petition, saying that all questions of conduct were irrelevant. Sir John Arnold distinguished *Morley v Morley* on the ground that the husband in that case had not proposed to raise the question of the wife's conduct in any forthcoming proceedings for financial provision and had accepted that the wife was entitled to a periodical payments order. (See the quotation from his lordship's judgment set out in the note to the summary of *Morley v Morley* at 8–907.)

2. Compare *Parsons v Parsons* (8–909), in which the wife petitioned for divorce on the
    ground of five years' separation. Sir George Baker P allowed the husband to defend the
    wife's additional prayer for a divorce on the ground of constructive desertion, saying:
    '. . . the wife has elected, perhaps unwisely, to add a plea of desertion which the husband
    is entitled to deny and defend. He was not out of time with his answer.'
3. It might at first sight appear that the fact that the husband was not out of time with his
    answer was of great importance in *Parsons v Parsons*. (See the short passage from Sir
    George Baker P's judgment quoted above.) However, the authors would argue that a
    closer study of *Morley v Morley, Parsons v Parsons* and *Mustafa v Mustafa*, and a
    comparison of these three cases with those concerned with leave to file an answer out of
    time (*Huxford v Huxford* (8–904), *Collins v Collins* (8–905), *Spill v Spill* (8–906) and
    Rogers v Rogers (8–908)), discloses that the rule that leave is required in order to file an
    answer out of time does nothing more than enable the matter to be considered at an
    early stage. Leave to file an answer out of time will be granted if it is reasonable to do so.
    In *Huxford v Huxford*, leave was granted because both the petition and proposed cross-
    petition were on the grounds of adultery. In *Collins v Collins* the petition was on the
    ground of five years' separation. There being no stigma attached to a divorce on this
    ground, leave to file an answer out of time was refused because a cross-petition would
    serve no useful purpose. In *Spill v Spill* the petition was on the ground of the
    respondent's behaviour. However, whereas leave to file an answer out of time would
    normally be granted, the respondent failed to show adequate ground why he had
    changed his mind at such a late stage and now sought the court's leave. *Rogers v Rogers*
    was another case in which the petition was on the ground of the respondent's behaviour;
    the respondent was refused legal aid to defend the petition; but eventually he obtained
    evidence of adultery by the petitioner, and leave to file out of time was granted; Sir
    Gordon Willmer referred to *Collins v Collins*, in which leave to file a cross-petition out
    of time had been refused. That was a case in which the petition had been on the ground
    of five years' separation, whereas in *Rogers v Rogers* the wife was making allegations of
    misconduct on the part of the husband and it was only right that the husband should be
    allowed to reply with allegations of misconduct on the part of the wife. Indeed, in
    Collins v Collins it was specifically stated that the position would have been different had
    the petition been one alleging adultery, as in *Huxford v Huxford*. Viewed in this light,
    the decisions in *Morley v Morley, Parsons v Parsons* and *Mustafa v Mustafa* are on all
    fours with the cases on leave to file out of time. All of these cases can be reconciled with
    one another on the basis that it is public policy that a defendant to a cause of action
    should be allowed to speak up in his defence if any useful purpose is to be served by his
    doing so, but that it is contrary to public policy that more matters should be canvassed
    in litigation than are necessary in order to achieve the aims of justice.

8–911 Greyson v Greyson

(1979) 10 Fam Law 89, CA

*Issues of conduct raised in proceedings for ancillary relief – registrar's discretion to
order transfer to High Court.*   Ormrod LJ said that it was a matter for the registrar
to decide whether he would hear the issue or whether the proceedings would be
better tried by a High Court judge. The advantage of the rule (rule 80 of the
Matrimonial Causes Rules 1977) was that it helped to prevent registrars' lists
from becoming cluttered up with applications for financial relief involving long
drawn out recriminations.

8–912 Practice Direction 4th June 1981

[1981] 2 All ER 642

. . . the following procedures laid down by the Registrar's Direction of 12th
February 1980, [1980] 1 All ER 592, are still useful and should be continued . . .
(d) Where an issue of conduct is raised on the affidavits, an appointment for
directions should be taken out at which the registrar will enquire whether the
issue is being pursued and, if so, will order particulars to be given of the precise
allegations relied on.
    The Registrar's Direction of 12th February 1980 is hereby cancelled.

CHAPTER 9
Relevance of existing agreement between the parties

The contents of this chapter are closely related to those of Chapter 10 'The clean break'. However, there is an important distinction to be drawn between the two concepts of pre-existing agreements and the clean break. The similarity between the two concepts is obvious; both can arise out of the natural and sensible desire on the part of litigants, their advisers and the courts to achieve a degree of finality and certainty insofar as it is possible. The important distinction, we submit, is as follows:

1. There is a general principle that the court's jurisdiction cannot be ousted. For example, the parties cannot contract out of the provisions of sections 23 and 24 of the Matrimonial Causes Act 1973. The importance of existing agreements is that they may well affect the manner in which the court's jurisdiction or discretion is exercised.

2. The principle of the 'clean break' co-exists separately. It is one of two fundamental principles on which the court's jurisdiction is exercised, the first being the public interest that spouses should provide for themselves and their children, the second principle, of equal importance, being that of the clean break. See *Minton v Minton*, per Lord Scarman (10–205).

Bearing that distinction closely in mind it will be seen that whenever private agreements have been considered by the courts, they have been considered from the starting point that the court's jurisdiction under sections 23 and 24 of the 1973 Act cannot be ousted. This important concept has its origins in the House of Lords' decision in *Hyman v Hyman* (9–001) decided in 1929. The fact that the concept is just as valid under the modern legislation is demonstrated by *Wright v Wright* (9–005), *Jessel v Jessel* (9–023) and *Edgar v Edgar* (9–026).

Although it is always important to remember that the court's jurisdiction cannot be ousted, it would be wrong to assume that private agreements cannot be of paramount significance, as the recent case of *Edgar v Edgar* illustrates. In that case, the court dismissed a wife's application for a lump sum because, prior to the divorce, the wife had signed a deed of separation which contained a clause debarring her from claiming a lump sum or any transfer of property order. It should be noted that *Edgar v Edgar* provides a clear example of the court regarding the existence of an agreement as an element of conduct which must be taken into account under the provisions of section 25 of the 1973 Act. It was said that the wife must offer 'prima facie evidence of material facts which show that justice requires that she should be relieved from the effects of her covenant'. Another element of the decision clearly involves an investigation of the circumstances in which the separation agreement had come about. For example, the court satisfied itself that there was no evidence which reflected adversely on the husband's conduct in the negotiations; the bargain had been freely entered into with the benefit of legal advice; the husband did not put pressure on the wife to accept the terms of the deed and he had in no way exploited his position as a wealthy man. The assumption must be that considerations such as these will be taken into account in any case in which it is argued that an existing agreement ought to affect the exercise of the court's discretion. A further example of a case in which all these considerations were applied is *Dean v Dean* (9–020). Again, the court referred to an examination of the agreement as a necessary exercise within the scope of Section 25. It was suggested that the conduct of the parties included the fact of and the nature of an agreement voluntarily arrived at between the parties. Provided that the agreement had been reached at arm's length and the parties had been separately advised, the agreement itself would be prima facie evidence of the reasonableness of its terms.

CASE SUMMARIES

9–001 Hyman v Hyman

[1929] All ER Rep 245, HL

The clean break – jurisdiction to award maintenance cannot be ousted by private agreement. By a deed of separation the husband covenanted for himself and his personal representatives that he would pay two lump sums to the wife, together with a weekly sum by way of maintenance during her lifetime. The wife covenanted not to institute proceedings for maintenance over and above the maintenance covenanted to be paid under the deed. The two lump sums were duly paid and the husband regularly paid the agreed maintenance. Subsequently, the wife obtained a decree nisi. She then commenced proceedings for maintenance, which the husband defended, relying on the deed of separation. The questions arising on the deed were heard as a preliminary issue by the judge, who ordered that the wife was not precluded from prosecuting her claim for maintenance by reason of the deed. Thus husband appealed. Both the Court of Appeal and the House of Lords upheld the judge's decision.

Applied in *Wright v Wright* (9–005), *Jessel v Jessel* (9–023) and *Edgar v Edgar* (9–026).

Note. For an explanation see *Minton v Minton* (10–205): the jurisdiction to award maintenance cannot be ousted by any private agreement between the parties, but it is otherwise when the agreement is brought before the court and an order of the court is made giving effect to its terms dismissing the wife's application for periodical payments: see *L v L* (10–201). However, in cases in which the wife's application for periodical payments is not dismissed the court retains jurisdiction to review the question of maintenance for the wife: see *Wright v Wright* (9–005) and *Jessel v Jessel* (9–023).

9–002 L v L

[1961] 3 All ER 834, CA

The clean break – jurisdiction to award maintenance cannot be ousted by private agreement – but it is otherwise when the agreement is brought before the court and an order is made giving effect to its terms dismissing the wife's application for periodical payments – no jurisdiction to entertain second application. See case summary 10–201.

Note. Compare *Wright v Wright* (9–005) and *Jessel v Jessel* (9–023): in cases in which the wife's application for periodical payments is not dismissed the court retains jurisdiction to review the question of maintenance for the wife.

9–003 Cresswell v Potter

(1968) 121 NLJ 1160

Unconscionable bargain. This case was referred to by Balcombe J in *Backhouse v Backhouse* (9–019) [1978] 1 All ER 1158. Referring to the transfer by the wife of her interest in the matrimonial home to her husband, his lordship said (at page 1165): '...I have already held that there was no duress which coerced the wife into signing the transfer, but that still leaves the question, should the transfer be allowed to stand in full effect? Was it in particular an unconscionable bargain? This matter was considered by Megarry J in the unreported case of *Cresswell v Potter*. It is referred to in a note in the New Law Journal and I quote from that note although, in fact, I have available a transcript of the judgment, and I am satisfied that the note I am about to read is an accurate summary of the effect of that judgment:

> "The unreported case of *Cresswell v Potter*, decided by Megarry J in 1968, has indicated that the law of unconscionable bargains is not a mere living fossil, but is still operative, and capable of development in ways that directly concern the average practitioner. There a matrimonial home had been conveyed to a husband and wife as joint tenants at law and in equity. After the marriage had broken down the wife was handed a document to execute by an enquiry agent who acted on behalf of the husband and his solicitor. This document was described as a conveyance. By it, in return for an indemnity against the liabilities under a mortgage of the property but for no other consideration, the wife released and conveyed to the husband all her interest in the matrimonial home. She believed, according to her evidence, that she was signing a document that would make it possible to sell the property without affecting her rights in it. The enquiry agent, for his part, could remember very little about the execution of the document. Megarry J considered the three requirements laid down in *Fry v Lane* (1888) 40 Ch D 312, [1886–90] All ER Rep 1084: poverty and ignorance of the plaintiff; sale at an undervalue, and lack of independent advice. He considered that all three were satisfied.

> *"(a) Poverty and Ignorance*
> "The plaintiff wife fell within the modern equivalent of these, under the euphemisms of the twentieth century 'poor' being replaced by 'a member of the lower income group' and 'ignorant' by 'less highly educated'. Regard had also to be paid to the circumstances in which the extent of her education was to be judged: although her employment as a telephonist required considerable alertness and skill, she could properly be described as 'ignorant' in the context of property transactions in general and the execution of conveyancing documents in particular.

> *"(b) Sale at an undervalue*
> "Since the plaintiff wife in *Cresswell v Potter* only received a release from her liability under the mortgage in return for giving up all interest in the property, which had increased in value, there was clearly an undervalue.

> *"(c) Lack of independent advice*
> "There was no suggestion that the plaintiff had had any independent advice, and accordingly this third requirement was satisfied. The fact that the plaintiff knew how to get independent advice if she wanted it made no difference. The three requirements being satisfied, Megarry J set the conveyance aside..."'

9–004 Brister v Brister (sub nom. B (GC) v B (BA))

[1970] 1 All ER 913

Power to vary consent order on ground of mistake. Ormrod J (as he then was) held that the court was not precluded from entertaining the husband's application to vary the order on the ground that it was based on a mistake as to his means and a mistake as to the amount of his liability to income tax. His lordship distinguished *L v L* (9–002) saying, at page 916, that in *L v L* the wife had agreed to her application for maintenance being *dismissed*, whereas in the present case there had been nothing more than an assent that a particular sum was appropriate, with the consequent drawing up of an order for the payment of that sum without further enquiry.

His lordship continued (at page 917): '. . . the onus must be on the party seeking to vary the consent order to satisfy the court: first, that a mistake was made in consenting to the order; and secondly, that such mistake has resulted in an order which is clearly and substantially different from the order which would probably have been made in the absence of mistake. Mere assertion that the husband thought at the time that he would be able to afford to pay the agreed amount would obviously not do. Proof of a specific mistake, either by showing that the figures were wrongly stated or not fully disclosed, would probably be essential. The effect of a mistake on the other party must also be considered, even though it may not be possible to establish a formal estoppel in law.'

Note. The order concerned was an order for maintenance and was therefore capable of variation. Compare *L v L* (9–027) – no power to vary lump sum and property adjustment orders.

9–005 Wright v Wright

[1970] 3 All ER 209, CA

The clean break – no agreement can deprive court of jurisdiction to review question of maintenance for wife even when agreement approved by court – Hyman v Hyman (9–001) applied – agreement by wife not to apply for maintenance unless unforeseen circumstances rendered it impossible for her to work – agreement approved by court – subsequent application for maintenance. Following the divorce the wife found that her living expenses had increased. She therefore found it more difficult to maintain herself. Although she had not become unable to work she applied for maintenance, contrary to the terms of the agreement which had been approved by the court.

The Court of Appeal, applying *Hyman v Hyman*, held that *no agreement could deprive the court of its jurisdiction to review the question of maintenance for a wife*, notwithstanding the fact that the agreement might have been approved by the court. However, in the instant case, having regard to the circumstances in which the agreement had been arrived at, the onus was on the wife to offer at least prima facie proof that unforeseen circumstances had arisen before she could apply for maintenance. This she had failed to do, and her appeal against the judge's refusal to award her maintenance was dismissed.

Applied in *Edgar v Edgar* (9–026).

Note. Compare *L v L* (9–002), in which the agreement approved by the court and embodied in an order of the court was an agreement that the wife's application for maintenance would be *dismissed*. *L v L* was not referred to in the judgments.

9–006 Parkes v Parkes

[1971] 3 All ER 870, CA

No agreement when parties not ad idem. The husband petitioned for divorce on the ground of five years' separation. The wife opposed the petition on the ground of grave financial hardship. The parties' solicitors reached an apparent agreement whereby the petition would proceed undefended on terms that the husband would, inter alia, transfer the former matrimonial home to the wife absolutely, these terms being subject to the husband deducing a good title to the property. After the hearing the wife's solicitors, on examining the title deeds, found that the husband had conveyed a large part of the adjoining land to the woman he wished to marry. Brandon J accordingly granted a stay on the making of the decree absolute. The Court of Appeal upheld his decision. The parties were not agreed at all. The decree would not be made absolute until the court was satisfied that proper provision had been made for the wife.

Note. Although this case smacks of bad faith on the part of the husband and his advisers, the Court of Appeal treated it simply as a case of lack of consensus between the parties. Lord Denning MR said (at page 872): '... I entirely agree with what Brandon J has done. The wife's advisers only allowed the decree to go uncontested because they thought that a definite agreement had been reached under which proper provision had been made for the wife. They thought it had been done. But very shortly after the decree nisi was pronounced errors were found. The parties were not really agreed. One thought one thing, the other another, and it was all a mistake.'

9–007 Smallman v Smallman

[1971] 3 All ER 717, CA

Agreement subject to approval of court is binding on parties pending being brought before court for approval. Lord Denning MR said (at page 720): 'In my opinion, if the parties have reached an agreement on all essential matters, then the clause "subject to the approval of the court" does not mean there is no agreement at all. There is an agreement, but the operation of it is suspended until the court approves it. It is the duty of one party or the other to bring the agreement before the court for approval. If the court approves, it is binding on the parties. If the court does not approve, it is not binding. But, pending the application to the court, it remains a binding agreement which neither party can disavow. Orr LJ has drawn my attention to a useful analogy. Many contracts for the sale of goods are made subject to an export or import licence being obtained. Such a condition does not mean there is no contract at all. It is the duty of the seller, or the buyer, as the case may be, to take reasonable steps to obtain a licence. If he applies for a licence and gets it, the contract operates. If he takes all reasonable steps to obtain it, and it is refused, he is released from his obligation. If he fails to apply for it or to do what is reasonable to obtain it, he is in breach and liable to damages ...'

9–008 Hall v Hall

(1972) Times, 30 June

Agreed terms to be made rules of court. Ormrod J (as he then was) suggested that where, in a divorce suit, the terms of a compromise reached between the parties were complex, there was a good deal to be said for using the old probate practice: the parties should agree that the terms be made rules of court, and both parties should sign them. His lordship suggested that this practice should be followed as a routine measure whenever an involved order was agreed upon.

Note. See now *Practice Direction dated 26 September 1972* (9–009).

9–009 Practice Direction 26 September 1972

[1972] 3 All ER 704

Agreements between parties – lodgment of copy of terms – order approving terms.

1. In matrimonial causes where an agreement as to financial provisions has been arrived at it is frequently desired that the agreed provisions should be embodied in an order made on the hearing of the cause.

The inclusion of agreed terms in an order will usually be justified only where they are in a form capable of subsequent variation or enforcement. Thus where it is intended:—

    (a) that a party should submit to an order which it is within the statutory power of the Court to make; or

    (b) that a party should submit to an undertaking to the Court which, in the event of non-compliance, is to be enforceable by committal;

the terms of the order or undertaking must be fully set out in the order. With this type of undertaking care should be taken to see that it is in sufficiently precise terms to be enforceable.

2. The President has directed that in cases for hearing at the Royal Courts of Justice in which it is proposed to ask the Judge at the hearing of a cause to make an order embodying the terms of an agreement, or any part of them, the document setting out the agreed terms, signed by or on behalf of the parties, should be lodged with the Registrar of the Family Division at Room 770, Royal Courts of Justice, for consideration prior to the hearing and, whenever possible, at least seven days before the date of the hearing. Failure to lodge the terms in advance may result in difficulty in incorporating them in the order of the Court.

Where it is desired that terms of compromise should be filed and made a rule of Court in lieu of being embodied in an order, the same procedure should be followed, and the terms, signed as above, must contain a specific provision that they are to be filed and made a rule of Court.

3. Where the parties have reached a concluded agreement with the assistance of their legal advisers it is now rarely necessary or desirable for them to incur the considerable expense of referring such an agreement to the Judge prior to the hearing; but the procedure for so doing under section 7 (1) of the Divorce Reform Act 1969 and Rule 6 of the Matrimonial Causes Rules 1971 remains for use in exceptional cases.

4. Where, in applications for ancillary relief or as to arrangements for access to children, etc., the court is to be asked to make an order in terms agreed between the parties it is of assistance to the court as well as to the parties and their representatives, particularly if the terms are lengthy or detailed, for the provisions which it is sought to embody in the order to be set out in an agreed draft, signed by the parties or their legal advisers, and handed in at or before the hearing of the application.

5. The President's Direction dated 22 December 1966 is cancelled.

9–010 Lyle v Lyle

(1972) 3 Fam Law 41, 117 Sol Jo 70

Agreements not to be made in haste. The husband presented a petition for nullity. The wife intended to defend the petition but instead, on the day of the hearing following discussion, she presented a petition for divorce on the ground of two years' separation with consent. It was agreed that the husband's petition would be dismissed and that the wife would receive £250 immediately from the husband, £750 when she vacated the former matrimonial home and £9,000 upon the decree being made absolute.

The wife applied for rescission of the decree nisi, alleging that her former counsel and solicitors had exerted improper pressure upon her. Brandon J dismissed her application. She had received every possible help from her former counsel and solicitors and also substantial benefits from the agreement. The husband's application to have the decree made absolute was granted.

However, his lordship said that it was undesirable that agreements in divorce suits which affected the future status of spouses and regulated their financial position should be reached in any kind of a hurry. It was important for both parties to have time for reflection, particularly where a spouse who had opposed divorce came round to accept the idea. Counsel and solicitors should be on their guard against rushed agreements.

Note. See also *Backhouse v Backhouse* (9–019) and *Edgar v Edgar* (9–026).

9–010A Chamberlain v Chamberlain

[1974] 1 All ER 33, CA

Variation of agreed terms. The wife petitioned for divorce on the ground of cruelty. The petition came before Rees J on 19 January 1970, by which time the parties had agreed terms on which the petition could go undefended. These terms were notified to the court and approved by Rees J and, that being so, the petition went through undefended and a decree nisi was granted. The terms of the settlement which were agreed and approved before Rees J, so far as relevant, were as follows. The wife was to live in the former matrimonial home until remarriage or cohabitation with another man. In either event the house was to be sold and the proceeds divided equally between the parties. In the meantime, the husband was to pay the mortgage repayments and other outgoings. Some time after these terms had been agreed, and the decree made absolute, the husband lost his job and defaulted on the mortgage. The building society began foreclosure proceedings and obtained a possession order. It was suspended on the wife undertaking to pay the current outgoings, and £10 a month off the arrears which the husband had allowed to accumulate.

In view of the difficult financial position in which the wife found herself, she applied to the court for variation of the agreed terms. By the time her application came to be heard by the registrar, the husband had been able to find another job. The husband was in debt, but there was now the prospect that he would eventually be able to clear himself of his debts.

The registrar made a new order on the application to vary. He ordered that, when the house was sold, the proceeds of sale should be divided as to two-thirds to the wife and one-third to the husband, and that in the meantime *the wife* should pay the outgoings, including the mortgage instalments and arrears. He reduced the wife's maintenance to a nominal sum of 5p a year, and increased the children's maintenance.

This left the wife in a difficult financial position. Nevertheless, she managed to continue paying off the mortgage arrears at the rate of £10 per month. On appeal by the wife, the judge varied the registrar's order by extinguishing the husband's interest in the house altogether. He ordered the house to be settled on trust for sale on the wife for life and then on the children in equal shares absolutely.

The husband now appealed, on the ground that it was wrong that his interest in the property should be settled on the children. The Court of Appeal agreed, and again varied the order. The judge had been wrong to order a settlement on the children. The property would be settled on trust for sale, the sale not to take place until the children had ceased to receive full-time education or thereafter without the consent of the parties or order of the court, the proceeds of sale to be divided as to two-thirds to the wife and one-third to the husband.

Note. Compare *Thwaite v Thwaite* (9–028) – jurisdiction to set aside consent orders – see Appendix II.

9–011 Carr (GA) v Carr (DV)

[1974] 3 All ER 366

No power to backdate order for variation of maintenance agreement. By a maintenance agreement dated two days before the date of the decree absolute, the husband undertook to pay to the wife the sum of £1,050 in respect of arrears arising under a previous maintenance order. The husband also covenanted under the agreement that he would henceforth pay the wife monthly periodical payments of £1,500 per annum for herself plus a further £500 per annum in respect of their child. The husband paid the lump sum of £1,050, but paid only one monthly instalment of the agreed maintenance.

After a lapse of two years, the wife brought a claim in the Queen's Bench Division for the sum of £3,500 arrears then due, and she subsequently obtained summary judgment under Order 14. The husband appealed to Forbes J on the ground that the judgment should not have been given because an application was pending in the Family Division to vary the maintenance agreement, and on the ground that the order for variation sought could be made retrospectively.

Forbes J decided to leave the matter for decision by a judge of the Family Division. He set aside the judgment, and ordered the husband to pay £250 of the arrears to the wife's solicitors.

The husband filed an affidavit indicating that very soon after the maintenance agreement had been entered into his financial circumstances had altered, and Hollings J agreed that there might well be grounds for varying the maintenance agreement. [No agreement between the parties can deprive the court of its right to review the question of maintenance – see *Wright v Wright* (9–005) – unless it is an agreement consenting to the *dismissal* of the application for maintenance and the court makes an order to that effect – see *L v L* (9–002).] However, the question which fell to be decided by Hollings J was not whether the maintenance agreement ought to be varied, but whether any order for variation of the maintenance agreement could be backdated. His lordship held that, on a true construction of section 35 of the Matrimonial Causes Act 1973, the court had no power to backdate an order varying a maintenance agreement. The court only had jurisdiction to make an order altering or revoking the agreement from the date of the order itself.

Notes

1. *Overruled in Warden v Warden* (1981) Times, 10 June, CA. A court making an order to vary a maintenance agreement may antedate the order to meet the justice of the case. See Appendix II.
2. Leave of the court is required to sue for arrears of maintenance due under a court order where the arrears became due more than twelve months previously. See section 32 of the Matrimonial Causes Act 1973. Section 32 makes no mention of arrears due under maintenance agreements. But before the enactment of the modern legislation it was a generally accepted practice that more than one year's arrears due under court orders would not be enforced except in special circumstances (see *Luscombe v Luscombe* [1962] 1 All ER 668). Therefore, by analogy, it is presumably arguable that the same non-statutory principle will apply to arrears due under maintenance agreements today. However, the point was not taken in *Carr v Carr*.
3. Arrears of maintenance due under court orders are not recoverable by action in the Queen's Bench Division.
4. There are no proceedings in the Family Division equivalent to proceedings for summary judgment under Order 14 in the Queen's Bench Division: see *Temple v Temple* (9–015).

9–012 D v D

(1974) Times, 3 October, 118 Sol Jo 715

Increase in value of former matrimonial home no ground for variation of agreement.   Sir George Baker P said that the fact that the house had increased in value over the years, since the making of the agreement relating to the property at the time of the divorce, did not justify any variation of the agreement.

9–013 Brockwell v Brockwell

(1975) 6 Fam Law 46, CA

Agreement to transfer interest in matrimonial home to spouse in return for granting of divorce taken into account under the heading of conduct.   The matrimonial home had been purchased in the joint names of the husband and the wife. The wife, who had committed adultery, asked the husband to divorce her, but he was reluctant to do so. Eventually the parties came to an agreement, evidenced in writing, whereby the husband agreed that he would petition for divorce on the ground of the wife's adultery and the wife would transfer her interest in the matrimonial home to the husband. The agreement was entered into with the benefit of legal advice and there was no disparity of bargaining power between the parties. The wife was not under any pressure from the husband to enter into the agreement; any pressure there was came from her own emotional feelings. Furthermore, the husband subsequently acted on the agreement by bringing the divorce proceedings. Following the divorce the wife attempted to resile from the agreement and to claim (inter alia) a lump sum order.

Stamp LJ referred to *Wright v Wright* (9–005), and said that there was nothing in the Matrimonial Causes Act 1973 enabling parties to contract out of sections 23 and 24 of the Act, or to preclude the court from performing the duties imposed upon it under section 25 [see Appendix I]. However, the agreement was something to which considerable attention should be paid by the court in considering whether to exercise its discretion to award a lump sum payment.

Unfortunately, the judge had not made it clear in his judgment whether he meant that in all the circumstances he did not think it right to award a lump sum (in which case Stamp LJ would have no quarrel with the judgment); or whether he was saying that in view of the agreement he was precluded from doing so. The judge had not had the advantage of having *Wright v Wright* called to his attention, and it could be that he had taken the view that his discretion to award a lump sum was strictly curtailed by the agreement. If the judge had taken this latter view, then Stamp LJ was of the opinion that the judge had been wrong. The wife ought to have the benefit of the doubt. A new trial would be ordered before a High Court judge.

Ormrod LJ, concurring, said that he considered the agreement a very important piece of conduct to be taken into account under section 25 of the 1973 Act.

Note. In *Edgar v Edgar* (9–026) [1980] 3 All ER 887, CA, having quoted from *Hyman v Hyman* (9–001) and *Wright v Wright* (9–005) (in which the principle laid down in *Hyman v Hyman* was followed) Ormrod LJ referred to his own judgment in *Brockwell v Brockwell*, saying (at page 892):

> 'That case, of course, arose under the current Matrimonial Causes Act 1973 and, in an attempt to integrate the *Hyman v Hyman* principle with the new provisions relating to the exercise of the discretion in financial matters set out in section 25 of the Act, I suggested in my judgment in that case that an agreement not to claim a lump sum should be taken into account under the heading of conduct and added: "... when people make an agreement like this it is a very important factor in considering what is the just outcome of the proceedings." I see no reason to resile from that statement.'

The relevant passage from Ormrod LJ's judgment in *Brockwell v Brockwell* was quoted in full by Bush J in *Dean v Dean* (9–020) [1978] 3 All ER 758 at 764:

> 'But it must be a matter entirely for the judge to look at all the facts and the financial situation of each party and take into account the fact that they made this agreement which to my mind is a very important piece of conduct under s. 25 of the 1973 Act, because what the court is required to arrive at eventually is such an order as will be just and practicable having regard, among other things, to the conduct of the parties, and clearly when people make an agreement like this it is a very important factor in considering what is the just outcome of the proceedings. It may or may not represent what they themselves felt to be fair at the time when they made the agreement, and that is as good a guide to justice perhaps as anything.'

9–014 McDonald v Windaybank

(1975) 120 Sol Jo 96

Agreement to accept fixed sum in return for transfer of half interest in matrimonial home unenforceable for lack of memorandum in writing as required by Law of Property Act 1925, section 40. By a deed of gift the house had been conveyed into the joint names of the parties on trust for sale as beneficial joint tenants. The beneficial interest in the property was accordingly owned by the parties equally. On the breakdown of the marriage the parties agreed that the property was then worth £3,500, and that on any sale, after paying off the mortgage, the wife would receive about £500. In the subsequent proceedings the husband contended that a verbal agreement had been reached that the wife would accept a fixed sum of £500 in return for her interest in the house, either when she asked for it or when it was sold, and that he would be free to live in the property in the meantime.

Following the divorce the wife remarried. She claimed her half interest in the property. She served a notice severing the joint tenancy and, by an originating summons in the Chancery Division, sought an order for sale. The value of the house had greatly increased in the meantime.

Templeman J said that the husband had failed to discharge the onus resting on him of showing that the wife had agreed to accept £500 and no more. But even had he succeeded on the facts, he would still have had to overcome the technical point that, by virtue of section 40 of the Law of Property Act 1925, such an agreement would have to be evidenced in writing if it were to be enforceable. Order for sale granted.

Notes

1. Compare *L v L* (9–027), in which an agreed valuation of the former matrimonial home was placed before the court and a property adjustment order made under section 24 of the Matrimonial Causes Act 1973 based on that valuation. On the sale of the property for substantially more than the agreed valuation, the husband applied for an adjustment of the distribution of the proceeds of sale. Balcombe J held that there was no power to vary a property adjustment order. But even had there been such jurisdiction his lordship would have dismissed the husband's application. It was of benefit to all concerned that agreed valuations should be presented to the court. Those advantages would be lost if parties were able to come back to the court at a later date and say that the valuation was wrong.

2. See also *Backhouse v Backhouse* (9–019), and the cases referred to in that case summary, on the question of agreements made without the benefit of independent legal advice.

9–015 Temple v Temple

[1976] 3 All ER 12, CA

Enforcement of maintenance agreement – application for summary judgment in Queen's Bench Division – counter-application for transfer to Family Division. The wife brought a claim in the Queen's Bench Division for arrears due under a maintenance agreement, and applied for summary judgment under Order 14. At the hearing of the summons under Order 14, the master, learning that the husband had already commenced proceedings for divorce in the Family Division, including proceedings under section 17 of the Married Women's Property Act 1882, and that it was expected that there would be an application by the wife for ancillary relief, ordered the proceedings to be transferred to the Family Division. On appeal to a judge, the master's decision was reversed. The husband appealed to the Court of Appeal.

Cairns LJ said that, on balance, and as a matter of convenience, it was right that the action should continue in the Queen's Bench Division. There was no authority on the question of such transfers and it was ultimately a matter of discretion. His lordship said (at page 14): '... It is accepted that proceedings for summary judgment would not be appropriate to the Family Division. I think that the wife ought not to be deprived of the opportunity of obtaining summary judgment. I do not regard this issue as to the validity of the maintenance agreement as being one which is so intermingled with other issues which will arise on financial matters that they ought all to be tried together. If, indeed, the wife gets judgment summarily, then that part of the dispute between the parties will have been dealt with and the other financial matters can be considered in the light of it, including, among other things, the question of whether at this stage, if that maintenance agreement has been held to be a valid agreement, it should be varied.'

Notes

1. Cairns LJ said that although it was possible to enforce a judgment in the Family Division, no procedure existed in the Family Division equivalent to Order 14 proceedings in the Queen's Bench Division.

2. For an action on a maintenance agreement in which summary judgment was obtained in the Queen's Bench Division, see *Carr (GA) v Carr (DV)* (9–011).

3. Arrears of maintenance under court orders are not recoverable by action in the Queen's Bench Division.

4. The question whether or not the agreement was valid had not yet been determined. It would have been an adequate defence to the wife's application for summary judgment for the husband merely to make out a prima facie case that it was not a valid agreement. The case would then have had to have gone forward for trial by a judge on that issue. It would appear from the report that the husband might well have succeeded in making out a prima facie case, thereby well and truly throwing a spanner in the works. Had that happened, then perhaps both parties would have then agreed to the question being determined in the proceedings for ancillary relief in the Family Division, subject to the question of costs being agreed. Such are the pitfalls of Order 14 proceedings!

9–016 Pace v Doe

[1977] 1 All ER 176

Wife barred by remarriage from obtaining lump sum by way of application to vary maintenance agreement. By an agreement concluded prior to the decree nisi the husband transferred to the wife a freehold house subject to the existing mortgage and agreed to pay the mortgage repayments and maintenance for the wife and children. Following the making of the decree absolute the wife remarried and her maintenance ceased, but the husband continued to make the mortgage repayments until they were paid off. The wife applied under section 35 of the Matrimonial Causes Act 1973 to vary the maintenance agreement. She asked that the children's maintenance be increased and secured. By a further application she asked that the agreement be varied to provide a lump sum for herself and the children.

The first matter for consideration was whether there was still a subsisting agreement in existence capable of variation. Counsel for the husband argued that the agreement was now subsisting only in respect of the children, and that it was not enforceable by the wife because of an undertaking given by the wife on the making of an order for maintenance of the children not to seek to enforce payment of any sums under the terms of the maintenance agreement. However, Sir George Baker P said that, at the date of the summons for variation, although the wife had remarried and her periodical payments had ceased, the mortgage repayments were still being made, so the wife still had an interest in the agreement herself at the operative date. Furthermore, the children's maintenance remained, albeit in abeyance. The question now was whether the wife could take advantage of the fact that the agreement was still subsisting to have a further clause added for her own benefit, and the vital question was whether the wife by her remarriage had put herself completely out of court.

On this question, his lordship said that to make an original application to the court for a lump sum under section 23 of the Matrimonial Causes Act 1973 after remarriage is expressly prohibited by section 28 (3) of the Act, and it would be contrary to the philosophy of the Act to permit the wife to obtain a lump sum after remarriage by means of an application to vary the maintenance agreement. In his lordship's view, there was no jurisdiction to vary the agreement in such a manner after remarriage.

Note. Sir George Baker P added that, even if there *was* jurisdiction to vary the maintenance agreement by ordering a lump sum to be paid to the wife after her remarriage, he would not allow such a variation in the present case in view of the wife's remarriage.

9–017 Wales v Wadham

[1977] 2 All ER 125

Consent order valid notwithstanding wife's failure to disclose intention to remarry.   Following negotiations between the parties' solicitors, an agreement was subsequently reached between counsel whereby the husband would pay the wife a sum of £13,000 out of his share of the proceeds of sale of the former matrimonial home in full and final settlement of the wife's claim for maintenance, on the wife undertaking not to make any further claim for maintenance in the future. The agreement was embodied in a consent order made on the granting of the decree nisi. Following the making of the decree absolute the wife remarried. The wife had at no time revealed her intention to remarry. Neither party had sworn any affidavit of means before the consent order was made. On the husband learning of the wife's remarriage he brought an action claiming rescission of the agreement and a declaration that the consent order be set aside.

Tudor Evans J held that there were no grounds for rescission of the agreement, and therefore no grounds for setting aside the consent order. Firstly, the husband had not been induced to enter into the agreement by false representations by the wife that she would not remarry. Secondly, he had not entered into the agreement under a unilateral mistake of fact; he had entered into the agreement with the possibility of the wife remarrying in mind. And thirdly, the wife was not under any duty to disclose that she intended to remarry. She was not under a contractual duty to do so; the agreement was not a contract uberrima fides, and the agreement had been reached before the wife's duty to file an affidavit of means had arisen and was an agreement made without full disclosure by either party.

Notes
1. Counsel for the wife accepted that as soon as a duty to file an affidavit of means arises a firm intention to remarry must be disclosed.
2. Tudor Evans J said that there might be circumstances in which there is a duty to make full disclosure even before a duty to file an affidavit of means arises.

9–017A Harte v Harte

(1976) Times, 3 December, CA

Agreement to compromise appeal valid – appeal stayed.   The husband had obtained leave from the Court of Appeal to appeal against a financial provision order. Immediately thereafter, negotiations were started between the parties. They subsequently concluded an agreement for the settlement of the issues in dispute. The husband argued that no agreement had been reached and that, in any event, such an agreement would be unenforceable under section 34 of the Matrimonial Causes Act 1973 as an agreement restricting the right to apply to the court for financial provision.

The Court of Appeal held that the letters passing between the parties' solicitors amounted to a binding agreement. The agreement did not contain any provision restricting the right to apply to the court. Even if it had contained such a provision, only that provision would have been void; the rest of the agreement would still have been enforceable. Furthermore, there was now no need to obtain the sanction of the court to an agreement to compromise an appeal. In *Brockwell v Brockwell* (9–013), Stamp LJ had said that parties could not contract out of sections 23 and 24 of the 1973 Act, but he did not say that parties were unable to compromise appeals. The appeal would be stayed.

9–018 Ladbrook v Ladbrook

(1977) 7 Fam Law 213, 121 Sol Jo 710

Application to vary consent order – no power to vary order for sale – application for further capital provision refused.   At the time of the divorce the parties agreed that the former matrimonial home be sold and that the wife receive £9,000 out of the proceeds of sale or one-half of the net sale proceeds, whichever be the greater. A consent order was made to that effect without the wife making any application to the court for financial provision. No acceptable offer was made for the house, and the husband agreed to the sale being postponed while the child was still at school. The child was now at university, and the husband's application to enforce the order for sale was granted. The wife appealed; she applied for a lump sum order or a transfer of property order and for an order varying the agreement underlying the consent order.

Dunn J said that it had been conceded from the beginning of the hearing that the agreement was not a maintenance agreement and so could not be varied under section 35 of the Matrimonial Causes Act 1973. *Nor was there power under section 31 of the Act to vary an order for sale.* It was, however, open to the wife to apply for a lump sum or transfer of property order, under sections 23 and 24 because, as a respondent who had not filed an answer, she was entitled to make an application any time after divorce. But her counsel conceded that her applications under sections 23 and 24 were an attempt to circumvent the consent order. Counsel for the husband referred to *Brister v Brister* (9–004) and *Wright v Wright* (9–005), and argued that, even where there was jurisdiction to vary a consent order, the court would not readily do so. Dunn J held that the agreement had been freely negotiated at arm's length with both parties legally represented, and the parties should stick to their bargains. It would not be just to order the husband to make further capital provision. Appeal dismissed. No order on the wife's application.

9–019 Backhouse v Backhouse

[1978] 1 All ER 1158

Time of stress – inequality of bargaining power – lack of independent legal advice. Balcombe J said (at page 1165) that the time of marriage breakdown was a time of great emotional stress, and that the court should look with circumspection on any transfer of property made by one spouse to the other without the benefit of independent legal advice. His lordship held that in this case there had been no duress coercing the wife into signing the transfer of her joint interest in the former matrimonial home to the husband. However, because of the fact that at the time of the transfer she had not had the benefit of independent legal advice and of the fact that there had been inequality of bargaining power, his lordship said that he would accordingly disregard the transfer and approach the case on the basis that it had not been made. *Cresswell v Potter* (9–003) and *Lloyds Bank Ltd v Bundy* [1974] 3 All ER 757, CA applied.

Note. In *Hanlon v Law Society* [1980] 2 All ER 199 at 206, HL Lord Simon referred with approval to the passage from Lord Denning MR's judgment in the Court of Appeal that: 'The court takes the rights and obligations of the parties all together, and puts the pieces into a mixed bag. Such pieces are the right to occupy the matrimonial home or have a share in it, the obligation to maintain the wife and children, and so forth. The court then takes out the pieces and hands them to the two parties, some to one party and some to the other, so that each can provide for the future with the pieces allotted to him or her. The court hands them out without paying any too nice a regard to their legal or equitable rights but simply according to what is the fairest provision for the future, for mother and father and the children.'

9–020 Dean v Dean

[1978] 3 All ER 758

Duty of court to consider agreement under section 25 of the Matrimonial Causes Act 1973 before making order in terms of agreement under sections 23 or 24. Prior to the filing of the petition for divorce the parties had reached agreement as to financial provision. Each party had been separately advised. The husband's petition stated that draft minutes of agreement would be submitted to the court for approval.

Subsequently, minutes of agreement were drawn up in two parts, headed: 'Draft Minutes of Order to be submitted for approval by a Registrar with a view to incorporation in the Order made on Decree Nisi'. One part was signed by each party. The registrar had already given his certificate that the husband was entitled to a decree nisi under the special procedure. He duly amended it by adding the words: 'And to an order in the terms of the draft minutes of order signed by the [wife] on the 12th September 1977 and signed by the [husband] on the 21st September 1977, both as amended by me on the 30th September 1977'. The amendment by the registrar was merely to insert the common form of order relating to the children. Within two weeks after having signed her part of the minutes of agreement, the wife sent a telegram to her solicitors which read: 'Stop all court proceedings. Having second thoughts.' The registrar was told that the wife had changed her mind, and again amended his certificate by deleting the reference to the agreed order.

The petition came before the county court judge under the special procedure. The judge stood the suit over for 14 days, directing the wife to file an affidavit to show cause why the minutes of agreement should not be made an order of the court, and he transferred the issue to a judge of the Family Division. Decree nisi was subsequently pronounced without prejudice to the issue.

Bush J said that on the authority of *Smallman v Smallman* (9–007) an agreement subject to the approval of the court was binding on the parties unless the court refused to approve it. But on the making of any order under sections 23 or 24 of the Matrimonial Causes Act 1973, the court had a duty to consider the matter under section 25 of the Act (see Appendix I). Moreover, even where under the special procedure a registrar had certified that the petitioner was entitled to an order in agreed terms, the judge who had to pronounce the decree remained under a duty to consider the reasonableness of the agreement in accordance with section 25.

It was clear from the wording of the registrar's certificate that the registrar was only saying that in his view the husband was entitled to an order in the agreed terms in due course. The registrar did not make an order in the agreed terms. Indeed there was no jurisdiction to make the order until on or after the decree nisi. The judge having transferred the issue to the High Court for consideration by his lordship, it was now his lordship's duty to consider the whole matter under section 25.

In exercising his duty under section 25 his lordship had to have regard to the conduct of the parties in all the circumstances. The conduct of the parties in this context included the fact of and the nature of an agreement voluntarily arrived at between the parties. Where such an agreement had been reached at arm's length and the parties had been separately advised, the agreement itself would be prima facie evidence of the reasonableness of its terms, and would be taken into account when considering the conduct of the parties under section 25.

In performing its duty under section 25 (1) of the Act where there was an agreement between the parties, the court should adopt a broad approach, taking into account that the court had a duty to uphold agreements which had been validly arrived at and which were not against public policy.

Taking into account all the circumstances, the agreement made reasonable provision for the wife and she should be held to it. Accordingly, the wife not having shown cause to the contrary, the minutes would be incorporated in an order of the court.

Note. This agreement was made *subject to approval by the court*. But the ratio decidendi of the case was that whenever the court was asked to make an order under section 23 or 24 the mandatory effect of section 25 operated. (See also *Brockwell v Brockwell* (9–013), in which the agreement was *not* subject to the court's approval.) Counsel for the husband raised the fear that the courts would have an impossible task, particularly under the special procedure, if every proposed financial consent order had to be examined minutely. Bush J said that, in the general run of cases, all that was necessary was the attendance of solicitors or the parties at the appropriate stage ready to answer any relevant questions. Under the special procedure it might well be convenient for the registrar to certify that the petitioner was entitled to an order in the agreed terms, and that might be sufficient to satisfy the judge who, under the special procedure, pronounced the decree in open court without any of the parties being in attendance. But it did not relieve the judge who was making an order by virtue of section 23 or section 24 of his primary duty under section 25 to see that the proposed order was just.

9–021 Minton v Minton

[1979] 1 All ER 79, HL

The clean break – jurisdiction to award maintenance cannot be ousted by private agreement – Hyman v Hyman (9–001) explained – but it is otherwise when the agreement is brought before the court and an order is made giving effect to its terms dismissing the wife's application for periodical payments – L v L (9–002) approved – consent order – nominal order for periodical payments to cease on conveyance of house to wife – genuine final order equivalent to a dismissal of wife's application for periodical payments – no jurisdiction to entertain second application. See case summary 10–205.

9–021A Brown v Brown

(1978) 9 Fam Law 216, CA

The clean break – private agreement between parties upheld. In 1971 the husband commenced proceedings for divorce on the ground of the wife's adultery. Following protracted negotiations between the parties in which both were represented by solicitors, and in which the wife, in particular, was represented by a very experienced counsel, an agreement was concluded in May 1972 in which the wife agreed to accept a lump sum in full and final satisfaction of all claims against the husband. In June 1972 the suit was heard undefended and decree nisi pronounced. *Evidence of the agreement was given at the hearing but no order of the court was sought in the terms agreed and no order made dismissing the wife's claims for financial provision.* The decree was subsequently made absolute.

Some four years later, in August 1976, the wife made application for periodical payments, a lump sum order and a transfer of property order. In her application she undertook that if such relief were granted she would not seek to enforce the agreement of May 1972.

Bush J held that the registrar had been correct in taking the view that the agreement did not preclude the court from reviewing its terms. [See *Wright v Wright* (9–005).] However, his lordship went on to refer to an attendance note in which the wife's solicitor was recorded as having warned the wife prior to the making of the agreement that only in the direst circumstances would she be able to go back to the court and seek a variation of the agreement once it was concluded. The attendance note also recorded that the wife had said that she understood this, and that she wished to enter into the agreement in view of the fact that she preferred the lump sum to maintenance. His lordship also pointed out that the wife's attitude had not changed when she appeared before him. Before his lordship she had said that she wished to be independent and to cut all ties, and had again said that she would prefer a lump sum to an award of maintenance.

A further point at issue was that the agreement had been concluded prior to the clarification of the modern legislation provided by *Wachtel v Wachtel* (7–101), and the fact that, in those circumstances, counsel who had advised the wife had approached the matter on the basis of the Married Women's Property Act 1882 rather than on the basis of the modern legislation. In consequence, the husband's interest in a holiday home had not been taken into account; and the wife's interest in the former matrimonial home had been valued strictly in accordance with her rights of ownership acquired by virtue of her financial contributions towards the family purse without taking into account her contribution in kind to the family over the years. However, Bush J went on to say that he could not conceive that it was the function of the court to upset an agreement merely because one party had received advice which was thought to be good law at the time but which subsequently turned out to be wrong.

The wife appealed to the Court of Appeal. Orr LJ said that the crucial question was the relative weight to be given, on the one hand, to the fact that the agreement had been reached before the guidelines as to the effect of the modern legislation had been laid down in *Wachtel v Wachtel* and, on the other hand, to the principle that an agreement entered into with skilled advice on both sides ought not lightly to be upset. His lordship considered that Bush J had properly weighed these conflicting considerations and had come to a proper conclusion. Lawton and Cumming-Bruce LJJ agreed. The wife's appeal was dismissed.

9–022 de Lasala v de Lasala

[1979] 2 All ER 1146, PC

The clean break – consent order dismissing wife's application for periodical payments – no jurisdiction to entertain second application – Minton v Minton (9–021) applied.　See case summary 10–206.

9–023 Jessel v Jessel

[1979] 3 All ER 645, CA

The clean break – consent order – agreement to accept periodical payments order in settlement of all claims for periodical payments – undertaking not to apply to increase husband's liability – application to vary – order not a 'once and for all' order – jurisdiction retained by court to entertain application to vary continuing order for periodical payments – Minton v Minton (9–021) distinguished.　On the making of the decree nisi, an agreement that the wife should accept the agreed periodical payments order in settlement of all her claims to periodical payments, and her undertaking not to apply to increase the husband's liability, were made a rule of the court. Four years after the decree absolute, the wife applied for increased maintenance.

Lord Denning MR said that the original agreement restricting the right of the wife to make further application to the court was void, under what was now section 34 of the Matrimonial Causes Act 1973. *Minton v Minton* only applied when an application for periodical payments had been dismissed, or when there was a genuine final order equivalent to a dismissal, or containing no continuing provision for periodical payments. In the present case, there was a continuing order capable of variation under section 31 of the 1973 Act. The payments were to be for 'joint lives or . . . until further order'. The words 'until further order' kept the provision alive. It was doubtful whether making the agreement a rule of court could validate it if it was void. It was contrary to public policy that a maintenance agreement should be made unalterably binding on a wife: *Hyman v Hyman* (9–001). The only exception was *Minton v Minton* where there was a 'clean break' and 'once and for all' provision.

Note. For a discussion of the above statement by Lord Denning MR as to the cases in which the *Minton v Minton* principle of the clean break applies, see notes 3 and 4 to the summary of *Minton v Minton* at 10–205.

9–024 Tilley v Tilley

(1979) 10 Fam Law 89, CA

Variation of consent order for payment of lump sum by instalments.　Following the pronouncement of the decree nisi, a consent order was made vesting two properties in the wife in consideration of the wife making instalment payments to the husband. It was part of the agreed order that the husband's maintenance liability should be merely a nominal 5p per year. The wife fell into financial difficulties and applied for variation of the consent order, on the basis that she could not pay the balance of the instalments amounting to £3,500 now due without selling the roof over her head and rendering herself and the children homeless.

Donaldson LJ said that counsel for the husband had urged on the court the necessity of maintaining the sanctity of consent orders, particularly where consent was given with the aid of skilled advice. *However, the fact that execution of the order would render a family and, above all, the children homeless was the paramount consideration in this case.* The order would be varied by providing that there should be no further payments made to the husband, but that if there were any future application for maintenance for the children, any court faced with such an application ought to take into consideration the £3,500 which the husband would have in effect contributed towards their maintenance.

Note. For further details, see case summary 4–110.

9–024A Hulley v Thompson

[1981] 1 All ER 1128

Husband's continuing liability to maintain children notwithstanding consent order transferring his interest in matrimonial home to wife.   See Appendix II.

Note. See also *Tilley v Tilley* (9–024).

9–025 Allsop v Allsop

(1980) 124 Sol Jo 710, CA

Consent order set aside on ground of fraud.   In reliance on an affidavit sworn by the husband to the effect that he was overdrawn at his bank, the wife agreed to a consent order being made under which the husband was to pay an agreed lump sum to the wife. It was later discovered that the husband had a substantial sum in a joint account in another bank. The wife applied to have the consent order set aside. The husband swore a further affidavit admitting fraud, but he claimed that the registrar had no power to set aside the consent order. Ormrod LJ said that, generally, a final order could be set aside on the ground of fraud only by a separate action, which was necessary in order to prove the fraud. But where, as here, the fraud was admitted, there was no need for a fresh action. The registrar's order setting aside the consent order was upheld by the Court of Appeal.

Notes
1. Ormrod LJ said that the court had power to set aside an interlocutory order on the grounds of mistake, misrepresentation or fraud without a separate action being required: *Mullins v Howell* (1879) 11 Ch D 763.
2. For an example of a consent order being set aside on the ground of mistake, see *Brister v Brister* (9–004).
3. See also *Wales v Wadham* (9–017).

9–026 Edgar v Edgar

[1980] 3 All ER 887, CA

Agreement not to claim lump sum taken into account under heading of conduct.   Prior to the divorce the parties entered into a deed of separation under which the husband agreed (inter alia) to purchase a house for the wife in her own name and to confer other very substantial capital benefits upon her. The deed contained a clause whereby the wife agreed that if she obtained a divorce she would not claim a lump sum or any transfer of property order. The parties entered into the agreement after receiving independent legal advice. The husband did not put pressure on the wife to accept the terms of the deed and in no way exploited his position as a wealthy man.

The husband duly carried out his obligations under the agreement. The wife then filed a petition for divorce containing a prayer for full ancillary relief and pursued her claim for a lump sum payment under section 23 of the Matrimonial Causes Act 1973. The Court of Appeal dismissed her application for a lump sum.

Ormrod LJ, referring to *Hyman v Hyman* (9–001), said, at page 891, that the wife could not by her own covenant preclude herself from invoking the jurisdiction of the court, and that the court therefore had jurisdiction to entertain her application. His lordship then referred to *Wright v Wright* (9–005), in which the principle laid down by the House of Lords in *Hyman v Hyman* was applied notwithstanding the fact that the agreement had been approved by the court. However, continuing at page 893, his lordship said: 'I agree with Sir Gordon Willmer in *Wright v Wright* [1970] 3 All ER 209 at 214 that the existence of an agreement –

"... at least makes it necessary for the wife, if she is to justify an award of maintenance, to offer prima facie proof that there have been unforeseen circumstances in the true sense, which make it impossible for her to work or otherwise maintain herself."

Adapting that statement to the present case, it means that the wife here must offer prima facie evidence of material facts which show that justice requires that she should be relieved from the effects of her covenant in clause 8 of the deed of separation, and awarded further capital provision.'

Ormrod LJ said that he came to the conclusion that there was no evidence which reflected adversely on the husband's conduct in the negotiations, and no adequate explanation of the wife's conduct in seeking to resile from the agreement. Accordingly, having had regard to the conduct of the parties and to all the circumstances of the case under section 25 of the 1973 Act, there were no grounds for holding that justice required the court to relieve the wife from her covenant under the deed.

Oliver LJ, concurring, said that under the separation agreement the wife had achieved the independence she desired, a home of her own choosing and a not insubstantial income. This was something which had commended itself to her at the time, and it did not become unjust merely because she could have done better had she taken the professional advice she had been given. Her reasons for seeking to resile from the agreement appeared to be that she felt unable to offer her children amenities comparable to those which her wealthy husband was able to offer, and that she would like to buy a farm and to have a house in London. The bargain had been freely entered into with the benefit of legal advice, and she should be held to that bargain.

Notes

1. Ormrod LJ explained his reasoning behind his reference to conduct by referring to his judgment in *Brockwell v Brockwell*. See the authors' notes to the summary of that case at 9–013.

2. See also *Dean v Dean* (9–020) on the subject of the court's duty under section 25 of the Act in cases where the parties have reached agreement. In that case Bush J said that where an agreement has been reached at arm's length and the parties have been separately advised, the agreement itself would be prima facie evidence of the reasonableness of its terms, and should be taken into account when considering the conduct of the parties under section 25.

9–026A Chanel Ltd v FW Woolworth & Co Ltd

[1981] 1 All ER 745

Grounds for setting aside consent order – point at issue subsequently decided by Court of Appeal in another case – rehearing refused. Foster J said that a party was not entitled to a rehearing of an interlocutory matter unless there had been some significant change of circumstances or he had become aware of facts which he could not reasonably have known or found out by the time of the original hearing.

It had been open to the defendants at the original hearing to take the point subsequently decided by the Court of Appeal. They did not do so. The defendants would not be allowed to reopen the case.

Notes

1. See also *Brown v Brown* (9–021A) – agreement inter partes concluded prior to clarification of modern law – not the function of the court to upset agreement merely because party received advice which was thought to be good law at the time but which subsequently turned out to be wrong.
2. Compare *Thwaite v Thwaite* (9–028) – fresh evidence adduced – consent order set aside – see Appendix II.
3. Compare *Allsop v Allsop* (9–025) – consent order set aside on ground of fraud.
4. Compare *Brister v Brister* (9–004) – consent order set aside on ground of mistake of fact.

9–027 L v L

(1980) Times, 13 November

Agreed valuation of former matrimonial home – no power to adjust undervaluation after making of order for capital provision under sections 23 and 24 of Matrimonial Causes Act 1973. Balcombe J dismissed the husband's application for adjustment of the distribution of the net sale proceeds after the property had sold for £7,500 more than the agreed valuation. His lordship said that the court had no jurisdiction to vary lump sum orders or property adjustment orders. But even had the court had jurisdiction, his lordship would still have dismissed the application. Parties were not compelled to agree a valuation, but by doing so time and costs were saved. The parties had agreed a valuation, with all the advantages of so doing. Those advantages would be lost if parties were able to come back and say that the circumstances had changed because the valuation had now turned out to be an undervaluation.

Notes

1. Compare *Brister v Brister* (9–004), *Parkes v Parkes* (9–006) and *Allsop v Allsop* (9–025).
2. Compare *Tilley v Tilley* (9–024) – order for payment of lump sum by instalments – not a 'once-and-for-all' order – capable of variation.

9–028 Thwaite v Thwaite

[1981] 2 All ER 789, CA

Jurisdiction to set aside consent orders. See Appendix II.

Note. Compare *Chamberlain v Chamberlain* (9–010A) – variation of agreed terms.

9–028A Re Fullard

[1981] 2 All ER 796, CA

Agreement entered into with benefit of legal advice likely to preclude successful application under Inheritance (Provision for Family and Dependants) Act 1975. After negotiations following the divorce, the husband conveyed his half share in the former matrimonial home to the wife in return for an agreed payment of £4,500, amounting to one half of the value of the property. The agreement was reached with the benefit of independent legal advice. The husband died within 13 months after the making of the decree absolute, leaving £7,100. The greater part of his estate consisted of the £4,500 paid to him by the wife. The wife applied for financial provision out of the estate. The judge dismissed the application, and the wife's appeal was dismissed by the Court of Appeal.

The Court of Appeal held that the fact that the applicant had been divorced from the deceased and the terms of the financial arrangements made by them on the divorce were relevant when considering an application under the Inheritance (Provision for Family and Dependants) Act 1975.

Purchas J, however, went further. His Lordship said (at page 803 at letter h): '... the approach [the judge] made (which I respectfully adopt) is that where the parties have with the assistance of legal advisers clearly gone into the whole situation, it must weigh heavily with the court in considering the various criteria, and in particular the matters referred to under s. 3 (1) and (2) [of the 1975 Act] . . .'

Note. Ormrod LJ added that s. 15 of the 1975 Act provides a form of security against applications such as this, and that the court and legal advisers might be well advised to remember s. 15 when considering the terms of financial provision on divorce and, if they can persuade the other side to agree, to write in a consent order that neither party to the marriage shall be entitled on the death of the other party to apply for an order under the 1975 Act. However, notwithstanding the fact that no such order had been made on the divorce, the Court of Appeal held that this did not materially affect the question the court had to answer. The passage from Purchas J's judgment at page 803, letter h quoted above in part reads as follows: '. . . He [the judge] had in mind (and referred to) s. 15 of the 1975 Act and commented that nothing was done under that section to prevent the applicant from coming back to the court, but the approach he made (which I respectfully adopt) is that, where the parties have with the assistance of legal advisers clearly gone into the whole situation, it must weigh heavily with the court in considering the various criteria, and in particular the matters referred to under s. 3 (1) and (2).'

9–029 Warden v Warden

(1981) Times, 10 June, [1981] 3 All ER 193, CA

Power to backdate order for variation of maintenance agreement. See Appendix II.
  Note. Carr (GA) v Carr (DV) (9–011) overruled.

CHAPTER 10

The clean break

As was suggested in the previous chapter, the clean break principle operates as one of the two fundamental principles by reference to which the court may choose to exercise its jurisdiction. The principle as generally understood was perhaps best defined by Lord Scarman in *Minton v Minton* (10–205):

'There are two principles which inform the modern legislation. One is the public interest that spouses, to the extent that their means permit, should provide for themselves and their children. But the other – of equal importance – is the principle of "the clean break". The law now encourages spouses to avoid bitterness after family breakdown and to settle their money and property problems. An object of the modern law is to encourage each to put the past behind them and to begin a new life which is not overshadowed by the relationship which has broken down.'

However noble this concept is, it is already apparent that there is a degree of misunderstanding as to whether the clean break principle can be imposed by the courts on parties who have not come to any agreement. It is certainly now possible for parties to achieve absolute finality in respect of claims for themselves. For example, the court clearly operates the principle of the clean break when it dismisses an application by consent on terms referred to in an order, or when it makes an order the terms of which are based on the parties' agreement. *Minton v Minton*, now applied in *de Lasala v de Lasala* (10–206), is the clearest authority for the proposition that applications for financial orders (in respect of the parties themselves, but *not* children) cannot be re-opened when such a re-application is inconsistent with an earlier consent order of the court. However, the largest area of uncertainty concerning what is generally considered to be the clean break principle involves the recent uncertainty as to whether a wife's claim for periodical payments can be dismissed without her consent. There are conflicting decisions, all of them relatively recent, about this question. See *Dipper v Dipper* (10–209), *Dunford v Dunford* (10–103) and *Carter v Carter* (10–208). It is respectfully submitted that the preponderance of authority is to the effect that a claim for periodical payments may only be dismissed by consent. In any event, it is clear that in practice a general understanding that dismissal of a maintenance claim can only be achieved by consent does in fact operate as an inducement to parties to achieve a negotiated settlement which is consistent with a clean break (as widely understood). For example, a husband who has left the matrimonial home leaving the wife in occupation is much more inclined to abandon his interest in the capital invested therein if, in return, he has the knowledge that the wife is abandoning her claim for maintenance for all time. Whether this sort of negotiated outcome is at all possible obviously depends on many variable factors, for example, the size of the capital sum which is invested in the home and the likely value to a husband of being free of a maintenance order against him. (This latter often depends on the wife's prospects of remarriage, which may be known to her but not to him.)

The clean break principle (as now widely understood) can embrace rather different concepts, ranging from the absolute finality of orders to the (much wider) idea of attempting to achieve an order which means that the outcome of the matrimonial home is settled forthwith rather than delayed whilst children are being educated. But in actual practice, most cases do involve parties who have children of school age. In most of these cases the children are still residing in a house which in the overall context of the capital position is far and away too valuable for a husband to wish to forfeit his capital rather than pay maintenance. In these, unhappily typical, cases the wider concept of a clean break must be of little effect. In one other sense it is also important to remember that the clean break cannot normally apply in cases where there are children; it has always been the case that a party cannot by negotiated agreement forfeit the right of a child to a maintenance order (for the right exists in the child's own name). It follows that existing orders in respect of children will always be open to review by the courts. *See Carter v Carter.*

1 Capital provision

CASE SUMMARIES

10–101 Coleman v Coleman

[1972] 3 All ER 886

No jurisdiction to entertain second application for lump sum order after granting of previous application. Following the divorce the wife obtained an order that the husband pay her a lump sum of £2,000 from the proceeds of sale of the former matrimonial home, such sum to be made available as soon as possible after completion of the sale, together with a further lump sum of £5,500 from the sale proceeds, such sum to be made available to her through her solicitors and to be invested in a home to be occupied by her and the child of the family until such time as the wife remarried or the child attained the age of 18 years or left home. The £2,000 was paid, but the £5,500 was not because the wife wished to emigrate and to take the £5,500 with her. She applied for a further order that the husband should pay her such further lump sum as might be just.

Sir George Baker P said (at page 890) that the primary question was one of jurisdiction. Counsel for the husband submitted that the court, having made an order under section 2 (1) (c) of the Matrimonial Proceedings and Property Act 1970 [now re-enacted as section 23 (1) (c) of the Matrimonial Causes Act 1973 – see Appendix I] for a lump sum or sums, had no power to entertain a further application. Section 2 (1) provides:

> 'On granting a decree of divorce ... or *at any time thereafter* ... the court may ... make any one or more of the following orders, that is to say ... (c) *an order* that either party to the marriage shall pay to the other *such lump sum or sums* as may be so specified'.

His lordship continued (at page 891): '. . . The essence of the argument of the husband . . . is that, if the legislature intended to give the wife a right to claim a second order for a lump sum, it would have said so, and that section (2) (1) (c) of the 1970 Act gives the court power only to make *an order*, not orders; and that the sum or sums must be specified in one order . . .

'A lump sum payment is, of course, once and for all, in that it is not returnable by the wife if she should remarry after receiving it, or on any other contingency, at least in the absence of conditions of the kind placed on the £5,500 in the present case. It is also once and for all in the sense that she cannot come back for more in the absence of fraud or non-disclosure of the husband's assets.'

Continuing, at page 892, his lordship said: 'In support of the contention that the jurisdiction of the court is to make "an order" and no more than one order, counsel for the husband submits that this is the ordinary meaning of the phrase: "the court may . . . make . . . an order". If the intention had been otherwise there would be a provision that the power to make such an order should be exercisable *from time to time*, as is the power to order payment of a lump sum . . . for the benefit of or to a child . . .' [See now section 23 (4) of the 1973 Act – see Appendix I.]

'Counsel for the husband further relies on the decision of the Court of Appeal in *L v L* (10–201). There . . . Willmer LJ said:

"If, as I think, jurisdiction to entertain such a second application did not exist before, I cannot construe the provisions of the [Matrimonial Causes (Property and Maintenance) Act 1958] as conferring it. All that is provided by section 1 is that any power of the court to award maintenance under section 19 of the [Matrimonial Causes Act 1950] may be exercised *either* on pronouncing the decree of divorce, *or* at any time thereafter. That is to say, the section merely enlarges the time within which an existing power of the court may be exercised. I agree with the submission of counsel for the husband that, *if the legislature had intended to confer a new right to make a second application for maintenance in a case where a previous application had been dismissed, it would be reasonable to expect that such a provision would have been expressed in clear and unambiguous terms . . .*"

He [Willmer LJ] then contrasted once-for-all orders with those which could be made in respect of custody, maintenance and education of children "from time to time" under section 26 of the 1950 Act. Davies LJ, having referred to the argument that there was no limit to the number of applications which could be made by a wife for permanent maintenance said:

"[The] argument goes . . . that, if a wife has made, for example, fifteen applications for maintenance, each one of which has been dismissed . . . she is nevertheless entitled to make thereafter a subsequent application with a view to re-litigating the question all over again. *In effect, that would mean that the words 'at any time thereafter' would be almost equivalent to 'at any number of times thereafter'. In my judgment, that is plainly wrong.*"

Continuing (on page 893) Sir George Baker P said: '*It follows that the words "or at any time thereafter" in section 2 (1) in the 1970 Act must have been used by the legislature in the sense in which they were construed in L v L: see Maxwell on the Interpretation of Statutes.*' His lordship accordingly held that the purpose of the words 'lump sum or sums' in section 2 (1) (c) was merely to enable the court to provide for more than one lump sum payment in any order, and that they did not give the court power to make a second order. Accordingly, the court had no jurisdiction to entertain the wife's application.

Note. Compare *Tilley v Tilley* (9–024) – order for payment of lump sum by instalments – not a 'once-and-for-all' order – capable of variation.

10–102 Hanlon v Hanlon

[1978] 2 All ER 889, [1978] 1 WLR 592, CA

Desirability of crystallising parties' interests in former matrimonial home once and for all.   The matrimonial home had been purchased in the sole name of the husband, although during the 14 years of the marriage the husband and wife had contributed equally in money and work to the family. The parties had now lived apart for over five years. The wife remained in the house with the four children while the husband, a police officer, now lived in a flat provided rent-free by his employers. The judge at first instance ordered that the house be transferred into joint names on trust for sale in equal shares, the sale to be postponed until the youngest child, then 12, had attained 17.

Ormrod LJ said that it was not right to regard the interests of the husband and wife in the house as being equal because the wife had, in the five years since the separation, maintained it and looked after the family and would continue to do so until they left home, and had therefore made a very large contribution to the family. As one-half of the equity on the eventual sale of the house could not produce a sum sufficient to enable the wife to buy another home for herself and such of the children as were still with her, it would be wrong to make an order which would have the result of forcing the wife to leave the house when the youngest child attained the age of 17. As she was willing to forgo any further periodical payments for the two children who were under 17, the proper order was to transfer the house to the wife absolutely.

Ormrod LJ said (at page 895): '. . . It was suggested that this might be the kind of case which could be met by postponing the sale indefinitely until further order, and then distributing the proceeds of sale, not necessarily on a 50-50 basis; but I do not think that that, in this case, would be in the least satisfactory; it would leave the wife in a state of perpetual uncertainty and neither party would know where ultimately they were going to be. It seems to me far better that the parties' interests should be crystallised now, once and for all, so that the wife can know what she is going to do about the property and the husband can make up his mind about what he is going to do about rehousing.'

Notes
1. Regarding the subsisting order for periodical payments for the two minor children of £7 per week each, Ormrod LJ said (at page 894): '. . . *If she is prepared to forgo any further periodical payments for the two children (she cannot of course bind herself not to make application for maintenance* [for the children in the future] *and she cannot bind the children, but she can indicate that it is not her intention in certain circumstances to seek contribution from the husband . . .*) he will save a substantial sum of money.' It should be noted that Ormrod LJ was here speaking of *further periodical payments for the children,* not for the wife herself. Neither party can bind themselves not to make any further application for maintenance *for the children* and neither party can bind the children – see *Minton v Minton* (10–205). In *Hanlon v Hanlon* the order for the children's maintenance was not discharged but was merely reduced to a nominal sum. In this way, the wife would not be precluded from applying for variation of the order for their maintenance in the future. However, even if the order for the children's maintenance had been discharged, the wife would still have been able to apply afresh for an order for their maintenance in the future – see *Minton v Minton*.
2. The wife was earning as much as the husband and no order was made for the maintenance of the wife herself.
3. It would be wrong to interpret the passage in Ormrod LJ's judgment quoted above as authority that a wife cannot bind herself not to make application for maintenance *for herself* in the future. Firstly, this passage was dealing solely with the question of maintenance *for the children.* Secondly, the House of Lords has now expressly held, in *Minton v Minton,* that a wife *can* bind herself not to make any future application for maintenance *for herself.*
4. This passage in Ormrod LJ's judgment implies that the wife was prepared to forgo any further periodical payments for the two children, and that this influenced their lordships in coming to their decision to transfer the house to her absolutely. Although this is not

made clear in the report in the All England Law Reports, the headnote to the report in The Weekly Law Reports reads as follows: '... taking into account the substantial contribution made by the wife to bringing up the family, the fact that the husband had a roof over his head and a better financial future and that the wife was willing to forgo future periodical payments for the children, the proper order was that the house should be transferred to the wife absolutely and that the order for periodical payments should be reduced to a nominal amount.'

10–103 Dunford v Dunford

[1980] 1 All ER 122, CA

Desirability of crystallising parties' interests in former matrimonial home once and for all. The matrimonial home had been purchased in the parties' joint names with the aid of a 100 per cent mortgage. The parties separated, the wife remaining in the house with the children, the husband going into lodgings. The county court judge ordered the husband to transfer his half share to the wife subject to a charge of 25 per cent of the net sale proceeds should the wife vacate the property or die. The husband appealed, contending that the house should be sold on the youngest child completing her full-time education or on the wife's remarriage, and that he should be ordered to transfer to the wife not 50 per cent of his interest in the property but only such interest as would be necessary for the wife's future needs. The wife cross-appealed, contending that the husband's interest should be extinguished. The Court of Appeal approved the judge's order in respect of the matrimonial home.

Lord Denning MR said that when the matter had first come before the registrar the registrar had applied *Mesher v Mesher* (4–101) and had ordered that the house was not to be sold until the youngest child had finished her schooling. Presumably, after that time, it could be sold and the proceeds divided equally between the parties. His lordship continued (at page 124): 'That order left the parties in complete uncertainty as to the future. After six or seven years the house would have to be sold and the husband would take a half share of the proceeds, and the wife would be left with insufficient money to buy another house. The wife's solicitors appealed. The judge made a different order. He ordered that the whole of the interest in the house should be transferred to the wife within three months. He realised that if it were transferred, the wife would have to pay the mortgage instalments, the rates, and all the other outgoings on the house. But the judge realised that the wife might die or might sell the house some time in the future. If that should happen, the judge ordered that the husband should then have 25 per cent of the equity ...

'By making that order, the parties would know exactly where they stood with regard to the future. In so ordering, the judge applied the principle which is now flowing through these cases. It was indicated in the recent case of *Hanlon v Hanlon* (10–102) by Ormrod LJ. When it was suggested that there should be a postponement of the sale and then a distribution on a fifty-fifty basis, he said:

"... I do not think that that, in this case, would be in the least satisfactory; it would leave the wife in a state of perpetual uncertainty and neither party would know where ultimately they were going to be. It seems to me far better that the parties' interests should be crystallised now, once and for all, so that the wife can know what she is going to do about the property and the husband can make up his mind about what he is going to do about rehousing."

That principle was expressed again in the recent case of *Minton v Minton* (10–205) by Lord Scarman. He drew attention of the principle of the clean break. He said:

"The law now encourages spouses to avoid bitterness after family breakdown and to settle their money and property problems. An object of the modern law is to encourage the parties to put the past behind them and to begin a new life which is not overshadowed by the relationship which has broken down."

'There is only one variation which I think should be made to the order of the judge. He ordered that the order for periodical payments for the wife should be 5p per annum, a nominal sum. That should not be included in an order when you want a clean break . . . so I think in this case the order of the judge should be varied by striking out the order for periodical payments of 5p per year. In that way we have the "clean break". The wife knows exactly where she stands. The house is vested in her. She has the property in it, and she can keep the family together. She can keep it as a home for the family as they grow up. She can keep it going indefinitely, knowing exactly where she stands. But if it should happen that she should sell the house (or should die) then the husband is to have one-quarter of the net proceeds.'

Eveleigh LJ, agreeing, said: 'It is true that the husband is losing his share in the equity of the house, but it is a house where the mortgage is still at the original figure and the wife has the obligation of paying that off. The husband's capital prospects are very much greater than those of the wife. He has a superior earning capacity; and, in the not too distant future, when the children's payments come to an end, the difference between their earning capacity or their income will be even more pronounced.

'In those circumstances, I think that his prospects, as I say, of acquiring a house in due course are really quite good.'

Notes

1. In *L v L* (1980) Times, 5 February, Balcombe J, referring to the conflicting decisions of the Court of Appeal in *Dunford v Dunford* and *Carter v Carter* (10–208), stated that *Dunford v Dunford* was to be preferred. In *Dunford v Dunford* Lord Denning MR, applying the principle of the clean break, struck out the nominal order of 5p a year made by the judge. In *Carter v Carter* Ormrod LJ said that there was no jurisdiction to dismiss a wife's claim for periodical payments unless she consented, and accordingly allowed the wife's appeal against the decision of the county court judge who had dismissed her claim for periodical payments. Balcombe J said that guidance on the conflict could be obtained from the judgment of Lord Scarman in *Minton v Minton* (10–205); in *Minton v Minton* the principle of the clean break had been held to be in accordance with public policy; it followed that a court had jurisdiction to dismiss a wife's claim for periodical payments whether she consented or not if the court thought it right to do so.

2. But Balcombe J's decision in *L v L* has now been overruled by the Court of Appeal in *Dipper v Dipper* (10–209), and it is now settled law that the court has no jurisdiction to dismiss a wife's application for periodical payments without her express consent. In *Dipper v Dipper* Roskill, Ormrod and Cumming-Bruce LJJ said that the House of Lords in *Minton v Minton* did not decide that the court could *of its own volition* dismiss a wife's claim for periodical payments (the wife in *Minton v Minton* having *consented* to the order for nominal periodical payments coming to an end), that any attempt to extend *Minton v Minton* should be regarded with extreme caution, that the earlier decision in *Carpenter v Carpenter* (10–204) was binding on the court and that *Dunford v Dunford* had been decided per incuriam insofar as the nominal order for periodical payments had been struck out without the wife's consent.

10–104 Chambers v Chambers

(1979) 10 Fam Law 22

No capital provision after delay of over 20 years.   The parties separated in 1956. In 1977 the wife petitioned for divorce on the ground of five years' separation and applied for capital provision. She did not pursue the prayer in her petition for periodical payments. Wood J said that the policy now was that on breakdown of marriage there should if possible be a clean break. After a certain lapse of time a party should be entitled to take the view that there would be no revival or institution of financial claims against him. The wife's application was dismissed. See case summary 13–017.

Note. Compare *Pearce v Pearce* (10–106).

10–105 Tilley v Tilley

(1979) 10 Fam Law 89, CA

Variation of order for payment of lump sum by instalments – not a 'once-and-for-all' order – jurisdiction retained by court to entertain application to vary continuing order. See case summary (9–024).

10–106 Pearce v Pearce

(1980) 1 FLR 261, CA

Capital provision after delay of 10 years. The marriage was dissolved in 1969. The husband remained an undischarged bankrupt until 1977. In 1978 the husband inherited assets from his late father. The wife obtained leave to apply out of time for a lump sum payment. The husband appealed.

The Court of Appeal held that the principle of the clean break was inapplicable. Where children were involved there could not be a clean break in normal circumstances. The husband had provided no financial contributions to the wife or children since 1969, and the wife had had great difficulty raising the children unaided. She had a strong claim in justice for a lump sum payment.

Note. Compare *Chambers v Chambers* (10–104).

10–107 Carson v Carson

(1981) Times, 7 July, CA

No jurisdiction to entertain second application for transfer of property order under section 24(1)(b) after granting of previous application under section 24(1)(a). Six years previously the wife had obtained a settlement of property order in the form of *Mesher v Mesher* (4–101), the matrimonial home being settled on the parties in equal shares, the sale to be postponed until her death or remarriage or until each of the children attained 18 or completed their education, whichever was earlier. She was now in financial difficulties, and applied for a further transfer of property order transferring the entire beneficial interest in the property to her absolutely.

Counsel for the wife argued that the fact that there had been a settlement order under section 24 (1) (a) of the Matrimonial Causes Act 1973 did not preclude a later application for a transfer of property order under section 24 (1) (b). However, Ormrod LJ said that the application for a further order was in reality an attempt to obtain a second settlement of the same asset, which would run counter to section 31 of the Act, which gave no power to the court to vary property settlement orders.

The wife also made application for leave to appeal out of time against the original order, which was also refused. Ormrod LJ said that he had great sympathy for the wife's predicament, but it was only in exceptional cases that such appeals should be permitted, because by then everyone would have acted on the assumption that the original decision had been correct.

The case was a good example of the dangers of *Mesher* orders, said Ormrod LJ; on the wife being obliged to sell the matrimonial home she would find herself in a most unfavourable position with only half the proceeds of sale.

2 Maintenance

CASE SUMMARIES

10–201 **L v L**

[1961] 3 All ER 834, CA

Jurisdiction to award maintenance cannot be ousted by private agreement – but it is otherwise when the agreement is brought before the court and an order is made giving effect to its terms dismissing the wife's application for periodical payments – no jurisdiction to entertain second application for periodical payments order after dismissal of previous application.   Following the separation and divorce, the husband and wife subsequently agreed to commute the maintenance payments (which the husband had agreed to pay under a deed of separation) in consideration of a lump sum payment to the wife and on condition that the deed of separation be cancelled and the wife's prayer for maintenance contained in her petition be dismissed. The husband accordingly paid over the lump sum *and an order was made by consent dismissing the wife's application for maintenance,* she 'having accepted the said sum in full satisfaction of all present and future rights to maintenance for herself'. The wife later made a further application for maintenance. The Court of Appeal held that the court did not have jurisdiction to entertain the new application by the wife, who was bound by her agreement to accept the lump sum in satisfaction of all present and future rights to maintenance. *Hyman v Hyman* (9–001) distinguished.

Notes

1. The Court of Appeal in *L v L* accepted as well-established the proposition (for which *Hyman v Hyman* is usually cited) that the jurisdiction to award maintenance cannot be ousted by any private agreement between the parties. However, it was held that the position was otherwise when the agreement was brought before the court and an order of the court was made giving effect to its terms dismissing the wife's application for periodical payments. *Hyman v Hyman* was accordingly distinguished.
2. Their lordships held that the right granted to a wife to apply for periodical payments either on the pronouncing of a decree of divorce *or at any time thereafter* as conferred by the relevant legislation was merely a right to make a single application, not a succession of applications.
3. Accordingly, the first application for periodical payments having been dismissed, there was no jurisdiction to entertain a second application.
4. As to the relevance of the Court of Appeal's decision in *L v L* to the modern legislation, see *Coleman v Coleman* (10–101), in which *L v L* was applied.
5. See also *Minton v Minton* (10–205), in which the decision in *L v L* was expresssly approved by the House of Lords.
6. Compare *Wright v Wright* (9–005) and *Jessel v Jessel* (10–207): in cases in which the wife's application for periodical payments is not dismissed the court retains jurisdiction to review the question of maintenance for the wife.

10–202 **Smith v Smith**

[1970] 1 All ER 244, CA

No prospect of wife receiving maintenance in the future – application by wife that in lieu of maintenance husband's interest in matrimonial home be extinguished.   In 1962 the husband left the wife and went to New Zealand. He paid the wife £8 a week for two years, but from 1964 onwards he had not paid her anything. He was earning £18 a week in New Zealand, but there was no prospect of the wife's receiving maintenance from him in the future. The wife, having obtained a divorce on the ground of the husband's desertion, applied to vary the post-nuptial settlement of the jointly-owned matrimonial home. The Court of Appeal varied the settlement, extinguishing the husband's interest under the trust for sale, on the condition that no further applications by the wife for maintenance, secured provision or lump sum would be entertained.

Salmon LJ (as he then was) said (at page 247): 'The court has a very wide discretion under section 17 of the Matrimonial Causes Act 1965 [to vary post-nuptial settlements]. In the present case, the court was considering an application under that section, in conjunction with maintenance, that is to say, *the wife was asking for the variation in lieu of maintenance* because the husband was not paying nor likely to pay any maintenance, and any order for maintenance would be virtually impossible to enforce.'

Note. In *Carpenter v Carpenter* (10–204), Ormrod LJ stated that the order in *Smith v Smith* was equivalent to a dismissal of the wife's application for ancillary relief by consent. (See the original transcript of his lordship's judgment referred to in *Dipper v Dipper* (10–209) [1980] 2 All ER 722 at 726).

10–203 Griffiths v Griffiths

[1974] 1 All ER 932, CA

Wife's prospect of receiving maintenance reduced following husband's business misfortune – periodical payments order not sought by wife – wife's share of capital assets increased in order to secure her financial position. The parties' only capital asset was the former matrimonial home, which the husband had conveyed into the sole name of the wife some years ago in return for a nominal sum. Following the decree nisi she had sold it for £54,000 net, and purchased a cheaper property out of the proceeds. The wife was earning £1,500 a year and the husband had a potential earning capacity of some £5,000 a year. Until his business misfortunes had overtaken him, the husband had provided well for the family, but he was now unemployed (although he had prospects of future employment). The husband applied for a lump sum order. The wife cross-claimed for ancillary relief but did not ask for periodical payments.

Arnold J (as he then was) awarded the husband a lump sum of £11,500 out of the net sale proceeds of the house (approximately one-fifth). This left the balance of approximately four-fifths in the wife's hands. Sir John Arnold had arrived at the figure of £11,500 by taking the potential earning capacities of both parties and a notional return on invested capital, and so adjusting the capital position of the parties as to equalise the parties' incomes. He dismissed the wife's application for ancillary relief. (As noted above, she had not made any application for periodical payments.)

The husband appealed, suggesting a 50:50 division of the capital assets coupled with an award of periodical payments. Roskill LJ said (at page 942): 'It seems to me that this is a case in which it would be wrong to order periodical payments. The husband's earning position, as I have already pointed out, is doubtful – I use no stronger word – and it would be wrong, in my judgment, to put the wife at risk as to the receipt or non-receipt of future payments according to what may or may not materialise from the husband's business. *Furthermore, having regard to the whole of the past unhappy history of this case it seems to me that the sooner there is a complete and final financial break between the parties the better for both and indeed for everybody else concerned.*

'. . . *For my part, I can see no reason why an order for periodical payments should be made. The wife has not sought it in this court.* Counsel for the wife sought to support the learned judge's order of £11,500 on the ground that the husband was getting the benefit of freedom from any future liability of any kind for supporting his wife for the rest of her days. I think that point is well taken.'

However, their lordships considered that the total of £11,500 awarded to the husband did not adequately reflect the fact that the house had originally been provided and paid for by the husband and that the husband had worked hard to support his family during the marriage. Accordingly, an increased lump sum payment of £15,000 was substituted.

10–204 Carpenter v Carpenter

(1976) 6 Fam Law 110, CA

Application for periodical payments cannot be dismissed without party's consent.   In *Dipper v Dipper* (10–209) [1980] 2 All ER 722 Roskill LJ said (at page 726): '. . . There is a decision of this court . . . in *Carpenter v Carpenter* (1976) Court of Appeal Transcript 65A. That case has not been fully reported, but there is an abridged report of Ormrod LJ's judgment in 6 Fam Law 110. We sent for the original transcript of that judgment. I do not think it is necessary to read right through Ormrod LJ's judgment. The decision seems to me to be beyond question. Ormrod LJ said:

> "In my judgment, *Griffiths v Griffiths* (10–203) is no authority for the proposition for which it is cited in *Rayden on Divorce* (12th Edn., 1974, p. 789) ['The court itself may order such dismissal even if one or both parties objects thereto.'], and *Smith v Smith* (10–202) is plainly a case which is equivalent to dismissal of the wife's application for ancillary relief by consent because in that case it was indeed her proposal that her claim for ancillary relief should be dismissed, if the court was prepared to vary the settlement in the way she was seeking. So I do not think there is any authority at the moment which gives this court, or any court, or which suggests that this court, or indeed any court, can properly exercise its discretion to dismiss a wife's claim for ancillary relief unless she herself consents, because it is such a serious step to take."

With that judgment both Stamp LJ and Sir John Pennycuick agreed almost monosyllabically. That plainly represented the conclusions of all three members of the court. That decision is, in my view, binding on this court unless it has subsequently been held by the House of Lords to be wrong.'

Continuing at page 729, Roskill LJ said: 'The decision in *Carpenter v Carpenter* must, with great respect to Lord Denning MR and Balcombe J, be treated as binding on this court unless it can be shown to have been disapproved in *Minton v Minton* (10–205). I have read and re-read the argument and speeches in *Minton v Minton*. There are references to *Carpenter* in the report of the argument and there is also a reference to *Carpenter* in Lord Scarman's speech; there is no suggestion anywhere that *Carpenter* was wrongly decided.'

The House of Lords in *Minton v Minton* not having disapproved of the Court of Appeal's decision in *Carpenter v Carpenter*, the Court of Appeal in *Dipper v Dipper* accordingly held that the decision in *Carpenter v Carpenter* was binding on the court.

10–205 Minton v Minton

[1979] 1 All ER 79, HL

Jurisdiction to award maintenance cannot be ousted by private agreement – Hyman v Hyman (9–001) explained – but it is otherwise when the agreement is brought before the court and an order is made giving effect to its terms dismissing the wife's application for periodical payments – L v L (10–201) approved – consent order – nominal order for periodical payments to cease on conveyance of house to wife – genuine final order equivalent to a dismissal of wife's application for periodical payments – no jurisdiction to entertain second application.   Following the divorce a consent order had been agreed by the parties' legal advisers which provided (inter alia) that the husband would transfer the former matrimonial home into the wife's sole name, that on completion of the conveyance the wife would pay the husband a stated sum in full and final settlement for his beneficial interest in the house, that until the house was conveyed to the wife the husband would pay her nominal maintenance of 5p per annum *and that those payments should cease on completion of the conveyance*. The county court judge duly made the consent order in the terms of two draft orders agreed by the parties.

The husband complied with the order and conveyed the matrimonial home to the wife, *and on completion of the conveyance the order for the nominal periodical payments came to an end*. The bargain proved disastrous for the wife, who found herself deeply in debt, in poor health and having to look after the children of the marriage. She applied to another county court judge for an order varying the maintenance payable under the consent order.

The county court judge dismissed the wife's application for want of jurisdiction. The wife appealed to the Court of Appeal and, subsequently, to the House of Lords, which also dismissed her appeal.

Lord Scarman, giving the unanimous decision of the court, said (at page 85): '... He [counsel for the wife] submits that the Court of Appeal in *L v L* (10–201) should have held themselves bound, by the public policy recognised by this House in *Hyman v Hyman* (9–001), to declare that the court *has* jurisdiction to entertain a fresh application for maintenance notwithstanding that the applicant had consented to the dismissal of an earlier application or the discharge of an earlier order. The Court of Appeal [in *L v L*] dealt specifically with the point. *Willmer LJ* [in *L v L*] *accepted as well established the proposition, for which Hyman v Hyman is usually cited, that the jurisdiction to award maintenance cannot be ousted by any private agreement between the parties. But he said it was* "otherwise when the agreement is brought before the court and an order of the court is made giving effect to its terms". And he quoted with approval an observation of Jenkins LJ in *Russell v Russell* [1956] 1 All ER 466 that "The principle in *Hyman v Hyman*, be it remembered, is satisfied by any bargain which is brought before the court for approval and approved by the court". *Willmer LJ was, if I may say so with respect, plainly right in his approach to Hyman v Hyman*. Lord Hailsham LC [in *Hyman v Hyman*] put the principle of that decision into these words: "However this may be, it is sufficient for the decision of the present case to hold, as I do, that the power of the court to make provision for a wife on the dissolution of her marriage is a necessary incident of the power to decree such a dissolution, conferred not merely in the interests of the wife, but of the public, and that the wife cannot *by her own covenant* preclude herself from invoking the jurisdiction of the court or preclude the court from the exercise of that jurisdiction." *Hyman v Hyman* was concerned only with the effect of an agreement which purported to oust the jurisdiction of the court. It is no authority as to the extent of the court's jurisdiction. That question must depend on the true construction of the statute conferring the jurisdiction.'

His lordship continued (at page 87): '... *section 23 (1) of the* [Matrimonial Causes Act 1973] *does not empower the court to make a second or subsequent maintenance order after an earlier application has been dismissed. Counsel for the wife, however, submits that the present is not a case of dismissal: an order was made which included periodical payments and a property transfer order*. As I understand his argument, he again invokes the public policy, which he says is to be derived from *Hyman v Hyman*, that it is in the interest of the public as well as the spouse that the court, *having made an order*, should have a continuing jurisdiction to make another. Thus he seeks to draw a distinction between a dismissal and an order. I agree with him that on its proper construction the consent order in this case is more than a dismissal. It contains an express provision for a limited period of maintenance (the nominal order until conveyance) and a provision for the transfer of the home.

'*The short answer to the point, however, is that on the true construction of section 23 (1) the court does not have the jurisdiction. Once an application has been dealt with on its merits, the court has no future jurisdiction save where there is a continuing order capable of variation or discharge under section 31 of the 1973 Act* [see Appendix I]. *But the specious reliance on public policy calls for an answer. There are two principles which inform the modern legislation. One is the public interest that* spouses, to the extent that their means permit, should provide for themselves and their children. But the other, of equal importance, is the principle of "the clean break". The law now encourages spouses to avoid bitterness after family breakdown and to settle their money and property problems. An object of the modern law is to encourage the parties to put the past behind them and to begin a new life which is not overshadowed by the relationship which has broken down. It would be inconsistent with this principle if the court could not make, as between the spouses, a genuinely final order unless it was prepared to dismiss the application. The present case is a good illustration. The court having made an order giving effect to a comprehensive settlement of all financial and property issues as between [the] spouses, it would be a strange application of the principle of the clean break if, notwithstanding the order, the court could make a future order on a subsequent application made by the wife after the husband had complied with all his obligations. The difference between a dismissal of an application [for an order for periodical payments] by consent on terms recited or referred to in the order . . . and an order whose terms incorporate the parties' agreement [that a nominal order for periodical payments is to come to an end] is a mere formality. The substance of the transaction is in each case a final settlement, as between the parties, approved by the court.'

Viscount Dilhorne, agreeing with Lord Scarman's speech, added: '. . . A man may be prepared to consent to an order being made in favour of his former wife which made more provision for her than that to which he would be prepared to agree if faced with the possibility of later being required to pay more, and to consent, on the basis of finality, to provide more than the court might have ordered but for his consent. The principle of "the clean break", to which my noble and learned friend refers, I regard as of great importance, and I would deprecate a practice developing where, in a case in which the court is satisfied that adequate or generous provision has been consented to, the court nevertheless, in case something happened in the future, made an order for payment of a nominal amount so as to retain jurisdiction to increase the provision made. A court should have power to make a final order for provision for a spouse. It has in my opinion that power and in a proper case it should be exercised.'

The only dissenting judgment was that of Lord Fraser of Tullybelton who said: '. . . I respectfully agree that there are great advantages in the finality of a "clean break". But it is easy to envisage an exceptional case in which a totally unforeseeable change in the circumstances of one of the former spouses occurs soon after a final court order has been made disposing of the financial issues between them. Such a change might render the order so inappropriate as to appear harsh and unjust. The change might be for the better, as by unexpected inheritance of property, or for worse, as by a sudden serious illness. To cover such exceptional cases it would, in my view, be desirable that the jurisdiction of the court to vary any order should invariably be preserved as a matter of general law.' However, his lordship added, agreeing with the unanimous decision of the court: 'But I do not think that the legislation as it stands is capable of being construed so as to lead to the result that I regard as preferable.'

Notes

1. The authors would (with some hesitation) sum up the decision in *Minton v Minton* as follows: Where, on an application by a wife for periodical payments for her own maintenance (as opposed to maintenance for the children), the court makes an order *on terms agreed between the parties* either (1) *dismissing the application* on the agreed terms recited or referred to in the order, or (2) stipulating that a nominal order for periodical payments *is to come to an end on the happening of a specified event* as agreed between the parties, the order is in either case *a final settlement of the issue* and there is *a clean break* between the parties, and the court does not have jurisdiction to entertain any future application either (a) for a further order for periodical payments for the wife's maintenance (as opposed to a further application for maintenance for the children), or (b) for variation of the consent order after the husband has complied with his side of the bargain and the nominal order for periodical payments has come to an end on the happening of the specified event.

2. The difference between the two forms of consent order is a mere formality. The substance of the agreement approved by the court is in each case a final settlement of the issue. Lord Scarman said (at page 88): 'The difference between [1] a *dismissal* of an application for an order for periodical payments by consent on terms recited or referred to in the order [as in *L v L* (10–201) and *de Lasala v de Lasala* (10–206)] . . . and [2] an order whose terms incorporate the parties' agreement [that a nominal order for periodical payments *is to come to an end*, as in *Minton v Minton*] is a mere formality. The substance of the transaction in each case is a final settlement, as between the parties, approved by the court.'

3. In *Jessel v Jessel* (10–207) Lord Denning MR, although allowing the wife's application to vary the agreed periodical payments order, attempted to extend the principle of the clean break. His lordship said: '*Minton v Minton* only applies when there is a *genuine final order* which contains *no continuing order for periodical payments*, as for instance [1] when the wife has applied for periodical payments and her application has been *dismissed* [as in *L v L* (10–201) and *de Lasala v de Lasala* (10–206)], or [2], as in *Minton v Minton*, *a nominal order for periodical payments came to an end*.' Or, Lord Denning continued [3]: 'where the parties make *a "once-and-for-all" provision* in the shape of a house, or whatever it may be, for the wife, *with no provision for continuing payments at all*.' [as in *Hanlon v Hanlon* (10–102), cited as an example of the clean break by Lord Denning MR in *Dunford v Dunford* (10–103)].

   One may note (1) the difference between Lord Denning's statement: 'when the wife has applied for periodical payments and her application has been dismissed' and Lord Scarman's statement: 'a dismissal of an application *by consent on terms recited or referred to in the order*', and (2) the fact that Lord Denning's statement: 'or, as in *Minton v Minton*, a nominal order for periodical payments came to an end' also omits the words 'by consent'. In *Dunford v Dunford* Lord Denning MR and Eveleigh LJ imposed a clean break without the wife's consent by striking out the judge's order for nominal periodical payments.

   In *Dipper v Dipper* (10–209) [1980] 2 All ER 722, Roskill, Ormrod and Cumming-Bruce LJJ held (per Cumming-Bruce LJ at 734): 'The only principle of clean break to be collected from *Minton v Minton* is, if the parties have decided deliberately to make a clean break *by consenting to a settlement*, then the opportunity for a second application has *by agreement* been lost. Without such consent, on the language of section 23 (1) . . . the applicant has the opportunity to return at any time.' Their lordships accordingly held that the court has no jurisdiction of its own volition to dismiss a wife's application for periodical payments, i.e. without the wife's consent, and that *Dunford v Dunford* had been decided per incuriam insofar as the nominal order for periodical payments made by the judge had been struck out by the Court of Appeal without the wife's consent.

4. As for Lord Denning MR's third example of the clean break: 'where the parties make a "once and for all" provision in the shape of a house, or whatever it may be, for the wife, *with no provision for continuing payments at all*', this has yet to be further considered by the courts. There is support for Lord Denning's point of view in Lord Fraser of Tullybelton's dissenting judgment in *Minton v Minton*. Lord Fraser said: '. . . it would, in my view, be desirable that the jurisdiction of the court to vary any order should invariably be preserved as a matter of general law. It seems unsatisfactory that this jurisdiction should only be preserved in cases when the court anticipates the possible need for subsequent variation of its order, and provides for it by the device of making *a nominal order*. But I do not think that the legislation as it stands is capable of being construed so as to lead to the result that I regard as preferable.' Lord Fraser's opinion would seem to support Lord Denning's opinion that, if the court simply makes *no order for maintenance* in favour of the wife while dealing with all other issues on the principle of the clean break [as in *Hanlon v Hanlon* (10–102)] then the result will be just the same as if the wife had made an application for maintenance which had been *dismissed*. Lord Fraser came to the conclusion that the only way the court could anticipate the possible need for variation of its order was to provide for this by the device of making *a nominal order*.

   The position is unfortunately still uncertain at the time of writing. In *Dipper v Dipper* (10–209) [1980] 2 All ER 722 Ormrod LJ said at 732: 'I commented in *Carter v Carter* (10–208) on the dangers of making "No order" on these applications. I will not repeat in full what I said there, but I do not think it is safe for registrars and judges to make orders in that form because of the difficulty of interpretation which arises subsequently. Sometimes it means that the court wishes to keep the position open. Sometimes it is tantamount to a dismissal. It is best, in my view, if that form of order were not used at all.'

5. However, although Ormrod LJ was of the opinion that there are circumstances in which the decision of the court not to make any order for periodical payments can be equivalent to a dismissal, this must be read subject to the caveat that a clean break can not be imposed on a wife without her consent. In the authors' view, the granting of 'once-and-for-all' provision in the shape of a house, or whatever it may be, for the wife, coupled with the order 'No order for periodical payments', will only preclude the wife from making further application to the court if there was a clear agreement between the parties to that effect and it can be shown that it was the parties' intention that the order of the court was to confirm that agreement. The authors would therefore distinguish *Hanlon v Hanlon* (10–102) from *Minton v Minton*. In *Hanlon v Hanlon* the wife simply made no application for periodical payments for herself. She never agreed to debar herself from making application in the future. It may possibly be held in future cases that Lord Denning's citing of *Hanlon v Hanlon* in *Dunford v Dunford* (10–103) as an example of the clean break was erroneous – although the authors consider that *Hanlon v Hanlon* does represent a valid example of the application of the principle of the clean break to capital provision. For an example of the court refusing to imply a dismissal from the mere lack of any order for periodical payments see *Empson v Empson* (10–207A). The burden of establishing that there was a dismissal lies on the party alleging it: *Brown v Kirrage* (1980) 11 Fam Law 141, CA.

6. Lord Scarman said that the principle of the clean break does not apply as far as maintenance for the children of the family is concerned. Section 23 (4) of the Matrimonial Causes Act 1973 says that 'The power of the court under subsection (1) or (2) (a) [of section 23] to make an order in favour of a child of the family *shall be exercisable from time to time* . . .' His lordship said (at page 87): 'When Parliament wished to make it clear that no previous dismissal of an application or discharge or termination of an order could displace the court's power to make maintenance orders in favour of children, it added, by subsection (4), the words "from time to time" to the words "at any time thereafter" which it had used in subsection (1). No plainer indication could be given of the intention of Parliament.' There is no subsection equivalent to subsection (4) qualifying the words used in subsection (1) in respect of maintenance orders in favour of the parties to the marriage themselves. Although in *Dipper v Dipper* (10–209) [1980] 2 All ER 722 Ormrod LJ said (at the foot of page 731): ' . . . I do not think that any assistance can be obtained from contrasting the phrase "exercisable from time to time" in subsection (4) of section 23 with the phrase "or at any time thereafter" in subsection (1)', it is generally agreed that the principle of the clean break does not apply as far as maintenance for the children of the family is concerned. As Ormrod LJ pointed out in *Carter v Carter* (10–208), there is no one who can consent to an application for periodical payments for the children's maintenance being dismissed.

10–206 de Lasala v de Lasala

[1979] 2 All ER 1146, PC

Consent order dismissing wife's application for periodical payments – no jurisdiction to entertain second application – Minton v Minton (10–205) applied. At all material times the Hong Kong legislation in respect of financial provision for parties to a marriage was in the same terms as the English legislation.

By a deed of arrangement and annexed trust deeds the husband and wife agreed that the husband would not defend the wife's petition for divorce (which contained claims for maintenance, a lump sum and secured provision) and that he would make financial provision for her by the payment to her of a lump sum and the payment to trustees of further sums in trust to buy a residence for her use for life, and furniture for it. *It was a term of the agreement that the wife would consent to the dismissal of her claims for financial provision contained in her petition.*

On the granting of the decree nisi, the judge in the Supreme Court of Hong Kong made a *consent order* approving the financial arrangements as set out in the deed of arrangement and annexed trust deeds and, on the husband's execution of those arrangements, *dismissed the wife's application for financial relief contained in her petition.*

The wife later applied to the Supreme Court of Hong Kong for an order to set aside or vary the consent order. This was dismissed on the ground that the court had no jurisdiction, because the wife's original application for financial relief had been dismissed by the consent order.

There followed an appeal to the Court of Appeal of Hong Kong and, finally, to the Judicial Committee of the Privy Council, which held that there was no jurisdiction to entertain the wife's subsequent application for financial relief. The decision of the House of Lords in *Minton v Minton* (10–205) had been to the effect that it was the policy of the Matrimonial Causes Act 1973 to permit parties to a marriage to make a clean break in regard to financial matters, from which there could be no going back.

10–207 Jessel v Jessel

[1979] 3 All ER 645, CA

Consent order – agreement to accept periodical payments order in settlement of all claims for periodical payments – undertaking not to apply to increase husband's liability – application to vary – order not a 'once and for all' order – jurisdiction retained by court to entertain application to vary continuing order for periodical payments – Minton v Minton (10–205) distinguished. On the making of the decree nisi, there had been embodied in an order of the court the terms of an agreement between the parties, namely, that the wife accepted the agreed periodical payments in settlement of all her claims to periodical payments and that she agreed not to apply to the court to increase the award in the future. Four years later the wife applied for an increase.

Lord Denning MR said that it was contrary to public policy that a maintenance agreement should be made unalterably binding on a wife. The only exception to this rule arose where there was a 'clean break' and a 'once-and-for-all' provision for the wife. But where there was a continuing periodical payments order, as in this case, the principle of the clean break did not apply.

Notes

1. For further details, see case summary 9–023.
2. Compare *Tilley v Tilley* (9–024) – order for payment of lump sum by instalments – not a 'once-and-for-all' order – capable of variation.

10–207A Empson v Empson

(1980) 1 FLR 269, CA

Consent order silent as to periodical payments – jurisdiction to entertain later application. In March 1977 a consent order was made embodying all the terms the parties had agreed, but silent as to periodical payments. In November 1979 the wife sought an order for periodical payments. The Court of Appeal (Orr and Ormrod LJJ) held that, as there had been no express or implied dismissal of any claim by the wife for periodical payments, a claim could now be made, and leave to appeal against the judge's order was accordingly granted. However, as to the prospect of success of the appeal, that was another matter. There was a very strong argument for saying that it was an implied term of the consent order that the wife would not make any application for periodical payments in the future. Ormrod LJ said that it was clear that practitioners, registrars and judges will have to be extremely careful when making or approving consent orders if they are silent as to periodical payments. The court will have to satisfy itself before making a consent order whether it is intended to dismiss the wife's claim for periodical payments or whether it is intended to leave it open to the wife to apply in the future.

Note. See also the authors' notes to *Minton v Minton* (10–205).

10–208 Carter v Carter

[1980] 1 All ER 827, CA

Application for periodical payments cannot be dismissed without party's consent – wife consenting to dismissal of application for periodical payments provided husband's half share in former matrimonial home transferred to her absolutely – order for transfer of husband's share to wife subject to charge in husband's favour – lack of consent to dismissal of application for periodical payments. The wife's appeal against the judge's order was allowed. Ormrod LJ said that the wife had not consented to her application for periodical payments being dismissed in consideration of the former matrimonial home being transferred into her sole name subject to any charge on the property in the husband's favour. Furthermore, the judge had purported to dismiss the wife's application for periodical payments for the maintenance of the children; there was no one who could consent on behalf of the children.

10–209 Dipper v Dipper

[1980] 2 All ER 722, CA

Application for periodical payments cannot be dismissed without party's consent. After quoting the words of section 23 (1) of the Matrimonial Causes Act 1973 [see Appendix I] Roskill LJ said (at page 726) that he found nothing in the express language of the Act which suggested that the court had any power to dismiss an application for periodical payments of its own volition and without the consent of the applicant. The decision in *Carpenter v Carpenter* (10–204) was binding on the court.

His lordship continued (at page 728): '. . . I think *Minton v Minton* (10–205) decides that, where *by consent* an application has been dismissed by an order of the court, there is no power in the court to entertain a second or subsequent application under s. 23 (1) of the Act. That section gives no such power to the court. But *Minton v Minton* does not, in my view, decide that where a wife applies for periodical payments and the court is of the opinion that, at the time that application is heard, no order should be made in her favour, the court is thereupon empowered *of its own violition* to dismiss her application so as to preclude her from thereafter making a subsequent application in the event of a change of circumstances. Reading the arguments of counsel in that case, I do not see any suggestion that such an argument was advanced before their Lordships.'

Dealing with the conflicting decisions of *Carter v Carter* (10–208) and *Dunford v Dunford* (10–103), his lordship said (at page 729) that, insofar as the Court of Appeal in *Dunford v Dunford* struck out the nominal order for periodical payments without the wife's consent, *Dunford v Dunford* must be treated as having been decided per incuriam.

Notes

1. At page 729, Roskill LJ said that it seemed clear from Lord Denning MR's judgment in *Dunford v Dunford* that the earlier decision of the Court of Appeal in *Carpenter v Carpenter* had not been referred to.
2. *Dunford v Dunford* was not reported in *The Times* because *The Times* was not being published at the time of the decision on 28 June 1979. Accordingly, when the question of consent again came before the Court of Appeal in *Carter v Carter* on 14 December 1979, the decision in *Dunford v Dunford* was unknown. (See page 728).
3. Although the report of *Carter v Carter* does not refer to *Carpenter v Carpenter*, in giving the first judgment in *Carter v Carter*, Ormrod LJ repeated what he had said earlier in *Carpenter v Carpenter*. (See page 728).
4. Lord Scarman, in his review of the authorities during his speech in the House of Lords in *Minton v Minton*, referred to *Carpenter v Carpenter* without any indication of disapproval. Accordingly, *Carter v Carter*, in which the decision in *Carpenter v Carpenter* was followed, must be treated as having been correctly decided. *Dunford v Dunford*, in which the decision in *Carpenter v Carpenter* was not followed, must therefore be treated as having been decided per incuriam insofar as the nominal order for periodical payments was struck out without the wife's consent. (See page 729).

10–210 Moore v Moore

(1980) Times, 10 May, CA

Clean break of no application where wife has no earning capacity. Ormrod LJ said that the 'clean break' principle as expounded in *Minton v Minton* (10–205) had caused misunderstanding. In that case a clean break was possible because a comprehensive settlement of the parties' finances was possible; it was not applicable where the financial resources of the parties were insufficient. It was nonsense to talk about a clean break where there were young children; it could not apply as the parties had to continue to co-operate because of the children. Moreover, it did not apply where one party was earning and the other could not earn; the effect of a clean break in such cases would mean people living on social security.

In the present case the wife was severely handicapped in that she was raising a small child on her own. She was entitled to a substantive order for periodical payments.

10–211 S v S

(1980) Times, 10 May

Desirability of a clean break where parties can afford it. The value of the husband's assets had been agreed at £2.1m. The parties agreed there should be a clean break and the wife consented to the dismissal of her claim for periodical payments.
Notes
1. For further details, see case summary 16–104 – one-third approach inappropriate where capital assets so large.
2. See also *Page v Page* (10–212).

10–211A Hulley v Thompson

[1981] 1 All ER 1128

Husband's continuing liability to maintain children notwithstanding consent order transferring his interest in matrimonial home to wife and consent order that he should not pay any maintenance to the wife either for herself or for the children. See Appendix II.
Note. See also *Tilley v Tilley* (9–024).

10–212 Page v Page

(1981) Times, 30 January, CA

Relationships between the parties so embittered that periodical payments to be avoided – desirability of a clean break where parties can afford it. The parties were both in their seventies. The value of the husband's assets had been assessed at £359,137. The relationship between them was now so embittered, said Ormrod LJ, that periodical payments were to be avoided. Accordingly, the case was one for a lump sum provision and no periodical payments. The wife agreed in principle with that view. However, the lump sum of £165,000 awarded by the judge in final satisfaction of all the wife's financial claims was too high. The Court of Appeal substituted a figure of £90,000.
Notes
1. For further details, see Appendix II.
2. See also *S v S* (10–211).

10–213 Thwaite v Thwaite

[1981] 2 All ER 789, CA

Consent order dismissing wife's application for periodical payments – failure to carry out terms of consent order – wife's original application for ancillary relief still before the court – jurisdiction to set aside consent order. See Appendix II.

10–214 H v H (15 May 1981)

(1981) Times, 16 May

Short childless marriage between young parties – both capable of earning their own living – if the wife was prepared to consent to the dismissal of her claim for periodical payments the court was prepared to order the husband to make her a small lump sum payment.   See Appendix II.

PART 3

Section 25 (1) of the Matrimonial Causes Act 1973: its interpretation and effect

It is this section which provides the very wide framework and guidelines within which the court will exercise its power to make financial provision and property adjustment orders on or after the grant of a decree. In this part of the book are set out summaries of many of the cases in which the precise words of this section have been judicially considered and explained. Somewhat inevitably, many of the cases included here are also to be found elsewhere in the work. With one or two exceptions, the cases in which the word 'conduct' (which appears in the concluding paragraph to the section) has been judicially considered are not considered here, as this important element is separately considered in Chapter 8.

The very fact that many of the cases contained within Part 3 are repeated elsewhere is somewhat inevitable, when it is this very section which is the starting point for the court's consideration of nearly all aspects of its powers: such as whether or not to order a sale of the matrimonial home; whether or not and, if so, in what proportions, to divide capital, order the payment of lump sums and periodic mainten-ance, etc. It is quite apparent that the framework laid down by the section is not only broad but also extremely flexible. In no sense whatsoever is the section meant to supply a precise answer to the obvious questions from the client of 'what will I have to pay or give?' or, perhaps more pertinently, 'what will I be awarded?' The manner in which a court will choose to operate within the guidelines of the section is, then, largely unpredictable. It is well known that the hundreds of registrars who exercise the powers given to them by the 1973 Act, as a matter of personal habit, caprice or impulse, vary enormously in the degrees of emphasis which they place on the various considerations to which they are directed by the section. Perhaps for that reason, the decisions of the appellate courts or the High Court in which the precise words of the section have been explained are of particular importance in that they do inevitably act as a restraint on purely capricious or impulsive decisions.

Perhaps the most important fact to bear in mind, when attempting to understand what approach the court ought to adopt in exercising its powers, is that the word 'equality' is nowhere to be found in the section. (See the judgment of Ormrod LJ in *P v P* (13–015).) The court is in no sense directed to arrive at a result which, even broadly speaking, can be said to be an equal result as between the parties. It follows that, because most of the considerations which are to be applied in subparagraphs (a) to (g) have nothing to do with equality (e.g. the respective financial needs, obligations and responsibilities of the parties after separation, which may be enormously different), a court may, for example, divest a husband of his interest in a matrimonial home purchased by his sole financial contributions over many years because the future and financial needs of his former spouse and children so far outweigh his technical property rights. A rather vague way of expressing the task that the court is faced with performing within this flexible framework is embodied in the phrase 'doing broad justice between the parties'. (Perhaps that is no more than a convenient way of endeavouring to explain to disgruntled parties why they have been, or are likely to be, stripped of valuable capital assets because of the existence in their hands of, for example, a superior earning capacity.) However, there is nothing to prevent the court from 'doing rough justice on the basis of equality'—see *Trippas v Trippas* (13–002).

It should also be pointed out that in practice the court would be performing an awkward and wholly artificial task if in each and every case it considered all of the matters referred to in Section 25 in a piecemeal and disjointed 'step by step' approach. The approach of most courts would seem to be entirely the reverse, and the vast majority of cases may be properly prepared, argued and judged without any specific reference to section 25, with the broad hope or assumption that the court and the advocates have its various considerations in the background at all stages. Again, a perusal of all these cases ought to show that, in a typical situation where the court is faced with the task of determining shares in a matrimonial home and balancing the day-to-day financial needs of the parties and their children, there is an endless permutation of possible results. In practice, what the court frequently does is attempt to arrive at a result which would, on the face of it, appear to do 'broad justice' between the parties. The factors working towards the arrival at this result are the myriad variables which go towards tipping the scales in any contested litigation. In some cases the solution is glaringly obvious. In more finely balanced cases the result may well depend on the demeanour of the party or the persuasiveness of his or her advocate. It would appear that sometimes the result is first arrived at in the mind of the judge or registrar, and that only then, it would seem, merely as a secondary exercise, that the court goes on to express that decision as being in the light of any of the particular guidelines within section 25. In other words, section 25 with its numerous considerations is, in our submission, frequently used as a collection of judicial pegs on which to hang a result which may have been simply arrived at because of its obvious fairness, or because of any one of the more complex reasons which affect contested litigation.

In all these circumstances, we considered setting out the cases in this part of the book according to whether they mentioned subparagraphs (a) to (g) in that particular order. We rejected this as an artificial and unnecessarily repetitive exercise. The cases in Chapter 13 all make some useful references to section 25 in one sense or another. They are set out in chronological order, and therefore there is no particular line of consistency in terms of which particular part of the section is being dealt with. However, Chapters 11 and 12 provide an index for easy reference.

CHAPTER 11

'It shall be the duty of the court . . . to have regard to all the circumstances of the case . . .'

CASE SUMMARIES

11–001 Lombardi v Lombardi

[1973] 3 All ER 625, CA

Lapse of time since separation. See case summary 13–003.

11–002 H v H (financial provision: remarriage)

[1975] 1 All ER 367

Remarriage. See case summary 13–005.

11–003 Jones v Jones

[1975] 2 All ER 12, CA

Effect of physical attack on former spouse after decree absolute. See case summary 13–006.

11–004 Calderbank v Calderbank

[1975] 3 All ER 333, CA

All the circumstances of the particular case. See case summary 13–007.

11–005 Kokosinski v Kokosinski

[1980] 1 All ER 1106

Wife's contribution to the family in kind and to the running of the family business prior to the marriage ceremony when husband unable to marry her. See case summary 13–016.

11–006 Chambers v Chambers

(1980) 1 FLR 10

Lapse of time since separation – the principle of the clean break – parties to be encouraged to deal with all outstanding issues as reasonably expeditiously and succinctly as possible. See case summary 13–017.

11–006A Foley v Foley

[1981] 2 All ER 857, CA

The 'duration of the marriage' under s. 25 (1) (d) does not include premarital cohabitation, which is merely one of the other 'circumstances' to which the court is required to have regard, and the weight to be given to it is a matter for the court's discretion. See Appendix II.

11-007 Preston v Preston

(1981) Times, 25 June, CA

All the circumstances of the case. See case summary 13-018.

'. . . including the following matters, that is to say –'

1 '(a) the income, earning capacity, property and other financial resources which each of the parties to the marriage has or is likely to have in the foreseeable future'

CASE SUMMARIES

12–101 Browne v Pritchard

[1975] 3 All ER 721, CA

See case summary 13–008.

12–102 W v W (financial provision: lump sum)

[1975] 3 All ER 970

See case summary 13–009.

12–103 Daubney v Daubney

[1976] 2 All ER 453, CA

See case summary 13–010.

12–104 Martin v Martin (sub nom. **Martin (BH) v Martin (D)**)

[1977] 3 All ER 762, CA

See case summary 13–014.

12–105 P v P (financial provision: lump sum)

[1978] 3 All ER 70, CA

See case summary 13–015.

12–106 Preston v Preston

(1981) Times, 25 June, CA

See case summary 13–018.

2 '(b) the financial needs, obligations and responsibilities which each of the parties to the marriage has or is likely to have in the foreseeable future'

CASE SUMMARIES

12–201 H v H (financial provision: remarriage)

[1975] 1 All ER 367

See case summary 13–005.

12–202 Calderbank v Calderbank

[1975] 3 All ER 333, CA

See case summary 13–007.

12–203 Browne v Pritchard

[1975] 3 All ER 721, CA

See case summary 13–008.

12–204 S v S

[1977] 1 All ER 56, CA

See case summary 13–012.

12–205 Martin v Martin (sub nom. Martin (BH) v Martin (D))

[1977] 3 All ER 762, CA

See case summary 13–014.

12–206 P v P (financial provision: lump sum)

[1978] 3 All ER 70, CA

See case summary 13–015.

12–207 Preston v Preston

(1981) Times, 25 June, CA

See case summary 13–018.

3 '(c) the standard of living enjoyed by the family before the breakdown of the marriage'

CASE SUMMARIES

12–301 Calderbank v Calderbank

[1975] 3 All ER 333, CA

See case summary 13–007.

12–302 Martin v Martin (sub nom. **Martin (BH) v Martin (D)**)

[1977] 3 All ER 762, CA

See case summary 13–014.

12–303 Preston v Preston

(1981) Times, 25 June, CA

See case summary 13–018.

4 '(d) the age of each party to the marriage and the duration of the marriage'

CASE SUMMARIES

12–401 Campbell v Campbell

[1977] 1 All ER 1

See case summary 13–011.

12–402 West v West

[1977] 2 All ER 705, CA

See case summary 13–013.

12–403 Kokosinski v Kokosinski

[1980] 1 All ER 1106

See case summary 13–016.

12–403A Foley v Foley

[1981] 2 All ER 857, CA

See Appendix II.

12–404 Preston v Preston

(1981) Times, 25 June, CA

See case summary 13–018.

5 '(e) any physical or mental disability of either of the parties to the marriage'

CASE SUMMARIES

12–501 Jones v Jones

[1975] 2 All ER 12, CA

See case summary 13–006.

6 '(f) the contributions made by each of the parties to the welfare of the family, including any contribution made by looking after the home or caring for the family'

CASE SUMMARIES

12–601 Wachtel v Wachtel

[1973] 1 All ER 829, CA

See case summary 13–001.

12–602 H v H (financial provision: remarriage)

[1975] 1 All ER 367

See case summary 13–005.

12–603 West v West

[1977] 2 All ER 705, CA

See case summary 13–013.

12–604 P v P (financial provision: lump sum)

[1978] 3 All ER 70, CA

See case summary 13–015.

12–605 Kokosinski v Kokosinski

[1980] 1 All ER 1106

See case summary 13–016.

12–606 Preston v Preston

(1981) Times, 25 June, CA

See case summary 13–018.

7 '(g) ... any benefit (for example, a pension) which, by reason of the dissolution or annulment of the marriage, that party will lose the chance of acquiring'

CASE SUMMARIES

12–701 Trippas v Trippas

[1973] 2 All ER 1, CA

See case summary 13–002.

12–702 Preston v Preston

(1981) Times, 25 June, CA

See case summary 13–018.

8 '. . . and so to exercise those powers as to place the
parties . . . in the financial position in which they would
have been if the marriage had not broken down . . .'

CASE SUMMARIES

12–801 Trippas v Trippas

[1973] 2 All ER 1, CA

See case summary 13–002.

12–802 Harnett v Harnett

[1974] 1 All ER 764, CA

See case summary 13–004.

12–803 Calderbank v Calderbank

[1975] 3 All ER 333, CA

See case summary 13–007.

12–804 Preston v Preston

(1981) Times, 25 June, CA

See case summary 13–018.

CHAPTER 13

Section 25 (1) of the Matrimonial Causes Act 1973: case summaries referred to

CASE SUMMARIES

13–001 Wachtel v Wachtel

[1973] 1 All ER 829, CA

As was pointed out in the judgment of Lord Denning MR (at page 838), this section arose directly out of the Law Commission Report on Financial Provision in Matrimonial Proceedings (1969). Lord Denning MR went on to explain the effect of subsection 1 (f) in clear and straighforward terms which, it is respectfully submitted, remains the definitive expression of the effect of the statute in this particular instance. Lord Denning MR said: 'In the light thus thrown on the reason for [section 25 (1) (f)], we may take it that Parliament recognised that the wife who looks after the home and family contributes as much to the family assets as the wife who goes out to work. The one contributes in kind. The other in money or money's worth. If the court comes to the conclusion that the home has been acquired and maintained by the joint efforts of both, then, when the marriage breaks down, it should be regarded as the joint property of both of them, no matter in whose name it stands. Just as the wife who makes substantial money contributions usually gets a share, so should the wife who looks after the home and cares for the family for 20 years or more.'

Note. See also case summary 7–101.

13–002 Trippas v Trippas

[1973] 2 All ER 1, CA

The husband and wife married in 1941. Both parties worked during the marriage, the husband in the family business. In 1968 the parties separated and both began to cohabit with new partners. The matrimonial home was worth £10,000 and the husband bought out the wife's interest for £5,000. In 1969 the family business was sold for £350,000, the husband receiving £80,000 in cash and £95,000 in shares. The husband paid £5,000 to each of the two sons but nothing to the wife. The judge awarded the wife a lump sum of £8,000. The husband appealed contending that, since the case was not an appropriate one for periodical payments, neither was it a case for a lump sum order, the wife having thrown in her lot with the man with whom she was living and whom she might marry. The wife cross-appealed against the quantum of the lump sum.

Scarman LJ (as he then was) said (at page 8): '... one turns back again to the language of [s. 25 (1) (g)]; and one sees that the court has to have regard, on an application for an order, to "the value to either of the parties to the marriage of any benefit (for example, a pension)..." Those words are apt in the circumstances of this man and his business to cover the availability of this money which, by reason of the dissolution of the marriage, the wife has lost the chance of acquiring. Like Lord Denning MR I think the words of the statute cover exactly the situation that arose and place on the court the necessity of considering whether or not a lump sum should be ordered under [s. 23].

'Counsel for the husband's third point was that a lump sum award is unjust; and he emphasised that the wife now has the support of the man with whom she is living. The court must have regard to all the circumstances of the case. Not only must the court have regard to the past, it must also have regard to the present and to the future. If one studies the present and the future of these parties, the situation is that if a capital sum is made available to the wife, something very near equality can be achieved.

'... a lump sum of £10,000 awarded to the wife would create a situation as near equality as it is practical to get. There is nothing either in the so-called one-third rule or in the language of the ... Act which precludes this court from doing rough justice on the basis of approximate equality, provided it is, on the whole, just to both parties, as in my opinion it is in this case. If one looks at the very last words of [s. 25 (1)], the court is required to exercise its powers –

> "so as to place the parties, so far as it is practicable and, having regard to their conduct, just to do so, in the financial position in which they would have been if the marriage had not broken down and each had properly discharged his or her financial obligations and responsibilities towards the other".

I think a lump sum of £10,000 goes as far as is practicable towards doing just that.'

13–003 Lombardi v Lombardi

[1973] 3 All ER 625, CA

The parties married in 1951. There two children. Separation occurred in 1956 but there was no divorce until 1971. Since 1959 the husband had cohabited with a third party and, with the assistance of his cohabitee, had carried on a grocery business which had accumulated a substantial capital sum for them. In addition the husband had an endowment policy of £10,000, and his standard of living was said to be very comfortable. By contrast, the wife lived in one room for which she paid £3 per week, was in fear of eviction and had no capital. The husband was ordered to pay the wife £3 per week. The judge took into account the fact that the parties had lived together for only five years, and that it was only after the marriage had broken up that the husband, with the assistance of the third party, had achieved a certain degree of prosperity. The wife's appeal was dismissed.

Cairns LJ assessed the statutory guidelines of what is now s. 25 (1), and referred thus to the argument that the trial judge had been wrong in taking into account the long lapse of time since the marriage broke up (at page 629): 'I do not think it can be said as a matter of law that he was wrong to do so. That is one of "the circumstances of the case".'

Later on, it was said: 'Another way in which the judgment is criticised is that the judge was wrong to take into account that the husband's fortune had accrued to him since the parting. Again, I think that that is a proper circumstance to pay regard to. It was never suggested in this case ... that the position crystallised at the time of the parting and that thereafter any change in the husband's means was irrelevant. The increase in the husband's means is plainly relevant; but it is also, in my view, relevant to remember that it is something which has happened since the parting. And what is of much more importance here is that it is not merely something which has happened since the parting: it is something which has been brought about by the husband in co-operation and partnership with [the cohabitee] ...'

13–004 Harnett v Harnett

[1974] 1 All ER 764, CA

The husband sought to appeal against an order that the former matrimonial home should be sold and that the wife should receive £12,500 from the proceeds of sale, contending that under [s. 25] of the Act it was not necessary to show that there had been misconduct of a gross and obvious nature before the question of conduct could be taken into account. The conduct pointed to was an adulterous association by the wife with a 20-year-old youth who had lived with the parties periodically over six years as a member of the family.

Cairns LJ rejected this argument saying (at page 767): 'For my part, even assuming that it were open to this court today to say that the doctrine laid down in *Wachtel v Wachtel* was wrong, it would be most unfortunate that we should do so. If there is anything which is likely to cause difficulty for the profession and for the public, it is that two different divisions of the Court of Appeal should say different things in relation to a matter of this kind. Not only that, but I would add that, speaking for myself, and quite independently of the authority of *Wachtel v Wachtel*, I would reach the view that it is the intention of the . . . Act that conduct should be taken into account only in a very broad way – that is to say, only where there is something in the conduct of one party which would make it quite inequitable to leave that out of account having regard to the conduct of the other party as well as the course of the marriage. I say that because if one looks at [s. 25], conduct of the parties is not one of the list of matters which are to be considered by the court as matters of detail in arriving at the figures but finds its place only at the end in the words that the court is to exercise those powers so as to –

> "place the parties, so far as is practicable and, having regard to their conduct, just to do so, in the financial position in which they would have been if the marriage had not broken down . . ."

In that context, I for my part think it right to say that conduct should be considered only if there is some misconduct of a gross and obvious nature.'

13–005 H v H (financial provision: remarriage)

[1975] 1 All ER 367

The wife left the husband and went to live with the co-respondent, who was a wealthy man. After the making of the decree absolute the wife married the co-respondent. The wife applied for a property adjustment order, claiming that the former matrimonial home should be held in trust for the parties in equal shares until the youngest child attained its 18th birthday, or alternatively, that she should receive a lump sum payment. In support of her claim, it was argued that by reason of her contributions to the welfare of the family she had earned an accrued right to participate in the division of the family assets by virtue of section 25 (1) (f) of the Matrimonial Causes Act 1973, and that her marriage to a wealthy man should not affect such right nor have any bearing on her accrued entitlement.

Sir George Baker P determined that the main question for decision was the effect of the wife's remarriage to a man of means, with her new home conveyed in their joint names, on her claim for the settlement of the former matrimonial home in trust in equal shares. At page 371 the learned judge considered a passage from Lord Denning MR's judgment in *Wachtel v Wachtel* and referred to *Trippas v Trippas*. In the latter case the wife was living with another man whom she might marry. That did not affect her entitlement. He continued: 'The prospect, chance or hope of remarriage is I think irrelevant, but *the fact of remarriage, which does not admit of speculation, is in my judgment something which the court must consider in the course of its statutory duty under section 25* [of the Matrimonial Causes Act 1973] *to have regard to all the circumstances of the case.*'

And having reviewed earlier authorities, the learned judge concluded: '*To ignore remarriage entirely would be to ignore the financial needs of the parties in the foreseeable future: see s. 25 (1) (b).*'

13–006 Jones v Jones (sub nom. **Jones (MA) v Jones (W)**)

[1975] 2 All ER 12, CA

The Court of Appeal had to consider whether or not to have regard to the husband's conduct in attacking the wife with a knife after the decree had been made absolute, thereby inflicting a number of wounds, one of which caused a 75 per cent disability of the hand. One of the effects of the injury was that the wife was unable to work, and her future prospects of employment were doubtful.

It was held that the word 'conduct' in s. 25 (1) of the Matrimonial Causes Act 1973 is not limited to events which take place before the breakdown of the marriage or, indeed, before the decree is made absolute. Megaw LJ said (at page 17): 'I would not for one moment accept that it is not permissible, under the provisions of s. 25 (1) . . ., for a court to take that fact into account in deciding what are the appropriate shares, if any, of the parties in the family assets. I know of no authority which so requires or so suggests. I do not care, for myself, whether the relevance for this purpose of the effect of the husband's physical attack on his wife should be regarded as coming within the opening words of s. 25 (1) as part of "all the circumstances of the case" to which the court is required to have regard, or whether, on the other hand, it should be regarded as part of their "conduct" in the concluding words of the subsection . . . I would stress again that in my view the word "conduct" in that context is not to be treated as being confined to matrimonial misconduct.'

Although there was no specific reference made to subparagraph (e) this was clearly a case where the court had regard to a 'physical . . . disability' of a party to the marriage.

13–007 Calderbank v Calderbank

[1975] 3 All ER 333, CA

The wife appealed (inter alia) against an award of a lump sum of £10,000 to the husband. Cairns LJ specifically referred to s. 25 (1) (b), saying: 'The main attack on this judgment has been that the judge failed to consider whether the wife had an obligation to the husband to provide him with money for a new house. *Insofar as obligations and responsibilities are referred to in s. 25 (1) (b) I am of opinion . . . that the obligations and responsibilities there mentioned are obligations and responsibilities to persons other than the other spouse.*'

The learned judge then went on to differentiate between the meaning of the expression 'obligations and responsibilities' as contained in s. 25 (1) (b) and the same expression as contained in what he called the 'overall consideration' as expressed at the very end of the complete subsection, namely:

> '. . . and so to exercise those powers as to place the parties, so far as it is practicable and, having regard to their conduct, just to do so, in the financial position in which they would have been if the marriage had not broken down and each had properly discharged his or her financial obligations and responsibilities towards the other'.

Cairns LJ considered that, *in this last mentioned passage*, the phrase 'obligations and responsibilities' means legally enforceable obligations and responsibilities. What falls to be considered under this part of the subsection, according to the learned judge, are the obligations and responsibilities which any reasonable spouse dealing with the other spouse and living in circumstances of a normal family life would recognise as being owed to that other spouse.

Returning to the instant case, the learned judge considered that, if the marriage had not broken down and each spouse had properly discharged his or her obligations and responsibilities to the other, the husband would still be living in a house for which he would not have to pay. As it was no longer practicable that the husband should continue to live in that house, it was considered entirely appropriate that he should be awarded such lump sum as would provide a suitable house for his needs.

Much of the judgment of Lord Scarman contained lengthy expressions as to his understanding of the framework of section 25. For example at page 338 he said: 'Whatever be the position today as between husband and wife while they are still married, it is abundantly plain that fresh powers have been given to the court to make financial and property adjustment orders on divorce, nullity or judicial separation. There is nothing in the relevant sections of the Act to indicate that the husband and wife are not for the purposes of those sections to be treated on an equal basis. The relevant sections are ss. 21, 22, 23, 24 and 25. It will be observed that each of the sections refers to "the parties to a marriage" and confers on the court precisely the same powers in respect of each party of the marriage, be it the husband or the wife. There is therefore nothing in the sections to suggest that only in exceptional circumstances may the court make a financial order by way of periodical payment or lump sum in favour of the husband. Basically the principle of the sections is that each spouse comes to the court on a basis of equality. But of course the court has to have regard to s. 25, and the particular circumstances of the case. Counsel for the wife says, Yes; the court has the power to make an order in favour of either spouse, whether husband or wife; but, when one looks at s. 25 it is clear, he says, that what really matters is to discover what are the obligations or responsibilities of the parties to the marriage, and counsel for the wife submits that where those words are used in s. 25 they refer to legal obligations. He then reverts to his basic proposition that apart from statute there is no legal obligation on a wife to maintain the husband. I think that counsel for the wife's approach to the sections is misconceived and based on an erroneous construction of s. 25. Really counsel for the wife is saying that we must read s. 25 as stating impliedly, because it certainly does not say so expressly, that financial provision may be made for a husband only in exceptional circumstances. The section says nothing of the sort. *The section requires the court to look at all the circumstances of the case and to make an order that is appropriate to the particular circumstances of the two spouses whose case is under consideration.* I think the learned trial judge [Heilbron J] got it absolutely right when she said in the course of her judgment:

> "The factors to be taken into consideration under s. 25 are factors relating to both parties, but obviously considerations will vary according to whether the party seeking the transfer of property or lump sum is the husband or the wife."

Of course the court has to take into account the fact that one party is the husband the other is the wife. It has to take into account much else besides. It has to look to the income, earning capacity, property and other financial resources of the parties to the marriage. Who is the breadwinner, who the housekeeper? It has to look to the financial needs, obligations and responsibilities of the parties to the marriage both at the time that the matter is before the court and in the foreseeable future. It has to look to their standard of living, to their age, to any physical or mental disability and to contributions made by each to the welfare of the family, for example working in the home. Finally the court has to exercise its powers so as to place the parties, so far as it can and it is just to do so, in the financial position in which they would have been if the marriage had not broken down and each had properly discharged his or her financial obligations and responsibilities towards the other. In the present case the judge came to the conclusion that there was a need of the husband for some capital to enable him to acquire, no doubt with the aid of a mortgage, a house suitable to his station in life and suitable for the accommodation of the three children when they came to stay with him.'

It should also be noted that, without any specific reference to subparagraph (c), the court referred directly to the standard of living and life-style which the husband had been able to enjoy since his marriage, supported by the capital resources of the wife. To that extent, the size of the lump sum awarded was meant to reflect not only his basic need for a house, but also the need for him to maintain a standard of living which was not too drastically curtailed from that to which he was accustomed.

Note. See also references to the judgments in *Calderbank v Calderbank* by Ormrod LJ in *P v P* (13–015).

13–008 Browne v Pritchard

[1975] 3 All ER 721, CA

After a short marriage the wife left the husband and went to live with her new husband in a council house. The husband remained in the matrimonial home (which was in joint names) with two children by a former association. The wife sought an order that she was entitled to a half share in the matrimonial home.

The Court of Appeal upheld the county court judge's assessment of the wife's interest at one-third but further ordered that her interest should take the form of a charge on the property, not to be enforced until the younger child had reached 18.

Ormrod LJ (at page 725) referred to the different factors to be considered as directed by subparagraphs (a) and (b). In the instant case one consideration, namely 'resources' (in other words the wife's strict property rights), would produce a very different result unless balanced (or, as in this case, outweighed) by the often conflicting consideration of 'needs'. He continued: 'Property rights are now ancillary to the interests of the family. That is quite clear from the tenor of the legislation itself. It is even more clear from the sidenote to s. 24 of the 1973 Act which refers to "property adjustment orders". Section 25 contains detailed directions to the court how it is to exercise the extremely wide powers given to it to make property adjustment orders. Section 25 (1) (a) begins by referring to "resources" and then in para (b) to "needs". Whenever a court is dealing with families of limited resources, needs are likely to be much more important than resources when it comes to exercising discretion. In most individuals and most families the most urgent need is a home. It is therefore to the provision of homes for all concerned that the courts should direct their attention in the first place. Where, as in this case, it is found that the wife has a secure home in a council flat, then she has what in these days is a very valuable asset.'

13–009 W v W (financial provision: lump sum)

[1975] 3 All ER 970

The parties were married in 1964 and there were two children. The matrimonial home had been bought in 1970 in the husband's sole name. In 1972 the wife left, taking the children with her. In early 1973 the wife began to cohabit with a third party, S, and eventually had a child by him. Again in 1973, S bought a new house on a 100% mortgage; the wife made no contribution to the cost of purchase. The wife and S lived in the new home together with S's children and the illegitimate child. In ancillary proceedings the wife applied for a lump sum order. The equity in the house owned by the wife and S was valued at £1,400 and the equity in the former matrimonial home was valued at £8,100. There were no other capital assets. The wife contended that she was entitled to a one-third share in the equity of the matrimonial home, i.e. £2,700. It was further argued that in considering, under s. 25 (1) (a) of the Matrimonial Causes Act, what order would be appropriate, no account should be taken of her interest in the house owned jointly with S since it was open to the court to find that since she had made no contribution to its purchase, it was not intended that she should have a beneficial interest in the house.

Counsel for the wife sought to argue that, although there was in fact joint ownership of the new home with S (which Sir George Baker P, the judge, considered a powerful indication of financial entitlement to a half share), it was open to the court to say that this was not 'property' or 'other financial resources which [the wife] has or is likely to have in the foreseeable future', within s. 25 (1) (a).

The President rejected this argument, saying: 'It seems to me that there is something of value to this lady. It may be that she would not in the end manage to obtain a half share; but, she might.' The learned judge considered all the future contingencies and continued: '... she has at least the asset of the roof over her head. That asset may be converted into cash at some future time, but it is a continuing asset. She has, as it were, a licence to be in this house, and a licence which is irrevocable in the sense that her agreement is needed before it can be ended. I think that this is obviously something of value and that, having regard to the fact that it could be turned into cash and that she could have a share of that cash in the foreseeable future, it can fall within s. 25 (1) (a) of the 1973 Act.'

In fact (although the house owned with S was in joint names) the judge chose not to take into account the full half share. The wife's interest in her new home was in fact valued at £300, and the lump sum of £2,700 to which she was otherwise entitled (in respect of her interest in the former matrimonial home) was reduced by that amount.

Note. In *Leake v Bruzzi* (24–202) the Court of Appeal held that an express declaration of the parties' interests under a trust for sale is conclusive in the absence of fraud or mistake.

13–010 Daubney v Daubney

[1976] 2 All ER 453, CA

The question arose for determination in the Court of Appeal whether damages awarded to the wife during the currency of the marriage (which were in respect of personal injury, pain and suffering), should be taken into account in assessing the husband's application for a transfer of property order. [In this context see 1–501, 502 and 503.] Having considered all the earlier authorities on this point and having distinguished *Jones v Jones* (1–502), Cairns LJ said (at page 458): 'I am in the somewhat embarrassing position of forming a view as to where the balance of judicial opinion is, but I think that it is right to say that the balance is in favour of taking this money into account. At any rate, I am of opinion that there is no decision binding us to leave out of account the resources of the wife acquired through her damages and, with all respect to those who have expressed a contrary view, I am still convinced that it would be contrary to s. 25 (1) (a) of the 1973 Act to leave them out.'

13–011 Campbell v Campbell

[1977] 1 All ER 1

The case initially concerned an appeal by the wife against the level of the order of the registrar for periodical payments for herself and a child. The question arose as to what, if any, attention should be paid to a period of cohabitation before marriage in considering the length of the marriage.

Sir George Baker P said that the wife had not taken the point, which is so often taken in 'short marriage' cases by a wife, that the marriage was only short because the husband had ended it and she had accordingly been deprived of the opportunity of being a good wife over the years. The learned judge was not disposed to treat the marriage as anything but a short marriage, and therefore the length of the marriage was a matter to which consideration had to be given within s. 25 (1) (d) of the Act. It had been argued on behalf of the wife that a period of 3½ years of premarital cohabitation should be taken into account in assessing the length of the marriage. The argument clearly held no appeal whatsoever for the learned judge, who said (at page 6):

'There is an increasing tendency ... to regard and, indeed, to speak of the celebration of marriage as "the paperwork" ... Well that is, to my mind, an entirely misconceived outlook. It is the ceremony of marriage and the sanctity of marriage which count; rights, duties and obligations begin on marriage and not before. It is a complete cheapening of the marriage relationship which, I believe, and I am sure many share this belief, is essential to the well-being of our society as we understand it, to suggest that premarital periods . . . should, as it were, by a doctrine of relation back of matrimony, be taken as a part of marriage to count in favour of the wife performing, as it is put, "wifely duties before marriage".'

Note. See *Kokosinski v Kokosinski* (13–016) for an example of a case where a period of premarital cohabitation was deemed to be relevant.

13–012 S v S

[1977] 1 All ER 56, CA

The registrar (who was upheld by the county court judge) fixed upon a fraction of one-seventh of the joint income as periodical payments for the wife. In addition the husband was to pay a lump sum of £7,000.

The Court of Appeal adopted a fresh approach, and in doing so were guided by s. 25 (1) (b). According to Ormrod LJ the adoption of the one-seventh fraction was a purely arbitrary exercise. It had the disadvantage that it fixed the sum 'without any regard to the needs of the wife . . .' The learned judge continued (at page 60): 'In my view it is much easier, and better in these cases, to follow s. 25 of the Matrimonial Causes Act 1973 and to perform the exercise there required, namely to ascertain the means of the parties and their resources and the charges and obligations that they have to meet; and also to take account of the needs of the parties and then to have regard to such other matters as are set out there, such as contribution to the family welfare: obviously, in a case like this, that contribution was not very great and counsel for the wife in this court has made no attempt to place any great reliance, or indeed any reliance, on that aspect of it. The length of the marriage has to be taken into account also; and again counsel for the wife has readily conceded that this was quite a short marriage.

'So it seems to me that the primary consideration is to look at the needs of the wife, first of all; and, having made some assessment of the needs, then to check the resulting figure that emerges against the resources of the husband, and at that stage see what the ratio of the one to the other is and to consider – assuming an order for £x, the lump sum, and £y for the periodical payments order – how the two parties will stand in relation one to the other, and relate that to all the circumstances of the case, including the shortness of the marriage. If attention is concentrated primarily on need in this type of case, the consequent calculations become very much easier and very much more logical, and discussion on the case will become very much more constructive.'

Approaching the matter in that way the court arrived at the result that the husband should settle £11,000 on the wife on trust until her death or earlier remarriage in order to provide a suitable house, together with a lump sum of £2,000 to cover the cost of moving. There was also an order for periodical payments of £2,000 per annum less tax.

13–013 West v West

[1977] 2 All ER 705, CA

The parties married in 1970 at a time when the husband had not found a house which was acceptable to the wife, who went back to live with her parents. In August 1970 the husband, with the wife's agreement, purchased a house which was suitable as the matrimonial home but the wife refused to live in it. In 1975 the husband petitioned for divorce on the ground of five years' separation. By then there were two children, who were being brought up by the wife whilst continuing to reside in her parents' home. The parties had spent no more than a total of seven weeks in cohabitation during more than five years of marriage. Following the divorce the wife applied for financial provision for herself and the children. At the first instance hearing of the wife's application the judge found that the wife had been in desertion from the outset of the marriage by reason of her conduct in refusing to cohabit, and that her conduct was the main factor in reducing the duration of the marriage virtually to nil and the main factor causing the eventual breakdown. The judge referred to s. 25 (1) (d) and (f) of the Act and held that the wife's conduct justified a substantial reduction in the amount of her financial provision, and he therefore awarded her periodical payments amounting to about one-eighth of the parties' joint income.

The wife's appeal was dismissed. Ormrod LJ said (at page 711): 'The learned judge was perfectly justified in arriving at the conclusion which he did by applying the relevant paragraph of s. 25 (1) and, in particular paragraphs (d) and (f) of [the Act] . . . The duration of the marriage, to all intents and purposes in this case, was nil, and so far as caring for the family is concerned, she has never cared for her husband in any sense.'

13–014 Martin v Martin (sub nom. Martin (BH) v Martin (D))

[1977] 3 All ER 762, CA

The Court of Appeal dismissed the husband's appeal from the order of Purchas J that the matrimonial home should be held on trust for the wife's sole use during her lifetime, or until her remarriage or voluntary removal from the property, whichever occurred first. The husband already had a secure home with the third party with whom he was living.

Stamp LJ gave express approval to the approach which Purchas J had adopted at first instance in his application of the statutory guidelines of s. 25 (1). In doing so the learned appeal judge made four important observations on the interpretation of s. 25. They were (at pages 765–7):

1.   '*It is of primary concern in these cases that on the breakdown of the marriage the parties should, if possible, each have a roof over his or her head. That is perhaps the most important circumstance to be taken into account in applying s. 25 of the Matrimonial Causes Act 1973 when the only available asset is the matrimonial home.* It is important that each party should have a roof over his or her head whether or not there be children of the marriage.'
2.   As to s. 25 (1) (a):
      'After a careful review of a number of authorities [Purchas J] turned to consider and apply the provisions of s. 25 of the 1973 Act. In relation to s. 25 (1) (a), the income and earning capacity of each of the parties in the instant case disclosed that each had a reasonable earning capacity, and that the wife's earnings were such that the registrar made only a nominal order for periodical payments in her favour. I would interrupt the recital of the judge's judgment by remarking that if the wife is allowed to remain in occupation of the matrimonial home the risk that the husband will ever be ordered to make periodical payments to her is, as I see it, negligible. In the absence of the unlikely event of dramatic improvement in his fortunes he will as a practical matter be relieved by the effect of the judge's order of the risk of having to make periodical payments to the wife in the future, for she will have a roof over her head for as long as she requires it and will be under no liability to pay rent.'
3.   As to s. 25 (1) (b):
      'The learned judge continued by referring to s. 25 (1) (b) of the 1973 Act, relating to the financial needs, obligations and responsibilities which each of the parties to the marriage had or was likely to have in the foreseeable future. He pointed out that there was no evidence that the husband had any immediate need for a capital sum in order to support his present way of life, and that he had a secure roof over his head. He went on to say a little later in the judgment

that the wife, on the other hand, needed either the matrimonial home in which she was presently living or some alternative accommodation. He pointed out that the learned registrar had found that "even with the sale of the matrimonial home the net equity available to the wife would not enable her to purchase alternative accommodation".

'Counsel for the husband submitted that there was a good possibility of the wife obtaining council accommodation, but there is no evidence whatsoever that she has, or is indeed likely to obtain, such accommodation. Apart, however, from that, I would require a good deal of convincing that it would not be contrary to public policy to make an order for sale of the matrimonial home so as to put £5,000 into the pocket of the husband and, incidentally, approximately the same amount into the wife's pocket, in the belief that the wife would be rehoused in council accommodation.'

4. As to s. 25 (1) (c):

'The judge went on to consider the effect of s. 25 (1) (c) of the 1973 Act, pointing out that it was "relevant to have regard to the fact that the family before the breakdown of the marriage lived in modest, comfortable circumstances in their own house on which a reasonably small mortgage was being paid off". In this connection I would emphasise that had the marriage continued the parties would almost certainly, as the judge pointed out, have remained in the house and would not have been in a position to enjoy the equity comprised in the matrimonial home in the form of a liquid asset until they reached the age of retirement and perhaps moved into smaller or more modest accommodation.'

Stamp LJ then quoted with approval these words from the judgment of the trial judge:

'If it is appropriate to balance the incidence of the order upon each of the parties in studying whether it is just to make the order . . . then I would say, without hesitation, that in these circumstances the degree of hardship likely to fall on the wife if she is forcibly removed from the matrimonial home will greatly exceed the hardship inflicted on the husband by being "kept out of his money" which in this case means little in the context of the continuation of the marriage and the unavailability of the matrimonial home as a liquid asset.'

13–015 P v P (financial provision: lump sum)

[1978] 3 All ER 70, CA

Shortly after the parties' marriage in 1964 the wife's father bought a farm (and farmstock) for the parties who went to live thereon. The farm was vastly improved and turned into a successful business by the efforts of both parties, but by the husband in particular. In 1971 the freehold of the farm was conveyed to the wife alone by way of a gift from her father. Following a divorce the husband left the farm in 1977; he had no qualifications and prior to his departure had been entirely dependent on the farm for his livelihood. The wife continued to live there with the three children aged six, ten and eleven. The farm, including the farmhouse and stock, was valued at £102,000. On hearing the husband's application under s. 17 of the Married Women's Property Act 1882 (for a declaration of his interest) and under s. 23 and s. 24 of the Matrimonial Causes Act 1973 (for lump sum and transfer of property orders) the county court judge awarded the husband a lump sum of £15,000 payable by the wife in three instalments; there were also nominal orders for periodical payments by the husband for the wife and children.

The husband's appeal against the level of the lump sum awarded to him was dismissed. Ormrod LJ said (at page 73): '. . . Counsel . . . referred us to a passage in *Wachtel v Wachtel* (13–001) which refers to "family assets". The judgment in *Wachtel v Wachtel* quite rightly described that as a convenient shorthand phrase.

Counsel . . . tells us, however, that a great deal of energy is spent in the courts dealing with these matters debating whether or not a particular item is properly to be regarded as a family asset. I would only like to say once and for all that the phrase "family assets" does not occur in the 1973 Act and it has nothing to do at all with s. 25 of that Act. Section 25 requires the court to have regard to the items set out in it and "family assets" is nothing to do with it. It is a convenient phrase that came into existence in the days before the courts had the wide jurisdiction provided originally by the Matrimonial Proceedings and Property Act 1970. In my judgment, it is not now a phrase of any particular use.'

The very heart of Ormrod LJ's judgment and his precise application of section 25 appears at page 75:

'Turning to the real nub of this case, I should like to start by taking a passage to which we were referred in the judgment of Scarman LJ in *Calderbank v Calderbank* which I think is very important. In that passage Scarman LJ said this:

"At the end of the day after a very careful judgment the judge came to a fair and sensible decision, and, speaking for myself, I rejoice that it should be made abundantly plain that husbands and wives come to the judgment seat in matters of money and property on a basis of complete equality. That complete equality may, and often will, have to give way to the particular circumstances of their married life."

I wish to stress the following words:

"It does not follow that, because they come to the judgment seat on the basis of complete equality, justice requires an equal division of the assets. The proportion of the division is dependent on the circumstances. The assets have to be divided or financial provision made according to the guidelines set out in s. 25. Every case will be different and no case may be decided except on its particular facts."

That passage should be regarded as the guideline in all these cases, and I would stress today, as I have stressed before, that the word "equality" does not have any place, any more than the phrase "family assets" has any place, in s. 25 of the 1973 Act. It is a great mistake to approach these cases as if either of those phrases were to be found in the section.

'If one looks at this case in the round the picture, as I see it, is this: in all probability the wife will have to carry the burden of bringing up the children for the rest of their childhood. There is very little likelihood of her getting much, if any, financial assistance from her husband through no fault, I hasten to add, of his. But we are not here concerned with faults or blame or anything else. We are concerned here with the bare, basic realities of life. Who is going to provide the money to keep these children and bring them up properly? The answer is overwhelmingly clear: the wife is going to. So it would be quite impracticable to expect her to raise any larger capital sum than the learned judge has called on her to raise out of the farm business. No court would or should in a case such as this make a lump sum order which has the effect of making it impossible for the earner parent to continue to earn a living and so maintain the family and the children and so on.'

Notes

1. For reference to s. 25 (1) (a), see page 73 at letter h.
2. For reference to s. 25 (1) (b), see page 74 at letter b.
3. For reference to s. 25 (1) (f), see page 74 at letter f.

13–016 Kokosinski v Kokosinski

[1980] 1 All ER 1106

The parties began to cohabit in 1947, when the husband was already married in Poland. He did not become free to marry until 1969, and the parties married in

1971. By then the husband's engineering business had prospered. In 1972 a fresh matrimonial home was purchased. The wife and son moved into it, but the husband refused to join them. Relations between husband and wife then deteriorated rapidly. In 1977 the wife was granted a divorce. In 1979 the wife applied (inter alia) for a lump sum order so that she could buy a flat near her work. At the time of the application the wife was 56 and the husband 69. Both were still accommodated in properties acquired during the period of cohabitation. Both had appreciable though not substantial incomes. The husband had capital assets worth approximately £47,545. In answer to the wife's application, the husband contended that it would be inappropriate to grant a lump sum order because the court was bound by section 25 (1) (d) of the 1973 Act to have regard to 'the duration of the marriage', and the marriage had only lasted a few months, and was also bound by s. 25 (1) (f) to take into account the wife's 'contributions to the welfare of the family' only during the subsistence of the marriage, and should not take into consideration her conduct during the 25 years that the husband and wife were cohabiting prior to their marriage.

In awarding the wife a lump sum of £8,000 Wood J chose to distinguish *Campbell v Campbell* (13–011), saying (at page 1115): 'On the facts of that case it was abundantly clear that neither party was worthy of praise for his or her moral attitudes, nor for his or her contribution to a home, nor the upbringing of a family. Indeed there seemed to have been nothing to show for his or her efforts during their relationship. I note that Sir George Baker P stressed in the passage which I have quoted that his decision related to the particular circumstances of that case. I believe it was to s. 25 (1) (d) that Sir George Baker P's mind was being directed in argument.

'In approaching problems under ss. 21 to 25 of the 1973 Act, a number of propositions are clearly established by authority. The function and duty of the court is to reach a physical and financial resolution of the problems of that family which is fair, just and reasonable as between the parties. The court must look to the statutory guidance now provided by s. 25 of that Act. Secondly, in exercising this wide discretionary jurisdiction it is important that the court should be careful not to limit its discretion by a narrow construction of the statutory guidelines. It is quite impossible for any judge to foresee the multiplicity of circumstances which may be brought before him.

'Turning to s. 25 (1) (d) itself, the words "the duration of the marriage" in my judgment clearly mean what they say, but within that phrase it is clear that it is the period between ceremony of marriage and the final break-up of cohabitation which is likely to be the most material.

'I turn next to s. 25 (1) (f). In considering the problem before me the word from which I derive some guidance in that subsection is the word "family". Reading the 1973 Act as a whole, I take the view that "family" in that context indicates a reference to events post-marriage. In the many contexts in which that word is to be found in the Act, I do not think it can properly be construed to refer to a time prior to the ceremony of marriage.

'Section 25 further requires me to have regard to the conduct of the parties, and also to all the circumstances of the case. The latter phrase is very wide, but the word "conduct" has received judicial attention.

'It is argued, and indeed it is true, that the factor of "conduct" has for the most part been used in order to cut down the amount of financial relief which the court might otherwise have awarded to a party, and not for the purpose of increasing that amount. In my judgment there is nothing in the language of the section itself which supports this restricted view. My initial approach, therefore, is that any such restriction is unwarranted, and I then turn to authority.'

Wood J then went on to consider *Wachtel v Wachtel* (13–001), *Harnett v Harnett* (13–004), *Armstrong v Armstrong* (8–205) and *Jones v Jones* (13–006), and came to the following conclusion on the instant facts of this case (at page 1117): 'I find nothing therefore in the authorities to suggest that a broad and general approach to the words "conduct" and "in all the circumstances of the case" is undesirable or wrong.

'This wife has given the best years of her life to this husband. She has been faithful, loving and hard-working. She has helped him to build what is in every sense a family business. She has managed his home and been a mother to and helped him bring up a son of whom they are both justly proud. I believe that she has earned for herself some part of the value of the family business.

'Having set out those matters prior to the ceremony of marriage itself, which seem to me to be relevant, I ask myself whether I can do justice, that which is fair, just and reasonable between these parties, if I ignore the earlier history and the wife's behaviour during those earlier years. To put the question in a different form: would it really offend a reasonable person's sense of justice to ignore those events and that behaviour? I have no doubt that the answer from the reasonable man would be that they must be taken into account and, in my judgment, not only can I take these matters into account, whether under the phrase "conduct" or "in all the circumstances of the case" in s. 25, but that same section casts a duty on me to do so.'

In so far as this was a departure from the very clear line adopted by the Court of Appeal in *Campbell v Campbell*, Wood J at the end of his judgment sought to place some reservations on the generality of the principle which he had chosen to follow in this particular case. He said (at page 1119): 'Bearing in mind what was said by Sir George Baker P in the passage which I have cited from *Campbell v Campbell* it will be said by some that to recognise the relationship which existed before marriage as relevant to financial redistribution, is to encourage relationships outside marriage. To them I would answer that the occasions on which a court is likely to feel that justice requires such recognition are likely to be few, possibly very few. It would, however, not be helpful to speculate on situations which may never arise. In my judgment, on the particular facts of the present case my decision will do nothing to undermine the institution of marriage.'

Note. For further details of the facts of this case, see case summary 8–310.

13–017 Chambers v Chambers

(1980) 1 FLR 10

The parties were married in 1935 and there were three children. The wife left the husband in 1956 and went to live with a third party as man and wife. She continued to live with him until 1976 when the third party became so seriously ill that he was no longer able to live at home and support the wife. In 1977 the wife filed a petition for divorce on the basis of five years' separation; in ancillary proceedings she sought a lump sum payment to purchase a lease on a flat.

In rejecting the wife's application Wood J said (at page 13): 'If the petitioner had brought proceedings in 1957, there was no power in the court to grant a lump sum. This jurisdiction was introduced by s. 5 (1) of the Matrimonial Causes Act 1963. In all the circumstances then existing, I do not think that any order for maintenance would have been made by the court.

'Secondly, it is now the policy of the matrimonial legislation that on the breakdown of a marriage there should, if possible, be a clean break financially. By inference this indicates that the financial issues should be decided within a reasonably short time of the breakdown.

'Thirdly, after a certain lapse of time a party to a marriage is, in my judgment, entitled to take the view that there will be no revival or initiation of financial claims against him or her. The longer the lapse of time the more secure should he or she feel in the re-arrangement of financial affairs, and the less should any such claim be encouraged or entertained. Whether this notion is based upon some form of estoppel or upon public policy, it matters not. Where a marriage is irretrievably broken down, the parties are to be encouraged to deal with all outstanding issues as reasonably expeditiously and succinctly as possible. The financial claims must at least be initiated before re-marriage: s. 28 (3) of the Matrimonial Causes Act 1973.

'It is important, however, that I should remind myself that it is the provision of s. 25 of the Matrimonial Causes Act 1973 which must guide me in my decision. It seems to me that those provisions do not exclude the three considerations set out above, which must surely fall within the words "all the circumstances of the case".

'Directing myself accordingly, I have reached the decision that this application should be rejected.'

13–017A Foley v Foley

[1981] 2 All ER 857, CA

The 'duration of the marriage' under s. 25 (1) (d) does not include premarital cohabitation, which is merely one of the other 'circumstances' to which the court is required to have regard, and the weight to be given to it is a matter for the court's discretion. See Appendix II.

13–018 Preston v Preston

(1981) Times, 25 June, CA

The wife had worked as a model until after her first pregnancy. She had lived frugally, so helping the husband to build up business assets valued at £2.3m. It was conceded that the husband had no liquidity problem. The Court of Appeal held (Brandon LJ dissenting) that the award of a lump sum of £600,000 to the wife was not so excessively high as to warrant interference with the exercise of the judge's discretion.

Ormrod LJ said that in most cases it was not necessary to consider the extent of the court's powers under section 25 (1) of the Matrimonial Causes Act 1973, because the resources available imposed their constraint on the court's discretion. In most cases they were insufficient to meet the reasonable needs of both parties after separation.

In others, said his lordship, where the resources were larger, the practicality of realising assets without destroying or seriously damaging a husband's business imposed another constraint.

It was only in the rare case where the assets were very large and there was no serious liquidity problem that it became necessary to consider the ultimate limits of the court's discretionary powers under the section.

In the first place, the court should consider all the circumstances of the case and the factors set out in paragraphs (a) to (g).

It was wrong in principle to adopt a purely arithmetical approach by considering what proportion of the assets should be allocated to the wife. The suggestion in *Watchtel v Wachtel* (14–001), of one-half or one-third of the total assets, was no more than a guideline.

Second, the word 'needs' in paragraph (b) in relation to the other provisions in the section was equivalent to 'reasonable requirements', having regard to the other factors and the objective set by the concluding words of the section.

Third, the powers of the court ought not to be exercised for the benefit of adult children, by enabling the wife to set up a child in business; or to provide by will for a child who was unlikely to benefit under the husband's will or otherwise.

Fourth, active participation by the wife, either by working in the business or by providing finance, would greatly enhance her contribution to the welfare of the family under paragraph (f), and might lead to a substantial increase in the lump sum over and above her 'reasonable requirements'. That, in effect, recognised that she had earned a share in the total assets, and should be able to realise it and use it as she chose.

Fifth, the acceptance by the wife of a frugal standard of living throughout the marriage, enabling the husband to plough back into the business a large proportion of the profits and develop it into a considerable enterprise, was a factor which could properly be reflected in the lump sum.

The same effect was produced where the wife's earnings contributed to the husband's success, especially in the early stages where they might be an important element.

Paragraph (c) required the court to have regard to the standard of living of the family during the marriage, but it would be anomalous if that were taken as an indication for reducing the lump sum for a wife who had accepted a lower standard of living in the hope that she and the family would benefit later.

Sixth, advanced age might be an important factor in that the wife's requirements might be provided for by a smaller capital sum.

The section required the court to make a hypothetical assessment of the future financial position on two assumptions, (a) that the marriage had continued, and (b) that each party had behaved properly to the other in financial matters; and then to express the assessment in terms of a lump sum or its equivalent.

The logical difficulties inherent in the process were so great that only a very approximate result could be achieved.

On a true construction of section 25 there came a point where the amount required to fulfil its terms 'levelled off'. That point would obviously shift as the value of money changed. His lordship's view was that the provision made for the wife by the judge was too much, in the sense that he would not have awarded so large a sum. However, his lordship was unable to hold that the judge's decision was wrong.

Hollings J concurred, and the husband's appeal was dismissed.

Note. For the facts of the case, see the report on page 3 of *The Times*. These are omitted from the law report on page 28.

PART 4

Distribution of capital assets

All of the chapters within this Part (and the subsequent Part 5) of the work involve a categorisation of cases which have some connection with the concept of distribution of assets (both capital and revenue) according to a proportional division. The origin of the various subdivisions which these chapters represent was the concept which became known as the 'one-third ratio'. The inclusion of chapters which subdivide these numerous cases should be explained in the clearest terms. This particular subdivision is *not* in any way meant to be illustrative of the way a court would approach what might be called the 'average' case. In the ordinary case the starting point is not for the court to ask whether it is an appropriate case in which to apply a one-third ratio in the wife's favour, or more than a third etc. In the ordinary case the overriding feature will be the dispute as to the fate of the matrimonial home. The concepts by which the court will be guided are the provisions of section 25 of the Matrimonial Causes Act 1973 (See Part 3), the application of those provisions according to the needs and circumstances of the parties and, if possible, according to the principle of the clean break.

To that extent, it might be suggested that the repetition of numerous cases which are categorised along strictly proportional divisions is now artificial and meaningless. The categories of the next nine chapters are, it must be conceded, only of value if used as references or cross-references. However, there are still numerous occasions when a case involves substantial assets which exist quite independently of the matrimonial home. In cases such as these the question 'what will be my share?' is still of very considerable significance. It is in that situation that a 'directory' reference approach to the cases often serves as a general guideline when attempting to answer the question of what proportions the court is likely to have in mind.

It was the case of *Wachtel v Wachtel* (14–001) which in 1973 gave rise to what was to become known as the 'one-third ratio'. The court, faced with the task of distributing the family assets fairly, had to have, it was said, a starting point, and one-third of the combined resources of the parties was said to be 'as good and rational a starting point as any other'. Those words emanate from the report of the Law Commission which led to the reforming legislation of 1969 and 1970.

It is often difficult to persuade a spouse of the justification for the one-third ratio, particularly a wife who might be about to receive a distribution where she is 'on the wrong end of the ratio'. In *Wachtel v Wachtel* Lord Denning MR offered a practical justification for the one-third starting point in what is by far the commonest human situation, namely, where the husband will have a continuing liability towards the wife in respect of periodical payments for maintenance. However, the concept of flexibility is more important than the concept of the one-third ratio itself.

The judgment of Bagnall J in *Harnett v Harnett* (14–002) at first instance, in which he explained that where a wife has capital resources of her own these must be taken into account in determining what she should be given by the husband, is of note. Thus the basic arithmetical sum is arrived at: the assets of the parties are added together and the total is divided by three; if the wife's assets amount to less than one-third of the combined assets of the parties the husband will have to divest himself of sufficient to bring the wife's share of the family assets up to one-third of the combined total of the family assets.

There has been much argument as to the degree of importance of the one-third ratio, which at one time almost achieved the status of a statutory rule. At the time of writing, however, (mid 1981), the general attitude of judges seems to be to treat it as a ratio merely to be applied in the first instance as a starting point, rather than as a rule to be applied strictly and mathematically, if at all. As was said in one case, the one-third ratio may be a valuable starting point but it will not necessarily be the finishing point. The caveat emphasised at the beginning of this introduction must be borne in mind at all times; in the ordinary case the overriding feature will be the dispute as to the matrimonial home, and the concepts by which the court will be guided are the provisions of section 25 of the 1973 Act, rather than any mathematical formula.

CHAPTER 14

The one-third ratio

14–001 Wachtel v Wachtel

[1973] 1 All ER 829, CA

The one-third starting point – one third of capital assets now plus one third of revenue-producing assets for the duration of their joint lives.   Lord Denning MR said: '. . . In any calculation the court has to have a starting point. If it is not to be one-third, should it be one-half or one-quarter? A starting point at one-third of the combined resources of the parties is as good and rational a starting point as any other . . . In these days of rising house prices, she should certainly have a share in the capital assets which she has helped to create. The windfall should not all go to the husband. But we do not think it should be as much as one-half if she is also to get periodical payments for her maintenance and support. Giving it the best consideration we can, we think that the fairest way is to start with one-third of each. If she has one-third of the family assets as her own and one-third of the joint earnings her past contributions are adequately recognised and her future living standards assured as far as may be.'

Notes

1. The matrimonial home was in the husband's name (compare *Mesher v Mesher* (17–001) where the parties owned it in equal shares and where the family assets were split 50:50 – but see also *Browne v Pritchard* (14–005)).
2. The husband, who was living in the former matrimonial home, was ordered to pay the wife her one-third share as a lump sum immediately.
3. In *Eshak v Nowojewski* (17–007) Sir John Arnold P said that in a case in which there was no question of periodical payments, the general approach was to start with the idea of an equal division of the property, bearing in mind, however, that this would yield to a different solution if the particular circumstances demanded it (see, for instance, *Page v Page* (17–008) – large assets – 50:50 division of property inappropriate – see Appendix II).
4. Purely arithmetical approach criticised in *Preston v Preston* (14–016).

14–002 Harnett v Harnett

[1973] 2 All ER 593; affd. [1974] 1 All ER 764, CA

Where the wife has capital of her own, that must be taken into account in determining what she should be given by the husband.   The first instance decision (that the wife should convey the house owned by her to trustees, that the husband should pay her a lump sum of £12,500 and that the wife's house should be held on beneficial trusts for the benefit of the wife for a period until her death or until both children reached 25 or married, whichever was the earlier, and thereafter to be held for the benefit of the husband and wife in equal shares), the effect of which was to split the family assets two-thirds to the husband and one-third to the wife, was upheld in the Court of Appeal.

The judgment of Bagnall J in the court of first instance is of note. He said: '. . . where the wife has no capital assets and the husband's capital is of comparatively small value, a reasonable starting point is to regard the wife as entitled *at some time* to about a third of that value – though as the total value increases the proportion is likely to be lower. *Where the wife has some capital, that must be taken into account in determining what she should be given by the husband.*'

14–003 Flatt v Flatt

(1973) 4 Fam Law 20, 118 Sol Jo 183, CA

One-third of capital assets plus 'rent' in respect of use and occupation of house by husband pending payment of one-third share to wife.   Lord Denning MR said that the judge had decided the case before *Wachtel v Wachtel*, and had made an order of some complication. The better order was that the house should be held by the husband and wife in the proportion of two-thirds to the husband and one-third to the wife on trust for sale. If the house was not being sold the husband, who was living in the house, should pay a further £247 per annum to the wife for as long as he was in the house (as a form of rent).

14–003A Cumbers v Cumbers

[1975] 1 All ER 1, CA

Husband ordered to pay lump sum by weekly instalments.   The former matrimonial home had been purchased by the husband three months before the marriage. The wife had no proprietary right in the property. She had no case under section 17 of the Married Women's Property Act 1882. Following the separation it was sold, realising a sum of £1,600. The husband remarried and used the proceeds of sale for the purpose of buying another house for himself and his new wife.

Lord Denning MR said that it would not be right that the wife should be able to sell up the husband's new house. His lordship was of the opinion that this was a case in which some capital provision – a lump sum – should be ordered. But the sum of £800 awarded by the judge (half the proceeds of sale of the former matrimonial home) was too large. The one-third ratio was applied and the wife awarded a lump sum of £500, charged on the new house at interest and payable by weekly instalments.

Note. In *Browne v Pritchard* (4–104) Lord Denning MR said that a charge for a proportion of the net proceeds of sale was preferable to a charge for a fixed sum because values change so much these days, but that the charge should not be realised so long as the husband required the house as a home for the two boys who were living with him. Therefore, the wife in *Browne v Pritchard* had to wait for her money. A spouse in such circumstances could have to wait a very considerable time. For as Ormrod LJ said in *Hanlon v Hanlon* (4–106), a family will not simply dissolve on the 17th birthday of the youngest child. Thus one can see the logic of the order in *Cumbers v Cumbers*; it preserved a home for the husband and his new family, while allowing the wife access to her capital by instalments together with the benefit of interest on the balance outstanding in the meantime.

14–004 O'Donnell v O'Donnell (sub nom. O'D v O'D)
[1975] 2 All ER 993, CA

Wife worked in husband's hotel business and contributed to success of business. However, the scale and speed of the development of the business was largely due to the capital resources made available by the husband's father. One-third ratio applied. See case summary 1–202.

Notes

1. This was a case bordering on the 'large assets' type of case. See case summary 16–102.

2. Compare *S v S* (16–104) – large assets – one-third ratio would produce a sum which was too large – wife nevertheless awarded a sum considerably in excess of her needs in order to take into account her contributions towards the success of the husband's business.

14–005 Browne v Pritchard

[1975] 3 All ER 721, CA

Comparative positions of the parties at the end of the day – wife having advantage of living in council accommodation – wife's half share in matrimonial home reduced to one-third. Ormrod LJ summed it up by saying: 'Finally, let us compare the positions of these two adults. At the end of the day the wife will have a council flat plus £X,000. The husband will have no council flat or other accommodation, plus £2X,000. It does not require much consideration, I venture to think, to decide which of those two people will be the better off in five years' time when [the younger of the two children living in the house with the husband attains the age of 18 and] the house is sold. Quite obviously the wife. And so I think the order proposed is a fair and reasonable one and represents the best that the court can do in the circumstances.' See case summary 4–104.

   Note. See also *Dallimer v Dallimer* (5–106).

14–006 Dennis v Dennis

(1975) 6 Fam Law 54, CA

(1) *Calculation of the one-third ratio – mortgages to be deducted.* The husband's father gave the husband £90,000 in order to purchase a farm, which the husband duly purchased. The judge awarded the wife one-third of the then gross assets of £90,000, namely £30,000. The husband appealed.

   Since the hearing before the judge at first instance, the farm had been sold for £72,500, and the husband's total assets less debts now amounted to only £30,000. Sir John Pennycuick said that a party could only be ordered to pay something he was in a postion to pay; the position became manifest in the ordinary case of a matrimonial home subject to a mortgage; nobody could even consider anything other than the equity. Both he and Stamp LJ agreed that £10,000, being one-third of the husband's present net assets, was a reasonable and proper lump sum.

(2) *Calculation of the one-third ratio – assets acquired after breakdown of the marriage.* The £90,000 had been given to the husband after the separation. Sir John Pennycuick said that there was no doubt that the court could take into account an accession of wealth after the break-up of the marriage, and he cited *Trippas v Trippas* (1–301) as an example. Stamp LJ agreed.

14–007 Fielding v Fielding

[1978] 1 All ER 267, CA

Calculation of the one-third ratio – broad justice between the parties. The court had difficulty in calculating the one-third ratio owing to problems in valuing certain assets, and their Lordships seemed undecided whether to value them at the date of the separation or the date of the hearing before the judge at first instance. Abandoning any attempt to ascertain the strict property rights of the parties, and in an attempt to do broad justice between them, the court finally made a lump sum award to the wife representing approximately one-third of the joint assets.

   Sir John Pennycuick: '. . . There are obviously certain cases, relatively unusual, in which the strict property rights of the spouses are material and fall to be determined under the Married Women's Property Act 1882; but such cases are indeed unusual and the present case is emphatically not one of them.

   'In this case, as in many others, it is a pure waste of time and money to investigate in detail the property rights of the spouses. . . .'

14–008 Scott v Scott

[1978] 3 All ER 65, CA

'Small capital' situation – house required as home for children – one third of net sale

proceeds insufficient to rehouse wife in 14 years' time on youngest child attaining 18 – wife's share increased accordingly – one-third ratio of no assistance. See case summary 5–105.

14–008A P v P (financial provision: lump sum)

[1978] 3 All ER 70, CA

(1) *Business assets – the problem of liquidity – assets not to be treated as cash sums equal to their valuation figures.* See case summary 26–010A.

Notes
1. Regarding the problem of liquidity generally, see Chapter 16/2.
2. Regarding the whole question of business assets, see Chapter 1/4.
3. Regarding capital gains tax, see *Wallhead v Wallhead* (14–010) and *Hudson v Hudson* (14–014).

(2) *Quantification of the parties' strict interests in matrimonial assets under Married Women's Property Act 1882, section 17 irrelevant under modern legislation.* Shortly after the marriage the wife's father purchased a farm, which he subsequently conveyed into the sole name of the wife. The farm was vastly improved and turned into a successful business by the efforts of both parties, but by the husband in particular. Following the divorce, the husband applied under section 17 of the Married Women's Property Act 1882 for a declaration of his interest in the property, and under sections 23 and 24 of the Matrimonial Causes Act 1973 for a lump sum and transfer of property orders. Ormrod LJ said (at page 75): '. . . For my part I do not find it particularly helpful to try to ascertain and quantify [the husband's] so-called interests. It is useful to ascertain these interests in a broad way so that one can see the justice of each side's case, but I would prefer to avoid quantifying or seeking to quantify these rights in terms of figures, because the moment one quantifies them people begin to do arithmetic with the figures, and it is a well-known statistical fallacy that if you start with an estimate and you multiply it and divide it you multiply and divide the error as well.'

14–009 Dallimer v Dallimer

(1978) 8 Fam Law 142, CA

Asset acquired by wife after breakdown of the marriage – comparative positions of the parties – wife's half share in matrimonial home reduced to one-third. See case summary 5–106.

14–010 Wallhead v Wallhead

(1978) 9 Fam Law 85, CA

(1) *Calculation of one-third ratio – valuation of assets.* Although the marriage broke down in 1970 it was not dissolved until 1976. The Judge at first instance valued the husband's properties at their 1970 values. Orr LJ said that there was no evidence that the rise in their values since 1970 was due to any additional expenditure by way of improvements on the part of the husband. Accordingly, there was no reason why their 1977 values should not be preferred.

(2) *Calculation of one-third ratio – allowance to be made for capital gains tax.* The 1977 values totalled £108,000, but from this a sum of £20,000 was deducted to allow for capital gains tax before applying the one-third ratio, this being the amount of tax the husband would have to pay on a sale in order to provide a lump sum for the wife.

Note. But see also *Hudson v Hudson* (14–014).

14–011 Bennett v Bennett

(1978) 9 Fam Law 19, CA

One-third of capital assets insufficient to rehouse wife – wife's share increased accordingly – one-third ratio of no assistance. See case summary 5–108.

14–012 Richardson v Richardson

(1978) 9 Fam Law 86, CA

The husband was a senior civil servant earning £7,152 p.a. with investments of £1,100, a sum of £1,090 in the Trustee Savings Bank and investments under a monthly savings plan scheme amounting to £4,400. The wife was unemployed and had no capital. The former matrimonial home had been sold for £22,500 which had been placed on deposit in the parties' joint names. From this sum the husband had used £11,000 in order to buy himself a new house for £20,000 with the aid of a £9,000 mortgage. On the husband's retirement in three years' time he would receive a lump sum payment of £9,000.

Orr LJ said that the judge at first instance had been wrong to leave the value of the savings plan out of account. The savings plan was being built up in order to supplement the husband's pension and, had the marriage subsisted, the wife would have had the benefit of it together with the husband. Equally, attention should have been paid to the wife's loss of a widow's pension under the husband's pension scheme, and to the lump sum payment which the husband would receive on his retirement. But the share of the wife should not be greater than one-third.

All the above assets were taken into account: the investments of £1,100; the bank deposit of £1,090; the savings plan of £4,400; the equity in the husband's new house of £11,000; the remaining proceeds of sale of the former matrimonial home amounting to £11,500; and the sum of £9,000 payable on the husband's retirement; totalling £38,090. The one-third ratio was then applied. The wife's award was increased by the Court of Appeal from £7,750 to £12,000.

Note. The report does not disclose whether the Court of Appeal considered the ownership of the former matrimonial home. It would appear from the report that it was treated as being owned wholly by the husband.

14–013 Priest v Priest

(1978) 9 Fam Law 252, CA

Calculation of the one-third ratio – valuation of future expectations. Prospect of lump sum gratuity being payable to husband contingent on his completing 22 years' service in Royal Marines taken into account. Contingent expectation of receiving gratuity amounting to at least £5,229, with expectation of receiving a substantially larger gratuity contingent on his continuing to serve beyond 22 years. Contingent expectation valued at £5,229. Husband ordered to pay lump sum amounting to one-third of that figure, to be payable on receipt of gratuity.

Note. Compare *Milne v Milne* (3–105) – commutable pension rights – order for payment of share of whatever lump sum to which husband entitled on retirement, rather than fixed amount.

14–014 Hudson v Hudson

(1979) 10 Fam Law 23, CA

Calculation of the one-third ratio – whether allowance to be made for capital gains tax. The parties were agreed in principle that the wife should retain the matrimonial home, while the husband should retain the hotel which had formerly been run by the parties in partnership, subject to an 'equalisation payment' by the husband to the wife. There was no evidence that either party was contemplating the hotel being sold. Nevertheless, counsel for the wife conceded that in valuing the hotel allowance should be made for estimated capital gains tax on any sale. Ormrod LJ said that the equalisation payment to the wife would have been considerably higher had no such allowance been made. His lordship stated that he would like to reserve his own opinion on the point until it arose in a contested case.

Note. The point is that if business assets are to be replaced, roll-over relief will apply.

14–014A Curtis v Curtis

(1980) 11 Fam Law 55, CA

Lump sum of £4,000 of very little value where inadequate to rehouse recipient party.   See case summary 5–113A.

14–015 Eshak v Nowojewski

(1980) Times, 19 November, CA

Leasehold property – wasting assets.   The matrimonial home was a leasehold property. The lease had 60 years to run when the property was purchased in 1969. It was in joint names, but the husband had provided the deposit and had made all the mortgage repayments. During the marriage the wife had suffered from ill-health, and the judge had found that her domestic and financial contributions to the family had not been significant, although she had done what she could. The wife had now remarried and was living in secure accommodation provided by her new husband. The husband required the house as a home for the children and, after they had left home, as a home for himself. The judge had ordered the house to be sold and the sale proceeds divided on the youngest child attaining 18 or finishing full-time education. One of his reasons was that the property, being leasehold, was a wasting asset. For the husband, it was urged that the proper order would be an outright transfer of the property into his name alone.

The Court of Appeal ordered that the house would be settled on the husband for life and that thereafter it would be sold and the proceeds divided equally between the husband's estate and the wife or her estate. Sir John Arnold P said that it seemed that the judge had failed to attach due importance to the husband's need for housing after the children had grown up. It was true that the probable effect of postponing the sale was that there would be a severe reduction in the capital value of the house [and thus of the wife's half share] and that the wife might not receive her share in her lifetime. [She was 41 and the husband 38.] Nevertheless, given the circumstances, a case had been made for paying the fullest attention to the husband's future housing needs.

In other words, the wife's half share in the matrimonial home was treated as a family asset, available for redistribution. The effect of its redistribution by being settled on the husband for life was that, not only would she be deprived of any benefit from this asset until the death of the husband, but that by the time her asset was made available to her (assuming she survived the husband) it was likely to be worth considerably less than its current value.

14–015A Foley v Foley

[1981] 2 All ER 857, CA

A useful starting point in many cases – but in many others it will be obvious from the start that the proportion to be awarded will be nothing like one-third.   The wife appealed against the award of a lump sum of £10,000, contending that the judge had failed to take into account or give sufficient weight to a period of seven years' cohabitation prior to the marriage ceremony. It was further pleaded that the judge had been wrong in holding that one-third was not an appropriate starting point for computing the lump sum. Applying the one-third ratio, the wife would have received £14,000. But the marriage itself had only lasted five years, and the Court of Appeal upheld the judge's exercise of his discretion (see Appendix II).

Regarding the one-third ratio, Eveleigh LJ said (at the foot of page 861): 'But the second ground of appeal is that the learned judge should have started on the basis that one-third was the proper proportion for the wife. Counsel for the wife argued that, starting from one-third, the wife, on the facts of this case, should actually have received more than the £14,000 which a "one-third" calculation would have produced, and he referred the court to the authorities relating to the "one-third" proportion. As I see it, one-third in many cases is a very useful starting point for the court in deciding what should be the final figure. It is a useful proportion to take and then adjust one way or another as the case demands. But it is in no way a rule of law, as I see it. It is an aid to the mental process when arriving at the appropriate figure and there are many cases where the "one-third" figure would not enter the mind of the court, because it would be obvious from the start that the proportion would be nothing like that. For example, the young marriage that lasts but a day or two. It is an extreme case but it is not unknown in this court. So I do not find it possible to criticise the learned judge because he in fact said that he did not regard one-third as the starting point in this case.'

14–016 Preston v Preston

(1981) Times, 25 June, CA

Wrong in principle to adopt a purely arithmetical approach.   Ormrod LJ said that it was wrong in principle to adopt a purely arithmetical approach. The suggestion in *Wachtel v Wachtel* (14–001) of one-half or one-third of the total assets was no more than a guideline. The court should consider all the circumstances of the case and the factors set out in paragraphs (a) to (g) of section 25 (1) of the Matrimonial Causes Act 1973. See case summary 13–018.

CHAPTER 15

Wife's award increased

I Wife's financial contributions taken into account

A. *Wife's contributions to purchase/improvement of matrimonial home*

CASE SUMMARIES

15–101 Chamberlain v Chamberlain

[1974] 1 All ER 33, CA

Wife saving jointly owned matrimonial home from threat of possession by building society – husband defaulting on mortgage – wife making mortgage repayments and paying off arrears. The parties had originally agreed that the wife was to live in the property until remarriage or cohabitation with another man, and that in either event the house was to be sold and the proceeds divided equally. However, the husband had since lost his job. The building society commenced foreclosure proceedings, and the wife was now paying off the mortgage arrears. The agreed terms were varied, and the property ordered to be held on trust for sale as to two-thirds to the wife and one-third to the husband. For further details, see case summary 9–010A.

Notes

1. See also *Martin v Martin* (15–132) – husband's dissipation of assets following separation – wife's contribution to running of farming business both before and, particularly, after separation.
2. See also *President v President* (15–105).

15–102 Jones v Jones

[1975] 2 All ER 12, CA

Wife making all mortgage repayments following husband's departure from matrimonial home. After making of decree absolute, husband attacked wife with knife, severing tendons of right hand. Husband now in prison. Wife's future prospects of employment doubtful. Wife's financial position now exceptionally weak. Husband's share in matrimonial home extinguished. See case summary 13–006.

Note. Smith v Smith (23–902) followed.

15–103 Earley v Earley

(1975) Times, 20 June, CA

Wife bearing almost entire responsibility for mortgage repayments on jointly owned matrimonial home occupied by her. See case summary 7–202.

15–104 Bryant v Bryant

(1976) Times, 3 February, CA

Husband failing to pay mortgage – wife making mortgage repayments. The husband was a persistent maintenance defaulter. He had spent three terms in prison for disobeying court orders, and had been in prison at the time of the first instance decision. Husband's share in matrimonial home extinguished. Wife ordered to make mortgage repayments.

15–105 President v President

(1976) 126 NLJ 740, CA

Wife saving jointly owned matrimonial home from threat of possession by building society. The Court of Appeal did not favour a trust for sale with its attendant expense and complications for securing a one-third share for the husband when, on a sale of the house, the wife's two-thirds share would not permit her to buy another house and when the husband's one-third share would be subject to the Law Society's charge for legal aid costs, which would substantially diminish that share. The husband's appeal against an order transferring his half share to his wife was dismissed.

Notes
1. The wife would have to pay the future mortgage instalments and pay off the arrears.
2. The equity in the house was only £2,400.
3. The husband and wife were of equal earning power and, although the husband was ordered to pay £15 per week for the maintenance of the parties' two children, he was not ordered to pay any maintenance for the support of his wife. The wife's financial position was weak. *Smith v Smith* (23–902) was referred to.
4. The fact that a husband's one-third share will be subject to the Law Society's charge is a very material consideration where the sums of money involved are relatively small.
5. Compare *Chamberlain v Chamberlain* (9–010A).

15–106 Hanlon v Hanlon

[1978] 2 All ER 889, CA

Wife's very large contributions to family, both financial and in kind. Matrimonial home in husband's sole name. Parties contributing equally in money and work to family. Wife earning as much as husband. No order for periodical payments for her maintenance sought by wife. Wife willing to forgo periodical payments for maintenance of children. The clean break. Absolute transfer of property to wife. See case summary 10–102.

Note. Counsel for the husband argued that it was essential that the husband should, to use his own phrase, get on the 'property escalator' as soon as possible, and that the best way of doing this was for the wife to raise £5,000 on mortgage to pay to the husband so that he could purchase a house on mortgage. But there was no clear evidence that the husband had any intention whatever of giving up his police flat so long as his employment in the police force continued.

B. *Wife's contributions in family business*

CASE SUMMARIES

15–131 Strelley-Upton v Strelley-Upton

(1973) 4 Fam Law 9, CA

Wife's assistance in running husband's farming business. Lump sum award in favour of wife reduced on appeal owing to husband's inability to pay a higher figure. See case summary 1–402.

Notes

1. See also *Martin v Martin* (15–132)
2. For further cases on the inability of the husband to pay a higher figure, see Chapter 16/2.

15–131A O'Donnell v O'Donnell (sub nom. O'D v O'D)

[1975] 2 All ER 993, CA

Wife's assistance in running of family business – large assets. Husband in partnership with his parents. Capital resources made available by husband's father. Wife's contributions in family business. One-third ratio applied notwithstanding the fact that this resulted in what seemed a large award in its day. See case summary 1–202.

Note. A much more clear-cut example is now provided by *S v S* (15–136), in which the wife was awarded much more than she required specifically because of her contributions to the husband's business.

15–132 Martin v Martin

[1976] 3 All ER 625, CA

Husband's dissipation of assets following separation. Wife's contribution to running of farming business both before and, particularly, after separation. Husband burdening farm with mortgage which would oblige wife to sell farmhouse. Husband's dissipation of his share of capital assets. Husband ordered to transfer to wife the whole of his interest in farm and to pay her a lump sum in addition. Lump sum award reduced on appeal owing to husband's inability to pay a higher figure. See case summary 1–405.

Notes

1. See also *Chamberlain v Chamberlain* (9–010A) – husband defaulting on mortgage on matrimonial home – wife making mortgage repayments and paying off arrears.
2. For further cases on the inability of the husband to pay a higher figure, see Chapter 16/2.

15–133 Penman v Penman

(1976) 7 Fam Law 46, CA

Husband and wife in partnership in farming business – 50:50 division of assets. Wife ordered to pay husband a lump sum on account of his share in the partnership, being an estimate of what he would receive on a final division of the partnership assets. Award of lump sum suspended on appeal owing to wife's inability to raise the money. See case summary 1–406.

Notes

1. The case was actually on the issue of excluding the husband from the matrimonial home. The court was informed that the dispute as to the parties' property rights could be determined within six months. Lord Denning MR said that the question of a home for the children was the most important factor in this case. The property rights between the spouses were of comparative minor importance.
2. For a further case on the inability of a wife to pay a larger lump sum payment to a husband, see *P v P* (1–408).

15–134 Hudson v Hudson

(1979) 10 Fam Law 23, CA

Husband and wife in partnership in hotel business – 50:50 division of assets. See case summary 1–409.

Note. Compare *O'Donnell v O'Donnell* (15–131A), in which the partnership was between the husband and his parents, the wife merely contributing to the family business by working in the business.

15–135 Kokosinski v Kokosinski

[1980] 1 All ER 1106

Wife's assistance in running of family business during period, prior to marriage ceremony, when husband unable to marry her. See case summary 1–410. For further details, see case summary 8–310.

15–136 S v S

(1980) Times, 10 May

Wife's assistance in running of husband's farming business – large assets. The value of the husband's assets had been agreed at £2.1m. The husband offered the wife £200,000. Balcombe J said that, although such a sum was more than adequate for the wife's needs, to award her no more that this would be to fail to adequately take into account her very substantial contributions to the husband's business. His lordship accordingly increased the lump sum to £375,000. For further details, see case summary 16–104.

15–137 Preston v Preston

(1981) Times, 25 June, CA

Contribution to success of husband's business by frugal living – large assets. The wife had lived frugally, so helping the husband to build up business assets valued at £2.3m. Ormrod LJ said that the judge was entitled to take into account the wife's contribution, which the judge had clearly regarded as a significant factor. Award of £600,000 upheld. For further details, see case summary 13–018.

2 Wife's difficult housing situation

CASE SUMMARIES

15–201 Smith v Smith (sub nom. S v S)

[1975] 2 All ER 19, CA

See case summary 23–701. For further details, see case summary 23–902.

15–202 Hanlon v Hanlon

[1978] 2 All ER 889, CA

See case summary 23–704. For further details, see case summary 5–104.

15–203 Scott v Scott

[1978] 3 All ER 65, CA

See case summary 23–705. For further details, see case summary 5–105.

15–204 Cawkwell v Cawkwell

(1978) 9 Fam Law 25, CA

See case summary 23–707. For further details, see case summary 5–107.

15–205 Bennett v Bennett

(1978) 9 Fam Law 19, CA

See case summary 23–708. For further details, see case summary 5–108.

15–206 Blezard v Blezard

(1978) 9 Fam Law 249, CA

See case summary 23–711. For further details, see case summary 5–111.

15–207 Ward v Ward and Greene (sub nom. **Ward v Ward)**

[1980] 1 All ER 176, [1980] 1 WLR 4, CA

See case summary 23–712. For further details, see case summary 5–112.

15–208 Dunford v Dunford

[1980] 1 All ER 122, CA

See case summary 23–713. For further details, see case summary 5–113.

3 Uncertainty/inadequacy of husband's income

CASE SUMMARIES

15–301 Hunter v Hunter

[1973] 3 All ER 362, CA

The husband's income was little more than £21 a week. The wife and four children of the family were dependent on social security benefits. The husband fell into arrears with the mortgage repayments and the mortgagees foreclosed. The wife and children were now living in a council house and the husband was separately housed. The equity in the former matrimonial home was valued at between £2,500 and £3,000. The house had been conveyed into the sole name of the husband. The judge at first instance said: 'In view of the fact that the husband has not now sufficient means to support the wife, the only way in which the wife's half share in the *enjoyment* of the home can be preserved is by transferring a half share in the *ownership* of the home to the wife.' Award of half share in balance sale proceeds upheld by Court of Appeal. But for the one-half award, the weekly maintenance for the children would have been higher.

Note. Supplementary benefit is no longer payable to applicants whose available capital exceeds £2,000.

15–302 Buchanan v Buchanan

(1973) Times, 22 May, CA

The husband's future earning position was uncertain. The former matrimonial home was owned by his employers, but he had free capital of £38,000. One-third ratio not applied. Wife awarded £15,000.

Note. The original award was £25,000, reduced to £15,000 on appeal.

15–303 Griffiths v Griffiths

[1974] 1 All ER 932, CA

Wife's prospect of receiving maintenance reduced following husband's business misfortune. Periodical payments order not sought by wife. It was unreasonable of the husband to suggest a 50:50 division of the capital assets coupled with an award of maintenance.

The husband's future earning position was uncertain and it would have been wrong to put the wife at risk as to future payments. Accordingly the wife was allowed a larger share in the proceeds of sale of the matrimonial home than would otherwise have been appropriate. The proceeds of sale were ordered to be split four-fifths for the wife, one-fifth for the husband, so adjusting the parties' capital position as to equalise their income position. (The court was careful to make an order which adequately reflected the fact that the husband had originally provided the house, paid for it and had worked hard to support his family.) See case summary 10–203.

15–304 Smith v Smith (sub nom. S v S)

[1975] 2 All ER 19

The husband's net income was between £24 and £25 a week. That was as high as he could get at the moment, but he had prospects of promotion. He was paying the wife only £4 per week for herself and the child, who had suffered from serious kidney trouble since infancy. Latey J said that, on the face of it, a total contribution of £4 a week was a very low one. The wife was receiving £15 a week from the DHSS. But, said his lordship, when one looked at the husband's necessary living expenses, there was not a great deal more to spare. Wife's relative financial position exceptionally weak. Husband's share in jointly-owned matrimonial home extinguished. See case summary 23–902.

> Note. Followed in *Jones v Jones* (23–604). See also *Martin v Martin* (23–607), *President v President* (23–608) and *Ward v Ward and Greene* (23–610).

15–305 Bryant v Bryant

(1976) Times, 3 February, CA

Husband a persistent maintenance defaulter, in prison. Husband's interest in former matrimonial home extinguished.

> Note. See also *Weisz v Weisz* (23–605).

4 Wife's acceptance of clean break

CASE SUMMARIES

15–401 Smith v Smith

[1970] 1 All ER 244, CA

See case summary 10–202.

15–401A Griffiths v Griffiths

[1974] 1 All ER 932, CA

See case summary 10–203.

15–402 Hanlon v Hanlon

[1978] 2 All ER 889, CA

See case summary 10–102.

15–403 Dunford v Dunford

[1980] 1 All ER 122, CA

See case summary 10–103.

CHAPTER 16

Wife's award reduced

1 Large assets/wife's assets adequate for her needs

CASE SUMMARIES

16–101 Trippas v Trippas

[1973] Fam 134, [1973] 2 All ER 1, CA

Scarman LJ said (at page 143): 'This case takes the law a little further along the road signposted by the Divorce Reform Act 1969 and the Matrimonial Proceedings and Property Act 1970. It is a different case on its facts from *Wachtel v Wachtel* (14–001). In *Wachtel v Wachtel* the problem was how to deal under the new legislation with the matrimonial home. In this case the problem is how to deal with the capital (at least £80,000) arising from the sale in 1969 of the husband's interest in his business.

'When this husband and wife parted, they did come to an agreement about the matrimonial home. They knew at that time that the husband might in the reasonably near future find his family business the subject of a take-over bid. They discussed the possible implications of such event on the family finances; and it is clear from the evidence that at that time the husband, acting, I should have thought, very properly and very reasonably, said that there would be something for the wife. The event (in the shape of £80,000 plus shares) did occur some nine months or so after their parting. When it occurred he made a gift of £5,000 to each of his sons. I think it reasonable to infer that, had they been living together at that time, the wife could have expected in cash or in kind some sort of benefit accruing to her from the sale of the business.'

The wife was awarded a lump sum of £10,000, which left the husband with *free capital,* that is, his capital apart from his house, of £30,000, and the wife with free capital of £12,000. The wife's capital after adjustment amounted to less than one-third of the sum of their total assets, but her income position, as long as she remained in work, would be slightly better than that of her husband, the husband not being in employment.

16–102 O'Donnell v O'Donnell (sub nom. O'D v O'D)

[1976] Fam 83, [1975] 2 All ER 993, CA

Ormrod LJ commented on *Trippas v Trippas* (at page 88): 'This appeal . . . raises a number of difficult questions on the application of the greatly extended powers of the court to adjust the property rights of the spouses following a dissolution of the marriage.

'*Wachtel v Wachtel* [1973] Fam 72 and *Trippas v Trippas* [1973] Fam 134 are the leading authorities in this court on this subject. *Wachtel v Wachtel* is the prototype of a very large class of cases with which the courts are dealing every day . . .

'But *Wachtel v Wachtel* is not typical of all the cases in which the court has to exercise this discretion. It was essentially a case of two people starting their married life with little or nothing but their earning capacities, and together founding a family and building up by their joint efforts such capital as they were able to save. Typically, their main capital asset was the matrimonial home, bought on a mortgage and paid for out of income. These cases are true examples of equal partnership, and such expressions as "family assets" and "the wife earning her share" are wholly apposite to them.

'In other cases the situation is different. One or other, or perhaps both, spouses may bring into the marriage substantial capital assets, or may acquire such assets during the marriage by inheritance or by gift from members of their families. In such cases the expressions quoted above from the judgment in *Wachtel v Wachtel* and others to be found in it cannot be applied without modification. *In these cases it is necessary to go directly to the terms of section 25 of the Act for guidance.*

'. . . *Trippas v Trippas* [1973] Fam 134 affords some assistance as to the way in which the courts should approach cases which do not fall within the *Wachtel* class, although the situation on the facts in that case was a peculiar one. It confirms the views expressed in *Wachtel v Wachtel* that the Matrimonial Proceedings and Property Act 1970 was a reforming statute which altered the conceptual basis on which the discretion of the court is to be exercised in dealing with the financial position and property rights of the spouses after the dissolution of the marriage. Financial orders, under what is now section 23 of the Act of 1973, and property adjustment orders, under section 24, are to be exercised, in the words of Scarman LJ, at page 143, "in accordance with one policy – the policy set out in section 5" (now section 25) . . . Both Lord Denning MR and Scarman LJ held that section 25 (1) (g) could apply to acquisitions of capital subsequent to the breakdown of the marriage or to the divorce so that the court could take them into account in assessing the sum to be awarded to the former spouse. On the facts in *Trippas v Trippas* it was "plain that the wife had a good chance of receiving a financial benefit on the sale of the business" which was concluded after separation, and "Now that there has been a divorce, she should be compensated for the loss of that chance" (per Lord Denning MR at page 141) . . .

'*Trippas* also shows that in attempting to place the parties in the position in which they would have been had the marriage not broken down the court can have regard to the fact that the wife "would have benefited generally from the availability of capital to the husband", per Scarman LJ, at page 145, and that in suitable cases it is just and proper to make adequate capital provision for a wife after the dissolution of the marriage, even in a case where periodical payments are admittedly inappropriate on their respective incomes. The case is of little value, however, in so far as specific sums are concerned, because the court recognised that the evidence as to the husband's true financial position was unsatisfactory and probably incomplete.'

Note. In *O'Donnell v O'Donnell* the judge at first instance applied the one-third ratio, and the award was upheld by the Court of Appeal. Ormrod LJ stated (at page 91): 'In cases on the scale of the present one this ratio may produce results which are, or may seem to be, too high, but inflation has already altered values very considerably, bringing many cases into the class in which the one-third rule would not have been accepted in the past.'

16–103 Calder v Calder

(1976) Times, 29 June, CA

The value of the husband's assets in the United Kingdom amounted to £156,000. The husband's mother, now domiciled in Monaco, enjoyed a large income from two very substantial Canadian settlements. Until the divorce occurred she had been in the habit of making large gifts of money both to the husband and to the wife. The trustees in Canada had refused to disclose any information concerning the settlements, but the husband appeared to have a vested interest of one-third in one of the settlements (whose assets were not less than 200,000 Canadian dollars) provided he survived his mother, and also a contingent interest in the other settlement which could be of far greater value.

Ormrod LJ said that the appeal raised the problem, already touched on in *O'Donnell v O'Donnell* (16–102), of a wife's proper share of assets which came to the husband by inheritance, and that the case could not be resolved on the basis of allocating a proportion of the total wealth; however, in his opinion the judge at first instance had been wrong to ignore the husband's interest in the Canadian settlements because, on a balance of probabilities, he could become a wealthy man when the interests of the various life tenants eventually fell in. Sir John Pennycuick agreed. Stamp LJ in a concurring judgment said that the problem in this case was quite different from that in *Wachtel v Wachtel*.

16–104 S v S

(1980) Times, 10 May

Soon after the marriage the parties went to live in a house with 32 acres of farmland provided by the husband's parents and conveyed into his sole name. The wife helped in the fields and with the milking. Over the years the farming business prospered, and the husband bought more land until he now owned 672 acres of good farmland and rented a further 105 acres. The value of his assets had been agreed at £2.1m. After 30 years of marriage he left the matrimonial home. The parties agreed there should be a clean break and the wife consented to the dismissal of her claim for periodical payments.

Balcombe J said that the one-third starting point would be inappropriate. On that basis the lump sum would have been around £700,000. His lordship did not find the one-third approach of much assistance in a case where the capital assets were so large. However, the sum of £200,000 offered by the husband was too low. It was more than adequate for the wife's needs, but to award her such a sum would not adequately take into account her very substantial contributions to the farming business. Although the house and the original 32 acres had been provided by the husband's family, the wife's hard physical work in the early years of the marriage and her acceptance of a very simple lifestyle had contributed in no small way to the husband's ability to utilise the profits of the farm and buy more land.

The husband was ordered to make a lump sum payment of £375,000. This was considerably more than was necessary for the wife's needs, but it did recognise the wife's contribution in assisting to build up the husband's assets. Yet it was not so huge that it would cripple the husband to realise it.

16–105 Page v Page

(1981) Times, 30 January, CA

The value of the husband's assets had been assessed at £359,137. His income was about £20,000 per annum. The wife's capital was about £29,000 and her income £2,750 per annum. The parties were both in their seventies. The relationship between them was now so embittered, said Ormrod LJ, that periodical payments were to be avoided. Accordingly, the case was one for a lump sum provision and no periodical payments. The wife agreed in principle with that view. However, the lump sum of £165,000 awarded by the judge in final satisfaction of all the wife's financial claims was too high. Doing the best he could to find an appropriate figure, his lordship thought that the lump sum should be £90,000. With her own capital, that would provide about £120,000 for the wife, which would enable her to buy a house or to provide reasonable medical and nursing care. This was a little under one-third of the joint assets of the parties (£130,000), and less than the £124,000 which the husband had given to his secretary. But the problem was to decide the size of the lump sum by taking into account all the factors in section 25 of the Matrimonial Causes Act 1973 (see Appendix I), and an arithmetical approach would have arrived at too high a figure. All one could do in a case such as this was to take a series of hypothetical figures and assess them, bearing in mind section 25, and try them out until a figure was found which fitted the facts of the case.

Notes

1. The £124,000 which the husband had transferred to his secretary was brought into account in calculating the total of the husband's assets.
2. For further details, see Appendix II.

16–106 Preston v Preston

(1981) Times, 25 June, CA

The wife had worked as a model until after her first pregnancy. She had lived frugally, so helping the husband to build up business assets valued at £2.3m. It was conceded that the husband had no liquidity problem. The Court of Appeal held (Brandon LJ dissenting) that the award of a lump sum of £600,000 to the wife was not so excessively high as to warrant interference with the exercise of the judge's discretion.

Ormrod LJ said that in most cases it was not necessary to consider the extent of the court's powers under section 25 (1) of the Matrimonial Causes Act 1973, because the resources available imposed their constraint on the court's discretion. In most cases they were insufficient to meet the reasonable needs of both parties after separation.

In others, said his lordship, where the resources were larger, the practicality of realising assets without destroying or seriously damaging a husband's business imposed another constraint.

It was only in the rare case where the assets were very large and there was no serious liquidity problem that it became necessary to consider the ultimate limits of the court's discretionary powers under the section.

His lordship then considered the various relevant factors as laid down in section 25 (1) of the Act (see case summary 13–018) and stated that, on a true construction of section 25, there came a point when the amount required to fulfil its terms 'levelled off'. That point would obviously shift as the value of money changed. His lordship's view was that the provision made for the wife by the judge was too much, in the sense that he would not have awarded so large a sum. However, his lordship was unable to hold that the judge's decision was wrong.

Hollings J concurred, and the husband's appeal was dismissed.

2 Husband's available assets limited

CASE SUMMARIES

16–201 H v H (financial provision: remarriage)

[1975] 1 All ER 367

Need to provide for the husband's new family. Relative financial positions of the parties following remarriage. See case summary 6–401.

16–202 Cumbers v Cumbers

[1975] 1 All ER 1, CA

Need to provide a home for the husband's new family. See case summary 6–402. For a full summary, see 14–003A.

16–203 Dixon v Dixon

(1974) 5 Fam Law 58, CA

Essential not to cripple husband's earning capacity. See case summary 8–103. For a full summary, see 8–206.

16–204 Dopson v Cherry

(1974) 5 Fam Law 57, CA

Need to provide a home for the husband's new family. Relative financial positions of the parties following remarriage. See case summary 6–403.

16–205 Mentel v Mentel

(1975) 6 Fam Law 53, 119 Sol Jo 808, CA

Husband's inability to pay a higher figure without crippling him financially. Relative financial positions of the parties following remarriage of wife. See case summary 5–102A.

16–206 Daubney v Daubney

[1976] 2 All ER 453, CA

Need to provide a home for the husband's new family. Relative financial positions of the parties. See case summary 6–404.

16–207 Martin v Martin

[1976] 3 All ER 625, CA

Husband's dissipation of assets. Lump sum award in favour of wife reduced on appeal owing to husband's inability to pay a higher figure. See case summary 1–405.

16–208 Backhouse v Backhouse

[1978] 1 All ER 1158

Need to provide a home for the husband's new family. Relative financial positions of the parties following remarriage. See case summary 6–405. For a full summary, see 8–308.

16–209 Porter v Porter

(1978) 8 Fam Law 143, CA

Need to provide for the husband's new family. Relative financial positions of the parties. See case summary 6–406. For a full summary, see 1–407.

3   Wife provided for by third party

CASE SUMMARIES

16–301 White v White

(1972) Times, 10 March, 116 Sol Jo 219, CA

See case summary 6–201. For a full summary, see 8–201.

16–302 H v H (financial provision: remarriage)

[1975] 1 All ER 367

See case summary 6–202. For a full summary, see 6–105.

16–303 Dopson v Cherry

(1974) 5 Fam Law 57, CA

See case summary 6–203.

16–304 W v W (financial provision: lump sum)

[1975] 3 All ER 970

See case summary 6–204.

16–305 Mentel v Mentel

(1975) 6 Fam Law 53, CA

See case summary 6–205. For a full summary, see 5–102A.

16–306 Backhouse v Backhouse

[1978] 1 All ER 1158

See case summary 6–206.

16–307 Dallimer v Dallimer

(1978) 8 Fam Law 142, CA

See case summary 6–207. For further details, see 5–106.

16–308 Eshak v Nowojewski

(1980) Times, 19 November, CA

See case summary 6–208. For further details, see 5–114.

4   Short marriage

CASE SUMMARIES

16–401 Krystman v Krystman

[1973] 3 All ER 247, CA

See case summary 7–702.

16–402 Taylor v Taylor

(1974) 119 Sol Jo 30

See case summary 7–201.

16–403 Browne v Pritchard

[1975] 3 All ER 721, CA

See case summary 7–103A.

16–404 M v M

(1976) 6 Fam Law 243, CA

See case summary 7–303.

16–405 S v S

[1977] 1 All ER 56, CA

See case summary 7–462.

16–406 Warder v Warder

(1978) 122 Sol Jo 713

See case summary 7–464.

16–407 Foley v Foley

[1981] 2 All ER 857, CA

See case summary 14–015A.

5 Wife's misconduct taken into account

CASE SUMMARIES

16–501 Cuzner v Underdown

[1974] 2 All ER 351, CA

See case summary 8–101. For a full summary, see 8–204.

16–502 Armstrong v Armstrong

(1974) 118 Sol Jo 579, CA

See case summary 8–102. For a full summary, see 8–205.

16–503 Backhouse v Backhouse

[1978] 1 All ER 1158

See case summary 8–109. For a full summary, see 8–308.

16–504 Bateman v Bateman

[1979] 2 WLR 377

See case summary 8–110. For a full summary, see 8–309.

CHAPTER 17

50:50 division of assets

17-001 Mesher v Mesher (sub nom. Mesher v Mesher and Hall)

(1973) Times, 13 February, [1980] 1 All ER 126n, CA

Matrimonial home owned in equal shares. Intended remarriage by both parties. Income positions of husband's new family and wife's new family similar. Husband and third party living in house purchased in their joint names. Matrimonial home required as a home for children of the marriage living with wife. Settlement on trust for sale. Not to be sold so long as children under 17. Net proceeds of sale to be divided equally. See case summary 4-101.

Note. Mesher orders are not always appropriate – see *Carson v Carson* (17-009).

17-002 Hunter v Hunter

[1973] 3 All ER 362, CA

Matrimonial home conveyed into sole name of husband. Inadequacy of husband's income. Foreclosure by mortgagees. Wife now in council accommodation. Wife awarded half share in proceeds of sale. See case summary 15-301.

17-003 Goodfield v Goodfield

(1975) 5 Fam Law 197, CA

Both parties agreed that their beneficial interests in the house should belong to them in equal shares. There was one child of the family, now over 17 years of age, but still living with the wife in the house. The Court of Appeal ordered that the house be sold and that the proceeds of sale be divided equally, on the ground that the wife, with her one-half share of the proceeds of sale and her earning capacity, would be able to find herself adequate alternative accommodation.

Note. This case was distinguished in *Martin v Martin* (17-005) on the ground that the sale of the house would not leave the wife without a roof over her head.

17-004 McDonnell v McDonnell

(1976) Times, 17 February, CA

The Court of Appeal said that an order giving a spouse on dissolution of marriage a proportion of the value of the matrimonial home was to be preferred to a charge of a fixed amount. The court allowed an appeal by the husband that he transfer to his former wife his whole interest in the matrimonial home and that the wife execute a charge on the property in his favour without interest, not to be enforced until the youngest child attained 17. There was substituted an order that the house be vested in trustees for the parties in equal shares, the sale to be postponed until the youngest child attained 17.

Notes

1. The house had originally been conveyed to the husband alone, but during an

unsuccessful attempt at reconciliation in 1973 the husband had transferred the house into joint names. Shortly afterwards the wife commenced divorce proceedings.

2. Compare *Cuzner v Underdown* (8–204), where the wife's conduct in taking a transfer of the house while committing adultery was held to be obvious and gross misconduct and her half share was extinguished.

17–005 Martin v Martin (sub nom. Martin (BH) v Martin (D))

[1977] 3 All ER 762, CA

After a childless marriage lasting 15 years the husband left the matrimonial home, which he had bought during the first year of the marriage, and went to live with another woman who had a tenancy of a council house. The wife remained in the home. The equity in the house was worth approximately £10,000 and the parties' solicitors agreed that the equity belonged to the parties in equal shares. Purchas J ordered that the house should be held on trust for the wife during her life or until her remarriage or such earlier date as she should cease to live there, and thereafter upon trust for the parties in equal shares. The husband's appeal was dismissed.

Stamp LJ distinguished *Goodfield v Goodfield* (17–003) on the ground that an order for sale and division of the proceeds in that case did not involve leaving the wife without a roof over her head.

17–006 Hudson v Hudson

(1979) 10 Fam Law 23, CA

Husband and wife equal partners. Parties agreed in principle that the wife should retain the matrimonial home, while the husband should retain the hotel which had formerly been run by the parties in partnership, subject to an 'equalisation payment' by the husband to the wife. See case summary 1–409.

17–007 Eshak v Nowojewski

(1980) Times, 19 November, CA

The former matrimonial home had been purchased by the husband in joint names. Following the divorce the wife had remarried and was now provided for by her new husband. Sir John Arnold P said that, in a case like the present in which there was no question of periodical payments, the general approach was to start with the idea of an equal division of the property, bearing in mind, however, that this would yield to a different solution if the particular circumstances demanded it.

The husband required the house as a home for the children, of whom he had custody, and it was right to consider his housing needs after they had grown up also. But there was no reason why his share should be increased so as to give him the whole of the property. The house would be held on trust for sale for the husband for the duration of his life. After his death the proceeds of sale would be divided equally between his estate and the wife or her estate.

Note. See, however, *Page v Page* (17–008) – large assets – 50:50 division of property inappropriate – see Appendix II.

17–008 Page v Page

(1981) Times, 30 January, CA

Large assets – 50:50 division of assets inappropriate.   See Appendix II.

Note. In *Eshak v Nowojewski* (17–007) Sir John Arnold P said that in a case where there was no question of periodical payments, the general approach was to start with the idea of an equal division of the property, bearing in mind that *this would yield to a different solution if the circumstances of any particular case so required.*

17–009 Carson v Carson

(1981) Times, 7 July, CA

No power to vary Mesher order once made – 50:50 division of assets on sale of matrimonial home rarely appropriate. Ormrod LJ said the case was a good example of the dangers of *Mesher* orders (see case summary 17–001). On the wife being obliged to sell the house on the children attaining 18 or completing their education she would find herself in a most unfavourable position with only half the proceeds of sale.

Notes

1. For further details, see case summary 10–107.
2. Compare *Goodfield v Goodfield* (17–003).

CHAPTER 18

Wife ordered to transfer assets to husband

18–001 Calderbank v Calderbank

[1975] 3 All ER 333, CA

The wife's parents had died and she had inherited substantial assets. Her capital assets now amounted to £78,000. The husband had no capital assets. Although the husband had suffered from poliomyelitis which had left him physically weakened and he had participated only to a small extent in the kennel business run jointly by the husband and the wife, he was now earning between £3,500 and £4,000 a year, and his new wife was earning about £2,000 a year. Award of £10,000 approved.

Cairns LJ said (at page 340): '... In *Wachtel v Wachtel* it was held by this Court that in considering any periodical payment or a lump sum to be awarded to a wife after divorce the starting point should be that she should have one third of the joint income and one third of the joint assets ...

'No such starting point is appropriate where it is the husband who is the applicant for a lump sum ...

'The main attack on this judgment [of Heilbron J] has been that the judge failed to consider whether the wife had an obligation to the husband to provide him with money for a new house ...'

His lordship continued (at page 341): '... the overall consideration ... is contained ... in these words: "... and so to exercise those powers (that is powers to make financial provision in one way or another) as to place the parties, so far as it is practicable and, having regard to their conduct, just to do so, in the financial position in which they would have been if the marriage had not broken down and each had properly discharged his or her financial obligations and responsibilities towards the other".

'In my judgment, in all the circumstances of this case, if the marriage had not broken down and each spouse had properly discharged his or her obligations and responsibilities to the other, the financial position of the parties would have included a continuance of the situation of the husband living in a house for which he had not to pay. Since it is not now practicable that he should continue to live in that house, I think it was quite right for the learned judge to award him such lump sum as would provide a suitable house for his needs. £10,000 could not be considered as an excessive sum for that purpose ...'

As Cairns LJ commented earlier: '£10,000 is, after all, not a large proportion of £78,000.'

18–002 Penman v Penman

(1976) 7 Fam Law 46, CA

Husband and wife in partnership in farming enterprise.   See case summary 1–406.

18–003 P v P (financial provision: lump sum)

[1978] 3 All ER 70, CA

Husband and wife in partnership in farming enterprise.   See case summary 1–408.

18–004 Curtis v Curtis

(1980) 11 Fam Law 55, CA

Settlement of sufficient to purchase residence for husband for life with remainder to wife absolutely.   See case summary 5–113A.

PART 5

Distribution of revenue-producing assets

CHAPTER 19

The one-third ratio

CASE SUMMARIES

19–001 Ackerman v Ackerman

[1972] 2 All ER 420, CA

Calculation of the one-third ratio – deductions from husband's income. Phillimore LJ said: 'I would begin with the one-third rule – bearing in mind that it is not a rule. I must first deduct certain expenses from the husband's income. Mr. Jackson concedes the following, which on a yearly basis are: National Insurance £72, interest on and repayment of a bank loan £240, making a total of £312. Deducting these from his . . . salary leaves £3,188, which for convenience I treat as £3,200. I then add to £3,200 the wife's income of £600, making £3,800. Divided by three, this gives £1,266. Deducting £600 leaves £666 as her share on a strict application of the one-third rule.

'. . . I have come to the conclusion that the right figure for the wife's maintenance is £520 per annum, less tax, payable weekly. This, with the £600 a year that she derives from family allowance and her pension, should be adequate for her support. So far as the children are concerned, I have no doubt that the husband would not have agreed to £6 a week if he had realised that the wife was going to claim maintenance for herself . . .'

The payments for the children's maintenance, which were in addition to the payments for the wife's maintenance, were accordingly varied downwards.

Note. All the earnings quoted were gross earnings not net earnings (although none of the reports specifically states that this was so). But see now *Furniss v Furniss* (19–016) and *Stockford v Stockford* (19–017).

19–001A Barnes v Barnes

[1972] 3 All ER 872, CA

Calculation of the one-third ratio – social security benefits to be ignored except in 'small income' cases. Edmund Davies LJ said that, in the first place, regard should not be had to social security benefits. However, if this would leave the husband below 'subsistence level', then the court may have regard to the social security benefits available to the wife.

Notes
1. For further details, see case summary 22–002.
2. Compare *Walker v Walker* (19–012A).
3. In 'small income' cases the one-third ratio is of no assistance anyway – see *Scott v Scott* (19–010), *Clarke v Clarke* (19–012) and *Fitzpatrick v Fitzpatrick* (19–013).

19–002 Wachtel v Wachtel

[1973] 1 All ER 829, CA

Calculation of the one third ratio – one third for wife plus additional sum for child. *Ackerman v Ackerman* (19–001) was referred to in the judgment and the one-third ratio approved. Lord Denning MR said: 'In any calculation the court has to have a starting point. If it is not to be one-third, should it be one-half or one-quarter? A starting point at one-third of the combined resources of the parties is as good and rational a starting point as any other . . .'

The wife was awarded periodical payments of £1,500 per annum, which was one-third of their earning capacities (£6,000 plus £750) less the sum representing her potential earning capacity of £750. She was also awarded £300 per annum in respect of their child.

Note. For the rationale behind the one-third ratio see case summary 14–001. See also *Stockford v Stockford* (19–017), however.

19–003 Trippas v Trippas

[1973] 2 All ER 1, CA

Husband not in employment – award of lump sum to wife – husband left with investment income approximately equal to wife's total income from her earnings and invested capital – 'rough justice on the basis of approximate equality'. One-third ratio not applied. See case summary 16–101.

19–004 Lombardi v Lombardi

[1973] 3 All ER 625, CA

Calculation of the one-third ratio – discounting of earnings of third party.   The total income of the husband and the woman with whom he was living was a little over £3,000 per annum gross. The Court of Appeal attributed one-third of that sum to the assistance of the woman in the husband's business and accordingly assessed the husband's earnings as £2,000 per annum gross. The wife's income was £728 per annum gross, giving a total of £2,728 per annum. One-third of that is £909, and the difference between that and the wife's income from her employment of £728 is £181. This meant a starting figure of something between £3 and £4 a week. The periodical payments order of £3 per week was accordingly upheld by the Court of Appeal.

19–005 Griffiths v Griffiths

[1974] 1 All ER 932, CA

Uncertainty of husband's income – award of lump sum to wife – adjustment of capital position so as to equalise income position.   One-third ratio not applied. See case summary 15–303.

19–006 Flatt v Flatt

(1973) 4 Fam Law 20, 118 Sol Jo 183, CA

Calculation of the one-third ratio – use and occupation of property rent-free taken into account.   Lord Denning MR said that the husband had a salary of £1,800 a year. The wife's income was £675 a year. Usually the wife got a third of the joint income, giving credit for what she earned, so she should get £156 a year: (£1800 + £675 = £2475; one-third = £825; £825 – £675 = £150; £13 per month = £156 per annum). Lord Denning said that the judge had decided the case before *Wachtel v Wachtel* (19–002) and had made an order of some complication. The better order was that the house should be held by them in the proportion of two-thirds to the husband and one-third to the wife on trust for sale. If the house was not being sold the husband, who was living in the house, should pay a further £247 per annum for as long as he was living there (as a form of rent) which meant £403 a year; periodical payments of £33.50 a month to be secured on the property (£33.50 per month = £402 per annum).

Note. Compare *Sopher v Sopher* (19–007).

19-007 Sopher v Sopher

(1975) 6 Fam Law 12.

Calculation of the one-third ratio – use and occupation of property rent-free taken into account. The husband was by profession a chartered accountant. He was employed as an attaché by a firm of stockbrokers, his earnings comprising the commission he earned on share dealings, and which fluctuated greatly. He also engaged in share dealings on his own account, but had so far been unsuccessful, and his capital had been steadily decreasing. The wife earned £46 per week gross.

The husband estimated his future commission at £400–£500 per month. The judge at first instance took the figure of £400 per month and added a sum of £1,200 a year to allow for the fact that the husband was living rent-free in a substantial house owned by his new wife. He took the wife's income as £40 per week, recognising the fact that she had not worked during the marriage, and awarded periodical payments of £624 per annum to the wife, after applying the one-third ratio. The order was upheld by the Court of Appeal. The calculation was as follows:

$$
\begin{aligned}
\text{husband's income: } £400 \text{ per month} &= £4,800 \text{ p.a.} \\
&+ £1,200 \text{ p.a.} \\
&= £6,000 \text{ p.a.} \\
\text{wife's income: } £40 \text{ per week} &= £2,080 \text{ p.a.} \\
\text{TOTAL} \quad & £8,080 \text{ p.a.} \\
\tfrac{1}{3} &= £2,693 \\
\text{deduct wife's income} \quad & £2,080 \\
& £613 \text{ per annum}
\end{aligned}
$$

£613 p.a., rounded up to £624 p.a., gives a figure for monthly maintenance of £52.

Note. Compare *Flatt v Flatt* (19–006).

19-007A Gengler v Gengler

[1976] 2 All ER 81

One-third ratio merely a useful starting point. Applying the one-third ratio, the wife would have been entitled to no more than a nominal order. The husband appealed against the award of maintenance of £6 per week by the magistrates' court. Sir George Baker P said that the wife had inevitably suffered financial loss as a result of the husband's desertion, and the magistrates were perfectly entitled to refuse to take into account the whole of the wife's earnings, it being irrelevant that she had worked prior to the breakdown of the marriage. However, had the order for maintenance been made following divorce proceedings, the wife would have been unlikely to have obtained more than a small order – possibly a nominal order only. And, said his lordship, it would be unfortunate if, by choosing not to divorce the husband, she could thereby keep herself in a better position than if she brought divorce proceedings. Order reduced to £3 per week.

Latey J added that although the one-third calculation was a fair and useful starting point it would not necessarily be the finishing point.

Note. Sir George Baker's assertion that in applying the one-third ratio the husband's *gross* income should be added to the wife's *net* income was disapproved by the Court of Appeal in *Rodewald v Rodewald* (19–009). And see now *Furniss v Furniss* (19–016) and *Stockford v Stockford* (19–017).

19-008 Weisz v Weisz

(1975) Times, 16th December, CA

Wife awarded three-quarters of the capital assets to compensate for award of one-sixth of the joint income. The husband concealed the existence of a bank account and the extent of his income. The Court of Appeal upheld an order that he should transfer his interest in the former matrimonial home to the wife. He was further ordered to make a lump sum payment of an amount equal to one-half of the value of his two additional properties. The total of the award amounted to three-quarters of the capital assets and one-sixth of the joint income. Held (Sir John Pennycuick dissenting) the husband was clearly a dishonest man, and unless compelled to do so would not make any contributions for the wife and daughter. The award was one which gave the wife financial security immediately and one which had the merit of finality. The husband's appeal was dismissed.

19–009 Rodewald v Rodewald

[1977] 2 All ER 609, CA

(1) *Calculation of the one-third ratio – children's contributions to household expenses.* The two adult children of the marriage were living with the husband. The son was earning and paid the husband £7 a week towards the household expenses. The daughter was in receipt of supplementary benefit, and the husband received contributions towards the household expenses from her also. The Court of Appeal held it was wrong to assume that the two adult children were 'income producing assets'. Their contributions to the household ought not to be taken into account in the calculation of the one-third ratio. However, their contributions might justify a higher award of maintenance than the one-third calculation would suggest.

(2) *Calculation of the one-third ratio – employees' benefits in kind.* The husband, in addition to his job as a factory hand, worked part-time for a butcher, and received an estimated £5 worth of free meat each week. The Court of Appeal held that, although the free meat was clearly a regular asset coming into the family and the judge had been correct in bringing it into account when calculating the one-third ratio, he had been wrong to gross up the notional value of this asset. If one grosses up a notional figure one is apt to get a figure which is possibly unreal, and the result is likely to become increasingly unrealistic the larger it is.

(3) *Calculation of the one-third ratio – gross earnings to be used, not net.* The Court of Appeal reiterated that, in calculating the one-third ratio, the parties' gross incomes should be taken. *Wachtel v Wachtel* (19–002) applied. Dictum of Sir George Baker P in *Gengler v Gengler* (19–007A) disapproved. But see now *Furniss v Furniss* (19–016) and *Stockford v Stockford* (19–017).

19–010 Scott v Scott

[1978] 3 All ER 65, CA

'Small income' situation – one-third ratio of no assistance. The husband's gross income from his employment was £3,400 a year, out of which he had to pay National Insurance contributions of £197 a year. The wife had £2,000 capital, which was invested and produced £285 a year before tax. The registrar had ordered the husband to pay £11 a week periodical payments to the wife and £6 a week to each of the three children. The county court judge had affirmed the registrar's order.

Cumming-Bruce LJ said that when one came to the realities of the situation on the facts of the present case, reference to the one-third ratio as a starting point was of no assistance, because on these family finances the dominating feature was the necessity of providing for three young children and the requirement of providing a home for them by means of mortgage payments. Looking at the figures, the result of the order made below was that after paying the sums ordered for the maintenance of the former wife and the children the husband was left with £24.30, £11 of which he appropriated to his rent, and £13.30 which he had in his hands for all living purposes. He lived in a bedsitter, with the shared use of bathroom and kitchen, and he had £13.30 to manage on. The wife was living in the former matrimonial home, a three-bedroomed house, by herself and with the three children, and, taking the order as it stood, she had £29 a week out of which to pay everything except the mortgage, for which her husband paid. Did the order produce a result in which the husband, on the one hand in his home, the bedsitter, had a comparable standard of living to the wife and children in their home? A man in salaried employment of £3,400 a year, who had to pay rent for his bedsitter, and then to try to live on £13.30 a week was not enjoying a standard of living – if 'enjoyment' was the right word – comparable to the admittedly restricted standard of living of the wife and children. The sacrifice had to be redistributed somehow, although even when it was redistributed the households in neither home were likely to enjoy a standard of living which was much above the bread line. No assistance was derived from a consideration of subsistence levels. What he sought to do was to try to picture the reality of the standards of living in the one home and the other having regard to the needs of the grown-ups and the needs of the children. The registrar and the judge had gone wrong in failing to have regard sufficiently to the consequence of the order upon the comparable standards of living in the two households. The order for periodical payments ought to be varied and should be reduced by £6 a week.

19–011 Shallow v Shallow

[1978] 2 All ER 483, CA

(1) *Calculation of the one-third ratio – deductions from the husband's income.*   The registrar had ordered the husband to pay £12 per week to his former wife and £5 per week to each of his two children, plus the mortgage instalments and rates on the former matrimonial home, which together came to £8.50 per week. His total liability therefore amounted to £30.50 per week.

The husband's appeal to the county court judge, on the ground, inter alia, that the order would depress him below subsistence level, was dismissed. He appealed to the Court of Appeal.

Ormrod LJ said (at page 487): '. . . On the one-third basis the husband's gross weekly income is approximately £75 per week, from which national insurance contribution is to be deducted (£228 per annum or £4.25 per week) together with something for travelling and other expenses of earning his income leaving, say, £68. The wife has no income except £3 per week child benefit. The aggregate is therefore £71, one-third of which is £24, from which £3 is to be deducted, leaving £21 as the starting point for the wife's own order. This is close to the registrar's figure of £20.50 (made up as to £12, plus £8.50 mortgage repayments and rates) for the wife herself.'

Because the registrar's order of £30.50 per week (including £5 per week for each of the two children) would not depress the husband below 'subsistence level' as defined (see case summary 22–007 for the definition of the term), the Court of Appeal upheld the order.

(2) *Calculation of the one-third ratio – child benefit.*   See quotation above.

19–012 Clarke v Clarke

(1978) 9 Fam Law 15, CA

'Small income' situation – one-third ratio of no assistance.   Husband earned £45 per week gross. Wife and child were living on social security. The husband lived with his mother and paid her £12 per week for board and lodging. He was employed as a lorry driver; he said that he could not park his lorry near to his mother's house and needed a car to get to work. Ormrod LJ said that he found it extraordinary that the husband should argue that he should be left with enough money to run a car so as to encourage him to go to work. It was wrong for husbands to say that the state should maintain their wives and children unless

they were rich enough to provide for them without any appreciable inconvenience to themselves. However, the judge had been correct in reducing the registrar's order in favour of the wife from £7.50 to £6 per week. The order made by the judge of £6 per week for the wife and £5 per week for the child would be upheld, notwithstanding that this was far below the cost of maintaining the wife and child, who were receiving £30 per week in social security benefits.

19–012A Walker v Walker

(1978) Times, 3 March, 8 Fam Law 107

Calculation of the one-third ratio – rent and rates rebates to be ignored except in 'small income' cases.   The husband complained that the registrar's order left him with less to live on than the figure allowed by the Supplementary Benefits Commission to a single man for minimum subsistence. The registrar had not taken account of the rent and rates rebates to which the wife would have been entitled had she applied to the appropriate authorities. Purchas J said that it would not be right to decrease the maintenance payments to such an extent as to promote the husband above the minimum level acceptable, because this would be to subsidise not the wife but the husband from public funds. The husband's appeal was allowed only to the extent of reducing the order for maintenance of the wife to such a sum as would leave the husband with a net sum slightly in excess of the amount to which he would have been entitled were he in receipt of supplementary benefit.

Notes

1. As is pointed out in the note to this case in *Family Law*, this case follows the line taken in *Shallow v Shallow* (22–007) and *Tovey v Tovey* (22–008), i.e. that the court should disregard the availability of social security benefits unless the husband would thereby be reduced below subsistence level.
2. Compare *Barnes v Barnes* (22–002), in which Edmund Davies LJ said that, in the first place, regard should not be had to social security benefits; however, if this would leave the husband below subsistence level, then the court may have regard to the social security benefits available to the wife.
3. For further details, see case summary 22–008A.
4. In 'small income' cases the one-third ratio is of no assistance anyway – see *Scott v Scott* (19–010), *Clarke v Clarke* (19–012) and *Fitzpatrick v Fitzpatrick* (19–013).

19–013 Fitzpatrick v Fitzpatrick

(1978) 9 Fam Law 16, CA

'Small income' situation – one-third ratio of no assistance.   The wife was living in a council flat with the two children. The husband lived with a woman he intended to marry and her two children in a house they owned jointly. The wife had been unable to find part-time work. The husband was earning £74 per week gross. If the judge had applied the one-third ratio, the order in favour of the wife would have been far in excess of the £15 per week ordered by the registrar and upheld by the judge; but the effect of that order, coupled with the order for the payment of £5 per week in respect of each of the two children, was that the husband would be £2 per week better off if he gave up working and lived on social security benefits. The Court of Appeal thought it unlikely that the husband would give up his employment for the sake of £2 per week. Nevertheless, they came to the conclusion that the order of £15 per week was too high and reduced this to £12 per week.

Note. The report of this case in *Family Law* refers to the following cases on the 'liable relative' formula used by the Supplementary Benefits Commission and the definition of the term 'subsistence level': *Ashley v Ashley* (22–001), *Smethurst v Smethurst* (22–006), *Shallow v Shallow* (22–007) and *Tovey v Tovey* (22–008). See the notes in *Family Law* at volume 8, pages 78 to 81 and volume 9, pages 16 and 17.

19–014 M v M (sub nom. **Moon v Moon**)

(1979) 10 Fam Law 114

(1) *Calculation of the one-third ratio – single parent allowance payable by DHSS.*   Waterhouse J said that it was not appropriate for justices to take account of the single parent allowance (i.e. the additional allowance paid by the DHSS to single parent families over and above child benefit). This allowance was intended by the state to compensate for the special difficulty encountered when bringing up a family without the aid of a spouse. To include the amount in the income of a single parent would negate the purpose of the allowance.

> *Note.* Approved in *C v W* (19–015), where the report quotes from Waterhouse J's judgment and makes it plain that his lordship was speaking of the single parent allowance paid by the DHSS and not the single parent allowance for income tax purposes.

(2) *Calculation of the one-third ratio – child benefit.*   A transcript of the official court tape recording provided by Messrs. Cater Walsh & Co. of 10 Victoria Avenue, Halesowen, West Midlands reads as follows: 'There seems to have been some confusion in the minds of the justices about the amount of the wife's income derived from allowances. The realistic position is that *she now gets £4 per week per child as child benefit. In addition, she gets £2 per week as single parent allowance . . . I would add that I do not myself regard it as appropriate to take account of the single parent allowance in these calculations . . . If it is included in the wife's income, the whole purpose of the allowance is negatived. The proper approach in this case is to say that the mother is receiving £4 per week as the contribution from the state to the cost of bringing up each child. In total, she receives £8 per week. That is the relevant figure.*'

> *Note.* See also *Shallow v Shallow* (19–011).

19–015 C v W

(1980) Times, 16 February

Calculation of the one-third ratio – single parent allowance payable by DHSS. Bush J endorsed Waterhouse J's statement in *M v M* (19–014) that it was not appropriate to take into account the additional single parent allowance paid by the DHSS to single parent families (i.e. over and above child benefit, which is payable to all families).

19–016 Furniss v Furniss

(1981) Times, 28 October, CA

One-third approach based on gross incomes wholly unsatisfactory. See Appendix II.

19–017 Stockford v Stockford

(1981) Times, 5 November, CA

(1) *Wrong in principle to adopt a purely arithmetical approach.* See Appendix II.
(2) *Net income approach to be preferred.* See Appendix II.

CHAPTER 20

Wife's award increased

20–001 Trippas v Trippas

[1973] 2 All ER 1, CA

Husband not in employment – award of lump sum to wife – husband left with investment income approximately equal to wife's total income from her earnings and invested capital – 'rough justice on the basis of approximate equality'. One-third ratio not applied. See case summary 16–101.

20–002 Griffiths v Griffiths

[1974] 1 All ER 932, CA

Uncertainty of husband's income – award of lump sum to wife – adjustment of capital position so as to equalise income position. See case summary 15–303.

20–003 Gengler v Gengler

[1976] 2 All ER 81

One-third ratio merely a useful starting point. Applying the one-third ratio, the wife would have been entitled to no more than a nominal order. The husband appealed against the award of maintenance of £6 per week by the magistrates' court. Order reduced to £3 per week. See case summary 19–007A.

20–004 Rodewald v Rodewald

[1977] 2 All ER 609, CA

Children's contributions to household expenses – all the circumstances of the case. The husband's gross income from his work was £3,000 per annum. In addition he did part-time work for a butcher for which he received meat to the value of £5 a week. Two older children of the marriage lived with the husband and contributed towards the household expenses. The wife earned £1,680 a year gross.

Ormrod LJ said that if one took the husband's gross income at £3,000 a year, plus something for the meat, and the wife's gross income at £1,680 and applied the one-third ratio one got a nominal order as a starting point. But it was conceded by the husband that this was not a case for a nominal order but for a real order, and £4 a week would be about right. Husband's appeal against order for payment of £7 a week allowed. See case summary 19–009 – calculation of the one-third ratio – children's contributions to household expenses.

20–005 Ward v Ward and Greene (sub nom. Ward v Ward)

[1980] 1 All ER 176, [1980] 1 WLR 4, CA

Award large enough to enable wife to borrow in order to provide a roof over her head. See case summary 6–303.

CHAPTER 21

Wife's award reduced

1 Wife's income adequate for her needs

CASE SUMMARIES

21–101 Griffiths v Griffiths

[1974] 1 All ER 932, CA

Wife's prospect of receiving maintenance reduced following husband's business misfortune. Periodical payments order not sought by wife. Wife's share of capital assets increased in order to secure her financial position. Wife's earnings, together with investment income from her share of capital assets, adequate for her needs. Unreasonable of husband to suggest 50:50 division of capital assets coupled with award of maintenance. Wrong to put wife into position of having to rely on maintenance. See case summary 10–203.

21–102 Bennett v Bennett

(1978) 9 Fam Law 19, CA

The husband had resigned his job as a financial director two years ago following the appointment of a new managing director. He was unwilling to accept a lower paid appointment. When the case came before the county court judge, the judge warned him that unless he found employment the house would be transferred into his wife's name. Such an order was duly made and the husband appealed.

The Court of Appeal held that the judge had paid too little regard to the difficulties with which the husband was faced on losing an employment he had held for 19 years, and that it was natural for the husband to be unwilling to accept new employment at a substantially reduced level. Furthermore, in view of the wife's earnings, applying the one-third ratio, the husband would have to be earning a substantial salary for the wife to be entitled to anything other than a nominal order.

The Court of Appeal ordered the former matrimonial home to be sold and that the wife should receive two-thirds of the net sale proceeds or £17,000, whichever was the greater. A sum of £17,000 was sufficient to enable the wife, with the £4,000 capital she already had, to purchase a suitable home in the area.

21–103 Minton v Minton

[1979] 1 All ER 79, HL

The clean break. Consent order. Adequate or generous capital provision for wife in full and final settlement of all future claims for financial relief. Genuine final order equivalent to a dismissal of wife's application for periodical payments. See case summary 10–205.

Notes
1. The wife's consent is required before the court can make any order dismissing her application for periodical payments – see *Dipper v Dipper* (10–209).

296

2. The clean break is of no application where the wife's income is not adequate for her needs – see *Moore v Moore* (10–210).

21–104 S v S

(1980) Times, 10 May

Desirability of a clean break where parties can afford it. The value of the husband's assets had been agreed at £2.1m. The parties agreed there should be a clean break and the wife consented to the dismissal of her claim for periodical payments.

Notes
1. For further details, see case summary 16–104 – one third approach inappropriate where capital assets so large.
2. See also *Page v Page* (21–105).

21–105 Page v Page

(1981) Times, 30 January, CA

Relationship between the parties so embittered that periodical payments to be avoided. Desirability of a clean break where parties can afford it. See case summary 16–105. For further details, see Appendix II.

2 Husband's income limited

CASE SUMMARIES

21–201 Barnes v Barnes

[1972] 3 All ER 872, CA

The husband's two families – conflict of interests. See case summary 6–431. For a full summary, see 22–002.

21–202 Winter v Winter

(1972) 140 JP Jo 597

The husband's two families – conflict of interests. See case summary 6–432. For a full summary, see 22–003.

21–203 Smethurst v Smethurst

[1977] 3 All ER 1110

The husband's several families – conflict of interests. See case summary 6–434. For a full summary, see 22–006.

21–204 Scott v Scott

[1978] 3 All ER 65, CA

The husband's low standard of living. See case summary 19–010.

21–205 Tovey v Tovey

(1977) 8 Fam Law 80, CA

The husband's two families – conflict of interests. See case summary 6–435. For a full summary, see 22–008.

21–206 Walker v Walker

(1978) 8 Fam Law 107

The husband's low standard of living. See case summary 19–012A. For a full summary, see 22–008A.

21–207 Clarke v Clarke

(1978) 9 Fam Law 15, CA

The husband's low standard of living. See case summary 19–012.

21–208 Fitzpatrick v Fitzpatrick

(1978) 9 Fam Law 16, CA

The husband's two families – conflict of interests. See case summary 6–436. For a full summary, see 22–009.

21–209 Wagner v Wagner

(1978) 9 Fam Law 183, CA

The husband's two families – what would be fair in all the circumstances. See case summary 6–437.

21–210 Re L

(1979) 9 Fam Law 152

The husband's two families – what would be fair in all the circumstances. See case summary 6–438.

3 Wife provided for by third party

CASE SUMMARIES

21–301 Wachtel v Wachtel

[1973] 1 All ER 829, CA

Lord Denning MR said: 'So far as periodical payments are concerned, they are, of course, to be assessed without regard to the prospects of remarriage. If the wife does in fact remarry, they cease. If she goes to live with another man – without marrying him – they may be reviewed.' See case summary 6–131.

21–302 Campbell v Campbell

[1977] 1 All ER 1

No evidence of wife cohabiting with third party; no sufficient evidence of maintenance of wife by third party. See case summary 6–132.

21–303 Re L

(1979) 9 Fam Law 152

Maintenance of children – resources of wife's household. See case summary 6–232.

4 Short marriage

CASE SUMMARIES

21–401 Krystman v Krystman

[1973] 3 All ER 247, CA

See case summary 7–702.

21–402 Graves v Graves

(1973) 4 Fam Law 124, 117 Sol Jo 679

See case summary 7–231.

21–403 Chesworth v Chesworth

(1973) 4 Fam Law 22, 118 Sol Jo 183

See case summary 7–232.

21–404 W-S v W-S (sub nom. Whyte-Smith v Whyte-Smith)

(1974) Times, 25 October, 119 Sol Jo 46

See case summary 7–361.

21–405 M v M

(1976) 6 Fam Law 243, CA

See note 2 to case summary 7–303.

21–406 Campbell v Campbell

[1977] 1 All ER 1

See case summary 8–401.

21–407 McGrady v McGrady

(1977) 8 Fam Law 15

See case summary 7–706.

21–408 S v S

[1977] 1 All ER 56, CA

See case summary 7–431.

21–409 West v West

[1977] 2 All ER 705, CA

See case summary 13–013.

21–410 Abdureman v Abdureman

(1978) 122 Sol Jo 663

See case summary 7–463.

21–411 Warder v Warder

(1978) 122 Sol Jo 713

See case summary 7–464.

21–412 Khan v Khan

[1980] 1 All ER 497

See case summary 7–234.

21–413 H v H (15 May 1981)

(1981) Times, 16 May

See Appendix II.

5 Wife's misconduct taken into account

CASE SUMMARIES

21–501 Armstrong v Armstrong

(1974) 118 Sol Jo 579, CA

See case summary 8–102. For a full summary, see 8–205.

21–502 West v West

[1977] 2 All ER 705, CA

See case summary 8–108. For a full summary, see 13–013.

21–503 Bateman v Bateman

[1979] 2 WLR 377

See case summary 8–110. For a full summary, see 8–309.

21–504 J (HD) v J (AM) (sub nom. **Johnson v Johnson**)

[1980] 1 All ER 156

See case summary 8–112. For a full summary, see 8–504.

CHAPTER 22

Relevance of social security benefits

22–000 Ivory v Ivory

[1954] 1 All ER 898

The husband was now unemployed and in receipt of a grant from the National Assistance Board. He had applied to the justices for a reduction in the award of maintenance made against him. On appeal to the Divisional Court, Sachs J said that counsel for the husband had attempted to argue that there was, in effect, an absolute bar to the court's making more than a nominal award of maintenance when the husband's sole source of income was from national assistance, but in the end had conceded that the fact that his client's income was derived solely from such funds was simply one factor to be taken into account when assessing what was proper for his client to pay.

Note. See, however, *Williams v Williams* (22–005) in which Finer J said: 'The court, it is well established, will not allow a man to absolve himself from his maintenance obligation at the public expense . . . But here the husband is himself on supplementary benefit, which is pitched at a level which gives him nothing to spare. The court cannot ignore this . . .'

22–001 Ashley v Ashley

[1965] 3 All ER 554

On a complaint brought by the wife, the justices found that the husband had deserted her and had wilfully neglected to provide reasonable maintenance for her and for the two children of the marriage, whose legal custody they granted to her. The wife appealed against the order for maintenance in her favour on the ground that it was inadequate.

Sir Jocelyn Simon P said (at page 558): 'In the present case, the husband has a net income of £14 5s., and he is provided daily with a free meal six days a week. The maintenance awarded for the wife and children together amounted to 30 shillings a week. They are young children and the wife is unable to work. The husband is left with a net income, after paying maintenance, of £12 15s., plus the benefit he gets from the meals. So gross a disparity can only be explained by the fact that the wife and children are on national assistance and that the justices in those circumstances thought it right that she and the children should be brought up to subsistence level by the National Assistance Board.

'There are two things to be said about that. First, the husband at £12 15s. plus meals is substantially above subsistence level as measured by the National Assistance rates. Secondly, as Denning LJ said in *National Assistance Board v Parkes* [1955] 3 All ER 1 (at page 4): "A husband cannot shift his responsibility on to the rest of the community in that way."

'. . . The matrimonial court should consider all the circumstances of the case, including, certainly, the fact that national assistance is available and may be required; but it should not, as the conclusion of the adjudication, allow the husband to enjoy a substantially higher standard of living than the wife, or shift his responsibilities for his wife and children on to the community generally through the National Assistance Board. On the other hand, the matrimonial court must remember that the National Assistance Board does not supplement wages. [Family Income Supplement was not introduced until 1970.] They must therefore not make such an order as would bring the husband below subsistence level. If the order so limited leaves the wife and children still below subsistence level, the National Assistance Board may properly be looked to, to supplement their income. Both parties and the children will then unhappily be at no better than subsistence level; but the result will be just as between the husband and his wife and children on the one hand, and between the husband and the general community as symbolised by the National Assistance Board on the other.

'...the fact that the National Assistance Board will in all probability get the benefit of any order made in favour of the wife is wholly irrelevant.'

In the event, the Divisional Court allowed the wife's appeal and the order for maintenance was increased, because the husband could afford to pay more without reducing his income below subsistence level as measured by the National Assistance rates.

22–002 Barnes v Barnes

[1972] 3 All ER 872, CA

By an order made in June 1971, the county court judge had awarded the wife maintenance of £2 per week for each of the four children, making a total of £8 per week, and nominal maintenance of 5p per annum for herself. In July 1971 the husband had remarried, and by a further order made by the judge in March 1972 the earlier award had been reduced to a sum of £1.50 per week for each of the four children, making a total of £6 per week.

Edmund Davies LJ said that there was evidence to show that the wife was not one penny worse off as a result of the reduction in the first award, because there had been a corresponding increase in the social security benefit which she was receiving. He continued (at page 874): 'It was submitted by counsel for the husband that such benefit is to be regarded as coming within section 5 (1) (a) of the Matrimonial Proceedings and Property Act 1970 [See now section 25 (1) (a) of the Matrimonial Causes Act 1973 – see Appendix I], as being comprised within the "other financial resources which each of the parties to the marriage has or is likely to have in the foreseeable future". I find it difficult to regard such state benefits as coming within such a frame ...'

Having quoted from the judgment of the Divisional Court in *Ashley v Ashley* (22–001) with approval, he continued: '... the conclusion to which I have come is that *in the first place when the court is seeking to arrive at what would be a proper order, it is desirable that regard should not be had to social security benefits ...* But if the case is one in which the income of the parties is of modest proportions, and *if the total available resources of both parties are so modest that an adjustment of that totality would result in the husband being left with a sum quite inadequate to enable him to meet his own financial commitments, then the court may have regard to the fact that in proper cases social security benefits will be available to the wife and the children of the marriage.*'

In the event, the Court of Appeal varied the judge's order of March 1972, increasing the award of nominal maintenance for the wife to an award of £2 per week, the effect of which was to restore the total award of £8 per week.

22–003 Winter v Winter

(1972) 140 JP Jo 597

The wife had obtained a decree nisi against the appellant husband on the ground of his adultery. The husband had left the wife and four children and moved a few doors away to co-habit with the other woman, by whom, at the time of the hearing, he had had two further children. The husband was a self-employed forestry contractor who also dealt in scrap metal and acted as a lorry driver. His gross income was assessed (with some difficulty) by the court as varying from £15 to £25 per week gross, out of which he had to pay £4 for board and lodgings and maintain his co-habitee and her two children. The court thought it would not be unreasonable to leave in his hands £13 to £14 per week to maintain these commitments at subsistence level, this being the kind of figure (including rent allowance) which would be calculated as his requirements if the cohabitee and her children were themselves in receipt of supplementary benefit.

Payne J said that no order should be made against a husband which left him with an inadequate amount for the support of his second family: the result would be that in such circumstances the husband would decide to maintain his second family and to default on the court order, knowing that his first wife could look to the state for support, whereas his second wife or mistress could not. In the present case, the wife's entitlement to supplementary benefit for herself and the children, if the husband did not support her, would exceed any sum which could reasonably be assessed against the husband by way of contribution. Therefore, any sum which the court awarded would not in fact benefit the wife, but would represent a contribution from him towards the supplementary benefit. And although the first wife's income could always be made up by the DHSS to the appropriate maximum supplementary benefit figure, the income of the husband's second family would not similarly be made up because supplementary benefit was not payable to a woman if she was cohabiting with a man who was in full employment. It was for this reason that those courts in which the position was fully understood tended to ensure that the husband and his second family did not suffer undue hardship. The first wife's hardship was alleviated by the payment of benefit; the second woman's was not.

In the result the court varied the registrar's order from £7 per week for maintenance pending suit and £2 for each child (a total of £15) to £3 per week for the wife and £1 for each child (making £7 per week in all).

22–004 Billington v Billington

[1974] 1 All ER 546

In 1968 the husband was ordered by the justices to pay £1 per week maintenance to the wife. This order was subsequently varied, and in May 1972 an attachment of earnings order was made requiring £1.50 per week to be deducted from his wages. *The protected earnings rate* under the attachment of earnings order (i.e. the amount below which the husband's net wages were not to be reduced by the deduction of maintenance payments under the order) was fixed by the justices at £11 per week. *The normal deduction rate* specified in the attachment of earnings order was £1.50 per week.

Following the divorce the husband had remarried and now had three dependent children. In October 1972 he applied for an order for variation.

The justices found that his net weekly earnings were £18.58. His second family also had the benefit of family income supplement of £3.60 per week and family allowance of £1.90 per week, thus making a total income of £24.08 per week.

The normal requirements of the husband under the Supplementary Benefits Commission scale (i.e. subsistence level) amounted to £23.05 per week. *The resources* of the husband *other than his earnings* consisted of the family income supplement of £3.60 per week and the family allowance of £1.90 per week, totalling £5.50 per week. His present wife did not work. Taking the husband's *resources other than earnings* of £5.50 per week from his *normal requirements* of £23.05 per week left a *protected earnings rate* of £17.55 per week (cf. *the protected earnings rate* fixed by the justices of only £11.00 per week).

The husband's net earnings of £18.58 per week were therefore £1.03 above *the protected earnings rate* of £17.55 per week; so he could meet a *normal deduction rate* of £1 per week (cf. *the normal deduction rate* fixed by the justices of £1.50 per week).

As the appeal was by way of case stated the Divisional Court had no power to order a rehearing. It was, however, open to the husband to apply for variation of *the protected earnings rate* of £11 per week fixed by the justices and of *the normal deduction rate* of £1.50 per week fixed by the justices.

Sir George Baker P said that there is no principle which prohibits the justices from fixing a *protected earnings rate* below the figure prescribed by the DHSS as a person's *normal requirements* (i.e. subsistence level) but that in most cases it would be unreasonable to do so.

22–005 Williams (LA) v Williams (EM) (sub nom. Williams v Williams)

[1974] 3 All ER 377

In divorce proceedings the husband had been ordered to pay the wife £4 per week. The order had been registered in the magistrates' court. The husband had subsequently been made redundant and was now in receipt of supplementary benefit. The wife was also receiving supplementary benefit. The husband applied to the justices for a variation of the maintenance order on the ground that it was impossible for him to pay £4 per week to the wife out of the amount he was receiving from the Supplementary Benefits Commission. The justices were not satisfied that the husband had genuinely attempted to find employment and dismissed the application. The husband appealed.

The Divisional Court held firstly, that because the officials of the DHSS (who had a duty to investigate such matters) had not reduced or stopped the payments of supplementary benefit to the husband, it was possible to infer that he was genuinely and not voluntarily unemployed. That was a matter which the justices ought to have taken into account, and the case would be remitted to a fresh panel of justices for rehearing.

Secondly, that the justices ought also to have taken into consideration the fact that here was a husband who was himself on supplementary benefit; to make him pay maintenance to the wife would not benefit her but would only reduce the amount of the benefits paid to her, while it would reduce the husband to a standard of living below the supplementary benefit level.

Finer J said (at page 383): 'The court, it is well established, will not allow a man to absolve himself from his maintenance obligation at the public expense. In assessing a man's maintenance liability one generally excludes from the consideration the fact, as it so often is, that to make him pay maintenance will not improve the financial position of the wife at all, but only reduce the amount of supplementary benefit being paid to her. This is all very well where a man has income to spare. But here the husband is himself on supplementary benefit, which is pitched at a level which gives him nothing to spare. The court cannot ignore this, nor the fact that the commission are content to treat him as a proper case for the payment of the benefit.'

The case was remitted for rehearing before a fresh panel of justices, who reduced the maintenance to 1p per week.

Notes

1. Sir George Baker P said (at page 384): 'The wife appeared before the justices by counsel, as did the husband. The wife appears here by counsel, and I have no doubt both here and before the justices she had a legal aid certificate. Presumably the husband, too, was legally aided before the justices, although he appears in person today. I have been asking myself who in truth had legal aid, the wife or the Ministry? And the only answer that I can see to that is that it was the Ministry that had legal aid, because the wife has no interest in this whatsoever. She cannot be better or worse off . . . the Law Society ought to consider looking carefully at the granting of legal aid in such circumstances.'

2. Compare *Tovey v Tovey* (22–008).

22–006 Smethurst v Smethurst

[1977] 3 All ER 1110

The county court registrar made a maintenance order against the husband in favour of his third wife, ordering him to pay £9 a week. The order was registered at a magistrates' court. At the time when the order was made the husband was earning approximately £34 a week net and, as the registrar knew, was liable under a previous maintenance order to pay his second wife £3.50 a week. The third wife was in receipt of social security and so the order would not in fact benefit her because the maintenance would be paid to the DHSS. The husband applied to the magistrates' court where the order was registered to vary the order by reducing the amount payable on the ground that he could not afford to pay it. The husband had married a fourth wife and she and her child were fully dependent on him. At the date of the application to vary, the husband's net income was virtually the same as at the date of the original order. The justices varied the order by reducing the amount payable by £2.50, holding that the husband had insufficient resources to meet the original order together with his other commitments and it was more realistic that he should pay a sum which he could afford. The third wife appealed to the Divisional Court.

Sir George Baker P said that whatever way one tested the husband's ability to pay he could not, at the date of the original order, have afforded to pay £9 a week maintenance without falling below subsistence level. In particular, if the matter had been approached by considering the contribution which the Supplementary Benefits Commission could have required him to pay, it was likely that no contribution would have been required having regard to his income. It followed that in ordering maintenance of £9 a week the registrar had made a mistake as to the husband's ability to pay. The justices therefore had jurisdiction to consider the matter de novo, and had acted properly in varying the order by reducing the maintenance to an amount which left the husband with enough to live on, at least at subsistence level. The third wife's appeal was dismissed.

Sir George Baker P said (at page 1114): 'In this case, the wife is in receipt of social security. The benefit of this order will be a benefit not to her but to the Supplementary Benefits Commission. On enquiring about that, we were told by counsel for the wife that she is contemplating getting employment, and therefore wants to keep as large an order against the husband as is right. She thinks in some way it will benefit her then, but of course that situation would immediately spur the husband to seek a review, because her earnings would have to be taken into consideration, applying the one-third approach. Another way of looking at this matter is to consider whether, and if so how far, the husband is on or above subsistence level. If the Supplementary Benefits Commission were seeking a contribution from this man, they would apply the formula, which is to be found in the Finer report. The report [Report of the Committee on One-Parent Families (1974) Cmnd 5629] stated:

> "Nothing could exceed the confusion created by three modes of assessment of a liability, all different from each other, and two of them employed in courts of law acting in ignorance of the third mode which the Supplementary Benefits Commission use in making decisions which affect the very same group of people."

'I am not aware of this approach having been used before in the courts, but I see no reason why it should not be, and to my knowledge justices are considering it. The Supplementary Benefits Commission formula is as follows: the husband and his wife would have an allowance of £20.65 a week; the child would have the benefit of £4.35, and there would be a rent allowance of £8.64. In addition to that, the Supplementary Benefits Commission would allow the husband, as what I suppose might be called an "incentive allowance", one-quarter of his net income or £5 whichever be the greater. In the present case that would be £10, and the total of these four items is £43.64. So as the husband's net income is £40 a week, it would seem that the Supplementary Benefits Commission would not seek to recover anything from him in the present case, or at best a very small sum if, I do not know if this is right or not, they took his gross instead of his net income. I suspect they take his net, because they assess the quarter on his net earnings.

'So what is happening in the present case seems to me to be that this court is being asked to set aside the justices' variation and leave the original order, with the result that the Supplementary Benefits Commission will be receiving a sum, if it is paid, which is greater, considerably greater, than they themselves would seek to recover from the husband in the circumstances prevailing here. I think in this case that the mistake in the original order was a mistake as to the husband's ability to pay. Something must have gone wrong somewhere.'

Note. In *Shallow v Shallow* (22–007) the Court of Appeal pointed out the illogicality of equating the figure produced by the 'liable relative formula' with 'subsistence level'. Because the formula includes an 'incentive allowance' over and above the supplementary benefits to which the husband would be entitled if he were out of work, it is bound to be greater than 'subsistence level' as defined in *Ashley v Ashley* (22–001), *Barnes v Barnes* (22–002) and *Shallow v Shallow*. However, this is not to say that the Divisional Court in *Smethurst v Smethurst* was wrong to dismiss the third wife's appeal, because whatever way one tested the husband's ability to pay he could not, at the date of the original order, have afforded to pay £9 a week maintenance.

22–007 Shallow v Shallow

[1978] 2 All ER 483, CA

The county court judge dismissed the husband's appeal against the registrar's order for the payment of maintenance totalling £30.50 per week to the wife and two children, on the following grounds:
i)   The wife needed the amount ordered. (Her total income of £33.50 per week, including £3 per week child benefit, was only £3.60 above the supplementary benefit 'subsistence level' of £29.90 to which she would have been entitled, including the £3 per week child benefit, had she not been in receipt of maintenance.)
ii) The husband could afford the order. (He was left with a net income of £31.94 per week, which was £9.74 more than the supplementary benefit 'subsistence level' of £22.20 to which he would have been entitled had he been out of work.)
iii) The fact that the amount of the order left the husband with less to live on than the amount which the Supplementary Benefits Commission would have permitted him to retain in accordance with their 'liable relative formula' was irrelevant. That formula should be rejected because the wife needed the amount ordered and the husband could afford to pay it.

The husband appealed to the Court of Appeal, contending that in a low income case such as this the court should fix the amount of maintenance by adopting the 'liable relative formula' applied by the Supplementary Benefits Commission, in preference to the one-third ratio. The Court of Appeal dismissed the husband's appeal.

The one-third ratio produced, as a starting point, a figure of £21 per week for the wife's maintenance. Adding a sum of £5 per week in respect of each child (as the registrar had done) gave a figure of £31 per week, which was very close to the order of £30.50 made by the registrar.

The Court of Appeal held that, although the Supplementary Benefits Commission's 'liable relative formula' might be a useful alternative starting point to the one-third ratio in some cases, neither formula produced anything more than a starting point which was to be adjusted according to the circumstances to give effect to the principles laid down in section 25 of the Matrimonial Causes Act

1973 (see Appendix I).

And since the application of the 'liable relative formula' would have resulted in the husband being about £15 a week above 'subsistence level' whereas the wife and children would have been left about £2 a week below 'subsistence level' the judge had been right to reject the formula.

The possibility that the husband might give up his job and a net income (after payment of the amount due under the order) of about £32 per week for supplementary benefit of about £22 per week seemed to the court to be remote.

Ormrod LJ said (at page 485): 'On the figures, which have been agreed by counsel in this court (they differ appreciably from those used by the judge), the position is that the husband had a gross annual income of £3,960 a year which, after tax and allowances, leaves him with a net weekly income of £62.44. The order [of the registrar] in the aggregate amounts to £30.50, leaving the husband, who is a single man, with £31.94 to live on. Since [ignoring the child benefit of £3 per week payable to the wife] this is rather more than the wife has on which to keep herself and the two children, it is absurd to suggest that the husband has been reduced below the subsistence level . . . [The argument of counsel for the husband] really amounts to saying that the court ought to adopt the practice which the Supplementary Benefits Commission use to determine the liability of the 'liable relative' to contribute to the support of his dependants, and he based his submission on a decision of the Divisional Court earlier this year in a case called *Smethurst v Smethurst* (22–006) . . .

'The matter arose originally from the Report of the Committee on One-Parent Families [(1974) Cmnd 5629] which is conveniently referred to as the Finer Report . . . The Finer Report disclosed for the first time to the public the existence of [the 'liable relative formula'] used by the Supplementary Benefits Commission . . .

'*Smethurst v Smethurst* is the first case in which reference had been made to it . . .

'. . . Sir George Baker P [in *Smethurst v Smethurst*] appears to be equating the figure which was produced by the formula with "subsistence level", a phrase which at once calls to mind . . . *Ashley v Ashley* (22–001) in which it was said that, except in unusual circumstances, orders for maintenance or periodical payments should not reduce a husband below "subsistence level". Sir Jocelyn Simon P [in *Ashley v Ashley*] related "subsistence level" closely to the amount which would be payable in supplementary benefits to the husband if he had no other resources for the support of himself and his dependants, if any. [*Ashley v Ashley* was] approved in principle in more general terms by this court in *Barnes v Barnes* (22–002) . . . It is, however, unnecessary to pursue the point further because . . . the formula has nothing to do with subsistence levels. It produces, in fact, nothing more than a negotiating figure for the use of the commission's officers seeking contributions from "liable relatives". If a liable relative makes an offer which is more or less consistent with the product of the formula, the officers can accept it as reasonable and one which, experience shows, is more likely to be paid regularly than a higher sum imposed on the liable relative. If, on the other hand, the commission itself undertakes to enforce an order for periodical payments or maintenance made by a court, it seeks enforcement of the full amount of the order.

'The subsistence level, in the language of *Ashley v Ashley*, therefore remains what it was, namely approximately the current amount of supplementary benefit appropriate to a single man or a man with dependants, as the case may be.'

Note. The 'liable relative formula' includes an 'incentive allowance' over and above the supplementary benefits to which the husband would be entitled if he were out of work. Hence it is bound to produce a figure greater than 'subsistence level' as defined in *Ashley v Ashley, Barnes v Barnes* and *Shallow v Shallow*. For an explanation of the formula see *Smethurst v Smethurst* (22–006).

22–008 Tovey v Tovey

(1977) 8 Fam Law 80, CA

Following the separation, the husband had gone to live with an unmarried woman (whom he intended to marry) who had two children. A decree absolute of divorce had now been pronounced and the wife had obtained custody of the three children of the marriage. The husband's income was £51.50 per week gross, £39 per week net. The wife earned £7 per week as a part-time barmaid, drawing £40 per week from the DHSS.

The registrar had applied the Supplementary Benefits Commission's so-called 'liable relative formula' in assessing what maintenance the husband should pay, and had assessed the maintenance both for the wife and for the children at a nominal sum.

Ormrod LJ referred to the unanimous judgment of the Court of Appeal in *Shallow v Shallow* (22–007), in which his lordship had said that the 'liable relative formula' (like the one-third ratio) did no more than provide what his lordship had called a 'ranging shot'; the material question was how to apply section 25 of the Matrimonial Causes Act 1973 [see Appendix I], bearing in mind the decision of *Ashley v Ashley* (22–001) which had indicated that the court would not, *generally speaking*, reduce the husband below what was then called 'subsistence level', which had been *more or less equated with the sort of figure* which the husband *could expect to get* from the Supplementary Benefits Commission if he were out of work and not receiving unemployment benefit. If the husband were out of work he would be entitled to supplementary benefit at the rate of £39 per week, and that figure, his lordship said, must be taken as being *more or less* the minimum that he could live on; the minimum figure *was not a fixed figure*, but obviously a sum of £39 per week *was very near the minimum*.

The Court of Appeal approved the registrar's award of a nominal sum for the maintenance of the wife herself. However, regarding the children, Ormrod LJ said that the question was: Should the husband be able to off-load the whole of his obligation to his wife *and his three children* on to the State, simply by taking on the responsibility of providing for another woman and her two children? His lordship said that it seemed to him a startling proposition that a man who was in regular work should be required to make *no contribution at all* to the maintenance *of his own children*. It was true that it could be argued that he had relieved the DHSS from having to support another woman and her two children. However, it was undesirable as a matter of public policy that a man should not continue to contribute *even in a purely formal sense* towards the upkeep of his own children, *who were his primary liability*.

On the figures here, it was clear that the husband *could not afford anything much* for the children, but in his lordship's opinion the husband *should at least pay £1 per week* for each child.

Notes

1. In *Tovey v Tovey* Orr and Ormrod LJJ followed their own judgment in *Shallow v Shallow* in which, in a unanimous judgment of the Court of Appeal comprising Stamp, Orr and Ormrod LJJ, there had been demonstrated the illogicality of equating the figure produced by the 'liable relative formula' with 'subsistence level'. Because the formula includes an 'incentive allowance', over and above the supplementary benefits to which the husband would be entitled if he were out of work, it is bound to produce a figure greater than 'subsistence level' as defined in *Ashley v Ashley* and *Shallow v Shallow*. (For an explanation of the formula see *Smethurst v Smethurst* (22–006).)

2. While the only practical effect of the Court of Appeal's order in *Tovey v Tovey* from the wife's point of view was that the increased maintenance for the children of £3 per week (over and above the nominal sum awarded by the registrar) would reduce the wife's entitlement to supplementary benefit by £3 per week, the practical effect of the Court of Appeal's order from the husband's point of view was that the husband would be £3 per week better off if he gave up his employment and received the appropriate supplementary benefits. In *Williams v Williams* (22–005) Finer J said: 'The court, it is

well established, will not allow a man to absolve himself from his maintenance obligation at public expense. In assessing a man's maintenance liability one generally excludes from the consideration the fact, as it so often is, that to make him pay maintenance will not improve the financial position of the wife at all, but only reduce the amount of supplementary benefit being paid to her. This is all very well where a man has income to spare. But here the husband is himself on supplementary benefit, which is pitched at a level which gives him nothing to spare. The court cannot ignore this . . .' In *Tovey v Tovey* the husband was not himself on supplementary benefit, but his net income after deductions was no greater than the amount of supplementary benefit to which he would have been entitled had he been out of work. In other words, if 'subsistence level' is to be defined strictly in accordance with the Supplementary Benefits Commission's rates, the husband in *Tovey v Tovey* had no more income to spare than the husband in *Williams v Williams*. Yet the Court of Appeal in *Tovey v Tovey* ordered the husband to pay a sum of £1 per week for each of his three children, thus reducing him below the 'official' subsistence level by £3 per week, so that he would have been £3 per week better off if he gave up his employment and received the appropriate supplementary benefits. Compare *Fitzpatrick v Fitzpatrick* (22–009), in which Stamp, Orr and Bridge LJJ decreased an order for maintenance for the very reason that the practical effect of the order from the husband's point of view was that he would be £2 per week better off if he gave up his employment and received the appropriate supplementary benefits. It is perhaps of note that Orr LJ was sitting in the Court of Appeal not only in *Shallow v Shallow* and *Tovey v Tovey* but also in *Fitzpatrick v Fitzpatrick*, and that the judgments in all three cases were unanimous. What the case of *Tovey v Tovey* seems to indicate, therefore, is that the 'official' subsistence level is only a guide and not an absolute standard. Nevertheless, it is respectfully submitted that the decision in *Fitzpatrick v Fitzpatrick* is to be preferred to that in *Tovey v Tovey*.

22–008A Walker v Walker

(1978) Times, 3 March, 8 Fam Law 107

The husband complained that, after paying income tax, national health and insurance contributions, travelling expenses, mortgage repayments, rates and the maintenance for the wife and child of the family ordered by the registrar, he had less on which to live than the figure allowed by the Supplementary Benefits Commission to a single man for minimum subsistence.

The wife was in employment. After paying income tax, national health and insurance contributions, rent and rates, she had considerably more than the amount allowed by the Commission to a single parent with one child.

The registrar had not taken into account the rent and rate rebates to which the wife would have been entitled had she applied to the appropriate authorities.

Purchas J said that in his opinion the rebates were financial resources within the meaning of section 25 (1) (a) of the Matrimonial Causes Act 1973 (see Appendix I) and that they could not wholly be ignored by the court.

However, his lordship continued, one had to bear in mind Finer J's words in *Williams v Williams* (22–005): 'The court . . . will not allow a man to absolve himself from his maintenance obligations at the public expense.'

His lordship said that his approach to the case would be that the order should not depress the husband below a minimum subsistence level; but it would not be right and just that he should, by decreasing the payments to the wife, promote the husband to a position above the minimum level acceptable. If he did otherwise he would be subsidising not the wife but the husband from public funds.

The husband's appeal was allowed only to the extent of reducing the order for maintenance of the wife to such a sum as would leave the husband with a net sum, slightly in excess of the amount to which he would have been entitled were he in receipt of supplementary benefit (i.e. subsistence level).

Note. Compare *Barnes v Barnes* (22–002) in which Edmund Davies LJ said: 'It was submitted by counsel for the husband that [the social security benefit being paid to the wife] is to be regarded . . . as being comprised within the "other financial resources which each of the parties to the marriage has or is likely to have in the foreseeable future". I find it difficult to regard such state benefits as coming within such a frame . . .' However, the effect of both judgments is the same. In *Barnes v Barnes* Edmund Davies LJ continued: '... in the first place when the court is seeking to arrive at what would be a proper order, it is desirable that regard should not be had to social security benefits ... [But if this] would result in the husband being left with a sum quite inadequate to enable him to meet his own financial commitments, then the court may have regard to the fact that in proper cases social security benefits will be available ...'

22–008B Clarke v Clarke

(1978) 9 Fam Law 15, CA

The wife and child of the marriage lived wholly on social security, getting some £30 a week. Thus husband lived with his mother, paying her £12 a week for his keep. He earned £45 a week gross as a lorry driver, £39 a week net, which left him with £27 out of which to provide for the wife and child. He lived very close to his place of employment, but said that as a matter of convenience he left his lorry some two miles from where he lived because of parking problems, and that to cover that distance he used a motor car which he ran and needed for that purpose. On appeal, the judge reduced the registrar's order to £6 a week for the wife and £5 a week for the child. The husband appealed to the Court of Appeal.

The husband said that the effect of the order was to reduce his standard of living below a tolerable level, and suggested that if the order remained as it was he would have no inducement to work and would probably default on the payments. Ormrod LJ said that the order in favour of the wife and child was far below the cost of maintaining either. The idea that a man should be running a motor car, while paying his wife and child as little as this husband had suggested he should pay, was to invert all the normal priorities. There was no suggestion that the judge's order had reduced the husband below a 'subsistence level'. The husband's appeal was dismissed.

22–009 Fitzpatrick v Fitzpatrick

(1978) 9 Fam Law 16, CA

The wife lived in a council flat with the two children of the marriage. The husband lived with a Mrs. James, whom he intended to marry, together with her two children from her previous marriage, now dissolved. The decree had now been made absolute.

At the time of the appeal, the husband was earning £74 per week gross plus a small addition for overtime; Mrs. James, with whom he was living, was unable to work by reason of spinal arthritis. The wife had been unable to find part-time work.

The county court judge had pointed out that, if he were to apply the one-third ratio, the sum which the husband would have to pay for the wife's maintenance would be far in excess of the £15 per week ordered by the registrar, and the fact that the registrar's award of £15 per week for the wife and £5 per week for each child was benefiting not the wife but the DHSS was irrelevant. He would have liked to help the husband by reducing the registrar's award, but felt that he could not do so.

The husband appealed to the Court of Appeal on the ground (inter alia) that the judge should have adopted the Supplementary Benefits Commission's 'liable relative formula' as a guide-line, the husband's net income (including Mrs. James's child benefit) being £10 per week less than the weekly sum which he would be entitled to retain if the formula were applied.

A further ground of appeal was that, on the basis of the judge's order of £15 per week for the wife and £5 per week for each child, the husband and his second family were left with £47.65 per week (including the child benefit in respect of Mrs. James's children), which sum was approximately £2 per week less than the supplementary benefits (including child benefit) to which the family would be entitled if he were unemployed.

Orr LJ referred to *Shallow v Shallow* (22–007), in which the Court of Appeal has held that the 'liable relative formula' was no more than a 'ranging shot'. He would have dismissed the appeal had it rested solely on the argument based on the 'liable relative formula'. However, the effect of the judge's order was that the husband would be £2 per week better off if he gave up his employment and received the appropriate supplementary benefits; to that extent the effect of the order was to reduce him below subsistence level. Their lordships accepted that in the case of a man with this husband's work record it was unlikely that this small difference would in fact tempt him to give up his employment, but nevertheless came to the conclusion that the order made for the payment of £15 per week to the wife was in all the circumstances excessive, and reduced the order to £12 per week.

Note. In effect, although the Court of Appeal did not say as much, notice was taken of the husband's need to support Mrs. James and her two children from her previous marriage. The county court judge had said that Mrs. James's ex-husband should be principally responsible for his children's maintenance; but who *should be principally responsible* and who *is in fact maintaining* a dependent woman and her children are very often quite different. It is submitted that the judgment of the Court of Appeal in *Fitzpatrick v Fitzpatrick* supports the practical approach of Payne J in *Winter v Winter* (22–003) and that this approach should be followed in the future.

22–010 Wagner v Wagner

(1978) 9 Fam Law 183, CA

What would be fair in all the circumstances. Young childless couple married in November 1971 and divorced in May 1976. On the assumption that the wife was earning £30 per week and the husband £72 per week, a consent order of £1 per week was made in the wife's favour. In fact, the wife had not disclosed that she had stopped work, being pregnant by another man. She and the child were now living on social security.

The husband was now living with another woman who had given birth to a child of which he was the father. The judge having increased the wife's award to £10 per week, the husband appealed, contending that it was inequitable that the order should be increased when the wife's child was not his; alternatively, that in view of his finances the order was excessive.

Waller LJ said that it was not correct to state that there was any principle which applied in such a case; the court had to do what would be fair in all the circumstances. Taking all things into account, including the fact that whatever sum the court awarded it would make no difference to the wife because her sole income came from social security benefits, £10 per week was too much. However, £1 per week was too little. After considering the living expenses of the husband's family his lordship reduced the order to £3 per week. Brandon and Ormrod LJJ agreed.

Note. Under the order of £10 per week, taking into account the £2.30 child benefit payable to the mother of his child, the husband was left with £2.93 per week in his pocket. Reducing the order to £3 per week left him with £7.62.

22–011 M v M (sub nom. Moon v Moon)

(1979) 10 Fam Law 114

(1) *Single parent allowance payable by DHSS;* (2) *child benefit payable by DHSS.* See case summary 19–014.

22–012 C v W

(1980) Times, 16 February

Single parent allowance payable by DHSS. Bush J endorsed Waterhouse J's statement in *M v M* (22–011) that it was not appropriate to take to take into account the additional single parent allowance paid by the DHSS to single parent families (i.e. over and above child benefit, which is payable to all families).

22–012A Hulley v Thompson

[1981] 1 All ER 1128

Husband's continuing liability to maintain children.   See Appendix II.

22–013 Perrot v Supplementary Benefits Commission

[1980] 3 All ER 110, CA

A person carrying on business as a self-employed person may be engaged in 'remunerative full-time work' so as to disentitle him to supplementary benefit notwithstanding that the expenses in conducting the business exceed the remuneration received.

Section 1 of the Supplementary Benefits Act 1976 provides that, subject to the provisions of the Act, every person in Great Britain over the age of 16 whose *resources* are insufficient to meet his *requirements* is entitled to a *supplementary pension* if of pensionable age or to a *supplementary allowance* if under pensionable age. Section 6 (1) of the Act provides: 'Except as provided in the following provisions of this section and in section 9 (1) of this Act . . . for any period during which a person is engaged in *remunerative full-time work* he shall not be entitled to supplementary benefit.'

The Court of Appeal held that the words 'remunerative full-time work' meant full-time work which brings remuneration, or full-time work which is paid for, however inadequate the remuneration and however inadequate the resources of the claimant.

Note. Family income supplement is available where the claimant is engaged in full-time work *and there is at least one dependent child.*

22–014 Supplementary Benefits Commission v Jull

[1980] 3 All ER 65, HL

Maintenance order payable direct to child to be taken into account when calculating mother's entitlement to supplementary benefit.   Mrs. Jull was divorced. Her former husband had been ordered to make periodical payments of £21 a week to her and £12 a week direct to the child who lived with her. He had paid the child's order regularly but had not paid anything on Mrs. Jull's order, so that she had to have recourse to supplementary benefit. The Supplementary Benefits Commission took into account as part of her resources the £12 per week payable direct to the child. The result was that she received £6.70 less benefit than she would have received had the child's order not been taken into account. Woolf J held that the child's maintenance, because it was payable direct to the child, should not be included as part of Mrs. Jull's resources. Hence Mrs. Jull would be entitled to a further £6.70 benefit each week. The House of Lords allowed the Commission's appeal.

Notes

1. In June 1979 the Commission changed its policy and decided to take into account maintenance payable direct to children when assessing the mother's entitlement to benefit, so ending the advantage of direct payments of maintenance to children so far as supplementary benefits are concerned. The decision of the House of Lords upholds the Commission's new policy.
2. Under the Social Security Act 1980, the Supplementary Benefits Commission is abolished.
3. Paragraph 3 (2) of Schedule 4 to the Act reads: 'Where a person is responsible for, and is a member of the same household as, another person . . . (a) if the other person is a child . . . their requirements and resources shall be aggregated and treated as those of the first-mentioned person.'

22–015 Y v Supplementary Benefits Commission

[1980] 3 All ER 65, HL

Affiliation order payable to mother in respect of her illegitimate child to be taken into account when calculating mother's entitlement to supplementary benefit.   The House of Lords upheld the views of the Supplementary Benefits Commission that maintenance payments are resources to be taken into account whether they are payable to the mother for the child or payable direct to the child. For further details, see *Supplementary Benefits Commission v Jull* (22–014).

22–016 Brown v Brown

(1981) Times, 14 July

Husband cohabiting with a woman with resources not entitled to supplementary benefit – maintenance order against husband reduced to nominal sum in respect both of wife and children.   See Appendix II.

Note. This husband had no resources. Compare *Tovey v Tovey* (22–008), in which the husband was ordered to pay maintenance of £1 per week for each of the children of his first marriage out of his meagre resources.

PART 6

The matrimonial home

This section of the book deals principally with the court's wide powers to make property adjustment orders under Section 24 of the Matrimonial Causes Act 1973. Chapter 23 categorises the cases according to the different results that can be achieved by the exercise of those powers. Those powers, in more simple terms, may be subdivided into the power of sale (involving division of the proceeds), the power to postpone a sale until the occurrence of a certain event and the power to order a transfer or settlement of property or the variation of a settlement. The decision which of these powers to invoke (or in what proportions) depends to some extent on the nature of the result which would be the fairest overall. That in itself sometimes depends on the existing ownership and nature of the property, but nowadays it more commonly depends on an appraisal of the needs and circumstances of both parties and, in particular, any dependent children of either party. Again, it has to be stressed that the court's powers in respect of the matrimonial home are not exercised in a vacuum, but are exercised along with all the other aspects of matrimonial finance which are, of course, interrelated. To that extent, some degree of overlapping in the cases is unavoidable.

It is difficult, if not impossible, to lay down any clear guidelines as to how the court will approach the problems engendered by the matrimonial home in any one case. The variable factors which go to make up a complete picture in the ordinary case are numerous. The principal variable factors are the fact of occupation of the home by one of the parties at the time of the hearing, the ownership of the property, the needs, income and other resources of both parties, the presence and age of any children and the alternative accommodation available. For those obvious reasons, each case has to be treated as 'unique'. However, it is possible by categorising the results of reported cases to predict with some degree of certainty what the court is likely to regard as a fair result, as most of the variable elements fall into one category or another.

In *Wachtel v Wachtel* (23-102) Lord Denning MR set out to lay down guidelines for what he thought would be the appropriate outcome of contested cases according to whether some of the simpler variable factors were present or not. It is possible to follow the simple examples that he formulated and, with the benefit of eight years' hindsight, perform the same hypothetical exercise. *In Wachtel v Wachtel* the wife had left the matrimonial home, leaving the husband and two children in occupation. The simplest solution in that instance is to vest the house in the husband absolutely and compensate the wife for the loss of her share by the award of a lump sum. Generally, the most important consideration will be to ensure that everyone concerned has a home. According to Lord Denning

MR, the level of the lump sum should normally be such as the husband can raise by a further mortgage on the house without crippling him financially. Where the husband cannot afford to pay an immediate lump sum, the payment may be deferred or payment by instalments ordered, or the wife may be awarded a deferred charge on a share of the property or an equitable interest with postponement of sale. These solutions relate to the position where the husband is left with children. If the husband is left in occupation when there are no young children, he should normally expect the house to be sold unless he can raise sufficient capital to compensate by way of a lump sum the wife's legal or equitable interest in the house.

Lord Denning MR then posed the opposite position, where the wife is left in the house with children. The ordinary solution as proposed by the Master of the Rolls was that there should generally be an outright transfer to the wife, with the husband being compensated by a reduction in the award of periodical payments. This solution, it is fair to say, did not become immediately fashionable. The problems which might arise with this sort of order were too immediately obvious. There are inevitably cases where the wife would not be able to afford to pay the mortgage, even were she to receive a full maintenance order. Her position within the house without a maintenance order in her favour would be even more hopeless. Again, the paramount consideration is to ensure that everyone involved, but with priority to the children, has a home. Frequently the solution is to order the sale of the matrimonial home where that course will release sufficient capital to enable the wife to buy a smaller house for herself and the children with a lesser or no mortgage. Where that sort of order is inevitable if the wife and children are to be housed, the husband must expect to receive a vastly reduced share in the capital.

Another common situation arises where the wife is able to remain in the matrimonial home with the children, but only if she is receiving a full maintenance order in her own name as well as for the children. Obviously an outright transfer is of no value to her without the means to pay the mortgage. It is in such cases that a common practice of postponing sale for a limited period has arisen. An object which the court generally seeks to achieve is to enable the wife and children to remain in the home at least until the children have reached some specified age. This solution was adopted in *Mesher v Mesher* (23–301). The shares of the parties in the home can be declared to exist in any proportion, thereby preserving the utmost flexibility. This type of order became so common after 1973 that it is generally known as a *Mesher* order, and the case assumed, rightly or wrongly, a degree of authority which Ormrod LJ has referred to as 'biblical'. If the house remains in joint ownership with sale postponed, it will normally be the party enjoying occupation who is responsible for all outgoings, including mortgage interest. If the occupying party has repaid some of the capital element of the mortgage, he or she should be given credit for this on the eventual sale. All these matters were expressed in the *Mesher v Mesher* order [and see generally Chapter 25].

The dangers of *Mesher* orders are that the wife may not have the means to keep the house going, so leading to its sale, when the proceeds will be divided in accordance with the terms of the order. This may precipitate a second problem, namely, the difficulty of rehousing the wife when she is left with only a share of the sale proceeds. See *Carson v Carson* (23–715).

A significant development of the law occurred in 1977 with the case of *Martin v Martin* (23–402), in which it was forcibly suggested by Ormrod LJ that the form of order in *Mesher v Mesher* was never intended to become a general practice. The difficulties which the *Mesher* order may be storing up for future years were outlined. It is argued with some force that the mere postponement of sale in fact creates greater hardship for a wife when the eventual day arrives. It is an unfortunate fact that, in most cases, when the house is eventually sold and the husband has been paid his share, the wife will be left with a sum of money probably insufficient to rehouse herself. She may well find this a greater hardship than she would have done, say, fifteen years earlier when the order was made. It is an insoluble problem, but at least the *Mesher* order gives a wife several years to contemplate the problem and cater for it if she can and, in the meantime, provides complete security for the children. There will still be many cases where a *Mesher* order is the only appropriate solution.

In similar circumstances, rather than settling the property on trust for sale and postponing the sale until the happening of some specified event, the court may decide to transfer the husband's interest to the wife and give the husband a charge on the property, enforceable on the occurrence of the same sorts of events as in a *Mesher* order, i.e. the completion of the children's education or their achieving a specified age, or remarriage or cohabitation by the spouse in occupation. Again, the same dangers are apparent as with *Mesher* orders. But in addition, this sort of order can be unfair to the spouse out of occupation; if a spouse is to be given a charge on the property without interest, it is generally better that the charge should be a charge for a fixed proportion of the proceeds of sale than a charge for a fixed amount which will be eroded by inflation. See the summary of *Hector v Hector* at 26–007.

The effect of *Martin v Martin* was to firmly establish the principle that it is the 'primary concern in these cases that on breakdown of marriage the parties should, if possible, each have a roof over his or her head'. The judgment in *Martin v Martin* also included other clearly stated policy decisions, they being:

1. That it is, in general, against public policy to order a sale of a house on the assumption that a wife or husband would be rehoused in council accommodation, for that merely enables the parties to release their capital at public expense.

2. Whenever it is to be argued before the courts that a spouse will have sufficient means to purchase alternative accommodation out of his or her share of the equity (or will be in a position to obtain council accommodation), such argument should be supported by evidence.

Perhaps an even more significant development has occurred because of the increasing tendency of the courts to look carefully at the long-term consequences of a *Mesher* order. In *Hanlon v Hanlon* (23–609) the wife appealed against such an order which involved equal division of the proceeds of sale when the youngest child reached 17. The Court of Appeal transferred the house to her absolutely, and reduced the periodical payments payable to the children to a nominal amount. As was pointed out by Ormrod LJ, this was not, in spite of the years of practice in which *Mesher* orders have held sway, a novel result. It was a solution first contemplated by Lord Denning MR in *Wachtel v Wachtel* (see above). The solution adopted in *Hanlon v Hanlon*, and followed in *Dunford v*

Dunford (10–103) is, perhaps by no mere coincidence, the more consistent with the clean break principle. As Ormrod LJ expressed the position in *Hanlon v Hanlon*:

'It seems to me far better that the parties' interests should be crystallised now, once and for all, so that the wife can know what she is going to do about the property and the husband can make up his mind about what he is going to do about rehousing.'

CHAPTER 23

Guidelines on transfer/settlement etc. under Matrimonial Causes Act 1973

1 Order for payment of lump sum in lieu of share in the property

CASE SUMMARIES

23–101 White v White

(1972) Times, 10 March, 116 Sol Jo 219, CA

Husband remaining in former matrimonial home – new home provided for wife by her new husband. Wife now married to co-respondent whose house provided better accommodation than former matrimonial home; wrong to force husband and child of family to leave; but if husband to remain in residence he should pay wife something in respect of her interest under trust for sale; wife's interest extinguished; co-respondent's appeal against award of damages allowed, thereby in effect compensating wife for loss of her interest in property. See case summary 8–201.

Notes
1. Damages may not now be awarded against a co-respondent.
2. Dunn J had placed the whole blame for the breakdown of the marriage on the wife.

23–102 Wachtel v Wachtel

[1973] 1 All ER 829, CA

Husband remaining in former matrimonial home – the right approach – house to be vested in husband absolutely – wife to be compensated by award of lump sum. Lord Denning MR, reading the unanimous judgment of the court, said (at the foot of page 840): 'Take a case like the present when the wife leaves the home and the husband stays in it. On the breakdown of the marriage arrangements should be made whereby it is vested in him absolutely, free of any share in the wife, and he alone is liable for the mortgage instalments. But the wife should be compensated for the loss of her share by being awarded a lump sum. It should be a sum sufficient to enable her to get settled in a place of her own, such as by putting down a deposit on a flat or a house. It should not, however, be an excessive sum. It should be such as the husband can raise by a further mortgage on the house without crippling him.'

Note. See also the summary of this case at 4–301 – settlement of matrimonial home on wife and children – disapproved in *Chamberlain v Chamberlain* (4–303) and *Alonso v Alonso* (4–305).

23–103 Hector v Hector

[1973] 3 All ER 1070, CA

Wife remaining in former matrimonial home with children – the right approach – house to be vested in wife absolutely – husband to be compensated by award of lump sum. Husband's interest extinguished; husband awarded lump sum of £1,000 charged on property without interest; charge not to be enforced until death of wife, sale of house or youngest child attaining 16. The husband's appeal was dismissed.

Lord Denning MR said (at page 1072): '...As we indicated in *Wachtel v Wachtel* (23–102), when a husband leaves the wife, and the wife is left in the home bringing up the children, then the right thing is to transfer the home to the wife alone so that she has that security to bring up the family as they have been in the past. So it is right to order the transfer of the whole of the husband's interest in the property, legal and beneficial, to the wife...'

Notes

1. For further details, see case summary 23–901.
2. The judge had relieved the husband of any payment for the maintenance of the wife, by reducing the order for her maintenance to a nominal 5p a year. Only the maintenance order for the children remained.
3. See, however, *McDonnell v McDonnell* (23–107), *Alonso v Alonso* (23–303) and *Browne v Pritchard* (23–305) – charge for fixed sum not desirable – and compare *Cumbers v Cumbers* (14–003A) – lump sum payable by weekly instalments, with interest.

23–104 Dopson v Cherry

(1975) 5 Fam Law 57, CA

Husband remaining in former matrimonial home – new home provided for wife by her new husband. Wife's interest in former matrimonial home extinguished; wife awarded immediate lump sum of £3,000; further £2,000 to be raised on house; house not to be sold except on application to court. See case summary 6–203.

23–105 Earley v Earley

(1975) Times, 20 June, CA

Short childless marriage – house in joint names – the right approach – not merely to have regard to cash contributions – also to have regard to commitments such as mortgage repayments. Wife had borne almost entire responsibility for mortgage instalments and would continue to do so; husband's interest extinguished; husband awarded immediate lump sum of £750 less amount owed to wife's parents. See case summary 7–202.

23–106 Mentel v Mentel

(1975) 6 Fam Law 53, CA

Husband remaining in former matrimonial home – new home provided for wife by her new husband. Wife's interest in former matrimonial home extinguished; wife awarded immediate lump sum of £1,750. See case summary 5–102A.

23–107 McDonnell v McDonnell

(1976) Times, 17 February, [1977] 1 All ER 766, CA

Wife remaining in former matrimonial home with children – the right approach – charge for fixed sum not desirable. The Court of Appeal allowed an appeal by the husband from the order of Mrs. Justice Lane that the husband's interest in the former matrimonial home be extinguished and that the husband be awarded a lump sum of £10,000, charged on the property without interest, the charge not to be enforced until, at the latest, the youngest child attained 17 [i.e. as in *Hector v Hector* (23–103)]. Referring to *Browne v Pritchard* (23–305) with approval, Ormrod LJ said that it was generally better to allocate shares in the matrimonial home than to give one spouse a charge for a fixed amount which might be eroded by inflation when it came to be realised.

The husband's appeal was allowed to the extent of substituting an order that the house be vested in trustees for sale for the parties in equal shares, the sale to be postponed until, at the latest, when the youngest child was 17.

For further details, see case summary 23–905.

Note. Compare *Cumbers v Cumbers* (14–003A) – lump sum payable by weekly instalments with interest.

23–108 Potts v Potts

(1976) 6 Fam Law 217, CA

Husband remaining in former matrimonial home – purchase of new home for wife and children. One of the agreed facts was that a suitable house in the same locality as the former matrimonial home could be purchased for £8,100. Wife's interest in former matrimonial home extinguished; wife awarded immediate lump sum of £8,100. See case summary 4–104A.

23–109 Backhouse v Backhouse

[1978] 1 All ER 1158

Husband remaining in former matrimonial home – new home purchased by wife together with her new husband. Wife's interest in former matrimonial home transferred to husband by wife without benefit of legal advice; time of stress; inequality of bargaining power; case approached on basis that transfer had not been made (see case summary 9–019); wife awarded immediate lump sum of £3,500. See case summary 6–206.

23–110 Bennett v Bennett

(1978) 9 Fam Law 19, CA

New home provided for husband by co-respondent – purchase of new home for wife. Former matrimonial home owned by husband; wife's advisers agreed that a suitable house in the locality could be purchased for £17,000; order for immediate sale of former matrimonial home; wife awarded immediate lump sum of £17,000 or two-thirds of net proceeds of sale, whichever was the greater. See case summary 5–108.

2 Order for sale and division of sale proceeds

CASE SUMMARIES

23–201 Goodfield v Goodfield

(1975) 5 Fam Law 197, CA

Matrimonial home owned in equal shares – one half of net sale proceeds sufficient to rehouse wife – order for sale subject to wife having twelve months in which to find alternative accommodation. See case summary 5–102.

Note. The child of the family was aged 17. In twelve months the child would have reached his majority. Compare *Bennett v Bennett* (5–108), in which an immediate sale was ordered. Compare *Blezard v Blezard* (5–111), in which the sale was postponed until the youngest child had finished her education.

23–202 Bennett v Bennett

(1978) 9 Fam Law 19, CA

Matrimonial home owned by husband – one third of capital assets insufficient to rehouse wife – order for immediate sale but wife's share of capital assets increased as necessary. See case summary 5–108.

Note. Compare *Goodfield v Goodfield* (5–102), in which the order for sale was not to take place before one year from the date of the order.

3 Order for sale, postponed during education of children, etc.

CASE SUMMARIES

23–301 Mesher v Mesher (sub nom. Mesher v Mesher and Hall)

(1973) Times, 13 February, [1980] 1 All ER 126n, CA

Sale not to take place until child has reached age 17 or until further order. See case summary 4–101.

Note. The property was owned by the parties in equal shares. On sale the net sale proceeds were to be divided equally between them. As was pointed out by Ormrod LJ in *Carson v Carson* (23–715), this is not always appropriate because of the problem of rehousing the party living in the property on its eventual sale.

23–302 Chamberlain v Chamberlain

[1974] 1 All ER 33, CA

A home for grown-up children. Sale not to take place until youngest child has ceased full-time education *or thereafter without the consent of the parties or order of the court.* See case summary 4–102.

Note. The house had been conveyed into the parties' joint names, and the parties had originally agreed a 50:50 division of the matrimonial assets, but since then the husband had run into debt and had defaulted on the mortgage repayments; the wife was paying off the mortgage arrears. The first instance decision settling the husband's half share in the matrimonial home on the wife for life and then on the children was set aside. The house was ordered to be held on trust for sale, one-third to the husband and two-thirds to the wife. See case summary 4–303 – settlement of matrimonial home on wife and children disapproved.

23–303 Alonso v Alonso

(1974) 4 Fam Law 164, 118 Sol Jo 660, CA

Sale not to take place until youngest child has reached age 21 or ceased full-time education, whichever be the earlier. See case summary 4–305.

Notes

1. Compare *Allen v Allen* (23–304) – sale not to take place until youngest child *has reached age 17* or ceased full-time education, whichever be the earlier.
2. Compare *Scott v Scott* (23–306) – sale not to take place until youngest child has reached age 18 or ceased full-time education, *whichever be the later*.
3. The first instance decision settling the husband's half share in the matrimonial home on the children was set aside. The house was ordered to be held on trust for sale, one-third for the husband and two-thirds for the wife. See case summary 4–305 – settlement of matrimonial home on wife and children disapproved.
4. There were arrears of interest owing on a promissory note securing a loan to purchase the property. Furthermore, although the wife was receiving maintenance in respect of the children she was receiving none for herself. The wife, who was living in the house with the children, was ordered to discharge all outgoings, but the husband and wife were ordered to remain equally liable on the promissory note.
5. Buckley LJ said that the sort of solution adopted in *Hector v Hector* (23–103), whereby the husband's interest was transferred to the wife subject to a charge payable to the

husband at some future date, was open to considerable objections in a period of rapid inflation, which gave the party subject to the benefit of the charge no share in any increase in value between the date of the order and the date when the amount secured became payable. It limited that party to a lump sum which, by the time it was paid, was very much less valuable.

23–304 Allen v Allen

[1974] 3 All ER 385, CA

Sale not to take place until youngest child has reached age 17 or ceased full-time education, whichever be the earlier.   See case summary 4–103.

Note. Compare *Scott v Scott* (23–306) – sale not to take place until youngest child has reached age 18 or ceased full-time education, *whichever be the later*.

23–305 Browne v Pritchard

[1975] 3 All ER 721, CA

Charge in favour of wife amounting to one-third of net sale proceeds not to be enforced until six months after the younger of the two children residing in the property has reached age 18.   See case summary 4–104.
Notes
1.   The husband and the two children were living in the house. The wife was living in council accommodation. The award of a charge in the wife's favour amounting to only one-third of the net proceeds of sale, notwithstanding the fact that the house had been conveyed into the joint names of the parties, was upheld by the Court of Appeal in view of the fact that the wife was living in secure accommodation and would not require her share of the proceeds of sale for housing purposes. Accordingly, it would be free capital in her hands. See case summary 14–005.
2.   Lord Denning MR said (at page 723): 'The charge should not be for a fixed sum such as £1,885, because values change so much these days. It should be simply for one-third of the net proceeds of sale whenever that takes place.' Compare, however, *Cumbers v Cumbers* (14–003A) – lump sum payable by weekly instalments, with interest.

23–306 Scott v Scott

[1978] 3 All ER 65, CA

Sale not to take place until youngest child has reached age 18 or ceased full-time education, whichever be the later.   See case summary 4–107.
Notes
1.   Compare *Allen v Allen* (23–304) – sale not to take place until youngest child has reached age 17 or ceased full-time education, *whichever be the earlier*.
2.   On the sale of the property, the proceeds were to be divided in such a way as to enable the wife to be in a slightly better capital position than the husband, in order to compensate her for the fact that she would not be in as strong a position as the husband to raise a mortgage and rehouse herself. See case summary 4–107.

23–307 Cawkwell v Cawkwell

(1978) 9 Fam Law 25, CA

Sale not to take place until youngest child has reached age 17 or ceased full-time education.   See case summary 5–107.

Note. The matrimonial home was in the husband's name, but the wife had contributed towards the mortgage repayments and had thereby acquired an equitable interest in the property by virtue of her financial contributions. The judge considered that in view of her substantial contributions towards the family's finances the wife deserved more than a one-third interest under the one-third ratio. He ordered that the house be transferred to the husband and wife in equal shares, and that the wife be allowed to remain in occupation until the youngest child reached age 17. Because one-half of the net sale proceeds would be insufficient to rehouse the wife in five years' time on the youngest child attaining 17, the wife's interest was increased to two-thirds by the Court of Appeal.

23–308 Blezard v Blezard

(1978) 9 Fam Law 249, CA

Completion of education at present school.   Sale not to take place until child still receiving full-time education has reached age 18 in order that the child can complete her education at her present school. See case summary 4–109.

    Note. Three-fifths of the net sale proceeds would have been sufficient to rehouse the wife. The husband accordingly asked for an immediate sale. Orr LJ said that had there been no children he would have ordered an immediate sale, subject only to allowing the wife sufficient time to find a new home. However, in his lordship's opinion it was in the best interests of the children that they should remain in their present home and that the daughter should complete her education at her present school. For further details, see case summary 5–111.

4   Order for sale, postponed until remarriage of wife, etc.

CASE SUMMARIES

23–401 Goodfield v Goodfield

(1975) 5 Fam Law 197, CA

Matrimonial home owned in equal shares – one half of net sale proceeds sufficient to rehouse wife – *order for sale subject to wife having twelve months in which to find alternative accommodation – sale not to take place before then without consent of wife except on wife's earlier remarriage or death.*   See case summary 5–102.

    Note. Compare *Blezard v Blezard* (23–405) – sale not to take place before stipulated time except on wife's earlier remarriage *or cohabitation with another man.*

23–402 Martin v Martin (sub nom. Martin (BH) v Martin (D))

[1977] 3 All ER 762, CA

Matrimonial home owned in equal shares – one half of net sale proceeds insufficient to rehouse wife – *sale not to take place except on wife voluntarily ceasing to reside there or on her remarriage or death.*   See case summary 5–103.

23–403 Scott v Scott

[1978] 3 All ER 65, CA

Matrimonial home vested in husband's name – one third of net sale proceeds insufficient to rehouse wife in 14 years' time on youngest child attaining 18 – house ordered to be settled on trust for sale – *sale not to take place until youngest child has reached age 18 or ceased full-time education, whichever be the later, except on wife's ealier remarriage or death* – in the event of no remarriage or death leading to an early sale, the equity in the house to be divided between the parties in some 14 years' time – see judgment of Cumming-Bruce LJ at page 67 at letter f.

    Note. For further details, see case summary 5–105.

23–404 Bateman v Bateman

[1979] Fam 25, [1979] 2 WLR 377

Wife inflicted serious chest wound on husband with a knife – husband consenting to settlement of house purchased by him as matrimonial home on wife for life or until remarriage – house ordered to be settled on trust for sale – *sale not to take place except on wife ceasing to use home as her main place of residence or on her remarriage or death.* See case summary 8–309.

Note. The husband agreed that the matrimonial home should be settled on the wife for her life or until remarriage, and he had adequate capital and income to rehouse himself and the woman he intended to marry. Had this not been the case, perhaps the judge might have made an order that the house be sold when the children had finished their full-time education, in view of the wife's conduct. However, notwithstanding the wife's serious conduct, Purchas J said that, taking the conduct of both parties as a whole, he did not consider that this was a case in which the wife should be deprived of all financial provision – see case summary 8–309 for further details.

23–405 Blezard v Blezard

(1978) 9 Fam Law 249, CA

Matrimonial home owned in equal shares – three fifths of net sale proceeds sufficient to rehouse wife – order for sale on youngest child completing education – *sale not to take place before then except on wife's earlier remarriage or cohabitation with another man.* See case summary 5–111.

5   Order for sale, postponed indefinitely

CASE SUMMARIES

23–501 Chamberlain v Chamberlain

[1974] 1 All ER 33, CA

Sale not to take place until youngest child has ceased full-time education or thereafter without the consent of the parties or order of the court. See case summary 4–102.

Note. The house had been conveyed into the parties' joint names, and the parties had originally agreed a 50:50 division of the matrimonial assets, but since then the husband had run into debt and had defaulted on the mortgage repayments; the wife was paying off the mortgage arrears. The first instance decision settling the husband's half share in the matrimonial home on the wife for life and then on the children was set aside. The house was ordered to be held on trust for sale, one-third to the husband and two-thirds to the wife. See case summary 4–303 – settlement of matrimonial home on wife and children disapproved.

23–502 Flatt v Flatt

(1973) 4 Fam Law 20, 118 Sol Jo 183, CA

Sale not to take place without consent of husband. See case summary 23–903.

23–503 Martin v Martin (sub nom. Martin (BH) v Martin (D))

[1977] 3 All ER 762, CA

Sale not to take place except on wife voluntarily ceasing to reside there or on her remarriage or death. See case summary 5–103.

23–504 Dallimer v Dallimer

(1978) 8 Fam Law 142, CA

Sale not to take place except on husband voluntarily ceasing to reside there or on his death. See case summary 5–106.

23–505 Bateman v Bateman

[1979] Fam 25, [1979] 2 WLR 377

Wife inflicted serious chest wound on husband with a knife – husband consenting
to settlement of house purchased by him as matrimonial home on wife for life or
until remarriage – house ordered to be settled on trust for sale – *sale not to take
place except on wife ceasing to use house as her main place of residence or on her
remarriage or death*. See case summary 8–309.

Note. The husband agreed that the matrimonial home should be settled on the wife for
her life or until remarriage, and he had adequate capital and income to rehouse himself and
the woman he intended to marry. Had this not been the case, perhaps the judge might have
made an order that the house be sold when the children had finished their full-time
education, in view of the wife's conduct. However, notwithstanding the wife's serious
conduct, Purchas J said that, taking the conduct of both parties as a whole, he did not
consider that this was a case in which the wife should be deprived of all financial provision –
see case summary 8–309 for further details.

23–506 Kurylowicz v Kurylowicz

(1978) 9 Fam Law 119, CA

Sale not to take place without consent of wife. See case summary 5–109.

23–507 Chinnock v Chinnock

(1978) 9 Fam Law 249, CA

Sale not to take place without consent of husband. See case summary 5–110.

23–508 Dunford v Dunford

[1980] 1 All ER 122, CA

Sale not to take place without consent of wife. See case summary 5–113.

23–509 Eshak v Nowojewski

(1980) Times, 19 November, CA

Sale not to take place without consent of husband. See case summary 5–114.

6   Absolute transfer without any order for lump sum payment in lieu of share transferred

CASE SUMMARIES

23–601 Cuzner v Underdown

[1974] 2 All ER 351, CA

Wife had already committed adultery with co-respondent and was contemplating
leaving husband for co-respondent at a time when husband and wife had decided
to move house. Husband arranged for purchase of new house in joint names in
order to benefit wife on his death. Husband, informed of adultery prior to
completion of purchase, persuaded wife not to leave. Wife deserted husband six
weeks later. Husband obtained divorce on ground of wife's adultery. Wife
subsequently married co-respondent. Wife now claimed half share in new house

under MWPA 1882 and applied for order for sale in order to purchase house for herself, co-respondent and children of their family. *Wife's need of lump sum to solve impending housing crisis of co-respondent. Probability that any sale and payment of sufficient lump sum to wife would precipitate housing crisis for husband. Necessity of retaining home for husband's new family. Wife's interest extinguished.* See case summary 8–204.

23–602 Smith v Smith (sub nom. S v S)

[1975] 2 All ER 19, CA

Wife remaining in former matrimonial home with child who had suffered from serious kidney trouble since infancy. Likelihood that child would need wife's continuing help and care even after leaving school. Wife unable to work full-time because of need to look after child during school holidays. Inability to rehouse herself and child in the area if house sold. Wife's relative financial position exceptionally weak. Husband's interest extinguished. See case summary 23–902.

Note. Followed in *Jones v Jones* (23–604). See also *Martin v Martin* (23–607), *President v President* (23–608) and *Ward v Ward and Greene* (23–610).

23–603 Brisdion v Brisdion

(1974) 5 Fam Law 92, 119 Sol Jo 234, CA

Former matrimonial home a council house purchased from council. Deposit a nominal £5. Right of pre-emption in favour of council. Equity in house worth only £16.40. Husband's interest extinguished. See case summary 23–904.

23–604 Jones v Jones (sub nom. Jones (MA) v Jones (W))

[1975] 2 All ER 12, CA

Gross conduct. Husband attacked wife with knife, severing tendons of right hand. Wife unable to continue working as a nurse. Wife's financial position exceptionally weak. Husband's interest in former matrimonial home extinguished. See case summary 13–006.

Note. Smith v Smith (23–602) followed. Orr LJ said (at page 17): 'So far as concerns the wife's circumstances when the youngest child ceases to be dependent, it seems to me that the considerations in this case are very similar to those which arose in *Smith v Smith*, the only difference being that here the wife is unable to work by reason of the injuries inflicted on her, not of her having to care for a child; but the difficulties which she will face on the child ceasing to be dependent are, it seems to me, of the same kind that arose in *Smith v Smith*.'

23–605 Weisz v Weisz

(1975) Times, 16 December, CA

Husband concealed existence of bank account and extent of his income. Held: husband clearly a dishonest man, and unless compelled to do so would not make any contribution for wife and daughter. Husband's interest in former matrimonial home extinguished and ordered to pay additional lump sum payment to wife. See case summary 8–209.

Note. See also *Bryant v Bryant* (23–606).

23–606 Bryant v Bryant

(1976) Times, 3 February, CA

Husband a persistent maintenance defaulter, in prison. Husband's interest in former matrimonial home extinguished.

Note. See also *Weisz v Weisz* (23–605).

23–607 Martin v Martin

[1976] 3 All ER 625, CA

Husband's dissipation of assets. Wife left in unnecessarily weak position. Former matrimonial home situated on farm now being run successfully by wife. Need to sell house in order to pay off debts incurred by husband. Husband's interest in house and farm extinguished. See case summary 8–307.

Note. See also *President v President* (23–608).

23–608 President v President

(1976) 126 NLJ 740, CA

Wife saved former matrimonial home from threat of possession by building society. Wife's financial position weak. Husband's interest extinguished. See case summary 15–105.

Notes
1. *Smith v Smith* (23–602) referred to and followed.
2. See also *Martin v Martin* (23–607).

23–609 Hanlon v Hanlon

[1978] 2 All ER 889, CA

The clean break. Husband's interest in former matrimonial home extinguished in return for wife's agreement not to claim maintenance either for herself or for the children. See case summary 4–106.

Notes
1. Regarding the wife's acceptance of a clean break in this case, see case summary 10–102.
2. See also *Dunford v Dunford* (10–103), in which the same principle was applied, but in which the husband's interest was extinguished in return for a charge amounting to 25 per cent of the net sale proceeds, the charge only to be enforceable on the wife vacating the property or on her death.

23–610 Ward v Ward and Greene (sub nom. **Ward v Ward**)

[1980] 1 All ER 176, [1980] 1 WLR 4, CA (these notes taken from transcript of shorthand notes of Association of Official Shorthandwriters Limited)

Husband and co-respondent securely housed. Wife's financial position exceptionally weak. Husband's interest in former matrimonial home extinguished. See case summary 5–112.

Note. See also *Smith v Smith* (23–602).

7 The problem of rehousing the party living in the property

CASE SUMMARIES

23–701 Smith v Smith (sub nom. **S v S**)

[1975] 2 All ER 19, CA

Matrimonial home owned in equal shares. Wife remaining in house with child who had suffered from serious kidney trouble since infancy. Likelihood that child would need wife's continuing help and care even after leaving school. Wife unable to work full-time because of need to look after child during school holidays.

Inability to rehouse herself and child in the area if house sold. Wife's relative financial position exceptionally weak. Husband's share extinguished. See case summary 23–902.

Note. Followed in *Jones v Jones* (23–604). See also *Ward v Ward and Greene* (23–712).

23–701A Thompson v Thompson

[1975] 2 All ER 208, CA

Council tenancy. Wife and child adequately housed with wife's parents. Husband's housing difficulties the decisive factor. See case summary 5–101.

23–702 Goodfield v Goodfield

(1975) 5 Fam Law 197, CA

Matrimonial home owned in equal shares. One-half of net sale proceeds sufficient to rehouse wife living in property. Order for sale. Wife allowed twelve months in which to find alternative accommodation. See case summary 5–102.

23–702A Mentel v Mentel

(1975) 6 Fam Law 53, 119 Sol Jo 808, CA

Matrimonial home owned in equal shares. Wife living with new husband in secure accommodation. Husband's inability to raise sufficient on mortgage to purchase wife's half share. Order for sale refused. See case summary 5–102A.

23–703 Martin v Martin (sub nom. Martin (BH) v Martin (D))

[1977] 3 All ER 762, CA

Matrimonial home owned in equal shares. Husband living with another woman in council house. One-half of net sale proceeds insufficient to rehouse wife. Order for sale refused. See case summary 5–103.

23–704 Hanlon v Hanlon

[1978] 2 All ER 889, CA

Equitable interest in matrimonial home owned by the parties jointly by virtue of wife's financial contributions. Husband living in secure accommodation. One-half of net sale proceeds insufficient to rehouse wife in 5 years' time on sale of property on youngest child attaining 17. Desirability of crystallising parties' interests now. Husband's interest extinguished. See case summary 5–104.

Note. In the original pleadings, each spouse was claiming a transfer of the other's interest in the house. But there was never any real agreement that the wife owned a beneficial half share in the property. See Lord Simon's speech in *Hanlon v Law Society* [1980] 2 All ER 199 at 209, HL.

23–705 Scott v Scott

[1978] 3 All ER 65, CA

Matrimonial home purchased in husband's sole name. One-third of net sale proceeds insufficient to rehouse wife in 14 years' time on sale of property on youngest child attaining 18. Wife's share of sale proceeds to be increased accordingly. See case summary 5–105.

23–706 Dallimer v Dallimer

(1978) 8 Fam Law 142, CA

Matrimonial home owned in equal shares. Wife living in new home provided by co-respondent. Wrong to force husband to leave. See case summary 5–106.

23–707 Cawkwell v Cawkwell

(1978) 9 Fam Law 25, CA

Equitable interest in matrimonial home owned by the parties jointly by virtue of wife's financial contributions. One-half of net sale proceeds insufficient to rehouse wife in 5 years' time on sale of property on youngest child attaining 17. Wife's share of sale proceeds to be increased accordingly. See case summary 5–107.

23–708 Bennett v Bennett

(1978) 9 Fam Law 19, CA

Matrimonial home purchased in husband's sole name. New home provided for husband by co-respondent. One-third of capital assets insufficient to rehouse wife. Order for sale. Wife's share of capital assets increased as necessary. See case summary 5–108.

23–709 Kurylowicz v Kurylowicz

(1978) 9 Fam Law 119, CA

Matrimonial home owned by the parties jointly. Two-thirds of net sale proceeds insufficient to rehouse wife living in property. Order for sale refused. See case summary 5–109.

23–710 Chinnock v Chinnock

(1978) 9 Fam Law 249, CA

Matrimonial home owned by the parties jointly. Wife and children living in council house. Three-fifths of net sale proceeds insufficient to rehouse husband. Order for sale refused. See case summary 5–110.

23–711 Blezard v Blezard

(1978) 9 Fam Law 249, CA

Matrimonial home owned in equal shares. Three-fifths of net sale proceeds sufficient to rehouse wife living in property. Order for sale on youngest child completing education. See case summary 5–111.

Note. Orr LJ said that had there not been the interests of children to consider he would have ordered an immediate sale, subject only to allowing the wife sufficient time to find a new house. Compare *Goodfield v Goodfield* (23–702).

23–712 Ward v Ward and Greene (sub nom. Ward v Ward)

[1980] 1 All ER 176, [1980] 1 WLR 4, CA (these notes taken from transcript of shorthand notes of Association of Official Shorthandwriters Limited)

Matrimonial home owned in equal shares. Husband and co-respondent securely housed. One-half of net sale proceeds insufficient to rehouse wife. Wife's financial position exceptionally weak. Husband's share extinguished. See case summary 5–112.

Note. See also *Smith v Smith* (23–701).

23–713 Dunford v Dunford

[1980] 1 All ER 122, CA

Matrimonial home owned in equal shares. One-half of net sale proceeds insufficient to rehouse wife in 7 years' time on sale of property on youngest child completing education. Order for sale refused. Husband ordered to transfer his half share to wife subject to charge of 25 per cent of net sale proceeds in his favour should wife vacate the property or die. Desirability of crystallising parties' interests now. *Hanlon v Hanlon* (23–704) applied. See case summary 5–113.

23–713A Curtis v Curtis

(1980) 11 Fam Law 55, CA

Matrimonial home, now valued at £40,000, purchased wholly out of wife's money. Husband now aged 69 and living on retirement and disability pension. Settlement of sufficient to purchase alternative residence for husband for life with remainder to wife absolutely. See case summary 5–113A.

23–714 Eshak v Nowojewski

(1980) Times, 19 November, CA

Matrimonial home owned in equal shares. Wife living in new home provided by her new husband. 60 per cent of net sale proceeds insufficient to rehouse husband in 13 years' time on sale of property on youngest child attaining 18. Wrong to force husband to leave. See case summary 5–114.

23–715 Carson v Carson

(1981) Times, 7 July, CA

Matrimonial home purchased in husband's sole name. *Mesher* order: settled on trust for sale in equal shares, sale postponed during education of children. Wife now, six years later, in financial difficulties. Problem of rehousing wife on sale in further eight or nine years' time on youngest child completing education. Danger of *Mesher* orders now becoming apparent. Equal division of sale proceeds rarely appropriate. See case summary 10–107.

8 The problem of rehousing the party vacating the property

CASE SUMMARIES

23–801 Potts v Potts

(1976) 6 Fam Law 217, CA

The matrimonial home was owned by the parties in equal shares. The wife left the home taking the children with her and rented a one-bedroomed flat, where she and the two children of the family were still living at the time of the appeal before the Court of Appeal some five years later. The Court of Appeal considered that the wife's delay in pursuing her claim was of relevance, if only because the husband had now remarried and now had two children living with him in the house. The husband had made an offer to pay the wife a lump sum not exceeding £8,100 in order to enable her to purchase a suitable house in the locality. It being agreed that a suitable house could be purchased in the vicinity for such a sum, the Court of Appeal ordered that the wife's interest in the matrimonial home should be extinguished on payment of this amount. See case summary 4–104A.

23–802 Hanlon v Hanlon

[1978] 2 All ER 889, CA

The equitable interest in the matrimonial home was owned by the parties jointly by virtue of the wife's financial contributions. In the original pleadings, each party claimed a transfer of the other's interest in the property. However, there was never any real agreement that the wife owned a beneficial half share. (See Lord Simon's speech in *Hanlon v Law Society* [1980] 2 All ER 199, HL at page 209 at letter g.) The husband was a police officer, who now lived in a flat provided rent-free by his employers. The court found that one half of the net sale proceeds would be insufficient to rehouse the wife in five years' time on any sale of the property on the youngest child attaining 17. As she was willing to forgo any further periodical payments for the children and was not making any claim for periodical payments for herself, the Court of Appeal ordered that the house be transferred into the sole name of the wife and that the husband's interest be extinguished.

Counsel for the husband argued that it was essential that the husband should, to use his own phrase, get on the 'property escalator' as soon as possible, and that the best way of doing this was for the wife to raise £5,000 on mortgage to pay to the husband so that he could purchase a house on mortgage. But there was no clear evidence that the husband had any intention whatever of giving up his police flat so long as his employment in the police force continued. The wife's future prospects were much less good than those of the husband. He would be able to retire at 58 with a lump sum gratuity of over £4,000 and take other employment, certainly for another seven years and possibly for longer. He was a completely free agent so far as his life was concerned, living to all intents and purposes a bachelor existence. By having to contribute neither towards the wife's maintenance nor to that of the children he would be able to save up a deposit in order to purchase another house if he wished to do so. This was particularly so in view of the fact that he had 'the enormous advantage of living rent-free in a police flat'. (See the judgment of Ormrod LJ at page 892 at letter c.)

Note. In the authors' experience, police officers strongly disagree with Ormrod LJ! But in view of the 'clean break', the authors consider that the judgment of the Court of Appeal was equitable between the parties. It is an obvious advantage to a man to obtain a 'clean break' if his former wife will agree. See case summary 10–102.

23–803 Scott v Scott

[1978] 3 All ER 65, CA

The equitable interest in the matrimonial home was owned by the parties jointly by virtue of the wife's financial contributions. The wife was now residing there with the children. It was ordered to be settled on trust for sale pending the completion of their education, the net sale proceeds on its eventual sale to be divided as to 60 per cent for the husband and 40 per cent for the wife. Such an order would enable the wife, with the aid of her own capital of £2,000, to be in a slightly better capital position than the husband when the house was sold in about 14 years' time. It would compensate her for the fact that she would not be in as strong a position as the husband to raise a mortgage and rehouse herself. *The husband, who would then be 45, would have less difficulty in obtaining a mortgage.* The husband was now living in a bed-sitting room. The Court of Appeal sympathised with his present predicament, but the house had first to be appropriated for the use of the children and the parent who had the responsibility of bringing them up. See case summary 4–107.

23–804 Cawkwell v Cawkwell

(1978) 9 Fam Law 25, CA

The equitable interest in the matrimonial home was owned by the parties jointly by virtue of the wife's financial contributions. The wife was now residing there with the children. On any sale of the property in 5 years' time on the youngest child completing her education, a half share of the net sale proceeds would be insufficient to rehouse the wife. The Court of Appeal accordingly increased the wife's beneficial interest to two-thirds.

The husband was now living in a bed-sitting room. Orr LJ said that the Court of Appeal had pointed out in *Hanlon v Hanlon* (23–802) that a serious problem arose where a sale of the former matrimonial home would not produce sufficient to rehouse both parties. In *Hanlon v Hanlon* the husband was a police officer living in police accommodation. In addition, he would be entitled to a lump sum by way of gratuity on his retirement. Similarly, in *Martin v Martin* (23–503), the husband was living with a woman he intended to marry in a council house of which she was the tenant. Therefore, in both of these cases the husbands in effect had a degree of security of tenure. In the present case the husband had none. It would therefore be harsh to make an order giving the whole of the value of the house to the wife (as was done in *Hanlon v Hanlon,* and as was effectively done in *Martin v Martin,* the wife in *Martin v Martin* being allowed to remain in the house indefinitely). To increase the wife's interest to two-thirds would give her a better chance of obtaining secure accommodation when the house was sold and would also provide a modest capital sum for the husband which he might be able to use so as to obtain secure accommodation for himself. See case summary 5–107.

Note. It might be thought that, even so, the husband was harshly treated. But see *Dunford v Dunford* (23–805) – a husband's future prospects are generally better than those of a wife with children; such a husband has a better chance of providing for himself in the future than such a wife has by her own efforts.

23–805 Dunford v Dunford

[1980] 1 All ER 122, CA

The matrimonial home was owned by the parties in equal shares. The wife was now residing there with the children. On any sale of the property in 7 years' time on the youngest child completing her education, a half share of the net sale proceeds would be insufficient to rehouse the wife. The husband was ordered to transfer his half share to the wife, subject to a charge of 25 per cent of the net sale proceeds in his favour should the wife vacate the property or die.

The husband was now living in lodgings. Eveleigh LJ said: 'It is true that the husband is losing his share in the equity of the house, but it is a house where the mortgage is still at the original figure and the wife has the obligation of paying that off. *The husband's capital prospects are very much greater than those of the wife. He has a superior earning capacity; and, in the not too distant future when the children's payments come to an end, the difference between their earning capacity or their income will be even more pronounced.*

'In those circumstances, I think that his prospects, as I say, of acquiring a house in due course are really quite good.'

Note. The Court of Appeal has now held that *Dunford v Dunford* was wrongly decided in so far as it imposed a clean break on the wife by striking out the nominal order for the wife's maintenance without her consent. See case summary 10–103.

9 Case summaries referred to in Chapter 23

These are summaries of cases not adequately summarised elsewhere in this book. Where there is a reference in this chapter to a summary of a case in another chapter, the reader is referred to that case summary.

23–901 Hector v Hector

[1973] 3 All ER 1070, CA

In October 1971 in proceedings under the Married Women's Property Act 1882, section 17 it was declared that the house was jointly owned by the parties in equal shares. In November 1971 the wife obtained a decree nisi from her husband, who had left the wife and four youngest children in the house. The judge at first instance had ordered the husband to transfer the whole of his interest in the house, the equity of which was worth £4,000, to the wife and that there should be a secondary charge of £1,000 on the house to be paid to the husband on the death of the wife, the sale of the property or the youngest child attaining 16. The husband appealed.

Lord Denning MR said that the judge's order for the transfer of the house to the wife was undoubtedly the right order: see *Wachtel v Wachtel* (23–102). It was said that £1,000 was too small and that the house would increase in value, but the overriding consideration was the words at the end of section 5 (1) of the 1970 Act: 'and so to exercise those powers as to place the parties, so far as it is practicable and, having regard to their conduct, just to do so, in the financial position in which they would have been if the marriage had not broken down and each had properly discharged his or her financial obligations and responsibilities towards the other'.

Note. In *Alonso v Alonso* (23–303) Buckley LJ said that although that sort of solution was sometimes appropriate it was open to considerable objections in a period of rapid inflation, which gave the party subject to the benefit of the charge no share in any increase in value between the date of the order and the date when the amount secured became payable. It limited that party to a lump sum which, by the time it was paid, was very much less valuable.

Similarly, in *McDonnell v McDonnell* (23–107) Ormrod LJ, referring to *Browne v Pritchard* (23–305) with approval, said that it was generally better to allocate shares in the matrimonial home than to give one spouse a charge for a fixed amount which might be eroded by inflation when it came to be realised.

23–902 Smith v Smith (sub nom. **S v S**)

[1975] 2 All ER 19, CA

The former matrimonial home was owned by the parties in equal shares. Following the separation the wife remained in the house with the child of the family, a girl approaching 12, who had suffered from serious kidney trouble since infancy. It was likely that the child would need the wife's continuing help and care even after leaving school. In any event, the wife was unable to work full-time at present because of the need to look after the child during the school holidays. Were the house to be sold, her one-half share of the net sale proceeds would not enable her to rehouse herself and the child in the area. Indeed, with anything less than the full equity and with no settled full-time employment she would find it very difficult, if not impossible, to purchase a new home in the area.

The husband was living with his parents. He had prospects of promotion. He was engaged to marry. His fiancée was a secretary. His hope was that in five years' time, on the child of his first marriage attaining 17, the former matrimonial home would be sold and that he would get enough out of the sale proceeds to set himself and his second wife up in a home and raise a second family.

Latey J ordered that the husband's interest in the former matrimonial home be transferred to the wife, because the wife's relative financial position was exceptionally weak, but he ordered that the husband be relieved of his obligations to pay rates, repairs and mortgage outgoings. The husband appealed. On 20 March 1974 Davies, Stephenson and Roskill LJJ dismissed his appeal. The only report of the appeal decision is at [1974] Bar Library Transcript 74. The report in the All England Reports, which was published following the appeal, merely notes that the appeal was dismissed.

Note. Latey J reviewed *Wachtel v Wachtel* (23–102), *Mesher v Mesher* (23–301), *Hector v Hector* (23–103) and *Chamberlain v Chamberlain* (23–302), and extracted from them four guidelines:

1. The court's approach should be flexible and, with the provisions of [section 25 of the 1973 Act] in mind, should suit its decision and order to the appropriate facts of the case. In many cases *Wachtel* orders are appropriate but the decision in *Wachtel v Wachtel* did not lay down any universal or general rule binding the court.
2. The availability of the house as a home for the wife and children should ordinarily be ensured while the children are being educated.
3. When the children have ceased their education and the house is sold the husband and wife should receive their shares absolutely. The suggestion that properties should be settled on a wife and children was disapproved in *Chamberlain v Chamberlain*.
4. If the wife has remarried or is going to remarry her financial position on remarriage has to be considered. If it is guesswork whether she might or might not remarry, prospective remarriage should be ignored.

His lordship's guideline 3 must now be reconsidered in the light of *Martin v Martin* (23–703) and *Hanlon v Hanlon* (23–704) and the other cases referred to in Chapter 23/7 – The problem of rehousing the party living in the property. Perhaps it can be re-stated thus:

3. Even where there are no children of the marriage (or the children have completed their education) and where the only available asset is the matrimonial home, the most important circumstance to be taken into account in applying section 25 of the 1973 Act is that both parties should have a roof over their heads. But if a home can be provided for both parties out of the proceeds of sale of the matrimonial home then it should be sold, and the husband and wife should receive their shares absolutely.

23–903 Flatt v Flatt

(1973) 4 Fam Law 20, 118 Sol Jo 183, CA

The husband and wife married in 1930. They had one daughter, who was now married. In 1956 the husband bought the house in which they had lived since 1935 for £1,130 of which he paid about one-half from his savings, the balance being on mortgage. In 1964 the wife left the husband and went to live with the married daughter. She obtained a magistrates' order against the husband on the ground of constructive desertion. In 1972 the husband obtained a decree nisi on the ground of five years' separation.

Lord Denning MR said that in *Wachtel v Wachtel* (14–001) it had been indicated that in regard to capital assets like the matrimonial home, on a separation one-third of those assets was recognised as a starting point; that applied here, so that the house should be held by the parties as tenants in common in the proportion of one-third to the wife and two-thirds to the husband on a trust for sale with power to the court to postpone the sale as long as the husband wished to remain there. In respect of her one-third interest in the house the husband should pay the wife £247 a year so long as he was in the house having the whole benefit of it. Cairns and Stephenson LJJ concurred.

There is no calculation in the reports of how the court arrived at the figure for the husband to pay for his sole occupation in respect of the wife's one-third interest.

Note. Compare *Dallimer v Dallimer* (5–106).

23–904 Brisdion v Brisdion

(1974) 5 Fam Law 92, 119 Sol Jo 234, CA

The parties bought the council house of which they had been the tenants for £3,020 in March 1972 on a mortgage granted by the council repayable over 25 years. The husband paid a deposit of £5. The property was conveyed into the parties' joint names and the conveyance contained a pre-emption clause giving the council an option to repurchase at the price at which they had sold the property if the parties should desire to sell it within 5 years of the date of purchase. The husband paid the mortgage repayments until August 1973 when he left the matrimonial home. Thereafter, the wife, who continued to live in the house with the children, paid the mortgage repayments.

Megaw LJ said that as a result of the pre-emption clause in the conveyance the equity in the house was only £16.40. The wife accordingly claimed that the house was a worthless asset. The husband had objected to its transfer to the wife on the ground that it was unfair that she should get the benefit of the windfall which would result from the substantial increase in value which would arise after 1977 when the pre-emption clause ceased to operate. He had relied on the fact that the house had been bought in joint names, and had said that not only had he paid the mortgage repayments until August 1973 but that no doubt part of the £16 a week which he had voluntarily paid the wife after he had left had gone towards the mortgage repayments which the wife had been paying. The wife had to be treated as having contributed because she had looked after the children and run the house until the marriage broke down. In those circumstances, where the wife was left with the responsibility of bringing up three children and the youngest was only seven, she was effectively precluded from taking any full time work for a substantial number of years to come, and where, as here, the husband's contribution towards obtaining the property had been so small, the fair and proper order was that the wife should have the property transferred wholly to her; the part of the judge's order directing the husband to pay the mortgage instalments would be discharged. Orr LJ and Latey J agreed.

23–905 McDonnell v McDonnell

(1976) Times, 17 February, [1977] 1 All ER 766, CA

The former matrimonial home had been given to the husband by his family. It was a large five-bedroomed house. It was unencumbered. During an unsuccessful attempt at reconciliation in 1973 the husband had transferred it into the parties' joint names. Shortly afterwards the wife commenced divorce proceedings.

Mrs. Justice Lane made an order extinguishing the husband's interest in return for a charge of £10,000, representing one-third of its value, secured on the property without interest, the charge not to be enforced until, at the latest, when the youngest child attained the age of 17 [i.e. as in *Hector v Hector* (23–103)]. The husband's appeal was allowed.

Ormrod LJ said that it was generally better to allocate shares in the matrimonial home than to give one spouse a charge for a fixed amount which might be eroded by inflation when it came to be realised. His lordship referred to *Browne v Pritchard* (23–305) [1975] 3 All ER 721, in which Lord Denning MR had said (at page 723): 'The charge should not be for a fixed sum such as £1,885, because values change so much these days. It should be simply for one-third of the net proceeds of sale whenever that takes place.' In that case the Court of Appeal had accordingly decided that the charge for a fixed amount awarded by the judge should be replaced by a charge amounting to one-third of the net proceeds of sale.

The appeal was allowed to the extent of substituting an order that the house be vested in trustees for sale for the parties in equal shares, the sale to be postponed until, at the latest, when the youngest child attained 17.

Notes

1. The further appeal on the question of costs, reported at [1977] 1 All ER 766, CA, gives brief details of the facts of the case. The case again came before Ormrod LJ and Sir John Pennycuick. Ormrod LJ said (at the foot of page 769): 'The house was originally acquired by the husband, or provided by his family, and was in his sole name. In 1973 he transferred it into the joint names of himself and his wife ... [The report in *The Times* states that the house had been given to the husband by his family, that during an unsuccessful attempt at reconciliation in 1973 the husband had transferred it into the parties' joint names and that shortly afterwards the wife had commenced divorce proceedings.]

   '... before Lane J the issue was what was to happen to his share. She ordered the husband to transfer it to the wife subject to a charge in his favour in the sum of

£10,000. This represented one-third of the value of the house at that time. However, in *Browne v Pritchard,* a decision of this court, it was pointed out that, in a period of unstable money, charges for fixed sums might work injustice and that it would often be preferable to charge the property with a proportion of the proceeds of sale.'

The headnote reads: '... On the hearing of the appeal, the husband succeeded on the major issue, his share in the house; the court ordered that he should be entitled to one-half of the proceeds of sale ...'

2.   Compare *Cumbers v Cumbers* (14–003A) – lump sum payable by weekly instalments, with interest.

CHAPTER 24

Proceedings under Married Women's Property Act 1882, etc.

Where there are proceedings for divorce or judicial separation, all the issues will normally be dealt with in applications for ancillary relief rather than under section 17 of the Married Women's Property Act 1882. However, disputes about property will still have to be resolved where there is no divorce or judicial separation. Where there are section 17 proceedings and also proceedings for ancillary relief, they will generally be heard together. See *Practice Direction dated 29.1.1971* (26–002A).

However, even where there are proceedings for divorce or judicial separation there remain some limited cases in which section 17 might be invoked to some advantage. In some cases it may be necessary to start section 17 proceedings with a view to obtaining an order for sale when divorce proceedings have become extraordinarily prolonged and the need to sell a particular property has become urgent (but see now the Matrimonial Homes and Property Act 1981, Appendix III). Secondly, if a party has remarried before filing an application for ancillary relief then section 17 proceedings will be necessary. See *Nixon v Fox* (6–166) and *Jenkins v Hargood* (6–167).

1 Ascertainment of ownership of the beneficial interest

Owing to considerations of space and cost, the full summaries of these cases originally prepared by the authors for insertion in this chapter have been deleted from the manuscript. Short summaries of many of these cases will be found in Chapter 24/3, *but only in so far as they are relevant to the making of mortgage repayments following the separation of the parties*, this topic being of far more importance today than the ascertainment of the ownership of the beneficial interest in the property (see Lord Denning MR's statement in his judgment in the Court of Appeal in *Hanlon v Law Society* ([1980] 1 All ER 763 at 770) quoted with approval by Lord Simon in his judgment in the House of Lords at [1980] 2 All ER 199 at the foot of 206).

24–101 Wilson v Wilson [1963] 2 All ER 447, CA
24–102 Jansen v Jansen [1965] 3 All ER 363, CA
24–103 Button v Button [1968] 1 All ER 1064, CA
24–104 Pettitt v Pettitt [1969] 2 All ER 385, HL
24–105 Gissing v Gissing [1970] 2 All ER 780, HL
24–106 Falconer v Falconer [1970] 3 All ER 449, CA
24–107 Heseltine v Heseltine [1971] 1 All ER 952, CA

24-108 **Morris v Tarrant** [1971] 2 All ER 920
24-109 **Davis v Vale** [1971] 2 All ER 1021, CA
24-110 **Cracknell v Cracknell** [1971] 3 All ER 552, CA
24-111 **Hargrave v Newton** [1971] 3 All ER 866, CA
24-112 **Hazell v Hazell** [1972] 1 All ER 923, CA
24-113 **Cowcher v Cowcher** [1972] 1 All ER 943, CA
24-114 **Kowalczuk v Kowalczuk** [1973] 2 All ER 1042, CA
24-115 **Re Nicholson, Nicholson v Perks** [1974] 2 All ER 386
24-116 **Leake v Bruzzi** [1974] 2 All ER 1196, CA
24-117 **Bothe v Amos** [1975] 2 All ER 321, CA
24-118 **Coley v Coley** (1975) 5 Fam Law 195, CA
24-119 **Finch v Finch** (1975) 119 Sol Jo 793, CA
24-120 **Shinh v Shinh** [1977] 1 All ER 97
24-121 **Suttill v Graham** [1977] 3 All ER 1117, CA
24-122 **Brykiert v Jones** (1981) Times, 16 January, CA
24-123 **Dennis v McDonald** [1981] 2 All ER 632

2 Relevance of express declaration of trust

CASE SUMMARIES

24-201 Wilson v Wilson

[1963] 2 All ER 447, CA

Matrimonial home conveyed to the parties as joint tenants in equity. Declaration of trust of proceeds of sale contained in conveyance held to be binding on the parties.

24-202 Leake v Bruzzi

[1974] 2 All ER 1196, CA

Matrimonial home purchased while wife an infant, aged 19, and conveyed into sole name of husband. Trust deed, declaring that beneficial interest held on trust for the parties as joint tenants, held to be conclusive of question of title in the absence of fraud or mistake. *Wilson v Wilson* (24-201) followed.

24-203 Brykiert v Jones

(1981) Times, 16 January, CA

Matrimonial home conveyed to the parties as joint tenants in equity. House purchased in 1948. Parties separated in 1951 when wife left. Marriage not dissolved until 1972. Remarriage by both parties. Proceedings commenced in Chancery Division in 1979 under Law of Property Act 1925, section 30. The Court of Appeal held that there was no room for any constructive or implied trust of the wife's beneficial interest for the benefit of the husband. Declaration of trust of proceeds of sale contained in conveyance held to be binding on the parties. Wife entitled to one-half of proceeds of sale, after crediting husband with mortgage repayments.

Note. The authors are grateful to the Editor of the Times Law Reports for confirming that the proceedings were brought under the 1925 legislation, not the Matrimonial Causes Act 1973.

3 Relevance of mortgage repayments made following separation

CASE SUMMARIES

24–301 Wilson v Wilson

[1963] 2 All ER 447, CA

Matrimonial home owned in equal shares. Husband in occupation. Husband given credit for mortgage instalments paid since separation by deducting one-half of payments from wife's share and adding the deductions to his share. Compare *Leake v Bruzzi* (24–305).

24–302 Falconer v Falconer

[1970] 3 All ER 449, CA

Matrimonial home owned in equal shares. Wife in occupation. Following separation, husband paid one-half of mortgage instalments for two years, then ceased. Wife paid whole of instalments thereafter for further two years. Wife not given full credit for this on the ground that she had had the use and benefit of the house. Compare *Leake v Bruzzi* (24–305).

24–303 Davis v Vale

[1971] 2 All ER 1021, CA

Matrimonial home owned in equal shares. Husband in occupation, paying all mortgage instalments and receiving rent from sub-tenant. Rent received to be set against mortgage instalments paid. Husband to be given credit for half the balance. Compare *Leake v Bruzzi* (24–305).

24–304 Cracknell v Cracknell

[1971] 3 All ER 552, CA

Matrimonial home owned in equal shares. Husband in occupation. Husband given credit for mortgage instalments paid since separation by setting off against the wife's share one-half of the mortgage instalments paid by him since the separation.

Notes
1. Wife's conduct taken into account. See case summary 8–701.
2. In *Suttill v Graham* (24–310) Stamp LJ said that the decision in *Leake v Bruzzi* (24–305) was to be preferred.

24–305 Leake v Bruzzi

[1974] 2 All ER 1196, CA

Matrimonial home owned in equal shares. Husband in occupation. Husband given credit for half the mortgage repayments in respect of capital since the separation but not in respect of interest because he had had the use and benefit of the house.

Notes
1. Husband's conduct irrelevant. See case summary 8–702.
2. Approved in *Suttill v Graham* (24–310).

24–306 Bothe v Amos

[1975] 2 All ER 321, CA

Matrimonial home situated at business premises owned in equal shares. Wife's interest in assets and goodwill of family business assessed as at the date she left and renounced the partnership by her conduct.

Notes

1. Wife's conduct in breaking up business partnership taken into account. See case summary 8–703.
2. Wife's adultery irrelevant (ibid.).

24–307 Coley v Coley

(1975) 5 Fam Law 195, CA

Matrimonial home owned in equal shares. Husband in occupation paying all mortgage instalments out of rents from letting of rooms. Mortgage instalments paid out of resources belonging to the parties equally. Husband not given credit in respect of payments.

Note. Husband's conduct irrelevant. See case summary 8–704.

24–308 Finch v Finch

(1975) 119 Sol Jo 793, CA

Matrimonial home owned in equal shares. Husband in occupation. Husband's conduct taken into account. Husband's contributions towards mortgage ignored. See case summary 8–705.

24–309 Shinh v Shinh

[1977] 1 All ER 97

Matrimonial home conveyed into the parties' joint names on trust for sale. Husband in occupation. Preliminary point of law. Wife claimed she left home because of husband's conduct and that husband therefore not entitled to claim credit for mortgage repayments made by him since separation. Jupp J concluded that the conduct of the parties was a relevant issue. *Cracknell v Cracknell* (24–304) applied. See case summary 8–706.

Note. The Court of Appeal's decision in *Suttill v Graham* (24–310) would appear to cast doubt on Jupp J's conclusions.

24–310 Suttill v Graham

[1977] 3 All ER 1117, CA

Matrimonial home conveyed into the parties' joint names on trust for sale. Husband in occupation. Husband given credit for half the repayments of capital made by him since the separation, but not of interest because he had had the use and occupation of the house.

Notes

1. Wife's adultery irrelevant. See case summary 8–707. *Leake v Bruzzi* (24–305) to be preferred to *Cracknell v Cracknell* (24–304).
2. Husband given credit for capital repayments only. *Leake v Bruzzi* followed in preference to *Cracknell v Cracknell*.

24–311 Dennis v McDonald

[1981] 2 All ER 632

Unmarried couple. Family home owned in equal shares. Man in occupation. Repayment mortgage. During the early years of a repayment mortgage the major element of the payments is interest on the capital sum advanced. No credit to be given for either capital or interest elements in the mortgage payments made by the man since separation. No credit for half the repayments of capital because negligible. No credit for half the payments of interest because he had had the use and occupation of the house. *Leake v Bruzzi* (24–305) applied.

4 The presumption of advancement

CASE SUMMARIES

24–401 Falconer v Falconer

[1970] 3 All ER 449, CA

Lord Denning MR said that the presumption of advancement has no place or, at any rate, very little place, in the law today. He referred to the speeches of Lord Reid, Lord Hodson and Lord Diplock in *Pettitt v Pettitt* [1969] 2 All ER 385, HL.

Note. Compare *Tinker v Tinker* [1970] 1 All ER 540, CA in which the house was purchased in the wife's name in order to avoid any potential claim by creditors if the husband's business failed. The husband acted honestly in putting the house in the wife's name. But, said Lord Denning, he could not say that as against his wife it belonged to him, while as against his creditors it belonged to her. It must be one or the other. The presumption was that it was conveyed to the wife for her own use, and the husband could not rebut that presumption by saying that he only did it to defeat his creditors.

24–402 Crane v Davis

(1981) Times, 13 May

Judgment on admission of the fact of receipt money. The plaintiff, Miss Crane, without the benefit of legal advice, paid to the first defendant, Mr. Davis, two cheques which Mr. Davis used to purchase a house in the name of the second defendant, a company incorporated in Spain. Having commenced proceedings in the Chancery Division, the plaintiff applied for judgment under RSC Order 27, rule 3 on the admission by the defendants in their joint defence of the fact of receipt of the money.

The defendants argued that a gift by cheque could be validly effected by delivery to the donee without requiring any deed or other written instrument, that the payment was a gift and that the motion should be dismissed and the case allowed to go for trial.

Falconer J said that it mattered not whether the payment was by way of cheque or cash. There being no relationship by blood or marriage, there could be no presumption of advancement, and there was accordingly a resulting trust for Miss Crane. His lordship referred to *Seldon v Davidson* [1968] 2 All ER 755, CA in which the county court judge had ruled that, there being no presumption of advancement, it was for the defendant to begin, and to the judgments of Willmer and Edmund Davies LJJ in that case. Willmer LJ had said that payment of the money having been admitted, prima facie that payment imported an obligation to repay in the absence of any circumstances tending to show anything in the nature of a presumption of advancement, and Edmund Davies LJ had made observations to the same effect. His lordship held that Miss Crane was entitled to judgment on the admission of the fact of receipt of the money in the defence.

CHAPTER 25

Orders for payment of future outgoings

CASE SUMMARIES

25–101 Mesher v Mesher (sub nom. Mesher v Mesher and Hall)

(1973) Times, 13 February, [1980] 1 All ER 126n, CA

The matrimonial home, which had been purchased by the parties in their joint names, was ordered to be held on trust for sale in equal shares, and the wife, who was living in the house with the daughter and a man she proposed to marry, was ordered to discharge all outgoings, including mortgage interest, any capital repayments to be discharged equally by the husband and wife.

25–102 Chamberlain v Chamberlain

[1974] 1 All ER 33, CA

The matrimonial home, which had been purchased by the parties in their joint names, was ordered to be held on trust for sale, one-third for the husband, two-thirds for the wife, and the wife, who was living in the house, was ordered to pay all outgoings, including all future mortgage instalments.

Note. The husband had run into debt and defaulted on the mortgage repayments and the wife had been paying off the mortgage arrears.

25–103 Flatt v Flatt

(1973) 4 Fam Law 20, 118 Sol Jo 183, CA

The matrimonial home, which had been purchased by the husband with the aid of a mortgage, was ordered to be held on trust for sale, two-thirds for the husband and one-third for the wife. If the house was not being sold the husband, who was living in the house, should pay a further £247 per annum to the wife for as long as he was in the house (as a form of 'rent').

Note. Nothing further was said about the mortgage, but the house had been purchased in 1956, and the mortgage must have been paid off by the time the case came before the Court.

25–104 Alonso v Alonso

(1974) 4 Fam Law 164, 118 Sol Jo 660, CA

The matrimonial home, which had been purchased by the parties in their joint names, was ordered to be held on trust for sale, one-third for the husband and two-thirds for the wife, and the wife, who was living in the home, was ordered to discharge all outgoings.

Note. The husband and the wife were ordered to remain liable in equal shares on the promissory note securing a loan to the parties from the husband's aunt which had been granted to enable them to purchase the property.

25–105 Allen v Allen

[1974] 3 All ER 385, CA

The matrimonial home, which had been purchased by the husband with the aid of a mortgage, was ordered to be held on trust for sale in equal shares, and the wife, who was granted the right to occupy the property, was ordered to discharge all outgoings, including the mortgage repayments, as from the date the husband vacated the property.

25–106 Goodfield v Goodfield

(1975) 5 Fam Law 197, CA

Both parties had agreed before the hearing of the application for ancillary relief that the equity in the matrimonial home should be divided between them in equal shares. The Court of Appeal, reversing the county court judge's order that no sale should take place without the wife's express consent, ordered that the house should be sold within a year of the order; until such sale the wife was to be entitled to remain in occupation and was to pay all outgoings, including the mortgage instalments.

25–107 Browne v Pritchard

[1975] 3 All ER 721, CA

The matrimonial home, which had been purchased by the parties in their joint names, was ordered to be held on trust for sale, two-thirds for the husband, one-third for the wife. The husband, who was living in the house with the two elder children of the family, would remain liable in respect of the mortgage repayments.

Note. Since the hearing before the county court judge, the husband had become unemployed; the DHSS were paying the mortgage interest; the wife's new husband had deserted her; the wife was living in a council house, supported by social security payments.

25–108 Martin v Martin (sub nom. Martin (BH) v Martin (D))

[1977] 3 All ER 762, CA

The matrimonial home, which had been purchased by the parties in their joint names, was ordered to be held on trust for sale in equal shares, and the wife, who was living in the property, was ordered to pay all outgoings, including all future mortgage instalments.

25–109 Scott v Scott

[1978] 3 All ER 65, CA

The Court of Appeal ordered that the matrimonial home, which had been purchased in the husband's name with the aid of an unusually beneficial mortgage from the husband's employers, would be held on trust for sale and that the husband would have an equitable interest of 60 per cent and the wife 40 per cent; the wife would have the right to continue in occupation until the younger children (twins) had reached the age of 18 or ceased to be in full-time education. No order was made as to the mortgage repayments; hence the husband remained liable. It was argued before the Court of Appeal that when the house was no longer needed as a home for the children – in about 14 years' time – it was wrong that the husband's capital asset would be reduced by 40 per cent, in view of the fact that he had been the legal owner of the property and that the burden of the mortgage repayments would have been totally borne by him. The Court of Appeal rejected this submission, saying that the order was an attempt to place both parties in a comparable position for the purposes of finding accommodation when the house was sold in 14 years' time, and of providing a home for the children in the meantime.

Note. The fact that the mortgage had been granted to the husband by his employers at an unusually low rate of interest may have influenced the court in coming to its decision. If the wife had been made responsible for the mortgage repayments the husband's employers would presumably have discontinued the beneficial arrangement, which would have resulted in the husband having to pay more maintenance to the wife in order to enable her to obtain a conventional mortgage.

25–110 Bateman v Bateman

[1979] Fam 25, [1979] 2 WLR 377

Gross conduct: wife inflicted serious chest wound on husband with a knife. Nevertheless, the husband agreed that the former matrimonial home should be settled on the wife for her life or until her remarriage, and thereafter should pass to the children absolutely. Order: that the house be settled on trust for sale, postponed until the wife ceased to use the house as her main place of residence or remarried or died; that thereafter the house should be sold and the proceeds distributed as to 25 per cent to the wife if still alive and 75 per cent to be divided equally among the surviving children or their issue; that the husband should pay a lump sum of £3,000 as a contribution towards the urgent repairs required to the house; reduced maintenance of £1,000 per annum only, plus a further £800 per annum out of which the wife should make the mortgage repayments on the house and pay the maintenance of the property, on the basis that the children would eventually benefit from the proper maintenance of the house and should not be prejudiced by their mother's conduct.

25–111 Dunford v Dunford

[1980] 1 All ER 122, CA

The matrimonial home had been purchased by the parties in their joint names with the aid of a mortgage. The husband was ordered to transfer his interest in the property to the wife subject to a charge in his favour of 25 per cent of the net sale proceeds when sold on the wife's vacating the property or on her death. The wife would be responsible for the mortgage repayments and the rates.

CHAPTER 26

Practice

26–001 Miles v Bull

[1968] 3 All ER 632

Class F land charge of no effect against registered land. See case summary 5–201.
Notes
1. On applying to register a Class F land charge in the Land Charges Registry, application should also be made for an index map search, in order to determine whether the Class F land charge should be superseded by a notice or caution at the Land Registry. The application to register the Class F land charge should be accompanied by a letter to the effect that the application is being made before the result of the index map search is known.
2. See also *Whittingham v Whittingham* (26–011) – house never occupied as matrimonial home – Class F land charge of no effect – application for transfer of property order registrable as a pending action.
3. See also *Barnett v Hassett* (26–016) – it is a misuse of the Matrimonial Homes Act 1967 for a spouse who has no intention of occupying the matrimonial home to register a Class F land charge on the property solely in order to freeze the assets of the other spouse – registration set aside.
4. A spouse's rights of occupation under the 1967 Act cease on the making of the decree absolute, whereupon any Class F land charge registered in respect of those rights ceases to be of effect unless an order has been made prior to decree absolute extending those rights of occupation and allowing the Class F land charge to be renewed after decree absolute. In *Terry-Smith v Terry-Smith* (see Appendix II) the decree absolute was set aside in order to preserve the wife's right to apply under the 1967 Act for a transfer of tenancy order, on the ground that the husband's solicitors had applied for the decree absolute without drawing the court's attention to the wife's pending application under the Act. Might a decree absolute be set aside on the ground that it was pronounced without the court's attention having been drawn to a Class F land charge?

26–002 Practice Direction 27 January 1971 – Applications for transfer of property orders – mortgagees

[1971] 1 All ER 896

Mortgagee to have notice of application and an opportunity to be heard. '... In all cases where an application is made for a transfer of property order in relation to property which is subject to a mortgage, it is desirable that the mortgagee should have notice of the application and an opportunity to be heard. Although no express provision is made in the Matrimonial Causes Rules, the registrar's powers under Matrimonial Causes Rule 77 (6) enable him to give directions for the conduct of the proceedings, and registrars should exercise those powers to ensure that no person or corporate body is prejudiced by an order without having notice of the application and an opportunity to be heard before the order is made.'

26-002A Practice Direction 29 January 1971 – Matrimonial property – related applications

[1971] 1 All ER 895

Related applications for ancillary relief and under Married Women's Property Act 1882 and/or Matrimonial Homes Act 1967 – desirability of applications being heard together. '...It is suggested that judges and registrars dealing with related applications under the Married Women's Property Act 1882 and/or the Matrimonial Homes Act 1967 and for ancillary relief which arise at the same time should give consideration to the desirability of providing for hearing by the same tribunal by reference, retention or transfer as may be convenient in particular cases.'

26-003 Jones (DI) v Jones (ET)

[1972] 3 All ER 289

Husband's interest under trust for sale extinguished – form of order. The parties were married in 1956. On 17 April 1963 the husband as registered proprietor of the matrimonial home declared that he held the property in trust as to one equal half-part or share for himself absolutely and the remaining one equal half-part or share for the wife absolutely. On 7 May 1969 the wife was granted a decree of divorce on the ground of the husband's cruelty. In March 1971 it was ordered that the settlement be varied by 'extinguishing the respondent's rights under the said settlement as if he were now dead and the petitioner had survived him'. The Chief Land Registrar refused to register the wife as proprietor of the matrimonial home under the court order on the ground that there was no interest upon which the order could operate as the trust deed had declared that the interests of the husband and wife were those of beneficial tenants in common.

On the wife's application to amend the order to give effect to the court's intention:

Held, amending the order, that the common form of order that a settlement be varied by extinguishing the rights of one party thereunder as if he were now dead and the other party had survived him was undesirable and, unless there was a simple unsevered joint tenancy, inappropriate, and, therefore, *where the Family Division exercised its jurisdiction to vary settlements under section 4 (c) of the Matrimonial Proceedings and Property Act 1970, the appropriate method was to declare what new or altered trusts were to take effect in place of the superseded trusts.*

Per curiam. The Rules Committee should give consideration to the desirability of amending the Rules of the Supreme Court so as to give the Family Division jurisdiction to make vesting orders under section 44 (vii) of the Trustee Act 1925.

26-004 Practice Direction 14 December 1972 – Matrimonial property – registered land

[1973] 1 All ER 143

Office copy entries on the Register to be filed.

'1. On any application under Section 17 of the Married Women's Property Act 1882 or under Section 4 of the Matrimonial Proceedings and Property Act 1970 in which the ownership of, or transfer of, real or leasehold property is in question *the affidavit in support of the application should state whether the title to the property is registered or unregistered and, if the former, should quote the Land Registry Title Number.* Where necessary, in order to obtain this information the applicant should apply to the appropriate District Land Registry for a search of the public index map.

'2. *Where the title to the property is registered the applicant should, when filing the affidavit or as soon as possible thereafter, and in any case by the time of the first hearing before the Registrar, lodge an up-to-date office copy of the Register.* Such an office copy is normally issued only to, or on the written authority of, the registered proprietor.

'3. If such authority is not forthcoming, the court has power to make an order that the applicant be allowed to inspect the register of title, but, pending the making of rules giving jurisdiction to the county courts to make such orders, it may be necessary to transfer county court proceedings in which such an order is sought to the High Court before the order is made.

'4. The order should direct that the applicant be allowed to inspect the register of Title No.   , which will automatically allow him to obtain an office copy.'

26–005 Wachtel v Wachtel

[1973] 1 All ER 829, CA

Settlement of matrimonial home on wife and children disapproved.   Lord Denning MR, reading the unanimous judgment of the Court of Appeal, said (at page 841): '. . . suppose the husband leaves the house and the wife stays in it. If she is likely to be there indefinitely, arrangements should be made whereby it is vested in her absolutely, free of any share in the husband; *or, if there are children, settled on her and the children.*' See case summary 4–301.

Note. Disapproved in *Chamberlain v Chamberlain* (4–303) and *Alonso v Alonso* (4–305). See also *Marsden v Marsden* (4–302) and *D v D* (4–308).

26–006 Mesher v Mesher (sub nom. **Mesher v Mesher and Hall**)

(1973) Times, 13 February, [1980] 1 All ER 126n, CA

Settlement of matrimonial home – form of order.   That the matrimonial home to be held on trust for sale to hold the net proceeds of sale and rents and profits until sale in equal shares, provided that as long as the child of the marriage be under the age of 17 or until further order the house not be sold; the wife to be at liberty to live there rent-free, paying and discharging all rates, taxes and outgoings, including mortgage interest, and indemnifying the husband therefor; any repayments of capital to be borne in equal shares.

Notes

1. See also *Jones v Jones* (26–003), *Chamberlain v Chamberlain* (26–007A) and *Allen v Allen* (26–009).
2. Criticised in *Carson v Carson* (26–019). On the wife in *Carson v Carson* being obliged to sell the house on the children attaining 18 or completing their education she would find herself in a most unfavourable position with only half the proceeds of sale. In practice *Mesher* orders are not always appropriate.

26–007 Hector v Hector

[1973] 3 All ER 1070, CA

Charge for fixed sum not desirable.   Wife remaining in matrimonial home with children; husband's interest extinguished; husband awarded lump sum charged on property without interest; charge not to be enforced until death of wife, sale of house or youngest child attaining 16. See case summary 23–901.

Note. Disapproved in *McDonnell v McDonnell* (23–107), *Alonso v Alonso* (23–303) and *Browne v Pritchard* (23–305). Compare *Cumbers v Cumbers* (14–003A) – lump sum payable by weekly instalments, with interest.

26–007A Chamberlain v Chamberlain

[1974] 1 All ER 33, CA

Settlement of matrimonial home – form of order.   Order below varied by declaring that beneficial interest in 81 Somerset Avenue Chessington Surrey is jointly held, in the proportions of two-thirds to wife and one-third to husband, to be so held on trust for sale, such sale not to take place until every child of the family has ceased to receive full-time education, or thereafter without the consent of the parties or order of the court.

Notes

1. The order that the wife should pay all outgoings, including the mortgage repayments and the arrears which the husband had allowed to accumulate when he had been out of work, was not varied.

2. See also *Jones v Jones* (26–003), *Mesher v Mesher and Hall* (26–006) and *Allen v Allen* (26–009).

26–008 Alonso v Alonso

(1974) 4 Fam Law 164, 118 Sol Jo 660, CA

Settlement of matrimonial home – liberty to apply.   Buckley LJ said that it was desirable, in orders which attempted to legislate for a trust for sale which was not to be carried into effect for a number of years, that the order of the court should normally include liberty for either party to apply, for one could not be sure that events would turn out precisely as expected. All sorts of contingencies might occur. One party might go bankrupt, one might wish to live elsewhere or, if the house were subject to a mortgage, the mortgagees might exercise their power of sale. As a general practice, liberty to apply should be included in such orders so that the parties could come back to the court in the event of unforeseen or unexpected contingencies occurring, and so that an arrangement could be made to fit any new circumstances that had arisen. See case summary 23–303.

Note. See also *Practice Direction dated 4 March 1980* (26–014) – liberty to apply – application to be made in accordance with Rules of Court.

26–009 Allen v Allen

[1974] 3 All ER 385, CA

Settlement of matrimonial home – form of order.   An order under section 24 of the Matrimonial Causes Act 1973 that the matrimonial home be settled on the wife on trust for sale, with a direction that the sale should not take place until the younger child has attained the age of 17 years or finished full-time education and thereafter that the property be held on trust for the spouses in equal shares, will effectively exclude the husband during such time as the house is needed as a home for the children. See case summary 4–103.

Note. See also *Jones v Jones* (26–003), *Mesher v Mesher and Hall* (26–006) and *Chamberlain v Chamberlain* (26–007A).

26–010 Williams v Williams (sub nom. Williams (JW) v Williams (MA))

[1977] 1 All ER 28, CA

Law of Property Act 1925, section 30 – divorce proceedings already instituted – order for sale refused – case remitted to Family Division.   See case summary 5–134.

Note. See, however, *Bigg v Bigg* (5–133) in which an application for an adjournment of the section 30 proceedings pending the commencement of divorce proceedings was refused by the Court of Appeal, on the ground that the judge had considered the matter fully and had exercised his discretion in a proper manner.

26–010A P v P (financial provision: lump sum)

[1978] 3 All ER 70, CA

Valuation of farm.   Ormrod LJ said (at page 73): '. . . There is a very marked tendency in these s. 24 cases to treat valuation figures as if they were the equivalent of cash, but everybody knows in other contexts that they are not. The figure of £102,000 is purely a valuer's figure. How much it would amount to if this farm had to be sold and the business liquidated is quite another matter. It is therefore wholly unrealistic, in my judgment, to approach this case on the footing that this wife is equivalent to a person who has £100,000 invested in readily realisable securities or in cash or on deposit or whatever. A sum of £100,000 in liquid assets is one thing; £100,000 invested in a small farm in the West Country is something very different.'

26–011 Whittingham v Whittingham (National Westminster Bank Ltd intervening)

[1978] 3 All ER 805, CA

House never occupied as matrimonial home – Class F land charge of no effect – application for transfer of property order registrable as a pending action. On the breakdown of the marriage the wife and children went to live in a house owned by the husband. The house had never been occupied by the parties as a matrimonial home. The wife registered a Class F land charge against the property and applied for a transfer of property order under section 24 of the Matrimonial Causes Act 1973. In view of the fact that the property had never been a matrimonial home a consent order was made that the Class F land charge be vacated. The husband executed a legal charge over the property in favour of a bank. On taking the legal charge the bank discovered the existence of the Class F land charge, which had not been vacated, but was shown the consent order.

The wife applied to have the legal charge set aside. The registrar gave judgment in her favour. The basis of the registrar's decision was that the bank had not acted in good faith, because it had wilfully shut its eyes to the occupants of the property at a time when it should have investigated whether or not those occupants had any rights in the property. The bank appealed.

Balcombe J held that an application for a transfer of property order is a pending action which is registrable under the Land Charges Act 1972, even where the applicant has no present interest in the property and will have no interest in the property until a transfer of property order is made in his or her favour. It followed that because the wife's application had not been registered it was not binding on the bank. The wife's appeal was dismissed by the Court of Appeal.

Quaere. Where the Matrimonial Homes Act 1967 is of no application, either (as in this instance) because the house in question has never been occupied as a matrimonial home or (as in *Barnett v Hassett* (26–016)) because the aim is not to protect rights of occupation but to prevent the disposal of an asset by the other spouse, the answer would appear to be to apply for a transfer of property order in respect of the property and to register a pending action in the Land Charges Registry (or a caution in the Land Registry, as appropriate). See, however, *Calgary and Edmonton Land Co Ltd v Dobinson* [1974] 1 All ER 484. A summons in the Companies Court merely to restrain the company from disposing of land is not registrable as a pending action because it is not an action relating to an interest in land. The *Calgary* case was distinguished in *Whittingham v Whittingham* on the ground that the wife's application for a transfer of property order (which she had made so as to restrain the husband from disposing of the house in which she was living) was a claim to an interest in land; accordingly, her application was registrable as a pending action. Presumably, therefore, the registration of a pending action by a spouse without the filing of any application for a transfer of property order, solely in order to freeze the assets of the other spouse, would not be in support of an action relating to an interest in land; thus an application for vacation of the land charge would presumably succeed. (In *Heywood v BDC Properties Ltd (No 2)* [1963] 2 All ER 1063, CA an application for vacation of the registration of a pending action succeeded because neither party was making any claim to land against the other. Compare *Selim Ltd v Bickenhall Engineering Ltd* (1981) Times, 3 June, in which proceedings for leave to commence an action which might include a claim for forfeiture of a lease were held to be proceedings relating to an interest in land; the application for vacation of the registration of a pending action accordingly failed. Megarry V-C has very kindly confirmed to the authors that the report of the latter case in *The Times* contains an error; the report incorrectly states that the application in the *Heywood* case failed.)

26–012 Rushton v Rushton

(1978) 9 Fam Law 218, CA

Partial property adjustment order unsatisfactory.   The judge's order provided that the matrimonial home should be transferred from the husband's sole name into the joint names of the parties, but the order made no provision as to who had the right to occupy the property. The husband was employed in Kuwait, but to leave the matter without stipulating whether he had or had not a right to occupy the property was most unsatisfactory. In this case, the right order was a *Mesher v Mesher* (26–006) type of order. The wife should have the sole right to occupy the house until the younger of the two children attained the age of 18, whereupon it should be sold and the proceeds divided equally.

   Note. See also *Allen v Allen* (26–009).

26–013 Ward v Ward and Greene

[1980] 1 All ER 176, CA

Power of court to order sale of property.   There is no necessity to issue any pro forma summons under either the Married Women's Property Act 1882, section 17 or under the Law of Property Act 1925, section 30. What matters is whether the circumstances are such as to bring the case within one or other of the two latter Acts which gave the necessary power to the court to order a sale. If so, it is not necessary to the proceedings as being under those Acts.

   Note. And see now the Matrimonial Homes and Property Act 1981 – orders for sale of property – see Appendix III.

26–014 Practice Direction 4 March 1980 – Liberty to apply

[1980] 1 All ER 1008

Liberty to apply – applications to be made in accordance with Rules of Court.   'Judges and registrars of the Family Division have found that there is misunderstanding among practitioners as to the meaning of the above words. In one sense there is always liberty to apply since the Court can always be applied to by using the proper procedure, but *it is emphasised that, except in a few special cases, the words "liberty to apply" do not give the right to apply to the Court without using the procedures comprised in Matrimonial Causes Rule 122 and in the Non-Contentious Probate Rules, passim.*

   'Under a summons for directions there is always liberty to apply for further directions without taking out a further summons. The Court may give liberty to apply as to terms of compromise or as to the minor terms where property is settled. These examples are not exhaustive, but in general applications should not be made under liberty to apply without using the procedures laid down by the Rules referred to.'

26–015 L v L

(1980) Times, 13 November

Advantages of agreed valuations.   Balcombe J said that he had no jurisdiction to vary an order for the payment of a lump sum out of the proceeds of sale of the matrimonial home, which had sold for £7,500 more than the agreed valuation. Even if there had been jurisdiction his lordship would have dismissed the application. Parties were not compelled to agree a valuation, but by doing so time and costs were saved. The parties had agreed a valuation, with all the advantages of so doing. Those advantages would be lost if parties were able to come back and say that the circumstances had changed because the valuation had now turned out to be an undervaluation.

26–015A Terry-Smith v Terry-Smith

(1981) 125 Sol Jo 375

Matrimonial Homes Act 1967 – pending application for transfer of tenancy order – decree absolute set aside. See Appendix II.

26–016 Barnett v Hassett

(1981) Times, 4 March

Misuse of Class F land charge by use of procedure solely in order to freeze spouse's assets. It is a misuse of the Matrimonial Homes Act 1967 for a husband who has no intention of occupying the matrimonial home to register a Class F land charge on the property solely in order to enable him to freeze the wife's assets in pursuit of a claim against her, said Wood J. The wife's application to set the registration aside was granted.

Quaere. The answer would seem to be to apply for a transfer of property order and to register a pending action – see *Whittingham v Whittingham* (26–011).

26–017 Burrows v Burrows

(1981) Times, 10 March, CA

Interest on lump sum award. The county court has no statutory power to award interest on judgment debts, said Ormrod LJ. However, his lordship continued (obiter), it would be open to the judge in the divorce county court on granting a lump sum order to state *in the order* that if the sum was not paid within a certain time then interest could be charged.

Note. See *Hector v Hector* (26–007) and notes to that case summary.

26–018 Practice Direction 4 June 1981

[1981] 2 All ER 642

Valuation of property. Valuation to be made by agreed valuer or, in default of agreement, by independent valuer chosen by the President of the Royal Institution of Chartered Surveyors. See Appendix II.

26–019 Carson v Carson

(1981) Times, 7 July, CA

No power to vary Mesher order once made – Mesher orders not always appropriate. Ormrod LJ said that the case was a good example of the dangers of *Mesher* orders (see case summary 26–006). On the wife being obliged to sell the matrimonial home on the children attaining 18 or completing their education she would find herself in a most unfavourable position with only half the proceeds of sale. See case summary 10–107.

26–020 Matrimonial Homes and Property Act 1981

Rights of occupation – registered land – protection by registration of a notice at HM Land Registry. When the appropriate provisions of the Matrimonial Homes and Property Act 1981 come into force it will no longer be possible to register rights of occupation under the Matrimonial Homes Act 1967 against registered land by means of a caution. Such rights will be registrable only by means of a notice. Notices have been little used in the past. The procedural difficulty that a notice is only registrable if the land certificate is on deposit at the Land Registry will be overcome by the simple expedient of rendering production of the land certificate unnecessary. Quite when this administrative mumbo-jumbo is to take effect remains to be seen. See Appendix III.

Orders for sale of property – see Appendix III.

Matrimonial Causes Act 1973

(relevant sections referred to, derivations and amendments)

Financial provision orders in connection with divorce proceedings, etc.

23. (1) On granting a decree of divorce, a decree of nullity of marriage or a decree of judicial separation or at any time thereafter (whether, in the case of a decree of divorce or of nullity of marriage, before or after the decree is made absolute), the court may make any one or more of the following orders, that is to say –

(a) an order that either party to the marriage shall make to the other such periodical payments, for such term, as may be specified in the order;

(b) an order that either party to the marriage shall secure to the other to the satisfaction of the court such periodical payments, for such term, as may be so specified;

(c) an order that either party to the marriage shall pay to the other such lump sum or sums as may be so specified;

(d) an order that a party to the marriage shall make to such person as may be specified in the order for the benefit of a child of the family, or to such a child, such periodical payments, for such term, as may be so specified;

(e) an order that a party to the marriage shall secure to such person as may be so specified for the benefit of such a child, or to such a child, to the satisfaction of the court, such periodical payments, for such term, as may be so specified;

(f) an order that a party to the marriage shall pay to such person as may be so specified for the benefit of such a child, or to such a child, such lump sum as may be so specified;

subject, however, in the case of an order under paragraph (d), (e) or (f) above, to the restrictions imposed by section 29 (1) and (3) below on the making of financial provision orders in favour of children who have attained the age of eighteen.

[*Derivation*: Matrimonial Proceedings and Property Act 1970, ss. 2 (1), 3 (1) (a), (2)]

(2) The court may also, subject to those restrictions, make any one or more of the orders mentioned in subsection (1) (d), (e) and (f) above –

(a) in any proceedings for divorce, nullity of marriage or judicial separation, before granting a decree; and

(b) where any such proceedings are dismissed after the beginning of the trial, either forthwith or within a reasonable period after the dismissal.

[*Derivation*: Matrimonial Proceedings and Property Act 1970, s. 3 (1)]

(3) Without prejudice to the generality of subsection (1) (c) or (f) above –

(a) an order under this section that a party to a marriage shall pay a lump sum to the other party may be made for the purposes of enabling that other party to meet any liabilities or expenses reasonably incurred by him or her in maintaining himself or herself or any child of the family before making an application for an order under this section in his or her favour;

(b) an order under this section for the payment of a lump sum to or for the benefit of a child of the family may be made for the purpose of enabling any liabilities or expenses reasonably incurred by or for the benefit of that child before the making of an application for an order under this section in his favour to be met; and

(c) an order under this section for the payment of a lump sum may provide for the payment of that sum by instalments of such amount as may be specified in the order and may require the payment of the instalments to be secured to the satisfaction of the court.

[*Derivation:* Matrimonial Proceedings and Property Act 1970, ss. 2 (2), 3 (3), 4]

(4) The power of the court under subsection (1) or (2) (a) above to make an order in favour of a child of the family shall be exercisable from time to time; and where the court makes an order in favour of a child under subsection (2) (b) above, it may from time to time, subject to the restrictions mentioned in subsection (1) above, make a further order in his favour of any of the kinds mentioned in subsection (1) (d), (e) or (f) above.

[*Derivation:* Matrimonial Proceedings and Property Act 1970, s. 3 (5)]

(5) Without prejudice to the power to give a direction under section 30 below for the settlement of an instrument by conveyancing counsel, where an order is made under subsection (1) (a), (b) or (c) above on or after granting a decree of divorce or nullity of marriage, neither the order nor any settlement made in pursuance of the order shall take effect unless the decree has been made absolute.

[*Derivation:* Matrimonial Proceedings and Property Act 1970, s. 24 (1) (b)]

Property adjustment orders in connection with divorce proceedings, etc.

24. (1) On granting a decree of divorce, a decree of nullity of marriage or a decree of judicial separation or at any time thereafter (whether, in the case of a decree of divorce or of nullity of marriage, before or after the decree is made absolute), the court may make any one or more of the following orders, that is to say –

(a) an order that a party to the marriage shall transfer to the other party, to any child of the family or to such person as may be specified in the order for the benefit of such a child such property as may be so specified, being property to which the first-mentioned party is entitled, either in possession or reversion;

(b) an order that a settlement of such property as may be so specified, being property to which a party to the marriage is so entitled, be made to the satisfaction of the court for the benefit of the other party to the marriage and of the children of the family or either or any of them;

(c) an order varying for the benefit of the parties to the marriage and of the children of the family or either or any of them any ante-nuptial or post-nuptial settlement (including such a settlement made by will or codicil) made on the parties to the marriage;

(d) an order extinguishing or reducing the interest of either of the parties to the marriage under any such settlement;

subject, however, in the case of an order under paragraph (a) above, to the restrictions imposed by section 29 (1) and (3) below on the making of orders for a transfer of property in favour of children who have attained the age of eighteen.

[*Derivation:* Matrimonial Proceedings and Property Act 1970, s. 4]

(2) The court may make an order under subsection (1) (*c*) above notwithstanding that there are no children of the family.

[*Derivation:* Matrimonial Proceedings and Property Act 1970, s. 4]

(3) Without prejudice to the power to give a direction under section 30 below for the settlement of an instrument by conveyancing counsel, where an order is made under this section on or after granting a decree of divorce or nullity of marriage, neither the order nor any settlement made in pursuance of the order shall take effect unless the decree has been made absolute.

[*Derivation:* Matrimonial Proceedings and Property Act 1970, s. 24 (1) (b)]

Matters to which the court is to have regard in deciding how to exercise its powers under sections 23 and 24.

25. (1) It shall be the duty of the court in deciding whether to exercise its powers under section 23 (1) (a), (b) or (c) or 24 above in relation to a party to the marriage and, if so, in what manner, to have regard to all the circumstances of the case including the following matters, that is to say —

- (a) the income, earning capacity, property and other financial resources which each of the parties to the marriage has or is likely to have in the foreseeable future;

- (b) the financial needs, obligations and responsibilities which each of the parties to the marriage has or is likely to have in the foreseeable future;

- (c) the standard of living enjoyed by the family before the breakdown of the marriage;

- (d) the age of each party to the marriage and the duration of the marriage;

- (e) any physical or mental disability of either of the parties to the marriage;

- (f) the contributions made by each of the parties to the welfare of the family, including any contribution made by looking after the home or caring for the family;

- (g) in the case of proceedings for divorce or nullity of marriage, the value to either of the parties to the marriage of any benefit (for example, a pension) which, by reason of the dissolution or annulment of the marriage, that party will lose the chance of acquiring;

and so to exercise those powers as to place the parties, so far as it is practicable and, having regard to their conduct, just to do so, in the financial position in which they would have been if the marriage had not broken down and each had properly discharged his or her financial obligations and responsibilities towards the other.

[*Derivation:* Matrimonial Proceedings and Property Act 1970, s. 5]

(2) Without prejudice to subsection (3) below, it shall be the duty of the court in deciding whether to exercise its powers under section 23 (1) (d), (e) or (f), (2) or (4) or 24 above in relation to a child of the family and, if so, in what manner, to have regard to all the circumstances of the case including the following matters, that is to say —

- (a) the financial needs of the child;

(b) the income, earning capacity (if any), property and other financial resources of the child;

(c) any physical or mental disability of the child;

(d) the standard of living enjoyed by the family before the breakdown of the marriage;

(e) the manner in which he was being and in which the parties to the marriage expected him to be educated or trained;

and so to exercise those powers as to place the child, so far as it is practicable and, having regard to the considerations mentioned in relation to the parties to the marriage in paragraph (a) and (b) of subsection (1) above, just to do so, in the financial position in which the child would have been if the marriage had not broken down and each of those parties had properly discharged his or her financial obligations and responsibilities towards him.

[*Derivation:* Matrimonial Proceedings and Property Act 1970, s. 5]

(3) It shall be the duty of the court in deciding whether to exercise its powers under section 23 (1) (d), (e) or (f), (2) or (4) or 24 above against a party to a marriage in favour of a child of the family who is not the child of that party and, if so, in what manner, to have regard (among the circumstances of the case) –

(a) to whether that party had assumed any responsibility for the child's maintenance and, if so, to the extent to which, and the basis upon which, that party assumed such responsibility and to the length of time for which that party discharged such responsibility;

(b) to whether in assuming and discharging such responsibility that party did so knowing that the child was not his or her own;

(c) to the liability of any other person to maintain the child.

[*Derivation:* Matrimonial Proceedings and Property Act 1970, s. 5]

Financial provision orders, etc., in case of neglect by party to marriage to maintain other party or child of the family.

27. (1) Either party to a marriage may apply to the court for an order under this section on the ground that the other party to the marriage (in this section referred to as the respondent)—

(a) *has failed to provide reasonable maintenance for the applicant, or*

(b) *has failed to provide, or to make a proper contribution towards, reasonable maintenance for any child of the family.*

[Words in italics substituted by Domestic Proceedings and Magistrates' Courts Act 1978]

(2) The court shall not entertain an application under this section *unless* –

(a) *the applicant or the respondent is domiciled in England and Wales on the date of the application; or*

(b) *the applicant has been habitually resident there throughout the period of one year ending with that date; or*

(c) *the respondent is resident there on that date.*

[Words in italics substituted by Domicile and Matrimonial Proceedings Act 1973]

(3) Where an application under this section is made on the ground mentioned in subsection (1) (a) above then, in deciding –

(a) whether the respondent has failed to provide reasonable maintenance for the applicant, and

(b) what order, if any, to make under this section in favour of the applicant,

the court shall have regard to all the circumstances of the case including the matters mentioned in section 25 (1) (a) to (f) above and, so far as it is just to take it into account, the conduct of each of the parties in relation to the marriage.

[Subsection (3) substituted for original subsection (3) by Domestic Proceedings and Magistrates' Courts Act 1978]

(3A) Where an application under this section is made on the ground mentioned in subsection (1) (b) above then, in deciding –

(a) whether the respondent has failed to provide, or to make a proper contribution towards, reasonable maintenance for the child of the family to whom the application relates, and

(b) what order, if any, to make under this section in favour of the child,

the court shall have regard to all the circumstances of the case including the matters mentioned in section 25 (1) (a) and (b) and (2) (a) to (e) above, and where the child of the family to whom the application relates is not the child of the respondent, including also the matters mentioned in section 25 (3) above.

(3B) In relation to an application under this section on the ground mentioned in subsection (1) (a) above, section 25 (1) (c) shall have effect as if for the reference therein to the breakdown of the marriage there were substituted a reference to the failure to provide reasonable maintenance for the applicant, and in relation to an application under this section on the ground mentioned in subsection (1) (b) above, section 25 (2) (d) shall have effect as if for the reference therein to the breakdown of the marriage there were substituted a reference to the failure to provide, or to make a proper contribution towards, reasonable maintenance for the child of the family to whom the application relates.

[Subsections (3A) and (3B) substituted for subsection (4) by Domestic Proceedings and Magistrates' Courts Act 1978]

(5) Where on an application under this section it appears to the court that the applicant or any child of the family to whom the application relates is in immediate need of financial assistance, but it is not yet possible to determine what order, if any, should be made on the application, the court may make an interim order for maintenance, that is to say, an order requiring the respondent to make to the applicant until the determination of the application such periodical payments as the court thinks reasonable.

(6) Where on an application under this section the applicant satisfies the court of any ground mentioned in subsection (1) above, the court may make any one or more of the following orders, that is to say –

(a) an order that the respondent shall make to the applicant such periodical payments, for such term, as may be specified in the order;

(b) an order that the respondent shall secure to the applicant, to the satisfaction of the court, such periodical payments, for such term, as may be so specified;

(c) an order that the respondent shall pay to the applicant such lump sum as may be so specified;

(d) an order that the respondent shall make to such person as may be specified in the order for the benefit of the child to whom the application relates, or to that child, such periodical payments, for such term, as may be so specified;

(e) an order that the respondent shall secure to such person as may be so specified for the benefit of that child, or to that child, to the satisfaction of the court, such periodical payments, for such term, as may be so specified;

(f) an order that the respondent shall pay to such person as may be so specified for the benefit of that child, or to that child, such lump sum as may be so specified;

subject, however, in the case of an order under paragraph (d), (e) or (f) above, to the restrictions imposed by section 29 (1) and (3) below on the making of financial provision orders in favour of children who have attained the age of eighteen.

(6A) An application for the variation under section 31 of this Act of a periodical payments order or secured periodical payments order made under this section in favour of a child may, if the child has attained the age of sixteen, be made by the child himself.

(6B) Where a periodical payments order made in favour of a child under this section ceases to have effect on the date on which the child attains the age of sixteen or at any time after that date but before or on the date on which he attains the age of eighteen, then, if at any time before he attains the age of twenty-one an application is made by the child for an order under this subsection, the court shall have power by order to revive the first mentioned order from such date as the court may specify, not being earlier than the date of the making of the application, and to exercise its powers under section 31 of this Act in relation to any order so revived.

[Subsections (6A) and (6B) added by Domestic Proceedings and Magistrates' Courts Act 1978]

(7) Without prejudice to the generality of subsection (6) (c) or (f) above, an order under this section for the payment of a lump sum –

(a) may be made for the purpose of enabling any liabilities or expenses reasonably incurred in maintaining the applicant or any child of the family to whom the application relates before the making of the application to be met;

(b) may provide for the payment of that sum by instalments of such amount as may be specified in the order and may require the payment of the instalments to be secured to the satisfaction of the court.

Additional material

B v B (matrimonial proceedings: discovery)

[1979] 1 All ER 801

(1) *Wife entitled to go 'fishing' for information in the Family Division.* See judgment of Dunn J at page 809 letter j and page 810 letter b: '... The wife is entitled to go "fishing" in the Family Division within the limits of the law and practice.'

(2) *Husband director ordered to produce for inspection invoices, receipts, credit card accounts and receipts and other vouchers relating to entertainment and all other expenses incurred by husband whether in his own name or in the name of the company.*

(3) *Such documents, although in the legal possession of the company, had been in the actual physical possession of the husband. Therefore, even though he had held them merely as the servant or agent of the company, since they had been in his possession or custody and were relevant to the suit they must be disclosed by the husband.* See Dunn J's summary of his conclusions as to the law at page 811 letter c.

(4) *Where a husband is a controlling director of a "one man" company so that the company is his alter ego he can be forced to disclose relevant documents which have never been in his possession or custody, on the principle that all the company's documents are in his power in that he has an enforceable right to inspect them and obtain possession or control of them.* (ibid.)

(5) *However, in the instant case, the husband not having a controlling interest, that part of the registrar's order which ordered the husband to produce for inspection all invoices and vouchers of the company relating to directors' expenses (i.e. including those of his co-directors) would be deleted.*

(6) *Confidentiality of documents is of itself no ground for refusing production, but there is an implied undertaking by a party who obtains production of documents against any improper disclosure.* See page 810 at letter j.

Notes

1. A standard audit report to the members of a limited company states that in the opinion of the auditors 'the financial statements give a true and fair view of the state of the company's affairs at the Balance Sheet date and of its profit (or loss) for the year then ended...' Thus the auditors certify the profit (or loss), but not the constituent elements to arrive at the profit (or loss), as there is no requirement for the allocation of the company's various expenses to be commented upon.
2. A company is required to submit a return of expenses paid on behalf of directors (and other higher paid employees) to the Inland Revenue on a form P11D. (It is up to the director to claim on his tax return that part or all of the expenses were incurred by him on behalf of the company.) This return is not subject to audit by the company's auditors, although the Inland Revenue will examine its authenticity when carrying out a PAYE audit, which is infrequent in practice.
3. The wife's allegations should be laid before the Registrar by way of an affidavit sworn by a qualified accountant, setting out his reasons for believing that certain expenses (such as entertaining, motor and travelling, rent and rates, light and heat, telephone,

etc.) in the Trading and Profit and Loss Account appear excessive when compared to previous accounting periods and/or that he has reason to believe that the P11D does not disclose the full amount of all expenses paid by the company on behalf of the director (or higher paid employee).
4. The authors are indebted to Mr. Jonathan Grant, chartered accountant, for his invaluable assistance in court and in the preparation of the note to this case summary.

Hulley v Thompson

[1981] 1 All ER 1128

Husband's continuing liability to maintain children. On the making of the divorce, a consent order was made that the husband should transfer to the wife his half share in the matrimonial home and that he should not pay her any maintenance, either for herself or for the children of the family. The Supplementary Benefits Commission brought a complaint against the husband as a person liable to maintain the children. The magistrates decided that in exercising their discretion the terms of the consent order were a relevant consideration, and that having regard to the terms of the consent order no order should be made against the husband for the maintenance of the children. The SBC officer appealed.

The husband maintained before the Divisional Court that the transfer of his half share in the house to the wife should be treated as having been made in lieu of his liability to maintain the children, since it provided them with a roof over their heads. The court held that he remained liable to maintain them notwithstanding the terms of the consent order. Prima facie, his resources were sufficient to meet his liability, and the case would be remitted to the magistrates for reconsideration.

Waller LJ added, however, that it might well be that some reduction should be made in the extent of the husband's liability in the light of the consent order.

Page v Page

(1981) Times, 30 January, CA

Large assets – lump sum payment reduced by Court of Appeal from £165,000 to £90,000. An order directing a husband to pay his 78-year-old wife a lump sum of £165,000, as being the sum required to bring her capital up to one-half of the total assets of the parties, was held by the Court of Appeal to be wrong in principle.

Lord Justice Ormrod said that the order for payment of £165,000 was made in final satisfaction of all the wife's financial claims. The figure was arrived at by calculating the sum required to bring the wife's capital up to half of the assets of the parties. The judge, though he briefly referred to the provisions of section 25 of the Matrimonial Causes Act 1973, seemed to have dealt with the matter mainly on the arithmetical basis of ascertaining the value of the assets of the parties and then deciding on the appropriate denominator, which he took as 2. He was obviously much influenced by the fact that about the time when the wife filed her petition, the husband transferred £124,000 to a Mrs. R, the husband's secretary, who subsequently removed it out of the jurisdiction to the Isle of Man.

The sum was too high. The reason for dividing the assets equally was simply that it would be unjust to give the wife less, but it was clear from the judgment that the judge was comparing and contrasting her position with that of Mrs. R and, in effect, saying that if Mrs. R had had £124,000 the wife should get more. The husband's conduct in regard to the transfer of the sum was a highly relevant consideration, but the judge must have overlooked the fact that the husband had, very wisely, agreed that that sum should be treated as still part of his assets for the purpose of the case and, therefore, was included in the £359,137 upon which the judge based his calculation.

The judge did not exercise his discretion in accordance with section 25. There was nothing in the section which lent any support to the arithmetical approach to such cases, although in *Wachtel v Wachtel* ([1973] Fam 72), the Court of Appeal suggested that the 'one-third rule' provided a convenient starting point. The court must perform its duties under section 25 and consider each of the factors therein set out, bearing in mind the result of applying the one-third rule.

The first factor under section 25 was the resources of the parties. The judge assessed the husband's capital at £359,137. His income was about £20,000. The wife's capital was about £29,000, and her income £2,750.

On those figures there was enough capital to provide adequately for both of them in their old age. He was 74, and she 78. Consequently, when considering the next factor – needs and obligations of each party – a broad view could be taken. In a case such as the present 'needs' could be regarded as equivalent to 'reasonable requirements', taking into account the other factors such as age, health, length of marriage and standard of living.

Both parties needed an adequate and secure income which must come from investments, and access to capital to set up separate homes, or as a contingency fund to make up any shortfall in income or to meet the extra cost of illness and nursing care.

Their Lordships did not know what the wife proposed to do about a home or whether she would be physically able to live alone. However, with the available resources it was reasonable to make provision for her to be able to afford to be comfortable if she had to live in a nursing home. She would, therefore, require a substantial capital sum.

The relationship between the parties was so embittered that periodical payments were to be avoided. Accordingly the case was one for a lump sum provision and no periodical payments. The wife agreed in principle with that view.

It was not legitimate, however, under section 25 to take into account, as the judge did, the wife's wish to be in a position to make provision by will for her adult children who were in no way dependent on their parents or either of them.

The problem, therefore, was to decide the size of the lump sum, taking into account all the section 25 factors, including the contribution each had made to the welfare of the family.

Forty years of marriage represented a large contribution by the wife, and the husband too; but the present case was not one where the wife had been actively engaged in the husband's business either by working in it or by providing capital, though she must have helped him to save money to invest in his business activities. She had not, in that sense, 'earned' a share in the assets which in some cases gave the wife a considerable stake in them.

Doing the best he could to find an appropriate figure, his Lordship thought that the lump sum should be £90,000. With her own capital that would provide about £120,000 for the wife. That would be enough to enable her to buy a home or, if necessary, afford reasonable medical and nursing care.

Notes

1. Compare *Eshak v Nowojewski* (17–007), in which Sir John Arnold P, Oliver LJ and Dame Elizabeth Lane said that in a case in which there was no question of periodical payments (the wife in that case having remarried), the *general approach* was to start with the idea of an equal division of the property, while bearing in mind that this would yield to a different solution in the circumstances of any particular case.
2. See also *S v S* (16–104).

Thwaite v Thwaite

[1981] 2 All ER 789, CA

Jurisdiction to set aside consent orders.   Following the making of the decree nisi a consent order was made. On the wife undertaking to return the children from Australia (where they were living with her and a third party) to England and Wales, and on the husband undertaking to pay the children's school fees, the husband was ordered to convey his interest in the former matrimonial home to the wife within 28 days of the children returning to this country; all the wife's other applications for ancillary relief were to stand dismissed from the date of the conveyance. In addition, there was an order for periodical payments for each child. Liberty to apply was given to both parties.

In May 1979 the children returned to England. There was delay by the husband's solicitors in completing the conveyance of the house. In August, before the husband had executed the conveyance, the wife took the children back to Australia.

The husband declined to complete the conveyance on the ground that he had agreed to transfer the house to the wife only on the understanding that the wife was to make a home for the children there. His application to vary the consent order was dismissed by the registrar, who ordered him to complete the conveyance. There followed an appeal to the county court judge, and then to the Court of Appeal, which held:

(1) The registrar had been correct in dismissing the husband's *application to vary* the consent order. The consent order was a *final order* and there was no jurisdiction to vary it.

(2) But the judge had been right to allow the husband's appeal against the registrar's order that he complete the conveyance. There was jurisdiction to refuse to make such an order. The consent order was still executory. As the wife had broken her side of the bargain in a material respect, it would be inequitable to enforce the consent order.

(3) Furthermore, notwithstanding the fact that the consent order was a final order, the court had jurisdiction to hear an *appeal* against the consent order in the circumstances of the present case, on the ground that fresh evidence was now available which had not been available on the making of the consent order. The order had been based on the belief that the wife had a settled intention of making a home for herself and the children in the property. Fresh evidence had been adduced before the judge which had shown that she had no such settled intention. The judge was therefore entitled, in his discretion, to set the consent order aside and to make a new order for ancillary relief (as he had done).

(4) However, the judge's jurisdiction to set the consent order aside and to make a new order arose not from the liberty to apply (as the judge had held) but from the fact that the wife's original application for ancillary relief was still before the court in so far as the consent order was still executory.

Terry-Smith v Terry-Smith

(1981) 125 Sol Jo 375

Matrimonial Homes Act 1967 – pending application for transfer of tenancy order – decree absolute set aside. Without drawing the court's attention to the wife's pending application for a transfer of tenancy order under s. 7 of the 1967 Act, the husband's solicitors applied for decree absolute. The effect of the pronouncement of the decree was to bar the wife's application. Sir John Arnold P said that justice demanded that the application be allowed to continue. Decree absolute set aside.

W v W

(1981) Times, 21 March and 27 March

Husband's business associates ordered to produce documents. The wife suspected that the husband had made payments to his business associates in order to reduce his assets. She applied for an order under rule 77 (5) of the Matrimonial Causes Rules 1977 that the husband's business associates attend the court for cross-examination and to produce documents.

Balcombe J said that the court had no jurisdiction under rule 77 (5) to order a person who was not a party to the proceedings to produce documents. The court's powers under the rule [to order the production of documents] were limited to the parties to the action: *Wynne v Wynne and Jeffers* (6–362).

Nor did rule 77 (5) give the court power to order third parties *who had not given evidence-in-chief* to attend the court for cross-examination *only*. That would allow a procedure of interrogation which was contrary to established practice.

However, it was open to the wife to seek leave of the court to issue a writ of subpoena ad testificandum or a writ of subpoena duces tecum under RSC Order 32, rule 7: *Morgan v Morgan* (1–206). His lordship was prepared to grant leave under Order 32 rule 7, and ordered the husband's business associates to bring certain documents to the court.

Notes
1. The report in *The Times* of 21 March 1981 was corrected on 27 March 1981.
2. However, it is still difficult to reconcile the case as reported in *The Times* with *Wynne v Wynne* (6–362), where Bridge LJ stated that a co-respondent could be ordered to attend the court for the purposes of cross-examination.
3. See also *B v B* [1979] 1 All ER 801 – application for order for disclosure against husband's company refused.

H v H (15 May 1981)

(1981) Times, 16 May

Short childless marriage between young parties – desirability of the clean break.   The husband was now aged 35 and the wife 26. There were no children. They had cohabited intermittently over a period of six years prior to the marriage. On the several occasions when they had parted they had both considered themselves free to take another partner in the interval. The marriage had effectively lasted for only seven weeks.

Balcombe J said that to consider such a period of cohabitation as equivalent to a true period of marriage would be cynical in the extreme. Where, as here, there had been a very short marriage between two young persons, neither of whom had been adversely affected financially by the consequences of marriage and each capable of earning their own living, the approach adopted by the court was to give the party in the weaker financial position, usually the wife, periodical payments for a short time, and then to achieve a 'clean break', if necessary, facilitated by a small lump sum payment.

The wife had been in receipt of maintenance pending suit of £3,000 a year. If the wife was prepared to consent to the dismissal of her claim for periodical payments, the court was prepared to order the husband to make her a lump sum payment of £3,500 within 28 days.

Foley v Foley

[1981] 2 All ER 857, CA

Premarital cohabitation taken into account under 'all the circumstances of the case' but not counted as part of duration of marriage under section 25 (1) (d).   At the date of the hearing before Balcombe J the husband was 52 and the wife 40. They commenced cohabiting in 1962. Between 1963 and 1969 a daughter and two sons were born. They married in 1969 and separated in 1974. Balcombe J said that he had endeavoured to take into account all the circumstances of the case, but that in so far as section 25 (1) (d) referred to the duration of the marriage he was not prepared to treat it as a marriage which had subsisted for more than the five years which it actually subsisted. His lordship decided that £10,000 was the right figure to award as a lump sum in recognition of the wife's contribution to the family. The wife's appeal was dismissed.

Eveleigh LJ said that the two periods, cohabitation and marriage, were not the same. The degree of weight to be given to matters which occurred during those periods would be for the judge to decide in the exercise of his discretion. There might be cases where the inability of the parties to sanctify or legitimise their relationship called for sympathy, which would enable the court to take the period of cohabitation into account. *Kokosinski v Kokosinski* (8–402) was such a case. *Campbell v Campbell* (8–401) was not. [See also *H v H* (1981) Times, 16 May – see p. 362 ante.] Balcombe J had not said that the years of cohabitation were irrelevant but simply that they were not years of marriage, and his lordship saw no reason for interfering with his discretion.

H v H (2 June 1981)

[1981] LS Gaz R 786

Subpoena issued against family company.   Following divorce, the wife applied for financial provision. The husband maintained that the wife possessed considerable assets and that the wife held shares in a private family property company of which she was the secretary and her mother the chairman. Information supplied by the wife about the company was inconclusive to ascertain the true value of the company

Anthony Lincoln J granted leave to issue a subpoena duces tecum to be issued against the company by its proper officer for the production of the material documents relating to the rents received by the company.

The chairman of the company applied to have the subpoena set aside on the ground that it was oppressive.

Anthony Lincoln J said that counsel for the chairman of the company had conceded that the material sought was relevant. It was said that the wife's holding in the company was under 3% of the total share capital and that it would be wrong to open the company's books and divulge the company's secrets to the husband. Reliance had been placed on *Morgan v Morgan* (1–206). In the present case what was being sought was information about the present value of an asset in which the wife had an existing interest not about some asset which might come to the wife in the future. The balance sheets alone were not sufficient to ascertain the true value of the assets of the company. The production of the material documents relating to the rents received by the company would avoid costly and wide-ranging cross-examination at the hearing. It was not oppressive to the company or its shareholder.

Application refused.

Practice Direction 4 June 1981

Pretrial reviews: ancillary relief

[1981] 2 All ER 642

'The experiment in operation from 1 April 1980 to secure the settlement of financial applications at a pretrial review has resulted in a success rate so low as not to justify its continuance. Consequently pretrial reviews on such applications will not take place as from 1 July next. Nevertheless *the following procedures laid down by the Registrar's Direction of 12 February 1980* ([1980] 1 All ER 592, [1980] 1 WLR 245) *are still useful and should be continued.*
a) After affidavits have been filed mutual discovery should take place without order 14 days from the last affidavit, unless some other period is agreed, with inspection seven days thereafter.
b) Where a dispute arises as to the value of any property, a valuation should be made without order by an agreed valuer, or in default of agreement, by an independent valuer chosen by the President of the Royal Institution of Chartered Surveyors. The valuation should be produced to the registrar at the hearing.
c) If a dispute arises as to the extent of discovery or as to answers in a

questionnaire, an appointment for directions should be taken out. Where the registrar considers that to answer any question would entail considerable expense and that there is doubt whether the answer would provide any information of value, he may make the order for the question to be answered at the questioner's risk as to costs. The registrar may refuse to order an answer to a question if he considers that its value would be small in relation to the property or income of the party to whom the question is addressed.

d) Where an issue of conduct is raised on the affidavits, an appointment for directions should be taken out at which the registrar will inquire whether the issue is being pursued and, if so, will order particulars to be given of the precise allegations relied on.

The Registrar's Direction of 12 February 1980 is hereby cancelled.'

Warden v Warden

[1981] 3 All ER 193, (1981) Times, 10 June, CA

Power to backdate order for variation of maintenance agreement. The husband and wife entered into the maintenance agreement in 1975. The husband lost his job, and was now in financial difficulties. In 1980, the wife obtained judgment for arrears of maintenance in proceedings under Order 14 of the Rules of the Supreme Court. The master took the view that the husband had no defence, because of the decision in *Carr (GA) v Carr (DV)* (9-011) that the court could not backdate any variation of a maintenance agreement. Execution was stayed pending the husband's appeal. Balcombe J came to the same conclusion as Hollings J in *Carr v Carr*, but the Court of Appeal allowed the husband's further appeal. Ormrod LJ said that, if Hollings and Balcombe JJ were right, then any injustice resulting from the agreement up to the date of variation could not be dealt with. There were no explicit words in section 35 of the Matrimonial Causes Act 1973 leading to that conclusion, and his lordship would not accept it. Dunn LJ and Waterhouse J concurred.

Hardy v Hardy

(1981) Times, 11 June, CA

Husband's very substantial expectations – wife's application for lump sum adjourned generally at her request. The husband petitioned for divorce on the ground of five years' separation. The wife made application under section 10 of the Matrimonial Causes Act 1973 for the court first to consider her position before granting the divorce. Evidence was filed which showed that, although the husband had no capital assets, he and his brother had very substantial expectations. The wife applied for her lump sum application to be adjourned generally, so that she could proceed with the application when the husband had assets. The registrar refused, and went on to consider the application for a lump sum. Having satisfied himself that on the present evidence a lump sum was not justified, he dismissed the wife's lump sum application. He made a declaration that the financial provision by the husband for the wife was reasonable and fair, and the decree was duly made absolute.

The Court of Appeal allowed the wife's appeal. Ormrod LJ said that there were no circumstances justifying the registrar's refusal to grant the application for the adjournment. It was essential in such a case that the wife's position should be protected. The wife's application for a lump sum was adjourned generally.

Brown v Brown

(1981) Times, 14 July

Maintenance of children – third party's earnings to be excluded. Purchas J allowed the husband's appeal from a magistrates' order that he pay £5 per week for each of his four children. The husband had become unemployed. He had no job and no money. He could only pay maintenance if he was put in funds by a third party, the woman with whom he lived who was earning £258 net a month. Because he was living with a woman with resources his entitlement to supplementary benefit had ceased. The justices were not entitled to take into account the income of a mistress as a financial resource of the husband. The husband's appeal was allowed and a nominal order of 5p a week substituted for each child.

Note. This case is the converse of *Re L (Minors)* (6–233), in which the roles were reversed.

Macey v Macey

(1981) Times, 14 July

Third party's earnings to be excluded – but to be taken into account in the overall picture. Wood J allowed the husband's appeal from a magistrates' order that he pay £15 per week to the wife and £12.50 per week for each of his two children. The husband lived in a house which was owned jointly by himself and a third party, the husband's mistress. His lordship held that the justices had erred in law in taking into account the joint income of the husband and his mistress.

However, the presence of a second wife or mistress might be relevant in two ways, said his lordship. The husband might be under a legal or moral obligation to support them, which would have some relevance on his ability to support the first wife and the children of the first marriage, or the husband might derive some benefit from the third party's income, which would mean that a greater part of his income would be available out of which to pay maintenance to his first wife and children.

In the circumstances, there was substituted a nominal order for the wife and an order that the husband pay £16.50 direct to each of the two children of the family.

Note. Wood J held that in applying s. 3 of the Domestic Proceedings and Magistrates' Courts Act 1978 magistrates should follow the same principles as followed by the higher courts in applying s. 25 of the Matrimonial Causes Act 1973.

Inland Revenue Statement of Practice No. 6/81 dated 8th September 1981 – Maintenance payments under court orders – retrospective dating

125 Sol Jo 644

'1. Section 2 of the Domestic Proceedings and Magistrates' Courts Act 1978 gives powers to magistrates' courts to make orders if they see fit for payment of maintenance direct to a child of a broken marriage. In these circumstances the payments become for tax purposes the income of that child. This provision took effect from 1 February 1981.

'2. Section 4 of that Act further provides that the payment ordered to be made shall not begin earlier than the date of the making of the application by the spouse for the order in question.

'3. Where an order, whether original or varying an existing order, does in fact provide for payments to the spouse or to the child for a period prior to the date of that order, the Inland Revenue will accept that such payments can be taken into account for tax purposes provided *a* the payments do not relate to a period before the date of application for the order or the variation order, as the case may be; *b* the parties agree; *c* there has been no undue delay by the parties in pressing the application.

'4. The practice referred to in para 3 will also apply to orders, whether original orders or variation orders, made by the High Court or county court'.

Furniss v Furniss

(1981) Times, 28 October, CA

One-third approach based on gross incomes wholly unsatisfactory. Ormrod LJ said that the net income approach was now the *only* satisfactory way of dealing with cases. The one-third approach based on the parties' gross incomes was wholly unsatisfactory. The court should apply s. 25 of the Matrimonial Causes Act 1973 and have regard to the needs of the parties. [See also *Stockford v Stockford* (19–017).]

Stockford v Stockford

(1981) Times, 5 November, CA

(1) *Wrong in principle to adopt a purely arithmetical approach.* Ormrod LJ said that the Court of Appeal had held in several cases that in all cases the court must apply the provisions of s. 25 of the Matrimonial Causes Act 1973. Those provisions had to be applied without superimposed judicial glosses, such as the 'one-third rule', said his lordship, referring to *Preston v Preston* (13–018).

(2) *Net income approach to be preferred.* Husband's available resources to be calculated by working out his liability to income tax on the basis of the proposed order for periodical payments, and deducting from his gross income the aggregate of his NI contributions, the amount of the order, his liability to income tax, and such mortgage liability as was reasonable having regard to his needs in accordance with s. 25 (1) (b) of the 1973 Act.

Matrimonial Homes and Property Act 1981

Orders for sale of property

(Sections in force 1 October 1981)

Powers of court to order sale of property in matrimonial proceedings

7. After section 24 of the Matrimonial Causes Act 1973 there shall be inserted the following section –

'Orders for sale of property

24A. (1) Where the court makes under section 23 or 24 of this Act a secured periodical payments order, an order for the payment of a lump sum or a property adjustment order, then, on making that order or at any time thereafter, the court may make a further order for the sale of such property as may be specified in the order, being property in which or in the proceeds of sale of which either or both of the parties to the marriage has or have a beneficial interest, either in possession or reversion.

(2) Any order made under subsection (1) above may contain such consequential or supplementary provisions as the court thinks fit and, without prejudice to the generality of the foregoing provision, may include –

  (a) provision requiring the making of a payment out of the proceeds of sale of the property to which the order relates, and

  (b) provision requiring any such property to be offered for sale to a person, or class of persons, specified in the order.

(3) Where an order is made under subsection (1) above on or after the grant of a decree of divorce or nullity of marriage, the order shall not take effect unless the decree has been made absolute.

(4) Where an order is made under subsection (1) above, the court may direct that the order, or such provision thereof as the court may specify, shall not take effect until the occurrence of an event specified by the court or the expiration of a period so specified.

(5) Where an order under subsection (1) above contains a provision requiring the proceeds of sale of the property to which the order relates to be used to secure periodical payments to a party to the marriage, the order shall cease to have effect on the death or re-marriage of that person.'

Amendments consequential on powers of court to order sale of property

8. (1) In section 25 of the Matrimonial Causes Act 1973 (which specifies the matters to which the court is to have regard in deciding how to exercise its powers under sections 23 and 24) in subsections (1), (2) and (3) for the words 'or 24' there shall be substituted the words '24 or 24A,' and at the end of that section there shall be added the following subsection –

'(4) Where a party to a marriage has a beneficial interest in any property, or in the proceeds of sale thereof, and some other person who is not a party to the marriage also has a beneficial interest in that property or in the proceeds of sale thereof, then, before deciding whether to make an order under section 24A above in relation to that property, it shall be the duty of the court to give that other person an opportunity to make representations with respect to the order; and any representations made by that other person shall be included among the circumstances to which the court is required to have regard under this section.'

(2) In section 31 of the said Act of 1973 (which provides for the variation and discharge of certain orders for financial relief) –

(a) at the end of subsection (2) there shall be inserted the following paragraph –
    '(f) any order made under section 24A (1) above for the sale of property';

(b) in subsection (6) for the words 'may be made by the person entitled to payments under the order' there shall be substituted the words '(and to any order made under section 24A (1) above which requires the proceeds of sale of property to be used for securing those payments) may be made by the person entitled to payments under the periodical payments order.'

(3) In paragraph 11 of Schedule 1 to the Domicile and Matrimonial Proceedings Act 1973 (which relates to the effect on an order for periodical payments of the stay of proceedings for divorce, judicial separation or nullity of marriage) after sub-paragraph (3) there shall be inserted the following sub-paragraph –

'(3A) Where any such order as is mentioned in paragraph (e) of section 23 (1) of the Matrimonial Causes Act 1973, being an order made under section 23 (1) or (2) (a) of that Act, ceases to have effect by virtue of sub-paragraph (2) or (3) above, any order made under section 24A (1) of that Act which requires the proceeds of sale of property to be used for securing periodical payments under the first mentioned order shall also cease to have effect.'

Note. The Matrimonial Homes and Property Act 1981 amends the Matrimonial Homes Act 1967 and makes provisions regarding the rights of husbands and wives to possession or occupation of the matrimonial home; it also enables orders for the sale of property to be made in certain circumstances under the Matrimonial Causes Act 1973. The Act, which received the royal assent on 2 July 1981, comes into force on a day or days to be appointed.

Section 1 and Sch. 1 amend the Matrimonial Homes Act 1967 in relation to its application where a matrimonial home is held on trust. Section 2 makes it clear that, for the purposes of the 1967 Act, a spouse is entitled to occupy the matrimonial home despite the fact that it is mortgaged. The 1967 Act applies to polygamous marriages: s. 3. Provisions relating to the registration of rights of occupation under the 1967 Act are contained in s. 4. Section 5 makes minor statutory amendments, including an amendment to the Domestic Violence and Matrimonial Proceedings Act 1976 which provides that a mortgagee's right to possession does not affect a spouse's entitlement to occupation under the 1976 Act. Section 6 and Sch. 2 re-enact with modifications provisions of the Matrimonial Homes Act 1967 regarding the transfer in matrimonial proceedings of tenancies subject to the Rent Acts and certain other enactments.

The court may make an order under the Matrimonial Causes Act 1973 for the sale of property of either spouse where an order for financial relief, except unsecured periodical payments, is made in divorce, nullity or judicial separation proceedings: s. 7. Section 8 makes various statutory amendments consequential on the court's power under s. 7. Sections 7 and 8 came into force on 1 October 1981.

Sections 9, 10 and Sch. 3 contain supplementary provisions and repeals. See Halsbury's Laws (4th Edn.), Vol. 22, paras. 1047–1057.

Index

Wife—*contd.*
   remarriage of—*contd.*
   failure to file application for relief prior
      to, 108, 109
   financial provision, 103, 104
   lump sum barred by, 108
   maintenance, relevance on application
      for, 104–106
   no evidence of likelihood of, 102
   possibility of, liberty to apply, 107, 108
   postponement of order for sale until,
      323, 324
   practice, 106–109
   possibility, relevance, 101–104
   wealthy man, to, relevance, 103, 104,
      130, 248

Wife—*contd.*
   resources of—
      earning capacity, other than, 32
      social security benefits, 33
   retirement, nearing, 36
   second, earning capacity of, 25
   third party providing for, 280, 281, 298
   whether under duty to work, 27
   working, whether dependant, 123
   young able-bodied, 31, 32
Witness
   exclusion of, in magistrates' court, 114
   mistress as, 118, 119